Cracking the

ACT®

with DVD

2013 Edition

Geoff Martz, Kim Magloire, and
Theodore Silver

Updated by Melissa Hendrix and
the Staff of The Princeton Review

PrincetonReview.com

Random House, Inc. New York

The Princeton Review, Inc.
111 Speen Street, Suite 550
Framingham, MA 01701
E-mail: editorialsupport@review.com

The Princeton Review is not affiliated with
Princeton University

ISBN 978-0-307-94536-5
ISSN 1934-4171

Editor: Selena Coppock
Production Editor: Berryville Graphics, Inc.

Printed in the United States of America on partially
recycled paper.

10 9 8 7 6 5 4 3 2 1

2013 Edition

Editorial
Rob Franek, Senior VP, Publisher
Selena Coppock, Senior Editor
Calvin Cato, Editor
Kristen O'Toole, Editor
Meave Shelton, Editor

Random House Publishing Team
Tom Russell, Publisher
Nicole Benhabib, Publishing Director
Ellen L. Reed, Production Manager
Alison Stoltzfus, Managing Editor

Acknowledgments

A test-preparation course is much more than clever techniques and powerful computer score reports; the reason our results are so great is that our teachers really care. Eleven years ago, a small group of Princeton Review instructors enthusiastically created a program to prepare students for the previous version of the ACT. We would like to thank John Cauman, Judy Moreland, Bill Lindsley, and Jim Reynolds for their commitment to the original ACT project.

The completion of this book would not have been possible without the help and dedication of several individuals. We would like to thank Melissa Hendrix in particular for her hard work revising and updating this edition.

Special thanks to Adam Robinson, who conceived of and perfected the Joe Bloggs approach to standardized tests and many other successful techniques used by The Princeton Review.

Contents

...So Much More Online!

More Lessons...

- Step-by-step guide to solving difficult problems
- Tutorials that put our strategies into action
- Useful information about ACT scores, college admissions, and score improvement strategies
- Interactive, click-through learning for English, Math, Reading, and Science
- Overview of the question types you will find on the ACT
- Two full-length practice tests

...then College!

- Detailed profiles for hundreds of colleges help you find the school that is right for you
- Information about financial aid and scholarships
- Dozens of Top 10 ranking lists including Quality of Professors, Worst Campus Food, Most Beautiful Campus, Party Schools, Diverse Student Population, and tons more from our annually revised book, *Best 377 Colleges*.

Register your book now!

- Go to PrincetonReview.com/cracking
- You'll see a Welcome page where you should register your book using the ISBN printed on the back cover of your book, right underneath the price. It's a 13 digit number, starting with "978." Type this number into the window.
- Next you will see a Sign Up/Sign In page where you will type in your e-mail address (username) and choose a password.
- Now you're good to go!

princetonreview.com/cracking

Part I
Orientation

Chapter 1
Introduction to
the ACT

So, you have to take the ACT? What will you need to do first? This chapter presents an overview of the ACT as a whole and discusses registration requirements, when to take the test, how to have your scores reported to colleges (or how not to), and the ways in which colleges use your scores.

THE ACT

The Princeton Review has a reputation for test bashing that is richly deserved. In general, we don't have many nice things to say about the tests we tackle or the organizations that write them. So it's a pleasure to take on what we feel is (by comparison) a fair and good-hearted test, written by intelligent people.

The ACT measures what it says it does—academic achievement. It doesn't pretend to measure your analytic ability or your intelligence. The people at ACT admit that you can increase your score by preparing for the test. They even put out their own coaching book.

So if we ever seem to be poking fun at the test or the people who write it, we want you to remember that it does not lessen our underlying affection and respect for the exam and its authors.

If there is any flaw in the ACT, it is that, in its attempt to be fair, it has become a little, well, predictable. Of course, when we say that the ACT is a completely predictable test, we mean it in the nicest possible way. We *like* predictable tests, and so should you.

The ACT Is a ~~Standardized~~ *Predictable* Test

From now on, whenever you see the word *standardized*, think *predictable* instead. The ACT tests the same information the same way, year after year. For example, there are always 14 plane geometry questions on the ACT, not 13, not 15, exactly 14. There are exactly 10 questions on punctuation. You can count on it. Even the way the test asks the questions is predictable, based on the need for a standardized product.

The review in this book is based on the very specific knowledge you need to do well on this test. The test-taking strategies we have developed are designed to take advantage of the ACT's predictability.

Do I Need to Prepare if I Have Good Grades?

Let's take the hypothetical case of Sid. Sid is valedictorian of his class, editor of the school paper, and the only teenager ever to win the Nobel Prize. To support his widowed mother, he sold more seeds from the back of comic books than any other person in recorded history. He speaks eight languages in addition to being able to communicate with dolphins and wolves. He has recommendations from Colin Powell *and* Bill Gates. So if Sid had a bad day when he took the ACT (the plane bringing him back from his Medal of Freedom award presentation was late), we are pretty sure that he is going to be just fine anyway. But Sid wants to ensure that when his colleges look at his ACT score, they see the same high-caliber student they see when they look at the rest of his application, so he carefully reviews the types of questions asked and learns some useful test-taking strategies.

I Have Lousy Grades in School. Is There Any Hope?

Let's take the case of Tom. Tom didn't do particularly well in high school. In fact, he has been on academic probation since kindergarten. He has caused four of his teachers to give up teaching as a profession, and he prides himself on his perfect homework record: He's never done any, not ever. But if Tom aces his ACT, a college might decide that he is actually a misunderstood genius and give him a full scholarship. Tom decides to learn as much as he can about the ACT.

Most of us, of course, fall between these two extremes. So is it important to prepare for the ACT?

If you were to look in the information bulletin of any of the colleges in which you are interested, we can pretty much guarantee that somewhere you would find the following paragraph:

> Many factors go into the acceptance of a student by a college. Test scores are *only one* of these factors. Grades in high school, extracurricular activities, essays, and recommendations are also important and may in some cases outweigh test scores.

> (2013 University of Anywhere Bulletin)

Truer words were never spoken. In our opinion, just about *every* other element in your application "package" is more important than your test scores. The Princeton Review (among other organizations) has been telling colleges for years that scores on the ACT or the SAT are pretty incomplete measures of a student's overall academic abilities. Some colleges have stopped looking at test scores entirely, and others are downplaying their importance.

So Why Should You Spend Any Time Preparing for the ACT?

Out of all the elements in your application "package," your ACT score is the easiest to *change*. The grades you've received up to now are written in stone. You aren't going to become captain of the football team or editor of the school paper overnight. Your essays will be only as good as you can write them, and recommendations are only as good as your teachers' memories of you.

On the contrary, in a few weeks you can substantially change your score on the ACT (and the way colleges look at your applications). The test does not pretend to measure analytic ability or intelligence. It measures your knowledge of specific skills such as grammar, algebra, and reading comprehension. Mostly, it measures how good you are at taking this test.

Watch it on your DVD

Size Matters
Large schools process more applications, so they rely heavily on standardized test scores. Small schools have the time to read the rest of your application.

When It Comes to the ACT, *Nothing* Is Written in Stone

It doesn't matter how well you've done in school up to now. Good grades are not a guarantee that you will do well on the ACT. It doesn't matter if you've always been bad at taking standardized tests. Colleges aren't going to see any of your scores from earlier standardized tests. It doesn't matter if you hate math in general or English in general or science in general. The ACT doesn't measure math in general. It measures the math that is on the ACT.

By reviewing the very specific knowledge that the people who write the ACT think is important and by learning good test-taking strategies, you should be able to increase your ACT score significantly. This is not just our opinion. Even the people who write the test agree.

What Is the ACT?

The ACT is a multiple-choice standardized exam that is supposed to measure your knowledge of some of the subjects taught in high school. The ACT takes about three and a half hours and has one break. It is divided into four tests, which are always given in the same order. (ACT calls them tests, but we may also use the term "sections" in this book to avoid confusion.)

Watch it on your DVD

1. English Test (45 minutes—75 questions)

In this section, you will see five essays on the left side of the page. Some words or phrases will be underlined. On the right side of the page, you will be asked whether the underlined portion is correct as written or whether one of the three alternatives listed would be better. This is a test of grammar, punctuation, sentence structure, and rhetorical skills. Throughout each essay, commonly known as a "passage," there will also be questions about overall organization and style or perhaps about how the writing could be revised or strengthened.

2. Math Test (60 minutes—60 questions)

These are the regular, multiple-choice math questions you've been doing all your life. The easier questions, which test basic math proficiency, *tend* to come first, but the folks at the ACT try to mix in easy, medium, and difficult problems throughout the Math test. A good third of the test covers pre-algebra and elementary algebra. Slightly less than a third covers intermediate algebra and coordinate geometry (graphing). Regular geometry accounts for less than a quarter of the questions, and there are four questions that cover trigonometry.

Power Booking
If you were getting ready to take a history test, you'd study history. If you were preparing for a basketball game, you'd practice basketball. So if you're preparing for the ACT, study the ACT!

3. Reading Test (35 minutes—40 questions)

In this test, there will be four reading passages of about 750 words each—the average length of a *People* magazine article but maybe not as interesting. There is always one prose fiction passage, one social science passage, one humanities passage, and one natural science passage, and they are always in that order. After reading each passage, you have to answer 10 questions.

4. Science Test (35 minutes—40 questions)

No specific scientific knowledge is necessary for the Science test. You won't need to know the chemical makeup of hydrochloric acid or any formulas. Instead, you will be asked to understand six sets of scientific information presented in graphs, charts, tables, and research summaries, and you will have to make sense of one disagreement between two or three scientists. (Occasionally, there are more than three scientists.)

There may be one additional section on the ACT. During this section, you will pay for the privilege of being a guinea pig while the test writers at ACT try out some experimental questions on you. This section typically comes at the end of the test and is usually very easy to recognize, as it is much shorter than a regular section—just 10 to 15 minutes long. In other words, it's not a big deal. This section usually shows up on the June exam, and it won't count toward your score.

5. Optional Writing Test (30 minutes)

The ACT contains an "optional" writing test featuring a single essay. We recommend you take the "ACT Plus Writing," version of the test because some schools require it. While on test day you may think you don't need it, you might later decide to apply to a school that requires a writing score. The last thing you want is to be forced into taking the whole ACT all over again…this time *with* the writing test. The essay consists of a prompt "relevant" to high school students on which you will be asked to write an essay stating your position on the prompt. Two people will then grade your essay on a scale of 1 to 6 for a total score of 2 to 12. In this book, we will teach you how to write the best possible essay for the ACT.

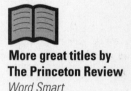

**More great titles by
The Princeton Review**
Word Smart

Where Does the ACT Come From?

The ACT is written by a company that used to call itself American College Testing but now just calls itself ACT. The company's main offices are in Iowa City, Iowa. The people at ACT have been writing a version of this test since 1959. Even if you aren't looking forward to taking the ACT this year, you would probably prefer it to the version they used to give. In the old days, the test included detailed questions about topics like the Constitution of the United States, electrostatic forces, and planets in the solar system.

The people at ACT also write a number of other tests, including a test for professional golfers and a test for dieticians. They provide a broad range of services to educational agencies and business institutions.

How Is the ACT Scored?

Scores for each of the four tests are reported on a scale of 1 to 36 (36 being the highest score possible). The four scores are averaged to yield your composite score, which is the score colleges and universities primarily use to determine admission. Next to each score is a percentile ranking. Percentile ranking refers to how you performed on the test relative to other people who took it at the same time. For instance, a percentile ranking of 87 indicates that you scored higher than 87 percent of the people who took the test and 13 percent scored higher than you.

Closed Loop

The ACT tests how well you take the ACT.

Some of the scores have subcategories. English is broken down into Usage/Mechanics and Rhetorical Skills. The subcategories may be of some marginal use to colleges; they are much more useful to you if you decide to take the test again, because they pinpoint your strengths and weaknesses. In these subcategories, scores are reported on a scale of 1 to 18 (18 being the highest score possible). They are also reported as percentiles.

If you decide to take the ACT Plus Writing test, you will receive standard ACT scores plus two additional scores. One will be a scaled score from 1 to 36, which combines your performance on the Writing test and the English test. The other will be a subscore, ranging from 2 to 12, which reflects how you did on your essay. Neither score contributes to your composite score. The Writing test costs an additional $15, which you will be charged when you sign up for the ACT. The ACT with the Essay section is more expensive than the ACT without the Essay section. Check www.act.org for current costs.

Three to seven weeks after you take the ACT, you and the colleges you have selected, if any, will receive your ACT scores in the mail. If you want, you can pay to see your scores a bit earlier (about 10 to 14 days after your test date).

More great titles by The Princeton Review

College Essays that Made a Difference

Who Actually Receives the Scores?

You might think that your scores will be mailed directly to your home, but this is not always the case. If you take the June administration of the test, scores are mailed to colleges and to you. For all other administrations, scores are sent to colleges and to your high school counselor, not directly to you, unless your high school has given ACT permission to send them to you. You then get the scores from the counselor. We've checked with ACT, and the people we talked to there said that if you choose not to provide a High School Code, your scores simply won't be sent to your high school. So, if you want your scores sent to your home (and not your high school), leave the High School Code blank. All colleges you list will get copies of your score regardless of whether you leave the High School Code blank.

There is one potential downside to not reporting your scores to your high school: If you're likely to receive a state-awarded scholarship on the basis of your ACT score, such a score is usually reported to the state's scholarship-awarding entity through—you guessed it—the high school. If you anticipate receiving such a score and are counting on such a scholarship (taking at least one test as a reality check is a good idea), go ahead and provide your High School Code. As the owners of your transcript, you and your parents can go to your high school and have a score removed from it later if you feel the score doesn't reflect your abilities. In any event, because ACT allows score choice (sending scores from just one testing date to colleges), the test scores on your high school transcript ultimately don't matter that much.

When Should You Take the ACT?

The test is given four times each year in New York and five times each year in most of the rest of the country, usually at 8:00 A.M. on a Saturday morning. In some states, there are six administrations each year (they include a September test date as well). Most students take the ACT in the spring of their junior year or in the fall of senior year. Check out www.act.org to determine which administrations are best for you. A good case can be made for taking it at the earlier date. For one thing, you'll have a better idea of where you stand. If your score is about what you want, you can spend the summer visiting colleges or getting started on your applications. If your score is lower than you want, you can use the summer to prepare to take the test again in the fall.

The cost of the ACT changes from time to time and depends on whether you decide to take the Writing test. In 2012–2013, the test without the writing portion is $35 and $50.50 with it. You can obtain a registration packet for the ACT at your high school guidance office, online at www.actstudent.org/forms/stud_req.html, or by writing or calling ACT at the address and phone number below.

ACT Registration
P.O. Box 414
Iowa City, IA 52243
319-337-1270

You can also register directly online via ACT's website at www.actstudent.org. But before you decide on a test date, there are other things that you should know.

Special Considerations

The ACT offers accommodations to students with special needs, learning or otherwise. You cannot, however, get accommodations without prior arrangement with ACT. A detailed description of the types of special accommodations available and of ACT's documentation requirements is available at www.act.org/aap/disab.

Some ACT Test Dates Are Better Than Others

On certain dates, the ACT offers what it calls "Test Information Release." If you take the ACT on one of these dates, you can, for $18.00 (as of 2011–2012), receive a copy of the test that you took and a photocopy of your actual answer sheet. We strongly advise that you take the test on one of these dates. It is not unheard of for ACT to make a mistake when scoring. You certainly won't find out about this unless you can see the test you took and your own answers. For example, it is possible to fill in an oval on the answer sheet darkly enough for the human eye to see, but not darkly enough for the machine that scores the test to read. In this case, if you point it out to them and pay another small, additional fee, the people at ACT will hand-score your test and change your grade if they indeed made a mistake.

Flying Standby
You don't have to register in advance for the ACT. It is possible to register on the spot on the day of the test for an additional fee, but you *must* bring a completed registration booklet. Also, be sure to arrive extra early if you're testing on standby, because just like on airplanes, there are a limited number of seats, and it's first-come, first-served.

What If I've Already Taken the ACT Once Before?

The nice folks at ACT allow you to decide which of your ACT scores they report to colleges. If you want to have full control over this, it is a good idea *not* to take advantage of the four free score reports ACT offers to send to colleges directly after the test. Why send colleges scores you might not want them to see? While it costs a few extra dollars to get ACT to send scores to schools later, it is well worth being able to send the colleges your best results.

How to Prepare for the ACT

The Princeton Review materials and test-taking techniques contained in this book should give you all the information you need to improve your score on the ACT.

Other popular coaching books contain several complete practice ACT exams. We strongly advise you *not* to waste your time taking these tests. In some cases, the questions in these books are not modeled on real ACT questions. Some of them cover material that is not even on the real ACT. Others give the impression that the ACT is much easier or more difficult than it really is. Taking the practice tests offered in these books could actually hurt your score.

One reason these coaching books do not use real ACT questions is that the folks at ACT won't let them. They have refused to let anyone (including us) license actual questions from old tests. You may have chosen our book because it contains two practice ACT exams. Rest assured that these tests are *modeled very closely after actual ACT exams*, with the proper balance of questions reflective of what the ACT actually tests.

Cynics might suggest that no one else can license ACT exams because ACT sells its own review book called *The Real ACT Prep Guide*. Although *The Real ACT* doesn't contain a very full review section and offers only limited test-taking strategies (after all, no one wants to rob his or her own house), we think ACT's book is well worth the price just for the three real tests it contains. We recommend that you either buy the book or ask your high school to send away to ACT for actual ACT tests. You can also buy real ACT tests on www.act.org. You should get a copy of *Preparing for the ACT Assessment* from your counselor. It's free, and it contains a complete, real ACT. The same test can be downloaded for free from ACT's website.

While we advise you to obtain these practice tests to further your preparation for the ACT, it is important that you use them properly. Many students like to think that they can prepare by simply taking test after test until they get the scores they want. Unfortunately, this doesn't work all that well. Why? Well, in many instances, repetitive test taking only reinforces some of the bad test-taking habits that we address in this book. You should use practice tests for the following three key purposes:

- to build up familiarity with the exam
- to learn how to avoid the types of mistakes you are currently making
- to master our techniques and strategies so you can save time and earn more points

The ACT vs. the SAT

You may have to take the ACT anyway, but most of the schools in which you're interested also accept the SAT. We think the SAT is nowhere near as fair a test as the ACT. Whereas the ACT says it measures "achievement" (which we believe *can* be measured), the SAT says it measures "ability" (which we don't think can be measured at all; and if it can, the SAT sure isn't doing it).

What Exactly Are the Differences?

The SAT tends to be less time-pressured than the ACT. However, many of the questions on the SAT are trickier than those on the ACT. The SAT Verbal sections have a stronger emphasis on vocabulary than do the ACT English and Reading tests. The SAT Math section tests primarily algebra and plane geometry and includes no trigonometry at all.

Both tests include an Essay section, although ACT has made this new essay optional because some colleges require it while others do not. ACT doesn't want to force students to take (and pay for) a test they don't need. The implication then is that many students can ignore the new Writing Test altogether depending on what the schools to which they are applying require.

To find out if the schools in which you are interested require the ACT essay, visit the ACT writing test page at www.actstudent.org/writing or contact the schools directly.

While we are obviously not tremendously fond of the SAT, you should know that some students end up scoring substantially higher on the SAT than they do on the ACT and vice versa. It may be to your advantage to take a practice test for each one and see which is more likely to get you a better score.

What Is The Princeton Review?

The Princeton Review is the world's leading test-preparation and educational services company. We run courses at hundreds of locations worldwide and offer web-based instruction at PrincetonReview.com. Our test-taking techniques and review strategies are unique and powerful. We developed them after studying all the real ACTs we could get our hands on and analyzed them with the most sophisticated software available. For more information about our programs and services, feel free to call us at **800-2Review**.

A Final Thought Before You Begin

The ACT does not measure intelligence, nor does it predict your ultimate success or failure as a human being. No matter how high or how low you score on this test initially, and no matter how much you may increase your score through preparation, you should *never* consider the score you receive on this or any other test a final judgment of your abilities.

**More great titles by
The Princeton Review**
*The Best 377 Colleges,
Complete Book of Colleges*

**Check out the Best Fit
College Search at**
PrincetonReview.com

Chapter 2
Triage

The ACT is a time-limited test. You can develop strategies to help you use the time you are given to your advantage. One simple strategy is to prioritize the questions rather than answer them in the order in which they appear. In this chapter, you'll learn how to use a two-pass, or triage, system for approaching the ACT efficiently and effectively.

How Questions Are Organized

Wouldn't it be great if all the questions on the ACT were arranged in order of difficulty? Then you could do the easiest questions first and move on from there. That way you wouldn't waste a lot of time trying to answer difficult questions before you had answered all the easy questions, which count for the same number of points anyway.

Unfortunately, the ACT is not organized that way.

According to the ACT writers we interviewed, the English section of the test is not in any order of difficulty. In the Math test, according to ACT literature, "most people find the first questions on the test easier… than the ones that come later," but these are only very rough guidelines. Many Princeton Review students find that some questions toward the end of the test are easier than many of the questions in the beginning.

Equality
Remember that easy questions are worth just as much as difficult questions, so do the easy ones first!

Oh. But What If…

But what if the Science Reasoning and Reading *passages* were arranged in order of difficulty? Some of the other test-preparation books maintain that they are. According to one ACT writer, this is true, "…only in an average sense. We believe in the philosophy that if students are running out of time, the questions they don't get to should be ones they would have difficulty with anyway. But students will find plenty of exceptions." So by its own admission, ACT does not use a definite order of difficulty in the Science Reasoning or Reading tests.

Oh. But…

But nothing! On the ACT, if you want to do the easy questions first, you're going to have to find them for yourself. We have a good way to think about this. We call it "triage."

TRIAGE

Triage is the medical term that describes the technique used by emergency-room doctors when they have several emergencies at the same time. To save the most lives, doctors separate patients into three groups: those who will die regardless of intervention, those who require immediate medical attention, and those who can afford to wait a little while. The routine patients are left until last.

In ACT triage, you adapt this strategy somewhat. See that really tough algebra problem sitting over there? Forget it; it's a goner. How about that problem on frequency and amplitude? That would take far too long, and even if you got it right, it would still only be worth one point. Now this problem involving basic arithmetic—this is something different altogether. It's an easy question, so you should do it right away.

See that tough, horrible-looking passage about European authoritarianism during the nineteenth century? Let's see if it's still breathing after we finish the one about Ronald Reagan's election in 1980.

Just One More Minute…

If you find yourself stuck on a question, waiting for divine inspiration, it's time to move on to another, easier problem. Save your time and live to fight another day (or question, that is). The temptation to get stubborn and stay with a particular problem can be very strong, especially when you've already invested some time on it. Nonetheless, you need to move on. Why stick with a question that's giving you problems when there are easier questions to be answered?

"Oh, Yeah!"

We've all had the experience of riding home in the car and suddenly slapping our hand to our forehead as we finally realized exactly how to do question number five. By using triage, you can sometimes have this sudden revelation *before* the test is over, when you can still do something about it. So how does triage work exactly?

Watch it on your DVD

For more help check out our academic tutoring offers at PrincetonReview.com

Now, Later, Never

Do you want to do the problem *now*? That is the question you should constantly be asking yourself during the exam. If you finish reading a problem and immediately know how to solve it, then of course you should do it right away.

But what if you finish reading a problem and you aren't really certain how to begin? If you think you might be able to figure it out on your second pass, circle the question number and move on. This might seem hard to do at first, but it is one of the central tenets of good test taking, and it gets easier with practice. You aren't necessarily skipping the problem forever. You're just putting it at the back of the line.

However, if the problem is a goner and you're sure you'll never figure it out, fill in your guess answer and forget it. There are other problems out there waiting for you; don't worry about the ones you just *can't* do.

Two Passes

First Pass, Second Pass
On the first pass, do the questions you know how to do and guess on the questions that you have no idea how to do. On the second pass, answer all the questions that are doable but likely to take you more time.

We want you to do each section in two passes. During the first pass, the object is to nail every single question you can answer. By answering all the questions of which you're sure, you will never have to hear the words, "Okay, pencils down," and know that there were several more questions you could have done if only there had been more time. You will have already done them.

What Happens if I Think I Know How to Do It, but Then I Realize I Was Wrong?

Nobody's right all the time. As soon as you realize you're stuck, you should put a big circle around the question and move on. This is the time when people tend to get stubborn. They think, "But I've already spent so much time on this question. It would be a waste to skip it now."

You Haven't Wasted the Time; You've Invested It

When you come back to this question on the second pass, you won't be starting from scratch. You'll already have read the question once. You may have made some notes in the margin. Perhaps reading it again will make you realize an important point you missed the first time. If not, throw it to the back of the line and count your blessings: You could still be back there working on question number five!

The Second Pass

After you've finished everything you can do on the first pass and bubbled in your Letter of the Day on all questions that you're sure you can't do, come back to the questions you circled for a second pass. Again, think ACT triage. Most of the "patients" in your emergency room have now been handled. Look over the remaining problems and ask yourself the same question: Which one do I want to do *now*? Obviously, none of them struck you as easy the first time or you would have answered on the first pass. On the contrary, among the remaining problems, some are probably more likely bets than others.

Sometimes when you read a question again, you suddenly realize what the point of the question really is. This will save you from having that "Oh, yeah!" revelation on the car ride home. But other times when you re-read a question, you suddenly realize that you will hate this question for the rest of your life and you never, ever want to see it again. Fine. Throw it to the back of the list and keep looking. These are "never" questions: Do them only if you have time to spare.

Sometimes you reject a question initially because you think it will take too much time. Well, now you have time. You've already locked in all the sure points, so maybe this is the question to do now.

Scoring More Points with ACT Triage

Deciding whether you will do a question *now*, *later*, or *never* is a crucial part of improving your results on the ACT. The whole point of ACT triage is to help you invest your time more profitably. By utilizing the two-pass approach and the concept of triage, you will, unlike most test takers, spend the majority of your time working on questions that seem easy or at least doable. As a result, you will score more points.

I've Done All the Questions I Know How to Do and All the Questions I Think I Know How to Do. Now What?

You guess. Guessing on the ACT is so important that we've given it its own chapter.

Time to Spare

Let's face it—the ACT is designed to be difficult to finish in the time given. Most students are not going to finish early. But what if you do? Do you lay your head down and catch a few z's? No way! Go back to the problems that you skipped the first time through or that you wondered if you'd done right. There's always something to check!

Chapter 3
Guessing and POE

There is no penalty for guessing on the ACT, so it is to your advantage to fill in an answer for every question. In this chapter, you'll learn how to take advantage of the multiple-choice nature of the ACT and get more points by understanding and using the Process of Elimination.

NO PENALTY FOR GUESSING

Imagine for a moment that you are a game show contestant. It's the final, big deal of the day. The host asks you, "Do you want curtain number one, curtain number two, or curtain number three?" As you carefully weigh your options, the members of the audience are screaming out their suggestions, but you can bet there is one suggestion no one in the audience is going to shout at you.

"Skip the question!"

It wouldn't make sense. You have a one-in-three shot of winning, and there is no penalty for guessing wrong. (Okay, you might have to cart home a lifetime supply of toilet paper.)

On the ACT, you don't even have to worry about the toilet paper because there is no guessing penalty at all.

You Must Fill in an Answer for Every Single Question on the ACT

There are 215 questions on the ACT. If you went into the test room, filled out your name, and then went to sleep for the entire test, your composite score would be just about what you might expect: 0.

If, however, you went into the test room, filled out your name, went to sleep for most of the time, then woke up and picked answer choice (B) or (G) 215 times, your composite score would be a 12!

We would not recommend random guessing as an overall strategy (unless all you need is a 12, and that's only the first percentile), but you can see that it is in your interest to guess on every question you either can't answer or don't get to in time.

Ah, but there's guessing, and then there's *guessing*.

How to Score Higher on the ACT

Try the following question:

> **1.** What is the French word for "eggplant"?

What? You don't know? Well then, you'd better guess at random. (By the way, there are no questions about vegetables, French or otherwise, on the ACT. We're just using this question to make a point.)

If you really don't know the answer to a question, of course, you should always guess. But before you choose an answer at random, take a look at the problem the way you would see it on the ACT.

> **1.** What is the French word for "eggplant?"
> **A.** のみもの
> **B.** すきやき
> **C.** Aubergine
> **D.** デザート

Suddenly the question looks a lot easier, doesn't it? You may not have known the correct answer to this question, but you certainly knew three answers that were incorrect.

POE

The Process of Elimination (POE for short) enables you to make your guesses really count. Incorrect answer choices are often easier to spot than correct ones. Sometimes they are logically absurd; sometimes they are the opposite of the correct answer. If you find a wrong answer, eliminate it. While you will rarely be able to eliminate all of the incorrect answer choices, it is often possible to eliminate one or two, and each time you can eliminate an answer choice, your odds of guessing correctly get better.

Try another question.

> **1.** What is the capital of Malawi?
> **A.** New York
> **B.** Lilongwe
> **C.** Paris
> **D.** Kinshasa

This time you could probably eliminate only two of the answer choices. However, that meant you were down to a fifty-fifty guess—much better than random guessing.

The Process of Elimination is a tremendously powerful tool. We refer to it in every single chapter of this book, and explain how to use it on a variety of specific types of questions.

Watch it on your DVD

Letter of the Day

Which makes more sense—guessing the same letter every time or switching around? If you think you're better off switching around, think again. As counter-intuitive as it may seem, you will pick up more points consistently if you always guess the same letter. Sure, you won't get all of your random guesses correct, but you'll get some points. On the contrary, if you vary your guess answer, you might get some correct, but you might miss all of them just as easily.

It doesn't matter what letter you pick as your Letter of the Day. Contrary to popular opinion, you won't get more questions right if you guess choice (C) rather than any other choice. Go crazy, guess choice (A) or (F) on the next ACT you take. Just be consistent.

Chapter 4
Taking the ACT

Preparing yourself both mentally and physically to take the ACT is important. This chapter helps you learn exactly what you're in for, so you can plan ahead and be as comfortable as possible on test day. We not only talk about what to do but also what *not* to do.

PREPARING FOR THE ACT

The best way to prepare for any test is to find out exactly what is going to be on it. This book provides you with just that information. In the following chapters, you will find a comprehensive review of all the question types on the ACT, complete information on all the subjects covered by the ACT, and some powerful test-taking strategies developed specifically for the ACT.

To take full advantage of the review and techniques, you should practice on the tests in this book as well as on real ACT questions. We've already told you how to obtain copies of real ACT exams. Taking full practice exams allows you to chart your progress (with accurate scores for each test), gives you confidence in our techniques, and develops your stamina.

The Night Before the Test

Unless you are the kind of person who remains calm only by staying up all night to do last-minute studying, we recommend that you take the evening off. Go see a movie or read a good book (besides this one), and make sure you get to bed at a normal hour. No final, frantically memorized math formula or grammatical rule is going to make or break your score. A positive mental attitude comes from treating yourself decently. If you've prepared over the last several weeks or months, then you're ready.

If you haven't really prepared, there will be other opportunities to take the test, so get some rest and do the best you can. Remember, colleges will see only the score you choose to let them see. No *single* ACT is going to be crucial. We don't think night-before-the-test cramming is very effective. For example, we would not recommend that you try going through this book in one night.

On the Day of the Test

Don't Leave Home Without 'Em
Here are some items you'll want to have on test day.
- admissions ticket
- photo ID or letter of identification
- plenty of sharpened No. 2 pencils
- a watch
- an acceptable calculator with new batteries

It's important that you eat a real breakfast, even if you normally don't. We find that about two-thirds of the way through the test, people who didn't eat something beforehand suddenly lose their will to live. Equally important, bring a snack to the test center. You will get a break during which food is allowed. Some people spend the break out in the hallways comparing answers and getting upset when their answers don't match. Ignore the people around you and eat your snack. Why assume they know any more than you do?

Warming Up

While you're having breakfast, do a couple of questions from an ACT on which you've already worked to get your mind going. You don't want to use the first test on the real exam to warm up. And please don't try a hard question you've never done before. If you miss it, your confidence will be diminished, and that's not something you want on the day of the test.

At the test center, you'll be asked to show some form of picture ID or provide a note from your school—on school stationery—describing what you look like. The time or time remaining is often *not* announced during the test sections, so you should also bring a reliable watch—not the beeping kind—and, of course, several No. 2 pencils, an eraser, and a calculator. Check www.actstudent.org/faq to see if your calculator model is permitted. If you haven't changed the batteries recently (or ever), you should do that before the test or bring a back-up calculator.

When you get into the actual room in which you'll be taking the exam, make sure you're comfortable. Is there enough light? Is your desk sturdy? Don't be afraid to speak up; after all, you're going to be spending three and a half hours at that desk. And it's not a bad idea to go to the bathroom *before* you get to the room. It's a long haul to that first break.

ZEN AND THE ART OF TEST TAKING

Once the exam begins, tune out the rest of the world. That girl with the annoying cough in the next row? You don't hear her. That guy who is fidgeting in the seat ahead of you? You don't see him. It's just you and the exam. Everything else should be a blur.

As soon as one test ends, erase it completely from your mind. It no longer exists. The only test that counts is the one you are taking right now. Even if you are upset about a particular test, erase it from your mind. If you are busy thinking about the last test, you cannot focus on the one on which you are currently working, and that's a surefire way to make costly mistakes. Most people aren't very good at assessing how they performed on a given section of the exam, especially while they're still taking it, so don't waste your time and energy trying.

Some Things to Remember
- Make sure you know where the test center is located and where you need to go once you are at the test center.
- Show up early; you can't show up right when the test is scheduled to begin and expect to get in.
- Lay out your pencils, calculator, watch, admission ticket, and photo identification the night before the test. The last thing you want to be doing on the morning of the test is running around looking for a calculator. Also, it's important to have your own watch because there's no requirement that the room you're in have a working clock.
- Bring a snack and a bottle of water just in case you get hungry. There's nothing worse than testing on an empty stomach.

Keep Your Answers to Yourself

Please don't let anyone cheat off you. Test companies have developed sophisticated anti-cheating measures that go way beyond having a proctor walk around the room. We know of one test company that gets seating charts of each testing room. Its computers scan the score sheets of people sitting in the immediate vicinity for correlations of wrong answer choices. Innocent and guilty are invited to take the exam over again, and their scores from the first exam are invalidated.

Beware of Misbubbling Your Answer Sheet

Probably the most painful kind of mistake you can make on the ACT is to bubble in choice (A) with your pencil when you really mean choice (B), or to have your answers be one question number off (perhaps because you skipped one question on the test but forgot to skip it on the answer sheet). Aargh! The proctor isn't allowed to let you change your answers after a section is over, so it is critical that you either catch yourself before a test section ends or—even better—that you don't make a mistake in the first place.

Write Now
Feel free to write all over your test booklet. Don't do computations in your head. Put them in the booklet; you paid for it. Go nuts!

We suggest to our students that they write down their answers in their test booklets. This way, whenever you finish a page of questions in the test booklet, you can transfer all your answers from that page in a group. We find that this method minimizes the possibility of misbubbling and it also saves time. Of course, as you get near the end of a test, you should go back to bubbling question by question.

If you get back your ACT scores and they seem completely out of line, you can ask the ACT examiners to look over your answer sheet for what are called "gridding errors." If you want to, you can even be there while they look. If it is clear that there has been an error, ACT will change your score. An example of a gridding error would be a test in which, if you moved all the responses over by one, they would suddenly all be correct.

Should I Ever Cancel My Scores?

We recommend against canceling your scores, even if you feel you've done poorly. If you have registered as we recommended and not sent the scores to any colleges and possibly not to your high school, then the score you receive won't go anywhere unless you send it on later. There is no need to panic and cancel your score without knowing what it is if no one will ever see it. You never know—perhaps you did better than you think. Furthermore, if you've taken the ACT two or more times (something we heartily recommend), you can choose which score you want colleges to see when you request reports from ACT.

If you do decide to cancel your scores, ACT allows you to do it only at the test center itself. However, you can stop scores from reaching colleges if you call ACT by 12:00 P.M., Central Time on the *Thursday* following the test. The number to call is 319-337-1270.

Part II
How to Crack the ACT English Test

Chapter 5
Introduction to the
ACT English Test

The English test is not a grammar test. It's also not a test of how well you write. In fact, it tests your editing skills: your ability to fix errors in grammar and punctuation and to improve the organization and style of five different passages. In this chapter, you'll learn the basic strategy of how to crack the passages and review the grammar you need to know.

WHAT'S ON THE ENGLISH TEST

Before we dive into the details of the content and strategy, let's review what the English test looks like. Remember, the five tests on the ACT are always given in the same order and English is always first.

There are five prose passages on topics ranging from historical essays to personal narratives. Each passage is typically accompanied by 15 questions for a total of 75 questions that you must answer in 45 minutes. Portions of each passage are underlined, and you must decide if these are correct as written, or if one of the other answers would fix or improve the selection. Other questions will ask you to add, cut, or re-order text, while still others will ask you to evaluate the passage as a whole.

WRITING

While the idea of English grammar makes most of us think of persnickety, picky rules long since outdated, English is actually a dynamic, adaptive language. We add new vocabulary all the time, and we let common usage influence and change many rules. Pick up a handful of style books, and you'll find very few rules that everyone agrees upon. This is actually good news for studying for the ACT: you're unlikely to see questions testing the most obscure or most disputed rules. However, few of us follow ALL of even the most basic, universally accepted rules when we speak, much less when we e-mail, text, or tweet.

The 4 C's: Complete, Consistent, Clear, and Concise

ACT test writers will never make you name a particular error. But with 75 questions, they can certainly test a lot of different rules—and yes, that's leaving out the obscure and debated rules. You would drive yourself crazy if you tried to learn, just for the ACT, all of the grammar you never knew in the first place. You're much better off with a common sense approach. We'll teach you the rules that show up the most often, and we'll show you how to crack the questions that test them. What about all the rest of the questions? That's where the 4 C's come in.

Good writing should be in **complete** sentences; everything should be **consistent**; the meaning should be **clear**. The best answer, free of any errors, will be the most **concise**. All of the rules we'll review fall under one or more of the 4 C's. But even when you can't identify what a question is testing, apply the 4 C's, and you'll be able to answer even the most difficult questions.

We'll explain in greater detail what the 4 C's mean in the grammar review and in the following lessons. But first, let's discuss your general strategies and overall approach to the English test.

HOW TO CRACK THE ENGLISH TEST

The Passages

As always on the ACT, time is your enemy. With only 45 minutes to review five passages and answer 75 questions, you can't read a passage in its entirety and then go back to do the questions. For each passage, work the questions as you make your way through the passage. Read from the beginning until you get to an underlined selection, work that question, and then resume reading until the next underlined portion and the next question.

The Questions

Not all questions are created equally. In fact, ACT divides the questions on the English test into two categories: usage and mechanics, and rhetorical skills. These designations will mean very little to you when you're taking the test. All questions are worth the same amount of points, after all, and you'll crack most of the questions the same way, regardless of what ACT calls them. Many of the rhetorical skills questions, however, are those on organization and style, and some take longer to answer than other questions do. Since there is no order of difficulty of the passages or of the questions, all that matters is that you identify your *Now, Later, Never* questions and make sure you finish.

The best way to make sure you finish with as many correct answers as possible is to use our 5-step Basic Approach.

Step 1: Identify the Topic

For each underlined portion, finish the sentence, and then look at the answers. The answers are your clues to identifying what the question is testing. Let's start off with this first question.

American <u>author Junot Diaz, was born in</u> the Dominican Republic.
₁

1. **A.** NO CHANGE
   B. author, Junot Diaz
   C. author Junot Diaz
   D. author, Junot Diaz,

Watch it on your DVD

Do any of the words change? No. What is the only thing that does change? Commas. So what must be the topic of the question? Commas.

Always identify the topic of the question first. Pay attention to what changes versus what stays the same in the answers.

Step 2: Use POE

You may have chosen an answer for #1 already. If you haven't, don't worry: we'll review all the rules of commas in the next lesson. But let's use #1 to learn the next step, POE. To go from good to great on the English test, you can't just fix a question in your head and then find an answer that matches. Instead, after you've identified what's wrong, eliminate all the choices that do not fix the error.

For question #1, the comma after *Diaz* is unnecessary and should be deleted. Cross off the answers that leave it in, choices (A) and (D).

> 1. A. ~~NO CHANGE~~
>   B. author, Junot Diaz
>   C. author Junot Diaz
>   D. ~~author, Junot Diaz,~~

Now compare the two that remain, choices (B) and (C). Do you need the comma after *author*? No, you don't need any commas, so choice (C) is the correct answer. Here's where you could have messed up if you didn't use POE: If you knew all along you didn't need any commas, you could have easily missed that new comma in choice (B) and chosen incorrectly. POE on English isn't optional or a backup when you're stuck. You have to first eliminate wrong answers and then compare what's left.

Let's go onto the next step.

Step 3: Use the Context

Even though you may struggle with time on the English test, you can't skip the non-underlined text in between questions in order to save yourself a few minutes. Take a look at this next question.

After Diaz won the 2008 Pulitzer Prize, many college literary courses <u>will add his</u>[2] works to the curriculum.

> 2. F. NO CHANGE
>   G. added
>   H. were adding
>   J. add

Don't forget to apply the first two steps. The verb in the answer choices is changing, specifically verb tense. How do you know which tense to use? Look at the beginning of the sentence: the phrase *After Diaz won* tells us we want past tense, so eliminate the choices that don't use past tense.

> 2. F. ~~NO CHANGE~~
>   G. added
>   H. were adding
>   J. ~~add~~

This is the 4 C's in action, or at least two of them: Between choices (G) and (H), choice (G) is most *concise*. The correct tense has to be *consistent* with the clues in the non-underlined portion. Between two choices that are technically grammatically correct, the more *concise* choice wins.

Don't skip from question to question. The non-underlined text provides context you need.

Let's move on to the next step.

Step 4: Trust Your Ear, But Verify

For question #2, you may have never even considered choice (H) as serious competition for choice (G). It just sounds wrong, doesn't it? Well, it turned out you were right. In fact, your ear is pretty reliable at raising the alarm for outright errors and clunky, awkward phrasing.

You should, however, always verify what your ear signals by confirming the actual error. Steps 1 and 2 will help with that: Use the answers to identify the topic, and use POE heavily.

But remember to be careful for errors your ear *won't* catch. Using the answers to identify the topic will save you there as well.

Let's try another question.

One college class chose Diaz's *The Brief Wondrous Life of Oscar Wao* as their favorite book of the semester.

3. **A.** NO CHANGE
   B. it's favorite book
   C. they're favorite book
   D. its favorite book

That sounded pretty good to us, how about you? But before we circle NO CHANGE and go on our merry way, look at the answers to identify the topic and confirm there is no error. Only the pronoun changes, so the question is testing pronouns. We'll go over all the rules about pronouns in Chapter 7, so we'll just give a short explanation here. *Their* is a plural pronoun, but *class* is singular. Cross off choices (A) and (C)— choice (C) isn't even the right type of pronoun, plural or not. Since we need a possessive pronoun, cross off choice (B) as well. Choice (D) is the correct answer.

Let's move on to our last step.

Step 5

Step 5: Don't Fix What Isn't Broken

Read the next question.

Among a generation of new American writers, Diaz has <u>emerged</u> as one of the freshest, most original voices.
        ₄

4. **F.** NO CHANGE
      G. been distinguished and deemed
      H. come on the scene as
      J. made a strong case to be called

Sounds okay, so go to Step 1, identify the topic. Remember that saved us with question #3. *Everything* seems to be changing in the answers for #4: What the question is testing isn't obvious at all. You can't confirm what you can't identify, so leave "NO CHANGE," and apply the 4 C's.

Does one of the answers fix something you missed?

Does one of the answers make the sentence better by making it more concise?

If the answer to both questions is No for all three other answers, the correct answer is choice (A), NO CHANGE.

NO CHANGE *is* a legitimate answer choice. Don't make the mistake of assuming that all questions have an error that you just can't spot. If you use the five steps of our Basic Approach, you'll catch errors your ear would miss, and you'll confidently choose NO CHANGE when it's the correct answer.

GRAMMAR REVIEW

This is not an exhaustive review of English grammar. It is an overview of the most common rules tested on the English test. We focus on the rules that show up the most AND that we know you can easily identify. In the next two chapters, we'll teach you how to crack those questions on the ACT. For now, we'll introduce you to the terms and rules you need to know.

Verbs

What's wrong with the following sentences?

1. Ryan play soccer.

2. Mary and Allison practices every day.

3. Next week, the team traveled to play its bitter rival.

4. Shivani has became the star of the team.

If you read thoughtfully, your ear probably caught all of the verb errors in these sentences. Remember, your ear will pretty reliably raise the alarm with many errors you'll encounter on the English test. You don't always need to know why a sentence is wrong to get the right answer, but the more you know why, the more you can count on getting that question right the next time it appears, and every time after that. Know the likely errors for verbs.

Subject-Verb Agreement

First, know your terms. A *subject* is the performer of an action. A *verb* is an action, feeling, or state of being. Verbs have to be consistent with their subjects. Singular subjects take the singular form of the verb, and plural subjects take plural forms of the verb.

*Ryan **plays** soccer.*

*Mary and Allison **practice** every day.*

Verb Tense

The tense of the verb changes with the time of the event.

Simple Tense

ACT tests your ability to choose from among the three simple tenses.

Past: *Last year, the team **finished** in last place.*

Present: *This year, the team **plays** a demanding schedule.*

Future: *Next week, the team **will travel** to play its bitter rival.*

Perfect Tenses

The perfect tenses provide additional ways to place an event in time. On the ACT, you may need to choose the past or future perfect to place the time of one event before another.

Past perfect: *I **had seen** the musical on Broadway before it opened in other cities.*

Present perfect: *Kelly **has danced** for several years.*

Future perfect: *Jim **will have left** by the time I will arrive.*

Irregular Verbs

ACT tests heavily the correct past *participle* of irregular verbs. Participle refers to the form the verb takes when it's paired with the helping verb *to have* to form a perfect tense. For regular verbs, the simple past tense and the past participle are the same.

*I **called** you last night. I **have called** you several times today.*

For irregular verbs, the two are different.

*Shivani **became** the star of the team,* or *Shivani **has become** the star of the team.*

Here is a list of some common irregular verbs.

Infinitive	Simple Past	Past Participle
become	became	become
begin	began	begun
blow	blew	blown
break	broke	broken
bring	brought	brought
choose	chose	chosen
come	came	come
drink	drank	drunk
drive	drove	driven
eat	ate	eaten
fall	fell	fallen
fly	flew	flown
forbid	forbade	forbidden
forget	forgot	forgotten
forgive	forgave	forgiven
freeze	froze	frozen
get	got	gotten
give	gave	given
go	went	gone
grow	grew	grown
hide	hid	hidden
know	knew	known
lay	laid	laid
lead	led	led
lie	lay	lain

Infinitive	Simple Past	Past Participle
ride	rode	ridden
ring	rang	rung
rise	rose	risen
run	ran	run
see	saw	seen
shake	shook	shaken
sing	sang	sung
speak	spoke	spoken
spring	sprang	sprung
steal	stole	stolen
swim	swam	swum
take	took	taken
teach	taught	taught
tear	tore	torn
throw	threw	thrown
wear	wore	worn
write	wrote	written

Pronouns

What's wrong with the following sentences?

1. The team nominated their goalie the most valuable player.

2. My friends and me took the train downtown.

3. Her and I worked on the group project together.

4. The crowd pushed Cesar and I onto the stage.

Pronoun Agreement

First, know your terms. *Pronouns* take the place of nouns. Pronouns have to be consistent with the nouns they replace in number and in gender.

	Female	Male	Things
Singular	she, her, hers	he, him, his	it, its
Plural	they, them, their	they, them, their	they, them, their

*The team nominated **its** goalie the most valuable player.*

Pronoun Case

Pronouns also need to be consistent with the function they perform in a sentence. There are three different cases of pronouns: *subject*, *object*, and *possessive*.

	1st person	2nd person	3rd person
Subject	I, we	you	she, he, it, they
Object	me, us	you	her, him, it, them
Possessive	my, mine, our, ours	your	her, hers, his, its, their, theirs

*My friends and **I** took the train downtown.*

***She** and I worked on the group project together.*

*The crowd pushed Cesar and **me** onto the stage.*

Modifiers

What's wrong with these sentences?

1. No one took her warnings serious.

2. Blizzard is a charmingly energetically puppy.

3. Farid is more busy than Wesley is.

4. Lara was the beautifulest girl at the prom.

Adjectives and Adverbs

Adjectives modify nouns. *Adverbs* modify everything else, including verbs, adjectives, and other adverbs. Most adverbs are formed by adding *-ly* to the end of an adjective.

*No one took her warnings **seriously**.*

*Blizzard is a charmingly **energetic** puppy.*

Comparisons and Superlatives

For most adjectives, an *-er* at the end makes a comparison, and an *-est* makes a superlative. But some adjectives need instead the word *more* for a comparison and the word *most* for a superlative.

*Farid is **busier** than Wesley is.*

*Lara was the **most beautiful** girl at the prom.*

In the following chapters, we'll show you how these rules appear on the ACT and how to crack those questions. We'll also discuss some of the more difficult and challenging concepts that you may face.

Summary

o   Identify what the question is testing by changes in the answer choices.

o   Use POE heavily.

o   Don't skip the non-underlined text: Use it for context.

o   Trust your ear, but verify by the rules.

o   NO CHANGE is a legitimate answer choice.

o   Good writing should be complete, consistent, clear, and concise.

Chapter 6
Complete

The ACT English test contains a number of questions that test sentence structure and punctuation. This chapter discusses how to identify ideas as complete or incomplete and then explains how to punctuate different ideas. In addition to covering punctuation, the chapter also covers how to change ideas with the addition or removal of conjunctions.

COMPLETE AND INCOMPLETE IDEAS

Many questions on the English test involve sentence structure and punctuation. The correct structure and punctuation all depend on whether the ideas are complete or incomplete.

A complete idea can stand on its own, whether it's the entire sentence or just one part. Let's look at some examples.

1. *Amanda throws strikes.*
2. *Go Bears!*
3. *Who won the game?*
4. *The team celebrated after they won the game.*

Think of a complete idea as one part of a conversation. You don't have to say a lot to hold up one side of a conversation, but you can't leave your listener hanging. You have to finish your sentence. You can give commands, and you can ask questions, too. Your listeners don't have to know what you're talking about: They just have to wait for you to finish to ask questions of their own. *What game are you asking me about? How did the team celebrate?*

In grammar terms, a complete idea must have a subject and a verb. Let's break down the examples above.

	Subject	Verb
1	*Amanda*	*throws*
2	You (understood)	*Go*
3	*Who*	*won*
4	*team* and *they*	*celebrated* and *won*

An incomplete idea can't stand on its own. Look at the following examples.

1. *The batter who hit second*
2. *Since you bought the hotdogs*
3. *To get a batter out*
4. *The team grabbed*

If anyone began a conversation with any of these, you would be waiting for the speaker to finish before you could speak. That's a sure sign all of the examples are incomplete: None of them is finished, and all would leave you hanging as a listener.

Now, in real life terms, we may think some of those examples could be fine as answers to these questions: *Who got the run? Why did you buy the sodas? Why did he pitch a fastball?* Remember, however, that in real life we don't always follow the conventional rules when we speak. So let's define an incomplete idea in grammatical terms:

An incomplete idea is always missing something, whether a subject and verb (example #3), the main idea (example #2), or the rest of an idea (examples #1 and #4). None of these could stand on its own, and each would need to link up with another idea to make a sentence. ACT tests heavily how to link ideas with punctuation and conjunctions, so let's see how that works.

For the Record
Semicolons can be used to separate items on a very complicated list, but ACT almost never tests this. Exclamation points and question marks show up only occasionally.

STOP PUNCTUATION

Imagine two trucks heading toward a busy intersection, one from the south and one from the west. If there were no traffic signals at the intersection, the two trucks would crash. Writing is just like traffic, depending on punctuation to prevent ideas from crashing into each other.

Two complete ideas are like two trucks and need the strongest punctuation to separate them. All of the punctuation in the box below can come in between only two complete ideas.

> **STOP Punctuation:**
>
> Period (.) Semicolon (;) Question mark (?) Exclamation mark (!)

Let's see how this works in a question.

Use the 4 C's: Be *Concise*.

After the thumping music started. The
<u>   </u>
                        1
<u>bird began</u> to dance.
        1

1. **A.** NO CHANGE
   B. started, the bird began,
   C. started; the bird began
   D. started, the bird began

Here's How to Crack It

Begin with Step 1 of the Basic Approach you learned in Chapter 5. Use the differences and similarities in the answer choices to identify the topic. Whenever a question is testing Stop punctuation, use the Vertical Line Test. Draw a vertical line where the Stop punctuation is to help you determine if the ideas before and after the line are complete or incomplete.

After the thumping music <u>started.|The</u>
                                   1
<u>bird began</u> to dance.
        1

After the thumping music started is incomplete. *The bird began to dance* is complete.

Since Stop punctuation can come in between *only* two complete ideas, go to Step 2 and use POE. Eliminate all the answers that don't fix the error, and compare those that are left.

1. A. ~~NO CHANGE~~
   B. started, the bird began,
   C. ~~started; the bird began~~
   D. started, the bird began

Using Steps 3 and 4, we can use the context of the rest of the sentence to confirm that we don't need the second comma that choice (B) offers. Choice (D) is the correct answer.

———————◯———————

GO PUNCTUATION

Let's go back to the traffic analogy. Imagine a road with a stop sign at every block. Those stop signs prevent accidents, but when rush hour hits, traffic backs up. Stop signs need to be used strategically, so that they don't cause more problems than they solve. Punctuation functions the same way: use it to prevent accidents, but don't slow down ideas and make the sentence longer than necessary, or just plain incomprehensible.

A sentence is a complete idea, regardless of how many complete and incomplete ideas it's made up of, so it will always end with Stop punctuation. Within a sentence, use punctuation only to avoid an error or to make your meaning clear. Use Stop punctuation in between two complete ideas. Use a comma to slow down, but not stop, ideas. If you don't need to stop or slow down, don't use any punctuation. Keep traffic moving, and keep ideas flowing.

Here's another example.

———————◯———————

I wondered how Snowball had learned to dance, and asked his trainer.
                     2

2. F. NO CHANGE
   G. to dance and asked his trainer.
   H. to dance; and asked his trainer.
   J. to dance. And asked his trainer.

Check for Commas
Look out for
- words and phrases in a series
- introductory phrases and words
- mid-sentence phrases that are not essential to the sentence

Here's How to Crack It

Use the Vertical Line Test whenever you see Stop punctuation, either in the sentence as written or among the answer choices. When you draw your line in between *dance* and *and*, the first idea is complete, and the second idea is incomplete. Eliminate choices (H) and (J). There is no reason to slow down the ideas at all, so eliminate choice (F). The correct answer is choice (G). By the way, this question isn't testing whether you can start a sentence with *and*—that's a good example of an outdated rule few enforce anymore, so ACT doesn't test it. Choices (H) and (J) are wrong because the idea to the right of the Stop punctuation is incomplete.

Commas

Commas work like blinking yellow lights: They slow down but do not stop ideas. Since the goal is to be concise, use a comma only for a specific reason. On the ACT, there are only four reasons to use a comma.

Stop

A comma by itself can't come in between two complete ideas, but it can when it's paired with what we call FANBOYS: *for, and, nor, but, or, yet, so.* A comma plus any of these is the equivalent of Stop punctuation. These words also impact direction, which might influence the correct answer.

> *The music changed suddenly, but Snowball picked up the new beat.*

Draw a vertical line on either side of *but* to help break the sentence into separate ideas. *The music changed suddenly* is complete. *Snowball picked up the new beat* is complete.

For the record, all conjunctions link things, but coordinating conjunctions—that is, FANBOYS—specifically come in between two ideas and are never a part of either idea.

Go

A comma can link an incomplete idea to a complete idea, in either order.

> *After Snowball stopped dancing, the trainer gave the bird another treat.*

> *Snowball rocked out to Lady Gaga, oblivious to the growing crowd of fans.*

Lists

Use a comma to separate items on a list.

> *Snowball prefers songs with a regular, funky beat.*

Regular and *funky* are both describing *beat*. If you would say *regular and funky* then you can say *regular, funky*.

> *Snowball seems to like best the music of The Backstreet Boys, Lady Gaga, and Queen.*

Whenever you have three or more items on a list, always use a comma before the "and" preceding the final item. This is a rule that not everyone agrees on, but if you apply the 4 C's, the extra comma makes your meaning *Clear*. On the ACT, always use the comma before the "and."

Unnecessary Info

Use a pair of commas around unnecessary information.

> *Further research has shown that parrots, including cockatoos, can dance in perfect synch to music.*

If information is necessary to the sentence in either meaning or structure, don't use the commas. If the meaning would be exactly the same but the additional information makes the sentence more interesting, use a pair of commas—or a pair of dashes—around the information.

Try the next questions.

Many people point to dog dancing competitions to argue that birds are not the only animals that can dance.

3. **A.** NO CHANGE
   B. argue, that birds are not the only animals,
   C. argue, that birds are not the only animals
   D. argue that birds are not the only animals,

Here's How to Crack It

The changes in the answers identify the topic of the question: commas. Remember, there are only four reasons to use a comma on the ACT, and if you can't name the reason you shouldn't use one. If you thought the sentence was fine, leave NO CHANGE, and confirm none of the answers fixed something you missed. Think of ACT's comma rules, and determine if any apply here. With neither STOP punctuation nor FANBOYS in play, it can't be two complete ideas or a list. If the Unnecessary Info rule is in play, choice (B) would mean that *that birds are not the only animals* isn't necessary, but the sentence would make no sense, so eliminate choice (B). The only other possible rule is GO, linking a complete idea to an incomplete idea. Neither choice (C) nor (D) offers a complete idea on one side of a comma, so eliminate both. The correct answer is choice (A), NO CHANGE.

Scientists now believe that the ability to mimic, which requires complex circuitry, for vocal learning, is necessary for an animal to keep a synchronized beat.

4. **F.** NO CHANGE
   G. mimic, which requires complex circuitry
   H. mimic, which, requires complex circuitry
   J. mimic which requires complex circuitry

Here's How to Crack It

The changes in the answers identify the topic of the question: commas. By reading to the end of the sentence, you catch the comma that isn't underlined. Since the Unnecessary Info rule requires two commas, not three, check that rule first. The extra information is *which requires complex circuitry for vocal learning,* and thus the correct answer is choice (G).

COLONS AND SINGLE DASHES

Colons and single dashes are very specific pieces of punctuation, and they are very flexible. They can link a complete idea to either an incomplete idea or another complete idea. The complete idea must come first, and the second idea will be a definition, explanation, or list. Since they are always used with at least one complete idea, use the Vertical Line Test whenever they appear in and out of answer choices.

Let's see two examples.

Need More Grammar Help?
Check out *Grammar Smart*

Parrots don't respond well to genres with the least noticeable upbeat; waltzes and salsa.
₅

5. **A.** NO CHANGE
   B. upbeat, waltzes, and salsa.
   C. upbeat: waltzes, and salsa.
   D. upbeat: waltzes and salsa.

Here's How to Crack It

Draw the vertical line in between *upbeat* and *waltzes*. The first idea is complete, but the second is incomplete. Eliminate choice (A). The list isn't *upbeat, waltzes, and salsa*, so eliminate choice (B). The list is only two things, so the comma in choice (C) is unnecessary. The correct answer is choice (D).

A waltz is particularly difficult—it follows a three-beat pattern.
₆

6. **F.** NO CHANGE
   G. difficult it follows a three-beat pattern.
   H. difficult, it follows a three-beat pattern.
   J. difficult, it follows, a three-beat pattern.

Here's How to Crack It

Draw the vertical line in between *difficult* and *it*. Both are complete ideas, so eliminate choices (G), (H), and (J). Choice (F) is correct.

Identical Punctuation

In question #6, a period, a semicolon, or a colon could have been used. Notice, however, that none of those appeared among the answer choices. ACT won't make you evaluate those subtle differences that might make one punctuation mark better than the others when they all perform essentially identical functions. Knowing which forms of punctuation are identical is a powerful POE tool. After all, you can't have two right answers, so if two or more choices are identical, they all must be wrong.

CONJUNCTIONS

Punctuation isn't the only way to link ideas. On some of the more difficult questions on sentence structure, you have to change the ideas by adding or deleting the conjunction.

Here are some of the more common conjunctions you may see.

> although, as, because, if, since, that, until, what,
> which, while, when, where, who, whom

Proper grammarians might object to calling *what, which, when, where, who,* and *whom* conjunctions, but the technical terms aren't important on the English test. It's not as if ACT makes you name any part of speech, and all that matters is that those words, when they are used in a sentence instead of a question, act just like conjunctions. They make an idea incomplete. (Look at how we used *when* in the next to last sentence in this paragraph!)

Add a conjunction to make an idea incomplete, or take one out to make the idea complete.

Let's see how this works in a few questions.

———————◯———————

The African grey parrot, which also <u>mimics</u> human speech and therefore can dance.
₇

7. **A.** NO CHANGE
   B. parrot which
   C. parrot that
   D. parrot

Here's How to Crack It

If conjunctions change in the answer choices, it is likely testing Complete. When you read to the end of the sentence, you're left hanging, waiting for the main point about African grey parrots. The sentence is incomplete, and the only way to fix it is to take out the conjunction. Choice (D) is correct. It's no coincidence that it's the most concise.

———————◯———————

Try another.

———————◯———————

<u>The videos of Snowball dancing have</u> sparked a serious area of study, researchers admit they appreciate the sheer entertainment value.
₈

8. **F.** NO CHANGE
   G. Although the videos of Snowball
   H. The videos appearing all over the internet of Snowball
   J. Since the videos of Snowball

Here's How to Crack It

If it sounded fine to your ear, using the answers to identify the topic will help you spot something you missed or verify that NO CHANGE is correct. If conjunctions change in the answer choices, it is likely testing Complete. Check if the entire sentence makes a complete idea and that all ideas within are joined correctly. There are two complete ideas in the sentence, separated only by a comma. A comma alone is GO punctuation, so eliminate choices (F) and (H). You need a choice with a conjunction added to the first idea, making it incomplete. Conjunctions vary by direction, which we'll discuss in the next lesson. The two ideas show a contrast—*serious* and *entertainment*—so choice (G) is correct.

———————◯———————

Complete Drill

In the drill below, you will find only questions that focus on sentence construction. Before you start, take a few moments to go back over the review material and techniques. Use the basic approach explained in Chapter 5. Answers are in Chapter 24.

When you see the gingerbread houses of Roskilde with their neatly thatched roofs, the gardens filled with flowers, blooms, and the happy smiles on the fresh-faced inhabitants, it is difficult to believe that this town was once the home of a more warlike people—the Vikings. Roskilde's main museum is devoted to those early inhabitants, the Vikings once wandered throughout Europe, and by some reports, may have traveled all the way to North America as well. The museum sits on a site at the edge of Roskilde fiord. Where the Viking ships were once launched on voyages of conquest and plunder. Until 20 years ago used only by the fishermen who still ply their trade in the fiord, since the craggy shoreline must now be shared with tourists who arrive in buses to watch local artisans build the Viking ships in the traditional manner.

My most memorable vacation as a child was a trip I took to the Grand Canyon with my grandfather. I was only eleven at the time, and had never been outside the city of Boston. My romantic picture of the West complete with cowboys and Indians was a little out of date, but the incredible scenery took my breath away. On our first day we decided that the best way to explore the vast beauty of the canyon would be to take a

1. A. NO CHANGE
   B. flowers and blooms,
   C. flowers; blooms
   D. flowers, blooms

2. F. NO CHANGE
   G. inhabitants the Vikings
   H. inhabitants. The Vikings
   J. inhabitants, the Vikings,

3. A. NO CHANGE
   B. fiord. Where,
   C. fiord, where
   D. fiord; where

4. F. NO CHANGE
   G. the craggy shoreline must now be shared with tourists who arrive in buses
   H. since the craggy shoreline must now be shared with tourists, who arrive in buses,
   J. the craggy shoreline must now be shared with tourists, who arrive in buses

5. A. NO CHANGE
   B. the time and had never been
   C. the time; never been
   D. the time. Never been

6. F. NO CHANGE
   G. West—complete with cowboys and Indians—
   H. West—complete with cowboys and Indians
   J. West; complete with cowboys and Indians,

7. A. NO CHANGE
   B. On our first day we,
   C. On our first day, we
   D. On, our first day, we

mule-packed trip down one of the trails. I rode along, on my
8

mules back, I noticed that each rock stratum displayed a
8

distinctive hue; gray and violet in some places, dark brown and
9

green in others. The rock layers of the Grand Canyon are

mostly made of limestone, freshwater shale and sandstone.
10

8. F. NO CHANGE
   G. I rode along on my mule's back,
   H. I was riding along on my mule's back,
   J. As I rode along on my mule's back,

9. A. NO CHANGE
   B. hue. Gray
   C. hue, gray
   D. hue: gray

10. F. NO CHANGE
    G. limestone, freshwater, shale, and sandstone.
    H. limestone, freshwater shale, and sandstone.
    J. limestone freshwater shale and sandstone

Summary

o   ACT writers like to test your knowledge of whether sentences are put together and punctuated correctly.

o   A complete idea can stand on its own as a complete sentence even though it may be part of a longer sentence. An incomplete idea can't stand on its own as a complete sentence and must be appropriately linked to a complete idea.

o   Stop punctuation includes a period, a semicolon, an exclamation mark, a question mark, and a comma plus FANBOYS. Stop punctuation can come in between only complete ideas.

o   Go punctuation includes a comma and nothing at all. Go punctuation can link anything except for two complete ideas.

o   Always put a comma before "and" at the end of a list with three or more items.

o   Always put a pair of commas around unnecessary info.

o   Colons and single dashes must follow a complete idea, but can precede a complete or incomplete idea.

o   Conjunctions make an idea incomplete.

Chapter 7
Consistent, Clear, and Concise

The key to an outstanding ACT English score is to focus on the topics that show up the most often *and* which are both easy to identify and simple to fix. In this chapter, we'll teach you how to crack questions on verbs, pronouns, apostrophes, and transitions. For each topic, following the rules makes good writing consistent, clear, and concise.

VERBS

A verb expresses an action, feeling, or state of being. The form of a verb depends on the number of the subject—singular or plural—the time of the event, and the presence of helping verbs. Whenever you spot the verb changing among the answer choices, use these three steps along with your Basic Approach.

1. Identify the subject. The verb must be consistent with its subject. Singular subject with a singular verb, and plural subject with a plural verb.
2. Check the tense. The tense must be consistent with the setting and the participle. Use the context of the non-underlined portion to determine if the verb should be past, present, or future.
3. Be concise. Pick the shortest answer free of any errors.

Here's an example.

Each of the first three taxis I saw were too far away to hail.
1

1. A. NO CHANGE
   B. are too far away
   C. is too far away
   D. was too far away

Here's How to Crack It

Use the changes in the answers to identify verbs as the topic ACT is testing. Both tense and number seem to be changing, so find the subject first. What was too far away? *Each* of the taxis. *Each* is singular, so eliminate the plural forms of the verb, choices (A) and (B). Now check the tense. *Saw* is past tense, so choose the past tense, choice (D).

Tricky Pronouns

Question #1 wasn't testing pronouns directly—the changes among the answer choices were verbs. To answer correctly, however, you had to know that the pronoun *each* is singular. The following pronouns are all singular.

anybody	either	nobody
anyone	everybody	somebody
each	everyone	someone

Your ear should reliably raise the alarm over a subject-verb agreement error, both for tricky pronouns and regular nouns. Consider the following examples.

*Somebody **love** me.*
*Everyone **like** ice cream.*
*Each **are** beautiful.*
*Nobody **do** it better.*

Your ear probably automatically fixed these.

*Somebody **loves** me.*
*Everyone **likes** ice cream.*
*Each **is** beautiful.*
*Nobody **does** it better.*

This is why your ear can frequently help you eliminate the wrong answers on verb questions. But remember Step 4 of the Basic Approach: trust, but verify your ear. Confirm the error by making sure you have correctly identified the subject. Another way ACT can make identifying the subject difficult is with prepositional phrases, another trap in question #1.

Prepositional Phrases

Another way ACT made question #1 confusing was by burying the subject to the left of the prepositional phrase. *Each **of the first three taxis** I saw were too far away to hail.* Prepositions are little words that show a relationship between nouns. Some examples are *at, between, by, in, of, on, to,* and *with.* A prepositional phrase modifies—that is, describes—a noun. ACT will add prepositional phrases to distract you from the subject, so be on the lookout for them. Always look to the left of the preposition to find your subject. Try the following examples. Does the subject agree with its verb?

Only one of the dresses fit me.
A selection of fruit, cheese, and nuts were served at the party.
The argument between Pat and Ron sadden all of us.
The books on the table is due back to the library.

Cross out the prepositional phrases to find the subject and confirm the verb.

*Only **one** ~~of the dresses~~ **fits** me.*
*A **selection** ~~of fruit, cheese, and nuts~~ **was** served at the party.*
*The **argument** ~~between Pat and Ron~~ **saddens** all of us.*
*The **books** ~~on the table~~ **are** due back to the library.*

Irregular Verb Participles

ACT can make verb tense difficult as well. Most tense questions are straightforward choices of past, present, or future. However, ACT loves to test the correct past participle for irregular verbs.

Let's try another ACT question.

I woken up at 10:30 to find that my <u> </u>
                 2
alarm clock had failed to go off.

2. **F.** NO CHANGE
   G. had woke up
   H. woke up
   J. waked up

Here's How to Crack It

The changes in the answers identify verbs as the topic. The subject, *I*, doesn't change the form, and all of the choices are in past tense. Use POE to get rid of all the wrong answers that do not use the correct form of the irregular verb, *to wake.* Use *woke* on its own but *woken* with *had* in front. Choice (H) is the only correct form.

Regular verbs follow a predictable pattern.

*Present: I **study** for the ACT every day.*
*Present perfect: I **have studied** for months.*
*Simple past: I **studied** all day yesterday.*
*Past perfect: I **had studied** for the SAT.*

Irregular verbs are the problem. While you can usually use your ear to find the correct participle, here is a small sample of some common irregular verbs. The *infinitive* is the form of the verb used with *to*; the simple past works on its own, without a helping verb; the *past participle* works with a form of the helping verb *to have*.

*Infinitive: Jacob would like **to become** a biotech engineer.*
*Present perfect: Hannah **has become** a star swimmer.*
*Simple past: Samara **became** a voracious reader.*
*Past perfect: Jonah **had become** tired of practicing.*

Let's try another ACT question.

———————○———————

My boss was mad that I had forgot to
<u>   </u>
                            3
<u>bring the report I had been preparing at home.</u>
                            3

3. **A.** NO CHANGE
   B. had forgotten to bring the report that I had prepared at home.
   C. had forgotten to bring the report that had been prepared at home by me.
   D. had forgotten to bring the report I had been preparing at home.

Here's How to Crack It

The changes in the answer choices identify verbs as the topic, specifically past participles. Choice (A) incorrectly uses the simple past *forgot* with the helping verb *had*, so you can eliminate it right away. Choices (B), (C), and (D) all fix that error, so compare the differences among them. Choice (B) is the most concise, and neither choices (C) nor (D) fixed something choice (B) missed. Both just made the sentence longer, so the correct answer is choice (B).

———————○———————

> ### You Don't Have to Be Perfect
> The perfect tenses change the time of an event in subtle ways. You will never need to identify by name a particular tense on the ACT, nor choose between the present and present perfect. Choose the past perfect to establish an order of one event happening in the past before another.

Need a refresher on irregular verbs? Check out the table in Chapter 5.

Passive Voice

In question #3, choice (B) was the most concise in part because it uses the active voice. Choice (C) is passive, which make the sentence much longer. Both active and passive voice are grammatically correct, they just describe one event in two different ways. Compare the following sentences:

Beatrice prepared the fine meal.

The fine meal was prepared by Beatrice.

Beatrice makes the meal in both sentences. Active voice preserves the performer of the action, *Beatrice,* as the subject. Passive voice promotes the receiver of the action, in this case *the meal,* to subject and changes the verb by adding the helping verb *was.*

How to Spot Passive Voice

Look for forms of the verb *to be* and the preposition *by.*

How to Crack It

Choose passive voice *only* when you're confident that the other three choices contain a grammatical error.

PRONOUNS

Pronouns take the place of nouns and make your writing more concise. On the ACT, several questions will test the correct usage of pronouns. Whenever you spot pronouns changing among the answers, use these two steps with your Basic Approach.

1. Find the original. The pronoun has to be consistent in number and gender with the noun it replaces and other related pronouns.
2. Check the case. Choose the correct pronoun based on its specific function in the sentence.

Let's try a few examples.

─────────────────○─────────────────

Have you ever had a day when you

wished <u>you could have</u> just stayed in bed?
₄

4. **F.** NO CHANGE
   G. you could of
   H. one could of
   J. one could have

Here's How to Crack It

Nothing seems obviously wrong, so leave choice (F) and use the answers to see if you missed something. Pronouns and verbs are changing—sort of; *of* is not a verb, even if it sounds like *have*. Eliminate choices (G) and (H). The pronoun should be consistent with the *you* in the non-underlined portion, so eliminate choice (J). Choice (F) is correct.

─────────────────○─────────────────

Try another.

─────────────────○─────────────────

The taxi driver <u>who finally picked up my</u>
₅

<u>boss and I</u> wouldn't take credit cards.
₅

5. **A.** NO CHANGE
   B. whom finally picked up my boss and I
   C. who finally picked up my boss and me
   D. which finally picked up my boss and myself

Revisit Chapter 5 for lists of different types of pronouns.

Here's How to Crack It

The changes in the answers identify pronouns as the topic of the sentence. There are two pronouns in the underlined portion, so consider both and follow your two steps. *Taxi driver* is a person, and which is only for things. *Myself* is correct only for emphasis (I myself don't know the answer) or when the subject and object are the same (I corrected myself). Cross off choice (D). Check the case for *who* and *I,* and don't worry—it's perfectly okay to check *I* first since everyone is scared of "who" versus "whom" (see "Who versus Whom" below). For case, cross off everything except for the pronoun and the verb. *Picked up I* is incorrect, because *I* is a subject pronoun, so eliminate choices (A) and (B). The correct choice is (C), and you didn't even have to worry about "who" and "whom." Now go learn about them so you don't have to depend on luck the next time.

Who Versus Whom

Who is the subject pronoun. *Whom* is the object pronoun. Why do they seem so hard to all of us? Very few movies and TV shows use *whom* when it's needed, and most of us do the same in our regular conversations.

How to Crack It

Whenever you see *who* and *whom* tested on the ACT, try *he* and *him* in their place. If you would say *he called me,* you would say *who called me.* If you would say *I called him,* you would say *whom I called.* Don't worry about how the words flip: just match your "m" pronouns and you're fine.

APOSTROPHES

Similar to pronouns, apostrophes make your writing more concise. They have two uses, possession and contraction.

Possession

To show possession with single nouns, add *'s*, and with plural nouns, add just the apostrophe. For tricky plurals that do not end in *s*, add *'s*.

Consider the following examples.

The new car of Peter = Peter's new car
The room of the girls = the girls' room.
The room of the men = the men's room.

To show possession with pronouns, never use apostrophes. Use the appropriate possessive pronoun.

__His__ car.
__Their__ room.
__Its__ door.

Contractions

Whenever you see a pronoun with an apostrophe, it's (it is) a contraction, which means the apostrophe takes the place of at least one letter.

Consider the following examples.

It is important. = __It's__ important.
They are happy to help. = __They're__ happy to help.
Who is the leader of the group? = __Who's__ the leader of the group?

Because these particular contractions sound the same as some possessive pronouns, these questions can be very tricky on the ACT. You can't use your ear—you have to know the above rules. Let's look at some sample ACT questions.

Revisit Chapter 5 to review a list of possessive pronouns.

Pronouns Most Frequently Misused
The ACT test writers will sometimes try to confuse you by presenting both a possessive pronoun and the same pronoun in a contraction as answer choices. Do you know the difference between these words: *whose, who's, its, it's*?

I watched in dismay as my laptop was

crushed beneath the <u>taxis wheels'</u>.
₆

6. **F.** NO CHANGE
   G. taxis' wheels.
   H. taxi's wheels'.
   J. taxi's wheels.

Here's How to Crack It

The changes in the answer choices identify apostrophes as the topic. Use POE heavily with apostrophes: eliminate all the answers that are wrong. If you just try to fix it in your head and find a match, you'll likely miss something. *Wheels* don't "possess" anything, so eliminate choices (F) and (H). There is only one taxi, so choose the singular, choice (J).

<u>Its'</u> screen was smashed to pieces.
₇

7. **A.** NO CHANGE
   B. Their screen
   C. It's screen
   D. Its screen

Here's How to Crack It

The changes in the answer choices identify apostrophes/pronouns as the topic. There is no such word as *its'*, so eliminate choice (A). The *laptop* (context from non-underlined portion in prior question) is singular, so eliminate choice (B). To determine if you need the possessive or a contraction, expand out to *it is*. *It is screen* makes no sense, so choose the possessive pronoun, choice (D).

TRANSITIONS

In Chapter 6, we used traffic as an analogy to explain punctuation. If good writing is like a pleasant drive, then transitions are road signs, preventing you from getting lost and helping you make important turns. Good transitions are consistent with the flow of ideas.

Many words can act as transitions. Some are specific to the context, where only one word will fit the precise meaning. But others are just slight variations, giving you directions: *turn around* or *keep going*. Here's a partial list.

Turn Around

although, but, despite, even though, however, nonetheless, nevertheless, or, yet

Keep Going

and, because, finally, furthermore, moreover, since, so, thus, therefore

---

Try an example.

I apologized for not having the report ready, <u>since she</u> had told me the report wasn't due for another week.
₈

8. **F.** NO CHANGE
   G. even though she
   H. because she
   J. and she

Here's How to Crack It

The changes in the answer choices are transition words, but they are also FAN-BOYS and conjunctions. Before you consider direction, make sure the sentence is complete and that all ideas within the sentence are joined correctly. All are correct and complete, but the sentence doesn't make sense because the direction is wrong. It is a transitions question. The two ideas on either side of the transition word disagree, so choose a *turn around* word. Only choice (G) makes sense.

CONCISE

All the 4 C's are important on the ACT. They are your framework for understanding the topics that you can identify and your strategy to conquer the questions whose topics you can't identify. But concise isn't just a strategy or a tool used to understand certain grammar rules. Sometimes, ACT tests it directly.

Try the following examples.

Next, my boss was furious that I was late.
9

9. **A.** NO CHANGE
   B. My boss
   C. Then, my boss
   D. Next my boss

Here's How to Crack It

The changes in the answer choices identify transitions as the topic, with possibly commas as well. Use POE. The words *then* and *next* mean the same thing used in this context. If both could be right, both must be wrong. Eliminate choices (A) and (C). *Next* should have a comma after it because it's an introductory idea, so eliminate choice (D) also. The correct answer is choice (B) because you do not need a transition word here.

ACT will frequently test concise in a transitions question. If you don't need a transition word for your sentence to be either complete or clear, don't use it. In the answer choices for question #9, note how *my boss* appeared in each, and one choice featured only *my boss* (and was correct). That is a reliable sign ACT is testing concise.

Try these additional questions.

I was already an hour and a half late for

work and not on time.
—————————
10

10. F. NO CHANGE
    G. work, and behind schedule.
    H. work and delayed in getting the morning started.
    J. work.

Here's How to Crack It

The appearance of *work* in every choice and by itself in one identifies the topic as concise. Use POE and pay attention to the non-underlined portion of the sentence for context. The narrator has already established she's late, so all of the other choices are unnecessarily wordy. The correct answer is choice (J).

I had left the lights on the previous

evening, and my car wouldn't start. Many
new cars have separate electrical boards for
—————————
11
the lights, so the battery won't drain.
—————————
11

11. A. NO CHANGE
    B. Batteries should be replaced every five years.
    C. I plan to buy a new car next year.
    D. DELETE the underlined portion.

Here's How to Crack It

The presence of DELETE is a sign the question might be testing concise, but it doesn't guarantee choice (D) is the answer. Read the answer choices through before making a decision. None of the other sentences add any useful info to the first sentence. Cross off the first three choices. In fact, the sentence *is* irrelevant to the passage, and Choice (D) is the correct answer.

There is no reliable pattern of how many times DELETE will be the correct answer on any given ACT. Always be biased toward DELETE. Unless deleting the underlined portion would create an error or drastically change the meaning, choose it.

Consistent, Clear, and Concise Drill

In the drill below, you will find questions focusing only on consistent, clear, and concise. Before you start, take a few moments to go back over the review material and techniques. Use the basic approach explained in Chapter 5. Answers are in Chapter 24.

Our Family Has Chemistry

There was always one big difference between my twin brother and I. He was good at subjects such as English and
<u>1</u>

history, while I was better at math and science. <u>We were always</u>
<u>thoughtful; he would be a professor and I would be a doctor.</u>
<u>2</u>
Because of this, I never felt particularly competitive with him
and was unconcerned when we accepted offers from the same

college. However, once we started, <u>we would find that things did</u>
<u>3</u>

not work out quite as <u>I would expect.</u>
<u>4</u>

I would never <u>believe</u> it if he hadn't told me himself, but all
<u>5</u>
of a sudden, my brother wanted to be a doctor, too. I can't say
that I was too happy about the situation, and I told him so. It was
fine if he wanted to "make a difference" and "help humanity,"
but as far as I was concerned, he could find his own way to do it.
Not surprisingly, he didn't see things that way; the next day, he
was sitting beside me in the front row of the lecture hall,

waiting for biology class to begin.

I wasn't too <u>worried because</u> I thought that a few days of
<u>6</u>
lectures on stoichiometry and the Krebs cycle would be enough
to send him running back to the English department for good.

1. A. NO CHANGE
   B. and me.
   C. and me were.
   D. and I had.

2. F. NO CHANGE
   G. Thoughtful as we were,
   H. I always thought that
   J. Although we were thoughtful,

3. A. NO CHANGE
   B. he found
   C. one had found
   D. I found

4. F. NO CHANGE
   G. had expected.
   H. was expecting.
   J. expect.

5. A. NO CHANGE
   B. of believed
   C. believed
   D. have believed

6. F. NO CHANGE
   G. worried, but
   H. worried, although
   J. worried, despite the fact that

However, as the weeks passed, this did not happen. I found that while we were struggling to maintain a B+ average, my brother was getting straight A's. To make matters worse, he seemed to be enjoying himself.

Determined to outdo him, I was thrown into my work. I went to the library every night, smuggling in big cups of coffee, and stayed until closing time.

I took a summer job working in a professors chemistry lab. By the end of the summer, I decided to apply to graduate school in chemistry instead of medical school.

7. **A.** NO CHANGE
   B. he was
   C. I was
   D. they were

8. **F.** NO CHANGE
   G. threw it
   H. threw myself
   J. was throwing everything

9. **A.** NO CHANGE
   B. professor's chemistry lab.
   C. professors chemistry's lab.
   D. professors' chemistry lab.

Summary

o Verbs, pronouns, apostrophes, and transitions are heavily tested on the ACT.

o All four are readily identifiable from changes in the answer choices, and all have relatively few rules to use to evaluate the question.

o The 4 C's can be applied to evaluate any question whose topic you can't identify. ACT also tests concise as its own topic.

o Be biased toward the choice that says DELETE, but do not assume it will be the correct answer all or even half the time.

Chapter 8
Rhetorical Skills

ACT categorizes the questions on the English test as either Rhetorical Skills or Usage and Mechanics. For most questions, the Basic Approach used to crack them is the same, regardless of how ACT labels them. Some questions, however, require a different approach. In this chapter, we'll teach you how to crack questions that ask for wrong answers, as well as questions on strategy and order.

EXCEPT/LEAST/NOT

You know a question is tricky when the right answer is wrong. That is, if the question asks you to identify the choice that is "NOT acceptable," you have to cross off three answers that work and choose the one that doesn't.

The EXCEPT/LEAST/NOT questions, or E/L/N for short, hide in plain sight, posing a challenge to spot. When most "questions" on the ACT feature only four answer choices, you could easily miss the presence of a bona fide question. Moreover, many of the topics on E/L/N will look familiar: Stop/Go punctuation and transition questions are two topics heavily tested in this format, so the four answers look pretty much the same way they always do.

For the Record
Not all EXCEPT/LEAST/NOT questions are Rhetorical Skills questions by ACT standards. Our argument is that when most of the "questions" are just four answer choices, the presence of a true question demands a different category and different approach.

POE provides your key to cracking these: eliminate all choices that *could* work. Cross off the EXCEPT/LEAST/NOT word and then use POE to cross off the answers that do work. NO CHANGE is almost never an option on these. Use the sentence as it is written as your standard of comparison for the answer choices. Let's try an example.

Be on the look out for E/L/N questions: expect as many as 3–4 *per passage*.

I gave my information to the director of

the animal shelter. She promised to contact
                    1
me if any French Bulldogs came in.

1. Which of the following alternatives to the underlined portion would be NOT acceptable?

    A. shelter; she promised
    B. shelter, and she promised
    C. shelter, she promised
    D. shelter, who promised

Here's How to Crack It

Cross out NOT. Since the sentence used Stop punctuation, use POE to eliminate first all answers that are Stop punctuation, choices (A) and (B). Before you worry about choice (D), which changes the wording, focus on the remaining choice with the exact same wording as the original sentence. Remember that a comma alone can never be Stop Punctuation, so choice (C) is grammatically wrong—and therefore the correct answer here.

Word Choice and Idioms

Two of the most popular and challenging topics ACT tests are word choice and idioms, either in regular or E/L/N format. Word choice refers to selecting the precise word that fits with the context. An idiom is an expression that requires a specific preposition. Idioms follow no grammatical rules—they are what they are.

Both word choice and idioms will be easy to spot by the changes in the answers, but neither fits our standards for being easy to fix. While they tend to be fairly common words and expressions, you'll either know them or you won't. ACT rarely if ever repeats any words or idioms, so there is no way to prepare for the particular ones that will show up on your ACT. Use POE heavily with these, and don't let them drag you down in your pacing.

Try additional examples.

I remember well the day I first saw

Wheezie at the animal shelter. In truth, I think

Wheezie is the one who <u>adopted</u> me.
      2
    2. Which of the following alternatives to the underlined word would be LEAST acceptable?

    F. selected
    G. assumed
    H. picked
    J. chose

Here's How to Crack It

Cross out LEAST. Use POE, trying each answer choice in place of *adopted*. Choices (F), (H), and (J) could all mean the same thing, but *assume* just doesn't work and is therefore the correct choice.

After an hour of play, chew toys, tennis

balls, and stuffed animals were strewn <u>around</u>
      3
the living room.
    3. Which of the following alternatives to the underlined word would be LEAST acceptable?

    A. on
    B. throughout
    C. all over
    D. about

Idioms are expressions that require the use of a specific preposition. Fortunately, you'll be familiar with many of the idioms on the test. The best way to spot them is to look for prepositions in the answer choices.

Here's How to Crack It

Cross out LEAST. This is testing an idiom, specifically which prepositions work with *strewn*. Use POE, trying each answer choice in place of *around*. Choices (B), (C), and (D) could all work with *strewn*, but *on* doesn't work and is therefore the correct choice.

------○------

STRATEGY QUESTIONS

Strategy questions come in many different forms, but they all revolve around the *purpose* of the text. Among the different types of Strategy questions, expect to see questions asking you to add and replace text, determine if text should be added or deleted, evaluate the impact on the passage if text is deleted, or judge the overall effect of the passage on the reader.

Let's see some examples.

------○------

Many dog owners turn to animal trainers when they find they can no longer control their pets. Most experts find that a poorly-trained dog has received plenty of affection but not enough discipline or exercise. ⁴

4. Which of the following sentences provides new, specific guidelines about the proper training of a dog?

F. Behavior that was cute in a twenty-pound puppy is alarming in a one hundred-pound adult dog.

G. Would-be dog owners should consider their own lifestyles and the temperament of a specific breed before adopting the animal.

H. Dogs should be walked at least three times a day and should never be given a treat without first obeying a command.

J. Small children should never be left unsupervised with a dog.

Here's How to Crack It

Identify the purpose of the proposed text. According to the question, one of these choices *provides new, specific guidance about the proper training of a dog*. We don't even need to go back into the passage: Find an answer choice that fulfills the purpose. Choices (F), (G), and (J) all may be true, but they do not offer any *specific* information about training a dog. Only choice (H) does that, and it is our correct answer.

Try another.

Wheezie's puppy playfulness masked the steely determination of a true French bulldog, and she stubbornly resisted all the lessons from our obedience class. [5]

5. At this point, the writer is considering adding the following true statement:

> My nephews trained Blizzard, a black lab with a sweet disposition, very easily.

Should the writer add this sentence here?

A. Yes, because it explains why the author felt so insecure about her difficulties training her dog.
B. Yes, because it provides an important detail about another breed of dog.
C. No, because it doesn't explain how Blizzard was trained.
D. No, because it distracts the reader from the main point of this paragraph.

Here's How to Crack It

Whenever a strategy question asks if you should add or delete new text, evaluate the reasons in the answer choices carefully. The reason should correctly explain the purpose of the selected text. Here, choice (D) is correct because there is no reason to add text that is irrelevant to the topic.

Most puppy books no longer recommend
using newspapers to housebreak dogs. I
bought three safety gates to block off the
kitchen from the rest of the house. I also
brought home a crate, baby blankets to make
it cozy, a stylish collar and matching leash,
several bags of food, and of course, plenty of
toys.

6. Given that all choices are true, which one provides the best opening to this paragraph?
   F. NO CHANGE
   G. When I was growing up, my family had an Irish Setter and four cats.
   H. I made sure I had all the supplies we'd need before bringing Wheezie home.
   J. Many people prefer cats as pets.

Here's How to Crack It

In many strategy questions, the purpose is to add a sentence to open or close a paragraph, or tie two paragraphs together. Use the context of the paragraph and read through to the end before deciding. Since the author mentions several things she's bought in preparation, choice (H) provides the best introduction to the paragraph.

ORDER

There are also several types of Order questions, but they all involve the correct placement of ideas. Some order questions will ask you to place correctly a modifier or additional text. Other questions will ask you to evaluate and possibly correct the order of sentences within a paragraph or the paragraphs themselves.

All order questions work best with POE. Ideas should be consistent and the meaning should be clear, but that meaning can be difficult to understand until ideas are in their proper place.

Let's look at a few examples.

French bulldogs can face a serious$\underset{7}{}$ number of health issues affecting the respiratory system, knees, and eyesight.

7. The best placement for the underlined word would be:

   A. where it is now.
   B. before the word *French* (revising the capitalization accordingly).
   C. before the word *health*.
   D. before the word *respiratory*.

Here's How to Crack It

Use POE, trying the word in the places suggested by each answer choice. The best answer is choice (C) because it modifies health issues and therefore includes all three listed. "Serious" to mean "a lot of" is slang, and thus appeals to your ear. But "large" is not a definition of serious, literally or figuratively, and none of the other definitions really apply to the figurative meaning of "large."

Order of Sentences

If there is a question on order of the sentences or placement of new text within a paragraph, all of the sentences in the passage will be numbered. NO CHANGE could be the answer to order of the sentences, but if you're reading along and get confused by a sudden shift in the action, that's a good sign the sentences are in fact out of order. Do not go back and reread, but instead wait until you get to the question.

Don't waste time trying to re-order all of the sentences yourself. Look for transition words that indicate an introduction, a conclusion, or a pair of sentences that should go back to back, and use POE.

Try an example.

---

[4]

[1] He recommended an excellent specialist to perform the surgery. [2] When the day came, I drove to the hospital, dreading the moment I'd need to leave her behind. [3] While we waited for her to be admitted, Wheezie sensed something was wrong and curled on my lap, trembling. [4] My vet broke the bad news that Wheezie would have to have surgery to correct the problems in her nasal passage and vocal chords.

8. Which of the following order of sentences will make the paragraph most logical?
   F. NO CHANGE
   G. 2, 3, 1, 4
   H. 4, 3, 2, 1
   J. 4, 1, 2, 3

Here's How to Crack It

Use POE. The surgery isn't properly introduced until the end, which means sentence 4 should be the introduction. Eliminate choices (F) and (G) and determine if sentence 3 or 1 should be next. Sentence 1 makes more sense, so the answer is choice (J).

Order of the Paragraphs

If there is a question on the order of the paragraphs, there will be a warning at the beginning of the passage, alerting you that the passages may or may not be in the correct order and identifying which question will ask about which paragraph.

Almost no one ever spots this warning. Treat these the same way you treat the order of the sentences. If you suddenly find yourself confused by an inexplicable shift in the action, check above the title if the warning is there. Alternatively, continue reading and working the questions and bet safely you'll encounter a question on the order of the paragraphs at the end of the passage.

AND IN THE END. . .

> Questions 9 and 10 ask about the passage as a whole.

Other than order of the paragraphs, two other questions routinely appear at the end and are always preceded by the announcement above.

Placement of New Info

The paragraphs will also be numbered for a question testing the placement of additional info.

---

9. Upon reviewing this essay and concluding some information has been left out, the writer composes the following sentence:

   > After a night spent winning the hearts of all of the attendants, Wheezie bounded out of the recovery room and into my waiting arms.

   This sentence should be:

   A. placed at the end of paragraph 4.
   B. placed at the end of paragraph 3.
   C. placed at the end of paragraph 2.
   D. placed at the end of paragraph 1.

Here's How to Crack It

OK, so this is a little unfair: we didn't give you the entire passage, and only the correct paragraph (4) was numbered. But we couldn't leave you hanging about Wheezie's fate. Even with a little bit of cheating on our part, the new information is consistent with the rest of the information in that paragraph, and choice (A) is the correct answer.

―――――――――――○――――――――――――

Grading the Passage

Questions at the end that ask you to evaluate the passage are another version of a strategy question. The question identifies the purpose of the passage and asks you to determine if the author succeeded. These are always at the end, so we waited to show you here.

―――――――――――○――――――――――――

10. Suppose that one of the writer's goals has been to address the role obedience classes can play in the healthy development of dogs. Would this essay fulfill that goal?

   F. Yes, because the essay implies the writer and her dog benefited from obedience classes.
   G. Yes, because the essay indicates French Bulldogs are not easily trained.
   H. No, because the essay is focused on one anecdote about one dog.
   J. No, because the essay indicates the dog displayed aggressive and territorial behavior.

Here's How to Crack It

With all strategy questions, identify the purpose in the question. With questions that use a Yes/No format, connect the purpose in the question to the reasons given in the answer choices. Choice (H) is the correct answer.

―――――――――――○――――――――――――

Rhetorical Skills Drill

In the drill below, you will find questions focusing only on Rhetorical Skills. Before you start, take a few moments to go back over the review material and techniques. Answers are in Chapter 24.

> The following paragraphs may or may not be in the most logical order. Each paragraph is numbered, and question 9 will ask you to choose where Paragraph 2 should most logically be placed.

[1]

The golden age of television means many things to many people, but to the small band of actors, writers, and directors who would rise to <u>prominence</u> in the late 50s and early 60s, without a doubt it meant the televisions shows such as

Playhouse 90, on which many of them worked for the first <u>live</u> time.

[2]

Despite the undeniable risks of live performances—or perhaps because of—the results rank among the greatest achievements in American entertainment. Many of its productions were later remade, both for television and film, including *Requiem for a Heavyweight, Judgement at Nuremberg,* and *Days of Wine and Roses.* ⊡3⊡ Many critics maintain none of the remakes could match the brilliance and electricity of the live performances displayed in *Playhouse 90.*

[3]

[1] Each week, a new "teleplay" was created from scratch—written, cast, rehearsed, and performed. [2] *Playhouse 90* was truly a remarkable training ground for the young talents. [3] Such future luminaries as Rod Serling, Sidney Lumet, Paddy Chayefsky, Marlon Brando, and Patricia Neal worked

1. Which of the following alternatives to the underlined word would be LEAST acceptable?
   A. fame
   B. projection
   C. stardom
   D. greatness

2. The best placement for the underlined word would be:
   F. where it is now.
   G. before the word *actors*.
   H. before the word *doubt*.
   J. before the word *television*.

3. The writer is considering deleting the preceding sentence. Should the sentence be kept or deleted?
   A. Kept, because it provides context for the reference to remakes in the next sentence.
   B. Kept, because it is crucial to understanding why *Playhouse 90* was a success.
   C. Deleted, because it does not match the objective tone of the essay.
   D. Deleted, because it contains information that has already been provided in the essay.

long hours reading scripts. [4] In some cases, when there were problems with the censors, it would have to be created

twice. 5

[4]

Due to the frantic pace, accidents happened frequently. David Niven once revealed that, during an early show, he inadvertently locked his costume in his dressing room two minutes before air time. As the announcer read the opening credits, the sound of axes splintering the door to Niven's dressing room could be heard in the background. 7

4. Which choice would most clearly indicate that the actors, writers, and directors became extremely skilled?

    F. memorizing their lines.
    G. honing their craft.
    H. constructing the set.
    J. skimming the want-ads.

5. Which of the following order of sentences will make the paragraph most logical?

    A. NO CHANGE
    B. 1, 2, 4, 3
    C. 2, 1, 4, 3
    D. 2, 3, 1, 4

6. Given that all choices are true, which one most effectively introduces this paragraph?

    F. NO CHANGE
    G. The ratings for *Playhouse 90* were unimpressive.
    H. Broadway has produced many famous actors as well.
    J. *Playhouse 90* ran on CBS from 1956 to 1961.

7. The writer is considering deleting the preceding sentence. If the writer were to make this deletion, the essay would primarily lose a statement that:

    A. explains the organization of the last paragraph.
    B. adds a much needed touch of humor to the essay.
    C. information that explains how one accident was resolved.
    D. nothing, since the information is provided elsewhere in the essay.

Questions 8 and 9 ask about the preceding passage as a whole.

8. Suppose that one of the writer's goals had been to write a brief essay describing an influential program in television's history. Would this essay fulfill that goal?
    F. Yes, because it explains that many future stars underwent valuable training working on *Playhouse 90*.
    G. Yes, because it mentions that *Playhouse 90* had the greatest number of viewers in its time slot.
    H. No, because it fails to mention any future stars by name.
    J. No, because even though many future stars received their start on *Playhouse 90*, few ever returned to television.

9. For the sake of the logic and coherence of this essay, Paragraph 2 should be placed:

    A. where it is now.
    B. before Paragraph 1.
    C. after Paragraph 3.
    D. after Paragraph 4.

Summary

o   The official categories of Usage and Mechanics and Rhetorical Skills do not matter if you use the same approach to crack.

o   Questions that come with actual questions—not just answer choices—do need a different approach.

o   For EXCEPT/LEAST/NOT questions, cross off the E/L/N word and use POE.

o   Strategy questions all involve a purpose.

o   Order questions involve the correct placement of words, sentences, and paragraphs.

Part III
How to Crack the ACT Mathematics Test

Chapter 9
Introduction to
the ACT
Mathematics Test

The second section of the ACT will always be the Math test. To perform your best, you'll need to become familiar with the structure and strategy of the ACT Math test. In this chapter, we discuss the types of questions you can expect to see and how you can use organizational strategy, estimation, and elimination skills to improve your Math score.

Watch it on
your DVD

WHAT TO EXPECT ON THE MATH TEST

You will have 60 minutes to answer 60 multiple-choice questions based on "…topics covered in typical high school classes." For those of you who aren't sure if you went to a typical high school, these questions break down into rather precise areas of knowledge.

There are usually

33 Algebra questions
- 14 pre-algebra questions based on math terminology (integers, prime numbers, etc.), basic number theory (rules of zero, order of operations etc.), and manipulation of fractions and decimals
- 10 elementary algebra questions based on inequalities, linear equations, ratios, percents, and averages
- 9 intermediate algebra questions based on exponents, roots, simultaneous equations, and quadratic equations

23 Geometry questions
- 14 plane geometry questions based on angles, lengths, triangles, quadrilaterals, circles, perimeter, area, and volume
- 9 coordinate geometry questions based on slope, distance, midpoint, parallel and perpendicular lines, points of intersection, and graphing

4 Trigonometry questions
- 4 questions based on basic sine, cosine, and tangent functions, trig identities, and graphing

What Not to Expect on the Math Test

The ACT does not provide any formulas at the beginning of the Math test. Before you panic, take a second look at the chart on the previous page. Because the ACT is so specific about the types of questions it expects you to answer, preparing to tackle ACT Math takes a few simple steps.

A NOTE ON CALCULATORS

Not all standardized tests allow calculators. Fortunately, ACT does. We're not about to give you the stodgy advice that you shouldn't use your calculator—quite the opposite, in fact. Your calculator can help to save a ton of time on operations that you may have forgotten how to do or that are easy to mess up. Adding fractions, multiplying decimals, doing operations with big numbers: why not use a calculator on these? The place where you have to be really careful with your calculator, though, is on the easy ones. Let's see an example.

1. What is the value of $3x^2 + 5x - 7$ when $x = -1$?
    A. −15
    B. −9
    C. −1
    D. 5
    E. 15

Here's How to Crack It

If you've got your calculator handy, use it. This problem is pretty straightforward, but a calculator can help to put everything together. BUT, make sure you're treating the −1 with the respect it deserves. What you punch into your calculator should look something like this:

$$3(-1)^2 + 5(-1) - 7$$

When working with negative numbers or fractions, make doubly sure that you use parentheses. If not, a lot of weird stuff can happen, and unfortunately all of the weird, wrong stuff that can happen is reflected in the wrong answer choices. If you ran this equation and found −9, choice (B), you got the right answer. Well done. If not, try to go back and figure out where you made your calculator mistake.

Types of Calculators

Throughout the rest of the Math chapters, we discuss ways to solve calculator-friendly questions in an accurate and manageable way. Because TI-89 and TI-92 calculators are not allowed on the ACT, we will show you how to solve problems on the TI-83. If you don't plan to use a TI-83 on the test, we recommend you make sure your calculator is acceptable for use on the test and that it can do the following:

- handle positive, negative, and fractional exponents
- use parentheses
- graph simple functions
- convert fractions to decimals and vice versa
- change a linear equation into $y = mx + b$ form

Use your calculator, but use it wisely. Be careful with negative numbers and fractions.

THE PRINCETON REVIEW APPROACH

Because the test is so predictable, the best way to prepare for ACT Math is with

1. a thorough review of the very specific information and question types that come up repeatedly.
2. an understanding of The Princeton Review's test-taking strategies and techniques.

In each Math chapter in this book, you'll find a mixture of review and technique, with a sprinkling of ACT-like problems. At the end of each chapter, there is a summary of the chapter and a drill designed to pinpoint your math test-taking strengths and weaknesses. In addition to working through the problems in this book, we strongly suggest you practice our techniques on some real ACT practice tests. Let's begin with some general strategies.

Order of Difficulty: Still Personal

The Math test is the only part of the ACT that is in Order of Difficulty (OOD). What this means is that the easier questions tend to be a bit earlier in the exam, and the harder questions are later. Usually, this means that #1 is a freebie and #60 is a doozy. None of the other tests have an OOD, unfortunately, so they are all about Personal Order of Difficulty (POOD). This OOD in and of itself is great to know when planning how you will attack this part of the ACT.

Now we all love easy questions, but hold on for a second. If you and I both get a B on a math test at school, is it necessarily because we got exactly the same questions right or wrong? Unfortunately, no. What makes for a hard question? Is it hard because it's a long word problem, or is it hard because it tests some arcane concept that your teacher went over for like five seconds? Only the very hardest questions will be both. So even on the Math test of the ACT, you still need to use your POOD. The things you might find easy or hard won't necessarily jibe with ACT's.

The Princeton Review's *1,296 ACT Practice Questions* offers the equivalent of 6 whole ACT practice tests.

Now, Later, Never

Now

Do the problems you're sure you can do quickly and accurately.

Later

If a problem looks time-consuming, save it for later. Do the Nows first.

Never.

Sometimes it's better to just walk away. If a problem has you totally stumped, answer with your Letter of the Day and move on.

Hard questions take a long time. Easy ones take a short time. That's obvious, but as we've seen, the definition of an "Easy" question is a tough one to pin down. That's why you'll want to be careful trusting ACT's Order of Difficulty on the Math test. The no-brainer approach is to open the test booklet and work questions 1 through 60 in order, but you can get a lot of extra points by out-thinking this test. You'll have a lot easier time drawing your own road map for this test than letting ACT guide you.

Clearly, a lot of the easy questions will be right in the beginning, but they won't all be. This is why when you arrive at each question, you'll want to first determine whether it is a Now, Later, or Never question. Do the Now questions immediately: they're the freebies, the ones you know how to do and can do quickly and accurately. Skip any questions you think might take you a bit longer, or which test unfamiliar concepts—save them for Later. Make sure you get all the points you can on the problems you know you can do, no matter what the question number.

Once you've done all the Now questions, go back to all the ones you left for Later. But here you should be careful as well. For both Now and Later questions, don't rush and make careless errors. On the other hand, don't get stuck on a particular problem. In a 60-minute exam, think of how much spending 5 minutes on a single problem can cost you!

Finally, there's no problem with leaving a few questions behind in the Never category. The good news here is that these problems are not necessarily totally lost. Fill them in with a Letter of the Day: choose one pair of letters and bubble in all the blanks this way. For example, always bubble in A or F, B or G, etc. ACT doesn't have a guessing penalty, so there's nothing to lose, and you can even get lucky and get a few free points.

USE PROCESS OF ELIMINATION (POE)

Remember the major technique we introduced in Chapter 3: POE, or process of elimination. ACT doesn't take away points for wrong answers, so you should always guess, and POE can help you improve those chances of guessing. Don't make the mistake of thinking that POE is a strategy reserved only for English, Reading, and Science. Math has its own kind of POE, one facet of which we like to call Ballparking.

BALLPARK

You can frequently get rid of several answer choices in an ACT math problem without doing any complicated math. Narrow down the choices by estimating your answer. We call this ballparking. Let's look at an example:

Cross Out the Crazy Answers
What's the average of 100 and 200?
A. 500
B. 150
C. a billion

3. There are 600 school children in the Lakeville district. If 54 of them are high school seniors, what is the percentage of high school seniors in the Lakeville district?

   A. .9%
   B. 2.32%
   C. 9%
   D. 11%
   E. 90%

Here's How to Crack It

Before we do any serious math on this problem, let's see if we can get rid of some answer choices by ballparking.

First, we need to figure out what percent 54 is of 600. It's pretty small, definitely way less than 50%, so we can eliminate choice (E) right off the bat. Now, think about easy percentages that you know—10 and 25%—and start from there. What's 10% of 600? Just move the decimal one place to the right to get it, and you'll find that 10% of 600 is 60. Therefore, if the number from the problem is 54, the answer must be less than 10%. Let's get rid of choice (D). Now, we know that 54 is pretty close to 60, so we want something close to 10% but slightly less, and the only possible answer is choice (C).

It may feel like we somehow cheated the system by doing the problem that way, but here's what ACT doesn't want you to know: the quick, easy way and the "real" way get you the same amount of points. Not all problems will be so easily ball-parkable, but if you think before you start frantically figuring, you can usually eliminate at least an answer choice or two.

WORD PROBLEMS

You've seen the breakdown of the topics that are tested on the ACT Math test. At a glance, it actually looks like the ACT should be kind of an easy test: you've definitely learned a lot of this stuff in school, a lot of it by the end of middle school. So what's the deal? Well, part of the deal is that ACT makes familiar stuff really unfamiliar by putting it into word problems. Word problems add some confusing steps that mask the often simple concepts trapped in the problems. Trap answers, partial answers, and weird phrasing abound in word problems. Is anyone else getting the feeling that this whole exam is about reading comprehension?

Word problems look a lot of different ways and test a lot of different math concepts, but if you keep these three steps in mind, you should be able to get started on most word problems:

> When dealing with Word Problems on the ACT Math test:
> 1. **Know the question.** Read the whole problem before calculating anything, and underline the actual question.
> 2. **Let the answers help.** Look for clues on how to solve and ways to use POE (Process of Elimination).
> 3. **Break the problem into bite-sized pieces.** When you read the problem a second time, calculate at each step necessary and watch out for tricky phrasing.

Let's try a problem:

---

8. Each member in a club had to choose an activity for a day of volunteer work. $\frac{1}{3}$ of the members chose to pick up trash. $\frac{1}{4}$ of the remaining members chose to paint fences. $\frac{5}{6}$ of the members still without tasks chose to clean school buses. The rest of the members chose to plant trees. If the club has 36 members, how many of the members chose to plant trees?

   F. 3
   G. 6
   H. 9
   J. 12
   K. 15

Here's How to Crack It

Step 1: Know the Question

This is actually a slightly tricky step on this one. First of all, the problem doesn't tell you until the very end that there are 36 students in this class. Without this piece of information, the fractions don't mean much of anything. Second, the question is asking for the number of members who chose to plant trees, and we're going to have to figure out a bunch of other things before we figure that out.

Step 2: Let the Answers Help

There aren't any crazy answers in this one, though if you noticed how much we're subtracting from 36, you're probably thinking that the answer will be one of the smaller numbers.

Step 3: Break the problem into bite-sized pieces

The starting point of this word problem actually comes at the end: this club has 36 members. Once you've got that, work the problem sentence by sentence, and pay particular attention to the language of the problem.

$\frac{1}{3}$ of the members chose to pick up trash.

A nice easy way to start. There are 36 members, and $\frac{1}{3}$ of 36 is 12, so 12 members pick up trash.

$\frac{1}{4}$ of the remaining members chose to paint fences.

This is just like the last piece, except for one HUGE exception, which comes from the word *remaining*. First, we'll need to figure out how many remaining members there are from the first step. There are 36 total members and 12 of them are picking up trash, so there are 24 members remaining. $\frac{1}{4}$ of 24 is 6, so 6 members paint fences.

$\frac{5}{6}$ of the remaining members still without tasks chose to clean school buses.

There's that word remaining again. There were 24 members in the last step, but 6 of them chose to paint fences, so now there are 18 *remaining* members. $\frac{5}{6}$ of 18 is 15, so 15 members clean school buses.

The rest of the members chose to plant trees.

There were 18 members left over in the last step, and 15 of them chose to clean school buses, which means there must be 3 students left to plant trees. Choice (F) is the correct answer. Look at those other answers, then look at the numbers you were dealing with in the problem: what a mess of partial answers!

If it seems like this took kind of a long time to do, don't worry, they won't all take this long. Most of these steps will come naturally after a while, and you'll have a solid base with which to begin any ACT Math problem in such a way that enables you to get to the answer as efficiently as possible.

———————◯———————

Summary

- o On the ACT Math test, you have 60 minutes to attempt 60 questions. The questions fall into the following categories:
  - 33 Algebra questions (14 pre-algebra, 10 elementary algebra, 9 intermediate algebra)
  - 23 Geometry questions (14 plane geometry, 9 coordinate geometry)
  - 4 Trigonometry questions

- o Use your Personal Order of Difficulty to determine if a question is for Now, Later, or Never.
  - Just because the Math is technically in order of difficulty doesn't mean you need to do it in order.
  - Never leave any blanks! Fill in the Never questions with your Letter of the Day.

- o Remember the basic approach for Word Problems:
  - **Know the question.** Read the problem all the way through and underline the question.
  - **Let the answers help.** Look for clues on how to solve. Use POE and ballparking.
  - **Break the problem into bite-sized pieces.** Every problem has lots of information: process each piece one at a time and be careful of tricky phrasing.

- o Finally, use your calculator liberally but wisely!

Chapter 10
Fundamentals

A solid base in the fundamentals of the math tested on the ACT is essential to getting a good score. We'll see a number of strategies that will help to work around some of the more advanced concepts, but there's often no way to work around questions that test the fundamentals.

VOCABULARY

Calculators can solve a lot of problems, but Vocabulary is one aspect of the math with which a calculator can't help. Let's review some of the main terms.

A Note on Calculators

This chapter will deal mainly with concepts rather than operations. As mentioned in the previous chapter, we encourage you to use your calculator liberally but wisely. The operations discussed in this chapter will be those for which a calculator might be unhelpful or extra confusing.

Basics

Use the numbers below to answer questions 1 through 6 that follow. Check your answers against the Answer Key at the end of this chapter on page 120.

$$-81, -19, -9, -6, -\frac{1}{4}, -0.15, 0, 1.75, 2, 3, 12, 16, 81$$

1. List all the *positive numbers*. _____
2. List all the *negative integers*. _____
3. List all the *odd* integers. _____
4. List all the *even* integers. _____
5. List all the *positive*, *even* integers in *consecutive* order. _____
   _____
6. List all the numbers that are neither *positive* nor *negative*. _____
   _____

Now try these questions.

7. What is the *reciprocal* of $-\frac{1}{4}$? _____

8. What is the *opposite reciprocal* of 2? _____
9. When a number and its reciprocal are multiplied, what is the product?
   _____
10. How many times does 2 go into 15 evenly? _____
11. How much is left over? _____
12. What is 15 divided by 2? _____

Let's try it the other way. Use the following list of terms to answer questions 13 through 18.

> Number, Integer, Positive, Negative, Even, Odd,
> Consecutive, Reciprocal, Remainder

13. Which terms describe the number 6? _____

_____

14. Which terms describe the number $-\dfrac{1}{5}$? _____

_____

15. Which terms describe the number 0? _____

_____

16. When 14 is divided by 3, it has a _____ of 2.

17. The _____ of $-\dfrac{1}{4}$ is -4.

18. The numbers 2, 4, 6 are listed in _____ order, but the numbers 3, 1, 14 are not.

Factors and Multiples

Factors and multiples are all about numbers that are divisible by other numbers. Start with examples, and the definitions will become easier.

Example:
- The factors of 10 are 1, 2, 5, 10.
- The first four positive multiples of 10 are 10, 20, 30, 40.

A Good Rule of Thumb

- The factors of a number are always equivalent to that number or *smaller*.
- The multiples of a number are always equivalent to that number or *larger*.

1. List the factors of 12. _____
2. List the first four multiples of 12. _____
3. List the factors of 30. _____
4. List the first four multiples of 30. _____
5. Is 12 a multiple or factor of 24? _____
6. Is 8 one of the factors of 64? _____
7. What is the greatest common factor of 27 and 45? _____
8. What is the greatest common factor of 9 and 36? _____
9. What is the least common multiple of 9 and 12? _____
10. What is the least common multiple of 24 and 48? _____

Prime

A prime number is any number with only two distinct factors: 1 and itself.

1. What are the single digit prime numbers? _____
2. What is the only even prime number? _____
3. Is 1 a prime number? _____

The prime factorization of a number is the reduction of a number to its prime factors. Find the prime factorization of a number by using a factor tree. Example:

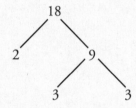

The prime factorization of 18 is $2 \times 3 \times 3$ or 2×3^2.

4. What is the prime factorization of 36?

5. What is the sum of all the prime factors of 36? _____
6. What is the product of all the distinct prime factors of 36? _____

ADVANCED TERMS

Real Numbers and Their Imaginary Friends

ACT uses the term "real" a lot, but it's usually only there to scare you. Sometimes, though, ACT will test it directly, so it's good to have at least a sense of what the term means.

1. How much would you like to earn in your eventual job? _____
2. How much scholarship money do you want from your eventual college? _____
3. What's the temperature in the Bahamas right now? (Ballpark it!) _____
4. How many slices of pizza could you eat in a single sitting? _____

Unless you have some interesting ideas about money and/or pizza, ALL of the numbers above are real. The only numbers that aren't real are imaginary—a negative number under an even root.

5. What is $\sqrt{1}$? _____
6. What is -1×-1? _____
7. What is $-1 \times -1 \times -1$? _____
8. What is $\sqrt{-1}$? _____
9. What real number could you square to get a product of –1? _____

That last question was a trick: there is no real number that you can square and get a negative product. The only way to get the square root (or any even root) of a negative number is to *imagine* it.

> $\sqrt{-1}$ is defined as the imaginary number *i*. All other imaginary numbers are something multiplied by *i*.

Rational Numbers and Their Irrational Friends

1. Write 0.5 as a fraction. _____
2. Write 3 as a fraction. _____
3. In the number 0.1666, what digit is coming next? _____
4. In the number, 0.191919, what digit is coming next? _____

A *rational* number is any number that can be written as a fraction: that includes integers and repeating decimals. An *irrational* is a number that cannot be written as a fraction because it goes on unpredictably. *Both* types of numbers are *real*.

Love Your Calculator for Real, but Be Rational

Your calculator can be a really handy tool for problems dealing with imaginary and irrational numbers. If you have a Texas Instruments calculator, the second function of the decimal is i. Use this function to solve the following problems.

5. $(2 + i)(2 - i)$? _____
6. $(3 + i)^2$? _____

To determine if a number is rational or irrational, it can help to try to convert it into a fraction. In the MATH menu, the first item is >*Frac*. This will convert a decimal to a fraction if the number is rational. For each question below, after you have typed in the number provided hit ENTER, then MATH>ENTER>ENTER. Give the result in the blank and identify whether it is rational or irrational.

7. 0.375 _____
8. 0.16666666666 (until the end of the screen) _____
9. π _____
10. 0.479109801431 _____

Exponents

Exponents are a shorthand way of indicating that a number is multiplied by itself. The exponent tells you how many times (for example, $5^4 = 5 \times 5 \times 5 \times 5$). Exponents are tricky when you have to combine them in some way. Here's a great way to remember all the rules.

Remember MADSPM!
- When you *multiply* two numbers with common bases, *add* the exponents.
- When you *divide* two numbers with common bases, *subtract* the exponents.
- When you raise an exponential number to a *power*, *multiply* the exponents.

Basic Rules

1. $(x^2)(x^3)$

2. $\dfrac{x^4}{x^3}$

3. $(x^4)^3$

4. $2x^2 \times 6x^3$

5. $(2x^2)^3$

6. $\dfrac{9x^6}{3x^2}$

7. $\dfrac{(x^2)(x^5)}{x^4}$

Special Rules

Follow the basic rules to see how some of these special rules are derived.

1. $\dfrac{x^4}{x^4}$

2. x^0

3. $\dfrac{x^2}{x^5}$

4. x^{-3}

5. x^1

6. 1^{513}

7. 0^{619}

8. $(-2)^2$

9. $(-2)^3$

10. -2^2

11. $\left(\dfrac{1}{2}\right)^2$

12. $\left(\dfrac{2}{3}\right)^2$

Roots

You can add or subtract square roots only when the numbers under the square root sign are the same.

Example:

$$4\sqrt{x} + 2\sqrt{x} = 6\sqrt{x}$$

$$4\sqrt{x} + 2\sqrt{2x} \text{ can't be combined!}$$

Multiplication and division are more flexible. Different values can be combined under the root, as long as the root has the same degree.

Example:

$$\left(\sqrt{x}\right)\left(\sqrt{y}\right) + \sqrt{xy}$$

$$\frac{\sqrt{x}}{\sqrt{y}} = \sqrt{\frac{x}{y}}$$

1. $\sqrt{x} + \sqrt{x} =$

2. $3\sqrt{x} + 5\sqrt{x} =$

3. $x\sqrt{3} + x\sqrt{5} =$

4. $\left(\sqrt{2x}\right)\left(\sqrt{y}\right) =$

5. $\left(\sqrt{x}\right)\left(\sqrt{xy}\right) =$

If ACT asks you to simplify exponents or roots with numbers instead of variables, use your calculator. But be extra careful with parentheses!

6. $4\sqrt{12} \times 2\sqrt{3} =$

7. $\dfrac{\sqrt{72}}{\sqrt{2}}$

8. $\left(\sqrt{529} - \sqrt{361}\right)^{\frac{1}{2}}$

Remember: the Answer Keys for the preceding drills can be found at the end of this chapter after the Summary page.

FUNDAMENTALS VOCABULARY DRILL

Absolute Value: _____

_____

Consecutive: _____

_____

Decimal: _____

_____

Difference: _____

_____

Digits: _____

_____

Distinct: _____

_____

Divisible: _____

_____

Even: _____

_____

Exponent/Power: _____

_____

Factor: _____

_____

Fraction: _____

_____

Greatest Common Factor: _____

_____

Imaginary: _____

_____

Integers: _____

_____

Irrational: _____

_____

Least Common Multiple: _____

_____

Multiple: _____

_____

Negative: _____

_____

Number: _____

_____

Odd: _____

_____

Opposite: _____

_____

Order of Operations: _____

_____

Positive: _____

_____

Prime: _____

_____

Product: _____

_____

Quotient: _____

_____

Real: _____

_____

Radical: _____

_____

Rational: _____

_____

Reciprocal: _____

_____

Remainder: _____

_____

Sum: _____

_____

GLOSSARY

Absolute Value:	The distance from zero on the number line
Consecutive:	In increasing order
Decimal:	A way of expressing a fraction in which numbers are divided by ten, hundred, thousand, and other powers of ten
Difference:	The result of subtraction
Digits:	The integers 0 through 9
Distinct:	Different
Divisible:	An integer can be divided by another integer evenly, with no fraction or decimal left over
Even:	Divisible by 2
Exponent/Power:	A number that indicates how many times to multiply a base by itself
Factor:	Integers that multiply together to make a given product
Fraction:	A way of expressing the division of numbers by stacking one over the other
Greatest Common Factor:	The largest factor common to two numbers
Imaginary:	The square (or any other even) root of a negative number
Integers:	All real numbers other than decimals or fractions
Irrational:	A number that can be expressed as a decimal but not a fraction
Least Common Multiple:	The smallest multiple common to two numbers
Multiple:	The product of an integer and another integer
Negative:	Less than 0
Number:	Everything
Odd:	NOT divisible by 2
Opposite:	Two numbers that have the same magnitude but are opposite in signs. That is, two numbers with the same distance from zero on the number line, but one is positive and the other negative.
Order of Operations:	Parentheses, Exponents, Multiplication, Division, Addition, Subtraction

Positive: Greater than 0

Prime: A number that has itself and 1 as its only factors

Product: The result of multiplication

Quotient: The result of division

Real: Zero, all positive and negative integers, fractions, decimals, and roots

Radical: Another word for the $\sqrt{}$ sign

Rational: A number that can be expressed as the ratio of two other numbers, making a fraction

Reciprocal: The inverse of a number—flip the numerator and denominator.

Remainder: The number left over when a number is not divisible by another number

Sum: The result of addition

Fundamentals Drill

In the drill below, you will find questions focusing only on fundamental skills. Before you start, take a few moments to go back over the review material and techniques. Answers are in Chapter 24.

1. What is the product of the distinct prime factors of 54?

 A. 2
 B. 3
 C. 6
 D. 11
 E. 54

2. If x is the least odd prime number and y is the least positive integer multiple of 10, what is the difference between x and y?

 F. 3
 G. 7
 H. 11
 J. 15
 K. 17

3. For all x and y, $(x^{-1}y^{-3})^{-2}(x^4y^7)^3 =$?

 A. $x^{10}y^{15}$
 B. x^5y^{10}
 C. x^3y^4
 D. $x^{14}y^{27}$
 E. $x^{-6}y^{18}$

4. In the complex numbers, where $i^2 = -1$, which of the following is equal to the result of squaring the expression $(i + 4)$?

 F. $4i$
 G. $16i$
 H. $15 + 8i$
 J. $i + 16$
 K. $17 - 18i$

5. What is the least possible sum of three distinct prime numbers between 10 and 20?

 A. 30
 B. 39
 C. 41
 D. 45
 E. 60

Summary

o   Learn the basics on the ACT Math test before you move on to more difficult concepts. The Fundamentals are the one thing on the ACT that you can't fake!

o   Know your vocabulary. The Math test requires its own Reading Comprehension.

o   Know your rules for 0:
   *   0 is an even number.
   *   0 is neither positive nor negative.
   *   Anything multiplied by 0 is 0.
   *   0 raised to any power is 0.
   *   Anything raised to the 0 power is 1.

o   A number's factors are always *smaller than* or the *same as* that number.

o   A number's multiples are always *larger than* or the *same as* that number.

o   A prime number has only two distinct factors: 1 and itself.
   *   1 is NOT a prime number.
   *   2 is the only even prime number.

o   Use your calculator well and wisely. A calculator is particularly helpful with:
   *   Imaginary numbers (represented as *i* in problems).
   *   Square roots that don't contain variables (and often those that do).
   *   Converting decimals or other expressions into fractions.
   *   Multiplying and dividing large numbers.

o   When combining numbers with exponents, remember MADSPM.

Answer Key
FUNDAMENTALS LESSON

Basics, page 104.
1. 1.75, 2, 3, 12, 16, 81
2. −81, −19, −9, −6
3. −81, −19, −9, 3, 81
4. −6, 0, 2, 12, 16
5. 2, 12, 16
6. 0
7. −4
8. $-\dfrac{1}{2}$
9. 1
10. 7
11. 1
12. 7 R 1 (7 *remainder* 1)
13. Number, Integer, Positive, Even
14. Number, Negative
15. Number, Integer, Even
16. Remainder
17. Reciprocal
18. Consecutive

Factors and Multiples, page 107.
1. 1, 2, 3, 4 , 6, 12
2. 12, 24, 36, 48
3. 1, 2, 3, 5, 6, 10, 15, 30
4. 30, 60, 90, 120
5. Factor
6. Yes
7. 9
8. 9
9. 36
10. 48

Prime, page 108.
1. 2, 3, 5, 7
2. 2
3. No, it does not have two *distinct* factors.
4. $2 \times 2 \times 3 \times 3$ or $2^2 \times 3^2$
5. 10 (2 + 2 + 3 + 3)
6. 6 (2 × 3)

Real Numbers and their Imaginary Friends, page 109.

5. 1
6. 1
7. −1
8. No answer, or Imaginary
9. None

Rational Numbers and their Irrational Friends, page 110.

1. $\dfrac{1}{2}$

2. $\dfrac{3}{1}$

3. 6
4. 1

Love Your Calculator for Real, but Be Rational, page 110.

5. 5
6. $8 + 6i$

7. $\dfrac{3}{8}$ Rational.

8. $\dfrac{1}{6}$ Rational.

9. No result. Irrational.

10. $\dfrac{479109801431}{10000000000000}$ Rational.

Basic Rules, page 111.

1. x^5
2. x^1, or x
3. x^{12}
4. $12x^5$. Don't forget the coefficients!
5. $8x^6$
6. $3x^4$
7. x^3

Special Rules, page 112.

1. x^0, or 1
2. 1
3. x^{-3}, or $\dfrac{1}{x^3}$
4. $\dfrac{1}{x^3}$
5. x
6. 1
7. 0
8. 4
9. -8
10. -4
11. $\dfrac{1}{4}$
12. $\dfrac{4}{9}$

Roots, page 113.

1. $2\sqrt{x}$

2. $8\sqrt{x}$

3. Can't be combined!

4. $\sqrt{2xy}$

5. $\sqrt{x^2 y} = x\sqrt{y}$

6. $8\sqrt{36} = 8(6) = 48$

7. $\sqrt{36} = 6$

8. $\left(\sqrt{529} - \sqrt{361}\right)^{\frac{1}{2}} = (23 - 19)^{\frac{1}{2}} = (4)^{\frac{1}{2}} = 2$

Chapter 11
No More Algebra

Once you have a solid foundation in basic operations and vocabulary, you are well-equipped to do a wide variety of problems. This chapter will look at some of the problems that test concepts you may have seen in Algebra classes, and it will show how to work around some of the toughest algebra problems.

ALGEBRA AND THE ACT

We've already seen in Chapter 10 some of the easier plug-and-chug algebra problems. Most questions that ACT considers "algebra" questions won't be so straightforward. ACT expects you to use algebra to solve word problems as well as plug-and-chug questions. Let's see how you can make this work in your favor.

HOW I LEARNED TO STOP WORRYING AND LOVE VARIABLES

Let's look at the following problem:

21. John has x red pencils, and three times as many red pencils as blue pencils. If he has four more yellow pencils than blue pencils, then in terms of x, how many yellow pencils does John have?

    A. $x + 4$

    B. $x + 7$

    C. $\dfrac{x}{6}$

    D. $\dfrac{x + 12}{6}$

    E. $\dfrac{x + 12}{3}$

Let's think about the bigger picture for a second here. We're all familiar with these x values from algebra class, but what we often forget is that x is substituting for some real value. Equations use x because that value is an unknown. The variable x could be 5 or 105 or 0.36491. In fact, the ACT writers are asking you to create an expression that will answer this question to find what that "certain number" is. And they want you to make it even harder on yourself by forgetting that x is a number at all.

PLUGGING IN

If you had $1 dollar and you bought 2 pieces of candy at 25 cents apiece, how much change would you have? 50 cents, of course. If you had d dollars and bought p pieces of candy at c cents apiece, how much change would you have? Um, letter of the day.

Numbers are a lot easier to work with than variables. Therefore, when you see variables on the ACT, you can usually make things a lot easier on yourself by using numbers instead. Whenever there are variables in the answer choices or the problem, you can use Plugging In.

Use Plugging In:

- when there are variables in the answer choices.
- when solving word problems or plug-and-chug questions.
- for questions of any difficulty level.

Let's go back to #21:

———————◯———————

21. John has x red pencils, and three times as many red pencils as blue pencils. If he has four more yellow pencils than blue pencils, then in terms of x, how many yellow pencils does John have?

   A. $x + 4$

   B. $x + 7$

   C. $\dfrac{x}{6}$

   D. $\dfrac{x + 12}{6}$

   E. $\dfrac{x + 12}{3}$

Here's How to Crack It

1. Know the Question. Underline "how many yellow pencils does John have?" We're not solving for x here, but for the number of yellow pencils. ACT just wants us to name the value "in terms of x."

2. Let the answers help. The answers help a lot here: each contains the variable x, which means we can Plug In.

3. Break the problem into bite-sized pieces. We know we can Plug In. Let's take it step by step from there:

We want to make the math easy on ourselves, so let's say $x = 3$, so John has 3 red pencils. Now that we've dispensed with the variable, let's work the rest of the problem.

John has 3 red pencils and *three times as many red pencils as blue pencils*. He therefore must have 1 blue pencil. He has *four more yellow pencils than blue pencils*, so he must have 5 yellow pencils.

So now we can answer the question with what is called our *target answer*. The question asks *How many yellow pencils does John have?*, to which our answer is 5. Circle this answer on your paper. Let's go to the answer choices and see which one gives us our target. Remember, $x = 3$.

Make sure to keep your work organized when Plugging In! Always circle your target answer.

A. $(3) + 4 = 7$ Not our target answer. Cross it off.

B. $(3) + 7 = 10$ Not our target answer. Cross it off.

C. $\dfrac{(3)}{6} = \dfrac{1}{2}$ Not our target answer. Cross it off.

D. $\dfrac{(3) + 12}{6} = \dfrac{15}{6}$ Not our target answer. Cross it off.

E. $\dfrac{(3) + 12}{3} = 5$

Only choice (E) works, so this is our correct answer. Look how easy that was, and not a bit of algebra necessary! Let's try another.

---

17. For all $x \neq 3$, which of the following is equivalent to the expression $\dfrac{3x^2 - 7x - 6}{x - 3}$?

  A. $3x + 2$

  B. $3x - 2$

  C. $3(x - 2)$

  D. $3(x + 2)$

  E. $x^2 - 2$

Here's How to Crack It

This looks a lot more like a standard plug-and-chug than the last problem did, but remember, we can always plug in when there are variables in the answer choices. This will be a tough problem to factor, so Plugging In will probably be your best bet, even if you're an ace with quadratic equations. The only thing the problem tells us is that $x \neq 3$, so let's say $x = 2$:

$$\frac{3(2)^2 - 7(2) - 6}{(2) - 3}$$

$$\frac{3(4) - 14 - 6}{-1}$$

$$\frac{-8}{-1} = 8$$

We now know that for the value we've chosen, the value of this expression is 8. That means **8** is our target answer. Let's plug our x value into the answer choices and find the one that matches the target:

  A. $3(2) + 2 = 8$ ✔ This matches our target answer, but when you Plug In, always check all 5 answers.

  B. $3(2) - 2 = 6 - 2 = 4$ Not our target answer. Cross it off.

  C. $3((2) - 2) = 3(0) = 0$ Not our target answer. Cross it off.

  D. $3((2) + 2) = 3(4) = 12$ Not our target answer. Cross it off.

  E. $(2)^2 - 2 = 2$ Not our target answer. Cross it off.

Only choice (A) worked, and it is the correct answer. So as we can see, Plugging In works for all kinds of algebra problems. Let's review what we've done so far.

WHAT TO DO WHEN YOU PLUG IN

1. Identify the opportunity. Can you plug in on this question?

2. Choose a good number. Make the math easy on yourself.

3. Find a target answer. Answer the question posed in the problem with your number, and circle your target answer.

4. Test all the answer choices. If two of them work, try a new number.

Let's try a tougher one.

---

36. In my dear Aunt Sally's math class, there are four exams. The first three exam scores are averaged, and the resulting score is averaged with the final exam score. If a, b, and c are the first three exam scores, and f is the final exam score, which of the following examples gives a student's final score in the class?

    F. $\dfrac{a+b+c}{3}+f$

    G. $\dfrac{a+b+c+3f}{6}$

    H. $\dfrac{a+b+c+f}{4}$

    J. $\dfrac{a+b+c+3f}{4}$

    K. $a+b+c+f$

Here's How to Crack It

This is a word problem, so remember the basic approach.

1. Know the question. Underline the question in this problem: *which of the following gives a student's final score in this class?*

2. Let the answers help. There are variables in each of these answer choices, which means we can Plug In, so these answers will help a lot. If you want to do a bit of POE, you might notice that the problem is asking for an average, so choice (K) can't work. Also, something funny will need to happen with the f variable, so you can eliminate choice (H).

3. Break the problem into bite-sized pieces. If you rush through this problem, it's very easy to mess up. Let's go piece by piece as we did in the earlier problem.

The first three exam scores are averaged.

There's no reason to give realistic exam scores here: we can pick whatever numbers we want, so let's use numbers that make the math easy. We know from this problem that the first three exam scores are represented by *a*, *b*, and *c*, so let's say *a = 2*, *b = 3*, and *c = 4*. The average of these three numbers can be found as follows: $\dfrac{2+3+4}{3} = \dfrac{9}{3} = 3$.

The resulting score is then averaged with the final score.

The resulting score is 3, and we need to plug in some final score, *f*. Let's use another easy number and say *f = 5*. In averaging these two numbers together, we find $\dfrac{3+5}{2} = \dfrac{8}{2} = 4$. Thus we have our target answer: a student's final score with these exam scores will be 4.

Let's go to the answer choices and look for the one that matches the target. Remember, *a = 2*, *b = 3*, *c = 4*, and *f = 5*.

F. $\dfrac{2+3+4}{3} + 5 = \dfrac{9}{3} + 5 = 8$ **x**

G. $\dfrac{2+3+4+3(5)}{6} = \dfrac{24}{6} = 4$ ✔

H. $\dfrac{2+3+4+5}{4} = \dfrac{14}{4} = 3.5$ **x**

J. $\dfrac{2+3+4+3(5)}{4} = \dfrac{24}{4} = 6$ **x**

K. $2+3+4+5 = 14$ **x**

Choice (G) is the correct answer, and no tough algebra necessary!

Hidden Plug-Ins

Both of the above questions have had variables in the answer choices, which is a dead giveaway that we can Plug In. The good news is that that's not the only time. In any problem in which there are hypothetical values or values relative to each other, Plugging In will work. Let's have a look at a problem.

---

25. If $x - z = 6$ and $y = 3x - 2 - 3z$, then $y = ?$

A.   2
B.   4
C.   14
D.   16
E.   18

Here's How to Crack It

There aren't any variables in the answer choices, but notice all values in the problem are defined relative to one another. Let's Plug In.

Using the first equation in the problem, let's make the numbers easy on ourselves and say $x = 8$ and $z = 2$. Using these values, let's find the value for the expression given in the problem: $y = 3(8) - 2 - 3(2) = 24 - 2 - 6 = 16$, choice (D).

It may feel like we just pulled these numbers out of thin air, but try any two numbers that work in the equation $x - z = 6$, and you'll find that it always works.

PLUGGING IN THE ANSWERS

So we've seen that Plugging In is a great strategy when there are variables in the question or the answers. How about when there aren't? Does that mean we have to go back to algebra? Of course not! On most problems on the ACT, there are a variety of ways to solve. Let's look at another one that helps to simplify the math in algebra-related problems.

> 2. If $600 were deposited in a bank account for one year and earned interest of $42, what was the interest rate?
>
> F. 6.26%
> G. 7.00%
> H. 8.00%
> J. 9.00%
> K. 9.50%

Before we get started cracking this problem, we should note a few things about it. First of all, there aren't any variables, but you get the feeling that you're going to have to put the $600 and the $42 in relationship to some other number by means of an algebraic expression. Then, notice that the problem is asking for a very specific number, the interest rate, and that the answer choices give possibilities for that specific number in ascending order. All of this taken together means that we can Plug In the Answers.

Plug In the Answers (PITA) when:

- answer choices are numbers in ascending or descending order.
- the question asks for a specific amount. Questions will usually be "what?" or "how many?"
- you get the urge to do algebra even when there are no variables in the problem.

Let's see what this looks like.

---

2. If $600 were deposited in a bank account for one year and earned interest of $42, what was the interest rate?

   F. 6.26%
   G. 7.00%
   H. 8.00%
   J. 9.00%
   K. 9.50%

Here's How to Crack It

1. Know the question. As we've already identified, we need to find the *interest rate*.

2. Let the answers help. The way the answer choices are listed has already indicated that we'll be able to PITA on this problem, so we'll be using the answers a lot in this question.

3. Break the problem into bite-sized pieces. We're going to use the answer choices to walk through each step of the problem, working it in bite-sized pieces.

Because these answer choices are listed in ascending order, it will be best to start with the middle choice. That way, if it's too high or too low, we'll be able to use POE more efficiently.

Therefore, if we start with 8.00% as our interest rate, we can find what the annual interest on a $600 deposit would be by multiplying $600 × 0.08 = $48. Because the problem tells us that the deposit earned $42 of interest, we know choice (H) is too high, which also eliminates choices (J) and (K).

Let's try choice (G): you may find it helpful to keep your work organized in columns as shown below.

	Interest Rate	Rate per $600	= $42?
F.	6.26%		
G.	7.00%	$42	Yes! ✔
H.	8.00%	$48	X
J.	9.00%		
K.	9.50%		

We haven't introduced any of our own numbers into this problem, so once we find the correct answer, we can stop. The correct answer is choice (G).

Let's try a harder one.

———————————————◯———————————————

49. In a piggy bank, there are pennies, nickels, dimes, and quarters that total $2.17 in value. If there are 3 times as many pennies as there are dimes, 1 more dime than nickels, and 2 more quarters than dimes, then how many pennies are in the piggy bank?

    A. 12
    B. 15
    C. 18
    D. 21
    E. 24

Here's How to Crack It

1. Know the question. *How many pennies are in the bank?*

2. Let the answers help. There are no variables, but the very specific question coupled with the numerical answers in ascending order gives a pretty good indication that we can PITA.

3. Break the problem into bite-sized pieces. Make sure you take your time with this problem, because you'll need to multiply the number of each coin by its monetary value. In other words, don't forget that 1 nickel will count for 5 cents, 1 dime will count for 10 cents, and 1 quarter will count for 25 cents. As in the previous problem, let's set up some columns to keep our work organized and begin with choice (C).

Since ACT has already given us the answers, we will plug those answers in and work backwards. Each of the answers listed gives a possible value for the number of pennies. Using the information in the problem, we can work backwards from that number of pennies to find the number of nickels, dimes, and quarters. When the values for the number of coins adds up to $2.17, we know we're done.

If we begin with the assumption that there are 18 pennies, then there must be 6 dimes *(3 times as many pennies as there are dimes)*. 6 dimes means 5 nickels *(1 more dime than nickels)* and 8 quarters *(2 more quarters than dimes)*.

Now multiply the number of coins by the monetary value of each and see if they total $2.17.

	Pennies ($P)	Dimes($D)	Nickels($N)	Quarters($Q)	Total = $2.17?
C.	18 ($0.18)	6 ($0.60)	5 ($0.25)	8 ($2.00)	Total = $3.03

That's too high, so not only is choice (C) incorrect, but also choices (D) and (E). Cross them off and try choice (B).

	Pennies ($P)	Dimes($D)	Nickels($N)	Quarters($Q)	Total = $2.17?
A.	12 ($0.12)	4 ($0.40)	3($0.15)	6($1.50)	Total = $2.17 ✔
B.	15 ($0.15)	5 ($0.50)	4($0.20)	7($1.75)	Total = $2.60 X
C.	18 ($0.18)	6 ($0.60)	5 ($0.25)	8 ($2.00)	Total = $3.03 X
D.	21	Eliminated through POE			
E.	24	Eliminated through POE			

Only choice (A) works. No algebra necessary!

A Note on Plugging In and PITA

Plugging In and PITA are not the only ways to solve these problems, and it may feel weird using these methods instead of trying to do these problems "the real way." You may have even found that you knew how to work with the variables in Plugging In problems or how to write the appropriate equations for the PITA problems. If you can do either of those things, you're already on your way to a great Math score.

But think about it this way. We've already said that ACT doesn't give any partial credit. So do you think doing it "the real way" gets you any extra points? It doesn't: on the ACT, a right answer is a right answer, no matter how you get it. "The real way" is great, but unfortunately, it's often a lot more complex and offers a lot more opportunities to make careless errors.

The biggest problem with doing things the real way, though, is that it essentially requires that you invent a new approach for every problem. Instead, notice what we've given you here: two strategies that will work toward getting you the right answer on any number of questions. You may have heard the saying, "Give a man a fish and you've fed him for a day, but teach a man to fish and you've fed him for a lifetime." Now, don't worry, our delusions of grandeur are not quite so extreme, but Plugging In and PITA are useful in a similar way. Rather than giving you a detailed description of how to create formulas and work through them for these problems that won't themselves ever appear on an ACT again, we're giving you a strategy that will help you to work through any number of similar problems in future ACTs.

Try these strategies on your own in the drill that concludes this chapter.

Algebra Drill

For the answers to this drill, please go to Chapter 24.

1. What is the largest value of x that solves the equation $x^2 - 4x + 3 = 0$?

   A. 1
   B. 2
   C. 3
   D. 4
   E. 5

2. For all $\dfrac{x^2 + 6x - 27}{(x + 9)} = ?$

   F. $x + 9$
   G. $x - 3$
   H. $x + 3$
   J. $2x - 4$
   K. $2x + 3$

3. If 2 less than 3 times a certain number is the same as 4 more than the product of 5 and 3, what is the number?

   A. 7
   B. 10
   C. 11
   D. 14
   E. 15

4. A certain number of books are to be given away at a promotion. If $\dfrac{2}{5}$ of the books are distributed in the morning and $\dfrac{1}{3}$ of the remaining books are distributed in the afternoon, what fraction of the books remains to be distributed the next day?

   F. $\dfrac{1}{5}$

   G. $\dfrac{2}{5}$

   H. $\dfrac{1}{3}$

   J. $\dfrac{5}{7}$

   K. $\dfrac{8}{9}$

5. In the equation $a = \dfrac{3}{b}$, b is a positive, real number. As the value of b is increased so it becomes closer and closer to infinity, what happens to the value of a?

   A. It remains constant.
   B. It gets closer and closer to zero.
   C. It gets closer and closer to one.
   D. It gets closer and closer to three.
   E. It gets closer and closer to infinity.

Summary

o Remember the basic approach for Word Problems:
  - Know the question.
  - Let the answers help.
  - Break the problem into bite-sized pieces.

o Use Plugging In when there are variables in the answer choices or the problem. Keep the following pointers in mind:
  - Choose numbers that make the math easy.
  - Try all the answer choices.
  - On more complex problems, keep your variables straight!

o Use Plugging In the Answers (PITA) when answer choices are listed in ascending or descending order and when the question is asking for a specific number. Keep these pointers in mind:
  - Start with choice (C) or (H) to help with POE.
  - When you find the correct answer, STOP!

Chapter 12
Plane Geometry

The ACT test writers tell us there will be 23 geometry questions on the Math test, 14 of which supposedly cover plane geometry. It's better, however, to think of the topic breakdown in broader terms rather than these specific numbers. For one thing, many problems incorporate several concepts: you even need algebra to solve many geometry questions, so would the ACT test writers count a question like that in the algebra or plane geometry column?

What matters most is that you can identify the topics that can make a question Now, Later, or Never for you.

While occasionally ACT test writers may throw in a more advanced formula or complex shape, the majority of the questions test the basic rules on the basic shapes. This chapter will review a cross-section of those formulas and concepts, and give you a strategic approach to apply those rules on the ACT.

CRACKING THE GEOMETRY ON THE ACT

Plug-and-chug geometry questions can have so much information in them, they feel like word problems. So treat them like word problems. Let's review the basic approach to word problems. We'll then add some points specific to geometry.

Step 1: Know the Question

Know the question. Read the whole problem before calculating anything, and underline the actual question.

Step 2: Let the Answers Help

Let the answers help. Look for clues on how to solve and ways to use POE (Process of Elimination).

Step 3: Break the Problem into Bite-Sized Pieces

Break the problem into bite-sized pieces. When you read the problem a second time, calculate at each step necessary and watch out for tricky phrasing.

For geometry questions, Step 3 has two specific additions:

> Step 3a: Write all the information given in the problem on the figure. If there is no figure, draw your own.
>
> Step 3b: Write down any formulas you need and fill in any information you have.

Geometry BFFs: POE and Ballparking

Step 2 of the basic approach is particularly important to geometry questions. In the last few chapters, we've seen how POE and Ballparking can help to narrow down the answer choices when you're confused. Before you rush to calculate, Ballparking in particular will help you a ton on geometry problems because most figures are drawn to scale.

To Scale or Not to Scale?

That is the question. The ACT makes a big deal in the instructions about the fact that their figures are "NOT necessarily drawn to scale." Here's the thing, though: they usually are drawn to scale, or at least enough to use them in broad strokes. Use Ballparking to eliminate answers that are too big or too small, rather than to determine a precise value. Questions on angles and area especially lend themselves to Ballparking. The main place to be skeptical is on those problems that ask questions like, "Which of the following must be true?" Those are the ones whose figures can be purposely misleading.

In most other cases, if you know how to use the figures that are given (or how to draw your own), you can eliminate several wrong answers before doing any math at all. Let's see how this works.

How Big Is Angle *NLM*?

Obviously, you don't know exactly how big this angle is, but it would be easy to compare it with an angle whose measure you *do* know exactly. Let's compare it with a 90-degree angle.

Angle *NLM* is clearly a bit less than 90°. Now look at the following problem, which asks about the same angle *NLM*.

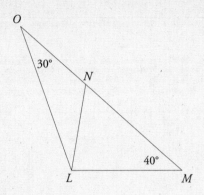

1. In the figure above, O, N, and M are collinear. If the lengths of $\overline{ON}$ and $\overline{NL}$ are the same, and the measure of angle LON is 30° and angle LMN is 40°, what is the measure of angle NLM?

A. 30°
B. 80°
C. 90°
D. 110°
E. 120°

Here's How to Crack It

Start with Step 1: Know the question. Underline "what is the measure of angle NLM?" and even mark the angle on your figure. You don't want to answer for the wrong angle. Now move to Step 2 and let's focus on eliminating answer choices that don't make sense. We've already decided that $\angle NLM$ is a little less than 90°, which means we can eliminate choices (C), (D), and (E). How much less than 90°? 30° is a third of 90. Could $\angle NLM$ be that small? No way! The answer to this question must be choice (B).

In this case, it wasn't necessary to do any "real" geometry at all to get the question right, but it took about half the time. ACT has to give you credit for right answers no matter how you get them. Revenge is sweet. What's more, if you worked this problem the "real" way, you might have picked one of the other answers: as you can imagine, every answer choice gives some partial answer that you would've seen as you worked the problem.

Let's Do It Again

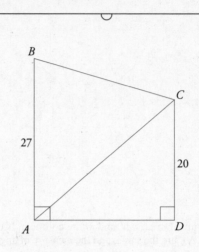

2. In the figure above, if $\overline{AB} = 27, \overline{CD} = 20$, and the area of triangle $ADC = 240$, what is the area of polygon $ABCD$?

   F.   420
   G.   480
   H.   540
   J.   564
   K. 1,128

Here's How to Crack It

Start with Step 1: Know the question. Underline "what is the area of polygon *ABCD*?" This polygon is not a conventional figure, but if we had to choose one figure that the polygon resembled, we might pick a rectangle. Try drawing a line at a right angle from the line segment $\overline{AB}$ so that it touches point *C*, thus creating a rectangle. It should look like this:

The area of polygon *ABCD* is equal to the area of the rectangle you've just formed, plus a little bit at the top. The problem tells you that the area of triangle *ADC* is 240. What is the area of the rectangle you just created? If you said 480, you are exactly right, whether you knew the geometric rules that applied or whether you just measured it with your eyes.

So the area of the rectangle is 480. Roughly speaking, then, what should the area of the polygon be? A little more. Let's look at the answer choices.

> **What Should I Do If There Is No Diagram?**
> Draw one! It's always easier to understand a problem when you can see it in front of you. If possible, draw your figure to scale so that you can estimate the answer as well.

Choices (F) and (G) are either less than or equal to 480; get rid of them. Choices (H) and (J) both seem possible; they are both a little more than 480; let's hold on to them. Choice (K) seems pretty crazy. We want more than 480, but 1,128 is ridiculous.

The answer to this question is choice (J). To get this final answer, you'll need to use a variety of area formulas, which we'll explore later in this chapter. For now, though, notice that your chances of guessing have increased from 20% to 50% with a little bit of quick thinking. Now what should you do? If you know how to do the problem, you do it. If you don't or if you are running out of time, you guess and move on.

However, even as we move in to the "real" geometry in the remainder of this chapter, don't forget:

> Always look for opportunities to Ballpark on geometry problems even if you know how to do them the "real" way.

GEOMETRY REVIEW

By using the diagrams ACT has so thoughtfully provided, and by making your own diagrams when they are not provided, you can often eliminate several of the answer choices. In some cases, you'll be able to eliminate every choice but one. Of course, you will also need to know the actual geometry concepts that ACT is testing. We've divided our review into the following four topics:

1. Angles and lines
2. Triangles
3. Four-sided figures
4. Circles

ANGLES AND LINES

Here is a line.

A line extends forever in either direction. This line, called l_1, has three points on it: A, B, and C. These three points are said to be **collinear** because they are all on the same line. The piece of the line in between points A and B is called a line **segment**. ACT will refer to it as segment AB or simply $\overline{AB}$. A and B are the **endpoints** of segment AB.

A line forms an angle of 180°. If that line is cut by another line, it divides that 180° into two pieces that together add up to 180°.

In the above diagram, what is the value of x? If you said 60°, you are correct. To find $\angle x$, just subtract 120° from 180°.

An angle can also be described by points on the lines that intersect to form the angle and the point of intersection itself, with the middle letter corresponding to the point of intersection. For example, in the previous diagram, $\angle x$ could also be described as $\angle LNP$. On the ACT, instead of writing out "angle LNP," they'll use math shorthand and put $\angle LNP$ instead. So "angle x" becomes $\angle x$.

If there are 180° above a line, there are also 180° below the line, for a total of 360°.

When two lines intersect, they form four angles, represented below by letters A, B, C, and D. $\angle A$ and $\angle B$ together form a straight line, so they add up to 180°.

Angles that add up to 180° are called **supplementary** angles. $\angle A$ and $\angle C$ are opposite from each other and always equal each other, as do $\angle B$ and $\angle D$. Angles like these are called **vertical** angles.

In the previous figure, what is the value of $\angle x$? If you said 80°, you're right. Together with the 100° angle, x forms a straight line. What is the value of $\angle y$? If you said 80°, you're right again. These two angles are vertical and must equal each other. The four angles together add up to 360°.

When two lines meet in such a way that 90° angles are formed, the lines are called **perpendicular**. The little box at the point of the intersection of the two lines below indicates that they are perpendicular. It stands to reason that all four of these angles have a value of 90°.

When two lines in the same plane are drawn so that they could extend into infinity without ever meeting, they are called **parallel**. In the figure below, l_1 is parallel to l_2. The symbol for parallel is $||$.

When two parallel lines are cut by a third line, eight angles are formed, but in fact, there are really only two—a big one and a little one. Look at the diagram below.

If $\angle A = 110°$, then $\angle B$ must equal 70° (together they form a straight line). $\angle D$ is vertical to $\angle B$, which means that it must also equal 70°. $\angle C$ is vertical to $\angle A$, so it must equal 110°.

The four angles $\angle E$, $\angle F$, $\angle G$, and $\angle H$ are in exactly the same proportion as the angles above. The little angles are both 70°. The big angles are both 110°.

Try the following problem.

1. In the figure above, line L is parallel to line M. Line N intersects both L and M, with angles a, b, c, d, e, f, g, and h as shown. Which of the following lists includes all the angles that are supplementary to $\angle a$?

    A. Angles b, d, f, and h
    B. Angles c, e, and g
    C. Angles b, d, and c
    D. Angles e, f, g, and h
    E. Angles d, c, h, and g

Here's How to Crack It

An angle is supplementary to another angle if the two angles together add up to 180°. Because $\angle a$ is one of the eight angles formed by the intersection of a line with two parallel lines, we know that there are really only two angles: a big one and a little one. $\angle a$ is a big one. Thus only the small angles would be supplementary to it. Which angles are those? The correct answer is choice (A). By the way, if you think back to the last chapter and apply what you learned there, could you have Plugged In on this problem? Of course you could have. After all, there are variables in the answer choices. Sometimes it is easier to see the correct answer if you substitute real values for the angles instead of just looking at them as a series of variables. Just because a problem involves geometry doesn't mean that you can't Plug In on it.

N

$a = 100°$ / $b = 80°$ L
$d = 80°$ / $c = 100°$

$e = 100°$ / $f = 80°$ M
$h = 80°$ / $g = 100°$

TRIANGLES

A triangle is a three-sided figure whose inside angles always add up to 180°. The largest angle of a triangle is always opposite its largest side. Thus, in triangle *XYZ* below, *XY* would be the largest side, followed by *YZ*, followed by *XZ*. On the ACT, "triangle *XYZ*" will be written as Δ*XYZ*.

The ACT likes to ask about certain kinds of triangles in particular.

An **isosceles** triangle has two equal sides. The angles opposite those sides are also equal. In the isosceles triangle above, if ∠*A* = 50°, then so does ∠*C*. If $\overline{AB}$ = 6, then so does $\overline{BC}$.

An **equilateral** triangle has three equal sides and three equal angles. Because the three equal angles must add up to 180°, all three angles of an equilateral triangle are always equal to 60°.

A **right triangle** has one inside angle that is equal to 90°. The longest side of a right triangle (the one opposite the 90° angle) is called the **hypotenuse**.

Pythagoras, a Greek mathematician, discovered that the sides of a right triangle are always in a particular proportion, which can be expressed by the formula $a^2 + b^2 = c^2$, where a and b are the shorter sides of the triangle, and c is the hypotenuse. This formula is called the **Pythagorean theorem**.

There are certain right triangles that the test writers at ACT find endlessly fascinating. Let's test out the Pythagorean theorem on the first of these.

$$3^2 + 4^2 = c^2$$
$$9 + 16 = 25$$
$$c^2 = 25, \text{ so } c = 5$$

The ACT writers adore the 3-4-5 triangle and use it frequently, along with its multiples, such as the 6-8-10 triangle and the 9-12-15 triangle. Of course, you can always use the Pythagorean theorem to figure out the third side of a right triangle, as long as you have the other two sides, but because ACT problems almost invariably use "triples" like the ones we've just mentioned, it makes sense just to memorize them.

The ACT has three commonly used right-triangle triples.

3-4-5 (and its multiples)

5-12-13 (and its multiples)

7-24-25 (not as common as the other two)

Don't Get Snared

- Is this a 3-4-5 triangle?

No, because the hypotenuse of a right triangle must be its *longest* side—the one opposite the 90° angle. In this case, we must use the Pythagorean theorem to discover side c: $3^2 + c^2 = 16$. $c = \sqrt{7}$.

- Is this a 5-12-13 triangle?

No, because the Pythagorean theorem—and triples—apply only to *right* triangles. We can't determine definitively the third side of this triangle based on the angles.

The Isosceles Right Triangle

As fond as the ACT test writers are of triples, they are even fonder of two other right triangles. The first is called the **isosceles right triangle**. The sides and angles of the isosceles right triangle are always in a particular proportion.

You could use the Pythagorean theorem to prove this (or you could just take our word for it). Whatever the value of the two equal sides of the isosceles right triangle, the hypotenuse is always equal to one of those sides times $\sqrt{2}$. Here are two examples.

> **Be on the Lookout…**
>
> for problems in which the application of the Pythagorean theorem is not obvious. For example, every rectangle contains two right triangles. That means that if you know the length and width of the rectangle, you also know the length of the diagonal, which is the hypotenuse of both triangles created by the diagonal.

The 30-60-90 Triangle

The other right triangle tested frequently on the ACT is the **30-60-90 triangle**, which also always has the same proportions.

You can use the Pythagorean theorem to prove this (or you can just take our word for it). Whatever the value of the short side of the 30-60-90 triangle, the hypotenuse is always twice as large. The medium side is always equal to the short side times $\sqrt{3}$. Here are two examples.

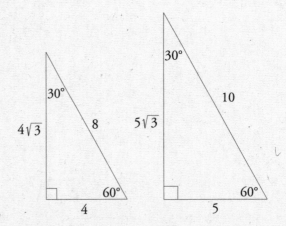

Because these triangles are tested so frequently, it makes sense to memorize the proportions, rather than waste time deriving them each time they appear.

Don't Get Snared

- In the isosceles right triangle below, are the sides equal to $3\sqrt{2}$?

No. Remember, in an isosceles right triangle, hypotenuse = the side $\sqrt{2}$. In this case, 3 = the side $\sqrt{2}$. If we solve for the side, we get $\dfrac{3}{\sqrt{2}}$ = the side.

For arcane mathematical reasons, we are not supposed to leave a radical in the denominator, but we can multiply top and bottom by $\sqrt{2}$ to get $\dfrac{3\sqrt{2}}{2}$.

- In the right triangle below, is x equal to $4\sqrt{3}$?

No. Even though it is one of ACT's favorites, you have to be careful not to see a 30-60-90 where none exists. In the triangle above, the short side is half of the *medium* side, not half of the hypotenuse. This is some sort of right triangle all right, but it is not a 30-60-90. The hypotenuse, in case you're curious, is really $4\sqrt{5}$.

Area

The **area** of a triangle can be found using the following formula:

$$\text{area} = \frac{\text{base} \times \text{height}}{2}$$

Height is measured as the perpendicular distance from the base of the triangle to its highest point.

In all three of the above triangles, the area is:

$$\frac{8 \times 4}{2} = 16$$

Don't Get Snared

- Sometimes the height of a triangle can be *outside* the triangle itself, as we just saw in the second example.
- In a right triangle, the height of the triangle can also be one of the sides of the triangle, as we just saw in the third example. However, be careful when finding the area of a *non-right* triangle. Simply because you know two sides of the triangle does not mean that you have the height of the triangle.

Similar Triangles

Two triangles are called similar if their angles have the same degree measures. This means their sides will be in proportion. For example, the two triangles below are similar.

Because the sides of the two triangles are in the same proportion, you can find the missing side, x, by setting up a proportion equation.

$$\begin{array}{cc} & \text{small triangle} \qquad \text{big triangle} \\ \dfrac{\text{short leg}}{\text{hypotenuse}} & \dfrac{2}{4} \quad = \quad \dfrac{4}{x} \\ & x = 8 \end{array}$$

ACT TRIANGLE PROBLEMS

In this chapter, we've pretty much given you all the basic triangle information you'll need to do the triangle problems on the ACT. The trick is that you'll have to use a lot of this information all at once. Let's have a look at a typical ACT triangle problem and see how to use the basic approach.

3. In the figure above, square *ABCD* is attached to △*ADE* as shown. If ∠*EAD* is equal to 30 and $\overline{AE}$ is equal to $4\sqrt{3}$, then what is the area of square *ABCD*?

   A. $8\sqrt{3}$
   B. 16
   C. 64
   D. 72
   E. $64\sqrt{2}$

Here's How to Crack It

Start with Step 1: Know the question. Underline "what is the area of square *ABCD*?" Move to Step 2 and look at the answers. We don't have any values for areas of other shapes within the figure, so there is nothing to Ballpark. But note the presence of $\sqrt{2}$ and $\sqrt{3}$ in the answers: they're an additional clue, if you haven't absorbed the info given, that either 30-60-90 and/or 45-45-90 triangles are in play.

The triangle in the figure is in fact a 30-60-90. Now move to Step 3: Break the problem into bite-sized pieces. Because angle *A* is the short angle, the side opposite that angle is equal to 4 and the hypotenuse is equal to 8. Now move on to Step 3a: mark your figure with these values. Now move to Step 3b: Write down any formulas you need. The area for a square is s^2. Because that hypotenuse is also the side of the square, the area of the square must be 8 times 8, or 64. This is choice (C). If you forgot the ratio of the sides of a 30-60-90 triangle, go back and review it. You'll need it.

POE Pointers

If you didn't remember the ratio of the sides of a 30-60-90 triangle, could you have eliminated some answers using POE? Of course. Let's see if we can use the diagram to eliminate some answer choices.

The diagram tells us that $\overline{AE}$ has length $4\sqrt{3}$. Remember the important approximations we gave you earlier in the chapter? A good approximation for $\sqrt{3}$ is 1.7. So $4\sqrt{3}$ = approximately 6.8. We can now use this to estimate the sides of square $ABCD$. Just using your eyes, would you say that $\overline{AD}$ is longer or shorter than $\overline{AE}$? Of course it's a bit longer; it's the hypotenuse of $\triangle ADE$. You decide and write down what you think it might be. To find the area of the square, simply square whatever value you decided the side equaled. This is your answer.

Now all you have to do is see which of the answer choices still makes sense. Could the answer be choice (A)? $8\sqrt{3}$ equals roughly 13.6. Is this close to your answer? No way. Could the answer be choice (B), which is 16? Still much too small. Could the answer be choice (C), which is 64? Quite possibly. Could the answer be 72? It might be. Could the correct answer be $64\sqrt{2}$? An approximation of radical 2 = 1.4, so $64\sqrt{2}$ equals 89.6. This seems rather large. Thus, on this problem, by using POE we could eliminate choices (A), (B), and (E).

FOUR-SIDED FIGURES

The interior angles of any four-sided figure (also known as a quadrilateral) add up to 360°. The most common four-sided figures on the ACT are the rectangle and the square, with the parallelogram and the trapezoid coming in a far distant third and fourth.

Your Friend the Triangle

Because a quadrilateral is really just two triangles, its interior angles must measure twice those of a triangle: 2(180) = 360.

A **rectangle** is a four-sided figure whose four interior angles are each equal to 90°. The area of a rectangle is *base* × *height*. Therefore, the area of the rectangle above is 8 (*base*) × 5 (*height*) = 40. The perimeter of a rectangle is the sum of all four of its sides. The perimeter of the rectangle above is 8 + 8 + 5 + 5 = 26.

A **square** is a rectangle whose four sides are all equal in length. You can think of the area of a square, therefore, as **side squared**. The area of the above square is 6 (*base*) × 6 (*height*) = 36. The perimeter is 24, or 4*s*.

A **parallelogram** is a four-sided figure made up of two sets of parallel lines. We said earlier that when parallel lines are crossed by a third line, eight angles are formed but that in reality there are only two—the big one and the little one. In a parallelogram, 16 angles are formed, but there are still, in reality, only two.

The area of a parallelogram is also *base × height,* but because of the shape of the figure, the height of a parallelogram is not necessarily equal to one of its sides. Height is measured by a perpendicular line drawn from the base to the top of the figure. The area of the parallelogram above is $9 \times 5 = 45$.

A **trapezoid** is a four-sided figure in which two sides are parallel. Both of the figures above are trapezoids. The area of a trapezoid is the *average of the two parallel sides × the height,* or $\frac{1}{2}$ (*base* 1 + *base* 2)(*height*), but on ACT problems involving trapezoids, there is almost always some easy way to find the area without knowing the formula (for example, by dividing the trapezoid into two triangles and a rectangle). In both trapezoids above, the area is 27.

Doh, I'm in a Square!
To help you remember the area of a four-sided figure (a square, a rectangle, or a parallelogram), imagine that Bart and Homer Simpson are stuck inside of it. To get its area, just multiply **B**art times **H**omer, or (*b*)(*h*), or the base times the height.

CIRCLES

The distance from the center of a circle to any point on the circle is called the **radius**. The distance from one point on a circle through the center of the circle to another point on the circle is called the **diameter**. The diameter is always equal to twice the radius. In the circle on the left below, *AB* is called a **chord**. *CD* is called a **tangent** to the circle.

The curved portion of the right-hand circle between points *A* and *B* is called an **arc**. The angle formed by drawing lines from the center of the circle to points *A* and *B* is said to be **subtended** by the arc. There are 360° in a circle, so that if the angle we just mentioned equaled 60°, it would take up $\frac{60}{360}$ or $\frac{1}{6}$ of the degrees in the entire circle. It would also take up $\frac{1}{6}$ of the area of the circle and $\frac{1}{6}$ of the outer perimeter of the circle, called the **circumference**.

The formula for the **area** of a circle is πr^2.

The formula for the **circumference** is $2\pi r$.

In the circle below, if the radius is 4, then the area is 16π, and the circumference is 8π.

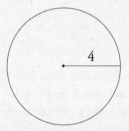

The key to circle problems on the ACT is to look for the word or phrase that tells you what to do. If you see the word *circumference*, immediately write down the formula for circumference, and plug in any numbers the problem has given you. By solving for whatever quantity is still unknown, you have probably already answered the problem. Another tip is to find the radius. The radius is the key to many circle problems.

1. If the area of a circle is 16 meters, what is its radius in meters?

   A. $\dfrac{8}{\pi}$

   B. 12π

   C. $\dfrac{4\sqrt{\pi}}{\pi}$

   D. $\dfrac{16}{\pi}$

   E. $144\pi^2$

Here's How to Crack It

Step 1: Know the question. We need to solve for the radius. Step 2: Let the answers help. We don't have a figure, so there's nothing to Ballpark. But no figure? Step 3a. Draw your own.

Step 3b: Write down any formulas you need and fill in the information you have. Set the formula for area of a circle equal to $\pi r^2 = 16$. The problem is asking for the radius, so you have to solve for r. If you divide both sides by π, you get

$$r^2 = \frac{16}{\pi}$$

$$r = \sqrt{\frac{16}{\pi}}$$

$$= \frac{4}{\sqrt{\pi}}$$

$$= \frac{4\sqrt{\pi}}{\pi}$$

The correct answer is choice (C).

2. In the figure above, the circle with center O is inscribed inside square $ABCD$ as shown. If a side of the square measures 8 units, what is the area of the shaded region?

   F. $8 - 16\pi$
   G. 8π
   H. 16π
   J. $64 - 16\pi$
   K. 64π

Here's How to Crack It

Begin with Step 1 and underline "what is the area of the shaded region?" Step 2 brings us to the answers, and we see all of the answers have π in them. There is no obvious choice to Ballpark just yet, so move to Step 3. Break the problem into bite-sized pieces, but don't get hung up on "inscribed." Yes, that's an important term to know, but since we have the figure, it's irrelevant. Move to Step 3a and 3b: mark the side of the square "8" and write down the formulas for the area of a circle and square: πr^2 and s^2.

Is there a formula for the shape made by the shaded region? Nope. We just need the basic formulas for the basic shapes. $8^2 = 64$, so we at least know the shaded region is less than 64, the area of the square. But what's the link between the square and the circle? The side of the square equals the diameter. So if the diameter is 8, then the radius must be 4. Use that in the area formula, and $4^2\pi = 16\pi$. Subtract the area of the circle from the area of the square, and we get choice (J).

FUN FACTS ABOUT FIGURES

Read and review the following facts you need to know about plane geometry.

Angle Facts

- There are 90° in a right angle.
- When two straight lines intersect, angles opposite each other are equal.
- There are 180° in a straight line.
- Two lines are perpendicular when they meet at a 90° angle.
- The sign for perpendicular is ⊥.
- Bisect means to cut exactly in half.
- There are 180° in a triangle.
- There are 360° in any four-sided figure.

Triangle Facts

In any triangle

- The longest side is opposite the largest angle.
- The shortest side is opposite the smallest angle.
- All angles add up to 180°.
- Area $= \frac{1}{2}$ (base × height) $= \frac{1}{2}bh$
- The height is the perpendicular distance from the base to the opposite vertex.
- Perimeter is the sum of the sides.
- The third side of any triangle is always less than the sum and greater than the difference of the other two sides.

In an isosceles triangle

- Two sides are equal.
- The two angles opposite the equal sides are also equal.

In an equilateral triangle

- All three sides are equal.
- All angles are each equal to 60°.

Four-Sided Figure Facts

In a quadrilateral
- All four angles add up to 360°.

In a parallelogram
- Opposite sides are parallel and equal.
- Opposite angles are equal.
- Adjacent angles are supplementary (add up to 180°).
- Area = base × height = bh
- The height is the perpendicular distance from the base to the opposite side.

In a rhombus
- Opposite sides are parallel.
- Opposite angles are equal.
- Adjacent angles are supplementary (add up to 180°).
- All 4 sides are equal.
- Area = base × height = bh
- The height is the perpendicular distance from the base to the opposite side.
- The diagonals are perpendicular.

In a rectangle
- Rectangles are special parallelograms; thus, any fact about parallelograms also applies to rectangles.
- All 4 angles are each equal to 90°.
- Area = length × width = lw
- Perimeter = 2(length) + 2(width) = $2l + 2w$
- The diagonals are equal.

In a square
- Squares are special rectangles; thus, any fact about rectangles also applies to squares.
- All 4 sides are equal.
- Area = (side)^2 = s^2
- Perimeter = 4(side) = $4s$
- The diagonals are perpendicular.

Circle Facts

Circle
- There are 360° in a circle.

Radius (r)
- The distance from the center to any point on the edge of the circle.
- All radii in a circle are equal.

Diameter (d)
- The distance of a line that connects two points on the edge of the circle, passing through the center.
- The longest line in a circle.
- Equals twice the radius.

Chord
- Any line segment connecting two points on the edge of a circle.
- The longest chord is called the diameter.

Circumference (C)
- The distance around the outside of the circle.
- $C = 2\pi r = \pi d$

Arc
- Any part of the circumference.
- The length of an arc is proportional to the size of the interior angle.

Area
- The amount of space within the boundaries of the circle.
- $A = \pi r^2$

Sector
- Any part of the area formed by two radii and the outside of the circle.
- The area of a sector is proportional to the size of the interior angle.

Line Facts

Line
- A line has no width and extends infinitely in both directions.
- Any line measures 180°.
- A line that contains points A and B is called $\overleftrightarrow{AB}$ (line AB).
- If a figure on the ACT looks like a straight line, and that line looks like it contains a point, it does.

Ray
- • A ray extends infinitely in one direction but has an endpoint.
- • The degree measure of a ray is 180°.
- • A ray with endpoint A that goes through point B is called $\overrightarrow{AB}$. Pay attention to the arrow above the points and the order they are given; those will determine the direction the ray is pointing!

Line Segment
- • A line segment is a part of a line and has two endpoints.
- • The degree measure of a line segment is 180°.
- • A line segment, which has endpoints of A and B, is written as $\overline{AB}$.

Tangents
- • Tangent means intersecting at one point. For example, a line tangent to a circle intersects exactly one point on the circumference of the circle. Two circles that touch at just one point are also tangent.
- • A tangent line to a circle is always perpendicular to the radius drawn to that point of intersection.
- • If $\overline{AB}$ intersects a circle at point T, then you would say, "$\overline{AB}$ is tangent to the circle at point T."

PLANE GEOMETRY FORMULAS

Here's a list of all the plane geometry formulas that could show up on the ACT. Memorize the formulas for perimeter/circumference, area, and volume for basic shapes. ACT usually provides the more advanced formulas if they are needed.

Circles

- Area: $A = \pi r^2$
- Circumference: $C = 2\pi r = \pi d$

Triangles

- Area: $A = \frac{1}{2}bh$

- Perimeter: P = sum of the sides

- Pythagorean theorem: $a^2 + b^2 = c^2$

SOHCAHTOA

- $\sin(\theta) = \dfrac{\text{opposite}}{\text{hypotenuse}}$

- $\cos(\theta) = \dfrac{\text{adjacent}}{\text{hypotenuse}}$

- $\tan(\theta) = \dfrac{\text{opposite}}{\text{adjacent}}$

- $\csc(\theta) = \dfrac{1}{\sin}$

- $\sec(\theta) = \dfrac{1}{\cos}$

- $\cot(\theta) = \dfrac{1}{\tan}$

Quadrilaterals

Parallelograms

- Area: $A = bh$
- Perimeter: P = sum of the sides

Rhombus

- Area: $A = bh$
- Perimeter: P = sum of the sides

Trapezoids

- Area: $A = \dfrac{1}{2}h\left(b_1 + b_2\right)$
- Perimeter: P = sum of the sides

Rectangles

- Area: $A = lw$
- Perimeter: $P = 2(l + w)$

Squares

- Area: $A = s^2$
- Perimeter: $P = 4s$

Polygons

- Sum of angles in an n-sided polygon: $(n-2)180°$
- Angle measure of each angle in a regular n-sided polygon:

$$\dfrac{(n-2)180°}{n}$$

3-D Figures

- Surface area of a rectangular solid: $S = 2\left(lw + lh + wh\right)$
- Surface area of a cube: $S = 6s^2$
- Surface area of a right circular cylinder: $S = 2\pi r^2 + 2\pi rh$
- Surface area of a sphere: $S = 4\pi r^2$
- Volume of a cube: $V = s^3$
- Volume of a rectangular solid: $V = lwh$
- Volume of a right circular cylinder: $V = \pi r^2 h$
- Volume of a sphere: $V = \dfrac{4\pi r^3}{3}$

GLOSSARY

Arc:	Any part of the circumference
Bisect:	To cut in half
Chord:	Any line segment connecting two points on the edge of a circle
Circumscribed:	Surrounded by a circle as small as possible
Collinear:	Lying on the same line
Congruent:	Equal in size
Diagonal (of a polygon):	A line segment connecting opposite vertices
Equilateral triangle:	All sides are equal and each angle measures 60°
Inscribed (angle in a circle):	An angle in a circle with its vertex on the circumference
Isosceles triangle:	A triangle with two equal sides
Parallel:	Two distinct lines that do not intersect
Perpendicular:	At a 90° angle
Plane:	A flat surface extending in all directions
Polygon:	A closed figure with two or more sides
Quadrilateral:	A four-sided figure
Regular polygon:	A figure with all equal sides and angles
Sector:	Any part of the area formed by two radii and the outside of the circle
Similar:	Equal angles and proportional sides
Surface area:	The sum of areas of each face of a figure
Tangent:	Intersecting at one point
Vertex/Vertices:	A corner point. For angles, it's where two rays meet. For figures, it's where two adjacent sides meet.

Geometry Drill

For the answers to this drill, please go to Chapter 24.

1. In △*ABC* above, ∠*A* = ∠*B,* and ∠*C* is twice the measure of ∠*B*. What is the measure, in degrees, of ∠*A*?

    A. 30
    B. 45
    C. 50
    D. 75
    E. 90

3. In the figure above, right triangles *ABC* and *ACD* are drawn as shown. If $\overline{AB} = 20$, $\overline{BC} = 15$, and $\overline{AD} = 7$, then $\overline{CD}$ =?

    A. 21
    B. 22
    C. 23
    D. 24
    E. 25

4. If the area of circle *A* is 16π, then what is the circumference of circle *B* if its radius is $\frac{1}{2}$ that of circle *A*?

    F. 2π
    G. 4π
    H. 6π
    J. 8π
    K. 16π

2. In the figure above, $l_1 \parallel l_2$. Which of the labeled angles must be equal to each other?

    F. *A* and *C*
    G. *D* and *E*
    H. *A* and *B*
    J. *D* and *B*
    K. *C* and *B*

5. In the figure above, $\overline{MO}$ is perpendicular to $\overline{LN}$, $\overline{LO}$ is equal to 4, $\overline{MO}$ is equal to $\overline{ON}$, and $\overline{LM}$ is equal to 6. What is $\overline{MN}$?

    A. $2\sqrt{10}$
    B. $3\sqrt{5}$
    C. $4\sqrt{5}$
    D. $3\sqrt{10}$
    E. $6\sqrt{4}$

Summary

o Use the basic approach.
- **Step 1:** Know the question. Read the whole problem before calculating anything, and underline the actual question.
- **Step 2:** Let the answers help. Look for clues on how to solve and ways to use Process of Elimination (POE). Ballparking works well on geometry questions on area and angles.
- **Step 3:** Break the problem into bite-sized pieces. When you read the problem a second time, calculate at each step necessary and watch out for tricky phrasing. On geometry, this means:
- **Step 3a:** Write all the information given in the problem on the figure. If there is no figure, draw your own.
- **Step 3b:** Write down any formulas you need and fill in any information you have.

o There are several things to know about angles and lines.
- A line is a 180° angle.
- When two lines intersect, four angles are formed, but in reality there are only two distinct measures.
- When two parallel lines are cut by a third line, eight angles are formed, but in reality there are still only two (a large one and a small one).

o There are several things to know about triangles.
- A triangle has three sides and three angles; the sum of the angles equals 180°.
- An isosceles triangle has two equal sides and two equal angles opposite those sides.
- An equilateral triangle has three equal sides and three equal angles; each angle equals 60°.
- A right triangle has one 90° angle. In a right triangle problem you can use the Pythagorean theorem to find the lengths of sides.
- Some common right triangles are 3-4-5, 6-8-10, 5-12-13, and 7-24-25.

- ACT test writers also like the isosceles right triangle, in which the sides are always in the ratio $s : s : s\sqrt{2}$, and the 30-60-90 triangle, in which the sides are always in the ratio $s : s\sqrt{3} : 2s$.
- Similar triangles have the same angle measurements and sides that are in the same proportion.

- The area of a triangle is equal to $\dfrac{(\text{base} \times \text{height})}{2}$, with height measured perpendicular to the base.

○ Four-sided objects are called quadrilaterals and have four angles, which add up to 360°. There are several important things to remember.
- The area of a rectangle, a square, or a parallelogram can be found using the formula *base* × *height* = *area,* with height measured perpendicular to the base.
- The perimeter of any object is the sum of the lengths of its sides.
- The area of a trapezoid is equal to the average of the two bases times the height.

○ For any circle problem, you need to know four basic things:
- radius
- diameter
- area (πr^2)
- circumference (πd or $2\pi r$)

○ Don't forget that you can plug in on geometry questions that have variables in the answer choices.

Chapter 13
Word Problems

Now that you've refreshed some of the essential geometry concepts, we will see how to integrate those concepts with your test-taking strategy. In addition, we'll see some other Word Problem strategies that will help you to complete problems quickly and accurately.

PLUGGING IN: NOT JUST ALGEBRA

Remember what the main requirements are for a Plugging In problem. You need variables in the answer choices or question: that's it. It doesn't say anywhere that the problem needs to be a pure algebra problem. What is a pure algebra problem anyway? Don't forget: part of what makes this test so hard is that ACT piles concept on top of concept in its problems. In other words, geometry problems often *are* algebra problems.

WORD PROBLEMS VS. PLUG-AND-CHUG QUESTIONS

We prefer a simple definition of a word problem: it has to tell a story. But as we discussed in Chapter 12, plug-and-chug geometry questions can have so much information in them, they feel like word problems. So treat them like word problems, and let's refresh the basic approach we discussed in Chapter 12.

Step 1: Know the Question

Know the question. Read the whole problem before calculating anything, and underline the actual question.

Step 2: Let the Answers Help

Let the answers help. Look for clues on how to solve and ways to use POE.

Step 3: Break the Problem into Bite-Sized Pieces

Break the problem into bite-sized pieces. When you read the problem a second time, calculate at each step necessary and watch out for tricky phrasing.

For geometry questions, Step 3 has two specific additions:

> **Step 3a:** Write all the information given in the problem on the figure. If there is no figure, draw your own.
>
> **Step 3b:** Write down any formulas you need and fill in any information you have.

Let's see a short, straightforward example:

———————◯———————

1. A circle with center *O* has a radius *r*. What is the area of a circle with a radius three times larger?

   A. $3\pi r$
   B. $9\pi r$
   C. $3\pi r^2$
   D. $6\pi r^2$
   E. $9\pi r^2$

Here's How to Crack It

Step 1: **Know the question.** We need to find the area of this new larger circle, not the larger radius.

Step 2: **Let the answers help.** First of all, we're looking for the area, which means something will have to be squared, so we can eliminate choices (A) and (B), which can't be right. Now, notice that each of these answer choices has a variable in it. If you're thinking Plugging In, you're thinking right.

Step 3: **Break the problem into bite-sized pieces.** Let's pick an easy value for *r*, like *r* = 2.

Step 3a: **Write all the information given in the problem on the figure.** There's no figure here, so draw 2 circles.

Step 3b: **Write down any formulas you need and fill in any information you have**. The formula for the area of a circle that we'll need is $A = \pi r^2$.

If the original radius is 2, then the larger radius, which is three times larger, must be 6. Therefore, the area of the larger circle must be $A = \pi(6)^2 = 36\pi$. We've got a target answer, so let's try it in the answer choices. Remember, we've already eliminated choices (A) and (B).

   A. ~~$3\pi r$~~
   B. ~~$9\pi r$~~
   C. $3\pi(2)^2 = 12\pi$ X
   D. $6\pi(2)^2 = 24\pi$ X
   E. $9\pi(2)^2 = 36\pi$ ✔

Choice (E) is the correct answer. Have another look at those answer choices and think of all the ways you could make mistakes on this problem. Plugging In saves the day again by minimizing the possibility for algebra errors.

———————◯———————

ARITHMETIC

When it comes to writing word problems, ACT test writers can draw on both algebra and geometry, as we've seen. But lots of word problems, and even some plug-and-chugs, will test a variety of arithmetic concepts. The rest of this chapter will review those topics.

PERCENTAGES, PROBABILITIES, AND RATIOS: DIDN'T WE JUST DO THIS?

Percentages, probabilities, and ratios can get mighty complex in your math classes at school. Do you want the good news or the bad news? Well, the bad news is that ratios, percentages, and probabilities will all appear on the ACT Math test, but the good news is that they're all testing the same basic concept: parts to wholes.

Let's say you're taking batting practice. You are thrown 100 pitches and you hit 20 of them. Ignoring the fact that you're probably not ready for the MLB, let's put this into some math language. Once we get the basics down, we'll try some more advanced problems.

First, what percent of the pitches did you hit? Well, that's easy on this one because we're dealing with 100. But you can always find percentages with this simple part-to-whole formula:

$$\frac{part}{whole} \times 100\%$$

Once we put the numbers in, we'll get this: $\frac{20}{100} \times 100\% = 0.2 \times 100\% = 20\%$. If you hit 20 of the 100 pitches, you hit 20% of them.

Next, what is the probability that you were to hit any given pitch? Remember, this is just a matter of parts to wholes, so we can find this probability as follows: $\frac{part}{whole} = \frac{hits}{pitches} = \frac{20}{100} = 0.2$. In other words, there's a 0.2, or $\frac{1}{5}$, probability you hit any given pitch during batting practice.

Ratios are a little different. Usually these will ask for the relationship of some part to some other part. If we're still using our batting practice statistics, we might want to know something like, What's the ratio of the pitches you hit to the pitches you missed?

Even though we're not dealing with the whole this time, we'll find the ratio the same way, but instead of $\frac{part}{whole}$, we'll use $\frac{part}{whole} = \frac{hits}{misses} = \frac{20}{80} = \frac{1}{4}$. The ratio of hits to misses is $\frac{1}{4}$, or 1 to 4, or 1:4.

If it feels like we just did the same thing three times, it was supposed to. As we've seen a few times already, just because things have different names doesn't mean that they are unrelated. Let's try some problems.

Percentages

---

1. At a restaurant, diners enjoy an "early bird" discount of 10% off their bills. If a diner orders a meal regularly priced at $18 and leaves a tip of 15% of the discounted meal (no tax), how much does he pay in total?

    A. $13.50
    B. $16.20
    C. $18.63
    D. $18.90
    E. $20.70

Here's How to Crack It

Step 1: **Know the question.** We want the price of the discounted meal plus tip.

Step 2: **Let the answers help.** We are reducing a number by 10%, then increasing it by 15%, so it's not likely that the final number will be much less or much greater than $18. Let's eliminate choices (A) and (E).

Step 3: **Break the problem into bite-sized pieces.**

First, we'll need to figure out what the discounted price of the meal is. There are a number of ways to do this, but if you find this $\frac{part}{whole}$ method useful, you could find the discount this way:

$$10\% = discount$$

$$\frac{10}{100} = \frac{discount}{\$18}$$

$$discount = \$1.80$$

The price of the discounted meal, then, is $18 − $1.80 = $16.20. Let's find the tip the same way.

$$15\% = tip$$

$$\frac{15}{100} = \frac{tip}{\$16.20}$$

$$tip = \$2.43$$

The price of the discounted meal plus tip, therefore, is $16.20 + $2.43 = $18.63 . The correct answer is choice (C).

Another Way to Deal with Percents

A percentage is a fraction in which the denominator equals 100. In literal terms, the word *percent* means "divided by 100," so any time you see a percentage in an ACT question, you can punch it into your calculator quite easily. If a question asks for 40 percent of something, for instance, you can express the percentage as a fraction: $\frac{40}{100}$. Any time you are looking for a percent, you can use your calculator to find the decimal equivalent and multiply the result by 100. If four out of five dentists recommend a particular brand of toothpaste, you can quickly determine the percent of doctors who recommend it by typing $\frac{4}{5} \times 100$ and hitting the [ENTER] key. The resulting "80" just needs a percent sign tacked onto it. To properly translate all percent questions, it is helpful to have a decoding table for the various terms you'll come across.

English	Math Equivalent
percent	/100
of	multiplication (×)
what	variable (*y*, *z*)
is, are, were	=
what percent	$\frac{y}{100}$

Percentage Shortcuts

In the last problem, we could have saved a little time if we had realized that $\frac{1}{5} = 20$ percent. Therefore, $\frac{4}{5}$ would be 4×20 percent or 80 percent. Below are some fractions and decimals whose percent equivalents you should know.

Another fast way to do percents is to move the decimal place. To find 10 percent of any number, move the decimal point of that number over one place to the left.

$$10\% \text{ of } 500 = 50$$

$$10\% \text{ of } 50 = 5$$

$$10\% \text{ of } 5 = .5$$

To find 1 percent of a number, move the decimal point of that number over two places to the left.

$$1\% \text{ of } 500 = 5$$

$$1\% \text{ of } 50 = .5$$

$$1\% \text{ of } 5 = .05$$

You can use a combination of these last two techniques to find even very complicated percentages by breaking them down into easy-to-find chunks.

- 20% of 500: 10% of 500 = 50, so 20% is twice 50, or 100.
- 30% of 70: 10% of 70 = 7, so 30% is three times 7, or 21.
- 32% of 400: 10% of 400 = 40, so 30% is three times 40, or 120.
- 1% of 400 = 4, so 2% is two times 4, or 8.

Therefore, 32 percent of 400 = 120 + 8 = 128.

> ## The Big Four: Fraction/Percent Equivalents You Should Know
>
> $$\frac{1}{5} = .2 = 20\%$$
>
> $$\frac{1}{4} = .25 = 25\%$$
>
> $$\frac{1}{3} = .\overline{33} = 33\frac{1}{3}\%$$
>
> $$\frac{1}{2} = .5 = 50\%$$

Let's have a look at another ACT percentage problem.

――――――○――――――

2. When 15% of 40 is added to 5% of 260, the resulting number is:

   F. 19
   G. 40
   H. 95
   J. 180
   K. 260

Here's How to Crack It

Let's try this one using the decoding table. Although this isn't really a word problem, that doesn't mean we shouldn't be careful and break it into bite-sized pieces.

First, 15% of 40. Remember, % translates ÷100 and "of" translates to multiplication. Therefore, we can rewrite 15% of 40 as $\frac{15}{100} \times 40$. Put this expression in your calculator to find that $\frac{15}{100} \times 40 = 6$.

Now, 5% of 260. Use the same translations to find $\frac{5}{100} \times 260 = 13$. We've done the tough part, so let's substitute what we've found back into the problem: *When 6 is added to 13, the resulting number is*: Now that's a problem we can handle! 6 + 13 = 19, choice (F).

――――――○――――――

Probability

———————○———————

3. Herbie's practice bag contains 4 blue racquetballs, one red racquetball, and 6 green racquetballs. If he chooses a ball at random, which of the following is closest to the probability that the ball will NOT be green?

   A. 0.09
   B. 0.27
   C. 0.36
   D. 0.45
   E. 0.54

Here's How to Crack It

Step 1: **Know the question.** Make sure you read carefully! We want the probability that the chosen ball will NOT be green.

Step 2: **Let the answers help.** Green balls account for slightly more than half the number of balls in the bag, so the likelihood that the ball will NOT be green should be slightly less than half. That eliminates choices (A), (B), and (E). Not bad!

Step 3: **Break the problem into bite-sized pieces.** This is a pretty straightforward $\frac{part}{whole}$ problem: $\frac{part}{whole} = \frac{NOT\,green}{all} = \frac{5}{11}$. The only slight difficulty is that the answers are not listed as fractions, but it's nothing a calculator can't help. Find $5 \div 11 = 0.45$, choice (D).

———————○———————

Ratios

4. If the ratio of $2x$ to $5y$ is $\frac{1}{20}$, what is the ratio of x to y?

    F. $\frac{1}{40}$

    G. $\frac{1}{20}$

    H. $\frac{1}{10}$

    J. $\frac{1}{8}$

    K. $\frac{1}{4}$

Here's How to Crack It

The difficulty of this problem is all in the setup. Just remember that you're comparing parts to wholes, and you'll be fine:

$$\frac{2x}{5y} = \frac{1}{20}$$

To isolate $\frac{x}{y}$ on the left side of this equation, let's multiply both sides of the equation by $\frac{5}{2}$.

$$\frac{5}{2} \times \frac{2x}{5y} = \frac{1}{20} \times \frac{5}{2}$$

$$\frac{x}{y} = \frac{5}{40}$$

$\frac{5}{40}$ reduces to $\frac{1}{8}$. The answer is choice (J).

If you got stuck on this one, look at those answer choices: you could've used PITA!

Let's see how ACT might test ratios in a word problem.

—————————— ◯ ——————————

5. If 3.7 inches of rain fall on Vancouver during the first 4 days of November, and the rain continues to fall at this pace for the rest of the month, approximately how many feet of rain will fall during December? (Note: The month of December has 31 days.)

    A.   2.4
    B.   3.7
    C.   9.5
    D.   28.7
    E.   114.7

Here's How to Crack It

Step 1: **Know the question.** It's in the last line: *how many feet of rain will fall in December?* But be careful: the value given in the problem is in inches. We're going to have to do some converting!

Step 2: **Let the answers help.** Since we know the problem is asking how many *feet* of rain will fall, and the problem tells us that 3.7 *inches* of rain will fall in 4 days, we can do some ballparking. The number of inches will increase, but it will be reduced again when we convert it into feet. Choice (E) is definitely too big, and choice (D) probably is, too.

Step 3: **Break the problem into bite-sized pieces.** There are going to be two main parts to this problem: first, we want to figure out how much rain will fall in 31 days, then we want to convert it to feet. We can do this by using ratios.

The ratio given in the problem is 3.7 inches every four days, or in math terms, $\dfrac{3.7 \text{ in}}{4 \text{ days}}$. The ratio will remain the same no matter how many days there are, so let's use this ratio to find how many inches of rain will fall in December.

$$\frac{3.7 \text{ in}}{4 \text{ days}} = \frac{? \text{ in}}{31 \text{ days}}$$

We can rearrange the terms to find

$$? \text{ in} = \frac{(3.7 \text{ in})(31 \text{ days})}{4 \text{ days}} = 28.675 \text{ in}$$

But we can't stop here! Remember, the problem is asking for a value in feet. (It's a good thing we did some early POE, isn't it?)

We'll use the same process, and this time we already know the ratio of inches to feet: $\dfrac{12 \text{ in}}{1 \text{ ft}}$. As we did above, let's use this ratio to find our answer:

$$\frac{12 \text{ in}}{1 \text{ ft}} = \frac{28.675 \text{ in}}{? \text{ ft}}$$

Rearrange the equation to find

$$? \text{ ft} = \frac{28.675 \text{ in}(1 \text{ ft})}{12 \text{ in}} \approx 2.4 \text{ ft}, \text{ choice (A)}.$$

AVERAGES

There are only three parts to any average question. Fortunately for you, the ACT must give you two of these parts, which are all you need to find the third. The average pie is an easy way to keep track of the information you get from questions dealing with averages. If you have the total, you can always divide by either the average or the number of things in the set (whichever you are given) to find the missing piece of the pie. Similarly, if you have the number of things and the average, you can multiply the two together to arrive at the total (the sum of all the items in the set).

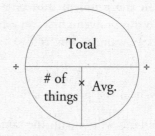

For example, if you want to find the average of 9, 12, and 6 using the average pie, you know you have 3 items with a total of 27. Dividing the total, 27, by the number of things, 3, will yield the average, 9. Your pie looks like this:

Although you probably could have done that without the average pie, more difficult average questions involve multiple calculations and lend themselves particularly well to using the pie. Let's take a look at one:

3. Over 9 games, a baseball team had an average of 8 runs per game. If the average number of runs for the first 7 games was 6 runs per game, and the same number of runs was scored in each of the last 2 games, how many runs did the team score during the last game?

   A.   5
   B.   15
   C.   26
   D.   30
   E.   46

The Missing Number
The ACT loves to leave out totals on average problems. You aren't done until you've found it.

Here's How to Crack It

Step 1: **Know the question.** *How many runs did the team score during the last game?*

Step 2: **Let the answers help.** Eliminate choice (A). Even though the average for the first 7 is higher than all 9, the runs scored in the last two games can't be that few. Similarly, choice (E) is probably too big. If you don't trust your sense of numbers and you're not comfortable Ballparking here, however, leave both. It's a complicated question on a more advanced topic.

Step 3: **Break the problem into bite-sized pieces.** Let's use bite-size pieces to put the information from the first line of this problem into our trusty average pie.

What is the sum of everything for these 9 games? 9×8, or 72.

Now let's put the information from the second line into the average equation.

What is the sum of everything for these 7 games? 7×6, or 42.

If all 9 games added up to 72, and 7 of these games added up to 42, then the remaining 2 games added up to $72 - 42$, or 30. In case you are feeling smug about getting this far, the ACT writers made 30 the answer for choice (D).

But of course you know that they only want the runs they scored in the last game. Because the same number of runs was scored in each of the last two games, the answer is $\frac{30}{2}$ or 15, choice (B).

The Weighted Average

ACT writers have a particular fondness for "weighted average" problems. First, let's look at a regular unweighted average question.

> If Sally received a grade of 90 on a test last week and a grade of 100 on a test this week, what is her average for the two tests?

Piece of cake, right? The answer is 95. You added the scores and divided by 2. Now let's turn the same question into a weighted average question.

> If Sally's average for the entire year last year was 90, and her average for the entire year this year was 100, is her average for the two years combined equal to 95?

The answer is "not necessarily." If Sally took the same number of courses in both years, then yes, her average is 95. But what if last year she took 6 courses while this year she took only 2 courses? Can you compare the two years equally? ACT likes to test your answer to this question. Here's an example.

---

1. The starting team of a baseball club has 9 members who have an average of 12 home runs apiece for the season. The second-string team for the baseball club has 7 members who have an average of 8 home runs apiece for the season. What is the average number of home runs for the starting team and the second-string team combined?

   A. 7.5
   B. 8
   C. 10
   D. 10.25
   E. 14.2

Here's How to Crack It

The ACT test writers want to see whether you spot this as a weighted average problem. If you thought the first-string team was exactly equivalent to the second-string team, then you merely had to take the average of the two averages, 12 and 8, to get 10. In weighted average problems, the ACT test writers always include the average of the two averages among the answer choices, and it is always wrong. 10 is choice (C). Cross off choice (C).

The two teams are not equivalent because there are different numbers of players on each team. To get the true average, we'll have to find the total number of home runs and divide by the total number of players. How do we do this? By going to the trusty average formula as usual. The first line of the problem says that the 9 members on the first team have an average of 12 runs apiece.

So the sum of everything is 9 × 12, or 108.

The second sentence says that the 7 members of the second team have an average of 8 runs each.

So the total is 7 × 8, or 56.

Now we can find the true average. Add all the runs scored by the first team to all the runs scored by the second team: 108 + 56 = 164. This is the true total. We divide it by the total number of players (9 + 7 = 16).

The answer is 10.25, or choice (D).

CHARTS AND GRAPHS

Since calculators were added to the arsenal you're allowed to bring with you when you take the ACT, more and more of the test has been composed of questions on which calculators are of little or no use, such as questions based on charts and graphs. On this type of question, your math skills aren't really being tested at all; what ACT is interested in is your ability to read a simple graph (not unlike on the Science Reasoning test, which we'll get to later in Part V). All of the questions we have seen in this format have been very direct. If you can read a simple graph, you can always get them right. What's most important on questions like these is paying attention to the labels on the information. Let's take a look at a graph.

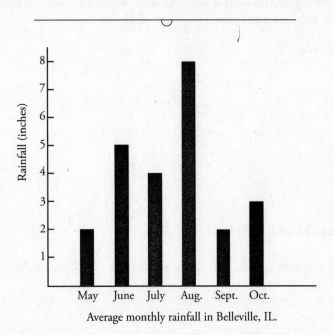

Average monthly rainfall in Belleville, IL.

3. Between which two months was the change in total rainfall the greatest?

    A. May and June
    B. June and July
    C. July and August
    D. August and September
    E. September and October

Here's How to Crack It

The ACT test writers want to see if you can decipher the information presented in the graph. Before you read the question then, you need to take a look at the graph. What is measured here? It says on the bottom: Average monthly rainfall in Belleville, IL. You should look at the values along the left side and bottom of the graph as well. When you do, you'll see that the rain is measured in inches (left-hand side), and the measurements were made each month (bottom).

Now for the question. To determine which two months had the greatest change, we need to compare the change between each pair of months, discarding the smaller ones until we have only one left. The difference from May to June is about 3, and that's larger than June to July and September to October, so choices (B) and (E) are out. July to August is larger still, though, so choice (A) is out, leaving only choices (C) and (D). It should be pretty apparent that the August to September change is larger than the July to August change, though, so the correct answer must be choice (D).

———————○———————

Although most questions involving graphs on the Math test are this simple, you may see slightly more complicated variations. Here's another question based on the same bar graph.

———————○———————

Average monthly rainfall in Belleville, IL.

24. Based on the information presented in the graph above, what is the approximate average monthly rainfall in Belleville, IL, for the period given?

    F.   2
    G.   3
    H.   4
    J.   5
    K.   8

Here's How to Crack It

As with the last question, the first thing you want to do is examine the graph and figure out what information is being given to you and how it is being presented. Because you already did that for this graph, we'll skip that step on this one.

This question combines graph reading with average calculation, so the next thing you'll have to do is estimate the rainfall for each month. Because the question uses the word *approximate*, you don't have to worry too much about making super-exact measurements of the heights of the bar graphs. Eyeballing it and rounding to the closest value given on the left-hand side will be good enough to get you the right answer. Do that now before you read the next sentence.

To us, it looks like about 2 inches fell in May and September, and around 3 fell in October. July saw about 4, June roughly 5, and August about 8. Your estimates should be the same as ours. If they're not, go back now and figure out why not. You probably need to be a little more careful in your estimating. Use another piece of paper as a guide if necessary (you can use your answer sheet in this manner when taking the real ACT).

Now it's just a matter of calculating the average. Find the total first.

$$2 + 2 + 3 + 4 + 5 + 8 = 24$$

There are 6 months, so divide the total by 6 to find the average.

So the answer is 4, or choice (H).

COMBINATIONS: CAN YOU SLOT ME IN?

Combination problems ask you how many different ways a number of things could be chosen or combined. The rules for combination problems on the ACT are straightforward.

1. Figure out the number of slots you need to fill.
2. Fill in those slots.
3. Find the product.

Seem confusing? It's not. Let's look at an example. This is what most combination problems on the ACT will look like:

6. At the school cafeteria, students can choose from 3 different salads, 5 different main dishes, and 2 different desserts. If Isabel chooses one salad, one main dish, and one dessert for lunch, how many different lunches could she choose?

   F. 10
   G. 15
   H. 25
   J. 30
   K. 50

Here's How to Crack It

We've got three slots to fill here, one for each item: salad, main dish, dessert. And the number of possibilities for each is pretty clear. Set up the slots and take the product:

$$\underset{\text{Salad}}{\underline{3}} \times \underset{\text{Main}}{\underline{5}} \times \underset{\text{Dessert}}{\underline{2}} = 30$$

The correct answer here is choice (J).

On a more difficult problem, you may run into a combination with more restricted elements. Just be sure to read the problem carefully before attempting it. If the question makes your head spin, leave it and return to it later, or pick your Letter of the Day and move on. For good measure, though, here's what one of those tougher ones might look like.

7. At the school cafeteria, 2 boys and 4 girls are forming a lunch line. If the boys must stand in the first and last places in line, how many different lines can be formed?

   A.   2
   B.   6
   C.   48
   D. 360
   E. 720

Here's How to Crack It

These restrictions might make this problem seem daunting, but this is where the slot method is really helpful. We have six spots in line to fill, so draw six slots:

___   ___   ___   ___   ___   ___

It even looks like the line the boys and girls are standing in! Do the restricted spots first. The problem tells us that the two boys *must stand in the first and last places in line.* This means that either of the boys could stand in first place, and then the other boy will stand in last. This means that we have two options for the first place, but only one for the last.

_2_   ___   ___   ___   ___   _1_

Now do the same with the unrestricted parts. Any of the four girls could stand in the second spot.

_2_   _4_   ___   ___   ___   _1_

Now, since one of the girls is standing in the second spot, there are only three left to stand in the third spot, and so on, and so on.

_2_   _4_   _3_   _2_   _1_   _1_

Now, as ever, just take the product, to find that the correct answer is choice (C), 48.

_2_ × _4_ × _3_ × _2_ × _1_ × _1_ = 48

Let's try one more that tests a few things.

––––––––––––––––––––––––○––––––––––––––––––––––––

8. Elias has to select one shirt, one pair of pants, and one pair
   of shoes. If he selects at random from his 8 shirts, 4 pairs of
   pants, and 3 pairs of shoes, and all his shirts, pants, and shoes
   are different colors, what is the likelihood that he will select
   his red shirt, black pants, and brown shoes?

   F. $\dfrac{1}{3}$

   G. $\dfrac{1}{4}$

   H. $\dfrac{1}{15}$

   J. $\dfrac{1}{32}$

   K. $\dfrac{1}{96}$

Here's How to Crack It

Step 1: **Know the question.** The problem is asking what the probability is that he
will select this one group of clothes from all possible combinations of clothes.

Step 2: **Let the answers help.** The answers offer the important reminder that we're
looking for a probability. We know that it will be only one arrangement out of a reasonably large number of them, so we should at least get rid of choices (F) and (G).

Step 3: **Break the problem into bite-sized pieces.** First, we should find the total
number of possible combinations. Then we can deal with the probability.

We have three slots to fill here, and we want to find the product of the three:

$$\underset{\text{Shirts}}{\underline{8}} \times \underset{\text{Pants}}{\underline{4}} \times \underset{\text{Shoes}}{\underline{3}} = 96 \text{ arrangements}$$

Of the 96 possible arrangements, an ensemble of red shirt, black pants, and
brown shoes is only one. Therefore, we can go to our $\dfrac{part}{whole}$ ratio to find

$\dfrac{part}{whole} = \dfrac{\text{red, black, brown}}{\text{ALL arrangements}} = \dfrac{1}{96}$, choice (K).

––––––––––––––––––––––––○––––––––––––––––––––––––

Word Problems Drill

For the answers to this drill, please go to Chapter 24.

1. The ratio of boys to girls at the Milwood School is 4 to 5. If there are a total of 27 children at the school, how many boys attend the Milwood School?

   A. 4
   B. 9
   C. 12
   D. 14
   E. 17

2. Linda computed the average of her six biology test scores by mistakenly adding the totals of five scores and dividing by five, giving her an average score of 88. When Linda realized her error, she recalculated and included the sixth test score of 82. What is the average of Linda's six biology tests?

   F. 82
   G. 85
   H. 86
   J. 87
   K. 88

3. In the process of milling grain, 3% of the original is lost because of spillage, and another 5% of the original is lost because of mildew. If the mill starts out with 490 tons of grain, how much (in tons) remains to be sold after milling?

   A. 425
   B. 426
   C. 420.5
   D. 440
   E. 450.8

4. A rectangular box has a base measuring a by a meters and height of b meters. Which of the following represents the surface area of the box?

   F. $6ab$
   G. a^2b
   H. $a^2 + 2ab$
   J. $2a(a + 2b)$
   K. $2(a^2 + b^{2)}$

5. In the word HAWKS, how many ways is it possible to rearrange the letters if none repeat and the letter W must go last?

   A. 5
   B. 15
   C. 24
   D. 120
   E. 650

Summary

o   Plugging In works on all kinds of problems, not just Algebra. Always look for opportunities to simplify the math by Plugging In!

o   Percentages and Probabilities are all based on a relationship of PART to WHOLE. Ratios are based on a relationship of PART to PART. Probabilities can be found by taking the part (the number of things that meet some given criteria) divided by the whole (all possibilities, including those that don't meet the critieria.)

o   Percentages can typically be found by multiplying $\frac{part}{whole} \times 100\%$.

  •   When dealing with percentages, remember to convert Math into English with the handy chart.

English	Math Equivalent
percent	/100
of	multiplication (×)
what	variable (*y*, *z*)
is, are, were	=
what percent	$\frac{y}{100}$

  •   Ratios are typically a relationship of one *part* to some other *part*.

o   On Combination problems
  1.   Figure out the number of slots you need to fill.
  2.   Fill in those slots.
  3.   Find the product.

o   On Average problems, use the average pie.
  1.   Divide the total by the number of things to find the average.
  2.   Divide the total by the average to find the number of things.
  3.   Multiply the number of things by the average to find the total.

Chapter 14
Graphing and Coordinate Geometry

We've covered most of what you'll need to get a great score on the ACT Math test. This chapter will give a brief overview of Coordinate Geometry. While it's not tested as heavily as Plane Geometry, Coordinate Geometry offers many fast plug-and-chug opportunities. Though we will be discussing the basic rules and formulas you need, we will always have an eye on how we can crack some of these problems more strategically as well.

COORDINATE GEOMETRY

As we saw in the first Math chapter, coordinate geometry will account for about 9 questions in any given exam. While ACT makes a big deal about how separate this is from plane geometry, really the major difference between the two is that you need more graph paper to do coordinate geometry. We'll cover the basics of graphing and its related functions, but don't forget, you know a lot of this stuff from the earlier geometry chapter already!

Graphing Inequalities

Here's a simple inequality:

$$3x + 5 > 11$$

As you know from reading the algebra chapter of this book, you solve an inequality the same way that you solve an equality. By subtracting 5 from both sides and then dividing both sides by 3, you get the expression

$$x > 2$$

This can be represented on a number line as shown below.

The open circle at 2 indicates that x can include every number greater than 2, but not 2 itself or anything less than 2.

If we had wanted to graph $x \geq 2$, the circle would have to be filled in, indicating that our graph includes 2 as well.

An ACT graphing problem might look like this.

An Open Circle
On the number line, a hollow circle means that point is *not* included in the graph.

A Solid Dot
On the number line, a solid dot means that point is included in the graph.

1. Which of the following represents the range of solutions for inequality $-5x - 7 < x + 5$?

Here's How to Crack It

The ACT test writers want you first to simplify the inequality and then figure out which of the answer choices represents a graph of the solution set of the inequality. To simplify, isolate x on one side of the inequality.

$$
\begin{array}{r}
-5x - 7 < x + 5 \\
\underline{-x \qquad -x} \\
-6x - 7 < \quad 5 \\
\underline{+7 \qquad +7} \\
-6x \quad < \quad 12
\end{array}
$$

Flip Flop
Remember that when you multiply or divide an inequality by a negative, the sign flips.

Now divide both sides by -6. Remember that when you multiply or divide an inequality by a negative, the sign flips over.

$$
\frac{-6x}{-6} < \frac{12}{-6}
$$
$$
x > -2
$$

Which of the choices answers the question? If you selected choice (B), you're right.

Graphing in Two Dimensions

More complicated graphing questions concern equations with two variables, usually designated x and y. These equations can be graphed on a Cartesian grid, which looks like this.

Every point (x,y) has a place on this grid. For example, the point A $(3,4)$ can be found by counting over on the *x*-axis 3 places to the right of (0,0)—known as the **origin**—and then counting on the *y*-axis 4 places up from the origin, as shown below. Point *B* (5,–2) can be found by counting 5 places to the right on the *x*-axis and then down 2 places on the *y*-axis. Point *C* (–4,–1) can be found by counting 4 places to the left of the origin on the *x*-axis and then 1 place down on the *y*-axis.

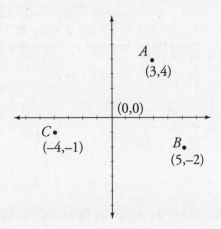

The grid is divided into four quadrants, which go counterclockwise.

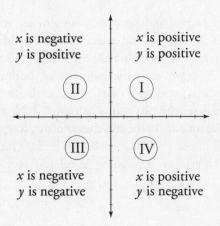

- In the first quadrant, *x* and *y* are both positive.
- In the second quadrant, *x* is negative but *y* is positive.
- In the third quadrant, *x* and *y* are both negative.
- In the fourth quadrant, *x* is positive but *y* is negative.

Note: This is when your graphing calculator (if you have one) will really get a chance to shine. Practice doing all the ACT coordinate geometry questions on your calculator now and you'll blow them away when you actually take the test.

Graphic Guesstimation

A few questions on the ACT might involve actual graphing, but it is more likely that you will be able to make use of graphing to *estimate* the answers to questions that the ACT test writers think are more complicated.

———————————————————

1. Point *B* (4,3) is the midpoint of line segment *AC*. If point *A* has coordinates (0,1), then what are the coordinates of point *C*?

   A. (−4,−1)
   B. (4, 1)
   C. (4, 4)
   D. (8, 5)
   E. (8, 9)

Here's How to Crack It

You may or may not remember the midpoint formula: The ACT test writers expect you to use it to solve this problem. We'll go over it in a moment, along with the other formulas you'll need to solve coordinate geometry questions. However, it is worth noting that by drawing a rough graph of this problem, you can get the correct answer without the formula.

On your TI-83, you can plot independent points to see what the graph should look like. To do this, hit [STAT] and select option [1: Edit]. Enter the *x*- and *y*-coordinate points in the first two columns; use [L1] for your *x*-coordinates and [L2] for the *y*-coordinates. After you enter the endpoints of the line, hit [2nd][Y=] to access the [STAT PLOT], menu. Select option [1: Plot1]. Change the [OFF] status to [ON] and hit [GRAPH]. You should now see the two points you entered. Now you can ballpark the answers based on where they are in the coordinate plane. Keep in mind that you can also plot all the points in the answers as well. Just be sure you keep track of all the *x*- and *y*-values. If you don't have a graphing calculator, use the grid we've provided on the next page.

B is supposed to be the midpoint of a line segment *AC*. Draw a line through the two points you've just plotted and extend it upward until *B* is the midpoint of the line segment. It should look like this:

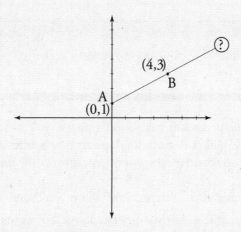

The place where you stopped drawing is the approximate location of point *C*. Now let's look at the answer choices to see if any of them are in the ballpark.

A.   (−4,−1): These coordinates are in the wrong quadrant.
B.   (4, 1): This point is way below where it should be.
C.   (4, 4): This point does not extend enough to the right.
D.   (8, 5): Definitely in the ballpark. Hold on to this answer choice.
E.   (8, 9): Possible, although the *y*-coordinate seems a little high.

Which answer choice do you want to pick? If you said choice (D), you are right.

THE IMPORTANT COORDINATE GEOMETRY FORMULAS

By memorizing a few formulas, you will be able to answer virtually all of the coordinate geometry questions on this test. Remember, too, that in coordinate geometry you almost *always* have a fallback—just graph it out.

And always keep your graphing calculator handy on these types of problems. Graphing calculators are great for solving line equations and giving you graphs you can use to ballpark. Be sure you know how to solve and graph an equation for a line on your calculator before you take the ACT.

The following formulas are listed in order of importance:

The Slope-Intercept Formula

$$y = mx + b$$

By putting (x,y) equations into the formula above, you can find two pieces of information that ACT likes to test: the **slope** and the y-intercept. Most graphing calculators will put an equation into y-intercept form at the touch of a button.

To find the x-intercept
Set y equal to zero and solve for x.

The **slope** is a number that tells you how sharply a line is inclining, and it is equivalent to the variable m in the equation above. For example, in the equation $y = 3x + 4$, the number 3 (think of it as $\frac{3}{1}$) tells us that from any point on the line, we can find another point on the line by going up 3 and over to the right 1.

In the equation $y = -\frac{4}{5}x - 7$, the slope of $-\frac{4}{5}$ tells us that from any point on the line, we can find another point on the line by going up 4 and over 5 to the left.

The **y-intercept**, equivalent to the variable b in the equation above, is the point at which the line intercepts the y-axis. For example, in the equation $y = 3x + 4$, the line will strike the y-axis at a point 4 above the origin. In the equation $y = 2x - 7$, the line will strike the y-axis at a point 7 below the origin. A typical ACT $y = mx + b$ question might give you an equation in another form and ask you to find either the slope or the y-intercept. Simply put the equation into the form we've just shown you.

1. What is the slope of the line based on the equation
$5x - y = 7x + 6$?

   A. −2
   B. 0
   C. 2
   D. 6
   E. −6

Here's How to Crack It

Isolate y on the left side of the equation. You can have your graphing calculator do
this for you, or you can do it by hand by subtracting $5x$ from both sides.

$$
\begin{array}{r}
5x - y = 7x + 6 \\
-5x \qquad -5x \\
\hline
-y = 2x + 6
\end{array}
$$

We aren't quite done. The format we want is $y = mx + b$, not $-y = mx + b$. Let's
multiply both sides by −1.

$$(-1)(-y) = (2x + 6)(-1)$$
$$y = -2x - 6$$

The slope of this line is −2, so the answer is choice (A).

The Slope Formula

You can find the slope of a line, even if all you have are two points on that line, by using the slope formula.

$$\text{slope} = \frac{\text{change in } y}{\text{change in } x} \quad \text{or} \quad \frac{y_2 - y_1}{x_2 - x_1}$$

Parallel Tracks

If two lines have the same slope, those lines are *parallel* to one another.

If two lines have opposite reciprocal slopes, those lines are *perpendicular* to one another.

So how about if #1 on this page asked for the slope of a line parallel to the one given in the problem? How about perpendicular?

A *parallel* line would have a slope of $-\frac{1}{8}$.

A *perpendicular* line would have a slope of 8.

1. What is the slope of the straight line passing through the points $(-2,5)$ and $(6,4)$?

    A. $-\dfrac{1}{16}$

    B. $-\dfrac{1}{8}$

    C. $\dfrac{1}{5}$

    D. $\dfrac{2}{9}$

    E. $\dfrac{4}{9}$

Here's How to Crack It

Find the change in y and put it over the change in x. The change in y is the first y-coordinate minus the second y-coordinate. (It doesn't matter which point is first and which is second.) The change in x is the first x minus the second x.

$$\frac{y_2 - y_1}{x_2 - x_1} = \frac{5 - 4}{-2 - 6} = \frac{1}{-8}$$

The correct answer is choice (B).

If you take a look at the formula for finding slope, you'll see that the part on top ("change in y") is how much the line is rising (or falling, if the line points down and has a negative slope). That change in position on the y-axis is called the *rise*. The part on the bottom ("change in x") is how far along the x-axis you move and called the *run*. So the slope of a line is sometimes referred to as "rise over run."

In the question we just did, then, the rise was 1 and the run was −8, giving us the slope $-\frac{1}{8}$. Same answer, different terminology.

Midpoint Formula

If you have the two endpoints of a line segment, you can find the midpoint of the segment by using the midpoint formula.

$$\left(x[m], y[m]\right) = \left(\frac{x_1 + x_2}{2}, \frac{y_1 + y_2}{2}\right)$$

It looks much more intimidating than it really is.

To find the midpoint of a line, just take the *average* of the two x-coordinates and the *average* of the two y-coordinates. For example, the midpoint of the line segment formed by the coordinates (3,4) and (9,2) is just

$$\frac{(3+9)}{2} = 6 \text{ and } \frac{(4+2)}{2} = 3$$
$$\text{or } (6,3)$$

Remember the first midpoint problem we did? Here it is again.

1. Point B (4,3) is the midpoint of line segment AC. If point A has coordinates (0,1), then what are the coordinates of point C?

   A. (−4,−1)
   B. (4, 1)
   C. (4, 4)
   D. (8, 5)
   E. (8, 9)

The Shortest Distance Between Two Points Is…a Calculator?

If you want to draw a line between two points on your TI-83, you can use the Line function. To access this, you'll want to press [2nd] [PRGM] to access the [DRAW] menu. From there, select option [2: Line]. The format of the line function is Line (X1, Y1, X2, Y2); for example, if you wanted to view the line that passes through the points (−2,5) and (6,4), you would enter Line (−2,5,6,4). Hit [ENTER] to see your line.

Here's How to Crack It

You'll remember that it was perfectly possible to solve this problem just by drawing a quick graph of what it ought to look like. However, to find the correct answer using the midpoint formula, we first have to realize that, in this case, we already *have* the midpoint. We are asked to find one of the endpoints.

The midpoint is (4,3). This represents the average of the two endpoints. The endpoint we know about is (0,1). Let's do the *x*-coordinate first. The average of the *x*-coordinates of the two endpoints equals the *x*-coordinate of the midpoint. So $\frac{(0+?)}{2} = 4$. What is the missing *x*-coordinate? 8. Now let's do the *y*-coordinate. $\frac{(1+?)}{2} = 3$. What is the missing *y*-coordinate? 5. The answer is choice (D).

If you had trouble following that last explanation, just remember that you already understood this problem (and got the answer) using graphing. Never be intimidated by formulas on the ACT. There is usually another way to do the problem.

The Distance Formula

We hate the distance formula. We keep forgetting it, and even when we remember it, we feel like fools for using it because there are much easier ways to find the distance between two points. We aren't even going to tell you what the distance formula is. If you need to know the distance between two points, you can always think of that distance as being the hypotenuse of a right triangle. Here's an example.

1. What is the distance between points *A* (2,2) and *B* (5,6)?
   - A. 3
   - B. 4
   - C. 5
   - D. 6
   - E. 7

Here's How to Crack It

Let's make a quick graph of what this ought to look like.

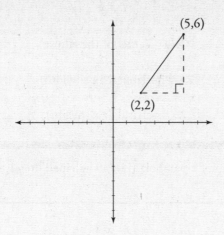

If we extend lines from the two points to form a right triangle under the line segment *AB*, we can use the Pythagorean theorem to get the distance between the two points. What is the length of the base of the triangle? It's 3. What is the length of the height of the triangle? It's 4. So what is the length of the hypotenuse? It's 5. Of course, as usual, it is one of the triples of which ACT is so fond. The answer is choice (C). You could also have popped the points into your calculator and had it calculate the distance for you.

Here's the distance formula if you must know (or know how to program into your calculator):

$$d = \sqrt{(x_2 - x_1)^2 + (y_2 - y_1)^2}$$

Isn't the triangle method so much easier?

Circles, Ellipses, and Parabolas, Oh My!

You should probably have a *vague* idea of what the equations for these figures look like; just remember that there are very few questions concerning these figures, and when they do come up, you can almost always figure them out by graphing.

The standard equation for a circle is shown below.

$$(x - h)^2 + (y - k)^2 = r^2$$

(h,k) = center of the circle

r = radius

The standard equation for an ellipse (just a squat-looking circle) is shown on the next page.

We include the ellipse formula because it has shown up on previous exams, but if you can't remember it, don't worry. It only shows up once in a blue moon, and you never need to reproduce it from memory.

$$\frac{(x-h)^2}{a^2}+\frac{(y-k)^2}{b^2}=1$$

(h,k) = center of the ellipse

$2a$ = horizontal axis (width)

$2b$ = vertical axis (height)

The standard equation for a parabola (just a U-shaped line) is shown below.

$$y = x^2$$

1. If the equation $x^2 = 1 - y^2$ were graphed in the standard (x,y) coordinate plane, the graph would represent which of the following geometric figures?

   A. square
   B. straight line
   C. circle
   D. triangle
   E. parabola

Graphing Circles on Your Calculator

To draw a circle on your TI-83, you first need to alter the Zoom settings. Press ZOOM and select option [5: ZSquare]. Next, hit 2nd PRGM to access the [DRAW] menu. Select option [9: Circle]. All you need to do is enter the coordinates of the circle's center and the value of its radius. If, for instance, you were trying to graph a circle with a center of (2,3) and a radius of 5, your screen would say the following: Circle (2,3,5). Hit ENTER to see the resulting graph. You can draw as many circles as you like, but to clear the graph you need to press 2nd[DRAW] and select option [1: ClrDraw].

Here's How to Crack It

If you're familiar with what the equations of the various elements in the answer choices are supposed to look like, you may be able to figure out the problem without graphing at all. (However, that's why you bought a graphing calculator in the first place....) Let's consider what we know about the equations of geometric figures. If an equation has only x and y, we know that the graph of the equation is a straight line. (Think back to the $y = mx + b$ problems we did earlier.) However, in this equation, both x and y are squared, so we can rule out choice (B). There is no equation for a square, so we can rule out choice (A). Similarly, there's no equation for a triangle, so choice (D) is out. If only one of the variables were squared, this might be a parabola, but in this problem both are squared, which means we can eliminate choice (E). We are left with choice (C).

Estimating Note

Of course, we could also just plug some numbers into the equation and plot them out on a homemade (x,y) axis in the scratchwork column of the test booklet. Let's try this on the grid below.

The easiest way to start is to let one of the variables equal 0. If $x = 0$, then y must equal 1. So one point of this equation is (0,1). If we let $y = 0$, then x must equal 1. So another point of this equation is (1,0). Plot out some other points of the equation. How about (–1,0) and (0,–1)? What kind of geometric figure does it appear that we have? If you said a circle, you are correct.

Graphing and Coordinate Geometry Drill

For the answers to this drill, please go to Chapter 24.

1. Which of the following represents the solution of the inequality $-3x - 6 > 9$?

A.

B.

C.

D.

E.

2. What is the midpoint of the line segment whose endpoints are represented on the coordinate axis by the points $(3,5)$ and $(-4,3)$?

F. $(-2, -5)$

G. $(-\frac{1}{2}, 4)$

H. $(1, 8)$

J. $(4, -\frac{1}{2})$

K. $(3, 3)$

3. What is the slope of the line represented by the equation $10x + 2x = y + 6$?

A. 10
B. 12
C. 14
D. 15
E. 16

4. What is the length of the line segment whose endpoints are represented on the coordinate axis by the points $(-2,-1)$ and $(1,3)$?

F. 3
G. 4
H. 5
J. 6
K. 7

5. What is the slope of the line that contains the points $(6,4)$ and $(13,5)$?

A. $-\frac{1}{8}$

B. $-\frac{1}{9}$

C. $\frac{1}{7}$

D. 1

E. 7

6. Which of the following gives the center point and radius of circle O, represented by the equation $(x - 3)^2 + (y + 2)^2 = 9$?

	Center	Radius
F.	$(-3, 2)$	3
G.	$(-3, 2)$	9
H.	$(2, 3)$	9
J.	$(3, -2)$	3
K.	$(3, -2)$	9

Summary

o   Coordinate geometry tests many of the same concepts you've seen elsewhere on the Math test.

o   If you are stuck on a coordinate geometry, sketch a graph and draw in a few points.

o   Many coordinate geometry questions can be solved by putting them into the format $y + mx = b$, where m is the slope of the line and b is the y-intercept.

o   Review the midpoint equation:

$$\left(x[m], y[m]\right) = \frac{x_1 + x_2}{2}, \frac{y_1 + y_2}{2}$$

o   You can avoid using the confusing distance formula by drawing a right triangle and using the Pythagorean theorem.

o   Every once in a while, ACT asks a question based on the equations of circles, ellipses, and parabolas. If you need a very high score, it might help to memorize these equations, but remember, these questions can frequently be done by using graphing to estimate the correct answer.

Chapter 15
Trigonometry

We've covered most of what you'll need to get a great score on the ACT Math test. This chapter will give a brief overview of one of the more advanced topics covered on the exam: Trigonometry. Though we will be discussing the identities and rules you need, we will always have an eye on how we can crack some of these problems more strategically as well.

A NOTE ON ACT MATH "DIFFICULTY"

As we noted in the first Math chapter in this book, "difficulty" is kind of a weird thing on the ACT. Is a problem difficult because it tests an unfamiliar concept? Or is it difficult because it tests a very familiar concept in a long word problem? We've seen that Plugging In and PITA can make some of the toughest problems pretty easy, so this part of the exam is more about POOD than ever. In this chapter, we will review trigonometry. Trigonometry is one of the more advanced topics on the ACT, and ACT wants to make you think it and the other advanced topics are very difficult. Some of these questions *are* difficult, tapping some of the most advanced topics of algebra II. But as you will see with trigonometry, most if not all of these questions can be answered correctly with a smart approach. We will review the relevant concepts, but we will also keep an eye on how to use the strategies from earlier chapters.

TRIGONOMETRY

It's easy to get freaked out by the trigonometry on the ACT. But remember there are only four questions on any given exam that deal with trig. What this means is that if you haven't learned trig before, it's not worth your time to try to do it now. If you are familiar with trig, on the other hand, here are a few topics that might come up. And don't worry, in four questions, there's no way all of these topics can come up!

Finally, as ever, remember that you don't get bonus points for doing anything the "real" way on the ACT. Always be on the lookout to use some of the great new techniques you've learned in this book.

SOHCAHTOA

There are four trig questions on any given ACT Math test, and typically two of them will ask about very basic trig concepts, covered by the acronym SOHCAHTOA. If you've had trig before, you probably know this acronym like the back of your hand. If not, here's what it means:

SOHCAHTOA

Sine is **O**pposite over **H**ypotenuse. Cosine is **A**djacent over **H**ypotenuse. Tangent is **O**pposite over **A**djacent. So in the triangle below, the sine of angle θ [*theta*, a Greek letter] would be $\frac{4}{5}$. The cosine of angle θ would be $\frac{3}{5}$. The tangent of angle θ would be $\frac{4}{3}$.

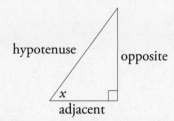

Sine, cosine, and tangent are often abbreviated as sin, cos, and tan, respectively.

The easier trig questions on this test involve the relationships between the sides of a right triangle. In the right triangle below, the angle x can be expressed in terms of the ratios of different sides of the triangle.

hypotenuse   opposite

x

adjacent

The **sine** of angle $x = \dfrac{\text{length of side opposite angle } x}{\text{length of hypotenuse}}$

The **cosine** of angle $x = \dfrac{\text{length of side adjacent angle } x}{\text{length of hypotenuse}}$

The **tangent** of angle $x = \dfrac{\text{length of side opposite angle } x}{\text{length of side adjacent angle } x}$

YOU'RE ALMOST DONE

There are three more relationships to memorize. They involve the reciprocals of the previous three.

$$\text{The cosecant} = \frac{1}{\text{sine}}$$
$$\text{The secant} = \frac{1}{\text{cosine}}$$
$$\text{The cotangent} = \frac{1}{\text{tangent}}$$

Let's try a few problems.

———————○———————

31. What is $\sin\theta$, if $\tan\theta = \dfrac{4}{3}$?

    A. $\dfrac{3}{4}$

    B. $\dfrac{4}{5}$

    C. $\dfrac{5}{4}$

    D. $\dfrac{5}{3}$

    E. $\dfrac{7}{3}$

> **Helpful Trig Identities**
>
> $$\sin^2\theta + \cos^2\theta = 1$$
>
> $$\frac{\sin\theta}{\cos\theta} = \tan\theta$$

Here's How to Crack It

It helps to sketch out the right triangle and fill in the information we know.

What kind of right triangle is this? That's right—a 3-4-5. Now, we need to know the sine of angle θ: opposite over hypotenuse, or $\dfrac{4}{5}$, which is choice (B).

———————○———————

43. For all θ, $\dfrac{\cos\theta}{\sin^2\theta + \cos^2\theta} = ?$

    A. $\sin\theta$
    B. $\csc\theta$
    C. $\cot\theta$
    D. $\cos\theta$
    E. $\tan\theta$

Here's How to Crack It

$\text{Sin}^2\theta + \cos^2\theta$ always equals 1. $\dfrac{\cos\theta}{1} = \cos\theta$. The answer is choice (D).

50. In a right triangle shown above, $\sec\theta$ is $\dfrac{25}{7}$. What is $\sin\theta$?

    F. $\dfrac{3}{25}$

    G. $\dfrac{5}{25}$

    H. $\dfrac{7}{25}$

    J. $\dfrac{24}{25}$

    K. $\dfrac{25}{7}$

Here's How to Crack It

The secant of any angle is the reciprocal of the cosine, which is just another way of saying that the cosine of angle θ is $\dfrac{7}{25}$.

Secant $\theta \dfrac{1}{\cos\theta}$ so $\dfrac{1}{\cos\theta} = \dfrac{25}{7}$, which means that $\cos\theta = \dfrac{7}{25}$. Are you done? No! Cross off (H) because you know it's not the answer.

Cosine means adjacent over hypotenuse. Let's sketch it.

As you can see, we now have two sides of a right triangle. Can we find the third side? If you said this was one of the triples we told you about before, you are absolutely correct, although you also could have derived this by using the Pythagorean theorem. The third side must be 24. The question asks for sin θ. Sine = opposite over hypotenuse, or $\dfrac{24}{25}$, which is choice (J).

HARDER TRIGONOMETRY

When graphing a trig function, such as sine, there are two important **coefficients**, A and B: A{sin (Bθ)}.

The two coefficients A and B govern the **amplitude** of the graph (how tall it is) and the **period** of the graph (how long it takes to get through a complete cycle), respectively. If there are no coefficients, then that means A = 1 and B = 1 and the graph is the same as what you'd get when you graph it on your calculator.

- Increases in A increase the amplitude of the graph. It's a direct relationship.

That means if A = 2, then the amplitude is doubled. If A = $\frac{1}{2}$, then the amplitude is cut in half.

- Increases in B decrease the period of the graph. It's an inverse relationship.

That means if B = 2, then the period is cut in half, which is to say the graph completes a full cycle faster than usual. If B = $\frac{1}{2}$, then the period is doubled.

You can add to or subtract from the function as a whole, and also to or from the variable, but neither of those actions changes the shape of the graph, only its position and starting place.

Here's the graph of sin x. What are the amplitude and period?

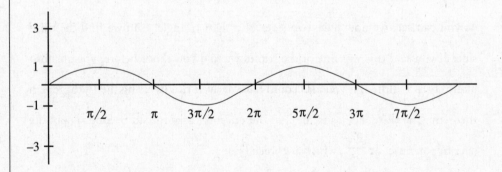

The simple function sin θ goes from –1 to 1 on the y-axis, so the amplitude is 1, while its period is 2π, which means that every 2π on the graph (as you go from side to side) it completes a full cycle. That's what you see in the graph above.

The graph below is also a sine function, but it's been changed. What is the function graphed here?

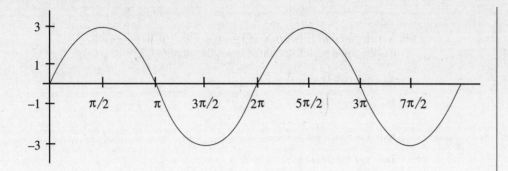

You have three things to check when looking at this graph: Is it sin or cos, is the period changed, and is the amplitude changed?

- This is a sin graph because it has a value of 0 at 0. Cos has a value of 1 at 0.
- It makes a complete cycle in 2π, so the period isn't changed. In other words, B = 1.
- The amplitude is triple what it normally is, so A = 3. The function graphed, therefore, is 3 sin θ.

How about here?

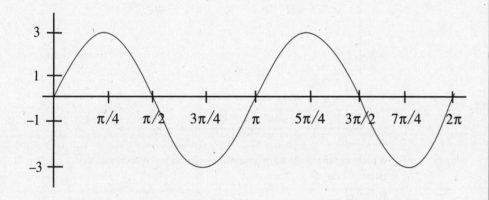

Once again, there are three things to check.

- This is a sin graph because it has a value of 0 at 0. Cos has a value of 1 at 0.
- It makes a complete cycle in π, so the period has changed—it's half of what it usually is. B has an inverse effect, which means B = 2.
- The amplitude is triple what it normally is, so A = 3. The function graphed, therefore, is 3 sin 2θ.

Let's try some practice questions.

49. As compared with the graph of $y = \cos x$, which of the following has the same period and three times the amplitude?

A. $y = \cos 3x$

B. $y = \cos \dfrac{1}{2}(x + 3)$

C. $y = 3 \cos \dfrac{1}{2}x$

D. $y = 1 + 3 \cos x$

E. $y = 3 + \cos x$

Here's How to Crack It

Recall that the coefficient on the outside of the function changes the amplitude and the one on the inside changes the period. Because the question states that the period isn't changed, you can eliminate choices (A), (B), and (C). The amplitude is three times greater, you're told; because there's a direct relationship between choice (A) and amplitude, you want to have a 3 multiplying the outside of the function. That leaves only choice (D) as a possibility.

52. Which of the following equations describes the equation graphed above?

F. $2 \cos x$

G. $1 + 2 \cos x$

H. $\cos 2x$

J. $1 + \cos 2x$

K. $1 + 2 \cos 2x$

Here's How to Crack It

At first it looks like this graph has an amplitude of 3, but if you look closer, you'll see that though the top value is 3, the bottom value is –1, which means that the whole graph has been shifted up. Because choices (F) and (H) don't add anything to the function (which is how you move a graph up and down), they're out. The period of this graph is half of what it usually is, so B = 2, which eliminates choice (G). Because the amplitude is changed also, you can eliminate choice (J). The answer is choice (K).

Trigonometry Drill

For the answers to this drill, please go to Chapter 24.

1. In $\triangle ABC$ below, the tan θ equals

A. $\dfrac{5}{12}$

B. $\dfrac{12}{13}$

C. $\dfrac{17}{12}$

D. $\dfrac{12}{5}$

E. 3

2. If the cotangent of an angle θ is 1, then the tangent of angle θ is

F. −1
G. 0
H. 1
J. 2
K. 3

3. If $x + \sin^2 \theta + \cos^2 \theta = 4$, then $x = ?$

A. 1
B. 2
C. 3
D. 4
E. 5

Summary

o   If you haven't had trigonometry in school, use your Letter of the Day on these trig problems. There are only 4!

o   Remember SOHCAHTOA!

$$\text{sine} = \frac{\text{opposite}}{\text{hypotenuse}} \; ; \; \text{cosine} = \frac{\text{adjacent}}{\text{hypotenuse}} \; ;$$
$$\text{tangent} = \frac{\text{opposite}}{\text{adjacent}}$$

o   For inverse functions, remember:

$$\csc\theta = \frac{1}{\text{sine}} \qquad \sec\theta = \frac{1}{\text{cosine}}$$
$$\tan\theta = \frac{1}{\text{tangent}}$$

o   Remember the special trig identities:

$$\sin^2\theta + \cos^2\theta = 1.$$

$$\frac{\sin\theta}{\cos\theta} = \tan\theta.$$

o   For more advanced trig problems, remember A{*sin* (Bθ)}, where *A* represents the amplitude and *B* represents the period of the function. These are usually the easiest to see on the graph.

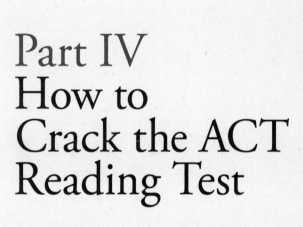

Part IV
How to
Crack the ACT
Reading Test

Chapter 16
Introduction to the ACT Reading Test

Reading on the ACT is not the same as reading for school. When you're reading for school, you have to *understand* what you've read and be able to discuss it. On the ACT, you only have to understand enough of the passage to answer the questions. You don't need to discuss the passage later. In fact, you'll just forget it. Therefore, rather than reading to remember, you'll want to direct your reading to find the right answers. This chapter shows you how to do just that.

The ACT Reading
Test Format
You read 4 passages and
answer 40 questions in
35 minutes.

OVERVIEW: CRACKING AND PACING THE READING TEST

The ACT Reading test presents 4 passages with 10 questions each. That's 40 questions total. You get 35 minutes for the whole section, which means you have about 9 minutes to cover each passage and the questions that follow it, *if* your pacing strategy requires you to work all 4 passages.

The passages are edited pieces of books and magazines, and according to ACT, they're "typical of what a college freshman might be required to read...." And the questions? ACT says they test your ability to "understand" the passages.

But That's Not Really True

No one ever achieved a great insight by spending eight or nine pressured minutes reading an isolated fragment of a book or an article. Serious writers don't intend their works to be read in fragments or in so hurried a fashion as reading tests require. (Imagine that you were asked to read a *fragment* of the history of the relations between the United States, Germany, and Japan during the twentieth century. Suppose, in particular, that you're asked to read only about their cooperative relations in the years 1985–1990. You'd be missing the history of their relationships during the years 1940–1945—World War II—which means you'd be missing a rather important piece of the story.)

Furthermore, serious readers take time to think about the things they read. How far would Albert Einstein have gotten if someone had interrupted his reading after 35 minutes to announce that he should "close his book because time is up"? As a college student, you'll be asked not only to read but also to think about what you read—and then to reread—and then to think some more. Any professor will tell you that understanding takes thought, and thought usually takes time.

When you take the ACT Reading test, you're not asked to understand. You're not asked to do anything you'll ever do in college. You're just asked to take a "reading test."

The ACT Reading Test: Cracking the System

You'll raise your reading score if you're "wise" to the test and if you think strategically. We're first going to show you how ACT reading questions are built. Then we'll show you how to use that knowledge to select correct answers. You'll learn to implement the techniques covered below.

1. Attack the passages in the order that best suits you.
2. See through the camouflage that hides correct answer choices.
3. Identify incorrect answer choices and eliminate them quickly.
4. Answer questions without really reading the passage.
5. Put all of these techniques together to approach every passage and question with a step-by-step strategy that leads systematically to the correct answers.

READING TEST TRIAGE: ORDERING THE PASSAGES

The Reading test has four passages, one each from the following fields:

- Prose Fiction (excerpts from short stories and novels)
- Social Sciences (history, economics, psychology, political sciences, and anthropology)
- Humanities (art, music, architecture, and dance)
- Natural Sciences (biology, chemistry, physics, and physical sciences)

Students differ in their abilities to tackle these different passage types, and it's important that you decide which passages are easiest and hardest for you. That way you can decide which passages to do first (the easier ones) and which to do last or never (the harder ones). The passages are always in the same order.

Prose Fiction Passages

The prose fiction passage is almost the opposite of the natural science passage. It tells a fictitious story and is supposed to be packed with hints and suggestions about characters and their motivations.

> Allen's grandmother was readying herself to leave. She was, in fact, putting the final touches on her makeup which, as always, looked to Allen as though someone had thrown it on her face with a shovel. As Mrs. Mandale placed her newly purchased bracelet over her wrist, a look of troubled ambivalence came over her. "Perhaps this bracelet isn't right for me," she said. "I won't wear it."
>
> Waiting now for 30 minutes, Allen tried to be tolerant. "It is right for you," he said. "It matches your personality. Wear it." The bracelet was a remarkable illustration of poor taste. Its colors were vulgar and the structure lacked any sign of thoughtful design. The truth is, it did match his grandmother's personality. All that she did and enjoyed was tasteless and induced in Allen a quiet hopelessness.

Fiction Passages

Most prose fiction passages are primarily concerned with the following five things:
- Who
- What
- When
- Where
- Why

Prose fiction questions often require that you "read between the lines" and draw inferences about the way characters feel or behave.

1. Allen most likely encouraged his grandmother to wear her bracelet because he:

   A. found it colorful and approved of its appearance.
   B. found its appearance pathetic and wished his grandmother to look pretty.
   C. was impatient with his grandmother for spending time worrying about the bracelet.
   D. felt the bracelet matched his grandmother's bright personality.

Some people have an ability for these kinds of passages and questions. Others find them unclear and confusing. If you find literature passages easiest, do them first. If you find them most difficult, do them last or never.

For the record, the answer is choice (C). Allen has been waiting and is trying "to be tolerant."

Social Science and Humanities Passages

Social science and humanities passages are sort of a cross between natural science and prose fiction. Often, the author has views about the subject he or she is discussing, and you might be asked to draw inferences about them. You might also be asked questions about details.

Religion is so fundamental a part of human existence that one might easily forget to ask how it started. Yet it had to start somewhere and there had to be a time when human beings or their apelike ancestors did not entertain notions of the supernatural. Hence the historian should want to probe the origins of religious belief.

It is doubtful that morality played a part in the beginnings of religious belief. Rather, religion is traceable to a far more fundamental human and animal characteristic. Storms, floods, famine, and other adversities inspired *fear* in the hearts of primitive peoples as well they should have. Curiously, humankind early took the position that it might somehow subject such catastrophes to its control. Specifically, it believed it might control them by obedience and submission and by conforming its behavior to their mandates. Worship, ritual, sacrifice of life, and property became means through which early peoples sought to cajole the powers and avoid the blights and miseries the peoples dreaded. As Petronius, in Lucretius's tradition remarked, "It was fear that first made the gods."

11. According to the passage, natural disasters contributed to the development of religion by:

   A. motivating human beings to acquire some command over their environment.
   B. making human beings distinguish themselves from animals.
   C. causing human beings to sacrifice their lives and goods.
   D. providing a need for ritual and tradition.

12. The author believes that the origins of religion:

   F. are extremely easy to ascertain and understand.
   G. should not be questioned by historians because religion is fundamental to civilized life.
   H. are directly tied to apelike subhuman species.
   J. should be the subject of serious historical inquiry.

The correct answer to 11 is choice (A) and the answer to 12 is choice (J).

Mark Twain had magnificent style, and with *The Adventures of Huckleberry Finn*, he built the gateway to American fiction. *Huckleberry Finn* treats extraordinarily serious themes, and it reflects the author's coming of age. Although they don't represent truly mature works, other Twain Mississippi River stories, published before Huck Finn, afford Americans a clear, collective picture of pre-Civil War life in the Mississippi Valley.

With the coming and going of the Civil War, however, Twain adopted a revised agenda, which was reflected in the style and subject matter of his writing. The postwar era demanded that he address himself to the nation's social squalor. His work was more intellectualized, artificial, and at times angry. The author himself had faced several personal tragedies in series, and these too might have contributed to the metamorphosis.

21. According to the passage, which of the following statements is true of *The Adventures of Huckleberry Finn*?

   A. It appeared after the publication of other Mark Twain stories describing life on the Mississippi River.
   B. It was the first full-length book that Mark Twain published.
   C. It would have been quite different if Mark Twain had not suffered personal tragedy.
   D. It had no serious themes and addressed no serious issues.

22. In the author's opinion, *The Adventures of Huckleberry Finn*:

   F. should not be read by children.
   G. contributed less to American literature than did Twain's postwar writings.
   H. is less adult in its subject matter than were Twain's postwar writings.
   J. reveals that Mark Twain had grown since writing his early Mississippi River stories.

Our answers here are choice (A) for 21 and choice (J) for 22.

Natural Science Passages

Natural science passages are filled with lots of details and technical descriptions.

> It is further noteworthy that the terrestrial vertebrate's most significant muscles of movement are no longer located lateral to the vertebral column as they are in the fish but rather in ventral and dorsal relation to it. This trend in terrestrial evolution is highly significant and means that the terrestrial vertebrate's principal movements are fore and back, not side to side. The trend is well documented in the whale, an aquatic animal whose ancestors are terrestrial quadrupeds. The whale, in other words, has "returned" to the sea secondarily after an ancestral stage on the land. Unlike the fish, and in accordance with its ancestry, it propels itself by moving the tail up and down, not side to side. In a sense, the whale moves itself by bending up and down at the waist. Indeed, that very analogy is recalled by the mythical mermaid figure who seems to represent a humanlike line returned to the water secondarily like the whale.

The questions usually track the text pretty closely and require you to make few inferences.

Reading Test Triage
If you have a knack for particular passage types, great. Do them first. If not, look at the topics, as well as the questions and answer choices. Some will be straightforward, while others will look more complicated. Use your time wisely.

31. Which of the following best represents a general trend associated with mammalian evolution?

    A. Enhancement of bodily movement from right to left and left to right
    B. Minimization of muscle groups oriented lateral to the vertebral column
    C. The development of propulsive fins from paired limbs
    D. Secondary return to the sea

Some people have a flair for the ACT's natural science passages, and some people find them extremely tedious and difficult. (And, by the way, it isn't necessarily good science students who do well with these passages nor poor science students who have trouble with them.) If among all of the passage types you find natural science the easiest, you should make it a rule to address the natural science passage first. If you find natural science passages the most difficult, however, save them for last.

The answer to 31 is choice (B).

TIME, TIME AGAIN

After working through the chapters in this book, you will have a good idea of which types of passages are easiest for you and which are hardest. When you take the Reading test, you should do the easiest (for you) passages first. Why? Because many people run out of time on the ACT Reading test. It's better to run out of time and have to guess on the passages that are the most difficult. You'll get more points at the beginning by working the easier passages first, and you'll lose fewer points by guessing on the hardest passage as time runs out.

How to Tell Which Passages You Find Easy and Hard

What do you do if you dislike all of the passages equally or show no particular—or, for that matter, consistent—knack for certain passage types? The subject matter of the passages may be dull, but in the end, you should base your ordering of the passages on

For More Great Titles by The Princeton Review
English and Reading Workout for the ACT

- **the user-friendliness of the topics themselves.**
  "Wait a minute!" you say. "I thought you said that if I show no particular knack for certain passage types…" True, but…
  Let's say you notice that a social science or humanities passage is historical in nature. Chances are that events will be presented in chronological order, making the passage easy to navigate. Or let's say you've recently learned about lasers in physics class and, lo and behold, the natural sciences passage is about lasers. Chances are that you'll be able to eliminate answers or even answer some of the questions based on what you've learned. You don't have to love a topic to take advantage of familiarity with it. In fact, being too enamored of a topic can work against you. Remember, you get points for answering questions correctly, not for understanding the passages, and certainly not for reading over them with great interest.
- **the user-friendliness of the questions and answer choices.**
  Many students who dislike all the passages find this an especially helpful guideline. Look at the questions. Do many of them direct you to particular lines in the passage, refer to dates, refer to proper nouns, or refer to italicized words? If so, a passage with several such questions will usually be much easier to manage. Look at the answer choices. Are they relatively straightforward, or do they resemble miniature novels? A passage with several longwinded questions and/or answer choices will always take more time to complete.

Take a quick look at the Reading in practice test 1. Try glancing at each passage—looking at either the topic or the questions and answer choices—and ask yourself which one looks easiest to you and which one you definitely want to leave for last. Ordering passages takes a little time at the beginning, but it can save you a lot of time (and gain you points) in the end.

Now that we've talked about the ordering of the passages and questions, let's talk about the whole point of this book—finding right answers.

THE RIGHT ANSWER MIGHT BE CAMOUFLAGED

Look at these two phrases.

"rationally conceived idea"

"concept born of reason"

The two phrases don't have a single word in common, but if you think about it, you'll probably agree that they mean the same thing. Lots of ACT reading questions test your ability to see that one sentence or phrase means more or less the same as another even though the wording is quite different. They test whether you can see that a sentence has been *paraphrased*, which means reworded.

Correct Answer Choices May Be Disguised
Look for answer choices that reword parts of the passage.

Read This Passage; It's Very Short

> Regardless of personal religious belief, no true student of history can emerge from study without a scholarly appreciation for the significant role of religion in the development of human civilization.

Now that you've read the passage, answer this question.

11. Which of the following represents the author's belief regarding religion and the study of history?

  A. Many historians develop a deep suspicion of totalitarian societies and the way in which they abuse human rights.

  B. Most historians have a profound distaste for ancient documents and torn papers.

  C. True historians develop an appreciation for the role of religion in the course of human development.

  D. Few historians develop insight into the manner in which political leaders gain power.

It's pretty easy to see that choice (C) is right, and that choices (A), (B), and (D) are wrong. Choice (C) features the author's words and accurately reflects his meaning. Choices (A), (B), and (D) are extreme and have nothing whatsoever to do with anything in the passage. This question is pretty straightforward. The wrong answers are clearly wrong, and the right answer is clearly right.

Many ACT Questions Aren't so Easy

ACT questions won't always provide you with a correct answer that reprints the author's own words. Instead, the author's statements will be camouflaged by *rewording*. That means you must be on the lookout for answer choices that don't seem right because the author's sentences have been reworded. Let's take the question we just answered and turn it into an ACT question by rewriting the answer choices.

11. Which of the following represents the author's belief regarding the role of religion in the study of history?

   A. Few historians have gained a complete appreciation for the development of religion.

   B. Historians should not allow their personal religious beliefs to affect the historical conclusions with which they emerge.

   C. Serious historians regard religious belief as an important force in man's social evolution.

   D. A true student of religious history should not ignore a general study of human development.

Choice (C) is still the correct answer, but that's not so easy to spot anymore. Unless you're on the lookout for camouflage, you might not appreciate the similarity between these two statements:

1. …no true student of history can emerge from study without a scholarly appreciation for the significant role of religion in the development of human civilization.

   and

2. Serious historians regard religious belief as an important force in man's social evolution.

These two statements don't have a single word in common. Yet, when you think about it,

"serious historians"	*is camouflage for*	"true student of history"
"important force"	*is camouflage for*	"significant role"
"man's social evolution"	*is camouflage for*	"development of human civilization"

Choice (C) presents the author's statements—camouflaged.

See Through the Camouflage

You'll raise your ACT score if you learn first to recognize camouflage and then to see through it. So let's practice. Each of the very short readings below comes from an ACT-type passage. We want you to

- read each one.
- think carefully about what it means.
- *with that meaning in mind* consider the meaning of each answer choice.
- determine which one constitutes the author's statements, camouflaged.

Let's try one.

The human condition is unequal, distributing its gifts and penalties according to a wildly haphazard scheme. A person is not what he deserves to be but simply what he is.

12. According to the passage, it is true that the human condition:

    F. is a precious gift and should not be treated haphazardly.

    G. does not allocate its burdens and benefits according to merit.

    H. will become more predictable as human beings learn to appreciate it.

    J. is sometimes unjust due to fundamental aspects of human nature.

Here's How to Crack It

What does the author say? The author says that life's pleasures and hardships are not given out fairly—according to what people deserve. Instead, they're given out randomly. The author is saying that you don't get what you deserve. You just get what you get.

With that in mind, let's look at the answer options and see which one makes the same statement in a different way.

What do the choices mean?

Choice (F) means that life is a very valuable thing and that people should not be careless with it. That's not what we're looking for.

Choice (G) says just what the author has said—in different words. Think about it.

"allocate"	*is camouflage for*	"distributing"
"burdens and benefits"	*is camouflage for*	"gifts and penalties"
"merit"	*is camouflage for*	"deserves"

Choice (H) means that people who appreciate life will find that it offers fewer surprises. The author did not say that.

Choice (J) means that human nature is the cause of life's unfairness. Interesting, but that's not what the author wrote.

Only choice (G) comes close to expressing the author's meaning. That's why it's right.

Try another.

———————————————○———————————————

> Poverty, deformity, illness, loss, weakness, and mistreatment impose themselves relentlessly on individual lives. That circumstance begs the historian to ask why humans have for the most part accepted the situation so peaceably.

13. The passage indicates that persistent poverty and illness:

  A. are caused partially by humanity's overriding concern with acceptance and peace.

  B. are due in some part to a faulty understanding of history.

  C. should make historians question the role of the individual in human affairs.

  D. should provoke historical inquiry into humanity's willingness to tolerate adversity.

Here's How to Crack It

What does the author say? The author says, first of all, that people have always had a lot of trouble in their lives. He then says that historians should try to figure out why they're so willing to put up with it.

What do the choices mean?

Choice (A) means that people have trouble because they're too concerned with peace. Ridiculous, but more important, it's not what the author wrote.

Choice (B) means that people have trouble because they don't understand history. Not so ridiculous, but the author made no such statement.

Choice (C) means that all of this trouble should make historians try to figure out the place of individuals in society. Whatever that means, it's not what we're looking for.

Now look at choice (D). It's just what the doctor ordered. It's the author's statement—camouflaged. Think about it.

"should provoke historical inquiry"	*is camouflage for*	"begs the historian to ask"
"willingness to tolerate adversity"	*is camouflage for*	"why humans…accepted the situation so peaceably"

So choice (D) is right.

———————————————○———————————————

Here's another one.

Religious belief allows the unlucky, on some very important level, to treat their misery as insignificant in the grand scheme of things, for they look to something higher: the approval of their god and the faith that they will not in the end be forsaken.

14. The passage states that religious belief helps people by:

    F. allowing them to accept the idea that they have been forsaken.

    G. providing them with faith that they will overcome their difficulties.

    H. diminishing the importance they might place on their day-to-day pain.

    J. emphasizing that spiritual strength is more significant than luck.

Here's How to Crack It

What does the author say? The author says that religious belief helps people whose lives are difficult. It causes them to focus on the wish to please their god, which means that they place relatively little importance on the troubles they face in their lives.

What do the choices mean?

Choice (F) means that religious believers don't mind being forsaken. Sorry, not what we're looking for.

Choice (G) means that religion helps people believe they'll get over their problems. Sounds good, but it's not the meaning we're after.

Choice (H) means that religious believers don't think their troubles are so important. That's what the author said! Choice (H) represents the author's statements camouflaged. Think about it:

"diminishing the importance"	*is camouflage for*	"treat…as insignificant"
"pain"	*is camouflage for*	"misery"

Choice (J) means that religious believers think spiritual strength is more important than luck. The author doesn't say anything like that. Only choice (H) reflects the author's meaning. That's why it's right.

Summary

o   There are always 4 passages and 40 questions on the ACT Reading test. The passages are always in this order: prose fiction, social science, humanities, and natural science.

o   Spend the first minute of the test determining which passage will be hardest for you—this is the one to leave until last. Playing to your strengths early in the test will gain you the most points.

o   Be wary of camouflaged answers. ACT test writers rarely use a direct quote from the passage in the correct answer.

o   Don't forget to always guess your Letter of the Day if there are questions that you can't answer or don't get to in time.

Chapter 17
Distractors

The ACT test writers are good at writing wrong answers that look right. To get you to pick these wrong answers, they utilize certain distracting techniques. This chapter shows you how to be on the lookout for deceptive answers that track the language of the passage very closely, for switches that say the opposite of the correct answer, for extreme answer choices, and for answers that sound too nice. They are usually incorrect.

GET WISE TO DISTRACTORS: USE PROCESS OF ELIMINATION

You'll raise your ACT Reading score if you're good at spotting not only right answers but also the wrong ones. In the standardized test business, wrong answers are called "distractors," and that's a perfect name for them. Distractors are designed to misdirect your thinking—to break your concentration, distract you, and throw you off course. Even if you have a pretty good grasp of the passage and the question you're trying to answer, distractors can make you lose sight of both. But if you're wise to distractors, you can quickly eliminate them and rapidly make your way to the right answer.

FOUR KINDS OF DISTRACTORS

You should know about the four kinds of distractors that show up on the ACT Reading test. We're going to show you how each one operates so you'll know how to use them to your advantage.

Distractor 1: Deceptive Answers

Many distractors steal words directly from the passages and use them to create a statement that does *not* reflect the content of the passages. These distractors use the authors' words but distort their meanings, so we call them *deceptive answers*.

Read this statement.

> *Tom loves going to the movies with Mary.*

It's easy to write a bunch of sentences that do not reflect the statement's meaning, even though they use the words "Tom," "love," "movies," and "Mary." For example, consider this

> *Tom fell in love with Mary at the movies.*

or this

> *Tom and Mary love movies.*

or this

> *Tom and Mary generally enjoy seeing movies about love.*

If you think about *meaning*, not one of these statements resembles the one with which we started. Each distorts the original by taking its words and rearranging them. Yet they all sort of "sound like" the original because they use the same words.

Each one of the deceptive answers we just read would make a good ACT distractor. Suppose you've just read an ACT passage that contains the statement we worked with: "Tom loves going to the movies with Mary." Now imagine that you get a question like this:

1. According to the passage, which of the following statements is true regarding Tom and Mary?

    A. Tom fell in love with Mary at the movies.
    B. Tom enjoys viewing motion pictures with Mary as his companion.
    C. Tom and Mary generally enjoy seeing movies about love.
    D. Both Tom and Mary love going to the movies.

Notice that choices (A), (C), and (D) use words that come straight from the passage. *They're all wrong.* Which one is right? Choice (B): It presents the author's meaning—in camouflage.

Don't Let Deceptive Answers Snare You
Don't be fooled by answer choices that misuse words and phrases from the passage.

Look at these four excerpts from ACT-like passages. Each one is followed by five statements. Three of the five are deceptive answer distractors. The other two accurately reflect the author's meaning; they *don't* distort. For each passage, decide which three statements are deceptive answers and which two are not.

Read this natural science excerpt.

As an explanation for the age and origin of the solar system, the nebular hypothesis lost ground at the turn of the twentieth century over questions about the distribution of angular momentum.

What does the author say?
- The nebular hypothesis was intended to explain the age and origin of the solar system.
- It lost influence at the beginning of the twentieth century.
- It happened because people raised questions about the distribution of angular momentum, and the nebular hypothesis did not provide adequate answers.

Use POE
Look for the following four types of distractors on the ACT Reading test:
- deceptive answers
- the switch
- extremes
- answer choices that sound too nice

Now evaluate these statements.

	Deceptive Answer	Not a Deceptive Answer
31. According to the nebular hypothesis, the solar system was created by distributions of angular momentum.	☐	☐
32. The nebular hypothesis came under question at the beginning of the twentieth century.	☐	☐
33. The nebular hypothesis was challenged because of issues related to angular momentum.	☐	☐
34. Knowledge about the solar system's angular momentum was first distributed in the twentieth century.	☐	☐
35. The nebular hypothesis was poorly understood until the twentieth century, when theories of angular momentum gained ground.	☐	☐

Here's How to Crack It

Statements 31, 34, and 35 are deceptive. They distort the author's meaning. The words come straight from the passage, but the meanings definitely do not. The author does not say

- the nebular hypothesis states that distributions of angular momentum created the solar system.
- someone first distributed knowledge about angular momentum in the twentieth century.
- people didn't understand the nebular hypothesis until the twentieth century.

Statements 32 and 33 are not deceptive answers. They do not distort. The author does say

- the nebular hypothesis was questioned (lost ground) at the beginning of the twentieth century.
- the nebular hypothesis was questioned because of concerns relating to angular momentum.

Important

Distortions are often words in the passage that are used out of context. Eliminate them.

Read this social science excerpt.

With revolutionary improvements in health care technologies, modern medicine's expansive arsenal has undoubtedly created an improved state of national health. Although the incidence of degenerative disease is on the rise, that is primarily because degenerative diseases are characteristic of old age and the population is living, on average, longer than did its parents and grandparents.

What does the author say?
- There has been great progress in medicine.
- It's true that there's more degenerative disease around than there used to be.
- That's because degenerative diseases usually affect the elderly, and people are living long enough to *get* these diseases.

Now evaluate these statements.	Deceptive Answer	Not a Deceptive Answer
11. Modern medicine has increased the individual's average life span.	☐	☐
12. Revolutionary health care techniques have produced degeneration in the state of national health.	☐	☐
13. Few people doubt that degenerative disease tends to increase longevity.	☐	☐
14. Today's health care technologies have bettered the national health.	☐	☐
15. With today's tools and techniques the physician can cure degenerative diseases that once caused early death.	☐	☐

Here's How to Crack It

Statements 12, 13, and 15 are deceptive answers. They distort the author's meaning. The words are familiar, but they've been rearranged to say something that has nothing to do with the passage. The author does not say

- modern medicine has had a negative effect on health care.
- most people think degenerative disease makes for longer life.
- modern medicine allows physicians to cure degenerative diseases.

Statements 11 and 14 are not deceptive answers. They do not distort. The author does say

- modern medicine has increased the average life span.
- modern medicine has improved the national health.

Read this prose fiction excerpt.

Mrs. Mandale's physician repeatedly reminded his patient of her diabetes and had ordered her on several occasions to lose weight. Hence, Allen found himself taking his grandmother once each week to her weight-watching group.

Mrs. Mandale was not among the heavier women in her group. She never announced her weight, however, because, "a true lady did not discuss such personal matters." The group was one of Mrs. Mandale's few pleasures, but she feared walking unaccompanied in the city at night and asked that Allen take her each week to "group." She pointed out that she had done much for him, that her very health was involved, and that he should be willing to extend himself for her.

What does the author say?
- Allen's grandmother has diabetes.
- For that reason, her doctor ordered her to lose weight.
- To lose the weight, she participates in a weight-watching group.
- She's not one of the heavier women in the group.
- Even so, she won't reveal her weight, because she thinks true ladies shouldn't discuss such personal issues.
- The weight-watching group is one of Mrs. Mandale's few pleasures.
- The weight-watching group is conducted at night, and Mrs. Mandale does not like to walk in the city by herself at night.
- Mrs. Mandale thinks she's done a lot for Allen so she asks him to take her to her weight-watching group each week.

Half-and-Half
Beware of answer choices that are half good, half bad. They're also deceptive. If an answer is half bad, it's all wrong.

Now evaluate these statements.

	Deceptive Answer	Not a Deceptive Answer
1. Mrs. Mandale is willing to reveal her weight only because she weighs less than others in her weight-watching group.	☐	☐
2. The doctor recommends that Allen's grandmother not walk alone at night.	☐	☐
3. Mrs. Mandale finds her weight reduction group more enjoyable than most of her other activities.	☐	☐
4. Mrs. Mandale thinks that other women in her weight-watching group are not as ladylike as she is.	☐	☐
5. Mrs. Mandale believes she has been a positive force in her grandson's life.	☐	☐

Here's How to Crack It

Statements 1, 2, and 4 are deceptive answers. They distort the author's meaning. The key words come straight from the passage, but the statements are distortions. The author does not say

- Mrs. Mandale is willing to reveal her weight.
- the doctor advised Mrs. Mandale against walking alone at night.
- Mrs. Mandale believes herself to be more of a lady than the other women in the group.

Statements 3 and 5 are not deceptive answers. They do not distort. The author does say

- the weight-watching group is one of the few pleasures Mrs. Mandale has.
- Mrs. Mandale thinks she has done a lot for her grandson.

Read this humanities excerpt.

Before the Civil War, Frances Ellen Watkins Harper was the best known of black abolitionist writers. Her greatest true novel, *Iola Leroy, or Shadows Uplifted,* appeared in 1892. The work was transitional: It treats both the pre-Civil War and post-Civil War periods. Although it describes the evils of slavery, its principal purpose was considerably different from some of the earlier novels for which Mrs. Harper became famous. In *Iola Leroy,* Mrs. Harper wished to promote justice and interracial tolerance. For that reason, the novel treats some issues with more idealism than realism.

Referring to her own novel, Mrs. Harper wrote: "I have woven a story whose mission will not be in vain if it awakens in the hearts of our countrymen a stronger sense of justice and a more Christlike humanity."

What does the author say?
- Mrs. Harper was a black abolitionist writer—the most famous of her time.
- Her greatest earlier novels dealt primarily with the evils of slavery.
- Her best novel was *Iola Leroy,* which was also called *Shadows Uplifted.*
- Dealing with the periods before and after the Civil War, *Iola Leroy* portrays the evils of slavery; Mrs. Harper primarily intended the novel to promote justice and tolerance among races.
- Because that was her purpose, she sometimes treated issues not in a realistic manner, but in an idealistic manner.

Now evaluate these statements.

	Deceptive Answer	Not a Deceptive Answer
21. *Iola Leroy* depicts situations occurring before and after the Civil War.	☐	☐
22. Frances Ellen Watkins Harper was not well known as an abolitionist until the appearance of her first true novel, *Iola Leroy*.	☐	☐
23. Although best known as abolitionist literature, Mrs. Harper's prewar novels usually concerned justice, not slavery.	☐	☐
24. Mrs. Harper was well known before the Civil War but in the postwar period her fame diminished considerably.	☐	☐
25. Frances Ellen Watkins Harper opposed slavery before the war and attempted to improve relations among blacks and whites after the war.	☐	☐

Here's How to Crack It

Statements 22, 23, and 24 are deceptive answers. They distort the author's meaning. The words come right out of the passage, but the meanings have nothing to do with it. The author definitely does not say

- *Iola Leroy* was Mrs. Harper's *first* true novel, or that Mrs. Harper was not well known until that novel appeared.
- Mrs. Harper's prewar novels concerned justice and not slavery.
- Mrs. Harper lost fame after the Civil War.

Statements 21 and 25 are not deceptive answers. They do not distort. The author does indicate that

- *Iola Leroy* concerned both the pre–Civil War and post–Civil War periods.
- Mrs. Harper was an abolitionist before the war and that her postwar novel *Iola Leroy* was intended to improve relations among the races.

Distractor 2

Distractor 2: Switches

Some ACT distractors take the truth and switch it around. We call this "the switch." Don't let it fool you. For instance, read this.

> 1. Professor Thorne generally explains a technological discovery first in terms of its history and then in terms of the science upon which it was founded.

We've learned that Professor Thorne discusses history *first* and science *second*.

Now look at this statement.

> 2. Professor Thorne generally explains a technological discovery first in terms of the science on which it was founded, and then in terms of its history.

Statement 2 looks like Statement 1, but it's backward. Professor Thorne is doing things in the wrong order: science first and history second. Statement 2 takes the truth and turns it around. That's the essence of "the switch."

But the ACT Test Writers Get Sneaky

When the ACT test writers throw a switch into the answer choices, they don't always write something like Statement 2, which takes the author's statement and literally reverses the order of its words. Sometimes they *change* the wording and at the same time, turn the meaning upside down. Read Statement 1 again, and then look at Statement 3 below.

> 3. After Professor Thorne describes the scientific aspects of a technological breakthrough, he explains the historical context in which the breakthrough was made.

It's not so easy to see at first, but Statement 3 is a switch. It doesn't use the words *first*, or *then*, and it begins with the word "after." But think about what it says. Professor Thorne discusses history *after* discussing science. That would mean that he discusses science first and history second. That's opposite to what you're told in the passage.

Now read this.

> 4. Irrespective of population, every state elects two members to the United States Senate. The most populous state and the least populous state thus have equal representation in that important legislative body. In contrast, the House of Representatives is population-based and the number of representatives elected by any state depends on the number of citizens residing in that state.

Here's a switch.

> **5.** Representation in the United States Senate is dependent on state population.

From Statement 4, we learned

- representation in the Senate is *not* based on population.
- representation in the House *is* based on population.

Statement 5 is exactly opposite to the original. It's a switch.

Eliminate the Switch

Let's say you're looking at a question. You spot two deceptive answers and eliminate them. That leaves you with two choices, and you aren't sure which is right. One thing you should do is determine whether one of them is a switch. If it is, then the *other* one is right. Here are two passage excerpts—each one followed by two to three questions. For each question, determine which answer choice is the switch.

Read this social sciences excerpt.

The Switch
Look out for
- changes in the wording in the answer choices
- a "flip" in the meaning of the sentence

Twenty or thirty thousand years ago, *Homo Sapiens* were uncommon animals, wandering alone or in small groups in a constant search for food. Primitive humans lived by the hunt, and modern nutritionists like to observe that with meat as a dietary
5 staple, they were seldom iron-deficient as are many farm-based populations today. But the absence of iron deficiency was perhaps the only advantage to the hunting lifestyle of the time. The hunter, it should be remembered, may find himself the hunted, and by anything approaching our own standards today, primitive
10 human life was unstable and incessantly hazardous.

In this regard, however, the advent of agriculture improved the human condition. Between ten and twenty thousand years ago, human beings discovered the use of herding and of growing, which apparently served as inspiration to man's mechanical facili-
15 ties. Relatively crude weapons of hunt were replaced by more refined farming implements. To be sure, farming is subject to the uncertainties of weather and climate, but it ultimately allows humans a greater degree of control over their food supply and relieves them from the dangers of the hunt.

11. In terms of the tools and implements made by primitive man, the passage suggests that:

    A. farming tools were less sophisticated than hunting weapons.

    B. [Already eliminated]

    C. agriculture is associated with more advanced tool-making skills.

    D. [Already eliminated]

Here's How to Crack It

Look at choice (A). It says farming tools are less sophisticated than hunting weapons. Now look at the passage, lines 16–17. It says that hunting implements were crude and that farming implements were more refined. Choice (A) has it backward—it's a switch. Eliminate it.

12. According to the passage, a life based on agriculture:

    F. [Already eliminated]

    G. provides humans with more iron than is provided by hunting.

    H. [Already eliminated]

    J. offers a greater degree of certainty than does a hunting lifestyle.

Here's How to Crack It

Look at choice (G). It says that agriculture provides more iron than does hunting. The author does discuss iron deficiency, but she says that hunters were *not* iron deficient, and that farmers *are.* Choice (G) is a switch. Eliminate it.

Read this natural science excerpt.

In certain critical respects the magnificence of science lies not in its discovery of what is true but in its identification of that which is not. Pivotal points in scientific learning are those at which some long-held assumption is openly examined
5 and exposed as a falsehood. Copernicus, Kepler, Galileo, and ultimately Newton established that the sun, not the earth, is the fixed center of the solar system and that the earth orbits the sun, thus invalidating the views of Aristotle and Ptolemy, which were largely unquestioned before that time.

10 Toward the turn of the last century, Michelson, Morley, Lorentz, and Einstein successfully challenged a host of assumptions about the absolute quality of space and time. Then, in the 1920s, theories put forward by Heisenberg, Schrodinger, and Dirac together created the science of quantum mechanics and
15 thus destroyed time-honored views about position and velocity. Even Einstein had difficulty accepting Heisenberg's theory, which

dealt a lethal blow to the cherished notion, advocated especially by LaPlace, that science could aspire to complete knowledge of the state of the universe and thus predict its future.

20   In 1929, Hubble, versed in the writings of Olbers one hundred years before him, showed that the universe was finite but expanding and more or less did away with the prevailing belief that the universe had to be either finite and static or infinite.

31. According to the passage, Ptolemy differed from Copernicus in that:

   A. Ptolemy envisioned a stationary earth and Copernicus did not.

   B. [Already eliminated]

   C. [Already eliminated]

   D. Ptolemy postulated that the earth followed an orbit about the sun and Copernicus did not.

Here's How to Crack It

Look at choice (D). It says that Ptolemy imagined the earth orbiting the sun and that Copernicus did not imagine the earth orbiting the sun. Now look at lines 5–9 of the passage. They tell us that Copernicus (and others) did *not* believe in a fixed earth. They thought the earth orbited the sun. That view invalidated Ptolemy's view. In other words, Ptolemy thought otherwise. He thought the earth was fixed and that the sun orbited the earth. Choice (D) is a switch. Eliminate it.

32. According to the passage, Heisenberg's theory:

   F. [Already eliminated]

   G. challenged traditional beliefs about position and velocity.

   H. described a universe that could be understood and predicted.

   J. [Already eliminated]

Here's How to Crack It

Look at choice (H). It says that Heisenberg's principle makes the universe seem predictable. Now read the passage, lines 16–19. They say that Heisenberg's theory *dealt a blow* to the idea that science could attain complete knowledge of the universe and predict its future. Heisenberg's principle *destroyed* the belief that science might completely understand the state of the universe. That means choice (H) is a switch. Eliminate it.

Sometimes the Switch Involves a Sneaky Word Substitution

Sometimes the switch involves the substitution of a wrong word (or name) for a right one. The answer choice looks correct but isn't because one word doesn't belong. Recall the natural science passage and look at the question below.

---

33. The Aristotelian conception of the solar system was:

    A. inconsistent with Newtonian and Galilean insights.
    B. at odds with Copernican and Ptolemic views.
    C. [Already eliminated]
    D. [Already eliminated]

Here's How to Crack It

Look at choice (B). It indicates that Aristotle's views were different from those of Ptolemy and Copernicus. Now look at lines 5–9 of the passage. They tell us that Copernicus, Kepler, Galileo, and Newton challenged the views of Aristotle and Ptolemy. In other words, Aristotle and Ptolemy believed one thing and the other four, including Copernicus, believed another. "Copernican" belongs in the answer choice, but "Ptolemic" does not. Choice (B) is a switch. Eliminate it.

Sometimes the Switch Gives You a Simple Shortcut to the Right Answer

If the answer choices happen to feature two statements that are basically opposites, then one of them is usually right (and the other, of course, is the switch). That means you can focus on these two and ignore the other two answer options unless neither of the first two is correct.

For instance, consider the natural science excerpt we just read, and look at the following answer choices:

---

34. Blah, blah, blah…:

    F. important in that it shows certain propositions to be true.
    G. important in that it shows certain propositions to be false.
    H. less precise than most scientists believe.
    J. extremely misleading to those who fail to question its premises.

Notice that choices (F) and (G) are opposites. Without even looking at the question, you can conclude that one of them will probably be the right answer. Why? Because the ACT test writers are predictable that way. They tend not to present opposing statements unless one of them is right. In this case, choices (H) and (J) are wrong, and you can eliminate them.

Now let's look at the question.

---

34. In the first paragraph, the author makes the point that natural science can be:

    F. important in that it shows certain propositions to be true.
    G. important in that it shows certain propositions to be false.
    H. less precise than most scientists believe.
    J. extremely misleading to those who fail to question its premises.

Here's How to Crack It

You know that either choice (F) or (G) is probably right, so focus on these two. In the first sentence of the paragraph, the author states, "In certain critical respects the magnificence of science lies not in its discovery of what is true but in its identification of that which is not." Choice (G) makes the same statement—in camouflage. Choice (F) is the switch. Choice (G) is correct.

Distractor 3: Extremes

If an answer choice indicates that something is *always* so, *invariably* so, or *never* so, then it's usually wrong. We call such choices *extremes,* and you should be very suspicious of them.

Words like *completely, perfectly,* and *absolutely* also signal an extreme choice.

Extremes tend to be wrong because they're usually *debatable,* and the ACT test writers know that. Think about these statements:

> *Patients who are chronically depressed never enjoy their lives.*

Never? *Ever?* It's pretty hard to prove the truth of such a statement.

It's one thing to say that depressed patients *have difficulty* enjoying their lives or that they *tend not* to enjoy their lives. But to say they *never* enjoy their lives just can't be correct.

Extreme Answer Choices
Look out for answer choices that are too extreme to be the correct answer. These are answer choices to eliminate. These answer choices include words such as *always, completely,* and *absolutely.*

A political leader should seek to make peace at all costs.

All costs? No matter what? That's pretty tough to defend. Such a statement is too one-sided to constitute a right answer on the ACT.

> *In order to lead a productive life, a citizen must devote all of his energy to his work.*

All of his energy? Come on. That statement is too easy to dispute, and the ACT test writers know it. They can't call it correct.

Extreme statements are easy to write and they're very useful to standardized test writers. When a standardized test writer has trouble thinking of a wrong answer choice for one of the questions, he or she often constructs an extreme.

Without reading any passage, consider this question and determine which answer choice is an extreme statement.

31. The author's claim that "cause is relative only to perspective" introduces his argument that:

   A. mental well-being depends on physical strength.
   B. how something is perceived depends on its nature.
   C. psychological health requires a perfect upbringing.
   D. psychiatric condition depends on numerous factors, environmental and internal.

Here's How to Crack It

Choice (C) is extreme. The idea that anything has to be "ideal" or "perfect" or "absolutely precise" or "completely objective" or "totally honest" is usually contrary to ACT philosophy. Eliminate it.

Look at this question and determine which answer choice or choices are extremes.

32. The author believes that practicing psychiatrists:

   F. cannot possibly help patients unless they are completely objective.
   G. are hopelessly confused over the genesis of mental illness.
   H. are scientists notwithstanding the uncertainties that surround psychiatry.
   J. should, for the time being, treat mental disease in terms of environment.

Here's How to Crack It
Choices (F) and (G) are extremes. The phrases "cannot possibly," "completely objective," and "hopelessly confused" should tip you off.

Read this next question and determine which answer choice or choices are extremes.

---

33. According to information presented in the third paragraph, an individual organism will not survive to reproductive age unless:

    A. all of its compensatory mechanisms are in ideal balance.
    B. it has adequate homeostatic and feedback responses.
    C. it is capable of complete adaptation to every form of stress.
    D. other individuals of the same species fail to reproduce.

Here's How to Crack It
Choices (A) and (C) are extremes. "Ideal balance," "complete adaptation," and "every...stress" are the tip-off phrases.

Distractor 4: Choices That Sound Too "Nice"
Some distractors will appeal to you simply because they sound "nice," even though they have little to do with the question or the passage. Such distractors might draw on something you already know, or on the surface they might just seem reasonable and correct. Think, for instance, about statements like the following:

> *Ultimately, the voting public knows its own best interest.*
>
> *Structure is important, but it should not be imposed in such a way as to stifle creativity.*
>
> *The ideal society is one that allows for individual difference, but at the same time creates a people united in interest.*
>
> *All people have a right to live and die with dignity.*

These thoughts are so "nice" and "sensible" as to seem practically beyond challenge. Some students read them and think, "This must be right." Sometimes these kinds of statements do represent the correct answer. But at other times they don't. When you find yourself drawn to such an answer choice, you should check back with the question and ask yourself whether the answer choice is just a sweet and easy sentiment or whether it really *answers* the question you are asked.

Too Nice
Don't automatically fall for answer choices that sound too "nice." Check to see if the statement was actually made in the passage. If not, eliminate that answer choice.

For example, look at this prose fiction excerpt and consider the question that follows:

"And then the men!" said Jonathan, "the men coming aboard drunk, and having to be pounded sober!…" "Well, what can you do?" he went on. "If you don't strike, the men think you're afraid of them…." Jonathan Tinker was plainly part of the horrible tyranny that we all know exists on shipboard; and his listener respected him the more that, though he had heart enough to be ashamed of it, he was too honest not to own it.

1. Jonathan's listener respected him because he believed:

   A. [Already eliminated]
   B. Jonathan did not attempt to conceal his participation in maritime abuse.
   C. Jonathan had a good heart and basically cared for his men.
   D. [Already eliminated]

Here's How to Crack It

Look at choice (C). What could be more correct than a good heart and an honest concern for other people? Choice (C) is tempting, but it isn't right. Nice or not, the author does not state that the listener's respect for Jonathan had anything to do with a good heart or a concern for his men. Read the last two lines of the passage. The listener respected Jonathan because he had the honesty to "own" his acts. He acknowledged his participation in the tyranny.

Read this social studies excerpt.

       The thought that older citizens might be denied health care on the basis of cost effectiveness is very troublesome and probably not acceptable to modern American society. Yet there is precedent for such policies in other westernized nations. In
5 Sweden, for example, where the overwhelming majority of health care is funded by the government, patients over the age of 55 are not eligible for long-term life-saving renal dialysis. The nation has made a decision to invest a certain amount of its resources in renal dialysis, and it does not consider it sensible to provide the
10 service to kidney patients over a certain age. Because Sweden is founded largely on egalitarian principles, a citizen over 55 is not permitted access to renal dialysis even if he is willing to pay for it on his own. The society does not believe that wealth should play a role in longevity. Recently, the United States has inaugurated
15 a number of systems aimed at controlling health care costs and avoiding waste. These include requirements that patients obtain a second opinion before undergoing surgery and utilize review systems aimed at shortening hospital stays. To date, however, no agency or insurer in the United States premises its willingness to
20 pay for health care on the age or the youth of the patient.

---

11. In Sweden, which of the following measures is designed to promote egalitarianism?

   A. [Already eliminated]
   B. The Swedish government denies certain life-saving medical resources to older citizens.
   C. [Already eliminated]
   D. The Swedish government attempts to provide the same health care to all citizens regardless of wealth or age.

Here's How to Crack It

Look at choice (D). Very, very attractive. What could be nicer than equal health care for all? But look at lines 4–14. In Sweden, we are told, citizens over 55 are denied access to renal dialysis. Choice (D) is wrong, and choice (B) is right.

Summary

o ACT test writers love distracting answers. They try to get you to you to pick one of their wrong answers by taking you off track.

o Be careful of deceptive answers, switches, and extreme answer choices, as well as answers that are too good to be true.

o Don't forget to always guess your Letter of the Day if there are questions that you can't answer or don't get to in time.

Chapter 18
The Four-Step System

The best way to beat the ACT system is to use a different one. The four-step system outlined in this chapter provides a way to look at the questions and passages methodically to maximize your points. Start by identifying any significant words in the questions. Scan the passage for these words, skim the passage and jot down notes, and then go back to the questions. We call this the loop.

Now that you've learned how to recognize right and wrong answer choices, we're going to teach you a four-step process that systematically leads you to the correct answers. We take time to explain each step slowly, so we can be sure you learn it. Because of that, you might at first think our system is lengthy or cumbersome. It isn't. It's streamlined and efficient. When we're all through, you'll see how speedily it works. (Think about how long it takes to tie a shoe. Now think about how long it would take to tell—not show—someone how to tie a shoe.)

We'll begin by answering the following simple question:

Why Are ACT Passages Hard to Follow?

You know how to read. So why is it so tough to read an ACT passage? It's tough, first of all, because the passage is pulled out of the middle of some larger work; you're reading it out of context. It's also tough to read an ACT passage because you don't know why you're reading it. You don't know what you're looking for or what you're supposed to "understand."

Stop thinking about the ACT for a second and suppose someone offers you a $20 per hour job. She points from her office window to a building sitting on a nearby lot. Then she hands you a key and says, "Check the place out and come back with a report."

That sounds easy enough, except for one thing.

You Don't Know What You're Looking For

What are you supposed to "check out?" The landscaping? The driveway? Are you looking for chipped paint? Leaky pipes? Broken windows?

You have no idea. So you roam around the place. An hour goes by and you roam back to your boss's office. She asks,

"Are there any mice in the basement?"

You tell her you don't know.

"In a whole hour you couldn't look in the basement and see if there were any mice?"

Of course you could have, but you didn't know she wanted you to. You had a simple job, and you blew it. Why? Because you never really knew what the job was. You didn't know what you were supposed to do.

The same sort of thing holds true for ACT reading passages. The passages are usually tough to read because you don't know what you're supposed to look for. They become much easier if you solve that problem. Having said that, we're ready to tell you about the first two steps of our system.

Step 1: Find the Lead Words and Phrases

Step 1 should take you about 30 seconds, and here's what it's all about. Before you read the passage, look at the questions (but not the answer choices) and underline any lead words they contain. Look, for instance, at the following question. (We'll help you ignore the answer choices by turning them all into "blah, blah, blah.")

11. Jeremy Bentham probably would have said that lawyers:

   A. blah, blah, blah…
   B. blah, blah, blah…
   C. blah, blah, blah…
   D. blah, blah, blah…

The question has some pretty ordinary words like "probably," "would," "have," and "that." We might find those words in a lot of different questions. The lead words special to this question are "Jeremy Bentham" and "lawyers." So when we say "lead words," we mean the words, phrases, or names that stand out and tell you what the question's about. Look at this question and underline the lead words or phrases.

12. The author states that the common law differs from the civil law in that:

   F. blah, blah, blah…
   G. blah, blah, blah…
   H. blah, blah, blah…
   J. blah, blah, blah…

There are of course some ordinary words like "author," "states," "from," "differs." This question's lead phrases are "common law" and "civil law."

Try three more.

21. According to the passage, Peters differs from Jefferson in that:

   A. blah, blah, blah…
   B. blah, blah, blah…
   C. blah, blah, blah…
   D. blah, blah, blah…

22. As discussed in the passage, the integrative movement produced:

   F. blah, blah, blah…
   G. blah, blah, blah…
   H. blah, blah, blah…
   J. blah, blah, blah…

33. According to the passage, edema and hypoproteinemia:

    A. blah, blah, blah…
    B. blah, blah, blah…
    C. blah, blah, blah…
    D. blah, blah, blah…

**Identify the
Lead Words**
As you read each question,
underline the key words or
phrases that tell you the
focus of the question.

- In question 21, the lead words are "Peters" and "Jefferson."
- In question 22, the lead phrase is "integrative movement."
- In question 33, the lead words are "edema" and "hypoproteinemia."

By the way, when you find lead words, don't worry about their meaning. You don't have to know who Peters is or what *edema* means. Your job at step 1 is to see that some name, word, or phrase is the focus of a question. Its meaning doesn't matter.

Some Questions Don't Have Lead Words

When you follow step 1, you're going to notice that some questions don't really have any lead words. Look at these three.

1. It can be most reasonably inferred that the author believes that:

    A. blah, blah, blah…
    B. blah, blah, blah…
    C. blah, blah, blah…
    D. blah, blah, blah…

2. Which of the following conclusions is drawn by the passage?

    F. blah, blah, blah…
    G. blah, blah, blah…
    H. blah, blah, blah…
    J. blah, blah, blah…

3. The author's discussion would best support which of the following statements?

    A. blah, blah, blah…
    B. blah, blah, blah…
    C. blah, blah, blah…
    D. blah, blah, blah…

As you can see, none of these three questions offers any critical words. "Writer," "opinion," "support," and "conclusion" are pretty ordinary. We might find them in lots of different questions. What do you do with these questions when you're pursuing step 1? You ignore them. Among the ten questions that follow a passage, usually 8 or 9 will offer you lead words. Those are the questions you're looking for when you follow step 1.

Take a look at the following ten questions (we've deleted the answer choices completely). Figure out which have lead words and which do not. We will revisit these questions as we cover the various techniques for the Reading test.

21. Which of the following conclusions is drawn by the passage?

22. As discussed in the passage, Quentin Bell believes that historians and critics:

23. The author expresses the idea that:

24. According to the passage, academicism and mannerism:

25. It can be most reasonably inferred that the author believes that:

26. According to the passage, Renoir differs from Daleur in that:

27. According to the passage, Cezanne's work is characterized by:

28. According to the sixth paragraph, the author implies that:

29. In the author's view, the phrase "modern sculpture" means sculpture that:

30. According to the author, subjectivism affected Rodin in which of the following ways?

Questions 22, 24, 26, 27, 29, and 30 have lead words: "Quentin Bell," "academicism," "mannerism," "Renoir," "Daleur," "Cezanne," "modern sculpture," "subjectivism." Questions 21, 23, 25, and 28 are more general. They don't have lead words. If you were to encounter these ten questions while pursuing step 1, you'd focus on 22, 24, 26, 27, 29, and 30. You'd ignore 21, 23, 25, and 28.

Step 2

Refer Back to the Passage for the Lead Words

Now that you have identified the lead words in the question, you can look for them in the passage.

Step 2: Scan the Passage for Lead Words

Step 2 of our system should take you about 30 seconds. In step 2, you *scan* the passage very quickly looking for the same lead words you noticed in step 1. You don't read the passage; you scan it. That means you pass your eyes over all of it, trying only to spot the lead words. Every time you see a lead word, underline it.

Here's part of the humanities passage followed by five of the questions we just reviewed with good lead words. We want you to

- First follow step 1: Look at the questions and notice the lead words.
- Then follow step 2: Scan the passage and underline those same lead words wherever you see them.

At step 2, you should also underline any words or phrases that seem to be very much like the lead words you find in the questions. For instance, if a question uses the phrase "modern art forms," and the phrase "modern styles of art" appears in the passage, you should underline it.

Rodin was surely a great artist, but he was not an innovator as was Cezanne; prevailing tides of subjectivism came over him. Rodin's mission was to reinvest sculpture with the integrity it lost when Michelangelo died. Rodin succeeded in this mission. His
50 first true work, *The Age of Bronze* (1877), marked the beginning of the end of academicism, mannerism, and decadence that had prevailed since Michelangelo's last sculpture, the *Rondanini Pieta*.

Yet it is largely Cezanne, not Rodin, who was artistic ances-tor to Picasso, Gonzalez, Brancusi, Archipenko, Lipchitz, and
55 Laurens, and they are unquestionably the first lights in the "new art" of sculpture. This "new art," of course, is the sculpture we call "modern." It is modern because it breaks with tradition and draws little on that which preceded it.

When I speak of "modern" sculpture, I do not refer to every
60 sculptor nor even to every highly talented sculptor of our age. I do not exclude, necessarily, the sculptors of an earlier time. Modern sculpture, as far as I am concerned, is any that consciously casts tradition aside and seeks forms more suitable to the senses and values of its time. Renoir and Daumier are, in this light, modern
65 sculptors notwithstanding the earlier time at which they worked. Daleur and Carpeaux are not modern, although they belong chronologically to the recent era.

Professor Quentin Bell argues that historians and critics name as "modern" those sculptors in whom they happen to be
70 interested and that the term when abused in that way has no historical or artistic significance. That, I think, is not right. The problem is that Professor Bell thinks "modern" means "now," when in fact it means "new."

22. As discussed in the passage, Quentin Bell believes that historians and critics:

F. blah, blah, blah…
G. blah, blah, blah…
H. blah, blah, blah…
J. blah, blah, blah…

24. According to the passage, academicism and mannerism:

F. blah, blah, blah…
G. blah, blah, blah…
H. blah, blah, blah…
J. blah, blah, blah…

26. According to the passage, Renoir differs from Daleur in that:

F. blah, blah, blah…
G. blah, blah, blah…
H. blah, blah, blah…
J. blah, blah, blah…

27. According to the passage, Cezanne's work is characterized by:

A. a return to subjectivism.
B. a pointless search for form.
C. excessively personal expressions.
D. rejection of the impressionistic philosophy.

29. In the author's view, the phrase "modern sculpture" means sculpture that:

A. blah, blah, blah…
B. blah, blah, blah…
C. blah, blah, blah…
D. blah, blah, blah…

30. According to the author, subjectivism affected Rodin in which of the following ways?

F. blah, blah, blah…
G. blah, blah, blah…
H. blah, blah, blah…
J. blah, blah, blah…

In the first question, you see the name Quentin Bell (whoever he is). In the second, you notice the words "academicism" and "mannerism" (whatever they mean). In question 26, the lead words are "Renoir" and "Daleur." In question 27, "Cezanne" is a great lead word. In question 29, the lead phrase is "modern sculpture." For question 30, you should notice the words "subjectivism" and "Rodin."

Take a Look, It's In a Book

So your underlined passage should look something like this.

Rodin was surely a great artist, but he was not an innovator as was Cezanne; prevailing tides of subjectivism came over him. Rodin's mission was to reinvest sculpture with the integrity it lost when Michelangelo died. Rodin succeeded in this mission. His
50 first true work, *The Age of Bronze* (1877), marked the beginning of the end of academicism, mannerism, and decadence that had prevailed since Michelangelo's last sculpture, the *Rondanini Pieta*.

Yet it is largely Cezanne, not Rodin, who was artistic ancestor to Picasso, Gonzalez, Brancusi, Archipenko, Lipchitz, and
55 Laurens, and they are unquestionably the first lights in the "new art" of sculpture. This "new art," of course, is the sculpture we call "modern." It is modern because it breaks with tradition and draws little on that which preceded it.

When I speak of "modern" sculpture, I do not refer to every
60 sculptor nor even to every highly talented sculptor of our age. I do not exclude, necessarily, the sculptors of an earlier time. Modern sculpture, as far as I am concerned, is any that consciously casts tradition aside and seeks forms more suitable to the senses and values of its time. Renoir and Daumier are, in this light, modern
65 sculptors notwithstanding the earlier time at which they worked. Daleur and Carpeaux are not modern, although they belong chronologically to the recent era.

Professor Quentin Bell argues that historians and critics name as "modern" those sculptors in whom they happen to be
70 interested and that the term when abused in that way has no historical or artistic significance. That, I think, is not right. The problem is that Professor Bell thinks "modern" means "now," when in fact it means "new."

Let's Do It Again

Here's another short passage followed by four questions. Follow steps 1 and 2 just as you did before.

Such relatively reliable insights as we have into the nature of Halley's comet's nucleus derive largely from the work done by the Giotto imaging team. Named for the spacecraft from which six key photographs of the comet were taken at distances

5   ranging from 14,430 to 2,730 kilometers, the team forged a single composite photograph under the directorship of H. Use Keler. As the photograph is normally held, north is up and the sun is at the left.

Discernibility of detail varies at different points in the

10   photograph. The greatest resolution, 100 meters, is found in the upper left portion of the image and the poorest resolution, 400 meters, is found at the lower right. This circumstance and other of the photograph's features largely reflect the "instructions" that were given to the Giotto camera, which had been systematically

15   programmed to track the brightest feature in its visual field. This, for example, explains why the greatest detail in the composite photograph is of the nucleus's uppermost aspect; it was photo-graphed when the comet was closest to Giotto.

The Giotto photographs have allowed investigators to con-

20   clude that the surface of the nucleus is rough. This conclusion emanates from the observation that the border area between light and dark portions of the comet is irregular. In addition, the light side reveals a large crater and a hill. The most noticeable of the comet's features relate to the movement of dust away from

25   selected portions of the comet's nucleus toward the sun. The re-sulting dust jets are brightly colored and likely arise from points and places that lack surface crust, which then would expose the deeper lying ices to the sun.

35. According to the passage, the nuclear surface of Halley's comet is believed to be:

    A. blah, blah, blah…
    B. blah, blah, blah…
    C. blah, blah, blah…
    D. blah, blah, blah…

36. As described in the passage, Giotto's camera was specifically programmed to:

    F. blah, blah, blah…
    G. blah, blah, blah…
    H. blah, blah, blah…
    J. blah, blah, blah…

37. As used in the passage, the word *resolution* (line 11) means:

    A. blah, blah, blah…
    B. blah, blah, blah…
    C. blah, blah, blah…
    D. blah, blah, blah…

38. The passage indicates that H. Use Keler:

    F. blah, blah, blah…
    G. blah, blah, blah…
    H. blah, blah, blah…
    J. blah, blah, blah…

For question 35, the lead phrases are "Halley's comet" and "nuclear surface." For question 36, it's "Giotto's camera." For question 37, it's "resolution." For question 38, it's "H. Use Keler."

Take a Look, It's In a Book

So your underlined passage should look something like this.

    Such relatively reliable insights as we have into the nature of <u>Halley's comet's nucleus</u> derive largely from the work done by the <u>Giotto</u> imaging team. Named for the spacecraft from which six key photographs of the comet were taken at distances
5 ranging from 14,430 to 2,730 kilometers, the team forged a single composite photograph under the directorship of <u>H. Use Keler</u>. As the photograph is normally held, north is up and the sun is at the left.

    Discernibility of detail varies at different points in the
10 photograph. The greatest <u>resolution</u>, 100 meters, is found in the upper left portion of the image and the poorest <u>resolution</u>, 400 meters, is found at the lower right. This circumstance and other of the photograph's features largely reflect the "instructions" that were given to the <u>Giotto camera</u>, which had been systematically
15 programmed to track the brightest feature in its visual field. This, for example, explains why the greatest detail in the composite photograph is of the nucleus's uppermost aspect; it was photographed when the comet was closest to <u>Giotto</u>.

    The <u>Giotto photographs</u> have allowed investigators to con-
20 clude that the <u>surface of the nucleus</u> is rough. This conclusion emanates from the observation that the border area between light and dark portions of the comet is irregular. In addition, the light side reveals a large crater and a hill. The most noticeable of the comet's features relate to the movement of dust away from
25 selected portions of the comet's nucleus toward the sun. The resulting dust jets are brightly colored and likely arise from points and places that lack surface crust, which then would expose the deeper lying ices to the sun.

How Steps 1 and 2 Help You

If you were actually to read a passage from beginning to end, you'd never know, as you read, which words or lines you're supposed to understand. Furthermore, when you then went to look at questions about Renoir, H. Use Keler, or the Giotto camera, you'd have to start hunting through the passage to find those words and to figure out what they're all about. By following steps 1 and 2, you help yourself in two important ways.

1. You avoid wasting time trying to read and comprehend the whole passage.
2. You identify those places in the passage likely to provide answers to the questions you're going to be asked. It's *those* portions of the passage that you'll read carefully when the time comes to answer questions.

Here's What We Mean

Below is a small piece of the sculpture passage with our underlining in it. There's also a question you've seen before, except this time it has answer choices. Read the question carefully and look at the answer choices. Then take a look back at the sentence and read *it* very carefully. Think about what it means and figure out which answer choice expresses the same thing—in camouflage. That's the right answer.

> Professor <u>Quentin Bell</u> argues that historians and critics name as "<u>modern</u>" those sculptors in whom they happen to be interested and that the term when abused in that way has no historical or artistic significance.

22. As discussed in the passage, Quentin Bell believes that historians and critics:

F. should be open-minded to new and innovative art forms.
G. misuse art and fail to understand its history.
H. are generally uninterested in modern art.
J. attach the phrase "modern art" to those sculptors that intrigue them.

The correct answer to this question is choice (J), and reading the whole passage definitely would *not* help you answer it any more quickly or accurately. The answer is wholly contained in a single sentence. The author says that Professor Quentin Bell (whoever he is) thinks historians and critics give the name "modern" to the sculptors in whom they happen to be interested. Choice (J) expresses that same thought—in camouflage.

You Won't *Always* Find the Answer in a Single Sentence

When you're looking for an answer, you might have to go to the underlined words and "read around" a little. You might have to read the sentences that appear immediately before and after the one that has your mark. Sometimes you'll have to read a whole paragraph.

Here again is the short passage about comets. It's followed by two questions you've already seen, except this time they have answer choices. Follow steps 1 and 2, and then answer the questions.

Such relatively reliable insights as we have into the nature of Halley's comet's nucleus derive largely from the work done by the Giotto imaging team. Named for the spacecraft from which six key photographs of the comet were taken at distances
5 ranging from 14,430 to 2,730 kilometers, the team forged a single composite photograph under the directorship of H. Use Keler. As the photograph is normally held, north is up and the sun is at the left.

Discernibility of detail varies at different points in the
10 photograph. The greatest resolution, 100 meters, is found in the upper left portion of the image and the poorest resolution, 400 meters, is found at the lower right. This circumstance and other of the photograph's features largely reflect the "instructions" that were given to the Giotto camera, which had been systematically
15 programmed to track the brightest feature in its visual field. This, for example, explains why the greatest detail in the composite photograph is of the nucleus's uppermost aspect; it was photographed when the comet was closest to Giotto.

The Giotto photographs have allowed investigators to con-
20 clude that the surface of the nucleus is rough. This conclusion emanates from the observation that the border area between light and dark portions of the comet is irregular. In addition, the light side reveals a large crater and a hill. The most noticeable of the comet's features relate to the movement of dust away from
25 selected portions of the comet's nucleus toward the sun. The resulting dust jets are brightly colored and likely arise from points and places that lack surface crust, which then would expose the deeper lying ices to the sun.

Reminder
Underline key words or phrases that resemble the critical words in the question. If you don't find the answer, read the sentences surrounding the underlined portion of the passage.

31. According to the passage, the nuclear surface of Halley's comet is believed to be:

   A. smooth, because the interface of light and dark shows high resolution.
   B. rough, because a visible border area is irregularly shaped.
   C. smooth at some points and rough at others, depending on the relative degrees of light and dark.
   D. undetectable, because even the most sophisticated instruments have limitations.

32. As described in the passage, the Giotto camera was specifically programmed to:

   F. send "instructions" to Halley's comet regarding detail and resolution.
   G. identify the portions of the comet that had relatively low light intensity.
   H. detect areas of Halley's comet that bordered on light and dark.
   J. photograph those areas of Halley's comet that gave off the most light.

Here's How to Crack It

The first question concerns the "nuclear surface" of "Halley's comet." That precise phrase does not appear in the passage, but the phrase "surface of the nucleus" shows up on line 21. That sentence and the one immediately following it give you the answer to the first question.

> The Giotto photographs have allowed investigators to conclude that the surface of the nucleus is rough. This conclusion emanates from the observation that the border area between light and dark portions of the comet is irregular.

These two sentences are telling you that Halley's comet has light and dark areas and that the border between these areas is irregular. When scientists noticed this they concluded that the surface of the nucleus was rough. You don't have to understand *why* that observation led to that conclusion. You just have to realize that these two sentences are telling you it did. Once you realize that, you know that the correct answer is choice (B).

The second question refers to "the Giotto camera." So when we first scanned the passage, we underlined the word "Giotto" everywhere it appeared. Look at the sentence that specifically mentions the "Giotto camera." What does it say?

> This circumstance and other of the photograph's features largely reflect the "instructions" that were given to the Giotto camera, which had been systematically programmed to track the brightest feature in its visual field.

The Giotto camera was systematically programmed to track the brightest feature in its visual field. Among the answer options, choice (J) is best. "Brightest feature" is camouflage for "areas...that gave off the most light."

Step 3: Skim and Scribble

Step 3 should take you about 60 seconds. In step 3, you skim the passage, and in the margin of each paragraph, you scribble a few words that describe its main idea. When we say "skim," we mean you should read fast—so fast that you're uncomfortable and not at all sure you comprehend the passage in detail. (Remember, you're not trying to understand the passage. You're trying to earn a high score on the ACT.) As you speed through each paragraph, you should

- direct a little more attention to the first two sentences than to the remainder.
- ask yourself, "What, basically, is this paragraph about?"

Then, in two or three words, scribble an answer in the margin. Here are three paragraphs from a humanities passage. Let's skim and scribble.

artist >
period

If we were to start fresh in the study of sculpture or any art, we might observe that the record is largely filled by works of relatively few great contributors. Next to the influences of these great geniuses, time periods themselves are of little significance.
5 The study of art and art history are properly directed to the achievements of outstanding individual artists, not the particular decades or centuries in which any may have worked.

movements

Nonetheless, when we study art in historical perspective we select a convenient frame of reference through which diverse styles
10 and talents are to be compared. Hence we write of "movements" and attempt to understand each artist in terms of the one to which he "belongs." Movements have limited use, but we should not talk of realism, impressionism, cubism, or surrealism as though they genuinely had lives of their own to which the artist was answerable.
15 We regard the movement as the governing force and the artist as its servant. Yet it is well to remember that the movements do not necessarily present themselves in orderly chronological series and the individual artist frequently weaves her way into one and out of another over the course of a single career.

artist switch
styles

20 Great artists are not normally confined by the "movements" that others may name for them. Rather, they transcend the conventional structure working now in one style, then in another, and later in a third. Picasso's work, for example, echoes many of the artistic movements, and other artists, too, moving from
25 one style through another. Indeed, artists are people, and any may decide to alter her style for no more complex a reason than that which makes most people want to "try something new" once in a while.

Skim the Passage
As you read the passage, underline key phrases in the passage or jot down notes next to each paragraph. Don't try to memorize information in the passage, just know the lay of the land.

Paragraph 1

The first paragraph seems to be about the fact that individual artists are more important than the time periods in which they work.

artist > periods

That's enough.

Paragraph 2

The second paragraph has something to do with artistic "movements." What should you scribble?

movements

Paragraph 3

The third paragraph tells us that great artists don't really conform to movements. They vary their styles over time. So for paragraph 3, you scribble

artists switch styles

Enough said, and enough scribbled.

With enough practice, skim and scribble should take you about one minute per passage.

Use Trigger Words

When you're skimming a passage, pay attention to words that signal a change in direction. In line 1 of the second paragraph, for instance, we see the word "nonetheless," which means the author is about to criticize, negate, or "take something away" from thoughts previously expressed. "Nonetheless" is what we call a *trigger word*. Trigger words tell you the author is about to "go somewhere," and you should watch where he's going. Sometimes a trigger word means the author is reaching some sort of conclusion (*therefore, hence*).

Trigger words help you figure out what a paragraph is all about. The "nonetheless" at the beginning of the second paragraph indicates that the author's going to say something that opposes what he said in the first paragraph. He says there's some purpose in thinking of art in terms of "movements," even though he has already said the individual artist is more important than the time periods in which they work.

> **Look for Trigger Words**
> Here are 15 trigger words and/or phrases:
> - *Despite* • *However* • *In spite of*
> - *Nonetheless* • *On the other hand*
> - *But* • *Rather* • *Yet* • *Ironically*
> - *Notwithstanding* • *But* • *Rather*
> - *Unfortunately* • *On the contrary*
> - *Therefore* • *Hence* • *Consequently*

Try Another Skim and Scribble

Look for Trigger Words

What are trigger words? Trigger words are words that signal a change in a sentence. Some of the most common trigger words are *but, although, despite*, and *however*.

Here are four paragraphs from the comet passage. Skim and scribble. See if you can do it in one minute.

On the other hand, the Giotto photographs reveal virtually nothing of the interior of the comet's nucleus or its rotational period. For instance, it is not known, even, whether the interior of the nucleus had a density greater than or less than 1 gram per
5 cubic centimeter, which is the density of water. Hans Rickman attempted to estimate the comet's density, hoping, with good reason, that this information would ultimately lead to better understanding of the nuclear interior. Rickman recognized that if he could gain estimates of the comet's mass and volume he
10 would be able to derive an estimate of density from the simple physical formulas relating mass, volume, and density: He would divide the volume into the mass and arrive at an estimate.

The comet's overall dimensions were already known to an approximation, and on this basis Rickman took the volume as
15 500–550 cubic kilometers. He then employed a rather ingenious method of estimating the nuclear mass. Rickman considered the fact that the comet was losing gas at all times and that the expulsion produced a thrust. He then reasoned, according to simple law, that mass times the thrust due to expelled gas had to equal
20 the product [rate at which mass was lost by expulsion of gas and dust] and the velocity of the expelled substance. Rickman then derived estimates of these values from the comet's motion and from the rate at which the comet visibly produced water. Rickman arrived at a value of 0.1 to 0.3 grams per cubic centimeter
25 for the density of Halley's nucleus.

Using an analogous technique, R. Z. Sagdeev and colleagues arrived at a value of 0.2 to 1.5 grams per cubic centimeter. Stanton J. Peale, however, wrote that he had little confidence in the estimates of mass and volume that had been used in connection
30 with the density calculations. He believed that little could be said about the nuclear density except that it was approximately equal to 1 gram per cubic centimeter.

Zdenek Sekanina and Stephen M. Larson studied the rotational period by first processing images of 1920 photographs in
35 an attempt to improve the image of spiral dust features. They assumed that the spiral dust characteristics were caused by emission from distinct parts of the nuclear surface and that these areas were visible when rotation brought them into sunlight and were invisible in the dark of the cometary night. On these premises,
40 the pair estimated that Halley has a rotation period of 2.2 days, and some spacecraft data have seemed to confirm the figure. However, Robert L. Millis and David G. Schleicher estimated a rotational period of 7.4 days by resorting to filters that allowed them to explore fluorescence of CN, C, and C_2 emissions and
45 the continuum emission from dust particles. Other investigators have reported additional approximations of Halley's rotational period but the issue remains, for the time being, clouded.

The first paragraph has something to do with the inside of the comet. Maybe it's about density, too. So we scribble

> *interior, density*

The second paragraph seems to provide details about what someone named Rickman did to calculate the density of the comet's interior.

> *Rickman, details, density*

The third paragraph concerns what other scientists said and did in response to Rickman's work.

> *other people*

The last paragraph has something to do with calculating the comet's rotational period.

> *rotational period*

So that's what we're talking about. It doesn't take long. Steps 1 through 3 together should take maybe one and a half to two minutes.

After Steps 1, 2, and 3

After you've spent about two minutes completing the three steps, go back to the questions.

The entire humanities passage about modern sculpture is on the next page. It's underlined and scribbled, and it includes ten questions. Even though we've already completed steps 1 to 3 for you, you should run through them again yourself so you're familiar with the underlining and scribbling. After you do that, we'll discuss step 4, which is called "practice the loop."

Our Steps So Far

- **Step 1—Notice Critical Words:** Look quickly at the questions. Notice critical words. Ignore questions that don't have critical words.
  Approximate Time: 30 seconds
- **Step 2—Scan and Underline:** Scan the passage and underline critical words.
  Approximate Time: 30 seconds
- **Step 3—Skim and Scribble:** Read the passage at racing speed, giving special attention to the first two or three sentences of each paragraph. For each paragraph, scribble in the margin a few words that describe the main subject.
  Approximate Time: 60 seconds

If we were to start fresh in the study of sculpture or any art, we might observe that the record is largely filled by works of relatively few great contributors. Next to the influences of these great geniuses, time periods themselves are of little significance. The study of art and art history are properly directed to the achievements of outstanding individual artists, not the particular decades or centuries in which any may have worked.

artist > period

Nonetheless, when we study art in historical perspective we select a convenient frame of reference through which diverse styles and talents are to be compared. Hence we write of "movements" and attempt to understand each artist in terms of the one to which he "belongs." Movements have limited use, but we should not talk of realism, impressionism, cubism, or surrealism as though they genuinely had lives of their own to which the artist was answerable. We regard the movement as the governing force and the artist as its servant. Yet it is well to remember that the movements do not necessarily present themselves in orderly chronological series and the individual artist frequently weaves her way into one and out of another over the course of a single career.

movements

Great artists are not normally confined by the "movements" that others may name for them. Rather, they transcend the conventional structure working now in one style, then in another, and later in a third. Picasso's work, for example, echoes many of the artistic movements, and other artists too, moving from one style through another. Indeed, artists are people, and any may decide to alter her style for no more complex a reason than that which makes most people want to "try something new" once in a while.

artists switch styles

In studying modern sculpture one is tempted to begin a history with Auguste Rodin (1840–1917), who was a contemporary of Cezanne. Yet the two artists did not, in artistic terms, belong to the same period. Their strategies and objectives differed. Although Rodin was surely a great artist, he did not do for sculpture what Cezanne did for painting. In fact, although Cezanne was a painter, he had a more lasting effect on sculpture than did Rodin.

Rodin and Cezanne

Cezanne's work constitutes a reaction against impressionism and the confusion he thought it created. He searched persistently for the "motif." Cezanne strived for clarity of form and was able to convert his personal perceptions into concrete, recognizable substance. He is justly considered to have offered the first glimmer of a new art—a new classicism.

Cezanne vs. Impressionism

Rodin was surely a great artist, but he was not an innovator as was Cezanne; prevailing tides of subjectivism came over him. Rodin's mission was to reinvest sculpture with the integrity it lost when Michelangelo died. Rodin succeeded in this mission. His first true work, *The Age of Bronze* (1877), marked the beginning of the end of academicism, mannerism, and decadence that had prevailed since Michelangelo's last sculpture, the *Rondanini Pieta*.

Rodin not innovator; recalled Michelangelo

Cezanne
influenced
"modern"
sculpture

50 Yet it is largely Cezanne, not <u>Rodin</u>, who was artistic ancestor to Picasso, Gonzalez, Brancusi, Archipenko, Lipchitz, and
Laurens, and they are unquestionably the first lights in the "new
art" of sculpture. This "<u>new art</u>," of course, is the sculpture we
call "<u>modern</u>." It is modern because it breaks with tradition and
draws little on that which preceded it.

"modern"
does not
necessarily
mean
"recent"

When I speak of "<u>modern</u>" sculpture, I do not refer to every
55 sculptor nor even to every highly talented sculptor of our age. I do
not exclude, necessarily, the sculptors of an earlier time. <u>Modern
sculpture</u>, as far as I am concerned, is any that consciously casts
tradition aside and seeks forms more suitable to the senses and
values of its time. <u>Renoir</u> and Daumier are, in this light, modern
60 sculptors notwithstanding the earlier time at which they worked.
<u>Daleur</u> and Carpeaux are not modern, although they belong
chronologically to the recent era.

Bell wrong;
"modern" ≠
now
"modern" =
new

Professor <u>Quentin Bell</u> argues that historians and critics
name as "<u>modern</u>" those sculptors in whom they happen to be
65 interested and that the term when abused in that way has no
historical or artistic significance. That, I think, is not right. The
problem is that Professor <u>Bell</u> thinks "<u>modern</u>" means "now,"
when in fact it means "new."

21. Which of the following conclusions is drawn by the passage?

   A. Cezanne had greater influence on modern sculpture
      than did Rodin.
   B. Rodin made no significant contribution to modern
      sculpture.
   C. Daumier should not be considered a modern sculptor.
   D. Carpeaux should be considered a modern sculptor.

22. As discussed in the passage, Quentin Bell believes that
    historians and critics:

   F. have no appreciation for the value of modern art.
   G. abuse art and its history.
   H. should evaluate works of art on the basis of their merit
      without regard to the artist's fame.
   J. attach the phrase "modern art" to those sculptors that
      intrigue them.

23. The author expresses the idea that:

   A. art should never be studied in terms of movements.
   B. true artists are seldom understandable in terms of a
      single movement.
   C. lesser artists do not usually vary their styles.
   D. great artists are always nonconformists.

24. According to the passage, academicism and mannerism:

    F. were readily visible in Rodin's earliest work.
    G. are partially manifest in the *Rondanini Pieta*.
    H. characterized the work of artists who followed Michelangelo.
    J. were primarily part of the Bronze Age.

25. It can be most reasonably inferred that the author believes that:

    A. Rodin was more innovative than Cezanne.
    B. Cezanne was more innovative than Rodin.
    C. Modern art is more important than classical art.
    D. Cezanne tried to emulate impressionism.

26. According to the passage, Renoir differs from Daleur in that:

    F. Daleur had no inspiration and Renoir was tremendously inspired.
    G. Renoir's work was highly innovative and Daleur's was not.
    H. Daleur was a sculptor and Renoir was not.
    J. Renoir revered tradition and Daleur did not.

27. According to the passage, Cezanne's work is characterized by:

    A. a return to subjectivism.
    B. a pointless search for form.
    C. excessively personal expressions.
    D. rejection of the impressionistic philosophy.

28. According to the sixth paragraph, the author implies that:

    F. mannerism reflects a lack of integrity.
    G. Rodin disliked the work of Michelangelo.
    H. Rodin embraced the notion of decadence.
    J. Rodin should have resisted the appeal of subjectivism.

29. In the author's view, the phrase "modern sculpture" means sculpture that:

    A. postdates the *Rondanini Pieta*.
    B. is not significantly tied to work that comes before it.
    C. shows no artistic merit.
    D. genuinely interests contemporary critics.

30. According to the author, subjectivism affected Rodin in which of the following ways?

    F. It ended his affiliation with mannerism.
    G. It caused him to lose his artistic integrity.
    H. It limited his ability to innovate.
    J. It caused him to become decadent.

Questions That Point

With the passage underlined and scribbled, go back to the questions, but don't go necessarily to question 21. Go first to the questions that point you to an answer. Look at questions 21–30 on the last passage. Questions 22, 24, 26, 27, 28, 29, and 30 point to the answer. Questions 22, 24, 26, 27, 29, and 30 have lead words. For those questions, we've already underlined the relevant sections of the passage and we know where to look.

- Question 28 sends us directly to the relevant paragraph.
- Questions 21, 23, and 25 don't point anywhere. We'll save them for last.

Now we're ready to answer questions.

Step 4: Practice the Loop

Step 4 should take you about 40 seconds per question if you're trying to finish all 4 passages.

- Go to the first question that points to an answer. Read it carefully. If it's relatively clear, make sure you remember the question before you go back to the passage. If the question is confusing, reword it so that you know what you're looking for.
- Return to the appropriate portion of the passage (either you've underlined it or the question sends you there).
- Read it carefully. Whenever possible, try to formulate your own answer to the question and jot it down.
- Go back to the question and pick the answer choice that most resembles your answer.

Now suppose something strikes you as correct. Be suspicious. Ask yourself if you're falling for a deceptive answer, a switch, or something too "nice." If you consider those possibilities and still think the answer is right, choose it and go to the next question.

Now suppose you're uncertain about the answer and when you come back to the question, nothing strikes you as right. Fine. Try to eliminate answers that are wrong. Look for a deceptive answer, a switch, an extreme statement, and eliminate it. (In the process, the right answer might strike you, in which case you'll choose it and move on.)

Practice the Loop
Once you've practiced using these techniques, you can put them together and form "the loop." Read the question, go to the passage, underline the appropriate words or phrases that relate to the question, and then go to the answer choices. As you read each answer choice, watch out for the distractors. If you're stuck, then take another pass through the loop.

If you don't settle on an answer, take a second pass through the loop.

- Come back to the question. Sometimes you've missed a clue in the question.
- Go back to the appropriate portion of the passage.
- Read it again. Understand it as best you can.
- Look at the choices that still remain (some were eliminated a few seconds earlier, during your first pass through the loop).

If one of the choices now strikes you as correct, choose it. If nothing strikes you as correct, see if you can eliminate it, and then guess among whatever answer choices remain.

We'll start with question 22 because question 21 doesn't point.

---

22. As discussed in the passage, Quentin Bell believes that historians and critics:

F. have no appreciation for the value of modern art.
G. abuse art and its history.
H. should evaluate works of art on the basis of their merit without regard to the artist's fame.
J. attach the phrase "modern art" to those sculptors that intrigue them.

Here's How to Crack It
We go to the relevant part of the passage, which we've already underlined.

> Professor <u>Quentin Bell</u> argues that historians and critics name as "<u>modern</u>" those sculptors in whom they happen to be interested and that the term when abused in that way has no historical or artistic significance.

- Read it carefully and try to understand it. Formulate an answer in your own words and write it down.
- Go back to the question and pick the answer choice that best matches what you came up with on your own.

In this case, one might easily answer this question by saying that Professor Bell argued that historians and critics use the word "modern" to describe anything in which they happen to be interested. Hey, that sounds a lot like choice (J), and thus, choice (J) is the correct response.

Suppose, however, that you couldn't come up with an answer of your own. Don't panic. Just start eliminating answer choices that are wrong. Choice (F) is an extreme statement ("no" appreciation). Eliminate it.

Choice (H) is very "nice" and very irrelevant. Eliminate it.

You're left with choices (G) and (J), but you're not sure which is right.

So take a second pass through the loop.

- Go back to the relevant part of the passage and read it again.
- Return to the question and try to choose again between choices (G) and (J).

Still not sure? Try to eliminate one of the choices. Choice (G) is a deceptive answer. (The author uses the word *abuse* but doesn't say that anyone abuses art or its history.) Eliminate choice (G). That leaves choice (J), so that's the answer you choose.

Altogether, you've spent 30 to 50 seconds answering question 22.

Use the loop to answer question 24.

24. According to the passage, academicism and mannerism:

    F. were readily visible in Rodin's first true work.
    G. are partially manifest in the *Rondanini Pieta*.
    H. characterized the work of artists who followed Michelangelo.
    J. were primarily part of the Bronze Age.

Here's How to Crack It

Go to the pertinent part of the passage.

> Rodin was surely a great artist, but he was not an innovator as was Cezanne; prevailing tides of subjectivism came over him. Rodin's mission was to reinvest sculpture with the integrity it lost when Michelangelo died. Rodin succeeded in this mission. His first true work, *The Age of Bronze* (1877), marked the beginning of the end of academicism, mannerism, and decadence that had prevailed since Michelangelo's last sculpture, the *Rondanini Pieta*.

- Read it carefully and try to answer it yourself. Jot down your answer.
- Go back to the question and find the answer choice that best matches what you jotted down.

Maybe you're not sure of the answer, but you realize that choices (F) and (J) are deceptive answers and eliminate them. You're left with choices (G) and (H).

Now you take a second pass through the loop.

- Read the question again. Any new insight?
- Go back to the relevant part of the passage and read it again.
- Return to the question.

The last sentence tells us that academicism, mannerism, and decadence were around *since Michelangelo produced his last sculpture*. Choice (H) says the same thing—in camouflage. Select choice (H) and move on.

26. According to the passage, Renoir differs from Daleur in that:

   F. Daleur had no inspiration and Renoir was tremendously inspired.

   G. Renoir's work was highly innovative and Daleur's was not.

   H. Daleur was a sculptor and Renoir was not.

   J. Renoir revered tradition and Daleur did not.

Here's How to Crack It
Read the important part of the passage carefully.

> When I speak of "modern" sculpture, I do not refer to every sculptor nor even to every highly talented sculptor of our age. I do not exclude, necessarily, the sculptors of an earlier time. Modern sculpture, as far as I am concerned, is any that consciously casts tradition aside and seeks forms more suitable to the senses and values of its time. Renoir and Daumier are, in this light, modern sculptors notwithstanding the earlier time at which they worked. Daleur and Carpeaux are not modern although they belong chronologically to the recent era.

- First, try to answer the question yourself. This one's fairly easy to answer on your own. The author clearly states that he views Renoir as modern and Daleur as not modern. Thus, choice (G) is the correct response.
- If you couldn't come up with your own answer, start eliminating bad answer choices.
- Choice (F) is a statement in the extreme. Eliminate it.
- Choice (H) is a switch. (The passage tells you that "Renoir and Daumier are modern sculptors." That means Renoir was a sculptor.) Eliminate it.
- Take a second pass. The author writes that modern sculpture is any that "casts tradition aside...." Then he writes that Renoir is a modern sculptor and Daleur is not. That means Renoir casts tradition aside and Daleur does not. Choice (G) says the same thing in camouflage, so choice (G) is right. [Choice (J) is a deceptive answer.]

Now use the loop to answer questions 27 to 30. When you're done, you can read on and compare your reasoning with ours.

———————————○———————————

27. According to the passage, Cezanne's work is characterized by:
   A. a return to subjectivism.
   B. a pointless search for form.
   C. excessively personal expressions.
   D. rejection of the impressionistic philosophy.

Here's How to Crack It

Go to the pertinent part of the passage.

> Cezanne's work constitutes a reaction against impressionism and the confusion he thought it created. He searched persistently for the "motif." Cezanne strived for clarity of form and was able to convert his personal perceptions into concrete, recognizable substance. He is justly considered to have offered the first glimmer of a new art—a new classicism.

- What does the passage tell us? Well, it says that Cezanne rejected impressionism and created a new style called "new classicism." That sounds a lot like choice (D).
- Not sure? Let's look at the other answer choices and see what we can eliminate.
- Choice (B) is extreme (and ridiculous). Eliminate it. With our eye on choices (A), (C), and (D), we take a second pass. The first sentence tells us that Cezanne reacted against impressionism. Choice (D) says the same thing—in camouflage.

Question 28: choice (J) is right.

- Choices (F), (G), and (H) are deceptive answers.

Question 29: choice (B) is right.

- Choices (A) and (D) are deceptive answers. (C) is a statement in the extreme.

Question 30: choice (H) is right.

- Choices (F), (G), and (J) are deceptive answers.

———————————○———————————

What If You *Can't* Settle on an Answer?

Simple. You guess. If you've taken two (or maybe three) passes through the loop and you still can't decide on an answer, look at the choices still remaining, take a guess, and move on. Remember: Having eliminated one or two choices, you've raised the odds that your guess will be right.

Three More Examples

We held questions 21, 23, and 25 for last because they don't point. Now it's time to answer them. For questions that don't point, you

- use the answer choices to tell you what the question is about.
- use your scribbles to get you to the right part of the passage.

Here are the answer choices for question 21.

> **A.** Cezanne had greater influence on modern sculpture than did Rodin.
> **B.** Rodin made no significant contribution to modern sculpture.
> **C.** Daumier should not be considered a modern sculptor.
> **D.** Carpeaux should be considered a modern sculptor.

Here's How to Crack It

Apparently, this question has a lot to do with the phrase "modern sculpture."

For Paragraph 8, we scribbled

"modern" does not necessarily mean "recent"

So you go to Paragraph 8. From there on, you follow the loop.

The correct answer is choice (A).

- Choice (B) is extreme.
- Choices (C) and (D) are both switches.

Let's look at question 23. Here are the answer choices.

> **A.** art should never be studied in terms of movements.
> **B.** true artists are seldom understandable in terms of a single movement.
> **C.** lesser artists do not usually vary their styles.
> **D.** great artists are always nonconformists.

Here's How to Crack It

Apparently, the question has something to do with movements and style. It calls our attention to Paragraphs 2 and 3 where we scribbled

> (2) *movements*
>
> (3) *artists switch styles*

It turns out that the answer is in Paragraph 3. It's choice (B).

- Choices (A) and (D) are extreme.
- Choice (C) is a distortion.

Lastly, look at question 25. Here are the answer choices.

> **A.** Rodin was more innovative than Cezanne.
> **B.** Cezanne was more innovative than Rodin.
> **C.** Modern art is more important than classical art.
> **D.** Cezanne tried to emulate impressionism.

Here's How to Crack It

This question appears to be focusing on the differences between Rodin and Cezanne.

For Paragraph 6, we scribbled

> *Rodin not innovator*

Read Paragraph 6 again. From there on, follow the loop. The best answer is choice (B).

- Choice (A) is the switch.
- Choices (C) and (D) are deceptive answers.

> **Steps 1–4**
> **Step 1—Find the Critical Words**
> *Approximate Time:* 30 seconds
> **Step 2—Scan the Passage for Critical Words**
> *Approximate Time:* 30 seconds
> **Step 3—Skim and Scribble**
> *Approximate Time:* 60 seconds
> **Step 4—Practice the Loop**
> *Approximate Time:* 40 seconds per question

Special Question Type: State of Mind

When you take the ACT, you'll probably get a few questions that ask you to describe attitudes or states of mind. Often, the answer choices are just one word.

Some Question Types Do Not Require You to Go Through the Loop
Why? The answer is not found in the passage. These question types are: Fact vs. Opinion, State of Mind, Vocab-in-Context, Except/Not/Least, and Roman Numeral

1. The author's attitude toward…blah, blah, blah…is best described as:

   A. skeptical.
   B. approving.
   C. concerned.
   D. hopeful.

In a literature passage, these questions pertain not to the author, but to some character. Read this final paragraph of a prose fiction passage and look at the question that follows it.

So they parted with a shake of the hand, Jonathan Tinker saying that he believed he should go down to the vessel and sleep aboard, if he could sleep, and murmuring at the last moment the hope of returning the compliment, while the contributor walked homeward, weary to the flesh, but, in spite of his sympathy for Jonathan Tinker, very elated in spirit. The truth is, and however disgraceful to human nature, let the truth be told, he had recurred to his primal satisfaction in the man as calamity capable of being used for such and such literary ends, and, while he pitied him, rejoiced in him as an episode of real life quite as striking and complete as anything in fiction.

1. As final response to his conversation with Jonathan Tinker, the contributor experienced a feeling of

   A. worry.
   B. amusement.
   C. gratification.
   D. disappointment.

Here's How to Crack It

If this kind of item throws you, it's probably because you start thinking about the distractors and lose sight of the question.

- Think about the person and the situation about which you're being asked.
- Turn the item into four true/false questions by saying to yourself:
TRUE/FALSE "This guy was _____."
Then fill in the blank with each of the answer choices.
- When you hit a statement that's true, you've got the ACT answer.

Let's try it.

- We think about the contributor as he is described in the last paragraph, and we say to ourselves (very quickly):
TRUE/FALSE "This guy was worried."
TRUE/FALSE "This guy was amused."
TRUE/FALSE "This guy was gratified."
TRUE/FALSE "This guy was disappointed."

Choices (A), (B), and (D) yield statements that sound false. There's nothing in the paragraph to suggest that this guy was worried or disappointed, and he's not particularly amused, either. (He didn't, for example, "chuckle," or "grin.") The paragraph tells us that the contributor experiences "satisfaction" and that he "rejoices." Choice (C) yields a statement that seems true.

———————————○———————————

Many decisions of the United States Supreme Court are inconsistent with the precedents by which they are theoretically balanced. It is true that the court has some freedom to overrule its own precedents, but in such cases it is expected to announce, forthrightly, that it has determined a particular precedent to be erroneous, and that such precedent is renounced.

Contrary to what should be so, however, there are a great many occasions on which the Supreme Court does in fact disavow its own precedents without acknowledging that it has done so. Instead, the Court contrives some implausible distinction between the precedent and the case before it and purports, dishonestly, to abide by a precedent it has in fact determined to repudiate.

11. In this passage, the author's attitude toward the United States Supreme Court is best described as one of:

    A. criticism.
    B. disbelief.
    C. appreciation.
    D. surprise.

Here's How to Crack It

- We consider what the author has said about the Supreme Court's attitude toward precedent. She objects to the dishonesty through which the court sometimes avoids precedent while pretending to honor it.
- We make four true/false questions.
  TRUE/FALSE "This woman is <u>critical</u>."
  TRUE/FALSE "This woman is in a state of <u>disbelief</u>."
  TRUE/FALSE "This woman is <u>appreciative</u>."
  TRUE/FALSE "This woman is <u>surprised</u>."

The correct answer is choice (A). The author thinks that if the Supreme Court decides not to abide by a precedent, it should do so honestly. Contrary to what should be so, the author explains, the court rejects precedents while pretending to honor them. She's making a criticism.

Special Question Type: Vocab-in-Context

On the ACT, you will encounter a couple of questions that ask you to define words or phrases that are used in the context of specific parts of the passages.

Many artists have spoken of seeing things differently while drawing, and have often mentioned that drawing puts them into a somewhat altered state of awareness. In that different subjective state, artists speak of feeling transported, "at one with their work," able to grasp relations that they ordinarily cannot see.

---

21. In line 79, the word *transported* is used to mean:

    A. moved from one place to another.
    B. engaged in artistic endeavor.
    C. in an altered state of consciousness.
    D. dreaming.

Here's How to Crack It

Go to the relevant section of the passage and read a couple of lines above and a couple of lines below where you see the word *transported*.

- Draw a line through the word *transported*, and based on your understanding of the lines surrounding it, try to replace it with a word or phrase of your own. In this case, the word *different* or the phrase from the passage, "altered state of awareness," would fit well, so the correct answer is choice (C).

- Having trouble coming up with your own word? No problem; just go to the answer choices and eliminate those that don't work.

- Choice (A) says "moved from one place to another," which is the primary definition of *transported* but has nothing to do with the passage. Eliminate it. Choice (B) says "engaged in artistic endeavor." This seems a little suspicious because the whole paragraph is about art. In essence, this is a deceptive answer choice. Eliminate it. Finally, choice (D) says *dreaming*. It's not a terrible answer choice, but does the passage actually tell us that artists go to sleep while working? No? Well, then, eliminate it.

Special Question Type: Except/Not/Least

If questions contain the words *except*, *not*, or *least*, you should leave them until you have answered all other questions. If you have time to return to them, your job is to identify the answers that are <u>not</u> supported by the passages.

In Scotland, bees are carried in carts to the Highlands and set free. In France and Poland, bees are carried from pasture to pasture and along rivers in barges so that they can collect the honey from the vegetation that grows along the rivers' banks. In Egypt they are taken up the Nile and floated slowly home again.

13. The passage mentions transportation of bees by river in all of the following countries EXCEPT:

   A. Scotland.
   B. France.
   C. Egypt.
   D. Poland.

Here's How to Crack It

- Skip this question until you have done all the others with the exception of any roman numeral questions. By the time you return to it, you probably will have read most of the passage.
- Look for a lead word in the question. Here, you're interested in the transportation of bees by river, so go back to the passage and see what the passage says on this subject.
- The passage says that bees are transported by river in France, Poland, and Egypt. Because you are looking for the answer choice that is not true, you can eliminate choices (B), (C), and (D), leaving only the correct answer, which is choice (A).

Special Question Type: Roman Numeral

A few questions on the ACT will provide you with three statements preceded by roman numerals (and not just in the Reading test). On these questions, your job is to determine which of the statements, according to the passages, are true.

---

16. According to the passage, bees:

    I. are attracted to pastures.
    II. are attracted to cultivated fields.
    III. are attracted to vegetation that grows along river banks.

    F. I only
    G. II only
    H. III only
    J. I and III only

Here's How to Crack It

- You should leave roman numeral questions for last.
- Look at both the question and the roman numeral statements for lead words.
- Take each roman numeral and check, one at a time, to see if the passage makes that statement.
- If you use the last passage and check it for mention of "pastures," you will find that bees do, in fact, like pastures. Because roman numeral I appears to be true, you can quickly eliminate choices (G) and (H) because they omit roman numeral I.
- Now all you need to do is make a second pass to check and see if the passage states that bees like vegetation that grows along river banks. According to the passage, bees collect honey from these plants, so both roman numerals I and III are true. Thus, choice (J) is the correct answer.

Summary

- By following a straightforward, four-step system, you can avoid wrong answers and find the right ones more easily.

- The first step is to find the critical words and phrases in the questions.

- The second step is to locate those critical words and phrases in the answer choices.

- Third, skim the passage and scribble a few words that describe the main idea of each paragraph. You aren't reading for comprehension but rather for a general idea.

- Last, practice the loop. Use the techniques to go through the questions as quickly and accurately as possible.

- Be aware of special question types, including Vocabulary-in-Context questions, EXCEPT/NOT/LEAST questions, and roman numeral questions.

- Don't forget to guess your Letter of the Day if there are questions that you can't answer or don't reach in time.

Part V
How to Crack the ACT Science Test

Chapter 19
Introduction to the ACT Science Test

The ACT Science test always comes fourth, after the Reading test and before the optional Writing test. Fatigue can negatively affect even the founding president of the I Heart Science Club. Even if the Science test were first, many students would find it the most intimidating and feel that they need to crack open their freshman bio textbooks. But this is not a test of science facts: It is instead a test of how well you look up and synthesize information from tables, graphs, illustrations, and passages.

To maximize your score on the Science test, you need to work the passages in a personal order of difficulty. We'll teach you how to order the passages, and we'll teach you how to employ a strategic and efficient approach that will earn you your highest possible score.

WHAT'S ON THE SCIENCE TEST

Remember when you had to study for that tough biology exam, memorizing dozens of facts about things like meiosis, mitosis, and mitochondria? When you sat down to take the test, you either knew the answers or you didn't. Well, that's not the case on the ACT Science test. Even though the word *science* appears in the title, this test doesn't look much like the tests you've taken in your high school science classes. Like the English and Reading tests, the Science test is passage based, but most of the passages present the really important content in figures rather than in text.

The Format
You have 35 minutes for 7 passages and 40 questions.

On the Science test, you have 35 minutes to spend on 7 passages and a total of 40 questions. There are 3 types of passages, but unlike in the Reading test, the order of the passages will vary every time. We'll go into more detail about the 3 types of passages later in this chapter.

What Do You Need to Know?

For the topics of the passages, ACT pulls content from biology, chemistry, physics, and the Earth/space sciences, such as astronomy, geology, and meteorology. While you won't be quizzed on specific facts, background familiarity with the topics certainly helps. If the passage is on genetics, you'll undoubtedly do better if you've recently finished that unit in school and know it cold. But the information you need in order to answer the questions is offered in the passage itself, most frequently presented in a table, graph, or illustration of some kind. The ACT Science test is an open-book test, and you do not need advanced knowledge of any science topic.

You may not need an encyclopedic knowledge of science facts. You *do* need good scientific reasoning skills, a personalized pacing strategy, and a smart, effective approach to working the passages. You also need to be flexible, ready to adapt your strategy or abandon a question you've already spent way too much time on: Guess, and move on. Of all the tests on the ACT, Science is the most time-sensitive. Even the biggest science geeks find themselves barely finishing.

Outside Knowledge

Most of the questions can be answered from the information presented in the passages or figures, but be prepared for 3 to 4 questions that require outside knowledge. The outside-knowledge questions are nothing to stress over, however. There is no way to predict what the outside-knowledge questions will be on the next ACT, so there is nothing you can do to prepare; you cannot, and *should not*, try to review everything you've never learned or already forgotten. Besides, the outside-knowledge questions tend to ask about fairly basic facts, commonly addressed in intro-level high school science courses.

For example, you may need to know that a honey badger is a mammal, or you may need to identify a chemical formula as bleach, or you may need to know where acid falls on the pH scale. In any case remember that for the overwhelming number of questions, everything that you need to answer them is right there in front of you. Use the basic approach we'll teach you in Chapter 21, and you'll do just fine.

On act.org, ACT identifies the skills you need for this test: "interpretation, analysis, evaluation, reasoning, and problem solving." We can boil this down to a more concise list.

You need to be able to

- look up data and trends
- make predictions
- synthesize information

But before you learn how to work the passages, you need to learn how to order them. To understand the reasoning behind the method, it's helpful to know the 3 categories of passages.

The Passages

All of the passages fall within 3 categories. The order of the passages will vary on each test, but the distribution of types of passages is always the same. To pick your order, it's less important what the passage is called than what it looks like. But it is important to know that there are 3 categories of passages and to know their similarities and differences. ACT has very formal-sounding names for the categories, so we made up our own.

1. Charts and Graphs (aka Data Representation)

3 Passages, 5 Questions Each

These passages will *always* come with figures: it's their purpose in life. You'll see one or more charts, tables, graphs, or illustrations. Charts and Graphs passages are intended to test your ability to understand and interpret the information that's presented. There are 3 Charts and Graphs passages per test, and each one has 5 questions, for a total of 15 questions.

2. Experiments (aka Research Summaries)

3 Passages, 6 Questions Each

These passages will *usually* come with figures. They're intended to describe several experiments, and they include more text than do the Charts and Graphs passages. But the results of the experiments are frequently presented in tables or in graphs, and you may have trouble distinguishing the Experiments passages from Charts and Graphs passages. That doesn't matter, however, because in Chapter 21 we'll teach you the basic approach that applies to both types of passages. You'll never need to identify one over the other when you're taking the test. For the record, however, Experiments passages come with more questions. There are 3 Experiments passages per test with 6 questions per passage, for a total of 18 questions.

3. Fighting Scientists (aka Conflicting Viewpoints)

1 Passage, 7 Questions

This passage *sometimes* comes with figures. Even when there are figures, however, the passage is fundamentally different from the Charts and Graphs passages and the Experiments passages. That means it also requires a different way to crack it, and we'll teach you how to do just that in Chapter 22. The Fighting Scientists passage involves much more reading than you'll need to do for the other 2 types. In fact, most of the Fighting Scientists passages will feel more like the passages on the Reading test, and you'll be able to use some of the skills you learned to crack the Reading test as you compare, contrast, and synthesize the different viewpoints.

When it comes to the topics, ACT may use arguments already resolved by the scientific community as well as more cutting-edge issues that are still contested. In either case, remind yourself again that the Science test is an open-book test, providing you the information you need to answer almost all the questions.

HOW TO CRACK THE SCIENCE TEST

Order the Passages

As always on the ACT, time is your enemy. With only 35 minutes to review 7 passages and answer 40 questions, you can't afford to spend too much time on the most difficult only to run out of time for the easiest. ACT doesn't present the passages in order of difficulty, but on every exam, some are easier than others while some are truly tough. What would happen if on your ACT, the most difficult came first and the easiest last? If you did them in order, you could likely run out of time without a chance to answer correctly all the questions on the easiest passage.

That's why you can't do the passages in the order ACT picks—unless that happens to match your Personal Order of Difficulty (POOD). If time is going to run out, you want it to run out on the hardest passage, not the easiest.

Now, Later, Never

We're using the term "easier" only because we're grading the passages on a curve. "Easy" is a loaded term.

Therefore it's more useful to think of the passages as those you'd do *Now*, those you'd do *Later*, and those you'd *Never* do.

Now Passages

Your goal with all the passages is to crack the main point. You don't necessarily need to know the topic but you do need to spot the conclusions the content offers: trends, patterns, and relationships. You will spot the main point faster when those conclusions are presented in figures rather than in text. The easier the figures are to "read," the faster you crack the main point.

As we explained above, this is not a test of science knowledge. Instead, it's a test of your scientific reasoning skills. That means spotting the trends and patterns of variables and the relationships between figures and viewpoints.

The best passages to do Now have the most obvious patterns as well as a few other common characteristics.

Look for

1. **Small graphs and tables:** A good Now passage can have only tables, only graphs, or both. Tables should be no more than 3–4 rows and columns, and graphs should have no more than 3–4 lines or curves.
2. **Easy-to-spot consistent trends:** Look for graphs with all lines/curves heading in the same direction: all up, all down, or all flat.
3. **Numbers in the figures:** To show a consistent trend, the figure has to feature numbers, not words or symbols.
4. **Short answers:** Look for as many questions as possible with short answers, specifically answers with numbers and short relationship words like *increase* or *decrease*.

In Chapter 20 we'll show in greater detail how trends and patterns deliver the main point.

Personal Order of Difficulty (POOD)

There is one additional important characteristic you need to look for: topics you know. Even if the figures are really ugly and confusing, if a passage is on a topic you just finished in school and know cold, you'll get the main point of the passage quickly, and that's the goal of choosing a Now passage.

Pace Yourself

Unless you're shooting for a 27 or higher on the Science test, you're better off choosing at least one passage as Never.

Take 35 minutes, and do fewer passages. You'll give yourself more time and increase your accuracy. As you steadily increase your scoring goals in practice, target the number of questions you need to reach your goal. The more aggressively you can move through the passages finding all the Now *questions* you can answer—no matter how difficult the passage may be—the better you'll score.

Be Flexible

As we've mentioned before, to earn your best score on the ACT, you have to be flexible, and nowhere is this more true than on the Science test. The Science test shows the greatest change in level of difficulty from one administration to the next. There is no way to predict how difficult the Science test will be, nor what the particular topics will be. Certainly, if you know more about the topic, you'll find even an ugly-looking passage more understandable. But that doesn't mean you're

Patterns
Look for trends *within* a figure. Look for relationships *between* figures and viewpoints.

Letter of the Day (LOTD)
Just because you don't work on a passage doesn't mean you don't bubble in answers. Never leave any bubbles blank on the ACT. Bubble in your Letter of the Day for all the questions on your Never passages.

relying on luck. The Princeton Review's basic approach works regardless of what the topics are. The goal is to practice using the basic approach so that the particulars of the passage are irrelevant.

However, you have to fight your own instincts, or at least retrain them into those of a great test-taker. Always be prepared to adapt your order based on what you see, both in practice and on a real test. If you choose a passage that looked good and then find yourself struggling, leave it and find another. Ignore the voice in your head that says, "Well, I've put so much time into this incredibly hard passage already, all that time would be a waste if I didn't finish the passage." Nothing could be further from the truth. You're throwing away perfectly good time if you stick with a passage that you're just not grasping.

You have to be just as strict with a tough question. When you're stumped, your first instinct may be to go back and read the passage or stare at the figure *again*, waiting for a flash of inspirational genius to suddenly make everything clear. Instead, focus on using POE to get rid of answers that can't be right. Even if you can cross off only one answer, guess from what's left and move on. If you stick with one tough question too long, you may be robbing yourself of 2–3 questions.

Process of Elimination (POE)

Just as in the other tests, POE is a powerful tool on the Science test. Particularly on tougher questions, use POE to eliminate wrong answers that are clearly contradicted by what you're looking at.

Let's see how POE works on the Science test.

1. An epidemiologist claims that a patient infected with chicken pox faces the greatest risk of mortality for any of the diseases studied. Do the results of Experiment 1 support her claim?

   A. Yes; the percentage of fatal chicken pox infections is greater than the percentage of fatal rabies infections.
   B. Yes; the percentage of fatal chicken pox infections is less than the percentage of fatal rabies infections.
   C. No; the percentage of fatal chicken pox infections is greater than the percentage of fatal rabies infections.
   D. No; the percentage of fatal chicken pox infections is less than the percentage of fatal rabies infections.

Hard Test = Generous Curve
Don't be scared of a hard Science test on any particular administration. Each test is curved against only the students who took that particular exam. If the Science test is hard, *everyone* will struggle with the hardest questions, and the curve will be more generous.

1 Point Earned, 3 Points Lost
Easy questions earn the same number of points as difficult questions. Don't waste time struggling with a hard question when you can move on and answer easy questions. You can always come back to the question if you have time.

POE
Each time you eliminate a wrong answer, you increase your chance of choosing the correct answer.

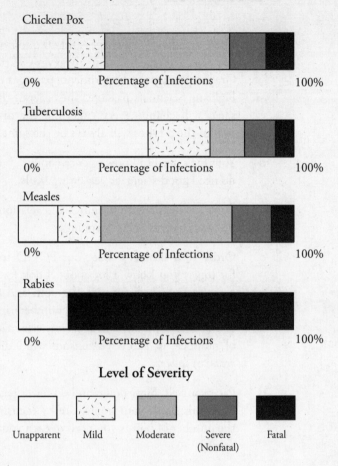

Infection Severity Incidence for Four Diseases

Chicken Pox

0%   Percentage of Infections   100%

Tuberculosis

0%   Percentage of Infections   100%

Measles

0%   Percentage of Infections   100%

Rabies

0%   Percentage of Infections   100%

Level of Severity

Unapparent   Mild   Moderate   Severe   Fatal
                                 (Nonfatal)

Here's How to Crack It

Don't waste time staring at the figure trying to look up the answer. Look at how descriptive the answer choices are: POE will be much faster. Ignore the "Yes" and "No," and focus on the reasons given. Do they accurately describe the figure? Choices (A) and (C) are disproven by the figure, so cross them off. The reason given in choices (B) and (D) is the opposite of the reason given in the other two, so both are proven by the figure. If you had no clue what *mortality* meant, you'd have a fifty-fifty chance of getting this right. If you do, you have to consider the claim and reason that chicken pox is less fatal than rabies and therefore poses less of a risk of mortality, i.e., death. The correct answer is choice (D).

Maybe you read the question, and a quick glance at the figure was all you needed to know the answer was "No." Great, cross off choices (A) and (B), and then compare what's different between choices (B) and (D). The point is to save time by looking at the answers and then the figure rather than staring at the figure and then the answers. The harder the figure, the more important POE is to your success.

Summary

- There are always 7 passages and 40 questions on the Science test. There are always 3 Charts and Graphs passages, 3 Experiments passages, and 1 Fighting Scientists passage. The order of the passages will change every time, but the distribution of the 3 types will always be the same.

- You don't need to know science content, but you do need good scientific reasoning skills.

- Look for trends within figures and relationships between figures and viewpoints.

- Order your passages. Use your POOD to look for topics you know a lot about. Look for Now passages, which feature small graphs and tables, easy-to-spot consistent trends, numbers instead of words or symbols, and short answers made up of numbers or short relationship words like *increase* or *lower*.

- Pace yourself. Slow down and do fewer passages, but work up to your goal score by focusing on the number of points you need to earn your goal score.

- Be flexible. Be ready to adapt your order, leave a tough passage, or guess on a tough question.

- Use Process of Elimination to cross off wrong answers and save time.

Chapter 20
Scientific Reasoning Skills

You don't need to know science facts for the ACT. For the most part the Science test is an open-book test, with the 7 passages offering the content you need to answer nearly all the questions. According to ACT you do need scientific reasoning skills. But all this really means is that you need some common sense. Science may seem intimidating, but it's based on a lot more common sense than you may think.

YOU KNOW MORE THAN YOU THINK

It's easy to feel very intimidated by the content and even the figures on the Science test. But all of science is built on common sense. The key to building good scientific reasoning skills is to realize you *already have* those skills. You use common sense every day to figure things out, to solve problems, to make conclusions. A scientist does the same. When you solve a problem, you think critically, and that's the basis of scientific reasoning.

How to Solve a Problem

Let's try an experiment. Say you put on a wool sweater and go out to dinner one night. At the restaurant you order some delectable shrimp for dinner, and then a beautiful bowl of strawberries for dessert.

The next morning, you wake up covered in red, itchy hives. What caused them? Do you jump to the conclusion it was the sweater? What about the shrimp? A lot of people have allergies to shellfish. But so, too, do a lot of people have allergies to strawberries. How are you supposed to know which one caused your hives? How do you know any of these options are the only possible culprits?

> ### Assumption = Guess
>
> An assumption is nothing more than a guess, and a lazy one at that, if you are willing to believe the riddle has been solved. A guess doesn't cut it in the scientific world: only proof does.

You don't. That's the first rule of scientific reasoning: Make no assumptions. You can't assume it was the sweater, the shrimp, or the strawberries. But you have to prove it was one and only one of these, if any. So how do you set about finding out which one?

You design an experiment. You first need to narrow the list of suspects down to the sweater, shrimp, and strawberries. Begin with a baseline. You need to see what happens on a day with none of the possible causes in play to compare to the days with them. Wear a cotton T-shirt and eat cauliflower and cantaloupe. Do you still have hives? Then the three suspects have all been vindicated. But if your hives have cleared up, you've confirmed your first hypothesis that it was indeed the sweater, the shrimp, or the strawberries.

> ### Hypothesis
>
> A hypothesis is a theory. An assumption is a guess with no proof. A hypothesis is more advanced than that. It's a theory that tries to explain what happened, but it requires proof.

Now you have to figure out which one of the three caused your hives. We need a day with one, and one only, of the possibilities, or *variables*, in play. That's the second rule of scientific reasoning: Change one variable at a time. On one day wear the sweater, but skip the shrimp and strawberries. On another lose the sweater and eat the shrimp but not the strawberries. On yet another replace the shrimp with the strawberries. On each day check for hives. The itchy red bumps *depend* on whatever *independent* variable is causing them.

That's all well and good. But what about everything else in your life? Notice we said you couldn't wear the sweater on the days you ate the shrimp and strawberries. But other than the sweater, *you have to wear the exact same clothes on the day you eat shrimp and on the day you eat strawberries.* It's not just what you wear. Everything else in your life has to be exactly the same. If on the day you wore the sweater, you worked out at the gym, but on the day you ate shrimp, you lay on your sofa all day watching TV, how much would you know? Not much. Certainly not much of anything with proof, and proof is what it's all about in science. The third rule of scientific reasoning is that you have to keep all the other variables in the experiment the same as you vary one and only one independent variable. In the hives experiment, this means that in order to conclusively prove the cause, you have to keep everything else the same on each day that you change one and only one independent variable. Do the same things. Wear the same clothes (except the sweater). Eat the same things (except the shrimp and strawberries).

Watch it on your DVD

And that's it. If you follow these three rules, you'll know what causes your hives.

Trends

In our first example, we looked at a dependent variable, hives, that were present only when an independent variable was present. You've undoubtedly faced other situations where different amounts of a variable seem to have an effect on another variable. The more you study, the better your grades. The more pints of ice cream you eat, the more pounds you gain. The more miles you run, the more pounds you lose.

Let's look at another situation. You sleep only 5 hours a night, staying up late and getting up early to study, but you're consistently scoring in the high 70s on your daily

math quizzes no matter how many hours you study. Suppose you had a hypothesis that if you slept more, your scores would improve. How would you design an experiment to test this? You already have a baseline of 5 hours and consistent scores in the high 70s. So beginning with the first night, you sleep longer and then see how you score the next day. The next night, you sleep even longer, and check your quiz score the next day. Can you do anything else differently? No, you have to keep all the other variables in your life the same. Each day you eat the same things and study the same number of hours. You even track quiz scores in the same unit to eliminate any possibility that there is any other reason why your quiz scores improve.

To be organized, you record all your data in a simple table.

Hours of sleep	Quiz scores
5	78
6	83
7	88
8	93

Table 1

As the number of hours of sleep increases, your quiz score increases. In this experiment the number of hours of sleep is the independent variable, and the quiz score is the dependent variable. You've established that your quiz score is ***directly*** proportional to the number of hours you sleep.

Let's look at another experiment. Suppose your hypothesis this time is that the more cups of coffee you drink, the fewer hours you sleep. How would you design the experiment? Same rules as always. First, you need a baseline. You need to get all the caffeine out of your system and cut your consumption down to 0 cups each day. You establish a consistent routine of the same diet, exercise, studying, sports practice, and so on. Then without changing any of those variables, you begin drinking coffee again—same size cup each day—increasing the number of cups and measuring the number of hours you sleep the following night.

Once again, you record your findings in a table.

Cups of coffee	Hours of sleep
0	8
1	7
2	6
3	5

Table 2

As the cups of coffee increase, the hours of sleep decrease. This time, the number of hours of sleep is the dependent variable, and the number of cups of coffee is the independent variable. You've established that the amount you sleep is ***inversely*** proportional to the amount of coffee you drink.

Many passages on the Science test feature passages whose main point is either a direct or inverse trend of the variables. In Chapter 19, we outlined characteristics of Now passages, for example, small tables and graphs with easy-to-spot consistent trends. When you look at the two tables above, the trend is pretty obvious from just a quick glance. You've already cracked the main point, and you will find all the questions that much easier to tackle as a result.

Graphs

Tables and graphs both show the trends of variables. Graphs are more visual, making the trends easier to spot.

If you graphed your data from Table 1, what would it look like?

Remember that in math, the horizontal axis is always x: It's the independent variable. The vertical axis is always y: It's the dependent variable. Science follows the same rules. This graph shows you that as x increases, y increases. They have a direct relationship.

Let's stick with using math to understand the graphs on the Science test better. Think about slope. It's the change in y over the change in x. In this graph, the slope is positive. Direct relationships are positive slopes.

$$\text{Slope} = \frac{rise}{run}$$

$$\frac{y_2 - y_1}{x_2 - x_1}$$

Let's graph Table 2.

This graph shows you that as x increases, y decreases. They have an inverse relationship, and the slope is negative. Inverse relationships are negative slopes.

Positive and Negative Slope

Using your math skills in coordinate geometry is a great way to see how much graphs tell you. We already pointed out that direct relationships have positive slopes, as shown by the graph of Table 1, and inverse relationships have negative slopes, as shown by the graph of Table 2. But the size of the slope tells you even more.

Let's take a look at another real-life example. You're sweltering in the middle of a heat wave, so it's time to fill your above-ground pool.

You pull out your hose to start filling the pool. The water fills at a constant rate of 1 gallon per hour, and it takes several hours to fill it.

As the number of hours increases (independent variable), the volume of the water, in gallons, increases (dependent variable). The following graph shows the direct relationship.

POSITIVE

The slope is positive 1 because the pool fills at a constant rate of 1 gallon per hour.

After a few days of enjoying your pool, the forecasts warn of an impending hurricane. For safety's sake, you have to drain the pool. You unplug the drain, and the water begins to flow out at the same 1 gallon per hour rate. The following graph shows the inverse relationship.

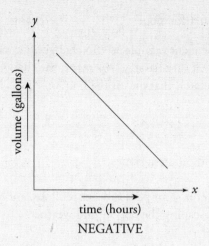

time (hours)

NEGATIVE

The slope is negative 1 because the pool drains at a constant rate of 1 gallon per hour.

It's very useful to spot a positive or negative slope on a graph in a Science passage. As we mentioned before, you've cracked the main point of the passage when you spot the relationship between the variables. But positive and negative linear graphs are not the only ones you'll see, and you'll also see different types of positive graphs and different types of negative graphs.

Let's dive back into the pool.

Flat Lines

At the last minute, the path of the hurricane heads out to sea and avoids landfall. In fact, your pool hasn't even finished draining when the storm changes direction. Now a new heat wave has descended, and you need to refill the pool. You turn your hose on and savor how great that water is going to feel at the end of a long, hot day. Unfortunately for you, you forget to replug the drain. Because you decide to spend the day in an air-conditioned movie theater, you don't even realize the pool isn't filling. Well, it is filling, but it is also draining at the exact same rate. Thus, the volume doesn't change.

time (hours)

The slope of this line is 0 because the volume doesn't change. As time passes, the number of hours keeps increasing, but the change in time has no effect on the volume.

Think about the formula for slope: $\dfrac{y_2 - y_1}{x_2 - x_1}$. The change in y is divided by the change in x. The independent variable (x) can change all it wants—as time marches on—but if the dependent variable stays **_constant,_** the change between y values is 0. When 0 is in the numerator, that means the fraction equals 0.

Shallow Lines

Different rates will yield different slopes.

Once you replug the drain, your pool finishes refilling, and you spend several days floating in your pool, escaping the hot, humid weather.

Water, however, has a nasty habit of evaporating. But the rate of evaporation is far slower than the rate at which the pool empties when the drain is unplugged. Still, if you don't use the hose to refill the pool, the volume of water will decrease over a number of days. Let's take a look at what that graph would look like.

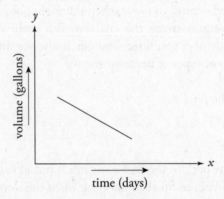

The slope is negative because as time increases, the volume decreases. Time and volume have an inverse relationship. But the effect that time has on volume is relatively small compared to the effects of an open drain.

Bring back the formula for slope: $\dfrac{y_2 - y_1}{x_2 - x_1}$. When the change in y is small compared to the change in x, you have a small numerator and a large denominator. Thus, you have a fraction smaller than 1. The smaller the fraction, the closer to parallel to the x axis the line will be. In fact, it's approaching a flat line, or a slope of 0.

The slope tells you a lot about the relationship between the independent variable (time) and the dependent variable (volume), namely that time has a very small effect on volume. If the effect were much less, the slope would be 0, which is to say that time would have no effect on volume.

Steep Lines

Back to the pool! You refill the pool to its full volume, but you decide it's time to rake around the pool with a deadly sharp rake. You swing a little wildly too close to the nylon pool and slice a huge gash in the side. Water starts gushing out, at a much faster rate than it empties when the drain is unplugged. Take a look at what the graph of your small accident looks like.

The slope is negative because as time increases, the volume of the water decreases. Time and volume have an inverse relationship. But compared to the rate of decrease when the drain is unplugged, the volume is decreasing at a faster rate. Compared to the rate of decrease from evaporation, the volume is decreasing at a much faster rate.

If you think about this with the formula of slope in mind, the change in y is very large and the change in x very small. Therefore, the numerator is larger than the denominator, leaving a fraction greater than 1. The bigger the fraction, the closer to parallel to the y axis the line will be. But the line will never be vertical. After all, time can't stand still, so there will always be a change in x. You know from your math review that the denominator can't be zero, so slope can't work if there is no change in x. Even if you had super powers to freeze time, the volume would freeze as well. So there is no way to have a change in y but no change in x.

Curves

In Science passages, not all graphs will feature straight lines. Just as in real life, not all situations are linear.

The heat wave passes, and summer turns to fall. But you're not ready to give up the pool, even as the days turn crisp. You decide to install a heat pump to make it a heated pool. You turn the pump on, and it gradually heats the chilly water to a perfect 78°F. However, the heat pump malfunctions, and the temperature continues to rise, faster and faster, until soon it's over 100°F.

Luckily for you, you witnessed all this safely from outside the pool. But let's take a look at what the graph would look like.

Steep Line = Big Slope
When the independent variable has to change by only a small amount to have a huge effect on the dependent variable, the slope will be steep.

The curve is obviously not linear, so slope doesn't apply. As the independent variable (time) increases, the dependent variable (temperature) increases, so the relationship between the variables is direct. But temperature increases *exponentially* faster, not in a constant, linear pattern. The amount that y changes with each change in x is different at different points on the graph.

Now let's think of this in math terms. What does the graph of $y = x^2$ look like? It's a parabola. Cut the parabola off at the origin and look only at the right half, and it will look just like the graph above.

TRENDS ON THE SCIENCE TEST

The key to cracking the Science test is to look for trends and patterns. Figures with consistent trends point to a Now passage because the figure has provided the main point of the passage, i.e., the relationship between the variables.

In the next chapter, we'll teach you a basic approach to cracking each passage, including passages that *don't* feature small tables and graphs with consistent trends. But we hope that this chapter has convinced you to look for passages featuring figures with consistent trends to do Now. You'll find even the hardest questions are easier to tackle when the figure tells you everything you need to know.

Look at each of the following figures. What are the relationships between the variables?

Dr. Frankenstein's Experiment

As the positive slope of the ordered pairs shows, it's a direct, linear relationship. The more abnormal the brain, the more deranged the behavior.

Try another.

This, too, is a direct, linear relationship. As temperature increases, volume increases.

What about the next one?

When the wind speed is 40 km/hr, what is the rate of sand movement? It's 0.3. When the wind speed is 50 km/hr, the rate of sand movement increases to 0.6, double the last reading even though the wind speed increased by only 10 km/hr. The relationship is direct, but the curve shows you it's an exponential relationship, not a linear one.

Try the next one.

Does time actually affect the size of a soda can? Of course not. As a result, we get a flat line.

Try one more.

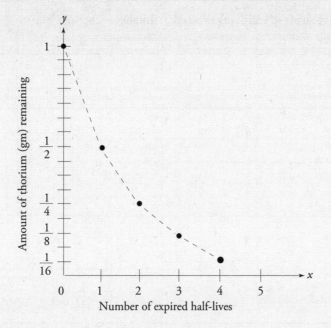

As the number of expired half-lives increases, the amount of thorium remaining decreases, so the two have an inverse relationship. But because the curve is headed downward, it's a negative relationship.

Do you need to know what "expired half-lives" and "thorium" are? No, you don't need to (but it's always helpful when you're familiar with the content). To answer the questions for this passage, everything you need to know comes from the relationships between the variables. The main point of the passage is just a summary of these relationships.

Tables

When we began this chapter, we showed you tables before switching to graphs. Everything we've discussed about graphs applies to tables. A table with consistent trends is just as helpful as a graph with consistent trends. The only difference is that tables are not as visual as graphs, so it's up to you to make them visual.

Look at the table below.

Number of half-lives expired for radioactive thorium	Amount of thorium (gm) remaining
0	1
1	$\frac{1}{2}$
2	$\frac{1}{4}$
3	$\frac{1}{8}$
4	$\frac{1}{16}$

This is the same information we saw in a graph. What direction is the number of half-lives headed? It's headed up. Draw an arrow to reflect the trend. What direction is the amount of thorium headed? It's headed down. Draw an arrow to reflect the trend. Your table should now look like this:

Number of half-lives expired for radioactive thorium	Amount of thorium (gm) remaining
0	1
1	$\frac{1}{2}$
2	$\frac{1}{4}$
3	$\frac{1}{8}$
4	$\frac{1}{16}$

You've just gotten a preview of the next chapter. Marking the trends in a figure is the first step in the basic approach to cracking Science passages.

Inconsistent Trends and No Relationships

Wouldn't it be great if you saw only tables and graphs with consistent trends on the ACT? Yes, it would, but there will be uglier figures as well. Now that you know how powerful consistent trends are, you can actually use that knowledge even when there is no consistency. The absence of consistency tells its own story.

As temperature increases, what does pH do? It barely increases at first, then makes a sharp jump before an equally sharp fall to a point that is lower than what it began. You may have immediately identified this as a **bell curve**. Is a bell curve consistent?

A bell curve is certainly not as consistent as a straight line or even a curve that moves in a positive or negative direction. There is some consistency, however. It increases, then decreases. The problem is that we can't make a prediction of what it will do next. That's the real beauty of consistent lines and curves: we can predict what will happen off the figure. But with a bell curve, we can't determine whether it will repeat its trend or if it will steadily decrease.

What about the next graph? What story does it tell?

aedes aegypti

There is no relationship at all between aedes aegypti and sarcoidosis. The incidence of sarcoidosis is *independent* of the aedes aegypti, not *dependent*. And unlike the relationship in a flat line, the incidence of sarcoidosis is not constant. Instead, it fluctuates wildly.

That's a good deal of information from a confusing figure with two strange variables. But would you want to do the passage with this figure Now or Later? Definitely Later.

Multiple Variables

In many Experiments passages, you'll see multiple tables and graphs. Take a look at the following tables (Tables 3 and 4).

Length (m)	Resistance (Ω)
0.9	7.5
1.8	15.0
3.6	30.0

Table 3

Cross-sectional area (mm²)	Resistance (Ω)
0.8	35.0
1.6	18.0
3.2	7.5

Table 4

First, mark the trends within each figure. In Table 3, as length increases, resistance increases. Length is the independent variable, resistance is the dependent variable, and the two have a direct relationship. In Table 4, as cross-sectional area increases, resistance decreases, and the two have an inverse relationship. What's the relationship between the figures? Look at the variable they have in common: resistance.

In Experiments passages—as well as in scientific studies in real life—it's common to test different independent variables to measure their effect on the same dependent variable. But recall our second and third rules of scientific reasoning skills:

2. **Change one variable at a time.** Vary each independent variable to see its effect on your dependent variable.

3. **Keep all other variables the same.** Your other independent variables *and everything else* has to be the same as you vary one and only one independent variable.

When length is varied, can cross-sectional area vary at the same time? No, it has to stay the same, that is, constant. And when cross-sectional area is varied, length has to stay constant.

On the Science test, you are likely to see a question that tests your ability to spot the constants.

———————————○———————————

1. Based on the results shown in Table 3 and Table 4 above, the cross-sectional area used in the first experiment (resulting in Table 3), was most likely:

   A. 0.8 mm².
   B. 1.6 mm².
   C. 3.2 mm².
   D. 4.8 mm².

Here's How to Crack It

Find the link between the two tables by looking at the variable they have in common, resistance. Look for a value of resistance that is the same in both tables. In Table 3, resistance is 7.5 Ω when length is 0.9 m. In Table 4, resistance is 7.5 Ω when cross-sectional area is 3.2 mm². Thus, we know that as length was varied, cross-sectional area was held constant at 3.2 mm², and as cross-sectional area was varied, length was held constant at 0.9 m. The correct answer is choice (C).

———————————○———————————

Graphs can also have multiple variables. Take a look at the following graph.

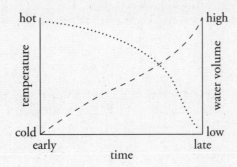

When there are multiple variables on a graph, you always need to be careful to look at the correct line and the correct axis. As time increases, temperature increases. As time increases, water volume decreases. Does that mean temperature and water volume have a relationship? Not directly, they don't. What's the variable they have in common? Temperature.

Try another question.

———————————◯———————————

2. According to the figure above what was the temperature when water volume was at its lowest?

   F. High
   G. Hot
   H. Low
   J. Cold

Here's How to Crack It

Find the link between the two axes by looking at the variable they have in common, time. Be sure to look at the correct curve on the correct axis. Water volume is the bubbled line, and when it's at its highest, the time on the x axis is early. When time is early, look at the dashed line for the temperature. When it's early, the temperature is cold.

The correct answer is choice (J).

———————————◯———————————

In the next lesson, we'll teach you how to use your scientific reasoning skills on ACT Science passages, which will feature plenty of tables and graphs with various trends and relationships.

Summary

o   Scientific reasoning is based on common sense.

o   The three rules of scientific reasoning skills are
    1.   make no assumptions.
    2.   change one variable at a time.
    3.   keep all other variables the same.

o   A hypothesis is a theory that needs proof to become a conclusion.

o   An independent variable creates or causes an effect on a dependent variable.

o   In a direct relationship, as x increases, y increases.

o   Direct linear relationships on a graph have positive slopes.

o   In an inverse relationship, as x increases, y decreases.

o   Inverse linear relationships on a graph have negative slopes.

o   A flat line means the dependent variable is constant, and the independent variable has no effect.

o   A steep slope means the independent variable has a drastic effect on the dependent variable.

o   A shallow slope means the independent variable has a slight effect on the dependent variable.

o   When the dependent variable changes by different amounts every time the independent variable changes, the result is a curved line.

Chapter 21
The Basic Approach

To earn your highest possible score on the Science test, you need an efficient and strategic approach to working the passages. In this chapter, we'll teach you how to apply your scientific reasoning skills to assess quickly the content of the passage and figures and make your way methodically through the questions.

HOW TO CRACK THE SCIENCE TEST

The most efficient way to boost your Science score is to pick your order of the passages and apply our 3-Step Basic Approach to the Charts and Graphs passages and Experiments passages. Follow our smart, effective strategy to earn as many points as you can.

Step 1: Work the Figures

Take 10–30 seconds to review the figures. In the last chapter we taught you how to look for and identify trends, patterns, and relationships. Your goal in Step 1 is to quickly identify the main point of the passage and the relationships between the variables that convey the main point. Consistent trends are the fastest to assess, but all trends and patterns tell a story. In Chapter 19, we gave you a way to spot the Now passages, which are chiefly characterized by consistent trends.

Now Passages
1. **Small tables and graphs:** No more than 3–4 curves on a graph, no more than 3–4 rows and columns on a table.
2. **Easy-to-spot consistent trends:** All lines headed in same direction, numbers in a table in easy-to-spot order.
3. **Numbers, not words or symbols:** Avoid tables and graphs with words or symbols.
4. **Short answers:** Numbers, or trend words like *increase* and *decrease* or *higher* and *lower*.

Graphs

Graphs visually represent the relationship between the variables. When you work a graph, identify the relationship, and take note of the variables and their units.

Look at the graph below.

Figure 1

1. Look at the direction of the curves: They are all headed up.
2. Take note of the variables and their units. Temperature, in °C, is on the x axis; solubility, in g solute/100 mL H_2O is on the y axis.
3. Identify the relationship. A positive slope means it's a direct relationship. As temperature increases, solubility increases.

Tables

For tables, you need to make the trends visual. Take a look at the table below.

Length (m)	Resistance (Ω)
0.9	7.5
1.8	15.0
3.6	30.0

Table 1

1. What is length doing? It's increasing. Mark it with an arrow.
2. What is resistance doing? It's increasing. Mark it with an arrow.
3. What are the units of the variables? m and Ω.
4. Identify the relationship. Both variables move in the same direction, so it's a direct relationship.

Here's what your table should look like.

Length (m)	Resistance (Ω)
0.9	7.5
1.8	15.0
3.6	30.0

↑ **Table 1** ↓

Try another table from the same passage.

Cross-sectional area (mm²)	Resistance (Ω)
0.8	30.0
1.6	15.0
3.2	7.5

Table 2

1. What is the cross-sectional area doing? It's increasing. Mark it with an arrow.
2. What is resistance doing? It's decreasing. Mark it with an arrow.
3. What are the units of the variables? mm² and Ω.
4. Identify the relationship. As the cross-sectional area increases, resistance decreases. It's an inverse relationship.

Here's what your table should look like.

Cross-sectional area (mm²)	Resistance (Ω)
0.8	30.0
1.6	15.0
3.2	7.5

↑ **Table 2** ↓

Last, identify the relationship between the tables. Each table has the variable **resistance** in common.

Step 2: Work the Questions
Once you've marked the figures, go straight to the questions.

Now, Later, Never

There is no set order of difficulty of the questions. Follow your Personal Order of Difficulty (POOD): if a question is fairly straightforward, do it Now. Most of the questions you consider straightforward will likely ask you to identify a trend, look up a value, or make a prediction. Now questions will have values or trend words like *increase* or *lower* in the answers. If a question strikes you as confusing or time consuming, come back to it Later. Occasionally, you'll judge a question tough enough you may Never want to do it. Pick a Letter of the Day (LOTD), and move on to the next passage. In Step 3, we'll address how smart use of Process of Elimination (POE) may eliminate the need for any Never questions on a Now passage. But for now, let's look at a sample Now question.

Acronyms Rule!
You've seen our favorite Princeton Review acronyms before and you'll see them again: POOD, LOTD, POE.

1. Based on the figure, as temperature increases, the solubility of $HgCl_3$:

    A. increases.
    B. decreases.
    C. increases, then decreases.
    D. decreases, then increases.

Here's How to Crack It

This question is asking you to identify a trend. You already cracked this question in Step 1, when you worked the figures and identified the trends. All the curves are headed up, so as temperature increases, the solubility of $HgCl_3$ increases. The correct answer is choice (A).

Try another.

---

2. According to Figure 1, KNO$_3$ and KCl have the same solubility at what temperature?

    F. Between 0° and 10°
    G. Between 10° and 20°
    H. Between 20° and 30°
    J. Between 30° and 40°

Here's How to Crack It

This question is asking you to look up a value in the figure. Find where KNO$_3$
and KCl have the same solubility. They have the same solubility when the lines
intersect, at a solubility of 30 g/100 mL H$_2$O. Draw a line down to the x axis to
see what the temperature is when solubility is 30; it's just over 20°, so the correct answer is choice (H).

Many questions on Science passages will entail nothing more than looking up a
trend or value in a figure. Both of these are great Now questions.

Let's try one more question from the same passage.

---

3. Based on the figure, at 100°C the solubility of HgCl$_3$ would
most likely be:

    A. less than 5 g/100 mL H$_2$O.
    B. between 10 g/100 mL H$_2$O and 20 g/100 mL H$_2$O.
    C. between 20 g/100 mL H$_2$O and 30 g/100 mL H$_2$O.
    D. greater than 30 g/100 mL H$_2$O.

Here's How to Crack It

If a question cites a specific value, first check to see if that value is in the figure. If
it's not, the question is asking you to make a prediction. Because the trend is consistent, you can predict what the curve will do. At 90°C, the solubility of HgCl$_3$ is
already over 30 g/100 mL H$_2$O. Thus at 100°C, the solubility will be greater than
30 g/100 mL H$_2$O. The correct answer is choice (D).

Read If and Only When You Need To

On most of the questions, particularly on Now passages, you will be able to
answer the questions by the figures. Whether it's a Charts and Graphs passage
or Experiments passage, waste no time reading any of the introduction, or in the
case of the Experiments passages, the descriptions of each experiment/study. If
you can't answer a question from the figures, read.

Let's take a look at some questions from an Experiments passage. We've already marked the tables from this passage.

———————————————○———————————————

Passage III

The *resistance* of a material that obeys Ohm's Law can be calculated by setting up a potential difference at the ends of a wire made of that material and then measuring the current in the wire; the resistance is the ratio of potential difference to current. Because resistance is dependent on length and cross-sectional area, scientists created a standard measure, *resistivity*, which is the measure of how strongly a material opposes the flow of current. In the experiments below, scientists examined the factors affecting resistance in an Ohmic material that they invented.

Experiment 1

In their first experiment, scientists examined the relationship between the length of a wire and its resistance. The resistivity of the wires used in this experiment was 27.5 ρ and the cross-sectional area of the wires was 3.2 mm^2.

Length (m)	Resistance (Ω)
0.9	7.5
1.8	15.0
3.6	30.0

↑ **Table 1** ↓

Experiment 2

In their second experiment, scientists examined the relationship between the cross-sectional area of a wire and its resistance. The resistivity of the wires used in this experiment was 27.5 ρ and the length of the wires was 0.9 m. The results are shown in Table 2.

Cross-sectional area (mm^2)	Resistance (Ω)
0.8	30.0
1.6	15.0
3.2	7.5

↑ **Table 2** ↓

Opposites
Whenever there is only
one pair of answers
that are exact opposites,
the correct answer is
frequently one of the two
opposites.

4. *Conductivity* measures a material's ability to conduct an electric current, and is defined as the reciprocal of a material's ability to oppose the flow of electric current. If the scientists wanted to increase the conductivity of the material they invented, they would:

F. increase the length.
G. decrease the cross-sectional area.
H. increase the resistivity.
J. decrease the resistivity.

When to Read
Read if and only when you can't answer a question from the figures. If a question introduces a new term that you can't identify as one of the variables on the figures, look for information about that term in the introduction and/or experiments.

Here's How to Crack It
The question defines a new term, **conductivity,** and asks how the scientists would increase the conductivity of their specific material. As part of the definition, the question states that conductivity is the reciprocal of a material's ability to oppose the flow of current. The tables do not feature an obvious variable for this quality, so you have to read the introduction and studies.

In the introduction, the term **resistivity** is defined as a material's ability to oppose the flow of electric current. The question adds the information that conductivity is the reciprocal of resistivity. Therefore, to increase the conductivity, the scientists would decrease the resistivity. The correct answer is choice (J). Notice that choices (H) and (J) are exact opposites. Whenever there is only one pair of exact opposites, the correct answer is frequently one of the pair.

Step 3: Work the Answers
On more difficult questions, POE will be much faster and more effective than scouring the text or figures to find an answer. If the answers are wordy—that is, anything but a simple value or trend word like *increase* or *lower*—use POE. Read each answer choice, and eliminate any that are contradicted by the figures.

Let's try a question from a different passage.

Passage I

The term *solubility* refers to the amount of a substance (solute) that will dissolve in a given amount of a liquid substance (solvent). The solubility of solids in water varies with temperature. The graph below displays the water solubility curves for four crystalline solids.

6. A solution is *saturated* when the concentration of a solute is equal to the solubility at that temperature. If a saturated solution of potassium chloride (KCl) at 10°C were heated to 80°C, would the solution remain saturated?

   F. Yes, because solubility decreases with increasing temperature.

   G. Yes, because concentration decreases with increasing temperature.

   H. No, because solubility is unaffected by increasing temperature.

   J. No, because concentration is unaffected by increasing temperature.

Here's How to Crack It

The question defines a new term, *saturated*, identifies KCl as saturated at a given temperature, and asks if KCl will remain saturated at a new temperature. If you're familiar with the topic of saturation, you may already know whether it's yes or no. If so, cross off the two answers you know to be wrong and examine the reasons given in the two remaining answers.

But if you didn't understand the new information and can't process what will happen at a new temperature, use POE on all four answers. Ignore the yes/no, and focus on the reasons given in each answer.

Choice (F) says that solubility will decrease with increasing temperature, but the figure disproves this. No matter what the new information in the question is, this cannot be the correct answer. Cross it off. Choice (G) brings in a new variable, *concentration*. Quickly check the introduction to see if concentration is defined. It's not, so you have to leave choice (G). You can't eliminate an answer about a variable that you know nothing about. You can eliminate choice (H), however, because the figure disproves the reason. Choice (J) revolves around concentration, so you have to keep that as well.

At worst, you have a fifty-fifty chance of getting this question right if you guessed from here and moved on. We can offer one extra tip to help sway you in your guess. Avoid an answer that provides either a value or describes a trend of an unknown variable if you have no proof of how that new variable will behave. Thus, between choices (G) and (J), the smart money is on (J), and it is the correct answer. Concentration is the number of grams of the substance per unit volume, and the concentration will not change with temperature.

POE and Pacing

POE is so powerful on Science, you should be able to eliminate at least one, sometimes two, wrong answers, and therefore have few Never questions, particularly on a Now passage.

Depending on your pacing, you may try to reason between the remaining answers. Don't spend more than another minute. Even if you get the question right, spending too much time on one question will likely cost 2–3 questions later on.

THE 3-STEP BASIC APPROACH AND LATER PASSAGES

The 3-Step Basic Approach works on all passages with figures, not just the Now passages featuring consistent trends in tables and graphs.

Take a look using the 3-Step Basic Approach at a Later passage in the following section.

Step 1: Work the Figures

Some ACT passages will feature an illustration, a diagram, or tables and graphs with no consistent trends. Take 10–15 seconds to review the figure. When there are no consistent trends, a figure doesn't reveal the main point as readily. You'll learn the main point as you work the questions and answers. Spend the limited time devoted to Step 1 looking for any patterns or terms.

Try this figure.

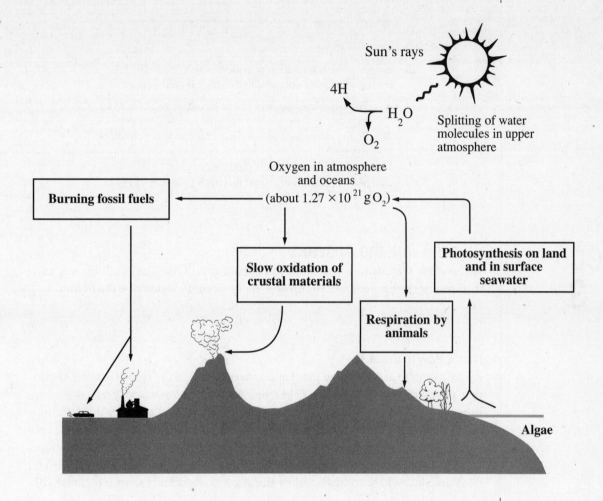

The terms **oxygen**, **fossil fuels**, **oxidation**, **respiration**, and **photosynthesis** all appear.

Step 2: Work the Questions

Even on Later passages, several questions will ask you to look something up in the figure. The more confusing the figure, however, the more likely you are to waste valuable time trying to figure everything out from staring at the figure, waiting for a flash of inspiration to hit. As we wrote before, spend 10–15 seconds looking for any patterns or terms. Your time is better spent moving to Steps 2 and 3. Working the questions and answers will help you crack the main point of the passage.

Try a question.

13. Based on the information provided, which one of the following statements concerning the oxygen cycle is true?

   A. Photosynthesis on land and in surface seawater uses up oxygen.
   B. Photosynthesis on land and in surface seawater produces oxygen.
   C. Respiration by animals produces oxygen.
   D. Slow oxidation of crustal materials produces oxygen.

Step 3: Work the Answers

The wordier the answers, the more you should use POE. Read each answer and then review the figure: Does the answer choice accurately describe the figure?

Here's How to Crack It

Pay attention to arrows. They provide a pattern that tells the story. Choice (A) says that photosynthesis uses oxygen, but the arrows lead toward oxygen, not away. Eliminate choice (A). Choice (B) is the exact opposite and matches the direction of the arrows. Keep it. Whenever there is only one pair of exact opposites, the correct answer is frequently one of the two opposites. Choice (C) and (D) both describe producing oxygen, but the arrows move away from oxygen, not toward it. Both descriptions are contradicted by the arrows. The correct answer is choice (B).

Basic Approach Drill 1

Use the Basic Approach on the passage below. For the answers to this drill, please go to Chapter 24.

The kinetic molecular theory provides new insights into the movement of molecules in liquids. It states that molecules are in constant motion and collide with one another. When the temperature of a liquid increases, there will be an increase in the movement of molecules and in the average kinetic energy. The figure below depicts the distribution of the kinetic energy of two volumetrically identical samples of water at different temperatures (T).

Water has attractive intermolecular forces that keep the molecules together. When enough heat is added to water, it will weaken these forces and allow some molecules to evaporate and escape the liquid as a gas. The activation energy (Ea) is the minimum energy necessary for molecules to escape the liquid and undergo a phase change.

Distribution of Kinetic Energy for Two Samples of Water

1. Which of the following statements best describes the changes observed in the graph?

    A. At T1, Sample 1 has a lower kinetic energy than does Sample 2.
    B. At T2, Sample 1 has a lower kinetic energy than does Sample 2.
    C. An increase in temperature leads to a decrease in kinetic energy.
    D. Water never undergoes a phase change.

2. Assume that water undergoes a phase change to a gas. Which of the following statements would be true?

    F. The attractive intermolecular forces of the escaping molecules are weak.
    G. The average kinetic energy of the water remains the same.
    H. The rate of movement of the gas molecules decreases.
    J. The gas will undergo no further phase changes.

3. Suppose a third sample of water is heated to a higher temperature than Sample 2. It is then found that a greater number of molecules escaped the liquid in Sample 3 than in Sample 2. Would these results be consistent with the results depicted in Figure 1?

    A. Yes, an increase in temperature leads to a decrease in the number of escaping molecules in the liquid.
    B. Yes, as the temperature increases, it leads to more molecules escaping the liquid.
    C. No, the temperature reading of Sample 2 would be five times as high as that of the third sample.
    D. No, the average kinetic energy of the water will decrease.

4. It can be inferred from the passage that when a substance undergoes a phase change from a liquid to a gas it will:

    F. evaporate.
    G. condense.
    H. disintegrate.
    J. remain the same.

5. Given the samples at T1 and T2, and the kinetic energies measured and shown in Figure 1, which temperature produces the highest single kinetic energy measurement?

    A. Both T1 and T2
    B. T2
    C. T1
    D. Neither T1 nor T2

Basic Approach Drill 2

Use the Basic Approach on the passage below. For the answers to this drill, please go to Chapter 24.

Amphibians are unique organisms that undergo drastic physical changes during the transformation from an immature organism into an adult form. This process, called metamorphosis, begins with the determination of cells at the tadpole stage. A study was conducted using tadpoles to determine the influence of thyroxine (a hormone) on metamorphosis.

As shown in the graph below, tadpoles were placed in solutions containing various concentrations of thyroxine. Increased levels of thyroxine correlated with increased rates of tail reabsorption and the appearance of adult characteristics such as lungs and hind legs.

Decrease in tail width in relation to varying levels of thyroxine solutions

Figure 1

1. Suppose that a tadpole was immersed in a 0.3 µg/ml solution for 72 hours. What would be the expected approximate decrease in tail width?

   A. 22%
   B. 30%
   C. 41%
   D. 50%

2. Which of the following generalizations about tadpoles is supported by the results of the study?

   F. They will not undergo metamorphosis if they are not given thyroxine.
   G. Metamorphosis in a normal tadpole takes at least five days.
   H. The most rapid disappearance of the tail is associated with the immersion of tadpoles in the most dilute thyroxine solution.
   J. Temperature plays a major role in metamorphosis.

3. After four days, the tadpoles are checked for development. In all samples other than the control, which of the following concentrations of thyroxine would the tadpoles be likely to show the LEAST development?

   A. 0.5 µg/ml
   B. 0.2 µg/ml
   C. 0.1 µg/ml
   D. All of the tadpoles would show the same development.

4. Based on the information in the passage, which of the following would be a correct order of the stages of tadpole development?

   F. Tadpole → adult → reabsorption of tail → cell determination
   G. Tadpole → cell determination → reabsorption of tail → adult
   H. Tadpole → reabsorption of tail → cell determination → adult
   J. Cell determination → tadpole → adult → reabsorption of tail

5. According to Figure 1, immersing the tadpoles in solutions containing various concentrations of thyroxine does not begin to affect the rate of tadpole metamorphosis until when?

   A. No time at all; the thyroxine affects the rate of metamorphosis immediately.
   B. 0–12 hours after immersion
   C. 12–24 hours after immersion
   D. 24–36 hours after immersion

Basic Approach Drill 3

Use the Basic Approach on the passage below. For the answers to this drill, please go to Chapter 24.

Each element is arranged in the periodic table according to its atomic number, which represents the number of protons in the nucleus. In every neutrally charged atom, the number of electrons equals the number of protons. The table below lists some of the properties of row 2 elements in the periodic table. *Electronegativity* is a measure of the relative strength with which the atoms attract outer electrons. Within a row of the periodic table, the electronegativity tends to increase with increasing atomic number, due to the tighter bonding between protons and electrons. The highest value for electronegativity is 4.0.

Element	Atomic number	Atomic radius	Electro–negativity	Characteristic
Li	3	1.52	1.0	metal
Be	4	1.13	1.5	metal
B	5	0.88	2.0	non-metal
C	6	0.77	2.5	non-metal
N	7	0.70	3.0	non-metal
O	8	0.66	3.5	non-metal
F	9	0.64	4.0	non-metal

1. Which of the following graphs best represents the relationship between atomic number and atomic radius for row 2 elements?

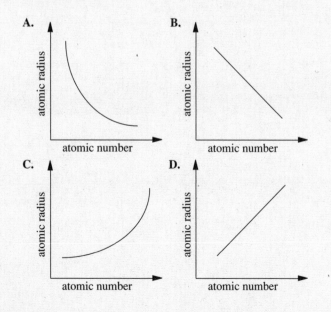

A. atomic radius / atomic number
B. atomic radius / atomic number
C. atomic radius / atomic number
D. atomic radius / atomic number

2. What conclusion could be appropriately drawn from the data regarding electronegativity in Table 1?

F. An element with high electronegativity has an even atomic number.
G. An element with high electronegativity will be a metal.
H. An element with high electronegativity will have little tendency to attract outer electrons.
J. An element with high electronegativity will be a non-metal.

3. What generalization can one make concerning the relationship between two properties of elements?

A. As the atomic radius decreases, the electronegativity decreases.
B. As the atomic radius decreases, the electronegativity increases.
C. All metals have higher electronegativity values than non-metals.
D. The atomic radius of F is larger than that of N.

4. Which of the following is true regarding the comparative electronegativity of fluorine (F) and lithium (Li)?

F. The electronegativity of F is greater than Li because F has fewer electrons in its outer shell.
G. The electronegativity of F is greater than Li because F electrons are more tightly bound.
H. The electronegativity of Li is greater than F because Li has a greater metallic character.
J. The electronegativity of F is greater than Li because Li has a greater metallic character.

5. Generally speaking, ionization energy follows the same trends as does electronegativity. Elements with a high electronegativity also have a high ionization energy. Which of the following is a correct order of elements with INCREASING ionization energies?

A. Li, N, F
B. F, N, Li
C. B, N, Be
D. Be, O, Li

Summary

o All Charts and Graphs passages and most Experiments passages come with figures.

o Use the 3-Step Basic Approach on passages with figures.

Step 1. Work the Figures. Look at the trends and patterns in the figure to identify the relationship between the variables. Mark trends in tables with arrows.

Step 2. Work the Questions. Do Now the straightforward questions that involve looking up a trend or value on the figure, or making a prediction of what a variable will do. Read if and only when you can't answer a question from the figures. Do Later any question that strikes you as more difficult or time consuming.

Step 3. Work the Answers. For tougher questions, POE should help you eliminate at least one wrong answer if not 3.

o Pace yourself. If you've eliminated at least one wrong answer, guess and move on to the next passage.

Chapter 22
Fighting Scientists

The third type of passage on the Science test is called "Fighting Scientists." There will be only 1 of these passages and it will be accompanied by 7 questions. Two, three, or possibly more conflicting views on a scientific phenomenon will be presented. Make a plan of the order in which you will read the scientists, and work one theory at a time before tackling the questions that require comparing and contrasting all the theories.

Think of it as a debate. Each debater proposes a hypothesis and then supports that hypothesis with facts, opinions, and assumptions. The ACT test writers want you to evaluate and compare the arguments made by each debater, but they don't care who wins the debate. We don't care either, but we do want you to answer correctly seven questions about the debate. In order to do that, you must understand each viewpoint and how it agrees and disagrees with the others. Some questions will ask about just one theory, but most of the questions will ask you to compare and contrast two or more. That's a lot to keep track of. Wouldn't it be easier to navigate this passage if you had a plan?

FOLLOW A PLAN

The Fighting Scientists passage has a lot in common with the Reading test, and you might recognize some of the same strategies we taught you to employ for Reading. Remember when we asked you how you would fare if your boss assigned you the task of checking out an empty building? How well do you do when you don't know what you're looking for? Not very well. How well would you fare if you dived right into a passage on the Reading test if you didn't know what you're looking for? Right. So how can you succeed on the Fighting Scientists passage if you don't know what you're looking for?

Step 1: Preview

Your first task is to map the order in which you will read the scientists. Just as on the Reading test, you should look at the questions first. In the Fighting Scientists section, the questions help you determine which hypothesis to read and which questions to answer first.

Let's try this with the questions on the next page. Read each question and mark it with a "1" if it asks about Hypothesis 1, a "2" if it asks about Hypothesis 2, and a "1 & 2" if it asks about both hypotheses.

1. Hypotheses 1 and 2 agree that the dinosaurs:

2. The basis of Hypothesis 1 is that a meteorite striking Earth was the primary cause of the dinosaurs' demise. Which of the following discoveries would best support this case?

3. Suppose a geologist discovered that the fossilized bones of dinosaurs contained traces of radioactive iridium. How would this evidence influence the two hypotheses?

4. The authors of the two hypotheses would disagree over whether the extinction of the dinosaurs was:

5. If current climatic changes turn out to be as dramatic as those described by the author of Hypothesis 2, which of the following would he say is most likely to occur?

6. Studies have shown that climatic conditions are interdependent. As conditions become less favorable for life in one locale, they improve in another. If fossil evidence were found which showed that this happened at the K-T boundary, how would it affect Hypothesis 2?

7. Both Hypothesis 1 and 2 would be supported by evidence showing that:

You should have a "1 & 2" next to questions 1, 3, 4, and 7. Question 2 should have a "1" next to it, and questions 5 and 6 should have a "2" next to them. What does this tell us? We should read Hypothesis 2 first.

Step 2: One Side at a Time

In order to compare and contrast multiple hypotheses, you need to understand each viewpoint and how it agrees and disagrees with the others. Reading and working the questions for one scientist at a time will give you the firm grasp of each theory you need.

Once the questions have provided a map, read the introduction to identify the disagreement.

> Approximately 65 million years ago (at the boundary between the Cretaceous and Tertiary periods, known as the K-T boundary), the dinosaurs became extinct.

> Here are two of the hypotheses that have been presented to explain their disappearance.

What will the hypotheses debate? They will debate what caused the extinction of the dinosaurs.

Next, read Hypothesis 2. You don't need to comprehend everything in the passage or remember every point of fact or argumentation, and until you read the other hypothesis, you have no basis for comparison. You do need to grasp the argument each is making, so as you read Hypothesis 2, find and underline the scientist's main point.

Hypothesis 2

This event at the K-T boundary was neither sudden nor isolated. It was a consequence of minor shifts in the earth's weather that spanned the K-T boundary. Furthermore, its effect was not as sweeping as some have suggested. While the majority of dinosaurs disappeared, some were able to adapt to the changing world. We see their descendants every day—the birds.

Alterations in the earth's *jet stream* (a steady, powerful wind that blows from west to east, circling the globe) shifted rains away from the great shallow seas that extended across much of what is now North America. As these late-Cretaceous seas began to dry up, a chain reaction of extinctions was set into motion. First affected was plant life. Next, animals that fed on plants began dying off. Ultimately, the lack of prey caused the demise of the dinosaurs. It was the mobility of the winged dinosaurs that saved them, allowing them to move to more favorable locations as conditions in their ancestral homes deteriorated.

What Are They Fighting About?

Some of the scientific theories you'll read about in a Fighting Scientists passage were settled a long time ago. In reading a passage arguing that Earth is the center of the universe, you may think, "Wait, Earth is NOT the center of the solar system—why in the world are they arguing about this?" For the ACT, the arguments presented are what count. Even though an argument may have been disproved a long time ago, it's still possible to evaluate it scientifically, and that's all you're being asked to do on this test.

What is the main point of Hypothesis 2?

According to Hypothesis 2, the extinction of dinosaurs was caused by a chain reaction prompted by changes in the weather.

Your Underlined Version Should Look Like This

Hypothesis 2

<u>This event at the K-T boundary was neither sudden nor isolated. It was a consequence of minor shifts in the earth's weather that spanned the K-T boundary.</u> Furthermore, its effect was not as sweeping as some have suggested. While the majority of dinosaurs disappeared, some were able to adapt to the changing world. We see their descendants every day—the birds.

Alterations in the earth's *jet stream* (a steady, powerful wind that blows from west to east, circling the globe) shifted rains away from the great shallow seas that extended across much of what is now North America. As these late-Cretaceous seas began to dry up, a chain reaction of extinctions was set into motion. First affected was plant life. Next, animals that fed on plants began dying off. Ultimately, the lack of prey caused the demise of the dinosaurs. It was the mobility of the winged dinosaurs that saved them, allowing them to move to more favorable locations as conditions in their ancestral homes deteriorated.

Did you notice that we didn't underline the details of the theory in the second paragraph? It's not that they are unimportant, but until we dive into the questions, we don't know what to pay attention to other than the main point. As we work the questions for Hypothesis 2, we'll gain a deeper understanding of the details of the theory.

Without further ado, let's go to the questions about Hypothesis 2.

---

5. If current climatic changes turn out to be as dramatic as those described by the author of Hypothesis 2, which of the following would he say is most likely to occur?

   A. A rapid extinction of most of Earth's life, beginning with sea dwellers such as krill (a microscopic crustacean) and progressing through the food chain.
   B. A gradual and complete extinction of Earth's life forms that moves through the food chain from the bottom up.
   C. An extinction of most life forms on Earth that is gradual and simultaneous, affecting predators as well as prey at roughly the same rates.
   D. A progressive extinction that begins with vegetation and eventually reaches to the top of the food chain, affecting most dramatically those life forms least suited to relocation.

Here's How to Crack It

The main point of Hypothesis 2 is that changes in the weather prompted a chain reaction of extinctions through the food chain until the dinosaurs were affected. We need to look for an answer that would predict a similar result from today's climatic changes. Use POE as you make your way through the answer choices.

Choice (A) is tempting because it mentions a progression "through the food chain," but the word "rapid" contradicts the first sentence of Hypothesis 2: "The event at the K-T boundary was neither sudden nor isolated." Choice (B) looks good, until we go back to the passage to confirm it and see that some dinosaurs survived, those that evolved into birds. Because of the word "complete," we have to eliminate it. Choice (C) is out because of the word "simultaneous," which we know from evaluating choice (A) is contradicted by the passage. The answer must be choice (D), and it paraphrases nicely what we underlined as the main point.

---

6. Studies have shown that climatic conditions are interdependent. As conditions become less favorable for life in one locale, they improve in another. If fossil evidence were found which showed that this happened at the K-T boundary, how would it affect Hypothesis 2 ?

F. It would strengthen the hypothesis by supporting one of the argument's assumptions.

G. It would weaken the hypothesis, because the area of improving climatic conditions should have provided a means for the survival of the dinosaurs well into the Tertiary period.

H. It would weaken the hypothesis by introducing additional evidence that the author could not have anticipated.

J. It would have no bearing on the hypothesis because the mobility of the winged dinosaurs would render such shifts irrelevant.

Here's How to Crack It

We've learned a lot about Hypothesis 2. We read it and underlined the main point, and then evaluated some of the nuances of the argument to eliminate wrong answers for question number 5. When you consider the import of this new fossil evidence, you should draw upon the deeper understanding you've gained. The correct answer to question 5 reminded us that those *least* suited to relocation are more impacted by the changes in weather. The author stated explicitly that some dinosaurs survived and evolved into birds. Those two facts together allow us to realize this new evidence would make Hypothesis 2 more credible. Eliminate choices (G), (H), and (J), and select choice (F) as the correct answer.

Step 3: The Other Side

Now it's time to read Hypothesis 1, but we know more than we did before reading Hypothesis 2 and thus should read more proactively. When you read the second theory, you should look for and underline the following:

- the main idea

- how this hypothesis disagrees from the first

- how this hypothesis agrees with the first

Hypothesis 1

For many years, scientists have speculated about the cause of the extinction of the dinosaurs. Fossil records confirm that dinosaurs as well as other life forms were suddenly wiped out. The natural cause of extinction is the inability of an organism to adapt to environmental changes, yet the extinction of all life forms is unlikely. Chemical analysis of clay found from this era attributes the sweeping extinction of dinosaurs to the collision of a huge meteorite with Earth. These fossil records confirm the presence of a high concentration of iridium, a rare heavy metal that is abundant in meteorites. It is believed that a meteorite hit the earth and created a huge crater, which threw up a dust cloud that blocked the sun for several months. This event led first to the destruction of much plant life and eventually all other life forms that consumed plants and/or herbivores, including the dinosaurs.

Write, Write, Write
Underlining and taking notes in the margins helps you keep track of the differences between the scientists.

What is the main point? Hypothesis 1 believes a meteorite struck Earth and wiped out the dinosaurs.

How do the two hypotheses differ? Hypothesis 2 believes the extinction was gradual; Hypothesis 1 believes it was sudden.

How do they agree? Both hypotheses mention the food chain.

If you didn't come up with those points, look at the underlined portions of the passage below.

Hypothesis 1

For many years, scientists have speculated about the cause of the extinction of the dinosaurs. <u>Fossil records confirm that dinosaurs as well as other life forms were suddenly wiped out.</u> The natural cause of extinction is the inability of an organism to adapt to environmental changes, yet the extinction of all life forms is unlikely. <u>Chemical analysis of clay found from this era attributes the sweeping extinction of dinosaurs to the collision of a huge meteorite with Earth.</u> These fossil records confirm the presence of a high concentration of iridium, a rare heavy metal that is abundant in meteorites. It is believed that a meteorite hit the earth and created a huge crater, which threw up a dust cloud that blocked the sun for several months. <u>This event led first to the destruction of much plant life and eventually all other life forms that consumed plants and/or herbivores, including the dinosaurs.</u>

Fighting Scientists
In a Fighting Scientists passage, you're given two or more opinions about a scientific phenomenon. Your job is to identify the differences between or among the viewpoints and the information the scientists use to support their points of view.

Now let's do the one question on Hypothesis 1 before we tackle the questions on both.

2. The basis of Hypothesis 1 is that a meteorite striking Earth was the primary cause of the dinosaurs' demise. Which of the following discoveries would best support this case?

F. The existence of radioactive substances in the soil.
G. The presence of other rare metals common to meteorites in the clay beds of the ocean from that period.
H. Fossil records of land-dwelling reptiles that roamed Earth for an additional 10 million years.
J. Evidence of dramatic changes in sea levels 65 million years ago.

Here's How to Crack It

What type of evidence would support Hypothesis 1? Any evidence that shows that dinosaurs were wiped out as a result of the impact of a meteorite. Would the presence of radioactive substances in the soil support Hypothesis 1? It could support the passage only if the radioactive elements were from meteorites (like iridium). Choice (F) did not specify that. Would the fact that some land-dwelling reptiles survived past this period support Hypothesis 1? No, so choice (H) is out. We can also get rid of choice (J) because it supports Hypothesis 2. What about choice (G)? What if other rare metals that are known to be found in meteorites were discovered? Would this support Hypothesis 1? Yes. The correct answer is choice (G).

Step 4: Compare and Contrast

We are now armed with a clear understanding of each hypothesis's main point, how the two differ, and how they agree.

1. Hypothesis 1 and 2 agree that the dinosaurs:

      I.   vanished because of a meteorite impact with the earth.

     II.   became extinct due to disruptions in their food chain.

   III.   became extinct due to some external force other than predation

   A.   I only
   B.   I and II only
   C.   II and III only
   D.   III only

Here's How to Crack It

We've already identified the area in which the two agree: the impact on the food chain. We can also eliminate choices that support only one of the theories. Statement 1 supports only Hypothesis 1, so it's out. Eliminate all answer choices with Statement 1 and we're left with choices (C) and (D) only. Because Statement II is in both answer choices, we know it must be correct. Of course, we'd identified the food chain as a point of agreement. Now let's check Statement III. Do both hypotheses state that dinosaurs became extinct because of some external force? Yes, so the correct answer is choice (C).

3. Suppose a geologist discovered that the fossilized bones of dinosaurs contained traces of radioactive iridium. How would this evidence influence the two hypotheses?

   A.   It would support both hypotheses.
   B.   It would support Hypothesis 2 and weaken Hypothesis 1.
   C.   It would support Hypothesis 1 and weaken Hypothesis 2.
   D.   It would not support Hypothesis 1 or Hypothesis 2.

Here's How to Crack It

Which of the hypotheses would be supported if a geologist found fossil bones that contained traces of radioactive iridium? Hypothesis 1 of course! The passage states that radioactive iridium is abundant in meteorites. If dinosaurs were exposed to the dust of meteorites, their bones would contain this metal. Hypothesis 2 didn't mention anything about iridium, so choice (C) is the correct answer.

---○---

4. The authors of the two hypotheses would disagree over whether the extinction of the dinosaurs was:

    F. a natural process.
    G. rapid.
    H. the result of a disruption on the food chain of the late-Cretaceous period.
    J. preventable.

Here's How to Crack It

The two hypotheses disagreed about the cause of the extinction, but they also disagreed on the pace. Hypothesis 1 believed it was sudden, whereas Hypothesis 2 believed it was gradual. Thus, choice (G) is the correct answer. Be careful with choice (H), because that's an issue on which both *agree*.

---○---

---○---

7. Both Hypothesis 1 and 2 would be supported by evidence showing that:

    A. pterodactyls (winged dinosaurs) survived well into the Tertiary period, adapted to changes in the earth's environment, and eventually evolved into a non-dinosaur life form.
    B. blockage of the sun's rays by particles measurable only on the microscopic scale can still have a significant effect on rates of photosynthesis.
    C. even apparently minor degradation of the plant population in a given ecosystem can have far-reaching effects on the animal population within that ecosystem.
    D. iridium is extremely likely to remain trapped in an ocean's bed when that ocean dries up.

Here's How to Crack It

On what point do the hypotheses agree? Look for an answer choice that provides evidence about the food chain. Eliminate any answer choice that supports only one hypothesis. Choice (A) is out because Hypothesis 1 never mentioned relocation or winged dinosaurs. Choice (B) looks good because it mentions photosynthesis, so keep it. Choice (C) looks much better because it explicitly mentions the effects of plants on animals. Choice (D) is incorrect because Hypothesis 2 never mentioned iridium and Hypothesis 1 never mentioned the ocean drying up. The test writers are trying to distract you with a switch, but you won't fall for it when you take the passages one at a time and learn each thoroughly before working the questions on both. The correct answer is choice (C).

---○---

Fighting Scientists Drill 1

How did the continents take on their current shape? Two differing views are presented below. For the answers to this drill, please go to Chapter 24.

Scientist 1

According to a theory based on plate tectonics, the land surface of Earth once comprised a single continent, termed *Pangaea*, which was surrounded by a single vast ocean. Pangaea broke apart because the surfaces of Earth floated on massive plates above the deeper mantle of the ocean's basin. Horizontal movement of the plates began to split up the land about 137 million years ago during the Jurassic period. The continents and the ocean basins moved along convection currents in the mantle, resulting in a continuous degeneration of Earth's physical features. The movement of these rigid plates produced zones of tectonic activity along their margins such as earthquakes, volcanoes, and mountain formations. Fossil records as well as geological evidence show similarities between widely displaced continents. For instance, the coastlines of South America and Africa contain similar rock formations and appear to fit together like a jigsaw puzzle.

Scientist 2

The continents and the ocean basins of Earth are permanent, fixed features of the planet. The hypothesis of plate tectonics is flawed because there is insufficient evidence to support it. The force of gravity is stronger than any known tangential force that can act on Earth's crust. The layers of crust that support the continents and ocean basins are strong enough to preserve Earth's physical features and are too strong to permit horizontal drift. Tectonic activity has always been present, but the hypothesis of plate tectonics explains such activity only in one late period of ancient history. In addition, it is not clear what kind of force could allow the continents, composed largely of granite, to move through areas of dense, iron-rich rock that comprise the ocean basins. Any geological evidence that supports such a theory may be because of the existence of similar conditions on different continents.

1. Which of the following statements is the most inconsistent with the beliefs of Scientist 1?

   A. Continents were once part of a large land mass.
   B. Continents split up and drifted apart.
   C. Ocean basins have not changed for millions of years.
   D. Geological evidence shows similarities between widely displaced continents.

2. Scientist 1 studied the fossils along the coast of South America and Africa and found identical fernlike plants on rocks of the same age. What claim could Scientist 2 make to refute the findings of Scientist 1?

   F. The dating and comparison of plant fossils is an exact science.
   G. The soil and climate conditions along the two coasts must have been very similar at the time the fossils were created.
   H. The ferns were extremely large.
   J. Ferns will only thrive in their original habitat.

3. A new zone of tectonic activity has been discovered in the large land mass of Eurasia. This zone shows geological evidence of having been active for several thousand years. Which scientist is supported by this finding and why?

   A. Scientist 1, because it proves that tectonic activity occurs on the planet.
   B. Scientist 1, because it shows that Pangaea and Eurasia are the same land mass.
   C. Scientist 2, because it proves that tectonic activity occurs in land masses and not solely in the ocean basin and along coastlines.
   D. Scientist 2, because it shows that the continents are made out of granite.

4. Both Scientist 1 and Scientist 2 are experts in plate tectonics. To what discipline of science do these scientists belong?

   F. Physics
   G. Geology
   H. Biology
   J. Chemistry

5. Which of the following claims would be supported by both scientists?

   I. Tectonic activity has always been a factor in the geology of land masses.
   II. The continents and the ocean basins are fixed features of the planet.
   III. Continental drift occurred in the Jurassic period.

   A. I only
   B. II only
   C. I and II only
   D. II and III only

Fighting Scientists Drill 2

How did life on Earth originate? Two differing views are presented. For the answers to this drill, please go to Chapter 24.

Hypothesis 1

In 1953, a graduate student attempted to recreate the conditions of primeval Earth in a sealed glass apparatus that he filled with methane, ammonia, hydrogen, and water. Sparks were released into the glass to simulate lightning, and heat was applied to the water. The result was the formation of organic compounds, known as amino acids, which are the building blocks of proteins. Since that time, others have shown how DNA may have been synthesized under various conditions as well. RNA, which is DNA's partner in the translation of genetic information into protein products, has been found to have the ability to reproduce itself under certain conditions. Thus, the origins of life are to be found in the "primordial soup" of the ancient earth that provided conditions for the simplest forms of organic matter to form and develop increasingly sophisticated means of organization. With the ability of compounds to make copies of themselves comes the opportunity for evolution by the mechanisms of heredity and mutation.

Hypothesis 2

Previous assumptions about the makeup of the "primordial soup" are inaccurate. It is not at all clear that methane and ammonia were present on the primeval earth or that conditions were as favorable as in the graduate student's experiment. The ability of RNA to reproduce itself is also limited to particular conditions that the primeval earth is unlikely to have provided. There is a possibility that, given enough time, random events could alone have resulted in the development of entire single-celled organisms, but some have likened that possibility to the chance that a tornado whirling through a junkyard could result in the formation of a 747 jetliner. During much of the time when the "primordial soup" was to have existed, Earth was a regular target of meteors that kept oceans boiling and the atmosphere inhospitable to organic development. Clearly much more research is needed before this theory can be widely accepted.

1. Which of the following statements about the conditions on primeval Earth could be used to support Hypothesis 2 ?

   A. Atmospheric conditions were too unstable to support the gases essential to the theories of the "primordial soup."
   B. Organic molecules were able to thrive under primeval Earth conditions.
   C. The origin of life began in the "primordial soup."
   D. The atmosphere contained methane, ammonia, hydrogen, and water.

2. To accept Hypothesis 1, one must assume that:

   F. Earth was bombarded by meteors during that time period.
   G. the conditions in the glass were analogous to the conditions on primeval Earth.
   H. proteins are the building blocks of amino acids.
   J. Earth lacked hydrogen in the atmosphere.

3. Which of the following shows how, according to Hypothesis 1, the building blocks of life were formed?

   A. Methane + Ammonia + Hydrogen + Water → Primordial Soup → Amino Acids
   B. Meteors → Primordial Soup → Amino Acids
   C. Amino Acids → Primordial Soup → DNA → Methane + Ammonia + Hydrogen + Water
   D. Primordial Soup → proteins → Amino Acids

Fighting Scientists Drill 3

Will Earth experience another ice age? For the answers to this drill, please go to Chapter 24.

Hypothesis 1

Scientists have long speculated whether glaciation will ever take place again. Given that glaciation is an unusual event, it is highly unlikely that such a phenomenon will ever repeat itself. Glaciation usually takes place under periods of extremely cool temperatures. However, it appears that the temperature on Earth has been milder and more stable than at any other period. In fact, it would take a 5°C drop in the average surface temperature in order for glaciation to occur. In addition, there would have to be a significant increase in precipitation.

Hypothesis 2

Although Earth has not experienced glaciation in a long time, the event, no matter how rare, can occur if the right conditions are met. Two factors that are critical to the growth of glaciers are precipitation and temperature. There are a number of areas, specifically land masses in the polar regions, that are currently cold enough to produce glaciers but do not have sufficient snowfall to develop glacier systems. However, if enough events occur simultaneously, they could bring on an ice age. For instance, if there is an increase in the level of snowfall in the winter in these polar regions, this could eventually lead to glaciation. On the other hand, the level of pollution in the atmosphere is also sufficient to gradually cool Earth. Under these conditions, it is quite clear that glaciation is only a matter of the right combination of events at the right time.

1. Which of the following discoveries would most clearly favor Hypothesis 2?

    A. Canada has more snowfall this year than any other year.
    B. When snow falls, it sticks to the ground.
    C. The more pollution in the air, the more the temperature drops.
    D. Earth's bodies of waters are becoming more polluted.

2. Which of the following statements is the strongest argument a supporter of Hypothesis 2 would use to counter Hypothesis 1?

    F. The temperature around polar regions fluctuates.
    G. The precipitation rate has been increasing in the Swiss Alps.
    H. Just because ideal conditions are rare does not mean they will not occur in the future.
    J. The temperature in the North Pole has gone up 2°C.

3. If Hypothesis 2 is correct and glaciation can take place in the future, what regions would be most affected?

    I. Heavily polluted regions
    II. Polar regions
    III. Humid regions

    A. I only
    B. II only
    C. I and II only
    D. II and III only

4. According to Hypothesis 2, what conditions could cause glaciation?

    F. Low levels of pollution leading to high precipitation.
    G. High levels of pollution leading to a blanketing effect that blocks out the sun and decreases the temperature dramatically.
    H. A lack of snowfall and low temperatures.
    J. A 5°C drop in the average surface temperature.

Summary

o   There is one Fighting Scientists passage on the Science test. In this passage, two, three, or more scientists present their differing views on a scientific subject.

o   Don't pick a side. The ACT test writers want you to evaluate and compare the arguments presented, not decide which one is correct. Even if you know something about the topic, answer the questions using only what is presented in the passage.

o   First, use the questions to make a map of the order in which you will read the theories and answer questions on each, one at a time.

o   Leave the questions on more than one theory for last.

o   Don't forget to guess your Letter of the Day if there are questions that you don't know how to do.

Part VI
How to Crack
the ACT
Writing Test

23 The Essay

Chapter 23
The Essay

The ACT includes an optional Essay section. Some schools are requesting an essay while others are not. We recommend that you take the essay when you take the ACT because you can't take the essay on its own later if you find that you need it; you'd have to take the whole ACT over again. The essay follows a predictable format, so preparation and practice help a lot.

THE KIND-OF OPTIONAL ESSAY

The ACT includes an "optional" essay component, but if you've already started to skip this section, stop for a moment. Although most students would not voluntarily choose to spend an extra half hour on a Saturday morning writing an essay for a standardized test, we **do** recommend that you write the essay. Why? There are two reasons.

- First, some schools require that you take the essay portion. You wouldn't want to have to take the entire test over again if you discover that your dream school wants an essay and you had decided not to write one.
- Second, writing the essay can make your college application look more attractive. Your essay score will appear on every score report you send to colleges, regardless of whether or not the school requires an essay. Every school to which you apply will see that you took the initiative to write the essay, which is a good thing.

Plus, it's not that difficult to get a good score on the essay, especially if you follow the guidelines in this chapter. An impressive score is an impressive score, optional or not.

OK, OK, I'LL WRITE THE ESSAY…
WHAT DO I HAVE TO DO?

The ACT essay will provide you with a prompt "relevant" to high school students—basically it's a topic on which the ACT test writers believe almost any typical high school student will have some opinion. Here's an example of a sample prompt.

The Children's Internet Protection Act (CIPA) requires all school libraries receiving certain federal funds to install and use blocking software to prevent students from viewing material considered "harmful to minors." However, some studies conclude that blocking software in schools damages educational opportunities for students, both by blocking access to Web pages that are directly related to the state-mandated curriculums and by restricting broader inquiries of both students and teachers. In your view, should the schools block access to certain Internet websites?

In your essay, take a position on this question. You may write about either one of the two points of view given, or you may present a different point of view on this question. Use specific reasons and examples to support your position.

Your job is to write an essay in which you take some sort of position on the prompt and develop your position through the use of appropriate supporting examples. You've probably written an essay like this in your high school English class. The only difference is that on the ACT you have a mere 30 minutes to read the prompt, brainstorm some examples, organize the essay, write it, and proofread it. You may be thinking that there's no way that you can write a great essay in such a short amount of time on a topic you've never seen before, and that is indeed true. But that's okay, because the ACT essay graders don't expect a perfect essay; they don't want to penalize you for minor spelling and grammar mistakes. Instead, graders will focus on the major components of your essay.

WHAT THE GRADERS ARE GRADING

If you think you have a tough job writing an essay in only 30 minutes, have some sympathy for the graders. They have to grade each essay in a matter of minutes. Imagine how you would feel if you spent an entire day grading thousands of essays on the same topic. By essay number 50 or so, you probably wouldn't care much if a student used "except" instead of "accept."

ACT Graders vs. English Teachers
The graders who grade for ACT aren't like your English teachers. They don't have the time to focus on the little details of each essay, and frankly, they don't care about your grade the way your English teacher does. So, don't sweat the small stuff. Focus on the big picture for the ACT: good thesis, organization, strong examples, and neatness.

ACT graders focus on the big picture. Your essay will be read by two graders, each of whom will assign it a score from 1 to 6 (for a total essay score from 2 to 12) based on how closely it adheres to the standards below. The essays are graded **holistically**, meaning the graders don't keep track of all the good things and bad things in an essay on a checklist or score sheet. Each reader simply reads the entire essay, and based on his or her overall impressions of the essay assigns it a grade.

According to the ACT guidelines, essay graders will base your score on your ability to do the following:

1. Take a position on the prompt   To score well on the ACT essay, you need a clear thesis statement. Essay graders will look for one when determining your score.

2. Maintain focus on topic   Once you come up with a thesis, stick to it. Avoid digressions in your essay—or even worse, changing or countering your thesis halfway through the paper.

3. Support your ideas   Good essays support their thesis statements with supporting examples. There is no magic number of examples. However, you do need to show that you understand the issue in the prompt, that you have a position on that issue, that you have a reason for that position, and that you can support that reason with evidence. You have to address the other side of the issue, but you don't want to argue it as strongly as your own side. Address the other issues and then point out why your examples are better.

4. Organize your ideas   This is one of the most important criteria. You must write an organized essay, meaning it needs to contain an introduction, body paragraphs, and a conclusion.

5. Use language clearly and effectively   The graders will look at stylistic issues, but those issues are not as important as the issues above. As a rule of thumb, graders will take issue with your grammar and language only if it detracts from their ability to identify the previous criteria.

HOW TO GET A GOOD SCORE

The way to get a good score on the essay is to make the graders' job easy: Show that you have a thesis, a clear essay structure, and some relevant examples. By following the guidelines presented here, you'll be able to write a clear, effective essay in the limited time available. Let's look at each step in the process. Be sure to practice each step individually, and then try to put all the steps together.

Step 1: Work with the Prompt

Our first task is to read the prompt. Here's the one we saw earlier.

The Children's Internet Protection Act (CIPA) requires all school libraries receiving certain federal funds to install and use blocking software to prevent students from viewing material considered "harmful to minors." However, some studies conclude that blocking software in schools damages educational opportunities for students, both by blocking access to Web pages that are directly related to the state-mandated curriculums and by restricting broader inquiries of both students and teachers. In your view, should the schools block access to certain Internet websites?

In your essay, take a position on this question. You may write about either one of the two points of view given, or you may present a different point of view on this question. Use specific reasons and examples to support your position.

After reading the prompt, you must decide what side of the argument you will defend. Even if you don't have a strong opinion either way, you still must pick a side. Although it is possible to write an essay that examines both sides of the issue at length, it is difficult to do that on the ACT because of the time limit. It's much easier to pick one side and defend it.

Key Words and Phrases

When reading the prompt, underline the key words and phrases. What are some of the key words in the prompt on the previous pages?

_____

_____

Some of the key words we see in the prompt are "school libraries," "blocking software," "prevent students," "harmful to minors," "damages educational opportunities," and "Internet websites." By identifying key words before you start to write, you can focus your essay and find the most pertinent examples.

On your test booklet, jot down something like this:

          Pro   Con

Decide which side you wish to defend—there is no right or wrong answer, so just pick the side that you think will be easier to support. Next, brainstorm two or three reasons why you chose the side you did. Fill them in under the appropriate heading.

         Pro   **Con**

_____   _____

_____   _____

_____   _____

At this point, you should have something that looks like this:

✓ Pro	Con
• Internet contains many offensive/objectionable sites • Dangerous spyware and adware can harm computers • School computers should be used only for school work	_____ _____ _____ _____

Of course, your reasons or examples may differ. The actual examples that you come up with do not matter, as long as they are related to the prompt. Now that you have your examples, you're halfway done. But before you move on, you need to think of an example or two for the other side of the argument. To get a top score on the essay, you have to consider both sides of the issue. So let's brainstorm an example or two for the opposing side.

Now you should have something like this:

✓ Pro	✓ Con
• Internet contains many offensive/objectionable sites • Dangerous spyware and adware can harm computers • School computers should be used only for school work	• Restricting access is a form of censorship • Students are deprived of opportunities to learn about certain topics

If you're having trouble coming up with appropriate examples, the prompt usually contains some good ideas.

Step 2: Structure Your Essay

Good ACT essays have a clear, logical structure. Your essay must contain an introductory paragraph, body paragraphs, and a conclusion. Although what you write in each paragraph of any given type will change, the structure of each paragraph should be fairly consistent.

Let's look at an introductory paragraph first.

Introductions

Your introductory paragraph should accomplish two major things.

1. Frame the discussion   You must tell the reader exactly what the topic of the essay will be. Introduce the topic by restating or, better yet, paraphrasing the prompt.

2. State your thesis   Establish which side of the issue you are on and why. Use the lines below to write your introduction, and then compare it with the sample paragraph that follows.

_____

_____

_____

_____

_____

_____

_____

_____

Here's our sample.

> The Internet has brought many changes to our world. Computers are used in businesses, homes, and of course, schools. However, with increased use of computers comes increased dangers. A new law, the Children's Internet Protection Act, requires schools to use blocking programs to restrict students' Internet access. Although some parents, students, and teachers believe that this law is a bad one, the dangers from the Internet make it clear that schools should block student access to certain Internet sites.

Notice that this introduction accomplishes the two basic goals mentioned previously. It paraphrases the prompt—expanding on it a bit by discussing the impact of the Internet and computers on everyday life—and introduces the question of whether schools should block student access to certain sites. Then the paragraph clearly states the author's position; in this case, the author agrees that schools should block student access.

That is all that is required in an introductory paragraph. Don't try to do too much with the first paragraph. Many writers make the mistake of trying to explain why they chose a particular side, but you should save that for the body paragraphs.

Body Paragraphs, Part I: Supporting Your Position

Body paragraphs are where you will give the reasons or support for your position. A good body paragraph will contain three major things.

1. A good transition/topic sentence   Transition sentences contribute to the flow and organization of the essay. Using transitions will help the grader follow your argument. Topic sentences show the grader that you are focused on your thesis.

2. A relevant example   Each body paragraph should discuss one and only one example. Otherwise, the paragraph becomes muddled and hard to follow. If you are using only one example, however, you'll want to break it up into logical paragraphs.

3. An explanation of how the example supports your position   It's not enough simply to throw a couple of examples into your essay and expect the grader to know what to make of them. Your job as a writer is to show the grader why the examples you chose support your position. Let's try to write a body paragraph. Using the lines below and one of the examples you've chosen (or one of ours) from the Pro/Con list, write a body paragraph. Then, compare it with the sample paragraph that follows.

_____

_____

_____

_____

_____

_____

_____

Here's our sample.

One convincing reason that schools should block access to certain Internet sites is that the Internet contains many offensive or objectionable sites. For example, there are sites on the Internet that contain racist and sexist jokes and content. Other sites might display material that is inappropriate for children. Because there is no censorship, there is no telling what sites a student can visit. This sort of material has no place in a school. If students see violent or offensive sites, they might be influenced. They could insult or hurt other students. For this reason, it is a good idea for schools to block access to certain sites.

Let's examine this body paragraph. The paragraph starts with a good topic sentence. The first sentence repeats the thesis, making it easy for the reader to follow the argument. Next, the author brings in an example—the presence of objectionable sites on the Internet. The following sentences expand on the example, presenting different sites that are inappropriate for a school setting. Finally, and most important, the last sentences tell the grader why the example supports the point—objectionable sites could lead students to insult or harm other students. Also, the last sentence again mentions the thesis. This helps the essay stay focused and makes the argument more forceful.

Practice writing body paragraphs for your remaining examples. For each one, try to start with a transition or topic sentence that restates the thesis. Then, present your example. Finally, state how your example supports your position. Try to end your body paragraph by restating the thesis again.

Writing to Your Grader
We're not talking about writing personal letters here. Rather, we're referring to modifying your writing style to make it fit what the grader wants to see. You do this all the time. When you get a new English teacher, you figure out how that teacher wants you to write your essays, and you tweak your style a little to meet expectations. You should do the same thing for the ACT graders. Figure out what they want to see and write that type of essay. It will help you get a better score.

Body Paragraphs, Part II: Attacking the Other Position

To get a good score on the ACT, you'll also have to write another type of body paragraph—one that discusses the "con," or opposite, side of the argument. This paragraph is similar to the supporting paragraph in structure. The only difference is that you will now attack the example and state why it is not an important consideration. Take a look at our sample paragraph first, and then try to write your own body paragraphs using one of the examples from the other side of the example.

Some people believe that it is wrong for schools to restrict access to certain Internet sites. These people think that restricting access is the same thing as censorship. However, this argument is incorrect. The school is not trying to control what students think or write. It is only trying to control what sorts of things a student can or cannot do at a school computer. This is well within the rights of the school. After all, schools can impose dress codes and dictate what classes students can take. It doesn't make sense to say that a school can determine what books a student reads or what clothes he or she wears, but cannot restrict access to certain Internet sites. Thus, this argument is not convincing.

The purpose of this paragraph is to look at the opposing side of the argument and then show the grader why the opposing side is wrong. The topic sentence clearly states the opposing position, and the next sentence gives a reason that some might consider the opposing side valid. The most important part of this paragraph comes in the third sentence. You must clearly indicate to the grader that you do not agree with this side. If you don't, your essay might seem to support both sides of the issue. Next, attack the opposing side by showing that the reason stated is inadequate, insufficient, or just plain wrong.

If you're having trouble attacking the other position, try one of the three techniques below.

1. The example is true, but... State the example, and then look for ways in which it could still be true but not relevant to the argument.

Example: Although it is true that restricting Internet access is a form of censorship, this is not relevant to the argument. The issue is whether students should be allowed to view the content at school.

2. The example is true, but not as important as... In this case, acknowledge that the example is relevant, but not as important as some other factor. A good way to attack a position is to compare the con example with the pro example and then state why the pro example is a more important consideration.

Example: It may be true that restricting Internet access is a form of censorship, but there is a more important consideration in this argument. Isn't it more important to keep the students safe than to worry about censorship?

3. The example is flawed because... Try to attack the actual example.

Example: Some people believe that restricting access to the Internet is a form of censorship. But this is flawed because the school isn't dictating what a student can think or write. It is only stating that students cannot view this material at school.

Now try it on your own. Use the lines here to write a body paragraph attacking one side of the argument.

_____

_____

_____

_____

_____

_____

_____

After you've written your body paragraphs, it's time to wrap things up.

Conclusions

Conclusions have only one purpose. Without looking below, try to guess what that purpose is.

1. A conclusion should restate the thesis   If you said the conclusion should conclude the essay, give yourself a prize. The conclusion should restate the thesis and sum up the essay. Go ahead and use the lines provided to write a conclusion paragraph. Then, compare your conclusion with the sample one.

_____

_____

_____

_____

_____

_____

_____

Here's our sample.

As this essay has shown, it is important and necessary for schools to block student access to certain Internet sites. The Internet has many potential dangers for a student, from objectionable sites to harmful computer viruses and bugs. A school that doesn't restrict access to the Internet puts itself at risk for far more serious issues.

This conclusion gets the job done. The first sentence restates the thesis and the next sentence repeats some of the major arguments of the essay. The final sentence of the conclusion is a good place to get a little sentimental or philosophical. It's the last thing the grader will see, so it's a nice touch.

Putting It All Together

The trick now is to string all of these individual paragraphs into a focused and coherent essay that addresses both sides of the issue, yet still clearly supports only one perspective. At first this seems like a daunting task, but if you practice using the outline below, you'll master it in no time.

Your essay should conform to the following outline:

   I.   Introduction paragraph
       A.   Paraphrase the prompt
       B.   State your thesis
  II.   Con body paragraph
       A.   Topic sentence
       B.   Con example
 III.   Pro body paragraph
       A.   Topic sentence
       B.   Pro example
 IV.   Pro body paragraph II
       A.   Topic sentence
       B.   Pro example II
  V.   Conclusion
       A.   Restate thesis

Here's what the essay looks like in its entirety.

The Internet has brought many changes to our world. Computers are used in businesses, homes, and, of course, schools. However, with increased use of computers comes increased dangers. A new law, the Children's Internet Protection Act, requires schools to use blocking programs to restrict students' Internet access. Although some parents, students, and teachers believe that this law is a bad one, the dangers from the Internet make it clear that schools should block student access to certain Internet sites.

Some people believe that it is wrong for schools to restrict access to certain Internet sites. These people think that restricting access is the same thing as censorship. However, this argument is incorrect. The school is not try-ing to control what students think or write. It is only trying to control what sort of things a student can or cannot do at a school computer. This is well within the rights of the school. After all, schools can impose dress codes and dictate what classes students can take. It doesn't make sense to say that a school can determine what books a student reads or what clothes he or she wears, but cannot restrict access to certain Internet sites. Thus, this argument is not convincing.

One convincing reason that schools should block access to certain Internet sites is that the Internet contains many offensive or objectionable sites. For example, there are sites on the Internet that contain racist and sexist jokes and content. Other sites might display material that is inappropriate for children. Because there is no censorship, there is no telling what sites a student can visit. This sort of material has no place in a school. If students see violent or offensive sites, they might be influenced. They could insult or hurt other students. For this reason, it is a good idea for schools to block access to certain sites.

Another good reason to restrict student access to the Internet is the presence of dangerous computer viruses, spyware, and other harmful computer programs. These programs can infect a computer via the Internet and affect the hardware of the system and all the computers that are attached to it. A student who visits certain restricted sites puts the entire computer network at risk. One infected computer can wipe out or ruin all the other computers in the school. Thus, it would be a very wise move for schools to restrict access to certain dangerous Internet sites.

As this essay has shown, it is important and necessary for schools to block student access to certain Internet sites. Although some people think restricting sites is censorship, the Internet has many potential dangers for a student, from objectionable sites to harmful computer viruses and bugs. A school that doesn't restrict access to the Internet puts itself at risk for far more serious issues.

Now it's your turn. Using the following prompt, write an essay. Don't time yourself; just focus on structuring your essay according to the guidelines.

In recent years, many schools have adopted a "Great Books"–based curriculum. These schools require students to study certain designated classic books of Western civilization, arguing that familiarity with these "Great Books" is essential to education. However, opponents of this curriculum argue that forcing teachers and students to use only the "Great Books," most of which are written by white, European authors, results in a biased view on the world. In your opinion, should schools adopt a "Great Books"–based curriculum?

In an essay, take a position on this question. You may write on either one of the views presented, or on a different point of view relevant to the question. Use examples and reasons to support your position.

_____

_____

_____

_____

_____

_____

_____

_____

_____

_____

_____

Step 3: Proofread

After you finish your essay, spend one or two minutes proofreading your essay if you have time. You don't have to catch every single grammatical and spelling mistake, but try to make sure there are no glaring errors. You can also edit as you go, but a quick review at the very end never hurts.

If you do find an error, erase it completely or cross it out with a single line and then neatly write the correction above it. Although you won't be graded on neatness, it is important. A neatly written essay makes for a happy grader, and a happy grader is a good thing.

OTHER THINGS TO KEEP IN MIND

Here are some other factors to consider when writing your essay. These factors are not nearly as crucial as the ones discussed earlier, but they can help boost your essay grade.

1. Length   ACT graders tend to reward longer essays. Try to write at least five paragraphs spanning one and a half to two pages. If your writing tends to be small, you may want to practice writing larger, especially because it will also make your essay a bit neater and easier to read. If your handwriting is large, make sure you write an extra page to compensate.

2. Sentence structure   Varying your sentence structure helps to improve the rhythm of your essay. If you write a really long sentence with lots of modifiers and dependent clauses, it sometimes helps to follow it with a shorter, more direct sentence. It really works. Don't try to be too fancy, though. The longer the sentence is, the more opportunity there is to confuse the reader or to make a grammatical mistake.

3. Diction   Diction refers to word choice. You certainly want to sprinkle some nice vocabulary words throughout your paper. But make sure to use and spell them correctly. If you're uncertain about the meaning or spelling of a word, it's best just to pick a different word. Using a big word incorrectly makes a worse impression than using a smaller word correctly.

4. Neatness   Make sure you indent each new paragraph. Align your essay using the lines on the paper. Don't go over the lines or write down the side of the page. Avoid messy cross-outs. Although the grader should not take these kinds of things into consideration when determining your grade, a neat, legible essay will be easier to read. Your grader will read hundreds, if not thousands of essays. A neat essay will make the grader happier.

PRACTICE ESSAY PROMPTS

Here are four sample essay prompts on which to practice. After you finish each essay, read it over—or better yet, have someone else read it—and use the Essay Checklist on page 390 to see how well your essay conforms to the ACT's grading standards. When you practice writing essays, it's best to limit your time to 30 minutes to experience how short the alloted time really is.

Practice Prompt #1

New laws are being proposed that would require schools to accommodate students who wish to transfer to a different school if the school falls below a certain level on statewide standardized tests. Supporters of this law believe that it is a student's right to transfer to a new school if his or her current school is not fulfilling its duties. Opponents argue that this law is impractical—what would happen if all the students requested transfers?—and unfairly weights test scores without considering other factors at a school. In your opinion, should students be allowed to transfer if schools score below a certain level on standardized tests?

In an essay, take a position on this question. You may write on either one of the views presented or on a different point of view relevant to the question. Use examples and reasons to support your position.

Practice Prompt #2

Colleges reward professors, who have significant research and teaching experience, with tenure. Once tenured, a professor holds his or her job without review and with little danger of being fired or replaced. Some people believe that high school teachers should be tenured as a reward for dedicated service. These people argue that tenure will attract highly qualified candidates to the profession and also allow teachers to do their jobs without fear of losing them. Opponents of this plan believe that tenure only leads to poor teaching. Without any fear of losing their jobs, teachers will not care as much about their students. In your opinion, should high school teachers receive tenure?

In an essay, take a position on this question. You may write on either one of the views presented, or on a different point of view relevant to the question. Use examples and reasons to support your position.

Practice Prompt #3

Many communities are considering adopting curfews for high school students. Some educators and parents favor curfews because they believe it will encourage students to focus more on their homework and make them more responsible. Others feel curfews are up to families, not the community, and that students today need freedom to work and participate in social activities in order to mature properly. Do you think that communities should impose curfews on high school students?

In an essay, take a position on this question. You may write on either one of the views presented or on a different point of view relevant to the question. Use examples and reasons to support your position.

Practice Prompt #4

In response to articles examining sensitive topics such as dating and partying, many schools are considering censoring their newspapers. Some schools believe that these topics are inappropriate for student-run papers, while others believe that, as long as what is printed is true, student papers should have the same freedoms as regular newspapers do. What is your opinion on this topic?

In an essay, take a position on this question. You may write on either one of the views presented or on a different point of view relevant to the question. Use examples and reasons to support your position.

Summary: An Essay Checklist

Now look at your essays and see if you applied the strategies presented in this chapter.

o The Introduction
   Did you
   • start with a topic sentence that paraphrases or restates the prompt?
   • clearly state your position on the issue?

o Body Paragraph 1
   Did you
   • start with a transition/topic sentence that discusses the opposing side of the argument?
   • give an example of a reason that one might agree with the opposing side of the argument?
   • clearly state that the opposing side of the argument is wrong or flawed?
   • show what is wrong with the opposing side's example or position?

o Body Paragraphs 2 and 3
   Did you
   • start with a transition/topic sentence that discusses your position on the prompt?
   • give one example or reason to support your position?
   • show the grader how your example supports your position?
   • end the paragraph by restating your thesis?

o Conclusion
   Did you
   • restate your position on the issue?
   • end with a flourish?

o Overall
   Did you
   • write neatly?
   • avoid multiple spelling and grammar mistakes?
   • try to vary your sentence structure?
   • use a few impressive-sounding words?

Part VII
Drill
Answers and
Explanations

Chapter 24
Drill Answers and Explanations

Complete Drill (Chapter 6)

1. **B** Draw a vertical line in between *flowers* and *blooms*. The ideas on both sides are incomplete, which eliminates choice (C). Among the answers that remain, the comma after *blooms* is needed because the list of the houses' features is coming to a close. You need the comma before the *and* immediately after the underlined portion ends. Eliminate choice (D). *Flowers* and *blooms* make a list of two things in the gardens, but as one feature buried in a list of items separated by commas, the use of *and* instead of a comma makes the groupings clear.

2. **H** Draw a vertical line in between *inhabitants* and *the*. Both ideas are complete, so they need Stop punctuation. Only choice (H) works.

3. **C** Draw a vertical line in between *fiord* and *Where*. The idea to the right of the vertical line is incomplete, which eliminates all Stop punctuation. Only choice (C) works.

4. **G** The entire sentence is incomplete. Delete the conjunction *since* to fix. In choice (J) the extra commas are unnecessary.

5. **B** Draw a vertical line after "time" and after "and," since comma + FANBOYS is stop punctuation. The idea before the line is complete, but the idea after the line is incomplete. Eliminate choices (A), (C), and (D).

6. **G** With the presence of the semicolon in choice (J), you could use the vertical line test, but it's better to consider the double dashes in choice (G) first. A pair of dashes sets off unnecessary info, just like a pair of commas. The information is unnecessary and choice (G) is the correct answer.

7. **C** Use a comma after an introductory idea. Both choices (C) and (D) have a comma between the incomplete and complete ideas, but you don't need a comma after "on." Eliminate choice (D).

8. **J** Commas and conjunctions are changing among the answers. Read to the end of the sentence: there are two complete ideas, separated by a comma. Change the first idea to incomplete by adding a conjunction. Only choice (J) uses a conjunction.

9. **D** Draw a vertical line. The idea to the left of the vertical line is complete, but the idea to the right is incomplete. Eliminate choices (A) and (B). The colon makes the meaning clearer than the comma.

10. **H** This is a list of three things, and each needs a comma after it, including one before the *and*. There is an extra comma in choice (G) that separates the adjective *freshwater* from its noun, *shale*.

Consistent, Clear, Concise Drill (Chapter 7)

1. **B** Always choose the object pronoun after a preposition. Choice (C) adds the verb *were*, creating an error.

2. **H** Choose the most concise choice: it makes the meaning clear.

3. D   Be consistent with the rest of the paragraph. The narrator is expressing his own thoughts.

4. G   The rest of the paragraph is written in the past tense, but the past perfect—the use of *had* with the past participle—is necessary when something happened before another event in the past.

5. D   The presence of the helping verb *would* works only with *believe* if the events are in the present or *have believed* if the events are in the past. *Of* is not a verb, and ACT is trying to trap your ear into thinking it's the same as *have*.

6. F   Choose the correct transition word to link the two ideas. The two ideas agree so only choice (F) makes sense.

7. C   Use the context to determine that the narrator is discussing his own grades.

8. H   Choose the correct form for *throw* and then choose the correct pronoun. *Myself* is correct here because the subject and object are the same. You could also eliminate choice (G) because there is no clear original for *it*.

9. B   Use POE carefully with apostrophes. The lab belongs to the professor, a singular noun, so all choices are incorrect except for choice (B).

Rhetorical Skills Drill (Chapter 8)

1. B   Cross off LEAST, and use POE. *Fame*, *stardom*, and *greatness* can all work the same way as *prominence* in the context of the sentence. *Projection* does not mean the same thing and is the correct answer.

2. J   Try out each answer choice. *Live television* is the intended meaning.

3. A   Evaluate the reasons given in the answers. The reason given in choice (A) could be true, but you have to read through the third paragraph to be able to judge. This makes this a good question to do later. In fact, the proposed clause does provide necessary context for the information given in the second and third sentences of the second paragraph.

4. G   Identify the purpose in the question. The correct choice must convey extreme skill. *Honing their craft* does just that, while all of the other choices contain no specific mention of skill.

5. D   Use POE. Sentences 2 and 3 should go back to back, with sentence 3 providing a list of the *young talents* mentioned in sentence 2. Eliminate choices (B) and (C), and compare the difference between choices (A) and (D). Sentence 1 should precede sentence 4, so choice (D) is correct.

6. F   Identify the purpose in the question. The correct choice must introduce the paragraph. Finish reading the paragraph and then return to the question. Since the topic involves problems with the live broadcast, choice (F) is the best introduction.

7.	C	To crack this type of strategy question, use POE and consider which choice correctly describes the sentence to be deleted. Choice (C) is the best description.

8.	F	Identify the purpose in the question and connect to the best reason among the answers. Choices (G), (H), and (J) offer reasons that do not support the purpose well, nor describe the content of the essay accurately.

9.	D	If you didn't see the warning at the beginning of the passage, you may have found the flow of the essay jarring. Even if you didn't, always use POE with order of paragraph questions. Look for topic and concluding sentences to make the flow of ideas consistent. The topic sentence of paragraph 2 makes a good transition after the discussion of accidents in paragraph 4.

Fundamentals Drill (Chapter 10)

1.	C	You'll need to find the prime factorization of 54, so use a factor tree. In using this tree, you'll find the prime factorization of $54 = 6 \times 9 = (2 \times 3) \times (3 \times 3) = 2 \times 3^3$. The *distinct* prime factors of 54, therefore, are 2 and 3. The product of these two numbers is 6, choice (C). If you chose (E), you may have missed the word *distinct*! Read carefully!

2.	G	Take this problem in bite-size pieces. If x is the least odd prime number, x must be 3. If y is the least positive integer multiple of 10, y must be 10. The difference between these two numbers is therefore $10 - 3 = 7$ or choice (G). If you selected choice (K), be careful, you may have thought that 20 was the first integer multiple of 10, but the first multiple of any number is that number itself!

3.	D	Remember MADSPM, and don't forget Order of Operations, or PEMDAS. Do the parentheses first, and remember, when you raise an exponent to a *power*, you *multiply* those exponents: $(x^{-1}y^{-3})^{-2}(x^4y^7)^3 = (x^2y^6)(x^{12}y^{21})$. Now, combine like terms, and remember, when you multiply numbers with exponents, you add those exponents to one another: $(x^2y^6)(x^{12}y^{21}) = x^{14}y^{27}$, choice (D).

4.	H	Although this problem involves an imaginary number, you can still use a traditional FOIL method to find the answer. You are asked to square the expression, so do so, and remember to multiply the First, Outer, Inner, and Last terms: $(i + 4)(i + 4) = i^2 + 8i + 16$. None of the answer choices look quite like this, but remember, $i^2 = -1$, so substitute this term: $i^2 + 8i + 16 = -1 + 8i + 16 = 8i + 15$, or choice (H).

5.	C	The prime numbers between 10 and 20 are as follows: 11, 13, 17, 19. You want the *least* sum of three *distinct* numbers, so the only possible answer is $11 + 13 + 17 + 41$, or choice (C). If you chose (B), you may have missed the word *distinct*.

Algebra Drill (Chapter 11)

1. **C** This might look like a traditional plug-and-chug problem, but the problem is asking for a specific value, and the answer choices are all real numbers. A great indication that you can PITA! This time, the problem is asking for the *largest*, so start with choice (E). Does the equation work if $x = 5$? $5^2 - 4(5) + 3 = 25 - 20 + 3 \neq 0$. Eliminate choice (E). Try choice (D), $4^2 - 4(4) + 3 = 16 - 16 + 3 \neq 0$. Try choice (C), $3^2 - 4(3) + 3 = 9 - 12 + 3 = 0$. It works, and because you're using PITA, you can stop once you've found a correct answer. If you selected choice (A), be careful, this is the *smallest* value of x that solves the equation!

2. **G** There are variables in the answer choices, so let's Plug In. Let's say $x = 2$ and plug this in to the equation: $\dfrac{(2)^2 + 6(2) - 27}{(2 + 9)} = \dfrac{4 + 12 - 27}{11} = \dfrac{-11}{11} = -1$, which means your target answer is -1. Try $x = 2$ in the answer choices to see which one gives this target answer. Only choice (G) works.

3. **A** This problem is very confusingly worded, so let's make sure we use PITA to keep all the work manageable. We'll start with choice (C) and work out from there, so our number is 11. "2 less than 3 times" 11 is $3(11) - 2 = 31$. "4 more than the product of 5 and 3" is $4 + (5 \times 3) = 19$. The problem tells us these numbers should be the same, and they're not here, so eliminate choice (C), and eliminate choices (D) and (E), because we know we need something smaller than 31. Try choice (B), 10. "2 less than 3 times" 10 is $3(10) - 2 = 28$, still too big. You can actually stop here, because there's only one answer choice left, but let's check it just to be on the safe side. Try choice (A), 7. "2 less than 3 times" 7 is $3(7) - 2 = 19$. Bingo! Choice (A) is the correct answer.

4. **G** There are no variables in this problem, but it deals with fractions of a "certain number," which means that this is a Hidden Plug-In. Let's plug something in for the number of books: it's usually a good idea to do some common multiple of the denominators, so let's say there are 30 books. $\dfrac{2}{5}$ of the books are distributed in the morning, which means $\dfrac{2}{5} \times 30 = 12$ books are distributed in the morning, leaving 18 books. $\dfrac{1}{3}$ of the remaining books are distributed in the afternoon, which means $\dfrac{1}{3} \times 18 = 6$ books are distributed in the afternoon, leaving 12 books. We're looking for the fraction of remaining books, so find $\dfrac{12}{30} = \dfrac{6}{15} = \dfrac{2}{5}$, choice (G).

5. **B** We need to find out what happens as b increases, and there's no easier way to do that than to try it out. Let's start with $b = 2$. If $b = 2$, $a = \dfrac{3}{2}$. We want to see what happens when b increases, so let's try $b = 3$. If $b = 3$, $a = \dfrac{3}{3} = 1$. We can see, then, even from these two numbers, that as b increases, a decreases, and we can eliminate choices (A), (D), and (E). Now, the remaining question is whether a gets closer to 1 or if it continues to get closer to 0. Try $b = 4$. If $b = 4$, $a = \dfrac{3}{4}$. It has continued decreasing past 1, so eliminate choice (C). Only (B) works.

Geometry Drill (Chapter 12)

1. **B** Although this is a geometry problem, it is asking for a specific value and giving a list of numerical answer choices as possibilities. This means you can use PITA. Start with choice (C). If $\angle A = 50$, then $\angle B = 50$, and because it is twice as large as $\angle B$, $\angle C = 100$. The sum of the three angles will then be $50 + 50 + 100 = 200$, which is too big, so you can eliminate choices (C), (D), and (E). Try choice (B). If $\angle A = 45$, then $\angle B = 45$, and because it is twice as large as $\angle B$, $\angle C = 90$. The sum of the three angles will then be $45 + 45 + 90 = 180$, which is exactly what you need, so the best answer is choice (B).

2. **F** When two parallel lines are intersected by a third line, it creates two kinds of angles: BIG angles and small angles. All the BIG angles are equal and all the small angles are equal. Because $\angle D$ is on a separate line, you don't know anything about it, so it can't possibly be correct, eliminating choices (G) and (J). The BIG angles, therefore, are A and C. The small angles are B and E. Only choice (F) matches like angles, so it is the only possible correct answer.

3. **D** Deal with the two right triangles separately. We already have the two legs of $\triangle ABC$, so use the Pythagorean theorem ($a^2 + b^2 = c^2$) to find the hypotenuse. In this case, $AB^2 + BC^2 = AC^2$, so $(20)^2 + (15)^2 = AC^2$, and $AC = 25$. Notice this is a special right triangle: it's a 3:4:5 with a multiplier of 5! Now that we have AC, we have two sides of the other right triangle and can find the third. This, too, is a special right triangle with sides 7:24:25, and since we have sides 7 and 25, the remaining side must be 24, or choice (D). If you don't spot these special right triangles, you can always use the Pythagorean theorem.

4. **G** If you have one piece of information about a circle, you find everything else you need. The area of circle A is 16π and because $A = \pi r^2$, the radius of circle A must be 4. If the radius of circle B is half that of circle A, then the radius of circle B must be 2. Then, find the circumference of circle B, with $C = 2\pi r = 2\pi(2) = 4\pi$, or choice (G).

5. **A** Separate the triangles and take this problem in bite-size pieces. You know two sides of the left triangle, so find the third with the Pythagorean theorem: $LO^2 + MO^2 = LM^2$. Substitute the values you know, $(4)^2 + MO^2 = (6)^2$, and $MO = 2\sqrt{5}$. Then, because we know MO is equal to ON, ON must also be equal to $2\sqrt{5}$. You can either use the Pythagorean theorem to find the third side, or note that this is a 45:45:90 triangle, which means its sides must be in a ratio of $x : x : x\sqrt{2}$, and the third side therefore must be $2\sqrt{5} \times \sqrt{2} = 2\sqrt{10}$, or choice (A).

Word Problems Drill (Chapter 13)

1. **C** The question is asking for a specific number and offering a list of numerical answer choices as options. Use PITA! Start with choice (C). If there are 12 boys in the class, then there must be $27 - 12 = 15$ girls. The ratio of boys to girls is therefore 12:15, which, when divided by 3, reduces to 4:5, exactly what you need! Choice (C) is the answer.

2. J Use an average pie to help Linda fix her mistake. She initially worked with only 5 items to get an average of 88. Multiply this average and this number of items to find the sum total of these five tests: $88 \times 5 = 440$. Now, add the sixth score to the total to find a new total of 522. Divide this number by the correct number of things, 6, to find an average of 87, choice (J). You're welcome, Linda.

3. E Read this problem carefully. Because both percentages are taken "of the original," add them together to find that 8% of the original amount is lost. Use the percentage translation to find how much is lost: *8% of 490 tons is how much?* In math terms, $\frac{8}{100} \times 490 = 39.2$ tons lost. The question asks for how much remains, so subtract $490 - 39.2 = 450.8$ tons, or choice (E).

4. J There's no figure in this problem, so draw one! This problem has variables in the answer choices, which is a dead giveaway that you can Plug In. Let's say $a = 2$ and $b = 3$. To find the surface area, simply find the area of all the surfaces, remember that there will be six in all. The surfaces will have areas of 4, 4, 6, 6, 6, and 6. Add them together to find $4 + 4 + 6 + 6 + 6 + 6 = 32$, your target answer. Go to the answer choices to find the one that matches this answer when $a = 2$ and $b = 3$. Choice (F) gives 36. Choice (G) gives 24. Choice (H) gives 16. Choice (J) gives 32. Choice (K) gives 26. Only choice (J) works!

5. C This problem is asking for arrangements, so start by creating the number of slots you will need:

   ____ ____ ____ ____ ____

   There is a restriction on the last in that only one letter, W, can go there, so fill this one in first:

   ____ ____ ____ ____   1

   Then, fill the rest in as normal, remembering that W is already taken, so there are only four letters left:

    4   3   2   1   1

   Now that you've got the slots filled in, go ahead and multiply the numbers to find the number of possible arrangements:

    4 × 3 × 2 × 1 × 1 = 24 possible arrangements, or choice (C).

Graphing and Coordinate Geometry Drill (Chapter 14)

1. E First, use POE to eliminate some answer choices. Since this is only a > sign, we can eliminate choices (B) and (D) right off the bat. Now, let's use Plugging In to narrow down the rest. First, let's try $x = -2$ $-3(-2) - 6 > 9$. This equation doesn't work, because 0 is NOT greater than 9, so eliminate any answer choices that include −2, leaving only choice (E).

2. G   Use the midpoint formula with the two given points. The midpoint formula is $\left(\dfrac{x_1+x_2}{2}, \dfrac{y_1+y_2}{2}\right)$, so plug the points into the equation to find $\left(\dfrac{3+(-4)}{2}, \dfrac{5+3}{2}\right)$, resulting in a midpoint of $\left(-\dfrac{1}{2}, 4\right)$, or choice (G).

3. B   In order to find the slope, put this equation into slope-intercept form, or $y = mx + b$. Combine the x-terms and subtract 6 from each side to find $12x - 6 = y$, in which the m term must be 12, or choice (B).

4. H   Plot your points on a graph and use them to draw a right triangle. The triangle will rise 4 units and run 3 units, meaning the legs of the triangle will be 3 and 4. You can then use the Pythagorean theorem to find the third side, or if you notice this is a 3:4:5 Pythagorean triple, the third side of the triangle must be 5, or choice (H).

5. C   Use the slope formula, $\dfrac{rise}{run}$ or $\dfrac{y_2 - y_1}{x_2 - x_1}$ with the given points to find that the slope is equivalent to $\dfrac{5-4}{13-6} = \dfrac{1}{7}$, or choice (C). If you selected choice (E), you may have switched the x- and y-terms!

6. J   The circle formula is $(x - h)^2 + (y - k)^2 = r^2$ where (h, k) is the center of the circle and r is its radius. Since $r^2 = 9$, the radius of the circle must be 3, eliminating choices (G), (H), and (K). Then, look at the first part of the equation, the $(x - 3)$ matches up without any manipulation with the $(x - h)$ part of the equation, so h must equal 3, eliminating choice (F). Only (J) is left, and we don't even need to solve for k!

Trigonometry Drill (Chapter 15)

1. D   Use SOHCAHTOA to find that $\tan\theta = \dfrac{opp}{adj}$. Your first impulse here may be to solve for the unknown side, but take a close look at where the θ is. Its adjacent side is 5, meaning the tangent of that angle must have a denominator of 5. Only choice (D) has it, so it's the only answer that can work. If you *do* solve for the unknown side, remember your Pythagorean triples: this is a 5:12:13 triangle, so the unknown side must be 12.

2. H $\cot\theta$ is defined as $\dfrac{1}{\tan\theta}$. Therefore, because $\tan\theta = 1$, substitute to find $\cot\theta = \dfrac{1}{\tan\theta} = \dfrac{1}{1} = 1$. Only choice (H) works!

3. C   Remember the special trig identity which states $\sin^2\theta + \cos^2\theta = 1$. Substitute this into the equation, $x + \sin^2\theta + \cos^2\theta = 4$ to find that $x + 1 = 4$ so x must be equal to 3. Choice (C) is the best answer.

Basic Approach Drill 1 (Chapter 21)

1. **B**   As you were reading the question, did you notice that choices (A) and (B) were the same except that the words "T1" and "T2" were switched? The answer choices are opposites, and one of them will probably be correct. Let's try choices (A) and (B) first. At T1, Sample 1 has a greater number of molecules in motion. The introduction clarifies that this corresponds to an increase in kinetic energy. The graph contradicts choice (A), so the answer appears to be choice (B). Now let's check the other two choices. Does an increase in temperature lead to a decrease in kinetic energy? No. The passage states that an increase in temperature leads to an increase in kinetic energy. So we can eliminate choice (C). Now let's look at choice (D). Is it true that water never undergoes a phase change? No; in fact, the text accompanying the graph says just the opposite. So we can eliminate choice (D). Also, remember to be cautious of extreme language such as "never." The correct answer is choice (B).

2. **F**   The question refers to the second paragraph, which mentions phase changes. What happens during a phase change? Two things happen: (1) Increased kinetic energy weakens the attractive intermolecular forces in the water, and (2) Some molecules escape the liquid as a gas. Now that we have reviewed this information, it's pretty easy to eliminate choices (G) and (H). Now let's look at choice (J). Did we read anything in the passage that told us about other phase changes? No. This answer is beyond the realm of the passage and can be eliminated. So the correct answer is choice (F), and again we've reached it by using POE.

3. **B**   The ACT test writers want to see if you can predict what will happen if you raise the temperature of water higher than that of Sample 2. What answer choices should you eliminate? Decide whether the correct answer should begin with a yes or a no. How do we do that? Just check the graph with the results for Samples 1 and 2. When you increase the temperature, will the sample have more or less kinetic energy? It will have more. That means we can rule out choice (D). We can eliminate choice (C) because the temperature reading of Sample 2 is lower than the third sample. Now compare choices (A) with (B) to see which one is correct. Does an increase in temperature lead to greater or fewer numbers of molecules escaping the liquid? Greater. Thus, the correct answer is choice (B).

4. **F**   The passage states that when a substance goes from the liquid to the gas phase, it will evaporate. When a substance has reached the temperature at which it undergoes the phase change, it will evaporate. That's how molecules will escape. Therefore, the answer is choice (F).

5. **C**   When you look at the figure, which line goes the highest? Which has the highest kinetic energy at any one point? Well, the curve for T1 goes higher than the curve for T2. T2 has the highest average kinetic energy, but that's not what this question asks us to find. Therefore, choices (A) and (B) can be eliminated. Choice (D) is a nonsensical answer choice. Choice (C) is the best answer.

Basic Approach Drill 2 (Chapter 21)

1. **B**   Do we see a solution of thyroxine that is 0.3 µg/ml? No. The ACT test writers want you to "guess-timate" where 0.3 µg/ml would fall on the table. This value would have to lie somewhere between 0.2 µg/ml and 0.5 µg/ml. The question requires that you make a guess within the values given. What do we call this skill? Interpolation! Now if we move across the *x*-axis to the value of 72 hours, and we move up to the range of values between 0.2 µg/ml and 0.5 µg/ml, we see that the *y*-values range from about 23 percent to 37 percent. The only one that falls in that range is choice (B)—30 percent.

2. **G**   Notice that they want to know what is true for tadpoles in general. Let's start with choice (F). This is a ridiculous answer choice. We know that all normal tadpoles undergo metamorphosis. If you're not sure, take a look at the graph. The control group in the graph represents normal tadpoles. They do have some decrease in tail width, although not a lot, in 120 hours or 5 days. (Notice that you needed to know that 5 days is the same as 120 hours.) Thus, choice (F) is incorrect. You can also rule out choice (H) because the figure clearly shows that high concentrations of thyroxine solutions lead to the greatest decrease in tail width. The passage doesn't mention anything about temperature, thus choice (J) is out. The correct answer is choice (G). We see that the control sample shows some reduction in tail size in 120 hours, so it must take longer for the process to be complete.

3. **C**   You must realize that as the tadpole develops, the tail is reabsorbed—or it shrinks. The graph compares percent decrease in tail width to hours. At 96 hours (4 days), the tadpoles showing the lowest percent decrease in tail width would be the least developed. Therefore, the answer must be choice (C), the tadpoles in 0.1 µg/ml.

4. **G**   Thyroxine affects the metamorphosis of the tadpole by influencing the process of cell determination from tadpole cells into mature adult cells. You don't have to understand this process—just realize that it occurs between tadpole and adult stages. Begin with choices (F), (G), and (H), because you need a tadpole to start the process. Using POE, the correct answer can be only choice (G).

5. **C**   Take a look at the figure provided. When do the lines start to differentiate from one another (showing different rates of tail reabsorption)? We can see that by 24 hours, the tadpoles placed in the various thyroxine solutions have each had a larger percent of their tails reabsorbed than the tadpoles in the control group. Choice (D) can be eliminated. Now look between 0 and 24 hours. At 0 hours and at 12 hours, the percent decrease in tail width is the same for all the tadpoles. Therefore, the change in metamorphosis rate must occur between 12 and 24 hours, so choice (C) is correct.

Basic Approach Drill 3 (Chapter 21)

1. **A** Finally, a question about drawing a graph! This question was easy because you only needed to look at the *x*- and *y*-axes. The atomic number of the elements was the independent variable, and the atomic radius was the dependent variable. What happens to the atomic radius as you increase the atomic number? It gets smaller. That means we can eliminate choices (C) and (D). Now we have to decide if it's a linear relationship or an exponential one. Just check the numbers. Notice that the numbers decrease by a smaller amount each time—so it's a curve, not a straight line. Thus, the correct answer is choice (A).

2. **J** You should look at relationships between electronegativity and one of the other properties of elements. Let's start with choices (G) and (J). Why? They are opposites (the switch again), so they can't both be true. If an element has a high electronegativity, is it a metal or a non-metal? It's a non-metal, so eliminate choice (G). Now we can check the other answer choices. Must an element with a high electronegativity have an even or an odd atomic number? Let's check. If you look at the two highest electronegative elements, O and F, one is even and one is odd. So choice (F) is not true. As for choice (H), we know that elements with high electronegativity pull their outer electrons (the passage defines electronegativity as a measure of that strength). Therefore, we can eliminate choice (H). The correct answer is choice (J).

3. **B** This question asks you to make a generalization about trends in the chart, with regard to the bigger picture. Let's take a moment to think about the answer choices. If we want to make generalizations about elements, would an answer that refers to specific elements be the correct one? Probably not. So we can probably eliminate choice (D). But let's look at choice (D) more closely to be sure. Is the atomic radius of F larger than that of N? No. Do all metals have high electronegativity values? No. Now notice that choices (A) and (B) state opposite trends. Use the chart to determine which is correct. As the atomic radius decreases, electronegativity increases. Thus, the correct is choice (B).

4. **G** The first part is easy. Look at the chart to tell you which has a greater electronegativity, Li or F. F, of course! So we can get rid of choice (J). Now why is the electronegativity of F greater than that of Li? We have to choose between choices (F) and (G). Can you determine which one of these is correct by using the information in the chart? No. Go back to the introduction and skim for information about electronegativity. The passage says specifically that within a row of the periodic table, the electronegativity tends to increase with increasing atomic number, due to the tighter bonding between protons and electrons. It's not the number that's important, but rather how tightly bound they are. F has a higher atomic number than Li and more electrons than Li, so, F's electrons are more tightly bound than Li's. Therefore, the best answer is choice (G).

5. **A** You must take new information given in the question and apply it to the chart given in the passage. Fortunately, this is very easy. Be careful; the question asks for increasing order of ionization energies. Because it follows the same trend as electronegativity, just find the answer that lists elements with increasing electronegativities. The answer can only be choice (A).

Fighting Scientists Drill 1 (Chapter 22)

1. C What are the beliefs of Scientist 1? His main point is that Pangaea (one continent) existed 137 million years ago. Now let's start by looking at each of the answer choices. Were the continents once part of one large land mass? Yes. We read that in the passage. What about choice (B)? Did the continents break up and drift apart? Definitely. Does the statement that the ocean basins remained fixed agree with the theory? No. If so, how would the continents drift apart? So choice (C) is inconsistent. Choice (D) is not inconsistent with the theory of Scientist 1. So the correct answer is choice (C).

2. G Scientist 2 needs to show how what Scientist 1 said fits with Scientist 2's hypothesis. It will also probably be something which disagrees with Scientist 1's argument. Choice (F) states that the techniques used to date and compare fossils are accurate. This is an argument Scientist 1 makes but that Scientist 2 doesn't mention. Cross it out. Choice (G) says that the soil and climate conditions were once the same—a nice paraphrase of what Scientist 2 says at the end of the argument. Keep choice (G) for now. Choice (H) supports Scientist 1 because extremely large ferns would have a hard time floating thousands of miles across the ocean. You can eliminate choice (J) because it doesn't support either scientist. Scientist 2 would infer that these ferns grew well in both places; choice (G) has to be right.

3. C Either scientist could use this information to support his theory if he could come up with a valid reason. Choice (A) says that Scientist 1 is supported because the finding shows tectonic activity. But we already knew about that and besides, that's a point on which the scientists agree. So eliminate choice (A). Choice (D) also gives us information that was already stated in Scientist 2's statement, so this choice is weak. Choice (B) is ridiculous because neither scientist believes that Pangaea exists today, so cross it out. At this point, choice (C) is looking pretty good. Scientist 2 could soundly reason that tectonic activity in a solid land mass demonstrates that this geological phenomenon does not lead to continental drift. The best answer is choice (C).

4. G The passage tells us about the formation of land masses, tectonic plates, and other geological evidence—namely fossils. You must be able to add this together and determine that the scientists know something about geology. So only choice (G) can be correct.

5. A You must know what each scientist supports. Let's go through the choices one by one. Statement I is supported by both scientists because both believe that tectonic activity exists and changes geological formations. (Scientist 1 thinks it's more important than does Scientist 2, but that doesn't matter here.) So Statement I is correct and we're down to choices (A) and (C). Let's keep checking. Only Scientist 2 supports Statement II and only Scientist 1 supports Statement III. Therefore, choice (A) must be the correct answer.

Fighting Scientists Drill 2 (Chapter 22)

1. **A** To do this, we must understand the argument. What's the main point of Hypothesis 2? The debater believes that the chance of RNA reproducing as the graduate student described is extremely small. Look for an answer choice that supports this argument. Choice (A) states that conditions in the atmosphere were too unstable to support the necessary gases. Does this statement support Hypothesis 2? Yes. How? Because it weakens Hypothesis 1. So choice (A) is correct. Choices (B), (C), and (D) are wrong because they support Hypothesis 1.

2. **G** What does Scientist 1 believe? That the experiment shows how the first organic compounds were made. Is choice (F) an assumption in this argument? No. It refers to Hypothesis 2. What about choice (G)? Yes. The scientist assumed that the experiment mimicked the conditions of primeval Earth. So choice (G) is correct. Choice (H) states that proteins are the building blocks of amino acids. That's wrong; as stated in Hypothesis 1, amino acids are the building blocks of proteins. So get rid of choice (H). Choice (J) is incorrect because Earth had to have hydrogen in order to form organic compounds.

3. **A** What does Hypothesis 1 say about amino acids? The passage tells us that amino acids are the building blocks of life, so let's start with the answer choices that list amino acids last. We can quickly eliminate choice (C). We can also eliminate choice (B) because the meteor theory was part of Hypothesis 2, not Hypothesis 1. And we're down to choices (A) and (D). We can also find in the passage that amino acids are the building blocks of proteins, so amino acids should be before proteins in the list. So by POE and understanding the passage, we arrive at the correct answer, choice (A).

Fighting Scientists Drill 3 (Chapter 22)

1. **C** We are looking for an answer that supports Hypothesis 2. Hypothesis 2 states that an increase in precipitation or an increase in pollution would lead to a significant drop in temperature. Choice (A) states that there is more snow in Canada this year, but we don't know if that's enough snow for glaciation. So we can eliminate it. Let's look at choice (B). If snow didn't stick to the ground, would there be an ice age? Choice (B) is silly; eliminate it. What about choice (C)? If there is a drop in temperature for every increase in the pollution rate, could that lead to glaciation? Yes. Let's look at choice (D). If the water became more polluted, would that necessarily lead to the next ice age? We're not sure. The passage states that pollution in the air, not necessarily in the water, leads to a decrease in temperature. So the correct answer is choice (C).

2. **H** For this question we're looking for an answer that could disprove Hypothesis 1. What is the main point of Hypothesis 1? The debater says that it is highly unlikely that Earth will experience another ice age. Why? Because he believes that the necessary conditions will not be met in the future. What is the best way to disprove this point? Just indicate that the conditions could change in the future

and then the chance for glaciation could increase. Which choice states that? Choice (H). Now let's look at choice (F). A fluctuation in temperature would not necessarily mean that the temperature was low enough for glaciation to occur. We therefore can eliminate this choice. Even if there was more snowfall in the Swiss Alps, we are not given an indication of how long it lasted. So you can get rid of choice (G). Now, if the temperature went up 5°C in the North Pole, it would be warmer, not colder, so choice (J) is out. So the correct answer is choice (H).

3. C   Let's start with Statement II, because it appears in the most answer choices. Based on the passage, would glaciation take place in polar regions? The passage tells us that polar regions would be one of the first locations in which glaciation would take place. Now that you can eliminate answer choices that don't include Statement II, you can eliminate choice (A). What about heavily polluted regions? Yes. The passage refers to the other possible cause of a temperature drop—pollution. We can eliminate choices (B) and (D) because they don't include Statement II. Therefore, choice (C) must be correct.

4. G   According to Hypothesis 2, there are two conditions that are critical to glaciation: temperature and precipitation. Choice (F) is incorrect because pollution doesn't cause precipitation. Choice (G) sounds good because it states that pollution leads to a major drop in temperature (it has one of the conditions). What about choice (H)? You can eliminate choice (H) because glaciation needs both low temperatures and high precipitation. Choice (J) supports Hypothesis 1, not Hypothesis 2, so we can eliminate it. The best answer is choice (G).

Part VIII
The Princeton Review ACT Practice Exam 1 and Answers and Explanations

Chapter 25
Practice Exam 1

ENGLISH TEST
45 Minutes—75 Questions

DIRECTIONS: In the five passages that follow, certain words and phrases are underlined and numbered. In the right-hand column, you will find alternatives for the underlined part. In most cases, you are to choose the one that best expresses the idea, makes the statement appropriate for standard written English, or is worded most consistently with the style and tone of the passage as a whole. If you think the original version is best, choose "NO CHANGE." In some cases, you will find in the right-hand column a question about the underlined part. You are to choose the best answer to the question.

You will also find questions about a section of the passage, or about the passage as a whole. These questions do not refer to an underlined portion of the passage, but rather are identified by a number or numbers in a box.

For each question, choose the alternative you consider best and fill in the corresponding oval on your answer document. Read each passage through once before you begin to answer the questions that accompany it. For many of the questions, you must read several sentences beyond the question to determine the answer. Be sure that you have read far enough ahead each time you choose an alternative.

PASSAGE I

I Am Iron Man

[1] The term "Iron Man" has many connotations, including references to a song, a comic book icon, even a movie. [2] Yet only one definition of the term truly lives up to its name: the Ironman Triathlon held annually in Hawaii a picturesque setting for a challenging race. [3] This grueling race demands amazing physical prowess and the ability to swim, bike, and run a marathon, all in less than 12 hours with no break. [4] Very few individuals are up to the task. [2]

1. **A.** NO CHANGE
   B. Hawaii,
   C. Hawaii, being
   D. Hawaii, it is

2. If the writer were to delete Sentence 4, the essay would primarily lose details that:
   F. emphasize how difficult the race truly is.
   G. mourn how few athletes are able to visit Hawaii in order to compete in the race.
   H. highlight that most athletes prefer the run to the swimming or biking components of the race.
   J. suggest that women are not truly competitive in the race.

Otherwise, Gordon Haller is a notable exception. Growing up in the 1950s, Haller developed an interest in many sports catgorized as endurance athletics, and welcomed their grueling physical demands. As he pursued a degree in physics he drove a

3. **A.** NO CHANGE
   B. As a result,
   C. In addition,
   D. However,

4. **F.** NO CHANGE
   G. athletics and welcomed their
   H. athletics, and welcomed there,
   J. athletics and, welcomed there

GO ON TO THE NEXT PAGE.

taxi to pay the bills, but competitive training proved his passion.
⁵
So when he heard about the race in 1978, the first year it was

held, he immediately signed up.

The race somewhat originated in an amusing way. The
⁶
members of two popular sports clubs, the Mid-Pacific Road

Runners of Honolulu, and the Waikiki Swim Club of Oahu, had
⁷
a long-standing and good-natured debate going over who made

better athletes: runners or swimmers. However, some local

bikers thought both clubs were wrong, while claiming that they,
⁸
in fact, deserved the title. Wanting to settle the dispute once and

for all, when they decided to combine three separate races
⁹

already held annually on the island into one massive test of
¹⁰
endurance. Thus, the Waikiki Roughwater Swim of 2.4 miles,

the Around-Oahu Bike race of 112 miles, and the Honolulu

Marathon of 26.2 miles were all combined to form the Ironman

Triathlon.

Haller was one of only fifteen competitors to show up that

February morning to start the race. He quickly scanned the few

pages of rules and instructions, and while reading those pages on
¹¹
the last page he discovered a sentence that would become the

race's famous slogan: "Swim 2.4 miles! Bike 112 miles! Run

26.2 miles! Brag for the rest of your life!" Haller took that to

5. A. NO CHANGE
    B. verified
    C   justified
    D. certified

6. The best placement for the underlined word would be:
    F. where it is now.
    G. before the word *in*.
    H. before the word *amusing* (changing *an* to *a*).
    J. before the word *way*.

7. A. NO CHANGE
    B. Runners, of Honolulu, and the Waikiki Swim Club
    C. Runners of Honolulu and the Waikiki Swim Club
    D. Runners, of Honolulu, and the Waikiki Swim Club,

8. F. NO CHANGE
    G. and while claiming
    H. they claimed
    J. claiming

9. A. NO CHANGE
    B. and
    C. where
    D. DELETE the underlined portion.

10. The best placement for the underlined phrase would be:
    F. where it is now.
    G. before the word *Wanting* (revising the capitalization accordingly).
    H. before the word *once*.
    J. after the word *endurance* (ending the sentence with a period).

11. A. NO CHANGE
    B. and
    C. and while perusing those pages
    D. and in those sheets of paper

GO ON TO THE NEXT PAGE.

heart, and at the end of the day, he <u>had became</u> the first Ironman

₁₂

champion in history. ⌷13

In the approximately thirty years since that very first race, the Ironman has become a tradition in Hawaii and now boasts approximately 1,500 entrants every year. <u>The competitors who</u>

₁₄
complete the race don't have to be the first across the finish line to claim success: just finishing is a victory unto intself.

12. **F.** NO CHANGE
   G. become
   H. became
   J. becamed

13. Which of the following true statements, if added here, would most effectively and specifically emphasize Haller's achievement as described in this essay?

   A. Twelve other people also finished the race that day.
   B. There were points in the race when Haller thought he couldn't possibly finish.
   C. No women raced this year, but that was soon to change.
   D. Haller's amazing physical strength had enabled him to do what no one else in the past had accomplished.

14. Which of the following alternatives to the underlined portion would be LEAST acceptable?

   F. The individuals
   G. That
   H. The athletes
   J. The people

Question 15 asks about the preceding passage as a whole.

---

15. If the writer were to delete the final paragraph of this essay, the essay would primarily lose information that:

   A. discusses the level of interest the race attracts in the present day.
   B. describes the way the current race is different from the race that Haller ran in 1978.
   C. describes how the victors respond when they cross the finish line.
   D. explains why 1,500 people would be willing to compete in such a difficult race.

GO ON TO THE NEXT PAGE.

1 ■ ■ ■ ■ ■ ■ ■ ■ ■ ■ 1

New Beginnings

[1]

As a junior in high school, I am very concerned about college. I'm trying to do everything right: <u>when I keep my</u> grades up, participate in a few extracurricular activities, prepare for standardized tests, even perform community service. I spend most days thinking about the <u>future hoping</u> that I'm on the right path, I do my best at everything I can.

[2]

[1] I'm interested in a career in <u>nursing,</u> I decided to try to secure a spot as a volunteer at the local hospital. [2] I accepted

his offer immediately, thinking to myself that here <u>lies</u> all the opportunities I could ever want! [3] It would be the best of both worlds: helping people while gaining valuable on-the-job

experience! [4] So I put on a nice <u>pair of slacks, a blouse,</u> and some comfortable shoes—don't all nurses wear comfortable shoes?—and went to visit the business office. [5] Fortunately, the hospital director was quite willing to let me help out, and he said I could start that summer as soon as I finished my finals. 21

[3]

The director gave me a brief tour of various departments as he told me about the primary focus of each, an <u>expert himself in every facet of hospital administration,</u> until we stopped right in front of the maternity ward. "This is where you're going to work," he said, ushering me through the brown double doors.

16. **F.** NO CHANGE
G. I keep
H. I am keeping
J. I have kept

17. **A.** NO CHANGE
B. future, hoping
C. future. Hoping
D. future praying

18. **F.** NO CHANGE
G. nursing, therefore,
H. nursing, so
J. nursing, but

19. **A.** NO CHANGE
B. lays
C. lay
D. lie

20. **F.** NO CHANGE
G. pair, of slacks, a blouse,
H. pair, of slacks, a blouse
J. pair of slacks a blouse

21. For the sake of the logic and coherence of this paragraph, Sentence 2 should be placed:
A. where it is now.
B. after Sentence 3.
C. after Sentence 4.
D. after Sentence 5.

22. **F.** NO CHANGE
G. expert, himself in every facet of hospital administration,
H. expert, himself, in every facet of hospital administration
J. expert himself in every facet of hospital administration

GO ON TO THE NEXT PAGE.

Practice Exam 1 | 413

Walking into the ward, my ears were immediately overwhelmed.
23
Women yelled and newborns wailed. Nurses rushed around to
23
adjust medical instruments that screamed for attention. I felt

suspicious in the center of so much action and wondered if I had
24
been too hasty in seeking out such a difficult service project.

[4]

Apparently my fear must have shown clearly on my

face as I looked around because the director said, "Don't worry.
25
You'll get used to the pace up here. You are going to help in the

nursery." With that, we walked down the busy hallway past
26
the numerous delivery rooms and into the most peaceful room
26
I've ever seen. The pastel colors provided a quiet backdrop to the
humming of machines and soft coos of sleeping infants. A

whispering nurse, the one in charge of the nursery, welcomed
27
me, thanked me for volunteering, and asked me to start folding

some baby blankets and placing it in the appropriate drawer. The
28
director gave me a questioning look, which I returned with a

quiet nod. [29] I got right to work.

23. **A.** NO CHANGE
B. my ears immediately felt overwhelmed, women
C. I was overwhelmed by the sounds. Women
D. hearing and overwhelmed. Women

24. Which choice would be most consistent with the figurative description provided elsewhere in this paragraph?
F. NO CHANGE
G. besieged
H. weak
J. defenseless

25. Which of the following alternatives to the underlined portion would be LEAST acceptable?
A. face while
B. face when
C. face at the same time that
D. face since

26. Given that all the choices are true, which one provides the most vivid description of the hospital hallway?
F. NO CHANGE
G. down a hallway filled with bright blue and pink balloons, beautiful flowers, and jubilant fathers
H. past a nurses' station and a handful of expectant fathers
J. under the yellowing ceiling of the dated hospital

27. **A.** NO CHANGE
B. nurse the one in charge of the nursery,
C. nurse the one in charge of the nursery
D. nurse, the one in charge of the nursery

28. **F.** NO CHANGE
G. place them
H. placed them
J. placing these

29. If the writer were to delete the phrase "which I returned with a quiet nod" from the preceding sentence and end the sentence with a period, the sentence would primarily lose:
A. a detail that expresses the narrator's ease while in the nursery.
B. a specific description of the narrator's anger toward the director.
C. information that indicates the narrator will quit the hospital as soon as the director leaves.
D. nothing at all, because this information had already been provided earlier in the passage.

GO ON TO THE NEXT PAGE.

Question 30 asks about the preceding passage as a whole.

30. Upon reviewing the essay and realizing that some key information has been left out, the writer composes the following sentence incorporating that information:

> Soon enough, I showed up for my first day at the hospital.

This sentence would most logically be placed before the first sentence in Paragraph:

- F. 1.
- G. 2.
- H. 3.
- J. 4.

PASSAGE III

Give a Snake a Break

Throughout much of history, snakes have had a reputation for being more deadly then they actually are. Negative associations abound: a "snake in the grass" is a seemingly innocent person intent on causing harm. 32 A "snake charmer" uses flattery to distract you from his shady intent. Nearly every reference to a snake that is popular in modern society bears this negative connotation. Despite this perception, the snake, with its ugly, slimy appearance, is one of the most unjustly maligned creatures on the planet.

31. A. NO CHANGE
    B. a reputation for being more deadly than
    C. a reputation as the most deadly than
    D. the deadliest reputation then

32. Given that all the following statements are true, which one provides the most relevant information at this point in the essay?
    F. "Snake oil" refers to fake medicine that promises impossible results.
    G. Most snakes are passive creatures that will never cause you injury.
    H. Snakes are carnivorous reptiles that can be found on every continent except Antarctica.
    J. Pet snakes have becomes increasingly common over the last decade.

33. A. NO CHANGE
    B. reference that is popular about a snake
    C. famous reference they have about a snake
    D. popular reference to a snake

34. F. NO CHANGE
    G. who's
    H. sporting it's
    J. with its'

GO ON TO THE NEXT PAGE.

Snakes are only rarely dangerous to humans. Their fangs, so

intimidating when the snakes are hissing, are designed not to

attack people but to hold small prey; small rodents, birds,

insects, etc. Only exceptionally large snakes, like pythons or

anacondas, pose a real threat. Most of the time, the typical snake

you encounter in your backyard is more afraid of you than you

are of it and will gladly avoid any contact with you.

Poisonous snakes—such as rattlesnakes, vipers, and

cobras—are most frightening to people, but they attack if they

are only provoked. While certainly venomous, these snakes pose

a threat mainly to smaller animals. Of the 5 million snake bites

that occur each year to humans around the world, only about 2.5

percent prove fatal. 38 Prompt treatment with one of the

available antivenoms do much to ensure the victim's survival.

Although you may get an infection at the wound site, you can be

effectively treated, seeing as you are still shaken from the

encounter, you will survive.

Why put up with snakes at all? Even if they don't normally

kill humans, most people still considering them a nuisance and

avoiding them like the plague. Individuals who dislike snakes for

this reason do not appreciate the great service snakes do for

humanity. The typical diet of a snake includes small rodents like

rats, mice, gophers, and prairie dogs, as well as lizards, birds,

fish, and insects. We may not like snakes, if they were

mysteriously wiped out of existence, however, we would be

virtually overrun with other vermin that would spread disease

and filth.

35.
A. NO CHANGE
B. fangs being
C. fangs, so they are
D. fangs, they are

36.
F. NO CHANGE
G. prey,
H. prey:
J. prey

37.
A. NO CHANGE
B. they will provoke and attack them.
C. they will attack humans only if provoked.
D. if provoked, they will attack them.

38. The writer is considering deleting the preceding sentence from this paragraph. If the writer made this deletion, the paragraph would primarily lose:
F. scientific proof that snakes are too dangerous to coexist with humans.
G. an example of the various locations where most fatalities take place.
H. a specific statistic to support a previous claim.
J. excessive detail that distracts the reader from the broader message of the passage.

39.
A. NO CHANGE
B. can do much
C. are able to do much
D. have much ability

40.
F. NO CHANGE
G. but because
H. and even if
J. however

41.
A. NO CHANGE
B. consider them a nuisance and avoid
C. considering them a nuisance and avoid
D. considered them a nuisance to avoid

42.
F. NO CHANGE
G. snake's if they
H. snakes, they
J. snakes; if they

GO ON TO THE NEXT PAGE.

So, next time you hear about someone putting down snakes, stand up for our legless friends. These snakes in the grass help us more than we might think.
⁴³
⁴³

43. The writer wants to provide a sentence here that will tie the conclusion of the essay to its beginning. Which choice does that best?

A. NO CHANGE
B. Snakes make excellent pets.
C. Let's reduce the incidence of snake bites around the world.
D. Wouldn't you rather see a snake in your yard than a rat?

> Questions 44 and 45 ask about the preceding passage as a whole.

44. The writer is considering deleting the last sentence of the first paragraph of the essay. If the writer were to make this deletion, the essay would primarily lose a statement that:

F. adds a bit of sarcasm to a rather humorous introduction.
G. identifies the overall point of the entire passage.
H. summarizes the list of examples previously provided by the author.
J. provides a list of animals more useful than the snake.

45. Suppose the writer's goal had been to write an essay focusing on the various ways in which humans were threatened by snakes. Would this essay fulfill that goal?

A. Yes, because the author gives specific statistical evidence that proves snake bites happen around the world.
B. Yes, because the essay focuses on many of the negative stereotypes associated with snakes.
C. No, because the essay primarily focuses on the fact that snakes are not harmful to humans.
D. No, because the essay points out that snakes feed primarily on rodents and other small animals.

PASSAGE IV

Zora Neale Hurston, Independent Woman

Zora Neale Hurston proves to be a study in contrasts: a black writer reaching a white audience, a woman struggling in a man's profession, an independent thinker living in a conformist era. Now, almost 50 years since her death, her hard work and
⁴⁶
fabulous novels still have much to teach the modern audience.

46. Which of the following alternatives to the underlined portion would be LEAST acceptable?

F. Presently,
G. Currently,
H. Instantly,
J. At the present,

She overcame the challenges she faced and demonstrated that
⁴⁷
perseverance makes anything possible.

47. Which of the following alternatives to the underlined portion would be LEAST acceptable?

A. faced, and in so doing,
B. faced and, thus,
C. faced that
D. faced, an action that

GO ON TO THE NEXT PAGE.

Hurston ascribed much of her deeply individualistic
personality to the experience of growing up in Eatonville,
48

Florida. The town was unique in that it was particularly hot in
49
the summer, but mild at other times of the year. Hurston always
49
said growing up in a community totally separate from the larger

white society allowed her a freedom that independence not
50
available to everyone in the south.

[1] Hurston began her undergraduate studies at Howard
University, but her obvious intelligence and talent soon earned
51
her a scholarship to Barnard College in New York City. [2]

Moving north in the 1920s thrust her into the midst of the
52
Harlem Renaissance, a black cultural movement that spawned

exceptional achievements in literature, books, poems, and plays,
53
art, and music. [3] Interacting with the likes of Langston
Hughes, W.E.B. DuBois, Billie Holiday, and Duke Ellington,
Hurston developed her skills as a writer and published numerous
54

short stories and poems. [55] [4] The most influential work that
came to define her career grew out of her attempt to capture the
black experience. [5] That novel, called *Their Eyes Were
Watching God*, traced three generations of a family living in

48. **F.** NO CHANGE
    G. personally individualistic
    H. freely independent
    J. truly egotistical

49. Given that all the choices are true, which one most effectively
    identifies why Eatonville has a history unlike any other city
    in the United States?
    A. NO CHANGE
    B. a fairly representative small town, founded in the mid-
    nineteenth century.
    C. the first all-black town to be incorporated in the country.
    D. not yet in existence at the start of the Civil War.

50. **F.** NO CHANGE
    G. and was
    H. it featured
    J. and

51. **A.** NO CHANGE
    B. intelligence, and talent
    C. intelligence, and talent,
    D. intelligence and talent,

52. **F.** NO CHANGE
    G. 1920s, thrust
    H. 1920s, thrust,
    J. 1920s; thrust

53. **A.** NO CHANGE
    B. literature, written records of stories once transmitted orally,
    C. literature, which includes all forms of written expression,
    D. literature,

54. **F.** NO CHANGE
    G. developed up
    H. develops up
    J. develops

55. At this point, the writer is considering adding the following
    true statement:

    Billie Holiday's music evokes such feeling and melan-
    choly that it's no wonder she became so popular.

    Should the writer add this sentence here?

    A. Yes, because it provides an interesting detail about one of
    the other Harlem Renaissance artists.
    B. Yes, because music was an important influence on Hur-
    ston's work.
    C. No, because it doesn't clearly identify which of Billie
    Holiday's songs were popular.
    D. No, because it distracts the reader from the main point of
    this paragraph.

GO ON TO THE NEXT PAGE.

Eatonville. [6] Her <u>interesting</u> representation of the southern
₅₆
dialect caused her Harlem Renaissance contemporaries to belittle

the work for what they saw as its propagation of inaccurate

stereotypes. [7] Hurston, however, remained true to <u>it,</u> convinced
₅₇
that the accuracy of her representation would ultimately prevail over

the political pressures her peers sought to inflict upon her. [58]

History has shown that Hurston was right. <u>However, modern</u>
₅₉
critics admire her authentic and skillful representation of the

language as well as her realistic portrayal of daily life in the

early twentieth century. She is universally <u>applauded, as one of</u>
₆₀
<u>the best writers of her era,</u> ranked with Toni Morrison, Maya
₆₀
Angelou, and Alice Walker as one of the most important African-

American writers of all time.

56. Which choice would most clearly indicate that the dialect referenced in the passage was a realistic representation of the actual way language was spoken in Eatonville?

   F. NO CHANGE
   G. unusual
   H. authentic
   J. fascinating

57. A. NO CHANGE
      B. her project,
      C. that thing,
      D. which,

58. The writer has decided to divide this paragraph into two. The best place to add the new paragraph break would be at the beginning of Sentence:

   F. 4, because it would indicate that Hurston's writing was most strongly influenced by Langston Hughes.
   G. 4, because it would signal the essay's shift in focus to one of Hurston's novels.
   H. 5, because all the remaining sentences in the paragraph provide a detailed summary of the plot of Hurston's novel.
   J. 5, because it would indicate that the essay is now going to focus on social conditions in Eatonville.

59. A. NO CHANGE
      B. Modern
      C. Thus, modern
      D. In addition, modern

60. F. NO CHANGE
      G. applauded as one of the best writers of her era and
      H. applauded as one of the best writers of her era
      J. applauded, as one of the best writers of her era, she is

PASSAGE V

Jimmy Carter, Humanitarian

[1]

Everyone has heard of Jimmy Carter. As president of the
United States from 1977 to <u>1981. He</u> oversaw a particularly
₆₁
turbulent time in American history. Americans taken hostage in

the Middle East, serious inflation woes, major gasoline shortages

around the country, and a tenuous relationship with a potential

61. A. NO CHANGE
      B. 1981 but he
      C. 1981, and he
      D. 1981, he

GO ON TO THE NEXT PAGE.

enemy—the Soviet Union—are hardly the stuff of pleasant
62
memories.

[2]

Yet even though Carter held Americas most, powerful office,
63

he will probably be remembered more for the work he has done
64
since he left the White House. His record on humanitarian issues

around the world sets him apart as a caring, dedicated person

who wants to see the underprivileged, those of low economic
65
or social status, benefit from the great wealth, power, and
65
generosity of this country.

[3]

One of the major issues Carter has focused on throughout his

career is peace in the Middle East. He questioned a national
66
energy policy designed to reduce American dependence long

before it was popular to do so on foreign oil and brokered a
67
peace treaty between Israel and Egypt. Likewise, he was among

the first to insist publicly on basic human rights for everyone

around the world, founding a non-profit organization, The Carter
68
Center, to work toward that end. In his opinion, this includes

extending modern health care to developing nations in order to

contain disease and improve quality of life around the world, in
69
many different countries.
69

62. **F.** NO CHANGE
G. enemy the Soviet Union—
H. enemy the Soviet Union
J. enemy—the Soviet Union

63. **A.** NO CHANGE
B. held America's most,
C. held America's most
D. held Americas, most

64. **F.** NO CHANGE
G. himself
H. him
J. itself

65. **A.** NO CHANGE
B. underprivileged, who may not have many resources,
C. underprivileged
D. underprivileged, who have less than others in society,

66. **F.** NO CHANGE
G. promoted
H. purchased
J. rejected

67. The best placement for the underlined portion would be:
A. where it is now.
B. after the word *designed.*
C. after the word *dependence.*
D. after the word *was.*

68. Which of the following alternatives to the underlined portion would NOT be acceptable?
F. world, and he found
G. world, and he founded
H. world, so he founded
J. world and founded

69. **A.** NO CHANGE
B. world.
C. world, both east and west of the United States.
D. world, including countries on every continent except Antarctica.

GO ON TO THE NEXT PAGE.

[4]

[1] Carter works actively to improve the standard of living at home here in the United States as well. [2] He and his wife Roslyn are enthusiastic supporters of Habitat for Humanity. [3] This volunteer-based organization devotes itself to building affordable but quality housing for those who otherwise might not be able to buy a home. [4] However, Carter does not focus abroad all his efforts. [5] Community workers come together on their own free time to construct, paint, and landscape simple homes, working side-by-side with the families that will occupy the residences. 72

[5]

For all these reasons, Carter deserves respect for dedicating his career to public service. Everyone can agree for his impressive philanthropy and acknowledge his obvious devotion to all of humanity.

70. **F.** NO CHANGE
    G. at home, not just abroad,
    H. at home, within the area over which he was president,
    J. at home,

71. **A.** NO CHANGE
    B. focus all his efforts abroad.
    C. focus all abroad his efforts.
    D. focus all his abroad efforts.

72. For the sake of the logic and coherence of this paragraph, Sentence 4 should be placed:

    F. where it is now.
    G. before Sentence 1.
    H. after Sentence 2.
    J. after Sentence 5.

73. **A.** NO CHANGE
    B. agree to
    C. agree by
    D. agree with

74. Which choice would best help this sentence to summarize key points made in the essay?

    F. NO CHANGE
    G. he should have been president for a second term.
    H. he has the right to express his opinions as much as any other American.
    J. he clearly didn't want the hostages to be harmed.

Question 75 asks about the preceding passage as a whole.

---

75. Upon reviewing notes for this essay, the writer comes across the following true statement:

    Habitat does more than build houses: it builds communities.

    If the writer were to use this sentence, the most logical place to add it would be at the end of Paragraph:

    A. 1
    B. 2
    C. 3
    D. 4

END OF TEST 1

STOP! DO NOT TURN THE PAGE UNTIL TOLD TO DO SO.

MATHEMATICS TEST

60 Minutes—60 Questions

DIRECTIONS: Solve each problem, choose the correct answer, and then darken the corresponding oval on your answer sheet.

Do not linger over problems that take too much time. Solve as many as you can; then return to the others in the time you have left for this test.

You are permitted to use a calculator on this test. You may use your calculator for any problems you choose,

but some of the problems may best be done without using a calculator.

Note: Unless otherwise stated, all of the following should be assumed:

1. Illustrative figures are NOT necessarily drawn to scale.
2. Geometric figures lie in a plane.
3. The word *line* indicates a straight line.
4. The word *average* indicates arithmetic mean.

---

1. On a level field, a telephone pole 24 feet tall casts a shadow 6 feet long, and at the same time of day, another nearby telephone pole casts a shadow 18 feet long. How many feet tall is the second telephone pole?

    A. 6
    B. 12
    C. 24
    D. 36
    E. 72

2. The membership fees for WebFilms consist of a monthly charge of $14 and a one-time new-member fee of $16. Sherwood made a credit card payment of $100 to pay his WebFilms fees for a certain number of months, including the new-member fee. How many months of membership did Sherwood include in his credit card payment?

    F. 4
    G. 6
    H. 7
    J. 12
    K. 14

3. If $y = -6$, what is the value of $\dfrac{y^2 - 4}{y - 2}$?

    A. −8
    B. −4
    C. 4
    D. 9
    E. 28

DO YOUR FIGURING HERE.

GO ON TO THE NEXT PAGE.

4. A school offered its students an optional field trip. If 15 or fewer students went on the field trip, the charge for each student would be $11.50. If more than 15 students chose to go on the field trip, the charge for each student would be $10.25. 18 students opted to go on the tour, but each pre-paid $11.50. The students agreed to put the extra amount toward dinner on the trip. How much total money will be put toward dinner on the trip?

F. $12.50
G. $14.75
H. $21.75
J. $22.50
K. $33.00

DO YOUR FIGURING HERE.

5. A 16-piece orchestra wants to choose one of its members to speak at performances. They decide that this member CANNOT be one of the 4 soloists in the group. What is the probability that Itzhak, who is NOT a soloist, will be chosen as the speaker?

A. 0

B. $\dfrac{1}{16}$

C. $\dfrac{1}{12}$

D. $\dfrac{1}{4}$

E. $\dfrac{1}{3}$

6. What is the perimeter, in feet, of a rectangle with width 8 feet and length 17 feet?

F. 25
G. 34
H. 50
J. 136
K. 272

7. Passes to the Renaissance Faire cost $9 when purchased online and $12 when purchased in person. The group sponsoring the fair would like to make at least $4,000 from sales of passes. If 240 passes were sold online, what is the minimum number of tickets that must be sold in person in order for the group to meet its goal?

A. 153
B. 154
C. 290
D. 334
E. 445

GO ON TO THE NEXT PAGE.

8. For what value of q is the equation $\dfrac{9}{q} = \dfrac{6}{10}$ true?

F.   3
G.   5
H.   13
J.   15
K.   19

9. If $-9(y - 13) = 16$, then $y = ?$

A. $-\dfrac{133}{9}$

B. $-\dfrac{29}{9}$

C. $-\dfrac{16}{9}$

D. $-\dfrac{1}{3}$

E. $\dfrac{101}{9}$

10. In the figure below, F, G, H, and J are collinear. $\overline{FG}$, $\overline{GK}$, and $\overline{HK}$ are line segments of equivalent length, and the measure of $\angle JHK$ is 120°. What is the degree measure of $\angle GFK$?

F.   30°
G.   45°
H.   60°
J.   120°
K.   150°

11. If $f(x) = 7x^2 - 9x + 4$, then $f(-3) = ?$

A.   −32
B.   −2
C.   32
D.   40
E.   94

GO ON TO THE NEXT PAGE.

12. What is the least common multiple of 25, 16, and 40?

  F.   27
  G.   32
  H.   320
  J.   400
  K. 16,000

DO YOUR FIGURING HERE.

13. While working on a problem on his calculator, Tex had meant to multiply a number by 3, but he accidentally divided the number by 3. Which of the following calculations could Tex then do to the result on the screen in order to obtain the result he originally wanted?

  A. Multiply by 3
  B. Multiply by 9
  C. Divide by 3
  D. Divide by 9
  E. Add the original number

14. The 8-sided figure below is divided into 12 congruent isosceles right triangles. The total area of the 12 triangles is 96 square centimeters. What is the perimeter, in centimeters, of the figure?

  F.   8
  G. $20 + 4\sqrt{2}$
  H.   48
  J. $40 + 8\sqrt{2}$
  K.   56

15. In $\triangle XYZ$, $\angle Y$ is a right angle and $\angle Z$ measures less than 52°. Which of the following phrases best describes the measure of $\angle X$?

  A. Greater than 38°
  B. Equal to 38°
  C. Equal to 45°
  D. Equal to 142°
  E. Less than 38°

GO ON TO THE NEXT PAGE.

DO YOUR FIGURING HERE.

16. Among the following arithmetic operations, which could the emoticon ☺ represent given that the equation $(8 ☺ 2)^3 - (4 ☺ 1)^2 = 48$ is true?

    I. Subtraction
    II. Multiplication
    III. Division

    F. I only
    G. III only
    H. II and III only
    J. I and III only
    K. I, II, and III

17. Which of the following equations represents the linear relation shown in the standard (x,y) coordinate plane below?

    A. $y = -5x$
    B. $y = -6x$
    C. $y = -2x + 2$
    D. $y = -5x + 6$
    E. $y = -2x + 6$

18. An integer, x, is subtracted from 6. That difference is then multiplied by 3. This product is 15 more than half the original integer. Which of the following equations represents this relationship?

    F. $3(6 - x) = \dfrac{x}{2} + 15$

    G. $3(6 - x) + 15 = \dfrac{x}{2}$

    H. $3(6 - x) = 15 - \dfrac{x}{2}$

    J. $x - 6 \times 3 = \dfrac{15}{2}$

    K. $6 + 3 = \dfrac{x}{2} + 15$

GO ON TO THE NEXT PAGE.

19. The employees of two factories, X and Y, are comparing their respective production records. Factory X has already produced 18,000 units and can produce 120 units per day. Factory Y has produced only 14,500 units but can produce 155 units per day. If d represents the number of days (that is, days during which each factory is producing its maximum number of units), which of the following equations could be solved to determine the number of days until X's total production equals Y's total production?

A. $18{,}000 + 120d = 14{,}500 + 155d$
B. $18{,}000 + 155d = 14{,}500 + 120d$
C. $(18{,}000 + 120)d = (14{,}500 + 155)d$
D. $(120 + 155)d = 18{,}000 - 14{,}500$
E. $(120 + 155)d = 18{,}000 + 14{,}500$

DO YOUR FIGURING HERE.

20. A ramp used to access the side entrance to the DPC Candy Store, which is located 7 meters above the ground, covers 24 meters along the level ground from the edge of the building. How many meters long is the ramp?

F. 13
G. 14
H. 17
J. 23
K. 25

21. The expression $9(y + 3) - 2(4y - 4)$ is equivalent to:

A. $y - 1$
B. $y + 15$
C. $y + 18$
D. $y + 23$
E. $y + 35$

22. If $a + 3b = 27$ and $a - 3b = 9$, then $b = ?$

F. 3
G. 9
H. 14
J. 18
K. 36

GO ON TO THE NEXT PAGE.

23. When $(2x + 4)^2$ is written in the format $ax^2 + bx + c$, where a, b, and c are integers, what is the value of $a + b - c$?

A. −20
B.   4
C. 20
D. 32
E. 36

DO YOUR FIGURING HERE.

24. What is the area, in square meters, of the figure below?

F. 336
G. 330
H. 225
J.   82
K.   56

25. The table below gives the values of two functions, g and h, for various values of x. One of the functions expresses a relationship that can be expressed by the formula $a + bx$, where a and b are real number coefficients. What is the value of that function for $x = 0$?

x	$g(x)$	$h(x)$
−3	4	
−2	2	3
−1	1	6
0		
1	1	
2		15
3		18

A. 0
B. 0.5
C. 1
D. 2
E. 9

GO ON TO THE NEXT PAGE.

26. What is the slope of the line represented by the equation $10y - 16x = 13$?

DO YOUR FIGURING HERE.

    F. −16

    G. $\dfrac{13}{10}$

    H. $\dfrac{8}{5}$

    J. 10

    K. 16

27. What is the sum of the 2 solutions of the equation $x^2 + 5x - 24 = 0$?

    A. −24
    B. −8
    C. −5
    D. 0
    E. 5

28. Two similar triangles have perimeters in the ratio 5:6. The sides of the larger triangle measure 12 in, 7 in, and 5 in. What is the perimeter, in inches, of the smaller triangle?

    F. 18
    G. 20
    H. 22
    J. 24
    K. 32

29. In early November in Winnipeg, Manitoba, the temperatures for each of nine consecutive days were −9°C, 3°C, −7°C, 2°C, 5°C, 1°C, 0°C, −8°C, −7°C. What was the median of the temperatures for these nine days in early November?

    A. −7°C
    B. 0°C
    C. 1.5°C
    D. 3°C
    E. 5°C

GO ON TO THE NEXT PAGE.

30. When asked the price, in dollars, of his fancy calculator, Albert responded, "If you take the square root of the price, then add $\frac{3}{8}$ the price, the result is 66." What is the price, in dollars, of Albert's calculator?

F. 169
G. 144
H. 121
J. 13
K. 12

DO YOUR FIGURING HERE.

31. The kinetic energy, *KE*, of an object travelling at *v* velocity can be modeled by the equation $KE = \frac{1}{2}mv^2$, where *m* is the mass of the object. If an object is moving at a velocity of 9, and it has a kinetic energy of 120, about how great is the object's mass?

A. Between 0 and 1
B. Between 1 and 2
C. Between 2 and 3
D. 6
E. 13

32. Let *x*, *y*, and *z* be distinct positive integers. What is the fourth term of the geometric sequence below?

$$2xz, \ 2x^2yz, \ 2x^3y^2z, \ \dots$$

F. $2x^2yz$
G. $2x^4y^3z$
H. $2x^3yz^2$
J. $4x^3y^2z$
K. $4x^4y^3z^2$

GO ON TO THE NEXT PAGE.

DO YOUR FIGURING HERE.

> Use the following information to answer
> questions 33–35.

A recent survey of book critics asked 30 critics how many stars
out of a possible 5 they gave to a recent novel from a popular author. The 30 critics' responses are summarized by the histogram
below.

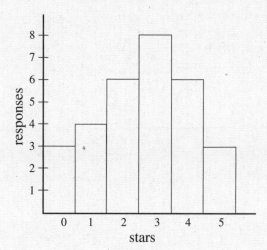

stars

33. What fraction of the critics gave the book a one-star review?

A. $\dfrac{1}{2}$

B. $\dfrac{3}{8}$

C. $\dfrac{17}{50}$

D. $\dfrac{3}{10}$

E. $\dfrac{2}{15}$

34. The group that took the survey wants to show the data in a
circle graph (pie chart). What should be the measure of the
central angle of the portion for one-star reviews?

F. 15°
G. 24°
H. 30°
J. 48°
K. 60°

GO ON TO THE NEXT PAGE.

35. To the nearest hundredth, what is the average star review for the 30 reviews?

A. 2.00
B. 2.33
C. 2.50
D. 2.63
E. 3.00

DO YOUR FIGURING HERE.

---

36. For all $x > 8$, $\frac{(x^2+7x+12)(x-2)}{(x^2+2x-8)(x+3)} = ?$

F. $\frac{-3(x-2)}{(x+3)}$

G. $\frac{-2(x-2)}{(x+3)}$

H. $\frac{(x-2)}{(x+2)}$

J. $\frac{11}{4}$

K. 1

37. A rock band, The Young Sohcahtoans, is trying to design a t-shirt logo. The measurements they have chosen are represented on the figure below. The angle to the right of the logo "TYS" has a degree measure of 35°, and the side of the figure has a measure of 10 in. Which of the following expressions gives the measure, in inches, of the diagonal top side of the figure?

A. 10 tan 35°

B. 10 cos 35°

C. 10 sin 35°

D. $\frac{10}{\sin 35°}$

E. $\frac{10}{\cos 35°}$

GO ON TO THE NEXT PAGE.

38. The endpoints of the diameter of a circle O are A and C. In the standard (x,y) coordinate plane, A is at $(4,3)$ and C is at $(-9,-2)$. What is the y-coordinate of the center of the circle?

F. -5

G. $-\dfrac{5}{2}$

H. $\dfrac{1}{2}$

J. 1

K. 2

DO YOUR FIGURING HERE.

39. On a sonar map in the standard (x,y) coordinate plane, the Yellow Submarine and the Sandwich Submarine are located at the points $(-7,4)$ and $(-2,6)$, respectively. Each unit on the map represents an actual distance of 5 nautical miles. Which of the following is closest to the distance, in nautical miles, between the two submarines?

A. 5
B. 19
C. 27
D. 30
E. 67

40. All of the following statements about rational and/or irrational numbers must be true EXCEPT:

F. the sum of any two rational numbers is rational.
G. the product of any two rational numbers is rational.
H. the sum of any two irrational numbers is irrational.
J. the product of a rational and an irrational number may be rational or irrational.
K. the product of any two irrational numbers is irrational.

41. For the imaginary number i, which of the following is a possible value of i^n if n is an integer less than 5?

A. 0
B. -1
C. -2
D. -3
E. -4

GO ON TO THE NEXT PAGE.

42. The table below gives the values of $f(x)$ for selected values of x in the function $f(x) = (x + 4)^2 - 1$, where x and y are both real numbers.

DO YOUR FIGURING HERE.

x	$f(x)$
−7	8
−5	0
−3	0
−1	8
0	15
1	24

For the equation above, which of the following values of x gives the greatest value of $f(x)$?

F. −4
G. −5
H. −6
J. −7
K. −8

43. The volume of the right circular cylinder shown below is 64π cubic inches. If its height is 4 in., what is its radius in inches?

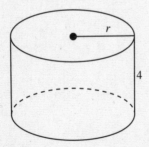

A. 2
B. 4
C. 8
D. 10
E. 16

GO ON TO THE NEXT PAGE.

44. Line segments $\overline{GH}$, $\overline{JK}$, and $\overline{LM}$ are parallel and intersect line segments $\overline{FL}$ and $\overline{FM}$ as shown in the figure below. The ratio of the perimeter of $\triangle FJK$ to the perimeter of $\triangle FLM$ is 3:5, and the ratio of $\overline{FH}$ to $\overline{FM}$ is 1:5. What is the ratio of $\overline{GJ}$ to $\overline{FG}$?

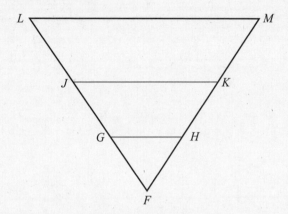

   F.   1:5
   G.   1:3
   H.   1:2
   J.   2:1
   K.   5:3

45. Avi is trying to draw a map of his most recent bike ride. He chose to place Market Street on the x-axis and Broad Street on the y-axis. He rode 60 m at an angle of 60° relative to Market Street, then rode 100 m at an angle of 45° relative to Market Street, and finally rode 35 m directly north on Broad Street. How many meters north of Market Street did Avi ride?

   A.   35
   B.   115
   C.   195
   D. $50\sqrt{2}+30\sqrt{3}$
   E. $35 + 50\sqrt{2}+30\sqrt{3}$

GO ON TO THE NEXT PAGE.

46. In the standard (x,y) coordinate plane, what is the area of the circle $(x - 3)^2 + (y + 2)^2 = 25$?

    F. 5π
    G. 10π
    H. 25π
    J. 125π
    K. 225π

47. In the standard (x,y) coordinate plane below, the base of a right triangle lies along the x-axis and is bisected by the y-axis. The vertex of the angle opposite the base is on the graph of the parabolic function $f(x) = 2x^2 - 4$. Let b represent any value of x such that $-\sqrt{2} < x < 0$. Which of the following is an expression in terms of b for the area, in square coordinate units, of any such right triangle?

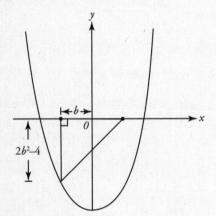

    A. $4b^4 - 16b^2 + 16$
    B. $4b^3 - 8b$
    C. $2b^3 - 4b$
    D. $2b^2 + b - 4$
    E. $b^2 - 4b + 4$

48. Which of the following expressions must be an even integer if x is an integer?

    F. $x + 5$

    G. $\dfrac{x}{4}$

    H. x^4

    J. $4x$

    K. 5^x

49. Which of the following ranges of consecutive integers contains the value of the expression $\log_9(9^{\frac{7}{3}})$?

    A. 0 and 1
    B. 1 and 2
    C. 2 and 3
    D. 5 and 6
    E. 7 and 8

GO ON TO THE NEXT PAGE.

Use the following information to answer questions 50–52.

The employees at Belinda's Paint Store are having a competition to see who can create the most new accounts over a period from January to June in a certain year. Data is missing because one of the employees began to erase it from the white board, thinking that the competition was over. The numbers in the chart below have been confirmed with the assistant manager's personal records.

	Month					
Employee	Jan.	Feb.	Mar.	Apr.	May	June
Don	64					
Maura	31	25		27	29	24
Cameron	23	19	22	17	20	22
Belinda	78	92	83	86		90

50. Which of the following is closest to the percent decrease in Cameron's new accounts from January to February?

F.   4.0%
G.   17.4%
H.   19.4%
J.   20.0%
K.   21.1%

51. At the beginning of the year, Maura wanted to average 30 new accounts per month for the first four months of the year. How many new accounts did she need to create in March in order to reach this goal?

A.   25
B.   27
C.   29
D.   31
E.   37

52. Additional records are uncovered that show that Don's sales decreased 5% each month from January to May because his responsibilities in the store mounted and he could not seek out new accounts as frequently. Which of the following is closest to the number of new accounts Don created in May?

F.   44
G.   52
H.   56
J.   72
K.   84

GO ON TO THE NEXT PAGE.

53. The amplitude of the trigonometric function shown below is defined as the average of the absolute values of the maximum value of $f(x)$ and the minimum value of $f(x)$. The trigonometric function graphed below can be described by the equation $f(x) = a \sin(bx + c)$, where a, b, and c are real numbers. Which of the following values describes the amplitude of this function?

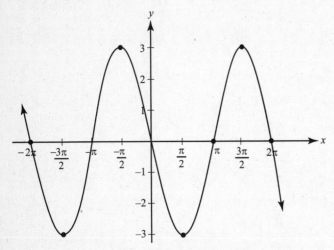

A. 1
B. 2
C. 3
D. π
E. 2π

54. A group of die-hard baseball fans has purchased a house that gives them a direct view of home plate, although their view of the rest of the field is largely impeded by the outfield wall. The house is 30 meters tall, and their angle of vision from the top of the building to home plate has a tangent of $\dfrac{7}{6}$. What is the horizontal distance, in meters, from home plate to the closest wall of the fans' house?

DO YOUR FIGURING HERE.

F. 35.0
G. 32.0
H. 25.7
J. 5.0
K. 4.3

55. Given the equation $|y^2 - 11| - 2 = 0$, which of the following is a solution but NOT a rational number?

A. $11\sqrt{13}$

B. $4\sqrt{13}$

C. $2\sqrt{13}$

D. $\sqrt{13}$

E. 3

GO ON TO THE NEXT PAGE.

56. Below is the graph that a specialty automobile manufacturer uses to plot the speed tests done on his new cars. The speed is recorded in units of $\frac{m}{s}$ and is conducted for a period of 9 seconds. A certain order of 3 of the following 6 actions describes the results of the speed test depicted in the graph below. Which order is it?

DO YOUR FIGURING HERE.

I.	Constant speed for 1 second
II.	Constant speed for 3 seconds
III.	Speed increase for 4 seconds
IV.	Speed increase for 9 seconds
V.	Speed decrease for 2 seconds
VI.	Speed decrease for 7 seconds

F. IV, II, VI
G. III, II, V
H. I, III, V
J. III, I, VI
K. V, I, II

57. As shown in the figure below, a compass has marks for every 10° and "North" and "South" are the endpoints of a line segment. If the point of the needle of this compass travels 42 mm as it moves in a clockwise direction from "East" to "North," how long is the needle to the nearest tenth of a millimeter?

A. 6.7
B. 8.9
C. 13.4
D. 14.0
E. 17.8

GO ON TO THE NEXT PAGE.

58. For θ, an angle whose measure is between 270° and 360°, $\cos\theta = \dfrac{5}{13}$. Which of the following equals $\tan\theta$?

F. $-\dfrac{5}{12}$

G. $-\dfrac{5}{13}$

H. $\dfrac{5}{13}$

J. $\dfrac{5}{12}$

K. $\dfrac{12}{13}$

59. Consider all positive integer values a and b such that the product $ab = 8$. For how many values does there exist a positive integer c that satisfies both $2^a = c$ and $c^b = 256$?

A. Infinitely many
B. 6
C. 4
D. 2
E. 0

60. A sphere is inscribed in a cube with a diagonal of $3\sqrt{3}$ ft. In feet, what is the diameter of the sphere?

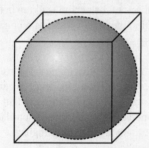

F. $3\sqrt{2}$

G. 2

H. $2\sqrt{2}$

J. 3

K. $3\sqrt{3}$

DO YOUR FIGURING HERE.

END OF TEST 2

STOP! DO NOT TURN THE PAGE UNTIL TOLD TO DO SO.

DO NOT RETURN TO A PREVIOUS TEST.

READING TEST

35 Minutes—40 Questions

DIRECTIONS: There are four passages in this test. Each passage is followed by several questions. After reading a passage, choose the best answer to each question and fill in the corresponding oval on your answer document. You may refer to the passages as often as necessary.

Passage I

PROSE FICTION: This passge is adapted from the novel A Well-Worn Jacket by Antonia Duke (© 2008 by Antonia Duke).

Monique was enjoying this afternoon more than she had anticipated. Often, the tryouts for the spring musical tested the limits of her patience and nerves, with one hopeful girl after the next taking turns strutting onto the tarnished wooden stage,
5 delivering a competent but uninspired version of some Rodgers & Hammerstein number, and then being politely excused by Mrs. Dominguez as the next name on the list was called.

However, this was to be Monique's third straight year in the musical, and the confidence that her seniority afforded her
10 around the more nervous newcomers allowed her to bask in the radiance of her own poise.

She had already sung her audition song an hour ago, commencing the day's ceremonies. This year, Monique used "God Bless the Child," a choice she found to be quite sophisticated
15 since Billie Holiday's version of it was familiar mostly to adults, and even then, mostly to adults of the previous generation. More importantly, it required a reserved performance, which Monique felt showcased her maturity, especially because most of the other auditioners chose songs that would show their enthusiasm, even
20 if it meant their technical mastery would not be on full display.

Normally, the first audition slot was dreaded by most. Mrs. Dominguez would ask if anyone wanted to volunteer to "get it over with," but no one would make a sound. Then, she would call the first name off her list and the room would drop into an
25 uncomfortably solemn silence as the first student walked nervously up to the stage. Monique often imagined during those moments that she was witness to a death-row inmate taking his inexorable march toward a quick curtain.

But not this year. Monique had decided to make a show
30 of her own self-confidence by volunteering to go first. Such a defiantly fearless act, she had figured, would probably instill even more fear into her competition because they would realize that Monique had something they clearly lacked. Mrs. Dominguez had seemed neither surprised nor charmed by Monique's
35 decision to go first. Although she was annoyed by Monique's escalating arrogance, she also acknowledged that Monique was

one of the more talented actors and was probably correct in assuming herself a shoo-in.

At this late stage of the afternoon, Monique felt like a mon-
40 arch, sitting in the back of the auditorium with her royal court of friends and admirers. They took care to sit far enough away from Mrs. Dominguez that they would not be caught in the act of belittling the other students' auditions.

To Monique, the endless parade of aspirants who sang their
45 hearts out for three minutes each were like jesters performing for her amusement. As Mrs. Dominguez read Esperanza Solito's name off her list, Monique and her entourage prepared themselves for a special treat.

Esperanza was one of the most awkward students at Thorn-
50 ton High. Her caramel-colored face was usually hidden behind thick tortoise shell glasses. Her wavy black hair exploded off her scalp like a snapshot of an atom bomb. She wore clothing that looked like it had spent years in a musty attic. Understanding her debased position on the social totem pole, Esperanza scur-
55 ried through the high school's hallways with her eyes looking narrowly at the back of the person walking in front of her, trying to disappear within the herd lest she be recognized by any malicious onlookers as easy prey.

Esperanza had been sitting alone in the front row, paying little
60 attention to the other auditions, working on geometry homework until her name was called. Shuffling her feet toward the center of the stage, Esperanza did not look up until she was there, and even then looked only at Mrs. Dominguez.

"Whenever you're ready," Mrs. Dominguez said politely,
65 sensing the potential for this audition to devolve into a painful target of ridicule.

As Esperanza began the opening notes to "The Star Spangled Banner," Monique and her friends looked at each other in total disbelief. Clearly, they thought, Esperanza had no theater
70 pedigree, or she would never stoop to singing such a trite, formulaic song. Standing perfectly still, Esperanza moved methodically through the tune with little flair or emotion. However, the

GO ON TO THE NEXT PAGE.

expectant smiles of mockery were quickly vanishing from the faces of all who listened.

75   Anticipating a tentative, mousy voice that would befit such a quirky presence as Esperanza's, the audience instead heard an unusually smooth, rich tone with full command of the multiple registers that the national anthem's melody requires. At the climactic "rocket's red glare," Esperanza's voice filled the room with
80 a calm resonance that forced one's heart to lift within one's chest as though some reluctant patriotism was determined to find its way out. The final phrase of the song, so often soaked in vibrato by melodramatic singers, was gently performed, with a touch that felt like a mother tucking in her baby to sleep.

85   Although Monique was loath to admit it and Esperanza was reluctant to want it, Esperanza had just set herself apart from the herd.

1. It can reasonably be inferred from the passage that Monique believed the song she chose for her audition:

   A. would be the most inspiring Rodgers & Hammerstein number she could choose.
   B. was the most sophisticated song in Billie Holiday's repertoire.
   C. would likely be more recognizable to Monique's parents than to her friends.
   D. would allow Monique to more effectively showcase her enthusiasm.

2. The passage initially portrays Monique and her friends as:

   F. concerned and nervous.
   G. confused and surprised.
   H. friendly and inclusive.
   J. aloof and disparaging.

3. According to the narrator, what did Esperanza do prior to singing "The Star Spangled Banner"?

   A. Looked only at Mrs. Dominguez
   B. Walked confidently up to the stage
   C. Watched the other auditions carefully
   D. Finished her geometry homework

4. The main purpose of the statement in line 29 is to:

   F. inform the reader that students' fears of going first were largely a thing of the past.
   G. present reasons for why this year's audition was the strangest yet.
   H. suggest that Monique's imagination no longer involved the same imagery.
   J. offer a contrast created by Monique's choice of audition slot.

5. It can be reasonably inferred from the passage that Esperanza Solito:

   A. was teased more than anyone else at her school.
   B. was not sitting near Monique and her friends during the auditions.
   C. had her audition immediately after Monique's audition.
   D. had previously explained her stage fright to Mrs. Dominguez.

6. According to the passage, Monique figured that volunteering to perform "God Bless the Child" as the first audition of the day would:

   F. bolster her confidence in her performance.
   G. make the other auditioners feel they could not compete with her.
   H. guarantee her a part in the play.
   J. impress and charm Mrs. Dominguez.

7. According to the passage, when Esperanza Solito got to the climax of "The Star Spangled Banner," she:

   A. raised her voice to emphasize the lines.
   B. demonstrated her patriotism.
   C. had a sudden bout of nerves.
   D. could be heard throughout the auditorium.

8. The passage states that Mrs. Dominguez suspected Esperanza's audition could be:

   F. vulnerable to ridicule.
   G. one of the most awkward.
   H. a special treat.
   J. neither surprising nor charming.

9. Which of the following details is used in the passage to describe how Monique and her friends responded to hearing Esperanza's audition?

   A. Their decision to sit comfortably behind Mrs. Dominguez
   B. Their preconceived notions about Esperanza's voice
   C. Their fading facial expressions of mockery
   D. Their fondness for patriotic songs

10. The passage most strongly suggests that Esperanza's choice of audition material was:

   F. good for a mousy voice.
   G. often partly sung with vibrato.
   H. an impressive, original choice.
   J. something Monique's friends had anticipated.

GO ON TO THE NEXT PAGE.

Passage II

SOCIAL SCIENCE: This passge is adapted from the article "Information Stupor-highway" by Cal Jergenson (© 2005 by Cal Jergenson).

Think about a remote control. Something so simple in function is seemingly capable of invisible magic to most of us. Only those with an engineering and electronics background probably have any real idea of *why* a remote control works. The rest of us
5 just assume it *should*. And the longer a given technology exists, the more we take it for granted.

Consider for a moment a split screen showing modern remote control users versus the first remote control users: the original users would be cautiously aiming the remote directly at
10 the television, reading the names of the buttons to find the right one, and deliberately pressing the button with a force that adds nothing to the effectiveness of the device. The modern users would be reclined on a sofa, pointing the remote any which way, and instinctively feeling for the button they desired, intuiting its
15 size, shape, and position on the remote.

Humans are known for being handy with tools, so it is no surprise that we get so comfortable with our technology. However, as we become increasingly comfortable with how to *use* new technologies, we become less aware of how they *work*.
20 Most people who use modern technology know nothing of its underlying science. They have spent neither mental nor financial resources on its development. And yet, rather than be humbled by its ingenuity, we consumers often become unfairly demanding of what our technology should do for us.

25 Many of the landmark inventions of the twentieth century followed predictable trajectories: initial versions of each technology (television, video games, computers, portable phones, etc.) succeeded in wowing the general public. Then, these wondrous novelties quickly became commonplace. Soon, the focus of
30 consumer attitudes toward these inventions changed from awed gratitude to discriminating preference.

Televisions needed to be bigger and have a higher resolution. Video games needed to be more realistic. Computers needed to be more powerful yet smaller in size. Cell phones needed to be
35 smaller yet capable of performing other tasks such as taking pictures, accessing the Internet, and even playing movies.

For children of the last twenty years born into this modern life, these technological marvels seem like elements of the periodic table: a given ingredient that is simply part of the universe.
40 Younger generations don't even try to conceive of life without modern conveniences. They do not appreciate the unprecedented technology that is in their possession; rather, they complain about the ways in which it fails to live up to ideal expectations.

"The videos that my phone can record are too pixelated."
45 "My digital video recorder at home doesn't allow me to program it from my computer at work." "It's taking too long for this interactive map to display on my portable GPS." "My robotic vacuum cleaner never manages to get the crumbs out of the cracks between the tiles."

50 If it sounds as though we're never satisfied, we aren't. Of course, our fussy complaints do actually motivate engineers to continually refine their products. After all, at the root of our tool-making instinct is the notion that "there must be a better way." Thus, the shortcomings of any current version of technology are
55 pinned on the limitations of its designers, and the expectation is that someone, somewhere is working on how to make the existing product even better.

The most dangerous extension of this mindset is its effect on our outlook on solving global climate problems. The firmly
60 substantiated problem of global warming threatens to quickly render the planet Earth inhospitable to most humans.

The solution? If you ask most people, you will hear that the solution resides in creating more efficient versions of our current technologies and devising alternative forms of energy
65 than those that burn fossil fuels.

Blindly confident that the creativity of human problem-solvers can wriggle us out of any dilemma, most people feel guiltless in continuing to live their lives with the assumption that someone else is working on these problems.

70 Unfortunately, having no real scientific perspective on the problems to be solved or the complexity of global weather patterns, most people are unduly optimistic about humanity's ability to think its way out of this problem. In a culture completely spoiled by the idea that technology can achieve whatever
75 goal it is tasked to perform, the idea that a global climate crisis may be beyond the reach of a clever technological solution is unthinkable.

Hence, the idea that we, as a culture, may need to reexamine our lifestyles and consumer habits is too alien to take seriously.
80 In contemporary society, the leaders who are most able to communicate the state of the world do not dare suggest to the public the unpopular ideas that "times will be rough," "sacrifices must be made," or "we may have to take some steps backwards."

As a result, the human race will continue defiantly with the
85 status quo and, ultimately, blame technology when problems arise. At that point, we'll all be searching for the "rewind" button on the remote control.

GO ON TO THE NEXT PAGE.

11. The passage states that original users of remote controls likely did all of the following EXCEPT:
    A. use more strength pressing the button than is necessary.
    B. aim the remote directly at the television.
    C. feel instinctively for the desired button.
    D. read the names of the buttons carefully.

12. In the passage, the author answers all of the following questions EXCEPT:
    F. How do most people think the global climate crisis should be solved?
    G. What was the most significant invention of the twentieth century?
    H. What idea underlies humanity's tool-making instinct?
    J. How do consumer attitudes about new technology change?

13. The descriptions offered by the author in the second paragraph (lines 7–15) are used to illustrate the concept that:
    A. consumer behavior toward new forms of technology changes over time.
    B. modern humans do not pay enough attention to instructions.
    C. the first consumers of new technology used new devices with ease and comfort.
    D. remote controls have become far more effective over the years.

14. The principal tone of the passage can best be described as:
    F. nostalgic.
    G. critical.
    H. sympathetic.
    J. frightened.

15. As it is used in line 79, the word *alien* most nearly means:
    A. extraterrestrial.
    B. repetitive.
    C. unusual.
    D. hilarious.

16. The author uses the statement "these technological marvels seem like elements of the periodic table" (lines 38–39) most nearly to mean that:
    F. children learn technology while they learn chemistry.
    G. consumers regard many technological inventions as unremarkable.
    H. space exploration gives us most of our technology.
    J. consumers complain when modern conveniences break down.

17. The phrase *the status quo* (line 85) most likely refers to:
    A. reexamining the scope and complexity of technology.
    B. making sacrifices to combat the global climate crisis.
    C. blaming technology for the problems we encounter.
    D. our current pattern of lifestyles and consumer habits.

18. One form of consumer behavior the author describes is a discriminating preference for:
    F. less realistic video games.
    G. needing to understand technology.
    H. more powerful computers.
    J. wanting to make sacrifices.

19. Among the following quotations from the passage, the one that best summarizes what the author sees as a potential danger is:
    A. "the shortcomings of any current version of technology" (line 54).
    B. "devising alternative forms of energy" (line 64).
    C. "the complexity of global weather patterns" (lines 71–72).
    D. "our outlook on solving global climate problems" (line 59).

20. The last paragraph differs from the first paragraph in that in the last paragraph the author:
    F. makes a prediction rather than making an observation.
    G. refutes a scientific theory.
    H. quotes experts to support his opinions.
    J. uses the word "we" instead of "I."

GO ON TO THE NEXT PAGE.

Passage III

HUMANITIES: The following passge is adapted from the article "Conquering Jazz" by Patrick Tyrrell (© 2006 by Patrick Tyrrell).

From the time I started playing instruments, I have been intrigued and slightly mystified by the world of jazz. I'm not talking about adventurous, atonal, confusing jazz that normal music listeners have a hard time following. I'm talking about the lively,
5 accessible, beautiful jazz that came of age in the swinging 1920s and 1930s: the simultaneously hip and regal symphonic swing of Duke Ellington and Count Basie; the carnival of contrapuntal melodies that inexplicably harmonize with each other in New Orleans' jazz; the buoyant, atmosphere-touching saxophone solos
10 of Charlie Parker and the young John Coltrane.

The one thing I had always heard about jazz but could never accept was that jazz was an improvised form of music. How could this be?

The trademark of beautiful jazz is the complexity of the
15 music. All the instrumentalists are capable of dizzying arrays of notes and rhythms. The soloists find seemingly impossible transitions from one phrase to the next that are so perfect one would think they had spent weeks trying to devise *just* the right route to conduct safe passage. To think they spontaneously craft
20 these ideas seems preposterous.

My first nervous jabs into the world of jazz came during college. I was in a rock band, but my fellow guitarist and bandmate, Victor, also played in a jazz ensemble. At our practices, I would sometimes show off a new chord I had just "invented" only to
25 have him calmly and confidently name it, "Oh, you mean C-sharp diminished?" Often, in between our band's simplistic rock songs, I would look over and see him playing chord shapes on his guitar I had never seen before. Were we playing the same instrument?

Of course, rock music, as well as most early classical mu-
30 sic, operates within a much simpler harmonic world than does jazz. There are 12 tones in Western music: A-flat, A, B-flat, B, C, D-flat, D, E-flat, E, F, G-flat, and G. There are major chords, which sound happy, and minor chords, which sound sad. Essentially, rock music requires only that you learn the major and
35 minor chord for each of the 12 tones. If you do, you can play 99 percent of all the popular radio songs from the 1950s onward.

Jazz uses the same twelve tones as do rock and classical, but it employs a much more robust variety of chords. Major sevenths, augmented fifths, flat ninths, and diminished chords all add to
40 the depth and detail of the music. These often bizarre-sounding chords toss in subtle hints of chaos and imbalance, adding a worldly imperfection to otherwise standard chord values. Jazz starts sounding better the older you get, just as candy starts tasting too sweet and a bit of bitterness makes for a more appealing flavor.

45 For the most part, Victor's elliptical personality prevented him from ever giving me straightforward explanations when I asked him to divulge the "magician's secrets" of jazz. But I did learn that jazz is only *partly* improvised. The musicians aren't inventing the structure of songs spontaneously, just the specific
50 details and embellishments. A sheet of jazz music doesn't look like a sheet of classical music. There aren't notes all over the page dictating the "ideas." There are just chord names spaced out over time, dictating the "topic of conversation."

There's a legendary book in the jazz world known as "The
55 Real Book." It's a collection of a few hundred classic songs. Open it up in any room full of jazz musicians, and they could play in synchrony for a week. For years, I wanted my own copy, but I had always been too afraid to buy it, afraid that I wouldn't know how to use the book once I had it. Then, at age 30, more
60 than a decade since Victor and I had gone our separate ways, I bought myself a copy. I resolved to learn how to play all the chords on guitar and piano. For the next few months, I quietly plucked away at these strange, new combinations. F-sharp minor-7 flat-5? Each chord was a cryptic message I had to decode and
65 then understand. It felt like being dropped off alone in a country where I didn't speak the language.

But I made progress. Chords that initially took me twenty seconds to figure out started to take only a few. My left hand was becoming comfortable in its role of supplying my right hand
70 with a steady bass line. Meanwhile, to my amazement, my right hand began to improvise melodies that sounded undeniably *jazzy*.

It seemed like the hard work of figuring out the exotic jazz chords had sent new melodic understanding straight to my hand, bypassing my brain entirely. I felt like a witness to performances
75 by detached hands; I couldn't believe that I was the one creating these sounds. I'm sure this feeling will not last, but for now I'm enjoying the rare and miraculous feeling of improvising music that I still consider beyond my abilities.

21. Which chord, if any, does the author eventually conclude is the most confusing jazz chord to play?

A. The passage does not indicate any such chord.
B. C-sharp diminished
C. Major sevenths
D. F-sharp minor-7 flat-5

GO ON TO THE NEXT PAGE.

22. As it is used in line 47, "magician's secrets" most nearly means:

   F. information on how to play jazz.
   G. forbidden bits of knowledge.
   H. instances of harmless trickery.
   J. the true nature of a private person.

23. As portrayed by the author, Victor responds to the author's *invented* chord with what is best described as:

   A. amazement.
   B. jealousy.
   C. confusion.
   D. nonchalance.

24. The author states that "The Real Book" was something he explored for a few:

   F. years.
   G. months.
   H. weeks.
   J. days.

25. The details in lines 40–44 primarily serve to suggest the:

   A. aspects of jazz's complexity that more mature listeners enjoy.
   B. lack of depth and detail found in rock and classical music.
   C. confusion and awkwardness of standard jazz chord values.
   D. unpleasantly bitter taste of candy that develops with age.

26. In the context of the passage, the author's statement in lines 68–71 most nearly means that:

   F. he was so overworked that his hands could still move, but his thoughts were turned off.
   G. he had accidentally trained his hands to resist being controlled by his brain.
   H. it was easier to decode the exotic jazz chords by pointing at them with his hands.
   J. his hand was capable of playing music that his mind was incapable of fully comprehending.

27. The author implies that F-sharp minor-7 flat-5 is an example of a chord that he:

   A. had little trouble decoding now that he had "The Real Book."
   B. had previously only seen during his travels abroad.
   C. knew how to play on guitar but not on a piano.
   D. initially found confusing and struggled to understand.

28. The passage supports which one of the following conclusions about Victor?

   F. He played music with the author until the author turned 30 years old.
   G. He gave his copy of "The Real Book" to the author as a gift.
   H. He was at one time a member of multiple musical groups.
   J. He invented a chord and named it C-sharp diminished.

29. The passage is best described as being told from the point of view of someone who is:

   A. reviewing the chain of events that led to his career in jazz.
   B. discussing reasons why jazz is less complicated than it seems.
   C. relating his impressions of jazz music and his attempts to play it.
   D. highlighting an important friendship that he had in college.

30. Assessing his early and later experiences with "The Real Book," the author most strongly implies that it was:

   F. pleasantly strange to begin with but annoyingly familiar by the end.
   G. initially difficult to decipher, but ultimately manageable following diligent practice.
   H. almost impossible to understand because its pages didn't look like sheets of classical music.
   J. very useful as a learning tool, but not useful for more profound study.

GO ON TO THE NEXT PAGE.

Passage IV

NATURAL SCIENCE: This passge is adapted from the article "Fair-Weather Warning" by Julia Mittlebury (© 2007 by Julia Mittlebury).

Could the sun be causing epidemics? Take cholera, for example, an often fatal disease caused by the bacterium *Vibrio cholerae* (*V. cholerae*). Every so often, coastal areas suffer massive outbreaks of cholera due to infected food or water. Where
5 do these outbreaks come from?

The bacterium that causes cholera is found in areas that contain the copepod, a certain type of crustacean. The copepod depends on zooplankton for nourishment, and these zooplankton in turn depend on phytoplankton for their nourishment. Phyto-
10 plankton use photosynthesis to feed on sunlight. Although one might need to go to the bottom of the food chain, the evidence shows that an increase in sunlight might mean an increase in the potential for cholera.

Interested in this correlation, Rita Calwell and her fellow
15 researchers at the University of Maryland are studying ways to use satellite measurements of sea temperatures, sea height, and chlorophyll concentrations in order to predict when conditions favoring a cholera outbreak are more likely. As sea temperatures rise, photosynthetic organisms such as phytoplankton become
20 more abundant. As sea levels rise, the phytoplankton, zooplankton, copepods, and, by extension, the cholera bacterium are all brought closer to the shore. This increases the likelihood of food and water contamination.

By monitoring the cholera food chain in reverse, Calwell and
25 her colleagues believe they can predict the emergence of cholera 4 to 6 weeks in advance. Calwell's model predicted the rate of infection during one recent cholera outbreak in Bangladesh with 95 percent accuracy. Unfortunately, because this field of study is so new and its insights are so speculative, local public health
30 officials have not yet begun to base any preventative measures on these satellite-based forecasts.

Just up the road from Calwell and the University of Maryland, Kenneth Linthicum is leading similar efforts at the NASA Goddard Space Flight Centre in Greenbelt, Maryland. He has
35 designed a model to analyze the spread of Rift Valley fever, a mosquito-spread virus that killed about 100,000 animals and 90,000 people back in December 1997.

Scientists observed that prior to the outbreak, the equatorial region of the Indian Ocean saw a half-degree increase in surface
40 temperature. Although half of a degree sounds like only a slight difference, the temperature of an ocean does not change easily. Warmer ocean water in this region corresponds with strong and prolonged rains, increased cloud cover, and warmer air over equatorial parts of Africa. These characteristics favor the pro-
45 liferation of mosquitoes and help keep them alive long enough for the virus to become easily transmittable.

In September 2007, Linthicum and his team became alerted to similar environmental changes. Over the next few months, they warned local health officials in Kenya, Somalia, and Tanzania that
50 conditions were ripe for a mosquito-based outbreak. As a result, only 300 lives were lost, an almost miraculous improvement from the devastation of the 1997 outbreak. While it is impossible to know if this outbreak would have been as far-reaching as that of 1997, it seems likely that the advance warning succeeded in
55 saving thousands, if not tens of thousands, of lives.

Similarly, a study by David Rogers at Oxford University has helped to predict outbreaks of sleeping sickness, a parasitic disease caused by West African tsetse flies. Here, Rogers first calibrated regional levels of photosynthesis to the size of a vein
60 in the wings of the flies. The vein size is a good measure of how numerous and robust the tsetse fly population is. Today, by reading the photosynthetic levels from satellite data, even researchers outside of West Africa can predict potential epidemics in the region.

65 This type of research is encouraging to many in the disease prevention field, because traditional methods involve slow, costly research. The newfound ability to cull massive amounts of meteorological data from satellites and to run that data through computer models has been much more efficient.

70 The goal of these models is to study the relationships between disease data and climate data. However, to do so requires decades', if not centuries', worth of high quality data to identify correlating factors with accuracy. Currently, the climatic data is much more reliable than the disease data. Nevertheless, excite-
75 ment about the potential usefulness of satellite-based predictions is persuading health agencies to compile and integrate their disease data more efficiently to give easier access to those trying to discover climate-disease links.

It may still take a good deal of time and energy before this
80 technology is ready for practical application. Critics claim that the number of variables underlying the spread of disease are too numerous and varied for a climate-based approach ever to be reliable. Fluctuations in the immunity of local populations, human and animal migrations, and the resistance to drugs used
85 to commonly treat certain diseases could confuse climate-based models. Advocates respond, though, that these non-climatic factors can similarly be incorporated into their research as long as the relevant data is collected, and the resulting models will have even better accuracy.

GO ON TO THE NEXT PAGE.

31. According to Calwell, scientists may be able to predict cholera outbreaks more than a month in advance by:

A. noticing increased activity in a known food chain.
B. using accurate climatic models derived from weather in Bangladesh.
C. measuring the decline of zooplankton with falling sea temperatures.
D finding connections between chlorophyll levels and diseased marine life.

32. According to the passage, levels of sunlight can influence cholera because:

F. phytoplankton feed on sunlight and contaminate the water.
G. the *V. cholerae* bacterium increases its photosynthetic rate.
H. sunlight promotes the growth of organisms upon which copepods depend.
J. many epidemics are caused by direct, prolonged exposure to sunlight.

33. According to the passage, the use of satellite data has aided the attempts of Oxford University researchers to predict outbreaks of sleeping sickness by providing information about:

A. the number of West African parasites.
B. which areas globally have the most photosynthesis.
C. the health and number of tsetse flies.
D. which flies have the biggest veins.

34. The passage states that Linthicum is conducting similar efforts to Calwell's in that Linthicum:

F. studies the climatic triggers of cholera.
G. works at the University of Maryland.
H. managed to save thousands of lives in 2007.
J. uses satellite data to build predictive models.

35. According to the passage, the use of satellite data to predict potential epidemics is encouraging because:

A. computer number-crunching is quicker and less expensive than traditional research methods.
B. it allows scientists to control the photosynthetic levels in West Africa.
C. satellites do not make the same mathematical errors that human forecasters often do.
D. there is already a large supply of long-term disease data available from satellites.

36. As it is used in line 44, the word *favor* most nearly means:

F. errand.
G. task.
H. promote.
J. request.

37. It can reasonably be inferred that the phrase *similar environmental changes* (line 48) refers to:

A. the beginning of the rainy season in Kenya.
B. the amount of bacteria circulating in the jet stream.
C. the proliferation of mosquitoes throughout central Africa.
D. warmer ocean water influencing rain and cloud cover.

38. The passage states that climatic satellite data has helped to do all of the following EXCEPT:

F. measure sea height.
G. predict tsetse fly populations.
H. forecast disease outbreaks.
J. raise the ocean temperature.

39. The phrase *confuse climate-based models* (line 85–86) refers directly to the fact that:

A. current models do not account for non-climate related factors.
B. drug resistance sometimes results in disorientation.
C. epidemics sometimes vanish more quickly than they arise.
D. researchers are not used to non-climate data.

40. It can reasonably be inferred from the passage that the information about the use of satellite-based data is presented primarily to:

F. demonstrate the various kinds of data that must be collected.
G. analyze the data's potential use in disease-prevention.
H. illustrate how few scientists do on-the-ground research.
J. show how West African tsetse fly populations have been predicted.

END OF TEST 3

STOP! DO NOT TURN THE PAGE UNTIL TOLD TO DO SO.

DO NOT RETURN TO A PREVIOUS TEST.

SCIENCE TEST

35 Minutes—40 Questions

Directions: There are seven passages in this test. Each passage is followed by several questions. After reading a passage, choose the best answer to each question and fill in the corresponding oval on your answer document. You may refer to the passages as often as necessary.

You are NOT permitted to use a calculator on this test.

Passage I

Two ways to measure the quality of soil are *bulk density* and the *soil organic matter test*, SOM (a measure of the active organic content). High quality soil provides structure to plants and moves water and nutrients, so plants grow in larger quantities, leading to higher crop yields at harvest.

Bulk density is measured as the dry weight of a sample of soil divided by the volume of the sample. A bulk density measure above 1.33 g/cm³ negatively affects soil quality. Figure 1 shows the bulk density levels for 5 different years at Fields A and B.

Table 1 shows how soil quality varies with SOM. Table 2 shows the average SOM at the end of each of the 5 years.

Table 1	
SOM	Soil quality rating
<0.25	poor
0.25 to 0.50	fair
0.51 to 0.75	good
>0.75	excellent

Table 2	
Field	Average SOM
A	0.89
B	0.28

Figure 2 shows the total crop yield at each field at the end of the 5 years.

Figure 1

Figure 2

GO ON TO THE NEXT PAGE.

1. Which set of data best supports the claim that Field A has *lower* soil quality than Field B?

   A. Figure 1
   B. Figure 2
   C. Table 1
   D. Table 2

2. If 8 tons or fewer in crop yields were considered a failed harvest, in which year and in which field would there have been a failed harvest?

   F. Field A in Year 1
   G. Field A in Year 3
   H. Field B in Year 4
   J. Field B in Year 5

3. Suppose a new crop rotation for Field B included legumes and other deep-rooted and high-residue crops. The SOM of this field will most likely change in which of the following ways? The SOM will:

   A. decrease, because soil quality is likely to increase.
   B. decrease, because soil quality is likely to decrease.
   C. increase, because soil quality is likely to increase.
   D. increase, because soil quality is likely to decrease.

4. Based on Figures 1 and 2, consider the average bulk density and the average crop yields for Fields A and B over the study period. Which site had the lower average crop yield, and which site had the higher average bulk density?

	Lower crop yield	Higher bulk density
F.	Field A	Field A
G.	Field B	Field B
H.	Field A	Field B
J.	Field B	Field A

5. As soil quality improves, the number of earthworms increases. Students hypothesized that more earthworms would be found in Field B. Are the data presented in Table 2 consistent with this hypothesis?

   A. Yes; based on SOM, Field B had a soil quality rating of fair and Field A had a soil quality rating of poor.
   B. Yes; based on SOM, Field B had a soil quality rating of excellent and Field A had a soil quality rating of fair.
   C. No; based on SOM, Field B had a soil quality rating of poor and Field A had a soil quality rating of fair.
   D. No; based on SOM, Field B had a soil quality rating of fair and Field A had a soil quality rating of excellent.

GO ON TO THE NEXT PAGE.

Passage II

Ferric oxide (Fe_2O_3) is more commonly known as rust. This is produced in a reaction between iron, a common metal, and water, H_2O.

$$2Fe + 3\,H_2O \longrightarrow Fe_2O_3 + 3H_2$$

Table 1 shows the amount of Fe_2O_3 produced over time from 15 g Fe submerged in different liquids: 100 mL distilled water, a salt solution made from dissolving 20 g of salt in 100 mL of distilled water, and a sugar solution made from dissolving 20 g of sugar in 100 mL of distilled water.

Table 1				
Solution	g Fe_2O_3 produced			
	Day 2	Day 4	Day 6	Day 8
Distilled water	0.34	0.40	0.59	0.72
Salt solution	0.56	0.81	1.23	1.84
Sugar solution	0.00	0.05	0.11	0.19

The distilled water trial was repeated four times, but for each trial, a total volume of 100 mL of water was buffered to different pH levels.

Figure 1

6. Based on Table 1, if the amount of Fe_2O_3 produced on Day 9 had been measured for the salt solution, it would most likely have been:

F. less than 0.56 g.
G. between 0.59 g and 0.72 g.
H. between 1.23 g and 1.84 g.
J. greater than 1.84 g.

7. In the experiments shown in Table 1 and Figure 1, by measuring the rate at which Fe_2O_3 was formed every day, the experimenters could also measure the rate at which:

A. H_2O was produced.
B. H_2 was produced.
C. Fe was produced.
D. FeO was produced.

8. Consider the amount of Fe_2O_3 produced by the salt solution on Day 2. Based on Table 1 and Figure 1, the water buffered to pH = 10.0 produced approximately the same amount of Fe_2O_3 on which of the following days?

F. Day 1
G. Day 3
H. Day 6
J. Day 10

9. According to Table 1, what was the amount of Fe_2O_3 produced by the sugar solution from the time the amount was measured on Day 6 until the time the amount was measured on Day 8?
A. 0.08 g
B. 0.11 g
C. 0.19 g
D. 0.30 g

GO ON TO THE NEXT PAGE.

10. Based on Table 1, which graph best shows how the amount of Fe_2O_3 produced by the sugar solution changes over time?

F.

G.

H.

J.

Passage III

Some physics students conducted experiments to study forces and springs. They used several identical springs attached to the bottom of a level platform, shown below in Figure 1.

Figure 1

The length of each spring was 0.30 m when there were no weights attached. The springs had identical spring constants. When weights were attached, the length of the springs increased as the force of the weights stretched the springs downward. The length the springs stretched was proportional to the force of the weight.

Experiment 1

The students attached different weights to two springs at once. When the springs stopped oscillating and came to a rest, the students measured their length. In Trial 1, a 10.0 N weight was attached to Spring A and Spring B, which were attached 0.25 m apart on the board. In Trial 2, a 15.0 N weight was attached to Spring A and Spring B. In Trial 3, a 20.0 N weight was attached to Spring A and Spring B. The effects of the weights on Springs A and B for the three trials are shown below in Figure 2.

Figure 2

Experiment 2

The students attached a 0.25 m board with a high friction surface to Spring B and Spring C (see Figure 3). The students then placed a 5.0 N weight at different locations along the board. Because of the high friction surface, the weights stayed in place when the board was at an angle.

Figure 3

In each of these 3 trials, a 5.0 N weight was placed at various distances along the board from the attachment with Spring B (see Figure 4). In Trial 4, the weight was placed so its center was 0.075 m along the board from the attachment with Spring B. In Trial 5, the weight was placed so its center was 0.125 m along the board from the attachment with Spring B. In Trial 6, the weight was placed so its center was 0.200 m along the board from the attachment with Spring B. The effects of the weight position on the lengths of Springs B and C for the 3 trials are also shown in Figure 4.

Figure 4

GO ON TO THE NEXT PAGE.

11. In a new study, suppose the students had placed a 10.0 N weight on Spring A only. Which of the following drawings most likely represents the results of this experiment?

A. 0.15 m

B. 0.30 m

C. 0.40 m

D. 0.50 m

12. In Experiment 2, as the distance between the 5.0 N weight and the attachment of the board to Spring B increased, the force exerted on Spring B:

F. increased only.
G. decreased only.
H. increased, then decreased.
J. decreased, then increased.

13. Which of the following statements is most likely the reason that the students used identical springs in Trials 1–3?

A. To ensure that the springs stretched similarly when a weight was attached.
B. To ensure that the springs did not share the weight evenly.
C. To compensate for the effects of oscillation on the results of the experiment.
D. To compensate for the weight of the board exerted on each of the springs.

14. Based on the results of Trials 1 and 5, the weight of the board used in Experiment 2 was:

F. 0 N.
G. 2.5 N.
H. 5.0 N.
J. 10.0 N.

15. In which of the following trials in Experiment 2, if any, was the force exerted by the weight and the board equally distributed between Springs B and C?

A. Trial 4
B. Trial 5
C. Trial 6
D. None of the trials

16. Assume that when a spring is stretched from its normal length, it stores the energy to return to its normal state as potential energy. Assume also that the greater the force of the weight stretching the spring, the more the spring will stretch. Was the potential energy stored by Spring C higher in Trial 5 or Trial 6?

F. In Trial 5, because the force of the weight on Spring C was greater in Trial 5.
G. In Trial 5, because the force of the weight on Spring C was less in Trial 5.
H. In Trial 6, because the force of the weight on Spring C was greater in Trial 6.
J. In Trial 6, because the force of the weight on Spring C was less in Trial 6.

GO ON TO THE NEXT PAGE.

Passage IV

Sodium chloride, or salt, is used to de-ice roads and sidewalks during the winter because it lowers the freezing point of water. Water with sodium chloride freezes at a lower temperature than water alone, so putting sodium chloride on icy sidewalks and roads can cause the ice to melt. Sodium chloride is highly effective as a de-icer and is given a *de-icer proof* of 100. Distilled water is ineffective as a de-icer and is given a de-icer proof of 0.

Different proportions of sodium chloride and distilled water were combined to create mixtures with de-icer proofs between 0 and 100.

Table 1		
De-icer proof	Volume of distilled water	Volume of sodium chloride
100	0 ml	50 ml
80	10 ml	40 ml
60	20 ml	30 ml
40	30 ml	20 ml
20	40 ml	10 ml
0	50 ml	0 ml

Experiment 1

A 125-g cube of ice, frozen from distilled water, was submerged in 500-mL of each de-icing mixture listed in Table 1. After 300 seconds, the portion of the cube that had not been melted was removed and weighed. The de-icing rate was calculated by determining the weight of ice melted per second. By doing this, it was possible to determine de-icer proof for a solution based on the rate at which ice was melted.

Experiment 2

The addition of magnesium chloride to a de-icer changes its de-icer proof. Different amounts of magnesium chloride were added to 500-mL samples of sodium chloride. Each de-icing mixture was tested under the same conditions as Experiment 1 and the measured de-icing rate was used to calculate the de-icer proof. The results are shown in Figure 1.

Figure 1

Experiment 3

The *temperature rating* (TR) is the minimum de-icer proof of a de-icing solution for a de-icer to have any effect on ice. 125-g cubes of ice were submerged in 500-mL samples of De-icers A and B and the samples were then placed in freezers at different temperatures. Table 2 shows the de-icer proof determined for each de-icer at each freezer temperature and the known TR for that temperature.

Table 2			
Freezer temperature	TR	Proof of:	
		De-icer A	De-icer B
−10°C	24.1	90.3	70.1
−25°C	36.9	78.9	64.9
−50°C	49.7	68.8	59.7
−75°C	52.3	56.6	51.7

17. Suppose a trial had been performed in Experiment 3 with a freezer temperature of −30°C. At this temperature, which of the following sets of proofs would most likely have been determined for De-icer A and De-icer B ?

	De-icer A	De-icer B
A.	68.8	59.7
B.	70.1	70.5
C.	75.5	61.8
D.	78.9	64.9

GO ON TO THE NEXT PAGE.

18. Based on Table 1, if 1 mL distilled water were added to 4 mL sodium chloride, the proof of this mixture would be:

   F.   4.
   G.   8.
   H.   40.
   J.   80.

19. Based on Experiment 3, as temperature decreases, the minimum proof for a de-icer to be effective:

   A.   increases only.
   B.   decreases only.
   C.   increases, then decreases.
   D.   decreases, then increases.

20. Which of the following expressions is equal to the proof for each de-icer mixture listed in Table 1?

   F. $\dfrac{\text{volume of sodium chloride}}{\text{volume of water}} \times 100$

   G. $\dfrac{\text{volume of water}}{\text{volume of sodium chloride}} \times 100$

   H. $\dfrac{\text{volume of sodium chloride}}{(\text{volume of water} + \text{volume of sodium chloride})} \cdot 100$

   J. $\dfrac{\text{volume of water}}{(\text{volume of water} + \text{volume of sodium chloride})} \cdot 100$

21. Based on Table 1 and Experiment 2, if 6 mL magnesium chloride were added to a mixture of 10 mL distilled water and 40 mL sodium chloride, the proof of the resulting de-icer would most likely be:

   A.   less than 60.
   B.   between 60 and 80.
   C.   between 80 and 112.
   D.   greater than 112.

22. Which of the 2 de-icers from Experiment 3 would be better to use to melt ice if the temperature were between −10°C and −75°C?

   F.   De-icer A, because its proof was lower than the TR at each temperature tested.
   G.   De-icer A, because its proof was higher than the TR at each temperature tested.
   H.   De-icer B, because its proof was lower than the TR at each temperature tested.
   J.   De-icer B, because its proof was higher than the TR at each temperature tested.

GO ON TO THE NEXT PAGE.

Passage V

Comets originate from regions of our solar system that are very far from the sun. The comets are formed from debris thrown from objects in the solar system: they have a nucleus of ice surrounded by dust and frozen gases. When comets are pulled into the earth's atmosphere by gravitational forces and become visible, they are called *meteors*. Meteors become visible about 50 to 85 km above the surface of Earth as air friction causes them to glow. Most meteors vaporize completely before they come within 50 km of the surface of Earth.

The Small Comet debate centers on whether dark spots and streaks seen in images of the Earth's atmosphere are due to random technological noise or a constant rain of comets composed of ice. Recently, images were taken by two instruments, UVA and VIS, which are located in a satellite orbiting in Earth's magnetosphere. UVA and VIS take pictures of the aurora borealis phenomenon, which occurs in the magnetosphere. The UVA and VIS technologies provide images of energy, which cannot be seen by the human eye.

The pictures taken by VIS and UVA both show dark spots and streaks. Scientists debate whether these spots and streaks are due to a natural incident, such as small comets entering the atmosphere, or random technological noise. The layers of Earth's atmosphere are shown in Figure 1.

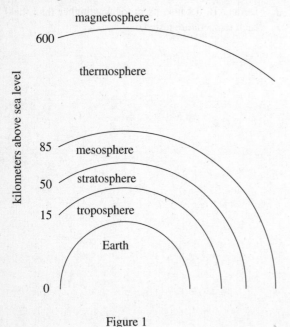

Figure 1

Two scientists debate whether there is a constant rain of comets burning up in Earth's magnetosphere.

Scientist 1

Small comets are pulled into Earth's atmosphere by gravitational effects and burn up in the magnetosphere. They are about 20 to 30 feet in diameter and burn up in the magnetosphere because they are much smaller than the comets that become meteors. Comets with larger radii will burn up in portions of the atmosphere much closer to Earth. About 30,000 small comets enter the Earth's magnetosphere every day. The dark spots and streaks on UVA and VIS images occur when the small comets begin to boil in the magnetosphere, releasing krypton and argon and creating gaseous H_2O, which interacts with hydroxyl, OH^-, radicals. Images taken by these instruments at different points in time show the same frequency of dark spots and streaks and give conclusive evidence in favor of the Small Comet theory. If the spots and streaks were due to random technological noise, then the frequency of their appearance would fluctuate.

Scientist 2

The dark spots and streaks in the UVA and VIS images are due to technological noise, not small comets. If the Small Comet Theory were true, and 20 small comets bombarded Earth's atmosphere per minute, there would be a visible bright object at least twice every five minutes. This is because, as objects enter the Earth's mesosphere, they burn up, creating large clouds of ice particles. As the ice particles vaporize, they have a brightness in the sky approximately equal to that of Venus. Because comets rarely enter Earth's atmosphere, such bright flashes are rare occurrences, far less than two times every five minutes, so the Small Comet theory cannot be correct. Further, since comets originate from regions of space beyond the orbit of the farthest planet, they contain argon and krypton. If the Small Comet theory were true and Earth were bombarded by 30,000 comets per day, there would be 500 times as much krypton in the atmosphere as there actually is.

23. According to Scientist 2, which of the following planets in our solar system is most likely the closest to the region of space where comets originate?

   A. Jupiter
   B. Venus
   C. Neptune
   D. Saturn

GO ON TO THE NEXT PAGE.

24. Based on Scientist 1's viewpoint, a comet that burns up in the thermosphere would have a diameter of:

- **F.** 5–10 ft.
- **G.** 10–20 ft.
- **H.** 20–30 ft.
- **J.** greater than 30 ft.

25. Which of the following generalizations about small comets is most consistent with Scientist 1's viewpoint?

- **A.** No small comet ever becomes a meteor.
- **B.** Some small comets become meteors.
- **C.** Small comets become meteors twice every five minutes.
- **D.** All small comets become meteors.

26. During the *Perseids*, an annual meteor shower, more than 1 object burning up in the atmosphere is visible per minute. According to the information provided, Scientist 2 would classify the Perseids as:

- **F.** typical comet frequency in the magnetosphere.
- **G.** unusual comet frequency in the magnetosphere.
- **H.** typical meteor frequency in the mesosphere.
- **J.** unusual meteor frequency in the mesosphere.

27. Given the information about Earth's atmosphere and Scientist 1's viewpoint, which of the following altitudes would most likely NOT be an altitude at which small comets burn up?

- **A.** 750 km
- **B.** 700 km
- **C.** 650 km
- **D.** 550 km

28. Suppose a study of the dark holes and streaks in the UVA and VIS images revealed krypton levels in the atmosphere 500 times greater than normal levels. How would the findings of this study most likely affect the scientists' viewpoints, if at all?

- **F.** It would strengthen Scientist 1's viewpoint only.
- **G.** It would strengthen Scientist 2's viewpoint only.
- **H.** It would weaken both Scientists' viewpoints.
- **J.** It would have no effect on either Scientist's viewpoint.

29. Scientist 1 would most likely suggest enhanced imaging technology that can take pictures of objects in the atmosphere be used to look at what region of the atmosphere to search for small comets?

- **A.** The region between 15 km above sea level and 50 km above sea level.
- **B.** The region between 50 km above sea level and 85 km above sea level.
- **C.** The region between 85 km above sea level and 600 km above sea level.
- **D.** The region between above 600 km above sea level.

GO ON TO THE NEXT PAGE.

Passage VI

A cotton fiber is composed of one very long cell with two cell walls. During a 2-week period of cell life called elongation, cotton fibers grow 3 to 6 cm. The level of hydrogen peroxide in cotton fiber cells during elongation is very high. Scientists wanted to study whether the level of hydrogen peroxide affected the length of the cotton fiber.

The amount of hydrogen peroxide is controlled by an enzyme called *superoxide dismutase* (SOD). This enzyme turns superoxide into hydrogen peroxide. Four identical lines of cotton fiber plants were created. Each line was able to express only one of three types of superoxide dismutase. The gene for SOD1 was incorporated into L1, the gene for SOD2 was incorporated into L2, and the gene for SOD3 was incorporated into L3.

Experiment

Five cotton plants of each line were grown in nutrient solution until cotton fibers completed the elongation period. The average length of cotton fibers and the average concentration of hydrogen peroxide were determined. This information is shown in Table 1.

Table 1			
	At the end of elongation period:		
Line	Average elongation period length (days)	Average amount of hydrogen peroxide (μmol/mg)	Average cotton fiber length (cm)
L1	8	2.1	3.6
L2	4	0.2	1.4
L3	20	5.6	5.9
L4	12	2.3	4.5

Next, because the scientists had determined the average elongation period, they measured the amount of hydrogen peroxide and the length of the cotton fibers halfway through their elongation period. This information is shown in Table 2.

Table 2			
	At the midpoint of elongation period:		
Line	Day of elongation period	Average amount of hydrogen peroxide (μmol/mg)	Average cotton fiber length (cm)
L1	4	4.1	2.7
L2	2	5.3	1.0
L3	10	12.4	2.0
L4	6	8.7	3.2

Finally, the scientists measured the amount of hydrogen peroxide and the length of cotton fibers on the first day of the elongation period. This information is shown in Table 3.

Table 3			
	On the first day of elongation period:		
Line	Day of elongation period	Average amount of hydrogen peroxide (μmol/mg)	Average cotton fiber length (cm)
L1	1	1.2	0.2
L2	1	6.0	0.5
L3	1	5.7	0.1
L4	1	1.9	0.2

30. For L2, as the elongation period moved from the first day to the end, the amount of hydrogen peroxide:
    F. increased only
    G. decreased only
    H. increased, then decreased
    J. decreased, then increased

31. Which of the following is a dependent variable in the experiment?
    A. The point in time during the elongation period
    B. The type of superoxide dismutase the plant could express
    C. The length of the cotton fiber
    D. The type of cotton plant

32. A cotton fiber is one very long cell with two cell walls. A cotton fiber is a special kind of what type of cell?
    F. Prokaryotic
    G. Animal
    H. Plant
    J. Bacterial

33. One plant had an average cotton fiber length of 0.5 cm, and the average amount of hydrogen peroxide in its fibers was 5.9 μmol/mg. Which of the following most likely describes this plant?
    A. It was from L1 and at the end of its elongation period.
    B. It was from L1 and at the midpoint of its elongation period.
    C. It was from L2 and at the beginning of its elongation period.
    D. It was from L2 and at the end of its elongation period.

GO ON TO THE NEXT PAGE.

34. The scientists used one of the four lines of cotton plants as a control. Which line was most likely the control?

   F. L1
   G. L2
   H. L3
   J. L4

35. Suppose the data for all the plants were plotted on a graph with the time of the elongation period on the x-axis and the average length of the cotton fiber on the y-axis. Suppose also that the best-fit line for these data was determined. Which of the following would most likely characterize the slope of this line?

   A. The line would have a positive slope.
   B. The line would have a negative slope.
   C. The line would have a slope equal to zero.
   D. The line would have no slope, because the line would be vertical.

GO ON TO THE NEXT PAGE.

Passage VII

Convection is a heat transfer process caused by moving liquid or gas currents from a hot region to a cold region. As a liquid or gas cools, it gets more dense. An example of a convection process is a cup of hot coffee: the liquid toward the top is cooled by the air, so it becomes more dense and sinks to the bottom of the cup; the hotter liquid toward the bottom of the cup is less dense, so it rises toward the top. See Figure 1, below.

Figure 1

The temperature of the liquid at the hot end of the insulated system is higher than the temperature at the cool end of the system. The difference (ΔT) between the hot liquid at the bottom and the cold liquid at the top changes depending on the starting temperature of the system. Table 1 gives ΔT for 500 mL of water in an insulated container with a height of 6.0 cm and a cross-sectional area of 4.0 cm^2 when the container is heated to different temperatures.

Table 1	
Heated temperature (°C)	ΔT (°C)
80	1
100	4
120	10
140	19

Figure 2 shows how ΔT changes with cross-sectional area for 500 mL of 100°C water in a container with a height of 6.0 cm. Figure 3 shows how ΔT changes with height for 500 mL 100°C water in a container with a cross-sectional area of 4.0 cm^2.

Figure 2

Figure 3

36. System 1 and System 2 are two convection systems. Based on Figure 2, if System 1 were the same height as System 2, but had two times the cross-sectional area and the systems were heated to the same temperature, the ratio of ΔT for System 1 to ΔT for System 2 would be:

F. 1:1
G. 1:2
H. 2:1
J. 3:1

GO ON TO THE NEXT PAGE.

37. For the systems described in the passage, if the containers were metal containers rather than insulated containers, heat would be transferred from the water to the container by which of the following heat transfer processes?

    I. Convection
   II. Conduction
  III. Radiation

A. I only
B. II only
C. I and III only
D. I and II only

38. Which of the following systems, if all were heated to the same temperature, would have the greatest ΔT ?

F.

G.

H.

J.

39. Based on the information in Table 1, if an insulated container of 500 mL of water with a height of 6.0 cm and a cross-sectional area of 4.0 cm^2 were heated to 120°C, which of the following pairs could represent the temperatures of the liquid at the top and bottom ends of the container?

	Bottom end	Top/Exposed to air end
A.	140°C	120°C
B.	140°C	110°C
C.	115°C	115°C
D.	120°C	110°C

40. The data in the passage supports the hypothesis that ΔT increases as which of the following increases?

F. Amount of insulation
G. Volume of liquid
H. Radius of the container
J. Air temperature

END OF TEST 4

STOP! DO NOT RETURN TO ANY OTHER TEST.

DIRECTIONS

This is a test of your writing skills. You will have thirty (30) minutes to write an essay. Before you begin planning and writing your essay, read the writing prompt carefully to understand exactly what you are being asked to do. Your essay will be evaluated on the evidence it provides of your ability to express judgments by taking a position on the issue in the writing prompt; to maintain a focus on the topic throughout your essay; to develop a position by using logical reasoning and by supporting your ideas; to organize ideas in a logical way; and to use language clearly and effectively according to the conventions of standard written English.

You may use the unlined pages in this test booklet to plan your essay. These pages will not be scored. *You must write your essay on the lined pages in the answer folder.* Your writing on those lined pages will be scored. You may not need all the lined pages, but to ensure you have enough room to finish, do NOT skip lines. You may write corrections or additions neatly between the lines of your essay, but do NOT write in the margins of the lined pages. *Illegible essays cannot be scored, so you must write (or print) clearly.*

If you finish before time is called, you may review your work. Lay your pencil down immediately when time is called.

DO NOT OPEN THIS BOOK UNTIL YOU ARE TOLD TO DO SO.

ACT Assessment Writing Test Prompt

Most schools have established honor codes or other rules to prevent students from cheating on exams and other school assignments. Many students admit to cheating, arguing that the practice has become so common—and is so rarely penalized—that it is the only way to survive in today's competitive academic world. Educators, however, feel that such behaviors only hurt the students, and that cheating in school is just the first step to more academic dishonesty, professional misconduct, and unethical business practices in the future. In your view, should high schools become more tolerant of cheating?

In your essay, take a position on this question. You may write about either one of the two points of view given or you may present a different point of view on this question. Use specific reasons and examples to support your position.

ACT Diagnostic Test Form

Use a No. 2 pencil only. Be sure each mark is dark and completely fills the intended oval. Completely erase any errors or stray marks.

1. YOUR NAME: _____
   (Print)　　　　　Last　　　　　　　　First　　　　　　　M.I.

SIGNATURE: _____ DATE: _____ / _____ / _____

HOME ADDRESS: _____
   (Print)　　　　　　　　　Number and Street

_____
City　　　　　　　　State　　　　　Zip

E-MAIL: _____

PHONE NO.: _____
   (Print)

SCHOOL: _____

CLASS OF: _____

IMPORTANT: Please fill in these boxes exactly as shown on the back cover of your tests book.

2. TEST FORM

_____

3. TEST CODE

⓪	⓪	⓪	⓪
①	①	①	①
②	②	②	②
③	③	③	③
④	④	④	④
⑤	⑤	⑤	⑤
⑥	⑥	⑥	⑥
⑦	⑦	⑦	⑦
⑧	⑧	⑧	⑧
⑨	⑨	⑨	⑨

4. PHONE NUMBER

⓪	⓪	⓪	⓪	⓪	⓪	⓪
①	①	①	①	①	①	①
②	②	②	②	②	②	②
③	③	③	③	③	③	③
④	④	④	④	④	④	④
⑤	⑤	⑤	⑤	⑤	⑤	⑤
⑥	⑥	⑥	⑥	⑥	⑥	⑥
⑦	⑦	⑦	⑦	⑦	⑦	⑦
⑧	⑧	⑧	⑧	⑧	⑧	⑧
⑨	⑨	⑨	⑨	⑨	⑨	⑨

5. YOUR NAME

First 4 letters of last name				FIRST INIT	MID INIT
Ⓐ	Ⓐ	Ⓐ	Ⓐ	Ⓐ	Ⓐ
Ⓑ	Ⓑ	Ⓑ	Ⓑ	Ⓑ	Ⓑ
Ⓒ	Ⓒ	Ⓒ	Ⓒ	Ⓒ	Ⓒ
Ⓓ	Ⓓ	Ⓓ	Ⓓ	Ⓓ	Ⓓ
Ⓔ	Ⓔ	Ⓔ	Ⓔ	Ⓔ	Ⓔ
Ⓕ	Ⓕ	Ⓕ	Ⓕ	Ⓕ	Ⓕ
Ⓖ	Ⓖ	Ⓖ	Ⓖ	Ⓖ	Ⓖ
Ⓗ	Ⓗ	Ⓗ	Ⓗ	Ⓗ	Ⓗ
Ⓘ	Ⓘ	Ⓘ	Ⓘ	Ⓘ	Ⓘ
Ⓙ	Ⓙ	Ⓙ	Ⓙ	Ⓙ	Ⓙ
Ⓚ	Ⓚ	Ⓚ	Ⓚ	Ⓚ	Ⓚ
Ⓛ	Ⓛ	Ⓛ	Ⓛ	Ⓛ	Ⓛ
Ⓜ	Ⓜ	Ⓜ	Ⓜ	Ⓜ	Ⓜ
Ⓝ	Ⓝ	Ⓝ	Ⓝ	Ⓝ	Ⓝ
Ⓞ	Ⓞ	Ⓞ	Ⓞ	Ⓞ	Ⓞ
Ⓟ	Ⓟ	Ⓟ	Ⓟ	Ⓟ	Ⓟ
Ⓠ	Ⓠ	Ⓠ	Ⓠ	Ⓠ	Ⓠ
Ⓡ	Ⓡ	Ⓡ	Ⓡ	Ⓡ	Ⓡ
Ⓢ	Ⓢ	Ⓢ	Ⓢ	Ⓢ	Ⓢ
Ⓣ	Ⓣ	Ⓣ	Ⓣ	Ⓣ	Ⓣ
Ⓤ	Ⓤ	Ⓤ	Ⓤ	Ⓤ	Ⓤ
Ⓥ	Ⓥ	Ⓥ	Ⓥ	Ⓥ	Ⓥ
Ⓦ	Ⓦ	Ⓦ	Ⓦ	Ⓦ	Ⓦ
Ⓧ	Ⓧ	Ⓧ	Ⓧ	Ⓧ	Ⓧ
Ⓨ	Ⓨ	Ⓨ	Ⓨ	Ⓨ	Ⓨ
Ⓩ	Ⓩ	Ⓩ	Ⓩ	Ⓩ	Ⓩ

6. DATE OF BIRTH

MONTH	DAY		YEAR	
◯ JAN				
◯ FEB				
◯ MAR	⓪	⓪	⓪	⓪
◯ APR	①	①	①	①
◯ MAY	②	②	②	②
◯ JUN	③	③	③	③
◯ JUL		④	④	④
◯ AUG		⑤	⑤	⑤
◯ SEP		⑥	⑥	⑥
◯ OCT		⑦	⑦	⑦
◯ NOV		⑧	⑧	⑧
◯ DEC		⑨	⑨	⑨

7. SEX

◯ MALE
◯ FEMALE

8. OTHER

1 Ⓐ Ⓑ Ⓒ Ⓓ Ⓔ
2 Ⓐ Ⓑ Ⓒ Ⓓ Ⓔ
3 Ⓐ Ⓑ Ⓒ Ⓓ Ⓔ

pScan iNSIGHT™ forms by Pearson NCS EM-255315-1:654321　　　Printed in U.S.A.

THIS PAGE INTENTIONALLY LEFT BLANK

The Princeton Review
Diagnostic ACT Form

Completely darken bubbles with a No. 2 pencil. If you make a mistake, be sure to erase mark completely. Erase all stray marks.

ENGLISH

1 Ⓐ Ⓑ Ⓒ Ⓓ	21 Ⓐ Ⓑ Ⓒ Ⓓ	41 Ⓐ Ⓑ Ⓒ Ⓓ	61 Ⓐ Ⓑ Ⓒ Ⓓ
2 Ⓕ Ⓖ Ⓗ Ⓙ	22 Ⓕ Ⓖ Ⓗ Ⓙ	42 Ⓕ Ⓖ Ⓗ Ⓙ	62 Ⓕ Ⓖ Ⓗ Ⓙ
3 Ⓐ Ⓑ Ⓒ Ⓓ	23 Ⓐ Ⓑ Ⓒ Ⓓ	43 Ⓐ Ⓑ Ⓒ Ⓓ	63 Ⓐ Ⓑ Ⓒ Ⓓ
4 Ⓕ Ⓖ Ⓗ Ⓙ	24 Ⓕ Ⓖ Ⓗ Ⓙ	44 Ⓕ Ⓖ Ⓗ Ⓙ	64 Ⓕ Ⓖ Ⓗ Ⓙ
5 Ⓐ Ⓑ Ⓒ Ⓓ	25 Ⓐ Ⓑ Ⓒ Ⓓ	45 Ⓐ Ⓑ Ⓒ Ⓓ	65 Ⓐ Ⓑ Ⓒ Ⓓ
6 Ⓕ Ⓖ Ⓗ Ⓙ	26 Ⓕ Ⓖ Ⓗ Ⓙ	46 Ⓕ Ⓖ Ⓗ Ⓙ	66 Ⓕ Ⓖ Ⓗ Ⓙ
7 Ⓐ Ⓑ Ⓒ Ⓓ	27 Ⓐ Ⓑ Ⓒ Ⓓ	47 Ⓐ Ⓑ Ⓒ Ⓓ	67 Ⓐ Ⓑ Ⓒ Ⓓ
8 Ⓕ Ⓖ Ⓗ Ⓙ	28 Ⓕ Ⓖ Ⓗ Ⓙ	48 Ⓕ Ⓖ Ⓗ Ⓙ	68 Ⓕ Ⓖ Ⓗ Ⓙ
9 Ⓐ Ⓑ Ⓒ Ⓓ	29 Ⓐ Ⓑ Ⓒ Ⓓ	49 Ⓐ Ⓑ Ⓒ Ⓓ	69 Ⓐ Ⓑ Ⓒ Ⓓ
10 Ⓕ Ⓖ Ⓗ Ⓙ	30 Ⓕ Ⓖ Ⓗ Ⓙ	50 Ⓕ Ⓖ Ⓗ Ⓙ	70 Ⓕ Ⓖ Ⓗ Ⓙ
11 Ⓐ Ⓑ Ⓒ Ⓓ	31 Ⓐ Ⓑ Ⓒ Ⓓ	51 Ⓐ Ⓑ Ⓒ Ⓓ	71 Ⓐ Ⓑ Ⓒ Ⓓ
12 Ⓕ Ⓖ Ⓗ Ⓙ	32 Ⓕ Ⓖ Ⓗ Ⓙ	52 Ⓕ Ⓖ Ⓗ Ⓙ	72 Ⓕ Ⓖ Ⓗ Ⓙ
13 Ⓐ Ⓑ Ⓒ Ⓓ	33 Ⓐ Ⓑ Ⓒ Ⓓ	53 Ⓐ Ⓑ Ⓒ Ⓓ	73 Ⓐ Ⓑ Ⓒ Ⓓ
14 Ⓕ Ⓖ Ⓗ Ⓙ	34 Ⓕ Ⓖ Ⓗ Ⓙ	54 Ⓕ Ⓖ Ⓗ Ⓙ	74 Ⓕ Ⓖ Ⓗ Ⓙ
15 Ⓐ Ⓑ Ⓒ Ⓓ	35 Ⓐ Ⓑ Ⓒ Ⓓ	55 Ⓐ Ⓑ Ⓒ Ⓓ	75 Ⓐ Ⓑ Ⓒ Ⓓ
16 Ⓕ Ⓖ Ⓗ Ⓙ	36 Ⓕ Ⓖ Ⓗ Ⓙ	56 Ⓕ Ⓖ Ⓗ Ⓙ	
17 Ⓐ Ⓑ Ⓒ Ⓓ	37 Ⓐ Ⓑ Ⓒ Ⓓ	57 Ⓐ Ⓑ Ⓒ Ⓓ	
18 Ⓕ Ⓖ Ⓗ Ⓙ	38 Ⓕ Ⓖ Ⓗ Ⓙ	58 Ⓕ Ⓖ Ⓗ Ⓙ	
19 Ⓐ Ⓑ Ⓒ Ⓓ	39 Ⓐ Ⓑ Ⓒ Ⓓ	59 Ⓐ Ⓑ Ⓒ Ⓓ	
20 Ⓕ Ⓖ Ⓗ Ⓙ	40 Ⓕ Ⓖ Ⓗ Ⓙ	60 Ⓕ Ⓖ Ⓗ Ⓙ	

MATHEMATICS

1 Ⓐ Ⓑ Ⓒ Ⓓ Ⓔ	16 Ⓕ Ⓖ Ⓗ Ⓙ Ⓚ	31 Ⓐ Ⓑ Ⓒ Ⓓ Ⓔ	46 Ⓕ Ⓖ Ⓗ Ⓙ Ⓚ
2 Ⓕ Ⓖ Ⓗ Ⓙ Ⓚ	17 Ⓐ Ⓑ Ⓒ Ⓓ Ⓔ	32 Ⓕ Ⓖ Ⓗ Ⓙ Ⓚ	47 Ⓐ Ⓑ Ⓒ Ⓓ Ⓔ
3 Ⓐ Ⓑ Ⓒ Ⓓ Ⓔ	18 Ⓕ Ⓖ Ⓗ Ⓙ Ⓚ	33 Ⓐ Ⓑ Ⓒ Ⓓ Ⓔ	48 Ⓕ Ⓖ Ⓗ Ⓙ Ⓚ
4 Ⓕ Ⓖ Ⓗ Ⓙ Ⓚ	19 Ⓐ Ⓑ Ⓒ Ⓓ Ⓔ	34 Ⓕ Ⓖ Ⓗ Ⓙ Ⓚ	49 Ⓐ Ⓑ Ⓒ Ⓓ Ⓔ
5 Ⓐ Ⓑ Ⓒ Ⓓ Ⓔ	20 Ⓕ Ⓖ Ⓗ Ⓙ Ⓚ	35 Ⓐ Ⓑ Ⓒ Ⓓ Ⓔ	50 Ⓕ Ⓖ Ⓗ Ⓙ Ⓚ
6 Ⓕ Ⓖ Ⓗ Ⓙ Ⓚ	21 Ⓐ Ⓑ Ⓒ Ⓓ Ⓔ	36 Ⓕ Ⓖ Ⓗ Ⓙ Ⓚ	51 Ⓐ Ⓑ Ⓒ Ⓓ Ⓔ
7 Ⓐ Ⓑ Ⓒ Ⓓ Ⓔ	22 Ⓕ Ⓖ Ⓗ Ⓙ Ⓚ	37 Ⓐ Ⓑ Ⓒ Ⓓ Ⓔ	52 Ⓕ Ⓖ Ⓗ Ⓙ Ⓚ
8 Ⓕ Ⓖ Ⓗ Ⓙ Ⓚ	23 Ⓐ Ⓑ Ⓒ Ⓓ Ⓔ	38 Ⓕ Ⓖ Ⓗ Ⓙ Ⓚ	53 Ⓐ Ⓑ Ⓒ Ⓓ Ⓔ
9 Ⓐ Ⓑ Ⓒ Ⓓ Ⓔ	24 Ⓕ Ⓖ Ⓗ Ⓙ Ⓚ	39 Ⓐ Ⓑ Ⓒ Ⓓ Ⓔ	54 Ⓕ Ⓖ Ⓗ Ⓙ Ⓚ
10 Ⓕ Ⓖ Ⓗ Ⓙ Ⓚ	25 Ⓐ Ⓑ Ⓒ Ⓓ Ⓔ	40 Ⓕ Ⓖ Ⓗ Ⓙ Ⓚ	55 Ⓐ Ⓑ Ⓒ Ⓓ Ⓔ
11 Ⓐ Ⓑ Ⓒ Ⓓ Ⓔ	26 Ⓕ Ⓖ Ⓗ Ⓙ Ⓚ	41 Ⓐ Ⓑ Ⓒ Ⓓ Ⓔ	56 Ⓕ Ⓖ Ⓗ Ⓙ Ⓚ
12 Ⓕ Ⓖ Ⓗ Ⓙ Ⓚ	27 Ⓐ Ⓑ Ⓒ Ⓓ Ⓔ	42 Ⓕ Ⓖ Ⓗ Ⓙ Ⓚ	57 Ⓐ Ⓑ Ⓒ Ⓓ Ⓔ
13 Ⓐ Ⓑ Ⓒ Ⓓ Ⓔ	28 Ⓕ Ⓖ Ⓗ Ⓙ Ⓚ	43 Ⓐ Ⓑ Ⓒ Ⓓ Ⓔ	58 Ⓕ Ⓖ Ⓗ Ⓙ Ⓚ
14 Ⓕ Ⓖ Ⓗ Ⓙ Ⓚ	29 Ⓐ Ⓑ Ⓒ Ⓓ Ⓔ	44 Ⓕ Ⓖ Ⓗ Ⓙ Ⓚ	59 Ⓐ Ⓑ Ⓒ Ⓓ Ⓔ
15 Ⓐ Ⓑ Ⓒ Ⓓ Ⓔ	30 Ⓕ Ⓖ Ⓗ Ⓙ Ⓚ	45 Ⓐ Ⓑ Ⓒ Ⓓ Ⓔ	60 Ⓕ Ⓖ Ⓗ Ⓙ Ⓚ

The Princeton Review
Diagnostic ACT Form

READING

1 Ⓐ Ⓑ Ⓒ Ⓓ	11 Ⓐ Ⓑ Ⓒ Ⓓ	21 Ⓐ Ⓑ Ⓒ Ⓓ	31 Ⓐ Ⓑ Ⓒ Ⓓ
2 Ⓕ Ⓖ Ⓗ Ⓙ	12 Ⓕ Ⓖ Ⓗ Ⓙ	22 Ⓕ Ⓖ Ⓗ Ⓙ	32 Ⓕ Ⓖ Ⓗ Ⓙ
3 Ⓐ Ⓑ Ⓒ Ⓓ	13 Ⓐ Ⓑ Ⓒ Ⓓ	23 Ⓐ Ⓑ Ⓒ Ⓓ	33 Ⓐ Ⓑ Ⓒ Ⓓ
4 Ⓕ Ⓖ Ⓗ Ⓙ	14 Ⓕ Ⓖ Ⓗ Ⓙ	24 Ⓕ Ⓖ Ⓗ Ⓙ	34 Ⓕ Ⓖ Ⓗ Ⓙ
5 Ⓐ Ⓑ Ⓒ Ⓓ	15 Ⓐ Ⓑ Ⓒ Ⓓ	25 Ⓐ Ⓑ Ⓒ Ⓓ	35 Ⓐ Ⓑ Ⓒ Ⓓ
6 Ⓕ Ⓖ Ⓗ Ⓙ	16 Ⓕ Ⓖ Ⓗ Ⓙ	26 Ⓕ Ⓖ Ⓗ Ⓙ	36 Ⓕ Ⓖ Ⓗ Ⓙ
7 Ⓐ Ⓑ Ⓒ Ⓓ	17 Ⓐ Ⓑ Ⓒ Ⓓ	27 Ⓐ Ⓑ Ⓒ Ⓓ	37 Ⓐ Ⓑ Ⓒ Ⓓ
8 Ⓕ Ⓖ Ⓗ Ⓙ	18 Ⓕ Ⓖ Ⓗ Ⓙ	28 Ⓕ Ⓖ Ⓗ Ⓙ	38 Ⓕ Ⓖ Ⓗ Ⓙ
9 Ⓐ Ⓑ Ⓒ Ⓓ	19 Ⓐ Ⓑ Ⓒ Ⓓ	29 Ⓐ Ⓑ Ⓒ Ⓓ	39 Ⓐ Ⓑ Ⓒ Ⓓ
10 Ⓕ Ⓖ Ⓗ Ⓙ	20 Ⓕ Ⓖ Ⓗ Ⓙ	30 Ⓕ Ⓖ Ⓗ Ⓙ	40 Ⓕ Ⓖ Ⓗ Ⓙ

SCIENCE REASONING

1 Ⓐ Ⓑ Ⓒ Ⓓ	11 Ⓐ Ⓑ Ⓒ Ⓓ	21 Ⓐ Ⓑ Ⓒ Ⓓ	31 Ⓐ Ⓑ Ⓒ Ⓓ
2 Ⓕ Ⓖ Ⓗ Ⓙ	12 Ⓕ Ⓖ Ⓗ Ⓙ	22 Ⓕ Ⓖ Ⓗ Ⓙ	32 Ⓕ Ⓖ Ⓗ Ⓙ
3 Ⓐ Ⓑ Ⓒ Ⓓ	13 Ⓐ Ⓑ Ⓒ Ⓓ	23 Ⓐ Ⓑ Ⓒ Ⓓ	33 Ⓐ Ⓑ Ⓒ Ⓓ
4 Ⓕ Ⓖ Ⓗ Ⓙ	14 Ⓕ Ⓖ Ⓗ Ⓙ	24 Ⓕ Ⓖ Ⓗ Ⓙ	34 Ⓕ Ⓖ Ⓗ Ⓙ
5 Ⓐ Ⓑ Ⓒ Ⓓ	15 Ⓐ Ⓑ Ⓒ Ⓓ	25 Ⓐ Ⓑ Ⓒ Ⓓ	35 Ⓐ Ⓑ Ⓒ Ⓓ
6 Ⓕ Ⓖ Ⓗ Ⓙ	16 Ⓕ Ⓖ Ⓗ Ⓙ	26 Ⓕ Ⓖ Ⓗ Ⓙ	36 Ⓕ Ⓖ Ⓗ Ⓙ
7 Ⓐ Ⓑ Ⓒ Ⓓ	17 Ⓐ Ⓑ Ⓒ Ⓓ	27 Ⓐ Ⓑ Ⓒ Ⓓ	37 Ⓐ Ⓑ Ⓒ Ⓓ
8 Ⓕ Ⓖ Ⓗ Ⓙ	18 Ⓕ Ⓖ Ⓗ Ⓙ	28 Ⓕ Ⓖ Ⓗ Ⓙ	38 Ⓕ Ⓖ Ⓗ Ⓙ
9 Ⓐ Ⓑ Ⓒ Ⓓ	19 Ⓐ Ⓑ Ⓒ Ⓓ	29 Ⓐ Ⓑ Ⓒ Ⓓ	39 Ⓐ Ⓑ Ⓒ Ⓓ
10 Ⓕ Ⓖ Ⓗ Ⓙ	20 Ⓕ Ⓖ Ⓗ Ⓙ	30 Ⓕ Ⓖ Ⓗ Ⓙ	40 Ⓕ Ⓖ Ⓗ Ⓙ

I hereby certify that I have truthfully identified myself on this form. I accept the consequences of falsifying my identity.

_____

Your signature

_____

Today's date

The Princeton Review
Diagnostic ACT Form

ESSAY

Begin your essay on this side. If necessary, continue on the opposite side.

Continue on the opposite side if necessary.

The Princeton Review
Diagnostic ACT Form

Continued from previous page.

_____

_____

_____

_____

_____

_____

_____

_____

_____

_____

_____

_____

_____

_____

_____

_____

_____

_____

_____

_____

_____

_____

_____

_____

_____

Chapter 26
Practice Exam 1:
Answers
and Explanations

English		Math		Reading		Science	
1. B	40. H	1. E	40. K	1. C	40. G	1. A	40. H
2. F	41. B	2. G	41. B	2. J		2. J	
3. D	42. J	3. B	42. K	3. A		3. C	
4. G	43. A	4. J	43. B	4. J		4. J	
5. A	44. G	5. C	44. J	5. B		5. D	
6. H	45. C	6. H	45. E	6. G		6. J	
7. C	46. H	7. B	46. H	7. D		7. B	
8. J	47. C	8. J	47. C	8. F		8. J	
9. D	48. F	9. E	48. J	9. C		9. A	
10. F	49. C	10. F	49. C	10. G		10. F	
11. B	50. J	11. E	50. G	11. C		11. D	
12. H	51. A	12. J	51. E	12. G		12. G	
13. D	52. F	13. B	52. G	13. A		13. A	
14. G	53. D	14. K	53. C	14. G		14. H	
15. A	54. F	15. A	54. F	15. C		15. B	
16. G	55. D	16. G	55. D	16. G		16. H	
17. C	56. H	17. D	56. G	17. D		17. C	
18. H	57. B	18. F	57. B	18. H		18. J	
19. D	58. G	19. A	58. F	19. D		19. A	
20. F	59. B	20. K	59. C	20. F		20. H	
21. D	60. G	21. E	60. J	21. A		21. C	
22. F	61. D	22. F		22. F		22. G	
23. C	62. F	23. B		23. D		23. C	
24. G	63. C	24. H		24. G		24. J	
25. D	64. F	25. E		25. A		25. A	
26. G	65. C	26. H		26. J		26. J	
27. A	66. G	27. C		27. D		27. D	
28. G	67. C	28. G		28. H		28. F	
29. A	68. F	29. B		29. C		29. D	
30. H	69. B	30. G		30. G		30. G	
31. B	70. J	31. C		31. A		31. C	
32. F	71. B	32. G		32. H		32. H	
33. D	72. G	33. E		33. C		33. C	
34. F	73. D	34. J		34. J		34. J	
35. A	74. F	35. D		35. A		35. A	
36. H	75. D	36. K		36. H		36. H	
37. C		37. D		37. D		37. B	
38. H		38. H		38. J		38. F	
39. B		39. C		39. A		39. D	

ENGLISH TEST

1. **B**   This sentence needs a comma after the complete idea and before the incomplete one. This brief pause clarifies that the incomplete idea is modifying Hawaii. Choices (C) and (D) introduce additional words that are unnecessary or create an error.

2. **F**   In Sentence 4, the writer provides additional support for how difficult the race is. If deleted, the passage would lose this emphasis, as choice (F) describes. Choices (G), (H), and (J) all introduce extraneous details that have not been provided by the passage.

3. **D**   This sentence requires a contrast to the previous paragraph. Only choice (D) provides that with *however*.

4. **G**   As written, this sentence incorrectly places a comma after the word *athletics*, which is not needed since an incomplete idea follows. This eliminates choices (F) and (H). Choice (J) is not correct because it places a comma after the word *and*, and uses the incorrect pronoun *there* to refer to sports' *physical demands*, which requires the possessive.

5. **A**   This sentence is correct as written, because *proved* as it is used means *became*. All the other options are synonyms of a different definition of *proved* and thus change the intended meaning of the sentence.

6. **H**   The word *somewhat* is referring to the *amusing way* in which the race started. Therefore, *somewhat* needs to be before the word *amusing* to correctly modify it, choice (H).

7. **C**   This sentence is providing the names of two sports clubs and the island on which they functioned. There is no need to separate anything here with a comma because it is a list of only two items, so that eliminates choices (A), (B), and (D). Only choice (C) correctly removes the commas.

8. **J**   *Claiming* describes the bikers and does not require a conjunction, eliminating choices (F) and (G). Choice (H) would create a comma splice.

9. **D**   The phrase before the comma is incomplete, and the word *when* introduces a second incomplete idea, leaving the sentence without any complete ideas. Therefore, the only possible answer is to delete the underlined portion, or choice (D).

10. **F**   The underlined phrase refers to the three separate races that were eventually combined into the single race of the Triathlon. Therefore, it should remain where it is now, choice (F).

11. **B**   As written, the underlined section is redundant because it references the pages he is reading, although they were just mentioned a few words before. This redundancy can be eliminated by selecting choice (B).

12. **H**   You can never join the helping verb *had* with the simple past tense *became*. This eliminates choice (F). Choice (G) is the present tense of the verb, and choice (J) is the incorrect form of the past tense, so both of those can be eliminated as well. Only choice (H) provides the correct form of the simple past tense.

13. D   Only choice (D) points out Haller's great achievement of winning the first Ironman. Choices (A) and (C) detract from his achievement by focusing on other competitors, and choice (B) discusses a moment of doubt Haller has.

14. G   Choices (F), (H), and (J) all provide specific, plural phrases that could represent the competitors to whom the sentence is referring. Choice (G) is a singular, ambiguous *that* that cannot refer to the competitors.

15. A   The final paragraph discusses how many compete in the race today, as well as how popular the race has become since its inception. This most closely aligns with choice (A).

16. G   The underlined portion is incorrect as written because the *when* makes the second part of the sentence incomplete. Therefore, choice (F) can be eliminated. Whenever there is a list, all the elements of that list must be parallel. None of the other items in the sentence as written end in –*ing*, so that eliminates choice (H). Nor are any of them in the past tense, which eliminates choice (J). Only choice (G) matches the others, and thus must be the correct answer.

17. C   As written, this sentence contains two complete ideas with no punctuation in between, which eliminates choice (A). Simply adding a comma does not fix the problem, so choice (B) cannot be correct. Changing *hoping* to *praying* does not help either, so choice (D) cannot be correct. Only choice (C), which separates the sentence into two by introducing a period, offers a viable solution.

18. H   A conjunction is needed to join the two halves of the sentence together, eliminating choices (F) and (G) (note: *therefore* is an adverb, not a conjunction). *But* is not the right conjunction to use because the two clauses do not disagree with each other. That eliminates choice (J). The only answer left is choice (H).

19. D   The subject of this sentence, *all the opportunities*, comes after the verb. However, the verb still must agree with it. Since the subject is plural, choices (A) and (B) are inappropriate because those are singular forms of the verb. Choice (C) is incorrect because the verb *lay* refers to placing an item down, like a book on the table, which is inappropriate in this context. The only acceptable answer is choice (D).

20. F   In a list, there should be a comma after every item, including the one before the *and*. The first item in this list is *a nice pair of slacks*, so the first comma is needed after that expression but nowhere inside of it. This eliminates all the answer except choice (F).

21. D   Sentence 2 refers to the narrator's acceptance of the volunteer position. This must logically follow the sentence that contains the director's offer of the position, Sentence 5.

22. F   The phrase *an expert himself in every facet of hospital administration* is an additional descriptive detail that is not essential to the sentence. Therefore, it should have a comma on both sides of it. The correct answer is choice (F).

23. C   The phrase preceding the comma at the beginning of this sentence must refer to the first noun following the phrase. As written, that noun is *my ears*, which cannot be correct because ears do not walk anywhere. Only choice (C) corrects the misplaced modifier by making *I* the subject.

24. G   In an earlier sentence in this paragraph, the narrator describes herself as *overwhelmed* by all the noise in the hospital. Therefore, as the sounds continue, she becomes more overwhelmed, or *beseiged*, as in choice (G).

25. D   The underlined section of the sentence refers to how the narrator's face revealed her fear at the same time that she looked around the ward. Choice (D) changes this meaning, so it is therefore the LEAST acceptable option.

26. G   This question calls for a vivid description of the hallway. Only choice (G) provides this, by giving specific details about all the family members and colorful decorations. Choice (F) just describes the hallway as busy, which is not particularly vivid. Choices (H) and (J) don't specifically refer to the hallway at all.

27. A   The phrase *the one in charge of the nursery* provides an extra detail that is not essential to the meaning of the sentence. As such, it needs to be set off by commas on both sides. Only choice (A) gives us this option.

28. G   The pronoun *it* should be referring to the blankets. However, *it* is singular, so choice (F) can be eliminated. *Them* is the appropriate pronoun to use, so choice (J) can be eliminated as well. Finally, *placing* doesn't match *start* as it needs to. Therefore, choice (H) can be eliminated and choice (G) must be the answer.

29. A   The final paragraph expresses the narrator's comfort in the nursery, especially as compared to the maternity ward. Therefore, when she gives the hospital director a nod, she is acknowledging the fact that she enjoys the new atmosphere. This most closely aligns with choice (A). At no point in the passage does the narrator express anger or the intention to quit, so choices (B) and (C) cannot be correct. Finally, nowhere else in the passage is the narrator nodding, so choice (D) can be eliminated as well.

30. H   This new information acts as an introduction to the narrator's first day working at the hospital. This most logically should be inserted at the beginning of Paragraph 3, in which the actual activities of her first day are described.

31. B   In this sentence, the author is making a comparison between the reputation snakes have and the reputation they deserve. Such a comparison will always be separated by the word *than*, which eliminates choices (A) and (D). Choice (C) can be eliminated because it changes the meaning of the sentence to imply that snakes have the deadliest reputation, which was not stated.

32. F   At this point in the essay, the author is identifying numerous negative associations related to the snake. Only choice (F) adds to this list. Choices (G), (H), and (J) do not contain anything particularly negative in their portrayals of the snake.

33. D   As written, the phrase *that is popular* refers to *a snake*, which is incorrect. The phrase should refer to the *reference*. The only choice which provides this concisely is choice (D).

34. F   Choice (G) contains the word *who's*, which is the contraction for *who is* and is inappropriate in this sentence. Choice (H) contains the word *it's*, a contraction for *it is* and likewise inappropriate. Choice (J) contains the word *its'*, which is never correct. The only remaining answer is choice (F).

35. A   This sentence is correct as written. The phrase following *fangs* is an unnecessary descriptive piece added to the sentence, which should be set off with commas. It is not necessary to introduce any additional words, because that would make the sentence a run-on.

36. H   The word *prey* is followed by a list of the items that fall into this category. A colon is needed before such a list, which makes choice (H) correct.

37. C   As written, the phrase *they are provoked* is ambiguous. Does it refer to the snakes or the people? Only choice (C) clarifies this ambiguity in a concise way.

38. H   The statistic quoted acts as support for the preceding sentence, arguing that snakes normally do not pose much threat to humans. Therefore, choice (H) is the correct response.

39. B   The underlined phrase needs a verb consistent with the singular subject of *Prompt treatment*. Only choice (B) is consistent and concise.

40. H   As underlined, the transition in this sentence is neither parallel nor logical, because the second half of the sentence is a separate idea that does not follow from the first. Only choice (H) provides a parallel transition.

41. B   As written, this sentence is not a complete thought. It needs verbs, and without helping verbs like *was* or *is*, the words *considering* and *avoiding* can't stand alone. Choices (A) and (C) don't fix the problem. Choice (D) incorrectly changes the sentence to past tense, as well as combines two clauses. Only choice (B) gives two present tense verbs, "consider" and "avoid," to fix the fragment in the original sentence.

42. J   As written, this sentence has complete ideas joined incorrectly. Two complete thoughts cannot be joined by a comma, which eliminates choices (F) and (H). Nor can two complete thoughts have no punctuation between them, so choice (G) must also be incorrect. Only choice (J) correctly uses a semicolon between the two thoughts.

43. A   The opening paragraph referred to all the common derogatory phrases associated with snakes. Therefore, since choice (A) refers to the *snake in the grass* referenced in that paragraph, it would achieve the writer's aim of referencing the opening paragraph. All the other choices refer to items mentioned elsewhere in the passage, not in the first paragraph.

44. G   The final sentence of the first paragraph refers to the snake as *unjustly maligned* despite its *ugly, slimy appearance*. The essay goes on to describe some of the misconceptions people have about snakes. Therefore, this sentence sets up the main idea of the passage as a whole, as choice (G) suggests.

45. C   Choice (C) is correct because the author takes a positive view of snakes: they do not hurt humans to the degree commonly believed, and they help society by keeping the population of undesirable rodents and other pests in check.

46. H   The underlined portion needs a word to indicate the present day. All the choices do this except choice (H), which changes the meaning.

47. C   Choice (C) changes the meaning to indicate that the challenges showed anything was possible, whereas the original meaning of the sentence indicates that Hurston's perseverance is what made anything possible. Therefore, choice (C) is not acceptable.

48. F   The underlined portion is correct as is, because it is the only choice that accurately reflects Hurston as an individualistic person, in keeping with the description of her provided in the previous paragraph. All the other choices change the meaning of the phrase in ways not supported by the passage.

49. C   This question calls for something historical in nature that makes Eatonville unique. Only choice (C) provides this. Choice (A) doesn't make the town unique, as many cities share a similar climate. Likewise, choices (B) and (D) discuss the town's founding but do not indicate that the town is different from any other community founded in the same era.

50. J   This sentence needs a simple conjunction to join the two items listed, *freedom* and *independence*. For this reason, choice (J) is the answer. Choice (F) makes no sense in the context of the sentence, because what follows *that* is not a separate clause. Choice (G) incorrectly introduces an unnecessary verb. Choice (H) makes the sentence two complete ideas linked incorrectly.

51. A   The underlined portion is correct as written, choice (A). This list of two items is essential to the meaning of the sentence, so it should not be set off with commas. Only information that could be removed without altering the meaning requires commas.

52. F   This sentence is correct as written. Choices (G) and (H) introduce a comma into the sentence that incorrectly separates the subject from the verb. Choice (J) incorrectly introduces a semicolon, which can only be used to connect two complete thoughts.

53. D   The correct choice is (D), because it correctly eliminates the redundancy in the underlined passage. The term *literature* means *books, poems, and plays*, so there is no need to repeat it, as choice (A) does. The same applies to choices (B) and (C), so they are likewise incorrect.

54. F   This sentence needs a verb in the past tense. This eliminates choices (H) and (J). Choice (G) cannot be correct, because *developed* does not require a preposition to follow it. Therefore, the correct answer must be choice (F).

55. D This additional information relating to Billie Holiday is not relevant at this point in a passage dedicated to Hurston. It provides interesting but superfluous detail, which most closely aligns with choice (D).

56. H This question wants a word that indicates the novel accurately reflects the actual dialect spoken. Choice (H) does this, because if something is authentic, it is true to the original. Choices (F), (G), and (J) positively comment on the dialect, but tell us nothing about how accurate it is.

57. B As written, the underlined *it* is ambiguous. The sentence needs to clearly identify what *it* is referring to. This eliminates both choices (A) and (C). Choice (D) cannot work, because *which* does not refer to Hurston's work. Therefore, choice (B) must be correct.

58. G Sentence 4 identifies one of Hurston's novels, and the following sentences provide additional information about the plot of that novel and the critical reception it received. Choice (G) most closely aligns with this summary. Choice (F) is incorrect because nothing in the remaining sentences indicates one specific influence. Choice (H) is incorrect because only one of the subsequent sentences provides a plot detail. Finally, choice (J) is incorrect because the remaining sentences focus on the novel, not Eatonville specifically.

59. B As written, the underlined portion is incorrect because the transition it uses indicates the sentence disagrees with the one that came before it. Therefore, choice (A) can be eliminated. However, choices (C) and (D) are incorrect as well, because there is no direct cause and effect relationship between the two sentences. Choice (B) is the best choice because no transition is necessary at all.

60. G The phrase *as one of the best writers of her era* is essential to the meaning of the sentence, which means it cannot be set off by commas. It does, however, need an *and* after it to join the two halves of the sentence together. Thus, choice (G) must be correct.

61. D As written, this sentence is incomplete and cannot be ended with a period. This eliminates choice (A). There is also no need to introduce a conjunction, because that does not fix the problem. Therefore, the correct answer must be choice (D).

62. F The phrase *Soviet Union* is extra information that is not essential to the meaning of the sentence. As such, it should have a dash on both sides of it, which only choice (F) provides.

63. C The word *Americas* is being used as a possessive, because it owns the *powerful office* that follows. Therefore, it should have an apostrophe before the *s*. This eliminates choices (A) and (D). The phrase *most powerful* is modifying the word *office* and does not need a comma. Therefore, choice (C) must be correct.

64. F The underlined portion is correct as written. A pronoun in the subject case is needed here, because it is the subject of the verb in the idea that follows.

65. C   The phrase *underprivileged* indicates that these individuals are not as fortunate as others in a given society. As such, it would be redundant to specify this again. Only choice (C) eliminates this redundancy.

66. G   This sentence indicates that Carter supported a national energy policy. Only choice (G) aligns with this information.

67. C   The phrase *on foreign oil* refers to what America depended upon. Therefore, it should be as close as possible to the word *dependence*, or choice (C).

68. F   All the answer choices refer to the creation of the Carter Center. However, choice (F) changes the meaning to imply that Carter discovered the Center, rather than started it.

69. B   The phrase *around the world* already refers to many different countries, so it would be redundant to specify those countries. Therefore, the correct answer is choice (B).

70. J   The first words in this phrase, *at home*, indicate that Carter works within the United States. There is no need to identify this again, making the sentence redundant. Therefore, the correct answer is choice (J).

71. B   As written, the placement of *abroad* incorrectly modifies the verb *focus*, which changes the intended meaning of the sentence. The word *abroad* refers to where Carter expends his efforts, or choice (B).

72. G   Sentence 4 functions as a transition between the previous paragraph and this paragraph. As such it should come first, as choice (G) suggests.

73. D   The correct preposition needs to be *with* in order to maintain the intended meaning of the sentence: someone concurring with Carter. Choices (A) and (C) use prepositions that never work with *agree*. Choice (B) changes the meaning to taking on an obligation.

74. F   This essay intends to identify some of the positive humanitarian goals Carter has sought to achieve in his career. Choice (F) most closely aligns with this goal. Choices (G) and (J) focus on his politics while ignoring his humanitarian interests, so they can be eliminated. Choice (H) comments on a right as an American, which has nothing to do with the rest of the passage.

75. D   The new sentence references Habitat for Humanity, which was discussed in Paragraph 4. Therefore, it would most logically be added to the end of that paragraph, or choice (D).

MATHEMATICS TEST

1. E Set up a proportion with the information you have and the information you are looking for:

$$\frac{\text{height}}{\text{length of shadow}} = \frac{24\,ft}{6\,ft} = \frac{x\,ft}{18\,ft}$$

Do the cross-multiplication to find that $x = 72$ feet, choice (E).

2. G Remember that Sherwood's $100 payment covers both his one-time new-member fee and a few months of a membership. Since the new-member fee is $16, this means that Sherwood put $100 − $16 = $84 toward his monthly fees. Since each month costs $14, Sherwood paid for $84 ÷ $14 = 6 months of membership.

3. B Although this looks like a problem in which you'll need to factor, you actually can just substitute the y value: $\frac{y^2 - 4}{y - 2} = \frac{(-6)^2 - 4}{(-6) - 2} = \frac{(36) - 4}{-8} = \frac{32}{-8} = -4$.

4. J Because the group ended up with more than 15 students, they overpaid. Figure out the total amount they should have paid and subtract it from the amount that they did pay: (18)($11.50) − (18)($10.25) = $22.50.

5. C When you are finding a probability, you need to figure out a basic part/whole relationship. In this case, there are 16 members in the orchestra, but only 12 of them are eligible to become speakers, so the "whole" (the denominator) must be 12. If you selected choice (B), you forgot to omit the 4 soloists. The likelihood that Itzhak would be chosen for this person is therefore $\frac{1}{12}$, because he represents one possibility out of the twelve eligible for the speaker position.

6. H In order to find the perimeter of a rectangle, remember that there are four sides. In this case the four sides add up as follows: 8 ft + 8 ft + 17 ft + 17 ft = 50 ft. If you selected choice (F), you may have only added two sides of the rectangle, and if you selected choice (J), be careful—this is the area!

7. B Work slowly through this problem. The group has sold 240 passes online at $9 each. This means that they have already made (240)($9) = $2160. In order to reach their goal, they will need $4000 − $2160 = $1840. Since the question asks how many in-person tickets they will need to sell, you can approximate how many tickets will get them $1840 by dividing: $1840 ÷ $12 = 153.333. Since there is no such thing as 0.333 tickets, you have to round up to get 154 tickets, choice (B).

8. J Do basic cross-multiplication here. $\frac{9}{q} = \frac{6}{10}$ becomes (9)(10) = 6q, so $q = \frac{(9)(10)}{6} = \frac{90}{6} = 15$.

9. E Make sure you keep all your negative signs straight and distribute properly. The original equation is −9(y − 13) = 16. First, distribute the (−9) to find (−9y + 117) = 16. Subtract the 117 from both sides to find (−9y) = −101. Divide each side by the (−9) to find $y = 11.2 = \frac{101}{9}$.

10. **F** Because Points *F, G, H,* and *J* are collinear, you can figure out $\angle GHK$ by subtracting $180° - \angle JHK = 180° - 120° = 60°$. Segments $\overline{GK}$ and $\overline{HK}$ are equivalent, so angles $\angle GHK$ and $\angle HGK$ are congruent, and $\angle HGK = 60°$. Again because they are collinear, $\angle HGK + \angle FGK = 180°$, so $\angle FGK = 120°$. Isolate this triangle to find $\angle GFK$. Because of the two congruent sides, $\angle GFK \cong \angle GKF$, so $\angle FGK + \angle GFK + \angle GKF = \angle FGK + 2(\angle GFK) = 120° + 2(\angle GFK) = 180°$, and $\angle GFK = 30°$.

11. **E** To find the answer, substitute (-3) for x throughout the equation $f(x) = 7x^2 - 9x + 4$. Once you've done this, you will find the following: $7(-3)^2 - 9(-3) + 4 = 7(9) + 27 + 4 = 63 + 27 + 4 = 94$. If you chose any of the other answers, you may not have distributed the negative properly.

12. **J** Use the answer choices and work backwards. Find the smallest number that divides evenly by 16, 25, and 40. This is 400: $400 \div 16 = 25$; $400 \div 25 = 16$; and $400 \div 40 = 10$. If you selected choice (K), be careful—this is a common multiple of all three numbers, but it is not the *least* common multiple.

13. **B** In order to cancel the original mistake, Tex will need to multiply by 3. Then, to get the number he wants, he will need to multiply by another 3. In total, he will be multiplying by 9, as in choice (B).

14. **K** There are 12 triangles, and the area of the whole figure is 96 cm², so each of the triangles has an area of 8 cm². Because each of the triangles is right isosceles, the base and height of each triangle are equivalent, so to find the length of each of these, use the area formula: $A = \frac{1}{2} = bh = \frac{1}{2}b^2$. Solve for b: $b = \sqrt{2A}$. The area of each triangle is 8, so you can find the base: $b = \sqrt{2A} = \sqrt{2(8)} = \sqrt{16} = 4$. You don't need to find the hypotenuse of the triangle, because this problem asks for the perimeter of the figure, so count up the sides (there are 14) to find that the perimeter is 56 cm.

15. **A** The sum of the measures of all angles in a triangle is 180°. $\angle Y$ is described as a right angle, which means its measure is 90°. The other two angles, therefore, will have to add up to 90° to complete the 180° in the triangle. If $\angle Z$ measures less than 52°, then $\angle X$ must be *greater* than $90° - 52° = 38°$. It cannot be *equal* to this value [as in choice (B)], because $\angle Z$ is described as *less than* 52°.

16. **G** Try the different operations listed. You will find that the only operation that makes the statement true is division. Replace all the emoticons with division signs: $(8 \div 2)^3 - (4 \div 1)^2 = (4)^3 - (4)^2 = 64 - 16 = 48$.

17. **D** First, identify a point on the graph. The easiest place to start is with the intercepts. The *x*-intercept is unclear, but the *y*-intercept passes through (0,6), eliminating choices (A), (B), and (C). Between the latter two choices, you can solve for the *x*-intercept, to find that in choice (D), $x = \frac{6}{5}$ and in choice (E), $x = 3$. Although the exact *x*-intercept is unclear on the graph, it is definitely less than 2, so you can eliminate choice (E).

18. F Translate the English in this problem into the math of the answer choices. The problem reads, "An integer, x, is subtracted from 6. That difference is then multiplied by 3." This translates into the following: $(6 - x) \bullet 3$ or $3(6 - x)$. The second part of the problem reads, "This product is 15 more than half the original integer." Therefore $3(6 - x)$ will equal "15 more than half the original integer": $15 + \frac{1}{2}x$ or $\frac{1}{2}x + 15$. Therefore, $3(6 - x) = \frac{1}{2}x + 15$.

19. A Find the total production of each company after d days. Factory X starts with 18,000 units and can produce 120 units per day, so its production after d days will be $18,000 + 120d$. Factory Y starts with only 14,500 units, but it can produce 155 units per day, so its production after d days will be $14,500 + 155d$. Since you are looking for the number of days after which the total production of each factory will be equal, set the two equations equal to one another: $18,000 + 120d = 14,500 + 155d$. That's all there is to it—you don't have to solve this!

20. K Use the Pythagorean theorem to find the length of the hypotenuse: $a^2 + b^2 = c^2$, where c is the hypotenuse. $c = \sqrt{a^2 = b^2} = \sqrt{7^2 + 24^2} = \sqrt{50,625} = 25$. Note that this is 7:24:25, a Pythagorean triple. If you remember a few of the basic triples, you can save yourself a lot of figuring.

21. E Make sure you are distributing properly: $9(y + 3) - 2(4y - 4) = 9y + 27 - 8y + 8 = y + 35$.

22. F Set up a system of equations to find a:

$a + 3b = 27$

$\underline{a - 3b = 9}$

$2a = 36$

If $2a = 36$, then $a = 18$. Use this value to find the value of b:

$18 - 3b = 9$

$3b = 18 - 9$

$3b = 9$

$b = 3$

23. B Make sure you FOIL the equation properly: $(2x + 4)^2 = 4x^2 + 8x + 8x + 16 = 4x^2 + 16x + 16$. In this case $a = 4$, $b = 16$, and $c = 16$, so $a + b - c = 4 + 16 - 16 = 4$. If you selected choice (C), you may have forgotten to FOIL. If you selected choice (E), you may done $a + b + c$ rather than $a + b - c$.

24. H Split the figure into two rectangles and find the area of each. See the figure below:

The smaller rectangle has sides of length 9 and 5, so its area by the formula $A = lw$ is 45. The larger rectangle has sides 30 and 6, so by the same formula, its area is 180. Add the two areas together to get $180 + 45 = 225$. If you selected choice (J), be careful—this is the perimeter.

25. E Look carefully at the values for each function. If a function can be graphed as $ax + b$, it is a linear function, and it will increase at constant increments. Function g decreases then increases in value. In fact, note the symmetry—this is a parabolic function, and can be graphed according to $ax^2 + bx + c$. Note that all the values in h increase by 3, so this is the function you want to work with. Since $h(-1) = 6$, $h(0)$ must equal 9.

26. H Put the equation into the slope-intercept form, $y = mx + b$. The m in this equation is the slope of the line. From the equation given, $10y - 16x = 13$, isolate the y term to get $10y = 16x + 13$, and divide through by 10 to get $y = \dfrac{16}{10}x + \dfrac{13}{10}$. Reduce to $y = \dfrac{8}{5}x + \dfrac{13}{10}$. The m term in this equation is $\dfrac{8}{5}$.

27. C First, simplify the expression: $x^2 + 5x - 24 = (x + 8)(x + 3)$. Now that you have the two expressions, find the solutions by setting each quantity equal to 0. If $x + 8 = 0$, then $x = -8$. If $x - 3 = 0$, then $x = 3$. Now find the sum of the solutions: $-8 + 3 = -5$. If you selected choice (E), you may have simplified correctly but found the roots incorrectly. If you selected choice (A), you found the product, not the sum.

28. G The perimeter of the larger triangle is 12 in. + 7 in. + 5 in. = 24 in. Since you know the ratio of the perimeters, you do not have to find each side of the smaller triangle; you can set up the following ratio:

$$\frac{5}{6} = \frac{x}{24}$$

$$\frac{5(24)}{6} = x$$

$$x = 20 \text{ in}$$

29. B To find the median of a list of numbers, those numbers must be listed in order. Make sure you rearrange the numbers given before you find the median. If you didn't rearrange the numbers, you may have picked (E). When you rearrange the numbers in this list, they are in this order: $-9°C$, $-8°C$, $-7°C$, $-7°C$, $0°C$, $1°C$, $2°C$, $3°C$, $5°C$. $0°C$ is the median. If you selected choice (A), be careful—this is the mode.

30. G You can set up an equation to find the price of the calculator. If we call the price of the calculator x, then the equation will look like this: $\sqrt{x} + \left(\frac{3}{8}\right)x = 66$. A simpler tactic is to try out the answer choices to see which works in this equation. You will find this to be 144: $\sqrt{144} + \left(\frac{3}{8}\right)144 = 66$.

31. C You need to solve for m in the equation given. The equation as written is $KE = \frac{1}{2}mv^2$. Once you've solved for m, the equation should look like this: $m = \frac{2KE}{v^2}$. Once you have this equation, substitute the values from the problem: $m = \frac{2KE}{v^2} = \frac{2(120)}{9^2} = \frac{240}{81} \approx 2.97$, between 2 and 3. If you selected choice (B), you may have forgotten to apply the $\frac{1}{2}$.

32. G A "geometric sequence" is one in which all subsequent numbers have a fixed ratio to one another. In order to figure out this ratio, look at how the numbers change. The first term $2xz$ is multiplied by xy to become the second term $2x^2yz$. This second term is multiplied again by xy to become $2x^3y^2z$. Multiply this term by xy to find the answer: $2x^4y^3z$. Note, process of elimination may be more effective here. Throughout the sequence given, neither 2 nor the z has changed, so you can eliminate choices (H), (J), and (K). The exponents have increased, not decreased, so you can eliminate choice (F).

33. E Use the histogram. Four critics gave the book a one-star review. There are thirty total critics, so the relationship you need is $\frac{4}{30} = \frac{2}{15}$.

34. J There are $360°$ in a circle, and, as the histogram shows, one-star reviews make up $\frac{2}{15}$ of all the reviews. As a result, the one-star reviews will make up $\frac{2}{15}$ of the whole circle: $\frac{2}{15} \times 360° = 48°$.

35. D Make sure you count every review. There are thirty of them, and the sum of the thirty reviews is 79. To find the average, divide $\frac{79}{80}$ to get 2.63, rounded to the nearest hundredth.

36. K Simplify the expression by factoring.

$$\frac{(x^2+7x+12)(x-2)}{(x^2+2x-8)(x+3)} = \frac{(x+3)(x+4)(x-2)}{(x+4)(x-2)(x+3)} = \frac{(x+4)(x-2)(x+3)}{(x+4)(x-2)(x+3)} = 1$$

37. D The logo in the t-shirt is a right triangle. You are given the 35° angle, so you need to determine which side you have and which side you need to find relative to this angle. On the figure, you have the 10-inch side, which is *opposite* this angle. You're looking for the top diagonal side of the triangle, which in this case is the *hypotenuse* of the triangle. Sine is the function that requires *opposite* and *hypotenuse* by the following formula: $\sin\theta = \frac{opp}{hyp}$. By this equation, $hyp = \frac{opp}{\sin\theta}$ and the top side = $\frac{10}{\sin 35°}$.

38. H The center of the circle will be the midpoint of the diameter. Use the midpoint formula to find the midpoint of the points (4,3) and (–9,–2): $\left(\frac{x_1+x_2}{2}, \frac{y_1+y_2}{2}\right)$. Insert the points to find $\left(\frac{4+(-9)}{2}, \frac{3+(-2)}{2}\right)$. If you selected choice (J), be careful—you may have forgotten to divide by 2, and if you selected choice (G), you mixed up the *x*- and *y*-coordinates.

39. C Use the distance formula to find the distance between the two points (–7,4) and (–2,6): $d = \sqrt{(x_2-x_1)^2+(y_2-y_1)^2} = \sqrt{(-7-(-2))^2+(4-6)^2} = \sqrt{(-5)^2+(-2)^2} = \sqrt{29}$

This value is approximately 5.385, but if you selected choice (A), you didn't complete the problem. Every unit on the map is equal to 5 nautical miles, and the problem is asking for the value in nautical miles. Multiply 5.385 by 5 nautical miles to find 26.92 nautical miles, which is closest to choice (C).

40. K On a "must be" question, the relationships must be true in all cases. If there is one case in which a relationship is not true, that answer choice is incorrect. Because this is an EXCEPT question, the incorrect relationship will be the correct answer. Choice (K) is often true, but not always. If you multiply $\sqrt{2}$, an irrational number, by itself, you get a rational number: 4.

41. B Because *i* is defined as the square root of negative one ($\sqrt{-1}$), its range of possibility when raised to certain powers is limited. $i = \sqrt{-1}$, $i^2 = -1$, $i^3 = -\sqrt{-1}$, $i^4 = 1$. If you continue the pattern, you will find that these are the only possible values for *i* raised to any power (including negative powers). Choice (B) is the only answer choice that lists one of these values.

42. K Note the symmetry in the chart. The equation given shows that this graph is a parabola, but even if you haven't made that deduction, the values in the chart show a general trend in the data. When *x* is –3 and –5, *y* = 0; when *x* is –1 and –7, *y* = 8. According to this data, you can infer that values less than –7 and greater than –1 will be greater than 8. Therefore, –8 will have a greater value than the others listed in the answer choices. If you have trouble reading the chart, you can always try out the values in the equation and see which gives you the greatest *f*(*x*).

43. B The formula for the volume of a right circular cylinder is $V = \pi r^2 h$. This question asks for the radius and gives V and h, so solve the equation for r: $r = \sqrt{\dfrac{V}{\pi h}}$. Substitute the values that you know to find r: $r = \sqrt{\dfrac{64\pi}{\pi(4)}} = \sqrt{16} = 4$. If you selected choice (E), you may have forgotten to take the square root of the radius. If you selected choice (C), you may have forgotten to include the height in your calculation.

44. J First, consider the relationships that you know. The ratio of the perimeter of $\triangle FJK$ to $\triangle FLM$ is 3:5, and the ratio of $\overline{FG}$ to $\overline{FG}$ is 1:5. Because all triangles share $\angle F$ and the lines are parallel, the three triangles are similar, which means all their sides—and therefore the perimeters—are proportional. From the proportions given, you can determine that the ratio of $\triangle FGH$ to $\triangle FJK$ to $\triangle FLM$ is 1:3:5; therefore, the ratio of $\overline{FG}$ to $\overline{FJ}$ to $\overline{FL}$ is also 1:3:5. Based on this ratio, you can substitute values for each of the segments to figure out the ratio of $\overline{GJ}$ to $\overline{FG}$. You can say that $\overline{FG} = 1$, $\overline{FG} = 3$, and $\overline{FG} = 5$. This enables you to calculate $\overline{GJ} = \overline{JF} - \overline{FG} = 3 - 1 = 2$. The ratio of $\overline{GJ}$ to $\overline{FG}$ is therefore 2:1. If you selected choice (H), make sure you read the question carefully—you may have switched the segments.

45. E You need to find the distance along the y-axis that Avi traveled in total. Isolate each part of Avi's ride. Note that each of these legs can be made into the hypotenuse of a right triangle. The first part of the ride creates a special 30-60-90 triangle, and the second part of the trip creates a special 45-45-90 triangle. See the figures below:

Therefore, the vertical height of the first part of the ride is $30\sqrt{3}$, and the vertical height of the second part of the ride is $50\sqrt{2}$. Don't forget to add the 35 m he rode along Broad St. at the end, to get a full vertical distance of $35 + 50\sqrt{2} + 30\sqrt{3}$. Choice (C) is the amount of the actual ride—read carefully; you just want the distance he traveled along the y-axis.

46. H The formula for a circle to which this problem is referring is $(x - h)^2 + (y - k)^2 = r^2$. In other words, the 25 in the equation $(x - 3)^2 + (y + 2)^2 = 25$ is the r^2. If $r^2 = 25$, then $r = 5$. With the radius, you can find the area of the circle with the basic formula $A = \pi r^2$. In this problem, since $r = 5$, the area will be $A = \pi(5)^2 = 25\pi$.

47. C Nearly everything you need is written on the figure. The only real piece of information you need from the text of the problem is that the y-axis bisects the base of the triangle. This tells you that the base of this triangle is $2b$. The height, according to the figure, is $2b^2 - 4$. With the base and height, you have all you need to find the area of the triangle with the standard formula $A = \frac{1}{2}bh$. Substitute the expressions to find $A = \frac{1}{2}(2b)(2b^2 - 4) = (b)(2b^2 - 4) = 2b^3 - 4b$. If you selected choice (B), you may have forgotten to divide by two.

48. J Because of the words "must be," the expression given must produce an even number in every instance. If you can find one instance in which an expression produces an odd number, you can eliminate that expression and answer choice. Since x can be any integer, there are many combinations you can try. In Choice (F), x could be 4, in which case $x + 5 = 4 + 5 = 9$, which is not even. In choice (G), x could be 1, which would make $\frac{x}{4} = \frac{1}{4}$, which is not even (nor is it an integer). If $x = 1$, choice (H) gives $x^4 = 1$, which is not even, and in choice (K), 5 raised to any integer power will always be odd. Only choice (J) generates an even number with every integer. This is because the product of an even number multiplied by either an even or an odd number will always be even.

49. C First, bring the exponent to the front of the expression: $\log_9(9^{\frac{7}{3}}) = \frac{7}{3}\log_9 9$. Once you're done, you can simplify the log portion of the expression. By the rules of logarithms, $\log_9 9$ can be rewritten as either $9^x = 9$ or $\frac{\log_9}{\log_9}$. As both expressions show, $\log_9 9 = 1$, which means you're left with $\frac{7}{3}$, between 2 and 3.

50. G In order to find the percent change, use the formula: % change $= \frac{difference}{original} \times 100\%$. In this case, Cameron's sales decreased from 23 to 19. In other words, he started at 23 (the original number), and he decreased to 19 (a difference of 4). Therefore, % change $= \frac{4}{23} \times 100 \approx 17.4\%$. If you selected choice (K), you may have calculated the increase from 19 to 23 rather than the decrease from 23 to 19.

51. E Maura wanted an average of 30 new accounts over the course of 4 months. This means that over the course of these four months, she had to create a total of 120 new accounts. Write this in an equation: Total = Jan. + Feb. + Mar. + Apr. Substitute what you know. $120 = 31 + 25 + \text{Mar.} + 27$. The total accounts needed in March will therefore be $120 - 31 - 25 - 27 = 37$.

52. G Don had 64 sales in January, and this value decreases by 5% each month. Do the calculations as follows, and don't round until you're done! February accounts $= (64) - (0.05)(64) = 60.8$. March accounts $= (60.8) - (0.05)(60.8) = 57.76$. April accounts $= (57.76) - (0.05)(57.76) = 54.872$. May accounts $= (54.872) - (54.872)(0.05) = 52.1284 \approx 52$ accounts.

53.   C   You can disregard the long equation of the function given in the problem. All you need to answer this question is the graph. As the problem says, the amplitude of this function is the "average of the absolute values" of the minimum and maximum values of $f(x)$. Pull this information from the graph. The graph goes up to $y = 3$ and down to $y = -3$. Take the average of the absolute values of these: $\frac{|3| + |3|}{2} = 3$. If you selected choice (E), be careful—this is the period.

54.   F   Start with the tangent relationship. The problem says that the tangent of the angle of vision is $\frac{7}{6}$. From SOHCAHTOA, you know that the tangent relationship is defined as $\tan\theta = \frac{opp}{adj}$, or, in terms of this problem, the tangent of the angle of vision is $\frac{\text{horizontal distance}}{\text{height of the building}}$. Set up a proportion: $\frac{7}{6} = \frac{\text{horizontal distance}}{\text{height of the building}}$. Fill in what you know: $\frac{7}{6} = \frac{\text{horizontal distance}}{30}$. Cross multiply to find that the horizontal distance from home plate to the building is 35 m. If you selected choice (H), you may have found the opposite relationship.

55.   D   If you selected choice (E), be careful—3 is a solution to this equation, but it is rational. This question asks for a solution that is NOT rational. To find the solutions, solve the equation for y. First, isolate the absolute value expression $|y^2 - 11| = 2$. Remember as you're solving this equation that you will have to create two different equations as you're removing the absolute value sign: $y^2 - 11 = 2$ and $y^2 - 11 = -2$. Solve each of these equations to find that $y^2 = 13$ and $y^2 = 9$, and therefore $y = \pm 3$ and $y = \pm\sqrt{13}$. The irrational solutions are $\pm\sqrt{13}$.

56.   G   A positive slope indicates a speed increase; a 0 slope indicates a constant speed; a negative slope indicates a speed decrease. The speed increases for 4 seconds, remains constant for 3 seconds, then decreases to 0 over 2 seconds. This is best described by choice (G). Note, if you're not sure how to read the graph, recall that the problem says the entire test takes 9 seconds. Therefore, whether speeds are increasing or decreasing, the times during which they do so will have to add to 9 seconds.

57.   B   Because the compass is a circle, it has a degree measure of 360°. "East" starts at 90° from "North," so the point of the needle will need to travel 270° to get back to "North" in a clockwise direction. In other words, the point of the needle will have to travel across $\frac{3}{4}$ of the circle as it goes from "East" to "North" in a clockwise direction. The problem states that the point of the needle travels 42 mm, so if you apply the ratio to this problem, you can say that 42 mm is $\frac{3}{4}$ of the circumference of the circle. Use this to find the full circumference: $42 = \frac{3}{4}C$ and $C = 56$ mm. Use this value to find the length of the needle, which is just the radius of this circle: $C = 2\pi r$. Solve the equation for r to find its value: $r = \frac{C}{2\pi} = \frac{56\,mm}{2\pi} \approx 8.9$.

58.   F   From 270° to 360°, the cosine function has a range of values from 0 to 1. In other words, it is always positive. Sine, by contrast, has a range of values from −1 to 0—it's always negative. Because the problem is asking for a tangent value from 270° to 360°, you know it must be negative because $\tan\theta = \dfrac{\sin\theta}{\cos\theta}$. Therefore, you can eliminate choices (H), (J), and (K). Then, because $\cos\theta = \dfrac{5}{13}$, the adjacent side, opposite side, and hypotenuse relative to the angle θ form the Pythagorean triple 5:12:13, respectively. You know that $\tan\theta = \dfrac{opp}{adj}$, and within the range from 270° to 360°, tangent is negative, so $\tan\theta = \dfrac{-5}{12}$.

59.   C   Since you need a and b such that $ab = 8$, your four possible pairs are $a = 1$, $b = 8$; $a = 2$, $b = 4$; $a = 4$, $b = 2$; $a = 8$, $b = 1$. Keep your work organized as you figure:

a	b	2^a	c	c^b
1	8	2	2	256
2	4	4	4	256
4	2	16	16	256
8	1	256	256	256

As this small chart demonstrates, there are four values of c that work in both expressions. If you selected choice (D), you may have forgotten that both $a = 1$, $b = 8$ and $a = 8$ and $b = 1$ are distinct and valid pairs.

60.   J   The formula for the length of the diagonal of a rectangular prism is $a^2 + b^2 + c^2 = d^2$ where a, b, and c represent the edges of the rectangular prism and d represents its diagonal. In the case of a cube, $a = b = c$, so the equation can be rewritten as follows: $3a^2 = d^2$. In this problem, $d = 3\sqrt{3}$, so $3a^2 = (3\sqrt{3})^2$. Therefore, $3a^2 = (9)(3)$ and $a = 3$. Therefore, the length of the edge of this cube is 3. Look at the figure—you can see from the figure that the length of the diameter of the sphere is equivalent to the length from one side of the figure to another, an edge. The diameter of the sphere is equivalent to an edge of the cube, so the diameter is 3, choice (J).

READING TEST

1. **C** Choice (C) is correct because the third paragraph states that "God Bless the Child" was *familiar mostly to adults*. Because of this, it is more likely that the song would be familiar to Monique's parents, who must be adults, than it would be to her friends, who are presumably high school students and not yet adults. Choice (A) is incorrect because the passage never identifies "God Bless the Child" as a Rodgers & Hammerstein number. Choice (B) is incorrect because the passage does not support the extreme claim that "God Bless the Child" is the *most* sophisticated Billie Holiday song. Choice (D) is incorrect because Monique's song choice is presented as a contrast to the overly enthusiastic choices of her peers.

2. **J** Choice (J) is correct because the passage initially describes Monique and her friends as *aloof*, because they isolate themselves in the auditorium and Monique acts like a monarch with a royal court, and *disparaging*, because they are anxious to belittle the other students during their auditions. Choice (F) is incorrect because, although the passage describes that most students are nervous about going first, this does not describe how Monique and her friends are presented. Choice (G) is incorrect because, although Monique and her friends react to Esperanza's song choice with *disbelief*, that is not how they are initially portrayed in the passage. Choice (H) is incorrect because Monique and her friends are portrayed as being unfriendly and excluding.

3. **A** Choice (A) is correct because the passage states that Esperanza did not look up until she got to center stage and then *looked only at Mrs. Dominguez*. Choice (B) is incorrect because the passage says she shuffled her feet on her walk to the stage, which is not a confident stride. Choice (C) is incorrect because the passage states she was *paying little attention to the other auditions*. Choice (D) is incorrect because the passage only states that she was *working* on her geometry homework, not that she finished it.

4. **J** The question is asking for the rhetorical effect of the statement *But not this year*. The previous paragraph establishes that students generally dread the first audition slot and relates the tense manner in which Monique used to view the first slot. The paragraph that follows this phrase explains that Monique had decided to embrace the first slot as a means of surprising her peers. Choice (J) is correct because it identifies the statement in question as a contrast between the status quo and Monique's surprising decision. Choice (F) is incorrect because the passage provides no evidence that most students have resolved their fears of going first, only that Monique has. Choice (G) is incorrect because the passage never establishes the extreme claim that this year's audition was the *strangest yet*. Choice (H) is incorrect because the passage does not go on to describe any different imagery Monique associates with the uncomfortable first slot but rather to say she is no longer uncomfortable with it at all.

5. B The passage describes in the sixth paragraph that Monique and her friends are *sitting at the back of the auditorium*. In the ninth paragraph the passage states that *Esperanza had been sitting alone in the first row*. Together, these facts justify choice (B). Choice (A) is incorrect because it makes the extreme claim that Esperanza is the *most* teased student, for which there is no evidence in the passage. Choice (C) is incorrect because the passage does not say that Monique and Esperanza auditioned consecutively, and the seventh paragraph implies that there was *an endless parade* of students who auditioned in between them. Choice (D) is incorrect because, although Mrs. Dominguez is sensitive to possible ridicule meeting Esperanza's audition, there is no evidence of a conversation taking place beforehand.

6. G Choice (G) is correct because the passage states that Monique figured going first would *instill fear into her competition because they would realize that Monique had something they clearly lacked*. Choice (F) is incorrect because, although going first is evidence of Monique's self-confidence, the passage does not say Monique chose to go first to increase her self-confidence. Choices (H) and (J) are incorrect because Monique's stated motivation for going first is to intimidate her rivals, not to increase her chances of getting a part or to gain any favor with Mrs. Dominguez.

7. D The passage states that at the *climactic* moment of "rockets' red glare," *Esperanza's voice filled the room with a calm resonance*. This makes choice (D) correct. Choice (A) is incorrect because it is not supported in the passage. Choice (B) is incorrect because while the passage states that her version of the song caused the people in the room to feel *some reluctant patriotism*, it does not suggest that Esperanza was patriotic herself. Choice (C) is incorrect because the passage contradicts it by saying that Esperanza was *calm*.

8. F When Mrs. Dominguez tells Esperanza she can begin to audition, the passage states that Mrs. Dominguez was *sensing the potential for the audition to devolve into a painful target of ridicule*. This makes choice (F) correct. Choice (G) is incorrect because this is how Esperanza is described in relation to Thornton High. Choice (H) is incorrect because this is what is anticipated by Monique and her friends. Choice (J) is incorrect because this relates to how Mrs. Dominguez viewed Monique's decision to audition first.

9. C Choice (C) is correct because the passage states that, once Esperanza was moving *methodically through the tune, the expectant smiles of mockery were quickly vanishing from the faces of all who listened*. Choice (A) is incorrect because the decision of where to sit was based on wanting to make comments about all the auditions and came before Esperanza's audition. Choice (B) is incorrect because their preconceived notions are described prior to Esperanza's audition, not as a reaction to the audition. Choice (D) is incorrect because the passage states that Monique and her friends were critical of Esperanza's song choice and even the resulting patriotism they felt is described as *reluctant*.

10. G   Esperanza sings "The Star Spangled Banner" for her audition. The twelfth paragraph explains that *the final phrase of the song* is *often soaked in vibrato*. This makes choice (G) correct. Choice (F) is incorrect because the passage states that Monique and her friends anticipated a "mousy" voice from Esperanza, but says nothing about "The Star Spangled Banner" being well suited to that type of voice. Choice (H) is incorrect because, although Esperanza's performance is ultimately impressive, the passage says that the song is *trite* and *formulaic*. Choice (J) is incorrect because when Esperanza begins singing her song, *Monique and her friends looked at each other in total disbelief.*

11. C   The third paragraph asks the reader to consider a contrast between an original user of a remote and a modern user. Choices (A), (B), and (D) are details provided to describe the original user. Choice (C) is a detail provided to describe the modern user. Hence, choice (C) is correct.

12. G   Choice (G) is correct because the author lists several important inventions of the twentieth century but does not identify any of them as the *most significant*. Choice (F) is incorrect because the author states that most people think the solution is new clean energy technology. Choice (H) is incorrect because the author attributes the root of tool-making to the mindset of *There's got to be a better way.* Choice (J) is incorrect because the author describes how consumers go from *awed gratitude to discriminating preference.*

13. A   The point that an example is used to illustrate is often found right before the example. In this case, the end of the first paragraph states that *the longer a given technology exists, the more we take it for granted.* The comparison between different users of remote controls is designed to illustrate this idea. Choice (A) best summarizes this concept and so is correct. Choice (B) is incorrect because the author never stresses a need to read instructions. Choice (C) is incorrect because modern users are described as using remote controls with ease and comfort. Choice (D) is incorrect because, while likely true, there is no support in the passage for the idea that remote controls have become *far more effective* than they were.

14. G   The passage focuses on the technology around us that often goes unappreciated, ultimately warning us that our unrealistic faith in technology may lead us into global climate trouble. Words and phrases like *spoiled, unduly optimistic*, and *unfairly demanding* indicate the author's attitude that most modern humans are somewhat in the wrong. Choice (G) is the safest match for this tone, which makes it the correct answer. Choice (F) is incorrect, because although the passage does look backward in time at certain spots, it is primarily focused on how the present is rather than a wish to return to the past. Choice (H) is incorrect because the author seems to be calling attention to the *dangerous extension of our mindset*, rather than sympathizing with it. Choice (J) is incorrect because the majority of the passage does not indicate the author's fear. The various references to shock and awe for new technology indicate amazement but not fright. The possible doomsday scenario toward the end of the passage does sound scary, but it functions only to demonstrate that modern humans have some problematic attitudes toward technology.

15. **C** The context for this sentence explains that, because we are spoiled by technology, we typically believe it can fix any problem. The notion that we might need to fix ourselves is unthinkable. Choice (C) is the correct answer because it best expresses that the suggestion that we need to change our own habits would be *unlike* our normal assumptions about technology. Choice (A) is incorrect because *extraterrestrial* literally means "not from earth," and the context does not suggest the idea is *that* exotic. Choice (B) is incorrect because the passage indicates this idea is seldom heard within our culture, so the notion that it is a repetitive idea is not supported. Choice (D) is incorrect because, although we do not take the idea in question seriously, it is because we are not accustomed to hearing the idea, not because the idea itself is funny.

16. **G** The point of this paragraph is that children born into a society that already possesses impressive technology do not tend to appreciate how impressive it is that this technology is human-made. They accept it as a given, much as one accepts the elements of the periodic table as the given substances found in the universe. Choice (G) is correct because it best expresses this idea. Choice (F) is incorrect because the passage does not suggest that children are literally learning about technology side-by-side as they learn about the periodic table. Choice (H) is incorrect because the reference to the *universe* does not provide any support for such an extreme claim as *most technology* comes from space exploration. Choice (J) is incorrect because it confuses the point of this paragraph, which is that children tend *not* to be impressed by the technology around them.

17. **D** The penultimate paragraph discusses how people in our culture assume that technology will solve our problems and do not want to hear about needing to change or reassess our lifestyles. Because leaders are too afraid to tell the public otherwise, the final paragraph says that we will continue as we have been. Hence, choice (D) is correct. Choice (A) is incorrect because it misses the correct meaning of the phrase, and *scope* and *complexity* were discussed in relation to assessing the global climate problem, not technology. Choice (B) is incorrect because this describes specifically what the passage explains we will *not* be doing. Making sacrifices would mean *changing* the status quo. Choice (C) is incorrect because the passage is saying that if we ever find ourselves in a disastrous situation as a result of maintaining our current lifestyles and habits, *then* we would blame technology. This would be a result of following the status quo but not the idea to which the phrase itself refers.

18. **H** *Discriminating preference* is used at the end of the seventh paragraph to foreshadow the ever-evolving demands of consumers for new technology. The eighth paragraph lists some of them. The passage states that *computers needed to become more powerful*. This makes choice (H) correct. Choice (F) is incorrect because the fifth paragraph contradicts that idea. Choice (G) is incorrect because the passage repeatedly suggests that most users of technology are happily oblivious to *how* it works. Choice (J) is incorrect because the second to last paragraph portrays this idea as something the public does not want to hear.

19.   D   The first half of the passage discusses the modern mindset toward technology. Then it says that the *most dangerous extension of this mindset* is how it relates to our ability to solve global climate problems. The second half of the passage explains why our attitude toward technology may worsen the situation. Choice (D) is correct because it precisely identifies the reason the author finds our overconfidence in technology to be potentially dangerous. Choice (A) is incorrect because this phrase refers to the flaws we consumers find with existing technology that we hope will be fixed. This is not directly relevant to the global warming problem with which the author associates the most danger. Choices (B) and (C) are incorrect because they refer to things that indirectly relate to the author's central concern. However, the author does not consider *devising new forms of energy* or *the complexity of global weather* to be dangerous in and of themselves.

20.   F   The passage ends with a severe prediction that humanity may ruin its habitat, all the while blaming technology for failing to rescue it. This makes choice (F) correct. Choice (G) is incorrect because the last paragraph does not contain any refutation of a theory. Choice (H) is incorrect because the last paragraph does not include an expert opinion. Choice (J) is incorrect because both paragraphs use "we."

21.   A   Choice (A) is correct because, although the author discusses having great difficulty and confusion in learning jazz chords, he does not ever identify one that is *most* confusing. Choices (B), (C), and (D) are incorrect because none of the chords are ever identified as the *most* confusing chords.

22.   F   In the context of the passage as a whole, the author discusses Victor as a source of knowledge about jazz. The author states he did not get *straightforward explanations* from Victor but that he *did learn* some things. Choice (F) is correct because, given the context of the passage, it refers to the most likely subject matter the author would be trying to get from Victor. Choice (G) is incorrect because the idea that knowledge about jazz would be *forbidden* is too strong. There is no evidence that the author was being purposefully excluded from learning about jazz. Choice (H) is incorrect because there is no context to support the idea that the author was asking about literal magic tricks. Choice (J) is incorrect because there is no context to support the idea that the author was trying to learn more about Victor as a person, nor does the passage ever describe Victor as *private*.

23.   D   Upon seeing the author's *invented* chord, Victor *calmly* informs the author of the chord's proper name. Choice (D) is correct because *nonchalance* indicates a relaxed, unimpressed manner, which is how Victor responds. Choice (A) is incorrect because Victor would not be amazed by a chord for which he already knows the technical name. Choice (B) is incorrect because Victor would not be jealous that the author could play a chord that was already familiar to Victor. Choice (C) is incorrect because Victor does not show confusion; he shows immediate recognition of what chord the author is playing.

24.   G   In the eighth paragraph, the author states that *for the next few months, I quietly plucked away* at the music found in "The Real Book." Hence, choice (G) is correct and choices (F), (H), and (J) are incorrect.

25. **A** The passage describes the more complex chord types of jazz and describes the effects of using them as introducing *subtle hints of chaos and imbalance, adding a worldly imperfection*, and becoming more enjoyable as one's age starts making things like candy taste too sweet and "imperfections" like bitterness make *for a more appealing flavor*. Choice (A) provides the best summary for these ideas. Choice (B) is incorrect because the description of jazz's complexity is not intended to be a critical comment about fundamental flaws in rock and classical music. Just because jazz's unique chords add *detail and depth to the music*, that doesn't mean the author thinks that other styles of music necessarily lack detail and depth. Choice (C) is incorrect because the passage does not specify anything about the confusion and awkwardness of *standard jazz chord values*; it describes what elements jazz chords add to *standard chord values*. Choice (D) is incorrect because the context explains that candy starts tasting unpleasantly *sweet* the older one gets.

26. **J** The end of the passage describes the author beginning to develop an ability to play jazz, but his newfound ability is still mentally surprising. Choice (J) summarizes this context best and is therefore correct. Choice (F) is incorrect because the passage does not support the idea that the author was *overworked*. Choice (G) is incorrect because, although the author is surprised by what his hands can do musically, there is no context to support that the author is actually losing the ability to *control* his hands. Choice (H) is incorrect because there is no information to support the idea that the author *pointing* at chords was part of his learning process.

27. **D** Choice (D) is correct because the eighth paragraph describes the author's initial attempts to work through the *strange, new combinations* he found in "The Real Book." He mentions F-sharp minor-7 flat-5 while speaking of chords that he *had to decode and then understand*. Choice (A) is incorrect because the context of this paragraph suggests that the author did indeed have some trouble with these unfamiliar chords. Choice (B) is incorrect because the remark about not knowing the language of a foreign country has no literal relation to this specific chord or the author's previous travels (about which we know nothing). Choice (C) is incorrect because the passage provides no evidence that the author knew how to play this chord on guitar.

28. **H** The fifth paragraph identifies Victor as a member of the author's rock band as well as a member of a jazz ensemble. This makes choice (H) correct. Choice (F) is incorrect because the passage states that at age 30, it had been *over a decade* since the author and Victor had gone their separate ways. Choice (G) is incorrect because the passage states that the author bought his own copy of "The Real Book." Choice (J) is incorrect because the passage does not say that Victor invented this chord, rather that he told the author the name of the chord the author presumed to have invented.

29. **C** The passage begins with the author's love for jazz. It transitions into his own experiences learning how to play jazz and culminates with his early successes in doing so. Choice (C) is correct because it encompasses the various points of focus throughout the passage. Choice (A) is incorrect because the passage only occasionally refers to a chain of events and never establishes that the author has a jazz career. Choice (B) is incorrect because the author does not try to show that jazz is uncomplicated; he describes the hard work he put into learning its complexity. Choice (D) is incorrect

because the central focus of the passage is the author's learning of jazz. Although the author's friendship with Victor relates to jazz, it is not the central focus of the author's discussion.

30.   G   In the last few paragraphs, the author describes the process by which he struggled to learn jazz. He begins by seeing jazz as *a cryptic message to decode* but later describes himself as *becoming comfortable* and possessing a *new melodic understanding*. These details make choice (G) correct. Choice (F) is incorrect because the author never says that the book becomes *annoyingly familiar* by the end. Choice (H) is incorrect because the author identifies a difference between jazz sheet music and classical sheet music, but this detail does not enter his discussion of his experiences with "The Real Book." Choice (J) is incorrect because the author has not suggested that he has moved on to other learning tools or more profound study.

31.   A   The third and fourth paragraphs discuss Calwell's work. Paragraph 4 explains that *by monitoring the cholera food chain in reverse*, Calwell is able to make predictions. This makes choice (A) correct. Choice (B) is incorrect because, while climatic models were used to predict an outbreak in Bangladesh, these models were derived from Oceanic data, not land-based measurements. Choice (C) is incorrect because, in addition to being too narrow a description of Calwell's method, the decline of zooplankton and falling sea temperatures would each suggest a reduced risk of a potential cholera outbreak. Choice (D) is incorrect because, while the passage states that cholera is found in areas that contain copepod, the passage never suggests that this marine life is diseased.

32.   H   The first few paragraphs explain the food chain that allows the cholera bacterium to grow. The bacterium grows around copepods, which feed on zooplankton, which feed on phytoplankton, which feed on sunlight. Hence, sunlight influences cholera by influencing the food chain on which the cholera bacterium depends. This makes choice (H) correct. Choice (F) is incorrect because the passage never says that phytoplankton *contaminate* the water. Choice (G) is incorrect because the passage does not state that *V. cholerae* uses photosynthesis at all. Choice (J) is incorrect because there is no support for this broad generalization about sunlight causing many epidemics. The first sentence of the passage is a rhetorical question, and the way in which the passage describes sunlight facilitating outbreaks has nothing to do with *direct, prolonged exposure*.

33.   C   The eighth paragraph explains that researchers at Oxford *calibrated regional levels of photosynthesis to the size of a vein in the wings of the flies*. The vein size measures *how numerous and robust the tsetse fly population is*. Therefore, the satellite data that measures photosynthesis is used to tell researchers how big the veins of tsetse flies are and hence how strong and prevalent their population is. This makes choice (C) correct. Choice (A) is incorrect because the passage does not say that the satellite data can be used to determine the total number of *parasites* in West Africa. Choice (B) is incorrect because measuring photosynthesis is done to gauge the size of tsetse fly populations in West Africa, not to find the global area with the *most* photosynthesis. Choice (D) is incorrect because the point of the data is not to find the flies with the biggest veins but to estimate the size of veins in tsetse flies.

34. J   The passage as a whole is presenting ways in which satellite data is being used to predict disease outbreaks, and both Calwell and Linthicum are offered as examples of those efforts. Hence, choice (J) is correct. Choice (F) is incorrect because Linthicum is studying Rift Valley fever, not cholera. Choice (G) is incorrect because Linthicum works at NASA in Greenbelt, Maryland. Choice (H) is incorrect because this does not indicate a similarity between Linthicum and Calwell since the passage never indicates that Calwell may have saved thousands of lives.

35. A   The ninth paragraph states that satellite data is more efficient than the traditional method of doing research for the reasons discussed in choice (A). Thus, choice (A) is correct. Choice (B) is incorrect because the passage does not indicate that scientists can *control* photosynthetic levels, just that they can measure them. Choice (C) is incorrect because the passage does not discuss the types of *mathematical errors* that human forecasters make. Choice (D) is incorrect because the tenth paragraph contradicts this idea by indicating there is not a lot of reliable disease data available.

36. H   The context of this word discusses conditions that would encourage or help mosquito populations to grow. *Promote* means to encourage or help, so choice (H) is correct. Choices (F) and (G) are incorrect because the weather is not performing an *errand* or a *task* for the mosquitoes. Similarly, choice (J) is incorrect because weather conditions would not *request* the growth of mosquito populations. The three incorrect answer choices relate more to the sense of *doing someone a favor* than to how the word is used in this context.

37. D   The sixth paragraph explains the weather conditions that facilitate the growth and spread of mosquito populations, which include increased rain, more clouds, and warmer air. The environmental changes Linthicum is studying are those that would precede a growth in mosquito populations. Hence, choice (D) is correct. Choice (A) is incorrect because the beginning of the rainy season in Kenya is not identified as the precursor to mosquito population growth. Choice (B) is incorrect because the passage never mentions bacteria in the jet stream. Choice (C) is incorrect because the environmental changes Linthicum is monitoring are those that precede mosquito population growth, not the population growth itself.

38. J   While it is true that satellite data has *measured* increases in ocean temperature, the passage never suggests or states that satellite data has actually *helped to* raise the ocean temperature. For this reason, choice (J) is correct. Choice (F) is incorrect because it is mentioned in the Calwell research. Choice (G) is incorrect because it is mentioned as part of the Oxford study. Choice (H) is incorrect because it is mentioned several times throughout the passage and represents the main point of the passage.

39. A   The context for this phrase is that fluctuations in certain variables would make climate-based models inaccurate predictors. The variables are labeled as *non-climatic factors* in the following sentence. This makes choice (A) the correct answer. Choice (B) is incorrect because there is no discussion of the effects of drug resistance. Choice (C) is incorrect because it does not address the source of confusion, which is a failure to incorporate certain variables into the model. Choice (D) is incorrect because it implies—without any textual evidence—that researchers are unfamiliar with non-climate data, although the passage suggests only that they are not currently using it in their models.

40. G   With the examples of Calwell, Linthicum, and Rogers, the author presents researchers who are using satellite-based data to predict disease outbreaks. The passage ends by assessing the value of these efforts. This makes choice (G) the correct answer. Choice (F) is incorrect because the passage does not itemize which satellite data *must* be collected, nor is the type of data the primary focus. Choice (H) is incorrect because the author does not stress that a small number of scientists do research by traditional methods. Choice (J) is incorrect because it is too narrow a purpose for an author who also discussed applications relating to predicting cholera and Rift Valley fever.

SCIENCE TEST

1. A   Higher bulk density means lower soil quality. Figure 1 shows that Field A consistently has a higher bulk density, so choice (A) is the correct answer. Table 1 does not contain any information about Field A or B, eliminating choice (C). Figure 2 and Table 2 show that the crop yields and average SOM for Field A are higher, which goes against what the question looks to prove, eliminating choices (B) and (D).

2. J   Figure 2 shows that Field B had a harvest of approximately 8 tons in Year 5. Of the values given in the figure, this is the only one that has a harvest less than or equal to 8 tons, thus making it a failed harvest.

3. C   Table 1 shows that as the SOM increases, the soil quality increases. Eliminate choices (A) and (D) because both show an inverse, rather than a direct, relationship. With the new information provided in the question, you can infer that legumes and *deep-rooted and high-residue crops* will increase the amount of organic matter in the soil, and thus lead to an increase in the soil organic matter (SOM) rating. Only choice (C) provides this relationship.

4. J   Figure 1 shows that Field A had a higher bulk density every year; therefore, regardless of the actual values, it can be assumed that the average bulk density was higher for Field A. Figure 2 shows that Field B had the lower crop yield in every year but Year 3. Therefore, it can be assumed that Field B has a lower average crop yield than Field A. The only choice that is correct for both parts of the question is choice (J).

5. D   Use Table 1 to judge the average SOM for Field A and Field B given in Table 2. Field A's average SOM of 0.89 rates as excellent and Field B's average SOM of 0.28 rates as fair. This means the hypothesis is not consistent with the data presented, so the correct answer is choice (D).

6. J   Based on Table 1, the salt solution increased the amount of rust every day. On Day 8, the sample had 1.84 g of rust, so on Day 9 the amount of rust would likely be higher than 1.84 g, choice (J).

7. B   The formula shows that when rust is produced, H_2 is also produced, so choice (B) is the only possible correct answer.

8. J   Table 1 shows that the salt solution produced 0.56 g Fe_2O_3 on Day 2. Figure 1 shows that the water buffered to pH = 10.0 had less than 0.50 g Fe_2O_3 until Day 8, so the only correct answer is choice (J).

9. A   Table 1 shows that the sugar solution produced 0.11 g Fe_2O_3 by Day 6 and 0.19 g by Day 8. The amount produced from Day 6 to Day 8, then, would have been 0.19 – 0.11 = 0.08 g.

10. F   Table 1 shows that the sugar solution had 0.00 g Fe_2O_3 on Day 2 and shows a steady increase. Choices (G) and (J) show the amount of Fe_2O_3 produced decreasing as time passes, so they cannot be correct. Choice (H) shows a big increase in Fe_2O_3 between Day 2 and Day 6, then a small increase between Day 6 and Day 8. Table 1 shows that the biggest increase in Fe_2O_3 was between Day 6 and Day 8, 0.08 g, so choice (H) cannot be correct. Only choice (F) shows 0.00 g on Day 1 and steady increases in g Fe_2O_3 produced, so this must be the correct answer.

11. D   Based on Experiment 1, shown in Figure 2, you can see that a 10.0 N weight shared between two springs caused Spring A to stretch to 0.40 m, so a 10.0 N weight on Spring A alone must cause it to stretch further. Choice (D) is the best answer.

12. G   Based on Experiment 2, shown in Figure 4, you can see that as the weight moved farther from Spring B, Spring B stretched less as the force on Spring B decreased. Choice (G) is the correct answer.

13. A   Because the students were attaching weights to two springs at once in Trials 1–3, it was important to use identical springs so that the effects on each spring would be the same. If they had used different springs, there would be no way of determining the relationship between the length of the spring and the weight. Choice (A) best describes this reason. Choice (B) does not make much sense, for the same reasons, so it should be eliminated. Choice (D) must be eliminated because it discusses the weight of the board, which is not used in Trials 1–3. Choice (C) discusses oscillation, which is only mentioned in the passage to state that the students waited until oscillation ceased before measuring. Once you are left with choices (A) and (C), choice (A) is clearly the better answer.

14. H   Experiment 2, Trial 5 shows the 5.0 N weight at exactly the midpoint of the board, and the springs stretched to 0.40 m. Experiment 1, Trial 1 has springs stretched to 0.40 m and a weight of 10.0 N. So the board in Experiment 3 must weigh 10.0 N – 5.0 N = 5.0 N, choice (H).

15. B   Experiment 2, Trial 5 is the only trial in Experiment 2 where the springs are stretched the same amount, choice (B).

16. H   If potential energy is highest when the springs are stretched the most, then the correct answer must be the trial wherein the spring was stretched the most, so you can eliminate choices (F) and (G) right away. Now, you need to find the answer that gives the correct reason for this phenomenon. Spring C was stretched the most because the force of the weight was greater, choice (H).

17. C   Based on Table 2, you know that the proofs for both de-icers decrease as temperature decreases, so you know that the proof at –30°C for each de-icer must be *less than* the proof at –25°C and *greater than* the proof at –50°C. Knowing this, you can eliminate choice (A) right away because the proofs are the same as the proofs at –50°C. You can eliminate choice (D) because the proofs are the same as the proofs at –25°C. Choice (B) shows the proof for De-icer B greater than the proof for De-icer A, but Table 2 shows that De-icer A always has a greater proof than De-icer B, so choice (B) cannot be correct. This leaves the correct answer, choice (C).

18. J   You can see from Table 1 that when 10 mL of distilled water is added to 40 mL of sodium chloride, the de-icer proof is 80. The de-icer proof changes based on the relative proportions of distilled water and sodium chloride. Choices (F) and (G) can be eliminated because proofs that small must be from de-icers that have almost all water. Because the proportion of water to sodium chloride is the same as in the problem, choice (J) is the correct answer.

19. A   The passage tells you that TR is the minimum proof for a de-icer to be effective at a particular temperature. Table 2 shows that as temperature decreases, TR increases only, so choice (A) is the correct answer.

20. H   Based on Table 1, you can see that when the amount of sodium chloride is 0, the de-icer proof is 0, so you can eliminate choice (J). You can also eliminate choices (F) and (G), because Table 1 shows de-icer proof values when the volume of distilled water or sodium chloride is 0, but those formulas involve division by 0, which isn't possible. This leaves you with choice (H), which a quick check of de-icer proof of 0 and 100 will show you is correct.

21. C   Table 1 shows you that a mixture of 10 mL of distilled water and 40 mL of sodium chloride produces a de-icer proof of 80. Figure 1 shows you that adding magnesium chloride increases the proof of a 100 proof de-icer, but that no matter how much magnesium chloride is added the proof never goes above 112. Based on this, you can eliminate choices (A) and (B) because they indicate that the proof would decrease and choice (D) because it indicates that the proof would exceed 112. The correct answer is choice (C).

22. G   The passage tells you that TR is the minimum proof for a de-icer to be effective, so the better de-icer will be one that has a proof higher than the TR for each temperature, so you should eliminate choices (F) and (H). Based on Table 2, you can see that only De-icer A had a proof higher than the TR for each temperature, so choice (G) is the correct answer.

23. C   Scientist 2 says that small comets originate from regions of the solar system beyond the farthest planet's, Neptune's, orbit, choice (C).

24. J   Scientist 1 says that small comets have a diameter of 20–30 ft and burn up in the magnetosphere. Since larger comets burn up in the parts of the atmosphere closer to the earth, a comet that burns up in the thermosphere must have a diameter of greater than 30 ft, choice (J).

25. A   Scientist 1 states that small comets are too small to be meteors. Scientist 1 also states that small comets burn up in the magnetosphere, but the passage says that meteors burn up between 50 and 85 km above Earth's surface, in the mesosphere. The correct choice, therefore is that no small comet ever becomes a meteor, choice (A).

26. J   The passage states that visible objects burning up in the atmosphere are called meteors, so you should eliminate choices that do not call the objects meteors, choices (F) and (G). Second, Scientist 2 tells you that meteors are seen "far less" often than twice every five minutes, so to see bright objects every minute is not typical, eliminating choice (H). This leaves the correct answer, choice (J).

27. D   Scientist 1 says that all small comets burn up in the magnetosphere. Figure 1 shows the magnetosphere is above 600 km, so the answer is choice (D). The other values given in the answer choices represent altitudes in or above the magnetosphere.

28. F   Scientist 1's viewpoint is that the dark spots are not mere noise; a change in the atmospheric conditions around these spots would support that viewpoint. Scientist 1 also states that the comets release krypton as they burn up, so the discovery of krypton around the spots confirms Scientist 1's viewpoint, choice (F). The other choices can be eliminated because none state that Scientist 1's viewpoint was strengthened.

29. D   Scientist 1 states that small comets all burn up in the magnetosphere. According to this hypothesis, only enhanced imaging technology that could take pictures of the magnetosphere would be useful for seeing small comets. Therefore, only enhanced imaging technology that could record data above 600 km above sea level would be effective, choice (D).

30. G   In Tables 1, 2, and 3, the amount of hydrogen peroxide decreases consistently from the first day (Table 3) to the end of the elongation period (Table 1), choice (G).

31. C   The dependent variable of the experiment is a variable that the experimenter is not intentionally manipulating or changing (which is the independent variable) or controlling (control groups or variables); it's the variable that the experimenter is trying to understand or predict. In this experiment, the experimenter manipulated the type of plant, the type of superoxide dismutase, and the point in time that measurements were taken. The length of the cotton fiber was neither intentionally changed nor controlled (represented as L1, L2, and L3). The introduction indicates that the *scientists wanted to study whether the level of hydrogen peroxide affected the length of the cotton fiber.* Choice (C) is the correct answer.

32. H   Only plant cells have cell walls, so the correct answer is choice (H). Choice (F), prokaryotic, refers to unicellular life forms without a membrane-bound nucleus; cotton plants are not unicellular, so choice (F) cannot be correct. Animal cells, choice (G), do not have cell walls, so this choice can be eliminated. Bacteria, choice (J), are also unicellular and cotton plants are not bacteria, so choice (J) cannot be correct. In addition, you could use "cotton" as the clue; because of the answer choices, "Plant" is the best approximation of what cotton is.

33. C   Take the information given, length of cotton fiber and amount of hydrogen peroxide, and find the most similar line and point in time. The correct answer is choice (C), L2 at the beginning of its elongation period.

34. J   The only cotton plant line which did not have its genetic structure altered was L4, so this was the control.

35. A   The *x*-axis will move in a positive direction, so determine how the average lengths change. For all the data, the lengths increase with increasing elongation periods. Thus you can conclude that the line will have a positive slope, choice (A).

36. H   Figure 2 shows that there is a linear relationship between cross-sectional area and ΔT. You can also see that as cross-sectional area increases, ΔT increases. If System 1 has a larger cross-sectional area than System 2, it must have a larger ΔT, so you can eliminate choices (F) and (G). The question tells you that System 1 has twice the cross-sectional area of System 2, so choice (H) is the correct answer. A quick check of Figure 2 confirms this: when cross-sectional area is 4 cm², ΔT is 6°C and when cross-sectional area is 8 cm², ΔT is 12°C.

37. B   Based on the definition given in the passage, convection would not transfer heat from the water to the metal containers. This eliminates all choices except for choice (B).

38. F   Figure 2 shows that ΔT increases with cross-sectional area. Figure 3 shows that ΔT increases with height. In particular, Figures 2 and 3 show that height affects ΔT more than cross-sectional area, although choice (H) has the greatest cross-sectional area, choices (F) and (G) have much greater height. Since choice (G) has a smaller height, the system with the greater ΔT is choice (F). Choice (F) is the best answer because it has larger values for both than any other choice.

39. D   Table 1 shows that for water in the setup described, ΔT should be 10°C. Find the differences in temperature in the answer choices given. Choice (A) has a difference of 20°C. Choice (B) has a difference of 30°C. Choice (C) has a difference of 0°C. Only choice (D) has the appropriate ΔT of 10°C.

40. H   The passage gives relationships between ΔT and only three variables: cross-sectional area, length, and starting temperature. None of these are possible choices, but radius is linked to cross-sectional area. As radius increases, area increases. Figure 2 shows that as cross-sectional area increases, ΔT increases, so the correct answer is choice (H). Insulation, amount of liquid, and air temperature are not discussed as being related to ΔT in the passage.

WRITING TEST

To grade your essay, see the Essay Checklist on the following page. The following is an example of a top-scoring essay for the prompt given in this test. Note that it's not perfect, but it still follows an organized outline and has a strong introductory paragraph, a concluding paragraph, and transitions throughout.

Today's high school student is presented with many opportunities to cheat. The Internet is a ready source of resources for the unscrupulous, even including papers already written on just about any topic imaginable. But the problem of cheating reaches farther than just homework assignments—students today also have chances to cheat during exams in school, as teachers cannot possibly monitor the behavior of every student in a classroom simultaneously. Because the pressure to get great grades and get into a good college is so high, the pressure to cheat is very high. Nevertheless, it is critically important that schools do not give up in the fight against cheating because cheating is unfair to the students who play by the rules, because the consequences of being caught only increase later in life, and because one of the purposes of school is to teach students values.

Contrary to popular belief, not every student cheats. In all likelihood, the percentage of students cheating regularly is much lower than 50 percent. But the damage these students do to the students who don't cheat is very real and very severe. Colleges are choosing students based on their GPA and their class rank (in part—there are obviously other factors). When students cheat, they get higher grades that they don't deserve. As these cheaters move up the class rank, they are pushing down students who deserve to be higher, hurting those students' college opportunities. Cheaters will often say "Who cares if I cheat—it doesn't hurt anyone else's grades." Maybe not, but the damage done is even worse—it's hurting other people's futures.

Because it's hard for teachers in high school to keep an eye on every student, cheaters believe that they won't get caught, and for a while they are probably going to be right. Cheaters learn tricks that work well in the high school environment. The problem is, though, that they will keep on cheating through life and eventually will get caught. Colleges and businesses take this sort of behavior much more seriously, and so the cost of being caught cheating becomes much higher. If the cheater gets caught in high school and learns not to continue this behavior in the future, it will be embarrassing, but the real cost will be much easier for him or her to bear. So, schools should work hard to catch cheating during high school and should treat it seriously.

Finally, schools have a responsibility to set an example to their students. Part of the school's job, whether students like it or not, is to teach them the values of right and wrong. If schools are perceived by the student body to be giving up in the face of cheating, that not only sends us the message that this sort of devious behavior is acceptable (which we know is not true), it also ruins the reputation of the administration in our eyes. We will no longer take the school seriously on any matter, which will have a long-term damaging effect on the school community.

Clearly, cheating is wrong. There is no disagreement on this point, even from those who cheat. Just as clearly, schools have to do their very best to prevent cheating from occurring. Of all the reasons given, the first is the most important: These people are stealing college opportunities from their classmates.

WRITING TEST

Essay Checklist

1. The Introduction
    Did you
    - o start with a topic sentence that paraphrases or restates the prompt?
    - o clearly state your position on the issue?

2. Body Paragraph 1
    Did you
    - o start with a transition/topic sentence that discusses the opposing side of the argument?
    - o give an example of a reason that one might agree with the opposing side of the argument?
    - o clearly state that the opposing side of the argument is wrong or flawed?
    - o show what is wrong with the opposing side's example or position?

3. Body Paragraphs 2 and 3
    Did you
    - o start with a transition/topic sentence that discusses your position on the prompt?
    - o give one example or reason to support your position?
    - o show the grader how your example supports your position?
    - o end the paragraph by restating your thesis?

4. Conclusion
    Did you
    - o restate your position on the issue?
    - o end with a flourish?

5. Overall
    Did you
    - o write neatly?
    - o avoid multiple spelling and grammar mistakes?
    - o try to vary your sentence structure?
    - o use a few impressive-sounding words?

SCORING YOUR PRACTICE EXAM

Step A

Count the number of correct answers for each section and record the number in the space provided for your raw score on the Score Conversion Worksheet below.

Step B

Using the Score Conversion Chart on the next page, convert your raw scores on each section to scaled scores. Then compute your composite ACT score by averaging the four subject scores. Add them up and divide by four. Don't worry about the essay score; it is not included in your composite score.

Score Conversion Worksheet		
Section	Raw Score	Scaled Score
1	_____/75	_____
2	_____/60	_____
3	_____/40	_____
4	_____/40	_____

SCORE CONVERSION CHART

Scaled Score	Raw Scores			
	Test 1 English	Test 2 Math	Test 3 Reading	Test 4 Science
36	75	59–60	40	39–40
35	72–74	57–58	––	38
34	71	56	39	37
33	70	54–55	38	––
32	69	53	37	36
31	68	51–52	––	35
30	66–67	50	36	34
29	65	49	35	33
28	64	47–48	34	32
27	62–63	45–46	33	31
26	60–61	42–44	32	29–30
25	58–59	40–41	31	27–28
24	56–57	38–39	30	26
23	53–55	35–37	29	24–25
22	51–52	33–34	27–28	22–23
21	47–50	32	26	20–21
20	44–46	30–31	24–25	18–19
19	41–43	28–29	22–23	17
18	39–40	26–27	21	15–16
17	37–38	22–25	19–20	14
16	34–36	18–21	17–18	13
15	31–33	14–17	15–16	12
14	29–30	10–13	13–14	11
13	27–28	08–09	11–12	10
12	25–26	07	09–10	09
11	23–24	05–06	08	08
10	20–22	04	06–07	07
09	17–19	––	––	05–06
08	15–16	03	05	04
07	12–14	––	04	––
06	10–11	02	03	03
05	07–09	––	––	02
04	06	01	02	––
03	04–05	––	––	01
02	02–03	––	01	––
01	00–01	00	00	00

Part IX
The Princeton Review ACT Practice Exam 2 and Answers and Explanations

Chapter 27
Practice Exam 2

ENGLISH TEST
45 Minutes—75 Questions

DIRECTIONS: In the five passages that follow, certain words and phrases are underlined and numbered. In the right-hand column, you will find alternatives for each underlined part. In most cases, you are to choose the one that best expresses the idea, makes the statement appropriate for standard written English, or is worded most consistently with the style and tone of the passage as a whole. If you think the original version is best, choose "NO CHANGE." In some cases, you will find in the right-hand column a question about the underlined part of the passage. You are to choose the best answer to the question.

You will also find questions about a section of the passage or the passage as a whole. These questions do not refer to an underlined portion of the passage, but rather are identified by a number or numbers in a box.

For each question, choose the alternative you consider best and blacken the corresponding oval on your answer document. Read each passage through once before you begin to answer the questions that accompany it. For many of the questions, you must read several sentences beyond the question to determine the answer. Be sure that you have read far enough ahead each time you choose an alternative.

PASSAGE I

Crocheting Makes a Good Hobby

Crocheting is the art of making fabric by twisting yarn or thread with a hook. Although many associate it by older women, [1]

crocheting can be a fun hobby for people of both genders and all [2] ages. Once you start crocheting, you won't be able to put down the hook; you'll have a hobby for life. [3]

1. **A.** NO CHANGE
   B. to
   C. by
   D. with

2. **F.** NO CHANGE
   G. for people of both genders, masculine and feminine,
   H. for male and female people of both genders
   J. for people of both genders, both males and females,

3. At this point, the author is considering adding the following true statement:

   > Irish nuns helped save lives with crocheting when they used it as a way to make a living during the Great Irish Potato Famine of 1846.

   Should the writer add this sentence here?

   A. Yes, because it is essential to know when crocheting became internationally prominent and how it did so.
   B. Yes, because the reference to the Great Irish Potato Famine demonstrates that the author is conscious of historical events.
   C. No, because the reference to the Great Irish Potato Famine is not relevant to the main topic of this essay.
   D. No, because many people who left Ireland in 1846 brought crocheting with them to the United States and Australia.

GO ON TO THE NEXT PAGE.

Time-honored and easily <u>taught</u> to all, crocheting is an easy
4
hobby to pick up. Instructional books are readily available, and

once you've learned a few basic <u>stitches. Picking</u> up the more
5
advanced ones is a snap. Once you learn how to crochet, you can

<u>purchase store-bought books that detail crocheting patterns</u> that
6
tell you exactly how to make the projects that interest you. Even
if you want to try several projects, the supplies required for

<u>it's</u> completion are minimal; all you need are a crochet hook,
7
yarn, and a pair of scissors. You don't need to worry about
making a big investment, either; fifteen dollars will buy you no
<u>fewer than</u> three starter kits!
8

[1] As you grow more proficient, you can expand your
supplies by purchasing hooks of different <u>types</u> to vary the
9
size of your stitches. [2] Crochet hooks are available in all

<u>sizes, ranging,</u> from very small to very large, with everything in
10
between. [3] Some are so big that you need to use two strands of
yarn. [4] Other hooks are very tiny, so small that you must use
thread. [5] These hooks are suitable for making smaller, more
delicate things such as lace doilies, tablecloths, and bedspreads.
[6] These hooks make big stitches, so you can finish a project
with them very quickly. [7] It is best to start with hooks that are
medium in size; these are the easiest to manipulate and require
only one strand of yarn. [11]

4. F. NO CHANGE
   G. teaches
   H. taughted
   J. teached

5. A. NO CHANGE
   B. stitches; picking
   C. stitches, picking
   D. stitches since picking

6. F. NO CHANGE
   G. buy books and other pamphlets at craft and book stores detailing certain specific patterns
   H. buy pattern books
   J. acquire store-bought pattern books

7. A. NO CHANGE
   B. its
   C. its'
   D. their

8. F. NO CHANGE
   G. fewer then
   H. less than
   J. less then

9. A. NO CHANGE
   B. types;
   C. types:
   D. types,

10. F. NO CHANGE
    G. sizes, ranging
    H. sizes; ranging
    J. sizes ranging,

11. For the sake of the logic and coherence of this paragraph, Sentence 6 should be placed:
    A. where it is now.
    B. after Sentence 1.
    C. after Sentence 3.
    D. after Sentence 7.

GO ON TO THE NEXT PAGE.

Because it seems like there are a million hooks to keep
₁₂
track of, crocheting makes a good hobby because it requires only
₁₂
time and patience, not attention or tremendous investment. You
can crochet while watching television, listening to music, or
visiting with other people. It is fun and relaxing and allows you
to express your creative side in an easy way. Also, you
₁₃
have finished a project, you have a cherished keepsake. Whether

you have made an afghan to keep you warm on cold winter
₁₄
nights or a lace tablecloth to add a touch of elegance to your
dining room, your creation is sure to be cherished for a long time
to come.

12. Given that all the choices are true, which one provides the most effective transition from the preceding paragraph to this one?
   F. NO CHANGE
   G. Because it can take a long time to finish a project,
   H. With such a simple and inexpensive set of materials,
   J. No longer a field dominated primarily by older women,

13. A. NO CHANGE
   B. Also, finally you
   C. Also, despite the fact you
   D. Also, once you

14. F. NO CHANGE
   G. at
   H. of
   J. within

Question 15 asks about the preceding passage as a whole.

15. Suppose the writer's goal had been to write an essay that demonstrates the commercial potential of crocheting. Would this essay successfully accomplish that goal?
   A. Yes, because it gives examples of end products of crocheting and shows the different kinds of materials needed to produce a wide range of products.
   B. Yes, because it discusses the supplies necessary to create crocheted products, and it shows the usefulness of many of them during the cold winter months.
   C. No, because it does not mention the market value of crocheted products or how one might go about selling them.
   D. No, because it describes other industries and hobbies that would be more commercially successful.

PASSAGE II

Seurat's Masterpiece

[1] How can I describe the wonder I felt the first time I saw my favorite painting, Georges Seurat's *A Sunday on La Grande Jatte*? [2] I had admired the work for years in art books, but I never thought I saw the actual painting, which was housed in
₁₆
Chicago, many miles from where I lived. [3] I finally got my

16. F. NO CHANGE
   G. would see
   H. had seen
   J. was seeing

GO ON TO THE NEXT PAGE.

chance to when I met someone else who loved the painting as
$\overline{17}$
much as I did. [4] We both had three days off at the same time,

so we decided to make a road trip to Chicago so we could see

the painting in all it's grandeur. [5] We packed our bags,
$\overline{18}$

jumped in the car, and headed on our way toward Chicago. 20
$\overline{19}$

[1] The first thing that struck me as we entered the room

where the painting was displayed; was the size of the painting.
$\overline{21}$
[2] A common size for canvases is 24 by 36 inches. [3] It was

enormous! [4] It covered a large part of an even larger wall. [5]

The painting's size amazed me since it was painted with dots, a

technique called pointillism. [6] To create a painting of such

magnitude using this technique seemed an almost impossible

task. [7] Seurat had done it, though, and had made it look easy! 23
$\overline{22}$

17. **A.** NO CHANGE
    B. at the moment
    C. just to
    D. DELETE the underlined portion.

18. **F.** NO CHANGE
    G. our
    H. its
    J. its'

19. **A.** NO CHANGE
    B. jumped in the car, and had headed
    C. jumped in the car, and head
    D. had jumped in the car, and headed

20. Upon reviewing this paragraph and noticing that some information has been left out, the writer composes the following
sentence, incorporating the information:

> Her name was Lisa; she lived in my dorm, and a mutual
> friend had introduced us to each other, knowing how
> much both of us loved art.

For the sake of the logic of this paragraph, this sentence should
be placed after Sentence:

    F. 2.
    G. 3.
    H. 4.
    J. 5.

21. **A.** NO CHANGE
    B. displayed:
    C. displayed,
    D. displayed

22. **F.** NO CHANGE
    G. task and difficult to complete.
    H. task, difficult to complete.
    J. task, overwhelming in its difficulty.

23. Which of the following sentences is LEAST relevant to the
development of this paragraph and therefore could be deleted?

    A. Sentence 2
    B. Sentence 4
    C. Sentence 5
    D. Sentence 6

GO ON TO THE NEXT PAGE.

Even more impressive, however, was the beauty of the
painting. Viewed from a distance, the colors looked muted,
capturing the idyllic mood of a summer day in the park.

When I approached the painting, though, its colors exploded into
myriad hues, illustrating the artist's skill in combining colors to
create a mood. Even the parts of the painting that appeared white
from a distance were vibrantly multicolored when viewed up
close. [26] The effect was incredible;

he sat and stared at the painting in wonder for a good portion of

the afternoon. [28]

My friend and I saw many other sights, on our trip to
Chicago, but the best part by far was being able to see our
favorite work of art. The image is forever imprinted in my mind

24. Given that all of the choices are accurate, which provides
the most effective and logical transition from the preceding
paragraph to this one?

F. NO CHANGE
G. One thing that struck me was
H. Many art critics have written about
J. The debate rages on over

25. Which of the following alternatives to the underlined portion
would NOT be acceptable?

A. As I approached the painting, though,
B. However, as I approached the painting,
C. I approached the painting, though,
D. However, when I approached the painting,

26. If the writer were to delete the phrase "from a distance" from
the preceding sentence, the paragraph would primarily lose:

F. an essential point explaining the author's love of the painting.
G. the first part of the contrast in this sentence, which the
author uses to describe viewing the painting.
H. a further indication of the length of the road trip taken by
the author and her friend.
J. nothing, because the information provided by this phrase
is stated more clearly elsewhere in the paragraph.

27. A. NO CHANGE
B. one
C. they
D. we

28. At this point, the writer is considering adding the following
true statement:

The Art Institute of Chicago contains many other
famous paintings, among them Edvard Munch's *The
Scream* and Grant Wood's *American Gothic.*

Should the writer make this addition here?

F. Yes, because it gives additional details essential to understanding the collection at the museum.
G. Yes, because it demonstrates a contrast between the author's favorite painting and those in this sentence.
H. No, because it provides information that is not relevant at
this point in the paragraph and essay.
J. No, because it is contradicted by other information presented in this essay.

29. A. NO CHANGE
B. sights, which
C. sights;
D. sights

GO ON TO THE NEXT PAGE.

at the museum gift shop, even when I'm not looking at the
<u>souvenir print I bought.</u>
30

30. The best placement for the underlined portion would be:

    F. where it is now.
    G. after the word *image*.
    H. after the word *looking*.
    J. after the word *bought* (ending the sentence with a period).

PASSAGE III

The Language of Cats

Many people believe that language is the domain of human beings. However, cats have <u>developed an intricate language not</u>
31
for each other, but for the human beings who

<u>have adopted them as pets.</u>
32

31. A. NO CHANGE
    B. developed, an intricate language
    C. developed an intricate language,
    D. developed; an intricate language

32. Which choice would most clearly and effectively express the ownership relationship between humans and cats?

    F. NO CHANGE
    G. like to have cats around.
    H. often have dogs as well.
    J. are naturally inclined to like cats.

When communicating with each other, <u>cats' "talk" is a</u>
33
<u>complex system of nonverbal signals.</u> In particular, their tails,
33

33. A. NO CHANGE
    B. a complicated system of nonverbal signals is used by cats to "talk."
    C. cats "talk" with a complex system of nonverbal signals.
    D. "talking" is done by them with a system of complex nonverbal signals.

rather than any kind of "speech," <u>provide</u> cats' chief means of
34
expression. They also use physical contact to express their feelings. With other cats, cats will use their voices only to express pain. <u>35</u>

34. F. NO CHANGE
    G. having provided
    H. has provided
    J. were provided by

35. If the preceding sentence were deleted, the essay would primarily lose:

    A. a redundant point made elsewhere in the essay.
    B. another description of the ways in which cats communicate nonverbally.
    C. an exception to the general trend described in this paragraph.
    D. a brief summary of the information contained in the essay up to this point.

<u>Next, incredibly,</u> all of that changes when a human walks
36
into the room. Cats use a wide range of vocal expressions when they communicate with a person, from affectionate meows to

36. F. NO CHANGE
    G. (Do NOT begin new paragraph) Incredibly,
    H. (Begin new paragraph) Next incredibly,
    J. (Begin new paragraph) Incredibly,

GO ON TO THE NEXT PAGE.

menacing hisses. Since <u>cats verbal expressions</u> are not used to
₃₇

communicate with other cats, it is <u>logical and reasonable</u>
₃₈
to conclude that cats developed this "language" expressly to
communicate with their human owners.

This fact is demonstrated more <u>clear since</u> observing
₃₉
households that have only one cat. An only cat is usually very
vocal, since the only creature around with whom the cat can
communicate is its owner. Cats with other feline companions,
though, are much quieter. If they want to have a conversation,
they need only go to their fellow cats and communicate in their
natural way. 40

Since cats learned to meow for the sole purpose of
communicating with human beings, owners should take the time
to learn what their different meows mean. If an owner
<u>knows, to name</u> just a few examples, which meow means the cat
₄₁
is hungry, which means the cat wants to be petted, and which
means the cat wants to have a little "conversation," the bond

between cat and owner will grow deeper. 42 Certainly, after a
time, owners will see that communicating with their pets, not
just cats, is every bit as important to forging good relationships

<u>as to communicate</u> with other humans. Once, as an owner,
₄₃
you know that the cat is not just

37. A. NO CHANGE
    B. cat's verbal expressions
    C. cats' verbal expressions
    D. cats verbal expressions,

38. F. NO CHANGE
    G. logical and well-reasoned
    H. logical to a startling degree
    J. logical

39. A. NO CHANGE
    B. clear when
    C. clearly since
    D. clearly when

40. At this point, the writer is considering adding the following
    true statement:

    > On the other hand, the natural way for most birds to
    > communicate is vocally, by way of the "bird song."

    Should the writer add this sentence here?

    F. Yes, because it shows that cats are truly unique in com-
        municating nonverbally.
    G. Yes, because it adds a relevant and enlightening detail
        about another animal.
    H. No, because it basically repeats information given earlier
        in the essay.
    J. No, because it does not contribute to the development of
        this paragraph and the essay as a whole.

41. A. NO CHANGE
    B. knows, to,
    C. knows to,
    D. knows to

42. If the writer wanted to emphasize that cats communicate vo-
    cally with their owners to express a large number of different
    emotions in addition to those listed in the previous sentence,
    which of the following true statements should be added at this
    point?

    F. Many animals communicate hunger similarly to cats.
    G. Cats will tell their owners when they feel pain, sadness,
        irritation, or love.
    H. Cats communicate these emotions differently to other cats.
    J. Humans have the easiest time communicating with other
        mammals.

43. A. NO CHANGE
    B. as being communicative
    C. as communicating
    D. through communicating

GO ON TO THE NEXT PAGE.

making senseless noises without any rhyme or reason but is
<u>   </u>
                          44
making an attempt to communicate, you can make an effort to

communicate back. After all, your cat isn't meowing just for the

sake of making noise; <u>however, cats are less communicative than</u>
                                                          45
<u>many other animals.</u>
      45

44. F. NO CHANGE
   G. making senseless noises
   H. senselessly making noises with no thought involved
   J. making senseless noises, having no idea what they mean,

45. Which choice would best summarize the main point the essay makes about cats' communication with their human owners?
   A. NO CHANGE
   B. rather, there's a good chance your cat is trying to tell you something.
   C. instead, your cat is probably trying to communicate with other cats by meowing.
   D. on the other hand, it is better to have more than one cat so they can undergo a natural development.

PASSAGE IV

Visiting Mackinac Island

Visiting Mackinac (pronounced "Mackinaw") Island is like

<u>taking a step back to the past in time.</u> Victorian
                          46

houses' and a fort dating back to the War of 1812 surround the
<u>   </u>
 47
historic downtown, where horses and buggies still pull

passengers down the road.

The only way to get to Mackinac Island is by boat or private
                                      48
plane, and you may not bring your car. Automobiles are

outlawed on the little, <u>isolated, Michigan, island,</u> so visitors can
                                      49

see the sights only by horse, carriage, or <u>by riding a bicycle,</u> or
                                                      50
on foot. Luckily, the island is small enough that cars are not

<u>necessary, Mackinac</u> measures only a mile and a half in
      51
diameter.

46. F. NO CHANGE
   G. moving in a past-related direction
   H. going back to the past, not the future,
   J. stepping back

47. A. NO CHANGE
   B. house's
   C. houses
   D. houses,

48. F. NO CHANGE
   G. your sweet self over to
   H. yourself on down to
   J. over to

49. A. NO CHANGE
   B. isolated Michigan island
   C. isolated Michigan island,
   D. isolated, Michigan, island

50. F. NO CHANGE
   G. by bicycle,
   H. riding on a bicycle,
   J. bicycle,

51. A. NO CHANGE
   B. necessary, furthermore, Mackinac
   C. necessary. Mackinac
   D. necessary Mackinac

GO ON TO THE NEXT PAGE.

There are many things to see while visiting Mackinac Island. The majestic Grand Hotel is a popular tourist spot, as are the governor's mansion and Arch Rock, a towering limestone arch formed naturally by water erosion. 52 Fort Mackinac, where they still set off cannons every hour, is also a popular place to visit. Visible from parts of the island are Mackinac Bridge—the longest suspension bridge ever built—and a picturesque old lighthouse.

Shopping is also a favorite pastime on Mackinac Island. The island's biggest industry is tourism, 53 For the island's many

tourists, the most popular item of sale on Mackinac Island is
                                                    54

fudge. The downtown streets are lined with fudge shops, where
                                                          55
tourists can watch fudge of all different flavors being made before lining up to buy some for themselves. These fudge shops

are so numerous and abundant that the local residents have even
       56

developed a special nickname for these tourists: I call the
                                                      57
tourists "fudgies."

Apart from sightseeing and shopping, Mackinac Island is a great place to just sit back and relax. In the summer, a gentle lake breeze floats through the air, when it creates a beautiful,
                                               58
temperate climate. It is peaceful to sit in the city park and watch the ferries and private boats float into the harbor. The privacy of

---

52. If the writer were to delete the phrase "formed naturally by water erosion" (placing a period after the word *arch*), this sentence would primarily lose:

F. a detail describing the unique formation of the Arch Rock.
G. factual information concerning the geological formations of the tourist attractions on Mackinac Island.
H. a contrast to the governor's mansion, which was constructed by human hands.
J. nothing; this information is detailed elsewhere in this paragraph.

53. Given that all the following are true, which one, if added here at the end of this sentence, would provide the most effective transition to the topic discussed in the sentence that follows?

A. so there are many souvenir stores, T-shirt shops, and candy and ice cream parlors.
B. so Mackinac Island has not been negatively affected by outsourcing.
C. which is a big change from the island's eighteenth-century use in the fur trade.
D. but it's not a tourist attraction like many others with theme parks and chain restaurants.

54. F. NO CHANGE
    G. for selling
    H. for sale
    J. of selling

55. Which of the following alternatives to the underlined portion would NOT be acceptable?

A. which
B. so
C. and
D. in which

56. F. NO CHANGE
    G. abundantly numerous
    H. numerous
    J. of an abundance truly numerous

57. A. NO CHANGE
    B. one calls
    C. it calls
    D. they call

58. F. NO CHANGE
    G. creating
    H. once it creates
    J. as if it had created

GO ON TO THE NEXT PAGE.

the island's environs certainly <u>don't give</u> it the hustle-bustle
₅₉
quality of a city, but the relaxing atmosphere makes Mackinac
Island the perfect place to visit to get away from the hectic pace
of everyday life.

59. A. NO CHANGE
B. isn't giving
C. hasn't given
D. doesn't give

Question 60 asks about the preceding passage as a whole.

---

60. Suppose the writer had intended to write an essay on the difficulty the residents of Mackinac Island have had prohibiting automobile traffic from the historic island. Would this essay have successfully fulfilled that goal?

F. Yes, because the automobile has become such an essential part of American tourist travel that the residents are clearly threatened.

G. Yes, because this essay discusses the fact that automobiles are outlawed and goes on to detail many of the reasons this was possible.

H. No, because the essay focuses instead on other aspects of Mackinac Island, mentioning automobiles in only one part of the passage.

J. No, because this essay describes the ways the residents of Mackinac Island have sought to bring automobiles back to the island, not to outlaw them.

PASSAGE V

Fun with Karaoke

[1]

[1] Karaoke is one of the most popular forms of
entertainment in the world. [2] What defies understanding,
though, is why so many ordinary people insist on getting up on
stage in public, humiliating themselves in front of both their
<u>friends; and peers.</u> [3] Whether practiced at home, in a
₆₁
restaurant, or at a party, karaoke is a form of entertainment

that <u>provides</u> people with a great time and a positive feeling. [4]
₆₂
It is understandable that people would enjoy singing in the

61. A. NO CHANGE
B. friends and peers.
C. friends, and peers.
D. friends and, peers.

62. Which of the following alternatives to the underlined portion would NOT be acceptable?

F. that has provided
G. , providing
H. , that is, providing
J. that having provided

GO ON TO THE NEXT PAGE.

privacy of their homes. [5] There are many different ways to respond to this question. ☐63

[2]

<u>Looking</u> more closely, and you'll see a main reason for
64
karaoke's success is its glitz and glamour. Karaoke provides people with a moment when they are more than just everyday folks—they are stars. Even though their performances may be heard only in dimly lit bars or busy <u>restaurants, but</u> karaoke
65
singers are still performing as if in a true concert with such

concert-hall <u>staples,</u> as microphones, lights, and applause. Even
66
though the singers' voices are not spectacular, the audience

<u>has known</u> that it's all for fun and responds anyway. And in the
67

end, everyone would like to be a rock star. <u>Karaoke is as close as
68
many people will get to fame and stardom, but this is not the
68
only reason for its enduring popularity.</u>
68

[3]

There is another, more obvious reason why karaoke is so popular and singing in public is such fun. The average person allows his or her singing to be heard only in the shower or in the car as the radio plays. Karaoke, <u>by contrast,</u> allows the average
69
person the opportunity to share that ordinarily solitary

experience with other people. <u>In lieu of</u> how good or bad their
70
voices are, people can experience the sheer joy of music with

63. For the sake of logic and coherence, Sentence 2 should be placed:
- **A.** where it is now.
- **B.** after Sentence 3.
- **C.** after Sentence 4.
- **D.** after Sentence 5.

64. F. NO CHANGE
- **G.** Having looked
- **H.** To look
- **J.** Look

65. A. NO CHANGE
- **B.** restaurants which
- **C.** restaurants,
- **D.** restaurants but

66. F. NO CHANGE
- **G.** staples:
- **H.** staples
- **J.** staples;

67. A. NO CHANGE
- **B.** is knowing
- **C.** knew
- **D.** knows

68. Given that all the choices are true, which one would most effectively conclude this paragraph while leading into the main focus of the next paragraph?
- **F.** NO CHANGE
- **G.** This is why AudioSynTrac and Numark Electronics were so successful in debuting the first singalong tapes and equipment back in the 1970s.
- **H.** Japan's lasting influence on karaoke is obvious all the way down to its name—the Japanese word karaoke translates roughly to "empty orchestra."
- **J.** Singing in front of people is more fun for many people than singing in the shower or in the car.

69. A. NO CHANGE
- **B.** furthermore,
- **C.** moreover,
- **D.** as a result,

70. F. NO CHANGE
- **G.** Regardless of
- **H.** However
- **J.** Because of

GO ON TO THE NEXT PAGE.

others, whose singing is mostly a private affair as well, through
      —
      71
karaoke.

[4]

The effect karaoke has on people may also provide an
explanation for its popularity: it helps bring people who are
ordinarily shy out of their shells. ｜72｜ Karaoke helps them
overcome stage fright, build their self-confidence, and conquer

their fears. The singers may feel nervous or silly if they first take
                                                                —
                                                                73
the stage, but when the audience breaks out into applause, the
singers are sure to feel rewarded.

[5]

Whatever the reason, karaoke continues to grow in
popularity. Last year, karaoke made no less than $7 billion in
                                              ——
                                              74
profit in Japan. Many dismiss it as a fad, but as long as karaoke
is fun and leaves people feeling good, it will not disappear.

71. A. NO CHANGE
B. who
C. whom
D. who's

72. If the writer were to delete the clause "who are ordinarily shy"
from the preceding sentence, the essay would primarily lose:
F. a detail that explains why karaoke is so popular in the
international community.
G. a detail meant to indicate that karaoke is popular among
those not normally inclined to sing in public.
H. information that emphasizes the possible psychological
benefits of karaoke for the chronically shy.
J. an indication that karaoke may be used at some future time
to help singers overcome stage fright.

73. A. NO CHANGE
B. when
C. unless
D. where

74. F. NO CHANGE
G. lesser than
H. fewer then
J. few than

Question 75 asks about the preceding passage
as a whole.

---

75. Upon reviewing notes for this essay, the writer comes across
some information and composes the following sentence incorporating that information:

While different regions of the United States prefer
different artists, the most popular karaoke requests
are invariably for country artists, varying from the
modern Carrie Underwood to the classic Johnny Cash.

For the sake of the logic and coherence of this essay, this
sentence should be:

A. placed at the end of Paragraph 3.
B. placed at the end of Paragraph 4.
C. placed at the end of Paragraph 5.
D. NOT added to the essay at all.

END OF TEST 1

STOP! DO NOT TURN THE PAGE UNTIL TOLD TO DO SO.

MATHEMATICS TEST

60 Minutes—60 Questions

DIRECTIONS: Solve each problem, choose the correct answer, and then darken the corresponding oval on your answer sheet.

Do not linger over problems that take too much time. Solve as many as you can; then return to the others in the time you have left for this test.

You are permitted to use a calculator on this test. You may use your calculator for any problems you choose, but some of the problems may best be done without using a calculator.

Note: Unless otherwise stated, all of the following should be assumed:

1. Illustrative figures are NOT necessarily drawn to scale.
2. Geometric figures lie in a plane.
3. The word *line* indicates a straight line.
4. The word *average* indicates arithmetic mean.

---

1. Point *X* is located at −15 on the real number line. If point *Y* is located at −11, what is the midpoint of line segment *XY*?

   A. −13
   B. −4
   C. −2
   D. 2
   E. 13

2. Given triangle *CDE* (shown below) with a right angle at point *E*, what is the length of leg *DE*?

   F. $\sqrt{2}$
   G. 2
   H. 6
   J. $\sqrt{164}$
   K. 16

DO YOUR FIGURING HERE.

GO ON TO THE NEXT PAGE.

3. Lucy is studying her ant farm. She needs to approximate the number of ants in the population, and she realizes that the number of ants, N, is close to 50 more than double the volume of the ant farm, V. Which of the formulas below expresses that approximation?

    A. $N \approx \frac{1}{2}V + 50$

    B. $N \approx \frac{1}{2}(V + 50)$

    C. $N \approx 2V + 50$

    D. $N \approx 2(V + 50)$

    E. $N \approx V^2 + 50$

DO YOUR FIGURING HERE.

4. Lisa has 5 fiction books and 7 nonfiction books on a table by her front door. As she rushes out the door one day, she takes a book at random. What is the probability that the book she takes is fiction?

    F. $\frac{1}{5}$

    G. $\frac{5}{7}$

    H. $\frac{1}{12}$

    J. $\frac{5}{12}$

    K. $\frac{7}{12}$

5. In the spring semester of her math class, Katie's test scores were 108, 81, 79, 99, 85, and 82. What was her average test score in the spring semester?

    A. 534
    B. 108
    C. 89
    D. 84
    E. 80

GO ON TO THE NEXT PAGE.

6. Given parallel lines *l* and *m*, which of the following choices lists a pair of angles that must be congruent?

DO YOUR FIGURING HERE.

    F.   ∠1 and ∠2
    G. ∠1 and ∠3
    H. ∠2 and ∠3
    J.   ∠2 and ∠5
    K. ∠3 and ∠5

7. Gregor works as a political intern and receives a monthly paycheck. He spends 20% of his paycheck on rent and deposits the remainder into a savings account. If his deposit is $3,200, how much does he receive as his monthly pay?

    A. $ 4,000
    B. $ 5,760
    C. $ 7,200
    D. $ 8,000
    E. $17,000

8. Given parallelogram *ABCD* below and parallelogram *EFGH* (not shown) are similar, which of the following statements must be true about the two shapes?

    F.   Their areas are equal.
    G. Their perimeters are equal.
    H. Side *AB* is congruent to side *EF*.
    J.   Diagonal *AC* is congruent to diagonal *EG*.
    K. Their corresponding angles are congruent.

9. A size 8 dress that usually sells for $60 is on sale for 30% off. Victoria has a store credit card that entitles her to an additional 10% off the reduced price of any item in the store. Excluding sales tax, what is the price Victoria pays for the dress?

    A. $22.20
    B. $24.75
    C. $34.00
    D. $36.00
    E. $37.80

GO ON TO THE NEXT PAGE.

DO YOUR FIGURING HERE.

10. Erin and Amy are playing poker. At a certain point in the game, Erin has 3 more chips than Amy. On the next hand, Erin wins 4 chips from Amy. Now how many more chips does Erin have than Amy?

    F.   1
    G.   4
    H.   7
    J.   11
    K.   14

11. If $y = 4$, then $|1 - y| = ?$

    A.   −5
    B.   −3
    C.   3
    D.   4
    E.   5

12. $(3a + 2b)(a - b^2)$ is equivalent to:

    F. $4a + b^2$
    G. $3a^2 - 2b^3$
    H. $3a^2 + 2ab + 2b^3$
    J. $3a^2 - 3ab^2 + a^2b^2$
    K. $3a^2 - 3ab^2 + 2ab - 2b^3$

13. For all real values of y, $3 - 2(4 - y) = ?$

    A. $-2y - 9$
    B. $-2y + 8$
    C. $-2y - 1$
    D. $2y - 5$
    E. $2y + 11$

14. Which of the following is equivalent to $(y^3)^8$?

    F. y^{11}
    G. y^{24}
    H. $8y^3$
    J. $8y^{11}$
    K. $24y$

15. If the first day of the year is a Monday, what is the 260th day?

    A.   Monday
    B.   Tuesday
    C.   Wednesday
    D.   Thursday
    E.   Friday

GO ON TO THE NEXT PAGE.

16. If a square has an area of 64 square units, what is the area of the largest circle that can be inscribed inside the square?

F. 4π
G. 8π
H. 16π
J. 64
K. 64π

DO YOUR FIGURING HERE.

17. What is the product of the solutions of the expression $x^2 - 5x - 14 = 0$?

A. -14
B. -2
C. 0
D. 5
E. 7

18. Factoring the polynomial $x^{12} - 9$ reveals a number of factors for the expression. Which of these is NOT one of the possible factors?

F. $x^6 + 3$
G. $x^{12} - 9$
H. $x^3 + \sqrt{3}$
J. $x^3 - \sqrt{3}$
K. $x - \sqrt{3}$

19. What is the value of $\dfrac{2x+4}{3x}$ when $x = \dfrac{1}{6}$?

A. $4\dfrac{1}{3}$
B. 2
C. $\dfrac{26}{3}$
D. 12
E. 24

20. If you drive 60 miles at 90 miles an hour, how many minutes will the trip take you?

F. 15
G. 30
H. 40
J. 60
K. 90

GO ON TO THE NEXT PAGE.

21. The area of a trapezoid is found by multiplying the height by the average of the bases: $A = \frac{1}{2}h(b_1 + b_2)$. Given the side measurements below, what is the area, in square inches, of the trapezoid?

A. $15\sqrt{2}$
B. 22
C. 24
D. $24\sqrt{2}$
E. $30\sqrt{2}$

22. If $x = -\frac{2}{3}$ and $x = \frac{1}{4}$ are the roots of the quadratic equation $ax^2 + bx + c = 0$, then which of the following could represent the two factors of $ax^2 + bx + c$?

F. $(3x + 2)$ and $(4x - 1)$
G. $(3x + 1)$ and $(4x - 2)$
H. $(3x - 1)$ and $(4x + 2)$
J. $(3x - 2)$ and $(4x + 1)$
K. $(3x - 2)$ and $(4x - 1)$

23. In the rhombus below, diagonal $AC = 6$ and diagonal $BD = 8$. What is the length of each of the four sides?

A. $\sqrt{7}$
B. $\sqrt{14}$
C. 5
D. 7
E. 10

GO ON TO THE NEXT PAGE.

24. A rectangular rug has an area of 80 square feet, and its width is exactly 2 feet shorter than its length. What is the length, in feet, of the rug?

F.   8
G. 10
H. 16
J. 18
K. 36

25. In the Cartesian plane, a line runs through points (1,–5) and (5,10). Which of the following represents the slope of that line?

A. $\dfrac{4}{15}$

B. $\dfrac{4}{5}$

C. 1

D. $\dfrac{5}{4}$

E. $\dfrac{15}{4}$

26. The equation of a circle in the standard (x,y) coordinate plane is given by the equation $(x + 5)^2 + (y - 5)^2 = 5$. What is the center of the circle?

F. $(-\sqrt{5},\ \sqrt{5})$
G. $(-5,\quad 5)$
H. $(\sqrt{5},\ -\sqrt{5})$
J. $(\ 5,\quad -5)$
K. $(\ 5,\quad 5)$

27. The graph below shows the function $f(x)$ in the coordinate plane. Which of the following choices best describes the *domain* of this function?

(Note: The domain is defined as the set of all values of x for which a function is defined.)

A. {0, 1, 2, 3, 4}
B. {0, 1, 2}
C. {x: 0 < x < 2}
D. {x: 0 < x < 4}
E. All real values of x

GO ON TO THE NEXT PAGE.

28. Amber decides to graph her office and the nearest coffee shop in the standard (x,y) plane. If her office is at point $(-1,-5)$ and the coffee shop is at point $(3,3)$, what are the coordinates of the point exactly halfway between those of her office and the shop? (You may assume Amber is able to walk a straight line between.)

F. $(1,-1)$
G. $(1, 4)$
H. $(2,-1)$
J. $(2, 4)$
K. $(2, 0)$

29. For a chemistry class, Sanjay is doing an experiment that involves periodically heating a container of liquid. The graph below shows the temperature of the liquid at different times during the experiment. What is the average rate of change of temperature (in degrees Celsius per minute) during the times in which Sanjay is applying heat to this container?

A. 4
B. 5
C. 8
D. 10
E. 20

30. If $\dfrac{a^x}{a^y} = a^5$, for $a \neq 0$, which of the following statements must be true?

F. $x \neq 0$ and $y \neq 0$

G. $x + y = 5$

H. $x - y = 5$

J. $xy = 5$

K. $\dfrac{x}{y} = 5$

31. What is the slope of the line given by the equation $8 = 3y - 5x$?

A. -5

B. $-\dfrac{5}{3}$

C. $-\dfrac{3}{5}$

D. $\dfrac{3}{5}$

E. $\dfrac{5}{3}$

DO YOUR FIGURING HERE.

32. When adding fractions, a useful first step is to find the least common denominator (LCD) of the fractions. What is the LCD for these fractions?

$$\frac{2}{3^2 \cdot 5}, \frac{13}{5^2 \cdot 7 \cdot 11}, \frac{2}{3 \cdot 11^3}$$

F. $3 \cdot 5 \cdot 7 \cdot 11$

G. $3^2 \cdot 5^2 \cdot 7 \cdot 11$

H. $3^2 \cdot 5^2 \cdot 11^3$

J. $3^2 \cdot 5^2 \cdot 7 \cdot 11^3$

K. $3^3 \cdot 5^3 \cdot 7 \cdot 11^4$

33. $\dfrac{1}{4} \cdot \dfrac{2}{5} \cdot \dfrac{3}{6} \cdot \dfrac{4}{7} \cdot \dfrac{5}{8} \cdot \dfrac{6}{9} \cdot \dfrac{7}{10} = ?$

A. $\dfrac{1}{720}$

B. $\dfrac{1}{360}$

C. $\dfrac{1}{120}$

D. $\dfrac{27}{49}$

E. 1

GO ON TO THE NEXT PAGE.

34. Dave is in Pikeston and needs to go to Danville, which is about 110 miles due south of Pikeston. From Danville, he'll head east to Rocketville, about 200 miles from Danville. As he sets out on his trip, a plane takes off from the Pikeston airport and flies directly to Rocketville. Approximately how far, in miles, does the plane fly?

DO YOUR FIGURING HERE.

   F. 310

   G. $\sqrt{310}$

   H. $\sqrt{27900}$

   J. $\sqrt{30000}$

   K. $\sqrt{52100}$

35. The figure below is a pentagon (5-sided figure). Suppose a second pentagon were overlaid on this pentagon. At most, the two figures could have how many points of intersection?

   A. 1
   B. 2
   C. 5
   D. 10
   E. Infinitely many

36. MicroCorp will hold its annual company picnic next week and will assign 3 planning duties to its employees. One person selected will reserve a venue, another will arrange catering, and a third will plan activities. There are 10 employees eligible to fulfill these duties, and no employee can be assigned more than one duty. How many different ways are there for duties to be assigned to employees?

   F. 7^3

   G. 9^3

   H. 10^3

   J. $9 \cdot 8 \cdot 7$

   K. $10 \cdot 9 \cdot 8$

GO ON TO THE NEXT PAGE.

37. In the (x,y) coordinate plane below, points P (6,2) and Q (1,4) are two vertices of $\triangle PQR$. If $\angle PQR$ is a right angle, then which of the following could be the coordinates of R ?

DO YOUR FIGURING HERE.

- **A.** (4,–3)
- **B.** (3, 0)
- **C.** (2, 1)
- **D.** (2, 4)
- **E.** (3, 9)

38. If $y = 0.25(100 - y)$, then what is the value of y?

- **F.** 200
- **G.** 75
- **H.** 25
- **J.** 20
- **K.** 18

39. If $0° \leq x \leq 180°$ and $4\cos^2 x = 1$, then $x = $?

- **A.** 0°
- **B.** 60°
- **C.** 90°
- **D.** 150°
- **E.** 180°

40. Danielle's living room is a rectangle with the dimensions 16 feet by 18 feet. If she partially covers the bare floor with a circular throw rug with a diameter of 12 feet, what is the approximate area of bare floor, in square feet, that remains exposed?

(Note: Assume the rug lies completely flat and does not touch any wall.)

- **F.** 113
- **G.** 144
- **H.** 175
- **J.** 288
- **K.** Cannot be determined without knowing the exact position of the rug

GO ON TO THE NEXT PAGE.

41. In the standard (x,y) coordinate plane, which of the following is the equation of the line perpendicular to the line $y = -2x + 2$ and that passes through the point $(0,-3)$?

A. $y = -2x - 3$

B. $y = -\dfrac{1}{2}x + 2$

C. $y = \dfrac{1}{2}x - 3$

D. $y = \dfrac{1}{2}x + 2$

E. $y = 2x - 3$

42. In the figure given below, what is $\sin \theta$?

F. $\dfrac{1}{2}$

G. $\dfrac{\sqrt{3}}{3}$

H. $\dfrac{\sqrt{3}}{2}$

J. 1

K. $\sqrt{3}$

43. If $a = 5$ and $b = -\dfrac{1}{4}$, which of the following expressions will be the greatest?

A. $a + b$
B. $a - b$
C. $a \times b$
D. $a \div b$
E. $|a \times b|$

GO ON TO THE NEXT PAGE.

DO YOUR FIGURING HERE.

44. When $\frac{x}{3} - 1 = -\frac{13}{12}$, which of the following must be true?

    F. $-12 < x < -3$
    G. $-3 < x < 0$
    H. $0 < x < 3$
    J. $3 < x < 4$
    K. $4 < x$

45. Which choice below is the complete solution set of $|2z - 3| \geq 7$?

    A. $z \geq 5$
    B. $z \leq -2$ or $z \geq 5$
    C. $-5 \leq z \leq 5$
    D. $z \leq -6$ or $z \geq 2$
    E. $z \leq -5$ or $z \geq 2$

46. Which trigonometric function (where defined) is equivalent to
$$\frac{\sin^2 x}{\cos x \tan x}?$$

    F. $\frac{\cos x}{\sin^2 x}$

    G. $\frac{1}{\cos x}$

    H. $\sin x$

    J. $\frac{1}{\sin x}$

    K. $\frac{1}{\sin^2 x}$

GO ON TO THE NEXT PAGE.

DO YOUR FIGURING HERE.

47. When $a \neq b$, the expression $\dfrac{ax - bx}{4a - 4b} < 0$. Which of the following describes the complete set of x values that make this inequality true?

   A. $x = -4$ only

   B. $x = 4$ only

   C. $x = -\dfrac{1}{4}$ only

   D. $x < 0$

   E. $x > 0$

48. The volume of a cone, which is derived by treating it as a pyramid with infinitely many lateral faces, is given by the formula $V = \dfrac{1}{3}\pi r^2 h$, where r is the radius of the base and h is the height. If the radius is halved and the height is doubled, what will be the ratio of the new volume to the old volume?

   F. 4:1
   G. 2:1
   H. 1:1
   J. 1:2
   K. 1:4

GO ON TO THE NEXT PAGE.

49. Al bikes a trail to the top of a hill and back down. He bikes up the hill in m minutes, then returns twice as quickly downhill on the same trail. What is the total time, in hours, that Al spends biking up the hill and back down?

A. $\dfrac{m}{60}$

B. $\dfrac{m}{40}$

C. $\dfrac{m}{30}$

D. $\dfrac{3m}{2}$

E. $2m$

DO YOUR FIGURING HERE.

50. Pippin the guinea pig is running on her wheel when, due to a manufacturing error, the wheel breaks free of its axis. Pippin remains in her wheel, running in a straight line until the wheel has rotated exactly 15 times. If the diameter of the wheel is 10 inches, how many inches has the wheel rolled?

F. 75

G. 150

H. 75π

J. 150π

K. $1,500\pi$

51. A circle is inscribed in a square, as shown below. If x is the distance from the center of the circle to a vertex of the square, then what is the length of the radius of the circle, in terms of x?

A. $2x$

B. $x\sqrt{2}$

C. x

D. $\dfrac{x\sqrt{2}}{2}$

E. Cannot be determined from the information given

GO ON TO THE NEXT PAGE.

52. A function is defined for x and y such that
$f_{(x,y)} = -2xy + y + x - 4$. So, for $x = 2$ and $y = 3$,
$f_{(2,3)} = -2 \times 2 \times 3 + 3 + 2 - 4 = -12 + 1 = -11$. If x and y
are to be chosen such that $f_{(x,y)} = f_{(y,x)}$, then which of
the following restrictions must be placed on x and y?

F. $x > 0$ and $y > 0$
G. $x < 0$ and $y < 0$
H. $x = y$
J. $xy < 0$
K. No restrictions are needed.

DO YOUR FIGURING HERE.

53. A pipe of radius 4 feet sends water to two smaller pipes of equal
size. If each of the smaller pipes allows exactly half as much
water to flow as the larger pipe, what is the radius of one of
the smaller pipes?

A. 2
B. 2π
C. $2\sqrt{2}$
D. $4\sqrt{2}$
E. $2\pi\sqrt{2}$

54. The cross-sectional view of a tent is shown below. If the
tent is 6 feet wide at its base, then which of the following
expressions could be used to calculate the height of the tent,
in feet?

F. $\dfrac{3}{\tan 80°}$

G. $3\tan 40°$

H. $\dfrac{3}{\tan 40°}$

J. $6\tan 40°$

K. $3\tan 80°$

GO ON TO THE NEXT PAGE.

55. Two girls walk home from school. Starting from school, Susan walks north 2 blocks and then west 8 blocks, while Cindy walks east 3 blocks and then south 1 block. Approximately how many blocks apart are the girls' homes?

A. 7.1
B. 10.4
C. 11.4
D. 12.7
E. 16.0

56. For all integer values of a and b such that $a > 0$ and $b < 0$, which of the following must also be an integer?

F. 3^{a+b}

G. 3^{a-b}

H. 3^{ab}

J. 3^{-a}

K. $3^{\frac{a}{b}}$

57. If x and y are real numbers and $0 < x < y < \dfrac{y}{x}$, which of the following gives the set of all values which $\dfrac{y}{x}$ could have?

A. ![number line with open circle at 1, arrow pointing right from -2 to 2]

B. ![number line with open circle at 0, arrow pointing right]

C. ![number line with open circles at 0 and 1]

D. ![number line with open circle at 1, arrow pointing left]

E. ![number line with open circles at -1 and 1]

GO ON TO THE NEXT PAGE.

58. A circular running track is being built in a fenced-in athletic field 100 feet wide and 150 feet long. If a border of 10 feet is needed between the outside edge of the track and the fence, what is the radius of the largest track that can be built?

    F.   40
    G.   45
    H.   65
    J.   90
    K. 110

DO YOUR FIGURING HERE.

59. If a sphere is cut by two different planes, dividing it into sections, how many sections is it possible to end up with?

    A. 2 only
    B. 2 or 4 only
    C. 3 only
    D. 3 or 4 only
    E. 2, 3, or 4 only

60. For all real values of a and b, the equation $|a - b| = 5$ can be interpreted as "the positive difference of a and b is 5." What is the positive difference between the 2 solutions for a ?

    F. b
    G. $b + 5$
    H. $2b$
    J. $\sqrt{b^2 - 25}$
    K. 10

END OF TEST 2

STOP! DO NOT TURN THE PAGE UNTIL TOLD TO DO SO.

DO NOT RETURN TO A PREVIOUS TEST.

READING TEST

35 Minutes—40 Questions

DIRECTIONS: There are four passages in this test. Each passage is followed by several questions. After reading a passage, choose the best answer to each question and fill in the corresponding oval on your answer document. You may refer to the passages as often as necessary.

Passage I

PROSE FICTION: The following passage is excerpted from the coming-of-age novel *The Year of the Unicorn* by Krista Prouty (©2008 by Krista Prouty).

It was always the same, every Christmas. My sister and I would wake up early, my parents would send us back to bed, and we would instead huddle in my room, discussing which gifts might be waiting for us downstairs. One year it was a bicycle
5 that I wanted, and I can still remember telling my sister exactly what it would look like: pink, with silver streamers and a spar-kly silver seat. Eventually we would hear our parents moving around downstairs and we would know that it was almost time. Once the scent of coffee made it to our rooms, we would hurl
10 ourselves downstairs since that signified that our parents were not only awake but caffeinated and ready for gift-giving.

The year that I was nine, and Lily was six, the gift that I had been craving was the Barbie Dream House. Another girl from my school had one and I had been lucky enough to be allowed
15 a glimpse of it after school one day. She was like a princess be-stowing largesse; allowing one or two people over after school most days, demonstrating the various clever mechanisms, then sitting quietly, contentedly, while we gazed in wonder for a few minutes. Then, she sent us on our way. I knew that if I could only
20 have a Dream House of my own, my life would be complete. It was a bigger gift than I usually requested but, logically, I felt, that meant I was all the more likely to have my wish granted.

One night I overheard my parents, after they thought Lily and I had gone to bed.

25 "Bill, what are we going to do about Christmas this year?" My mother's voice, quiet and unsettlingly uncertain, came from the kitchen.

"I don't know yet, Mel, but we'll figure something out. We always do, honey."

30 "I know. I just can't help but worry." Whatever my mother said next was drowned out by the running water—she must have been washing up after dinner. I crept back to my bedroom, a little bit troubled by what I had heard but, as is the way of children, soon forgot and went back to Barbie Dream House dreaming.

35 On the Christmas morning in question, Lily and I huddled in my room, waiting for the signal to appear. She wanted a new bike and kept asking me if Santa would get it for her, but all I could think about was my Dream House. Somehow, I had con-vinced myself that I was certain to get it, that life and the fates
40 could not possibly be cruel enough to deny me this. I could see the wallpaper that was printed on the plastic walls, the darling matching furniture, and the ingenious hand-operated elevator. It would smell like new plastic. I inhaled deeply, imagining myself showing my gift off to friends and foes alike. Instead of
45 new plastic, however, my nostrils quivered to the odor of freshly brewed coffee. It was time.

My eyes still full of the glories I expected, I barreled down the stairs, almost knocking Lily down in my haste. Both of my parents were standing in the kitchen, sipping coffee. I tore past
50 them, even though I knew that they would expect me to stop and wait for them to walk into the living room with me. My longing was simply too exquisite to wait any longer. I burst through the double doors into our living room, words of joy and gratitude ready on my lips, only to find—there was no Dream House. Fran-
55 tically, I began to paw through the boxes under the tree, certain that it had to be there, somewhere, blind to the movement of my parents and sister entering the room behind me, nervous smiles on both my parents' faces. Eventually I was forced to concede that the tree was not somehow harboring a Dream House under
60 its limbs. I looked up at my parents, grief and confusion painted large on my features.

"Hold up a minute, honey. Santa brought you one more gift that wouldn't quite fit under the tree. Bill, go ahead—show her."

As I watched my father head towards a corner where a
65 large blanket was draped over some bulky object, hope flickered back to life a bit. But the size was all wrong, as was the shape. Still smiling anxiously, my father pulled the blanket away from what appeared to be a huge dollhouse. If Barbie's Dream House was sleek and modern, this was awkward and old-fashioned. It
70 had a peaked roof and a patio, with what looked like handmade furniture and wallpaper that looked suspiciously like the paper my parents had hung in Lily's room last fall. Slowly, realization dawned—my father had made it for me.

GO ON TO THE NEXT PAGE.

Looking back, I can only recall the rest of that day hazily,
75 even though the events up until that moment are as clear today
as they were at the time. I remember the feeling of devastation
that I felt, as I realized that the other girls from school would
not, in fact, be blown away by my Christmas gift. I tried to be as
grateful as I could, understanding even then that my father had
80 probably spent countless hours working on the house, but my
disappointment was only too evident. I just couldn't understand
why they had given me this crude approximation instead of my
heart's desire. As an adult, I wish I could go back in time, whis-
per the reason to my younger self, try to be more appreciative
85 of my father's efforts, but that is not the way of the world. I still
have the house, though, and when I have children of my own, I
will tell them the whole story, and I hope they will understand
better than I did.

1. Which of the following statements does NOT describe one of
   the narrator's reactions to her Christmas gift?

   A. She is devastated by the realization that the other children
       at school will not be impressed by this gift.
   B. She wishes that her parents had bought her a real Barbie
       Dream House instead of a handmade one.
   C. She despises the house for its old-fashioned appearance
       and lack of modern conveniences, such as an elevator.
   D. She appreciates all the effort her father went to in order to
       give her this gift and tries to convey a sense of gratitude.

2. According to the passage, when the narrator smells coffee on
   Christmas morning, it means that:

   F. her parents are ready to proceed with the Christmas festivi-
       ties.
   G. she and her sister should hurry to the kitchen for breakfast.
   H. her father has finally finished preparing her Christmas gift.
   J. it is time to burst into the living room in front of her parents.

3. The narrator would most likely agree with which of the
   following statements about owning a Barbie Dream House?

   A. She would become a princess able to bestow largesse on
       other children.
   B. She would, at least for the moment, be content with her
       life.
   C. It would allow her to appreciate her parents' hard work
       and sacrifices.
   D. She would then be able to pass it on to her own children
       someday.

4. What is the main point of the first paragraph?

   F. The smell of coffee still reminds the narrator of the Christ-
       mases of her childhood.
   G. The narrator's family had a specific ritual that was
       followed every Christmas morning.
   H. Most years, the narrator and her sister would hurl them-
       selves into their gifts without warning.
   J. The narrator had once desperately wanted a pink and silver
       bicycle.

5. Which of the following statements most accurately expresses
   the narrator's feelings when she first sees the gift that her father
   made for her?

   A. She is disappointed that it is not the exact gift that she had
       hoped to receive.
   B. She gratefully acknowledges the long hours her father
       must have put into the gift.
   C. She admires the traditional architecture of the house and
       its attractive wallpaper.
   D. She looks forward to showing her new house off to all of
       the other girls at school.

6. The narrator's father can most accurately be characterized as:

   F. ignorant and cruel.
   G. thoughtful but lazy.
   H. concerned and hard-working.
   J. caring but inaccessible.

7. It can logically be inferred from the passage that the reason
   the narrator was not given the official Barbie Dream House
   for Christmas is because:

   A. it is too costly a gift for her parents to buy that year.
   B. she had already been given the pink and silver bicycle that
       she wanted.
   C. her father had always wanted to make his daughter a doll-
       house.
   D. her parents do not wish for their daughter to be happy.

8. According to the passage, the reason the narrator hopes to
   someday tell the children the story of her dollhouse is that she:

   F. wants them to be able to impress the other children at
       school as she once did.
   G. knows that, by that time, it is likely to be worth a great
       deal of money.
   H. remembers how much she appreciated the gift when it was
       given to her.
   J. hopes that they will be better able to understand the mean-
       ing behind the gift than she was.

GO ON TO THE NEXT PAGE.

9. A reasonable conclusion that the narrator draws regarding her dollhouse is that:

A. it is far more beautiful than was the plastic Barbie Dream House that she had initially desired.

B. without an elevator, it is less valuable than it would otherwise have been.

C. it was given to her with the intention that she keep it to pass on to her own children someday.

D. constructing it must have been time-consuming and labor-intensive.

10. The main point of the last paragraph is that:

F. the narrator would have been much happier if she had been given a Barbie Dream House.

G. it is not fair to give one child a long-desired gift and not give the same to another child.

H. the disappointments suffered in childhood affect people well into adulthood.

J. the passage of time can alter the way events from the past are viewed.

Passage II

SOCIAL SCIENCE: This passage is adapted from T. H. Watkins' The Great Depression (©1993, Little, Brown and Co.; Blackside Inc.).

One of the most durable and well regarded of all the New Deal's programs came from President Roosevelt himself, who had his own share of inventiveness. If the president cared about the fate of people, he also cared about the fate of trees, having
5 practiced the art of silviculture on his Hyde Park estate with such enthusiasm that on various official forms he was fond of listing his occupation as "tree farmer." It was in early March, 1933, that he proceeded to bring the two concerns together—enlisting young unemployed men in a kind of volunteer "army" to be put to
10 work in the national forests, national parks, and on other federal public lands. When he went to Congress for authorization of the program, he called the new agency the Civilian Corps Reforestation Youth Rehabilitation Movement, but before sinking under the weight of an acronym like CCRYRM, it was soon changed
15 to the Civilian Conservation Corps (known forever after as the CCC). Congress chose not to handle the details itself. It simply authorized the president to create the program and structure it as he saw fit by executive order; it was to last two years. Responsibility was divided up among the Labor Department, which was
20 to screen and select the enrollees, the War Department, which would house and feed them in their nonworking hours, and the Departments of Agriculture and Interior, which would design and supervise projects in regional and national forests, national parks, and other public lands. The men would be paid $30 a
25 month, anywhere from $23 to $25 of it to be sent to their families.

The CCC officially began on April 5, 1933, calling for an enrollment of 250,000 to be housed in 1,468 camps around the country. The cost for the first year was estimated at $500 million. The men had to be US citizens between the ages of seventeen
30 and twenty-seven (later, twenty-four), out of school, out of work, capable of physical labor, over 60 inches but under 78 inches in height, more than 107 pounds in weight, and had to possess no fewer than "three serviceable natural masticating teeth above and below." They would serve terms of no more than nine months
35 so that as many as possible could be accommodated over the course of time.

Among the earliest enrollees were some veterans who had returned to Washington, setting up camp and demanding payment of their bonuses for service during the war. While making
40 it clear that he opposed the payments on economic grounds, FDR provided tents, showers, mess halls, and latrines, and, waiving the age restriction for them, invited the members of this new Bonus Army to join his new agency. What was more, Eleanor Roosevelt dropped by one rainy day for a visit, slogging through
45 ankle-deep mud to meet and talk with the men. "Hoover sent the army," said one veteran of the previous summer's BEF disaster, "Roosevelt sent his wife." When it became clear that no bonus would be forthcoming, about twenty-five hundred of the men took Roosevelt up on his offer and joined the CCC.

50 In the summer of 1934, Roosevelt expanded the size of the CCC to 350,000 and would raise it to 500,000 in 1935. Congress continued to reauthorize it faithfully over the next seven years, and by the time it was closed out in 1942, the CCC had put more than three million young "soil soldiers" to work. In the national
55 forests alone they built 3,470 fire towers, installed 65,100 miles of telephone lines, scraped and graded thousands of fire breaks, roads, and trails, and built 97,000 miles of truck trails and roads, spent 4.1 million man-hours fighting fires, and cut down and hauled out millions of diseased trees and planted more than 1.3
60 billion young trees in the first major reforestation campaign in the country's history. For the National Park Service, they built roads, campgrounds, bridges, and recreation and administration facilities; for the Biological Survey (a predecessor of today's Fish and Wildlife Service), they conducted wildlife surveys
65 and improved wildlife refuge lands; and for the Army Corps of Engineers, they built flood control projects in West Virginia, Vermont, and New York State.

In return, the CCC, at its best, took at least some young men out of the urban tangle of hopelessness where so many resided,
70 introduced them to the intricacies and healing joy of the outdoors, and clothed and fed them better than many had been for years. Moreover, the program taught more than a hundred thousand to read and write, passed out twenty-five thousand eighth-grade diplomas and five thousand high-school diplomas, gave struc-
75 ture and discipline to lives that had experienced little of either, strengthened bodies and minds, and for many provided a dose of self-esteem they had never known.

GO ON TO THE NEXT PAGE.

11. The main idea of the passage is that:

    A. the CCC forced unemployed young men to work in the national forests, national parks, and on other federal public lands for no payment or bonus.

    B. it was only after President Roosevelt created the CCC that veterans had suitable employment during the Great Depression.

    C. research into the history of the New Deal shows that the idea for the CCC came from Congress.

    D. among the programs of the New Deal, the CCC employed young men to build public works projects on public lands in return for modest wages, food, clothing, and some education.

12. The main idea of the third paragraph (lines 37–49) is that:

    F. President Hoover had dispatched the army to meet with disgruntled veterans, but President Roosevelt sent his wife, Eleanor, to meet with the Bonus Army.

    G. when they realized President Roosevelt would not pay the bonus, many veterans abandoned the Bonus Army and accepted his invitation to join the CCC.

    H. President Roosevelt supplied shelter and food to the veterans before paying the bonus the veterans demanded.

    J. many of the veterans were above the age requirement of the CCC.

13. As it is used in line 7 to describe President Roosevelt, the term *tree farmer* most nearly means that Roosevelt:

    A. had supported his family by growing trees before he entered politics.

    B. believed in an agrarian economy over urban industrialization.

    C. continued his successful business selling trees while in office.

    D. had a great interest in trees and knew a good deal about them.

14. According to the passage, which of the following was a project the CCC performed for the National Park Service?

    F. Building fire towers
    G. Building campground facilities
    H. Installing telephone lines
    J. Conducting wildlife surveys

15. According to the passage, which of the following statements is true about the CCC?

    A. The agency provided enrollees with academic instruction.
    B. The agency provided enrollees with urban job training.
    C. The agency accepted only men with six teeth.
    D. The agency offered courses in nutrition and self-esteem.

16. Information in the fourth paragraph (lines 50–67) makes it clear that the CCC:

    F. was voluntary and therefore did not pay members anything.

    G. ran for more years and employed more men than was originally intended.

    H. employed 4.1 million men.

    J. battled fires in West Virginia, Vermont, and New York.

17. The passage most strongly suggests that before the 1930s, the national forests:

    A. received no federal support or aid for projects to clear diseased trees.

    B. included land reserved for wildlife refuges.

    C. had never undergone a major reforestation campaign.

    D. experienced more floods than forest fires.

18. According to the passage, when did the CCC change its name?

    F. After President Roosevelt received authorization from Congress.

    G. After Congress protested that CCRYRM was too difficult to say.

    H. In the same year the size expanded to 500,000 men.

    J. After the Bonus Army disbanded.

19. The passage states that the same year the CCC was authorized enrollees had to be:

    A. over 78 inches in height.
    B. in school.
    C. between the ages of seventeen and twenty-seven.
    D. between the ages of seventeen and twenty-four.

20. According to the passage, CCC programs in national parks and forests were:

    F. conducted far from where the members were fed and housed.

    G. under the control of the Departments of Agriculture and the Interior.

    H. supervised by the Labor Department.

    J. minimum-wage jobs.

GO ON TO THE NEXT PAGE.

Passage III

HUMANITIES: This passage is adapted from John Gattuso, ed., Native American (©1993, Houghton Mifflin Co.).

Northwest natives are carvers by tradition, but it was the natives of the far north, in what is now British Columbia and Alaska, who first carved totem poles. The history of these fascinating works is surprisingly brief, for it wasn't until the mid-18th
5 century, when European explorers first encountered these remote tribes, that the unique sculptures began to appear. Although the natives were already expert carvers of canoes, tools, longhouses, and furniture, they lacked the iron tools necessary to fell a massive tree in one piece and carve its entire length.

10 With the iron axes they got in trade for their baskets, boxes, and pelts, the coastal tribes of the far north could take advantage of the trees that grew so tall and straight in their wet climate. Initially, the poles were made to stand against the front of a house, with figures facing out and a door cut through the base, so all
15 would enter the house through the pole. In this case, the totem pole functioned as a family crest, recounting genealogies, stories, or legends that in some way identified the owner. Towards the end of the 19th century, the poles stood free on the beach or in the village outside the carvers' homes. Some villages were virtual
20 forests of dozens, sometimes hundreds, of poles.

The family that carved the pole gave a potlatch with feasting, games, and much gift-giving. The guests, in return, raised the pole. These gatherings were costly and required a great deal of preparation and participation. The custom frustrated whites
25 trying to "civilize" the Indians, especially missionaries who solved the problem by knocking the poles down. Employers, too, complained that their Indian workers were unreliable when a pole was being carved or a potlatch planned. Eventually, both the Canadian and United States governments banned potlatches,
30 and pole carving nearly died out. The ban was lifted in the 1950s.

The Tlingit, on the southeastern coast of Alaska, and the Haidas and Tsimshian of western Canada are known for their pole carving. On a tour in 1899, a group of Seattle businessmen visited the Tlingit village of Tongas and, finding no one there, took
35 one of the poles. They erected it in Seattle where, at a towering 50 ft., it became one of the city's most distinctive monuments. In 1938, Tlingit carvers copied the pole after the original was destroyed by fire, and it remains in Pioneer Square today.

Poles serve the important purpose of recording the lore of
40 a clan, much as a book would. The top figure on the pole identifies the owner's clan, and succeeding characters (read from top to bottom) tell their stories. Raven, the trickster, might tell the story of how he fooled the Creator into giving him the sun, or Frog might tell how he wooed a human woman. With slight
45 variations between villages, everyone knew these stories, and

potlatch guests dramatized them at the pole-raising with masks, drumming, and songs. And so the legends were preserved from one generation to the next.

There is a story behind almost every image on the pole. For
50 example, if an animal had the power to transform itself into other beings, the carver would portray it in all its forms. If Raven were sometimes bird, sometimes human, he would be carved with both wings and limbs, or have a human face with a raven's beak. Other images are used to describe the spirits' special abilities.
55 Eyes are frequently used to suggest acuteness or skill. So, for example, if an eye appears in an animal's ear, it might indicate that that animal has a sharp sense of hearing. And human figures in unexpected places, like an ear or nose, might mean that the animal has great powers.

60 Learning to read totem poles is like learning to read a language. They speak of history, mythology, social structure, and spirituality. They serve many purposes and continue to be carved by the descendants of the original carvers.

Today, Haida, Tlingit, Tsimshian, Kwakiutl and other na-
65 tive craftsmen carve, predominantly for the tourist trade, small "souvenir" totem poles in wood and black slate (or argillite). They also carve extraordinarily beautiful masks, effigies, boxes, house posts, and fixtures…

21. Which of the following statements best expresses the main idea of the passage?

   A. Many Native American tribes created totem poles with meaningful symbols, but these poles were less important than the canoes carved before the mid-18th century.
   B. Although the Tlingit village was deserted, the Seattle businessmen who took the totem pole were not right to take it without permission.
   C. The history of totem pole carving dates back to only the mid-18th-century, but these poles have played an important role in Native American culture since that time.
   D. The ban issued by the Canadian and United States governments against potlatches was lifted in the 1950s, but interest in totem-pole carving had diminished by that time.

22. Which of the following questions is NOT answered in the passage?

   F. In terms of geographical region, which were the first groups to carve totem poles?
   G. What is the tallest totem pole in North America?
   H. What is the predominant use of the small totem poles carved today?
   J. What prevented Native American tribes from carving totem poles before the 18th century?

GO ON TO THE NEXT PAGE.

23. The passage suggests that one of the main purposes of totem poles is the way in which they:

 A. demonstrate the artistic skill of the carvers.
 B. function as landmarks in major North American cities.
 C. document the history and mythology of various clans.
 D. complement the festivities of the potlatch.

24. The main function of the sixth paragraph (lines 49–59) is to:

 F. identify the origins of the stories behind every image on a totem pole.
 G. describe and explain some of the images that might appear on a totem pole.
 H. contrast the images on the totem poles of the Northwest natives with those of British Columbia and Alaska.
 J. explain the role of the Raven in Native American mythology.

25. All of the following are used in the passage as illustrations of the role totem poles play in Native American culture EXCEPT the:

 A. function of the top figure on the pole.
 B. descriptions of the Raven and Frog as characters on the pole.
 C. reference to the popularity of totem poles in the tourist industries of many tribes.
 D. placement of the Tlingit totem pole in Seattle's Pioneer Square.

26. The second paragraph (lines 10–20) establishes all of the following about the totem poles carved by the coastal tribes of the far north EXCEPT that they were:

 F. initially used as the entryways of houses.
 G. fashioned from tall, straight trees.
 H. used to identify the owners of the poles.
 J. produced only by clans with family crests.

27. One of the main points of the fifth paragraph (lines 39–48) is that the various characters on a totem pole are meant to represent:

 A. the owner of the totem pole.
 B. the lore of the owner's clan.
 C. Raven, the trickster, fooling the Creator.
 D. Frog wooing a human woman.

28. According to the passage, which of the following places is home to the Tlingit?

 F. Seattle
 G. Western Canada
 H. Pioneer Square
 J. Alaska

29. The author most likely includes the information in lines 60–63 to suggest that:

 A. totem poles are notable for reasons beyond physical beauty.
 B. totem poles have replaced books for Native American tribes.
 C. Native American tribes have no spoken or written language.
 D. the descendants of the original carvers of totem poles carve copies of older poles.

30. Which of the following words best describes the attitude of the employers referred to in the third paragraph (lines 21–30) in reaction to potlatches?

 F. Patient
 G. Accepting
 H. Irritated
 J. Civilized

Passage IV

NATURAL SCIENCE: This passage is adapted from the article "The Pioneer Mission to Venus" by Janet G. Luhmann, James B. Pollack, and Lawrence Colin (©1994, Scientific American).

Venus is sometimes referred to as the Earth's "twin" because it resembles the Earth in size and in distance from the sun. Over its 14 years of operation, the National Aeronautics and Space Administration's *Pioneer Venus* mission revealed that the rela-
5 tion between the two worlds is more analogous to Dr. Jekyll and Mr. Hyde. The surface of Venus bakes under a dense carbon dioxide atmosphere, the overlying clouds consist of noxious sulfuric acid, and the planet's lack of a magnetic field exposes the upper atmosphere to the continuous hail of charged particles
10 from the sun. Our opportunity to explore the hostile Venusian environment came to an abrupt close in October 1992, when the *Pioneer Venus Orbiter* burned up like a meteor in the thick Venusian atmosphere. The craft's demise marked the end of an era for the U.S. space program; in the present climate of fiscal
15 austerity, there is no telling when humans will next get a good look at the earth's nearest planetary neighbor.

The information gleaned by *Pioneer Venus* complements the well-publicized radar images recently sent back by the *Magellan* spacecraft. *Magellan* concentrated on studies of Venus's surface
20 geology and interior structure. *Pioneer Venus*, in comparison, gathered data on the composition and dynamics of the planet's atmosphere and interplanetary surroundings. These findings illustrate how seemingly small differences in physical conditions have sent Venus and the Earth hurtling down very different evo-
25 lutionary paths. Such knowledge will help scientists intelligently evaluate how human activity may be changing the environment on the Earth.

Well before the arrival of *Pioneer Venus*, astronomers had learned that Venus does not live up to its image as Earth's near-
30 twin. Whereas Earth maintains conditions ideal for liquid water and life, Venus's surface temperature of 450 degrees Celsius is hotter than the melting point of lead. Atmospheric pressure at the ground is some 93 times that at sea level on Earth.

Even aside from the heat and the pressure, the air on Venus
35 would be utterly unbreathable to humans. The Earth's atmosphere is about 78 percent nitrogen and 21 percent oxygen. Venus's much thicker atmosphere, in contrast, is composed almost entirely of carbon dioxide. Nitrogen, the next most abundant gas makes up only about 3.5 percent of the gas molecules. Both planets
40 possess about the same amount of gaseous nitrogen, but Venus's atmosphere contains some 30,000 times as much carbon dioxide as does Earth's. In fact, Earth does hold a quantity of carbon dioxide comparable to that in the Venusian atmosphere. On Earth, however, the carbon dioxide is locked away in carbonate
45 rocks, not in gaseous form in the air. The crucial distinction is responsible for many of the drastic environmental differences that exist between the two planets.

The large *Pioneer Venus* atmospheric probe carried a mass spectrometer and gas chromatograph, devices that measured
50 the exact composition of the atmosphere of Venus. One of the most stunning aspects of the Venusian atmosphere is that it is extremely dry. It possesses only a hundred thousandth as much water as Earth has in its oceans. If all of Venus's water could somehow be condensed onto the surface, it would make a global
55 puddle only a couple of centimeters deep.

Unlike the Earth, Venus harbors little if any molecular oxygen in its lower atmosphere. The abundant oxygen in the earth's atmosphere is a by-product of photosynthesis by plants; if not for the activity of living things, Earth's atmosphere also
60 would be oxygen poor. The atmosphere of Venus is far richer than the earth's in sulfur-containing gases, primarily sulfur dioxide. On Earth, rain efficiently removes similar sulfur gases from the atmosphere.

Pioneer Venus revealed other ways in which Venus is more
65 primordial than Earth. Venus's atmosphere contains higher concentrations of inert, or noble, gases—especially neon and isotopes of argon—that have been present since the time the planets were born. This difference suggests that Venus has held on to a far greater fraction of its earliest atmosphere. Much of
70 Earth's primitive atmosphere may have been stripped away and lost into space when our world was struck by a Mars-size body. Many planetary scientists now think the moon formed out of the cloud of debris that resulted from such a gigantic impact.

31. With regard to the possibility of returning to the planet Venus, information presented in the passage makes it clear that the author is:

    A. cheerful and optimistic.
    B. sarcastic and contentious.
    C. doubtful and pragmatic.
    D. uncertain and withdrawn.

32. Which of the following statements most accurately summarizes how the passage characterizes the state of scientific knowledge about Venus before the *Pioneer* mission?

    F. The scientific community was hesitant to return to Venus after an earlier mission had ended in disaster.
    G. Scientists saw Earth and Venus as near polar opposites in atmospheric conditions.
    H. The common belief that Earth and Venus were "twins" had been eroding under the weight of scientific evidence.
    J. Scientists knew little about the planet Venus because they were more interested in other planets.

GO ON TO THE NEXT PAGE.

33. Based on the passage, discoveries made in which two areas of study have caused scientists to re-evaluate their theories about Earth and Venus?

    A. Water content and bedrock composition
    B. Sulfuric gases and photosynthesis
    C. Carbon dioxide and climate change
    D. Atmosphere and surface temperature

34. The main point of the second paragraph (lines 17–27) is to:

    F. account for the failure of the *Magellan* mission and to show the superiority of the *Pioneer* mission.
    G. suggest that information from both the *Magellan* and *Pioneer* missions can bring the scientific community to a deeper understanding of Venus.
    H. show that the *Magellan* had sent back information regarding the physical characteristics while the *Pioneer* had not.
    J. hypothesize that the findings of the *Pioneer* mission will help scientists to approach problems more intelligently.

35. The passage indicates that if humans were to attempt to live on the planet Venus, survival would not be possible because:

    A. of the mistaken belief that Venus and Earth are "twin" planets.
    B. carbon dioxide is locked away in bicarbonate rocks, not in gaseous form.
    C. the atmospheric pressure, heat, and air are not suitable for human life.
    D. all of the water on Venus is condensed onto the surface.

36. According to the passage, some evidence gained before the *Pioneer Venus* mission suggesting that Earth and Venus are not near-twins stated that:

    F. Venus produces no lead on or underneath its surface.
    G. Earth was found to be much farther from the sun than was previously thought.
    H. the atmosphere of Venus contains 78 percent nitrogen and 21 percent oxygen.
    J. the surface temperature of Venus is 450 degrees Celsius and thus unlivable for humans.

37. As it is used in line 56, the word *harbors* most nearly means:

    A. sails.
    B. hides.
    C. holds.
    D. soaks.

38. According to the passage, "primordial" describes planets that:

    F. are oxygen-poor due to a lack of activity by living things.
    G. are not hospitable to humans because they have thick atmospheres and high surface temperatures.
    H. have preserved many of the characteristics present when the planets were formed.
    J. have been struck by large bodies which have altered the planets' atmospheres.

39. It can reasonably be inferred that the "activity of living things" described in line 59 directly refers to organisms on Earth that:

    A. produce oxygen by their own natural processes and influence the contents of Earth's atmosphere.
    B. remove sulfur gases from the atmosphere during heavy rainfall.
    C. lock away carbon dioxide in carbonate rocks and maintain a reserve of the gas.
    D. could easily live in oppressive atmospheres similar to the atmosphere of Venus.

40. According to the passage, the *Pioneer Venus* mission to Venus involved investigating details relating to the planet's:

    F. surface geology and interior structure.
    G. atmosphere as it has been changed by the influence of photosynthesis.
    H. similarities to the planet Earth.
    J. atmospheric contents.

END OF TEST 3
STOP! DO NOT TURN THE PAGE UNTIL TOLD TO DO SO.
DO NOT RETURN TO A PREVIOUS TEST.

SCIENCE TEST

35 Minutes–40 Questions

Directions: There are seven passages in this test. Each passage is followed by several questions. After reading a passage, choose the best answer to each question and fill in the corresponding oval on your answer document. You may refer to the passages as often as necessary.

You are NOT permitted to use a calculator on this test.

Passage I

Metallic *alloys*, solid mixtures of metal, are useful for coin production when they contain a high percentage of zinc. When electric current is applied to zinc in the presence of precious metal solutions of *silver nitrate*, *copper sulfate* or *potassium gold cyanide*, the precious metals *plate* (form a coating) on the zinc surface.

- Silver nitrate, formed when silver dissolves in *nitric acid*, reacts with zinc to form solid silver and *zinc nitrate*.
- Copper sulfate, formed when copper dissolves in *sulfuric acid*, reacts with zinc to form solid copper and *zinc sulfate*.
- Potassium gold cyanide contains reactive gold ions.

A chemist performed experiments on precious metal plating.

Experiment 1

The chemist obtained 4 coin-like samples of a high percentage zinc alloy. All samples were circular, had a radius of 1 cm, and had the same thickness. The mass of each coin was recorded. Each coin was wired via a battery to a strip of either pure silver or copper metal. Coins wired to silver were placed in dilute nitric acid and coins wired to copper were placed in dilute sulfuric acid. Electric current of either 1,000 milliamperes (mA) or 2,000 mA was applied for 30 minutes to each sample. The coins were removed and the increase in mass from precious metal plating was recorded in milligrams. Results of the experiment are shown in Table 1.

	Precious metal solution		Increased mass from plating (mg)
Coin sample	Identity	Electric Current (mA)	
I	silver nitrate	1,000	2.0
II	silver nitrate	2,000	4.0
III	copper sulfate	1,000	1.2
IV	copper sulfate	2,000	2.4

Table 1

Experiment 2

The chemist completely dissolved equal amounts of pure silver in 4 beakers of nitric acid. He then placed equivalent coin-like samples of zinc into the beakers for different lengths of time measured in minutes (min). The coin surfaces developed a silver metal coating without any electric current applied. The concentrations of silver coating on the coin and zinc nitrate in the surrounding solution were determined in parts per billion (ppb) and recorded in Table 2.

Table 2

Coin sample	Time (min)	Silver coating concentration (ppb)	Zinc nitrate concentration (ppb)
V	5	75	30
VI	15	125	55
VII	30	200	75
VIII	60	500	85

1. A comparison of the results for coin samples II and IV supports the hypothesis that zinc is plated more extensively when exposed to:

   A. silver nitrate and a current of 1,000 mA than silver nitrate and a current of 2,000 mA.
   B. copper sulfate and a current of 1,000 mA than copper sulfate and a current of 2,000 mA.
   C. silver nitrate than when exposed to copper sulfate.
   D. copper sulfate than when exposed to silver nitrate.

GO ON TO THE NEXT PAGE.

2. If the chemist were to repeat Experiment 1, but compress each coin sample to a radius of 0.5 cm to decrease the surface area exposed to the surrounding solution, how would the mass of precious metal plated most likely be affected?

   F. The mass of precious metal plated would decrease for all coin samples.
   G. The mass of precious metal plated would decrease for coin samples I and III and increase for coin samples II and IV.
   H. The mass of precious metal plated would remain constant for all coin samples.
   J. The mass of precious metal plated would increase for all coin samples.

3. According to the information in the passage, a zinc alloy coin sample exposed to which of the following conditions would result in the greatest concentration of zinc nitrate?

   A. 10 minutes in a solution with a high initial concentration of silver nitrate
   B. 10 minutes in a solution with a low initial concentration of silver nitrate
   C. 6 minutes in a solution with a high initial concentration of silver nitrate
   D. 6 minutes in a solution with a low initial concentration of silver nitrate

4. In Experiment 1, if the chemist had applied 1,580 mA to a 1 cm radius zinc alloy coin sample in a copper sulfate solution, approximately how much copper would have plated after 30 minutes?

   F. 0.6 mg
   G. 1.1 mg
   H. 1.9 mg
   J. 4.6 mg

5. In Experiment 1, which of the following variables was the same for all 4 zinc alloy coin sample trials?

   A. Change in mass from plating
   B. Electric current applied
   C. Type of precious metal solution used
   D. Initial radius of the sample

6. According to the passage, if a chemist wants to study the effect of plating zinc alloys with silver, the chemist should monitor the concentration of which of the following substances in the surrounding solution?

   F. Potassium gold cyanide
   G. Zinc nitrate
   H. Copper sulfate
   J. Sulfuric acid

GO ON TO THE NEXT PAGE.

Passage II

Organic compounds are molecules that frequently contain carbon (C), hydrogen (H), and oxygen (O) joined together by covalent bonds (symbolized by straight lines in chemical notation). As the number of bonds to oxygen atoms increases in a carbon chain, the overall molecule is increasingly oxidized. For example, aldehydes are more oxidized than alcohols, which are more oxidized than alkanes as shown in Table 1. The melting points of these compounds are listed in Table 2, and their *viscosities* (resistance to flow, or "stickiness,") are listed in Table 3.

Table 1

Carbons in the chain	Name prefix	Structure		
		alkane (suffix -ane)	alcohol (suffix -anol)	aldehyde (suffix -analdehyde)
4	but-			
5	pent-			
6	hex-			
7	hept-			
8	oct-			

Table 2

Carbons in the chain	Melting point (K)		
	alkane	alcohol	aldehyde
4	135	183	174
5	143	194	213
6	178	221	217
7	182	239	231
8	216	257	285

Table 3

Carbons in the chain	Viscosity (cP)		
	alkane	alcohol	aldehyde
4	0.01	3.0	0.4
5	0.24	5.1	0.5
6	0.29	5.4	0.8
7	0.39	5.8	1.0
8	0.54	8.4	1.2

GO ON TO THE NEXT PAGE.

7. Which organic compounds in Table 2 are solids at 215 K?

   A. All alkanes, alcohols, and aldehydes with 5 carbons or fewer.

   B. Alcohols and aldehydes with 6 or more carbons and octane.

   C. The 4- and 5-carbon alcohols and aldehydes, and all alkanes with 7 or fewer carbons.

   D. The 5-carbon pentane and pentanol compounds and the 4-carbon butane, butanol, and butanaldehyde.

8. According to Tables 1 and 3, which organic compound has the highest viscosity?

   F. Octanol

   G. Octanaldehyde

   H. Hexanol

   J. Butane

9. According to Table 3, how do the different types of 5-carbon molecules differ with respect to their viscosity?

   A. The alkane has a higher viscosity than the aldehyde and the aldehyde has a higher viscosity than the alcohol.

   B. The alkane has a higher viscosity than the alcohol and the alcohol has a higher viscosity than the aldehyde.

   C. The alcohol has a higher viscosity than the alkane and the alkane has a higher viscosity than the aldehyde.

   D. The alcohol has a higher viscosity than the aldehyde and the aldehyde has a higher viscosity than the alkane.

10. For each type of organic compound, what is the relationship between the length of the carbon chain to the melting point and viscosity? As the number of carbons in the chain increases, the melting point:

   F. decreases and the viscosity decreases.

   G. increases and the viscosity increases.

   H. increases but the viscosity decreases.

   J. decreases but the viscosity increases.

11. According to Table 2, the difference in melting point between an alkane and an alcohol with the same number of carbons is approximately how much?

   A. 25 K

   B. 35 K

   C. 45 K

   D. 65 K

GO ON TO THE NEXT PAGE.

Passage III

A mass suspended by a lightweight thread and swinging back and forth approximates the motion of a *simple gravity pendulum*, a system in which gravity is the only force acting on the mass, causing an acceleration of 9.8 m/sec². The time to complete one cycle of swinging back and forth is the *period* and is inversely related to gravitational acceleration.

Using the same type and length of thread, 2 cubes were suspended, lifted to the same starting angle, and let go. The amount of time required for each pendulum to complete one swinging cycle (1 period) was recorded with a timer capable of reading to the nearest 0.01 sec. The measured times were used to calculate acceleration.

Experiment 1

A cube of lead (11.3 grams) and a cube of tin (7.4 grams) were suspended from a 0.5 m length of thread. Both cubes had the same length. (Note: A cube's volume is proportional to its length cubed; its surface area is proportional to its length squared.) The cubes were set in motion from a fixed starting angle, and the period for each was recorded.

Table 1		
Trial	Measured period (sec)	
	lead cube	tin cube
1	1.48	1.51
2	1.45	1.47
3	1.46	1.42
4	1.49	1.45
5	1.39	1.53

The average periods were 1.46 sec and 1.48 sec for the lead and tin cubes, respectively. The average accelerations were 9.3 m/sec² for lead and 9.1 m/sec² for tin.

Experiment 2

The same procedures used in Experiment 1 were repeated using a thread length of 1.0 m and the same fixed starting angle. Results were recorded in Table 2.

Table 2		
Trial	Measured period (sec)	
	lead cube	tin cube
6	2.10	2.12
7	2.04	2.06
8	2.05	2.07
9	2.12	2.11
10	2.00	2.10

The average periods were 2.06 sec and 2.09 sec for the lead and tin cubes, respectively. The average accelerations were 9.3 m/sec² for lead and 9.0 m/sec² for tin.

Experiment 3

Given the results of the first 2 experiments, the accuracy of the timer was tested. The procedures of Experiment 1 were repeated using only the lead cube. The trials were recorded on digital video at 100 frames per second. The video was then reviewed to obtain precise measurements of the period for each trial and results are shown in Table 3.

Table 3	
Trial	Measured period (sec)
11	1.47
12	1.42
13	1.49
14	1.50
15	1.46

The average period recorded in Table 3 was 1.47 sec.

12. To demonstrate that a pendulum's acceleration is reduced by drag force from air resistance, which additional experiment can be performed in addition to those in the passage?

F. The cubes are suspended by 0.5 m and 1 m springs and set in motion by extending the spring 9.8 cm and letting go in a vacuum chamber with no air pressure.

G. The cubes are suspended by 0.5 m and 1 m threads and set in motion from the same starting angle in a vacuum chamber with no air pressure.

H. The cubes are suspended by 0.5 m and 1 m springs and set in motion by extending the spring 9.8 cm and letting go in a vacuum chamber at 1 atmosphere of pressure.

J. The cubes are suspended by 0.5 m and 1 m threads and set in motion from the same starting angle in a vacuum chamber at 1 atmosphere of pressure.

GO ON TO THE NEXT PAGE.

13. In Experiment 1, could a timer that reads to the nearest second be used to obtain similar results, and why?

    A. No, because the period of both pendulums was between 1 and 2 seconds.
    B. No, because the pendulums would have traveled farther in 1 second than they did in 1 period.
    C. Yes, because the period of both pendulums was approximately 1.5 seconds.
    D. Yes, because the pendulums would not have traveled as far in 1 second as they did in 1 period.

14. The results of the experiments indicate that forces other than gravity are acting on the pendulums because the calculated values of acceleration were:

    F. the same for pendulums of different lengths.
    G. the same for cubes of different mass.
    H. lower than the expected 9.8 m/sec² from gravity alone.
    J. greater than the expected 9.8 m/sec² from gravity alone.

15. Based on the passage, if a tin cube is suspended from a 2.0 m thread and set in motion multiple times from the same starting angle, the average measured period will most likely be:

    A. less than 1.48 sec.
    B. approximately 1.48 sec.
    C. approximately 2.09 sec.
    D. greater than 2.09 sec.

16. In Experiment 2, if an additional trial were conducted using the lead cube, the cube's measured period would most likely be nearest:

    F. 1.90 sec.
    G. 2.05 sec.
    H. 2.15 sec.
    J. 2.20 sec.

17. Experiments 1 and 2 were conducted using lead and tin cubes most likely to determine whether a pendulum's period was altered by the material attached to the string and the cube's:

    A. length.
    B. surface area.
    C. starting angle.
    D. mass.

GO ON TO THE NEXT PAGE.

Passage IV

Accepted classification systems of life do not include *viruses*. Although viruses possess certain features of cellular organisms, including genetic material that codes for making new viral particles, they cannot *replicate* (make copies of) themselves without first infecting a living cell. Biologists agree that viruses originated from genetic material called *nucleic acid*, but it is difficult to prove any single theory regarding how this occurred. Three hypotheses of viral origin are presented here.

Coevolution Hypothesis

Some biologists argue that viruses evolved alongside other organisms over billions of years. They suggest that simple molecules of *ribonucleic acid* (RNA), a *nucleotide* that forms the genetic code for proteins, joined to form more complex sequences. These RNA sequences developed enzyme-like abilities including the ability to self-replicate and insert themselves into other nucleotide sequences. While some RNA sequences became incorporated into membrane-bound cells, others were packaged inside proteins as the first viral particles that could replicate after infecting cellular organisms (see Figure 1).

ancestral self-replicating RNA

first coevolved viral particle

Figure 1

Cellular Origin Hypothesis

Some biologists claim that nucleotide sequences within *prokaryotic* (non-nucleated) and *eukaryotic* (nucleated) cellular organisms incorporated into a protein coating and escaped from the cell as a viral particle. Initially, DNA or RNA nucleotide sequences gained the code required for other cells to replicate them. Next, these sequences associated with proteins to form an outer *capsid*. Finally, the *virion* (viral particle) became capable of passing through the cell membrane and infecting other cells where it could be replicated. After the initial escape, viruses evolved independently from their initial host and ultimately could infect either prokaryotic or eukaryotic cells.

Regressive Evolution Hypothesis

An alternative explanation of viral origin is that viruses evolved from cellular organisms. Some cellular organisms, particularly certain bacteria, are *obligate intracellular parasites* because they must infect a host cell in order to reproduce. Regressive evolution suggests that some bacterial parasites gradually lost the structures required for survival outside of a cell. The result was a virus particle containing only nucleotides, a capsid (protein coating), and at times an outer membrane or envelope. This would account readily for viruses that contain complex *deoxyribonucleic acid* (DNA) similar to that found in bacteria and other cellular organisms (see Figure 2).

ancestral intracellular parasite bacteria

first regressive evolved virus

Figure 2

18. The development of which of the following is addressed in the passage by the Coevolution Hypothesis, but NOT by the Regressive Evolution Hypothesis?

F. Self-replication
G. Capsid
H. Deoxyribonucleic acid
J. Cell membrane transit

19. Supporters of all of the theories presented in the passage would agree with the conclusion that the first viruses:

A. evolved from bacteria.
B. could self-replicate outside a cell.
C. were enclosed within a membrane.
D. contained nucleic acid.

20. The Coevolution Hypothesis does NOT provide an explanation for the earliest virus particles possessing:

F. protein.
G. enzyme-like activity.
H. nucleotides.
J. DNA.

GO ON TO THE NEXT PAGE.

21. If the Cellular Origin Hypothesis is correct, which of the following conclusions can be made about modern T4 DNA viruses, which infect *Escherichia coli* bacteria, and modern PP7 RNA viruses, which infect *Pseudomonas aeruginosa* bacteria?

A. T4 and PP7 are more closely related to each other than to bacteria genetically.

B. T4 and PP7 are only distantly related genetically through a cellular organism.

C. T4 and PP7 both evolved from prokaryotic organisms.

D. T4 and PP7 both evolved from eukaryotic organisms.

22. The discovery of which of the following living organisms would provide the most support for the Regressive Evolution Hypothesis?

F. Extracellular parasites with DNA resembling a known virus

G. Extracellular parasites with unique RNA nucleotide sequences

H. Intracellular parasites with DNA resembling a known virus

J. Intracellular parasites with unique RNA nucleotide sequences

23. Supporters of all the theories presented would agree with which of the following conclusions about the origin of viruses?

A. Viral capsids contain a protein structure similar to the cell walls of modern bacteria.

B. The first viruses did not originate before the first cellular organisms.

C. RNA viruses are more advanced than DNA viruses.

D. The first virus contained DNA and was surrounded by an envelope similar to a cell membrane.

24. Which of the following questions is raised by the Coevolution Hypothesis, but is NOT answered in the passage?

F. Why were some RNA sequences packaged into protein structures and others incorporated into cell structures?

G. Why did obligate intracellular parasites lose their ability to survive outside of cells?

H. How could two different types of cellular organisms account for the origin of viruses?

J. How did virions develop the ability to pass through the cell membrane out of the cell?

GO ON TO THE NEXT PAGE.

Passage V

Wind causes *topsoil deflation*, a type of erosion that is affected by plant and organic cover as well as water content of the soil. Scientists performed 2 experiments using equal-sized fields containing the same volume of soil. The soil samples were primarily a mixture of sand and silt, but differed in the percentage of clay they contained. Soil X was composed of 5% clay and soil Y was composed of 40% clay. Large fans were used to simulate wind. Topsoil deflation was measured in kilograms per hectare (kg/ha) following 10 hours of wind.

Experiment 1

A mixture of compost and straw was used to represent plant and organic cover. The percentage of soil covered with the mixture was considered to approximate an equivalent percentage of natural vegetative cover. One field remained uncovered, and the other fields were covered with different percentages of compost and straw. The topsoil deflation from each field was recorded in Table 1.

Table 1				
Soil	Topsoil deflation (kg/ha) by percentage of organic cover			
	0%	25%	50%	75%
X	105,000	68,000	46,000	20,000
Y	65,000	42,000	28,500	12,000

Experiment 2

Rainfall was simulated using a sprinkler system. Sprinklers were turned on for either 4 hours or 8 hours for fields of each kind of soil. Two additional fields composed of each type of soil were left unwatered. Afterward, soil samples were taken from all of the fields to determine their water content percentage, which was recorded in Table 2. Wind was applied as in Experiment 1 and topsoil deflation for all fields was recorded in Table 3.

Table 2			
Soil	Water content of soil following various sprinkler times		
	0 hours	4 hours	8 hours
X	10%	13%	16%
Y	10%	14%	22%

Table 3			
Soil	Topsoil deflation (kg/ha) following various sprinkler times		
	0 hours	4 hours	8 hours
X	89,250	66,000	14,000
Y	53,400	40,100	10,300

25. According to the results of Experiments 1 and 2, topsoil deflation will be minimized by:

A. decreased organic cover, increased amount of rainfall, and the use of either Soil X or Y as topsoil.
B. decreased organic cover, decreased amount of rainfall, and the use of Soil Y as topsoil.
C. increased organic cover, increased amount of rainfall, and the use of Soil Y as topsoil.
D. increased organic cover, increased amount of rainfall, and the use of Soil X as topsoil.

26. If Experiment 1 were repeated using a soil containing 10% clay with 0% organic cover, which of the following would be the most likely topsoil deflation amount?

F. 110,200 kg/ha
G. 99,800 kg/ha
H. 70,700 kg/ha
J. 60,200 kg/ha

27. To further investigate the effect of water content on erosion from topsoil deflation, the scientists should repeat Experiment:

A. 1, using a different type of topsoil.
B. 1, using plastic covers over the fields.
C. 2, using no sprinklers.
D. 2, using fields exposed to various amounts of rainfall.

28. What assumption in experimental design is most important to consider when applying the findings of Experiment 1 to a practical situation?

F. The quantity of topsoil deflation is independent of the percentage of clay present in the soil.
G. The presence of straw on the soil does not accurately simulate vegetation and organic cover.
H. Air movement from fans provides an accurate simulation of the wind responsible for topsoil deflation.
J. Compost is more effective than water content in the prevention of topsoil erosion.

GO ON TO THE NEXT PAGE.

29. In Experiment 2, the water content in the two soil types was similar after 4 hours of sprinkling, yet the topsoil deflation was significantly different. Which of the following statements provides the best explanation for these findings?

A. Topsoil erosion is independent of the water content found in the soil.

B. Fields are susceptible to topsoil deflation only when water completely evaporates from the topsoil.

C. Soil with a lower percentage of clay is more prone to erosion from topsoil deflation than one with a higher percentage of clay.

D. Water is trapped in the topsoil by wind and this increases the rate of topsoil deflation.

30. If Experiment 2 were repeated with soil containing 10% clay, which of the following values would be expected for water content and topsoil deflation in a field following 8 hours of water sprinkling?

F. water content of 17%; topsoil deflation of 13,400 kg/ha

G. water content of 21%; topsoil deflation of 9,700 kg/ha

H. water content of 15%; topsoil deflation of 10,900 kg/ha

J. water content of 14%; topsoil deflation of 101,000 kg/ha

GO ON TO THE NEXT PAGE.

Passage VI

The oceans of Earth are exposed to various climates and consequently have different physical properties. Deep oceans can be divided into zones based on temperature gradient and penetration of sunlight. Figure 1 shows the zones of a typical deep-water ocean, the depth of the zone boundaries in meters (m), and the overall pressure at those depths in kilopascals (kPa). Figure 2 shows the water temperature in degrees Celsius (°C) in warmer tropical oceans and cooler temperate oceans at varying depths. Sound waves are used to measure water temperature at depth, and readings from two different ocean regions are recorded in Table 1.

Figure 2

Zone of Ocean	Depth (m)	Total pressure (kPa)
surface	0	101
continental shelf / mixed / epipelagic	100	1,107
	140	1,509
thermocline	200	2,112
mesopelagic	1,000	10,153
continental rise / bathypelagic	4,000	4.0×10^4
deep water / abyssopelagic	6,000	6.0×10^4
abyss / hadopelagic		

Figure 1

(Note: Figure is NOT drawn to scale)

Table 1			
Total pressure (kPa)	Depth (m)	Ocean temperature (°C)	
		Region 1	Region 2
101	0	24	21
200	9.8	22	20
300	19.8	14	11
400	29.7	11	9
500	39.7	10	8
600	49.6	9	8
700	59.6	7	6
800	69.5	5	3
900	79.5	4	2

GO ON TO THE NEXT PAGE.

31. According to Figure 1, the regions of several ocean zones overlap. Which of the following pairs of ocean zones share part of a common depth range?

   A. Bathypelagic and mesopelagic
   B. Bathypelagic and epipelagic
   C. Epipelagic and thermocline
   D. Epipelagic and mesopelagic

32. According to Figure 1, an oceanographic reading taken at a total pressure of 1,200 kPa is most likely from which of the following zones?

   F. Abyss
   G. Continental rise
   H. Mixed
   J. Continental shelf

33. According to Figure 2, a sonographic measurement of temperature would be unable to distinguish the difference between tropical and temperate oceans at which of the following depths?

   A. 250 m
   B. 500 m
   C. 625 m
   D. 750 m

34. According to Table 1, the relationship between depth and ocean temperature is best described by which of the following statements?

   F. The water temperature increased with increasing depth in Region 1 only.
   G. The water temperature decreased with increasing depth in Region 1 only.
   H. The water temperature increased with increasing depth in Region 2 only.
   J. The water temperature decreased with increasing depth in Region 2 only.

35. According to Figure 1 and Table 1, if water temperature measurements were taken at depths greater than 79.5, the total pressure at those depths would most likely:

   A. decrease to less than 101 kPa.
   B. increase to more than 900 kPa.
   C. stay at 900 kPa.
   D. increase to 101 kPa.

GO ON TO THE NEXT PAGE.

Passage VII

Although many forms of bacteria are helpful for human health, they can also cause illness and even death from severe infections. *Antibiotics* are a class of medicines used to combat bacterial infections. *Bacteriostatic* activity inhibits bacteria cell division and *bactericidal* activity kills bacterial cells. Both actions eliminate populations of bacteria over time. Several classes of bacteriostatic and bactericidal antibiotics are described in Table 1.

The effectiveness of several antibiotics against a bacterium known to cause common skin infections was tested. Drugs were introduced to the bacterial culture by themselves or in combination with sulfamethoxazole (forming SMX compounds). The effectiveness of these antibiotics at eliminating the responsible bacterium is shown in Figure 1.

Key

penicillin 250 mg	. . . .
doxycycline 100 mg	——
SMX/doxycycline 200/100 mg	- - - -
azithromycin 250 mg	– – –
sulfamethoxazole 400 mg	• • •
SMX/azithromycin 200/250 mg	– – – –
sulfamethoxazole 800 mg	·–·–·
SMX/trimethoprim 800/160 mg	·— ·—

Figure 1

Table 1				
Class	Example	Active against	Mechanism	Common uses
β-lactams	ampicillin	some gram-positive and gram-negative bacteria	disrupt cell wall synthesis; bactericidal	respiratory and skin infections
Tetracyclines	doxycycline	atypical gram-indeterminate bacteria	disrupt bacterial mRNA synthesis; mostly bacteriostatic	respiratory and genitourinary infections
Macrolides	azithromycin	gram-positive and atypical bacteria	disrupt bacterial protein synthesis; mostly bacteriostatic	atypical and respiratory infections
Aminoglycosides	gentamicin, streptomycin	gram-negative bacteria	disrupt bacterial protein synthesis; bactericidal	severe systemic infections
Quinolones	ofloxacin, gatifloxacin	broad spectrum of bacteria	disrupt bacterial DNA replication; bactericidal	respiratory, genitourinary, and gastrointestinal infections
Antifolates	sulfamethoxazole, trimethoprim	some gram-positive and gram-negative bacteria	disrupt bacterial DNA and RNA synthesis; mostly bacteriostatic	genitourinary and skin infections

GO ON TO THE NEXT PAGE.

36. According to the information in Table 1 and Figure 1, what can be concluded about the use of sulfamethoxazole as an antibiotic for common skin infections?

   F. Using sulfamethoxazole 800 mg is ineffective as an antibiotic.
   G. Increasing the dosage of sulfamethoxazole decreases its overall effectiveness as an antibiotic.
   H. As an antibiotic, the mechanism of action of sulfamethoxazole is unknown.
   J. Compounding antibiotics with sulfamethoxazole increases their effectiveness against common skin infections.

37. According to Figure 1, if an investigator administered a sulfamethoxazole dose of 600 mg, 20% of the original bacteria would remain after a treatment interval:

   A. greater than 120 min.
   B. between 90 and 120 min.
   C. between 60 and 90 min.
   D. between 30 and 60 min.

38. After treatment of a bacterial culture similar to that in the passage with 250 mg of penicillin for 2 hours, the culture will probably contain:

   F. less bacteria overall, but most will have survived.
   G. less bacteria overall, and most will have been killed.
   H. the same amount of bacteria overall, and most will have survived.
   J. the same amount of bacteria overall, and most will have been killed.

39. Is the statement "antibiotics compounded with sulfamethoxazole are more effective against common skin infections than when administered alone" supported by the information shown in Figure 1, and why?

   A. No, because penicillin is more effective against a common skin infection bacterium than sulfamethoxazole 400 mg.
   B. No, because azithromycin is more effective against a common skin infection bacterium than SMX/azithromycin.
   C. Yes, because sulfamethoxazole 800 mg is more effective against a common skin infection bacterium than SMX/azithromycin.
   D. Yes, because SMX/doxycycline is more effective against a common skin infection bacterium than doxycycline.

40. According to the passage, the most effective antibiotic against bacteria is one that results in the:

   F. lowest percentage of bacterial elimination in the shortest treatment interval.
   G. lowest percentage of bacterial elimination in the longest treatment interval.
   H. greatest percentage of bacterial elimination in the shortest treatment interval.
   J. greatest percentage of bacterial elimination in the longest treatment interval.

END OF TEST 4

STOP! DO NOT RETURN TO ANY OTHER TEST.

DIRECTIONS

This is a test of your writing skills. You will have thirty (30) minutes to write an essay. Before you begin planning and writing your essay, read the writing prompt carefully to understand exactly what you are being asked to do. Your essay will be evaluated on the evidence it provides of your ability to express judgments by taking a position on the issue in the writing prompt; to maintain a focus on the topic throughout your essay; to develop a position by using logical reasoning and by supporting your ideas; to organize ideas in a logical way; and to use language clearly and effectively according to the conventions of standard written English.

You may use the unlined pages in this test booklet to plan your essay. These pages will not be scored. *You must write your essay on the lined pages in the answer folder.* Your writing on those lined pages will be scored. You may not need all the lined pages, but to ensure you have enough room to finish, do NOT skip lines. You may write corrections or additions neatly between the lines of your essay, but do NOT write in the margins of the lined pages. *Illegible essays cannot be scored, so you must write (or print) clearly.*

If you finish before time is called, you may review your work. Lay your pencil down immediately when time is called.

DO NOT OPEN THIS BOOK UNTIL YOU ARE TOLD TO DO SO.

ACT Assessment Writing Test Prompt

Schools in some states have changed their school calendars so that they are now year-round schools. Advocates of year-round schooling argue that the traditional summer break is a waste of students' time that could otherwise be spent learning. Opponents charge that today's students are already overburdened with the stresses of school and need the summer to get a much-needed break. In your view, should the traditional three-month summer vacation from school be maintained?

In your essay, take a position on this question. You may write about either one of the two points of view given, or you may present a different point of view on this question. Use specific reasons and examples to support your position.

ACT Diagnostic Test Form

Use a No. 2 pencil only. Be sure each mark is dark and completely fills the intended oval. Completely erase any errors or stray marks.

1. YOUR NAME: _____
(Print)   Last   First   M.I.

SIGNATURE: _____ **DATE:** _____ / _____ / _____

HOME ADDRESS: _____
(Print)   Number and Street

_____
City   State   Zip

E-MAIL: _____

PHONE NO.: _____
(Print)

SCHOOL: _____

CLASS OF: _____

3. TEST CODE

⓪	⓪	⓪	⓪
①	①	①	①
②	②	②	②
③	③	③	③
④	④	④	④
⑤	⑤	⑤	⑤
⑥	⑥	⑥	⑥
⑦	⑦	⑦	⑦
⑧	⑧	⑧	⑧
⑨	⑨	⑨	⑨

IMPORTANT: Please fill in these boxes exactly as shown on the back cover of your tests book.

2. TEST FORM

_____

4. PHONE NUMBER

⓪	⓪	⓪	⓪	⓪	⓪	⓪
①	①	①	①	①	①	①
②	②	②	②	②	②	②
③	③	③	③	③	③	③
④	④	④	④	④	④	④
⑤	⑤	⑤	⑤	⑤	⑤	⑤
⑥	⑥	⑥	⑥	⑥	⑥	⑥
⑦	⑦	⑦	⑦	⑦	⑦	⑦
⑧	⑧	⑧	⑧	⑧	⑧	⑧
⑨	⑨	⑨	⑨	⑨	⑨	⑨

5. YOUR NAME

First 4 letters of last name				FIRST INIT	MID INIT
Ⓐ	Ⓐ	Ⓐ	Ⓐ	Ⓐ	Ⓐ
Ⓑ	Ⓑ	Ⓑ	Ⓑ	Ⓑ	Ⓑ
Ⓒ	Ⓒ	Ⓒ	Ⓒ	Ⓒ	Ⓒ
Ⓓ	Ⓓ	Ⓓ	Ⓓ	Ⓓ	Ⓓ
Ⓔ	Ⓔ	Ⓔ	Ⓔ	Ⓔ	Ⓔ
Ⓕ	Ⓕ	Ⓕ	Ⓕ	Ⓕ	Ⓕ
Ⓖ	Ⓖ	Ⓖ	Ⓖ	Ⓖ	Ⓖ
Ⓗ	Ⓗ	Ⓗ	Ⓗ	Ⓗ	Ⓗ
Ⓘ	Ⓘ	Ⓘ	Ⓘ	Ⓘ	Ⓘ
Ⓙ	Ⓙ	Ⓙ	Ⓙ	Ⓙ	Ⓙ
Ⓚ	Ⓚ	Ⓚ	Ⓚ	Ⓚ	Ⓚ
Ⓛ	Ⓛ	Ⓛ	Ⓛ	Ⓛ	Ⓛ
Ⓜ	Ⓜ	Ⓜ	Ⓜ	Ⓜ	Ⓜ
Ⓝ	Ⓝ	Ⓝ	Ⓝ	Ⓝ	Ⓝ
Ⓞ	Ⓞ	Ⓞ	Ⓞ	Ⓞ	Ⓞ
Ⓟ	Ⓟ	Ⓟ	Ⓟ	Ⓟ	Ⓟ
Ⓠ	Ⓠ	Ⓠ	Ⓠ	Ⓠ	Ⓠ
Ⓡ	Ⓡ	Ⓡ	Ⓡ	Ⓡ	Ⓡ
Ⓢ	Ⓢ	Ⓢ	Ⓢ	Ⓢ	Ⓢ
Ⓣ	Ⓣ	Ⓣ	Ⓣ	Ⓣ	Ⓣ
Ⓤ	Ⓤ	Ⓤ	Ⓤ	Ⓤ	Ⓤ
Ⓥ	Ⓥ	Ⓥ	Ⓥ	Ⓥ	Ⓥ
Ⓦ	Ⓦ	Ⓦ	Ⓦ	Ⓦ	Ⓦ
Ⓧ	Ⓧ	Ⓧ	Ⓧ	Ⓧ	Ⓧ
Ⓨ	Ⓨ	Ⓨ	Ⓨ	Ⓨ	Ⓨ
Ⓩ	Ⓩ	Ⓩ	Ⓩ	Ⓩ	Ⓩ

6. DATE OF BIRTH

MONTH	DAY		YEAR	
○ JAN				
○ FEB				
○ MAR	⓪	⓪	⓪	⓪
○ APR	①	①	①	①
○ MAY	②	②	②	②
○ JUN	③	③	③	③
○ JUL		④	④	④
○ AUG		⑤	⑤	⑤
○ SEP		⑥	⑥	⑥
○ OCT		⑦	⑦	⑦
○ NOV		⑧	⑧	⑧
○ DEC		⑨	⑨	⑨

7. SEX

○ MALE
○ FEMALE

8. OTHER

1 Ⓐ Ⓑ Ⓒ Ⓓ Ⓔ
2 Ⓐ Ⓑ Ⓒ Ⓓ Ⓔ
3 Ⓐ Ⓑ Ⓒ Ⓓ Ⓔ

THIS PAGE INTENTIONALLY LEFT BLANK

The Princeton Review
Diagnostic ACT Form

ENGLISH

1 Ⓐ Ⓑ Ⓒ Ⓓ	21 Ⓐ Ⓑ Ⓒ Ⓓ	41 Ⓐ Ⓑ Ⓒ Ⓓ	61 Ⓐ Ⓑ Ⓒ Ⓓ
2 Ⓕ Ⓖ Ⓗ Ⓙ	22 Ⓕ Ⓖ Ⓗ Ⓙ	42 Ⓕ Ⓖ Ⓗ Ⓙ	62 Ⓕ Ⓖ Ⓗ Ⓙ
3 Ⓐ Ⓑ Ⓒ Ⓓ	23 Ⓐ Ⓑ Ⓒ Ⓓ	43 Ⓐ Ⓑ Ⓒ Ⓓ	63 Ⓐ Ⓑ Ⓒ Ⓓ
4 Ⓕ Ⓖ Ⓗ Ⓙ	24 Ⓕ Ⓖ Ⓗ Ⓙ	44 Ⓕ Ⓖ Ⓗ Ⓙ	64 Ⓕ Ⓖ Ⓗ Ⓙ
5 Ⓐ Ⓑ Ⓒ Ⓓ	25 Ⓐ Ⓑ Ⓒ Ⓓ	45 Ⓐ Ⓑ Ⓒ Ⓓ	65 Ⓐ Ⓑ Ⓒ Ⓓ
6 Ⓕ Ⓖ Ⓗ Ⓙ	26 Ⓕ Ⓖ Ⓗ Ⓙ	46 Ⓕ Ⓖ Ⓗ Ⓙ	66 Ⓕ Ⓖ Ⓗ Ⓙ
7 Ⓐ Ⓑ Ⓒ Ⓓ	27 Ⓐ Ⓑ Ⓒ Ⓓ	47 Ⓐ Ⓑ Ⓒ Ⓓ	67 Ⓐ Ⓑ Ⓒ Ⓓ
8 Ⓕ Ⓖ Ⓗ Ⓙ	28 Ⓕ Ⓖ Ⓗ Ⓙ	48 Ⓕ Ⓖ Ⓗ Ⓙ	68 Ⓕ Ⓖ Ⓗ Ⓙ
9 Ⓐ Ⓑ Ⓒ Ⓓ	29 Ⓐ Ⓑ Ⓒ Ⓓ	49 Ⓐ Ⓑ Ⓒ Ⓓ	69 Ⓐ Ⓑ Ⓒ Ⓓ
10 Ⓕ Ⓖ Ⓗ Ⓙ	30 Ⓕ Ⓖ Ⓗ Ⓙ	50 Ⓕ Ⓖ Ⓗ Ⓙ	70 Ⓕ Ⓖ Ⓗ Ⓙ
11 Ⓐ Ⓑ Ⓒ Ⓓ	31 Ⓐ Ⓑ Ⓒ Ⓓ	51 Ⓐ Ⓑ Ⓒ Ⓓ	71 Ⓐ Ⓑ Ⓒ Ⓓ
12 Ⓕ Ⓖ Ⓗ Ⓙ	32 Ⓕ Ⓖ Ⓗ Ⓙ	52 Ⓕ Ⓖ Ⓗ Ⓙ	72 Ⓕ Ⓖ Ⓗ Ⓙ
13 Ⓐ Ⓑ Ⓒ Ⓓ	33 Ⓐ Ⓑ Ⓒ Ⓓ	53 Ⓐ Ⓑ Ⓒ Ⓓ	73 Ⓐ Ⓑ Ⓒ Ⓓ
14 Ⓕ Ⓖ Ⓗ Ⓙ	34 Ⓕ Ⓖ Ⓗ Ⓙ	54 Ⓕ Ⓖ Ⓗ Ⓙ	74 Ⓕ Ⓖ Ⓗ Ⓙ
15 Ⓐ Ⓑ Ⓒ Ⓓ	35 Ⓐ Ⓑ Ⓒ Ⓓ	55 Ⓐ Ⓑ Ⓒ Ⓓ	75 Ⓐ Ⓑ Ⓒ Ⓓ
16 Ⓕ Ⓖ Ⓗ Ⓙ	36 Ⓕ Ⓖ Ⓗ Ⓙ	56 Ⓕ Ⓖ Ⓗ Ⓙ	
17 Ⓐ Ⓑ Ⓒ Ⓓ	37 Ⓐ Ⓑ Ⓒ Ⓓ	57 Ⓐ Ⓑ Ⓒ Ⓓ	
18 Ⓕ Ⓖ Ⓗ Ⓙ	38 Ⓕ Ⓖ Ⓗ Ⓙ	58 Ⓕ Ⓖ Ⓗ Ⓙ	
19 Ⓐ Ⓑ Ⓒ Ⓓ	39 Ⓐ Ⓑ Ⓒ Ⓓ	59 Ⓐ Ⓑ Ⓒ Ⓓ	
20 Ⓕ Ⓖ Ⓗ Ⓙ	40 Ⓕ Ⓖ Ⓗ Ⓙ	60 Ⓕ Ⓖ Ⓗ Ⓙ	

MATHEMATICS

1 Ⓐ Ⓑ Ⓒ Ⓓ Ⓔ	16 Ⓕ Ⓖ Ⓗ Ⓙ Ⓚ	31 Ⓐ Ⓑ Ⓒ Ⓓ Ⓔ	46 Ⓕ Ⓖ Ⓗ Ⓙ Ⓚ
2 Ⓕ Ⓖ Ⓗ Ⓙ Ⓚ	17 Ⓐ Ⓑ Ⓒ Ⓓ Ⓔ	32 Ⓕ Ⓖ Ⓗ Ⓙ Ⓚ	47 Ⓐ Ⓑ Ⓒ Ⓓ Ⓔ
3 Ⓐ Ⓑ Ⓒ Ⓓ Ⓔ	18 Ⓕ Ⓖ Ⓗ Ⓙ Ⓚ	33 Ⓐ Ⓑ Ⓒ Ⓓ Ⓔ	48 Ⓕ Ⓖ Ⓗ Ⓙ Ⓚ
4 Ⓕ Ⓖ Ⓗ Ⓙ Ⓚ	19 Ⓐ Ⓑ Ⓒ Ⓓ Ⓔ	34 Ⓕ Ⓖ Ⓗ Ⓙ Ⓚ	49 Ⓐ Ⓑ Ⓒ Ⓓ Ⓔ
5 Ⓐ Ⓑ Ⓒ Ⓓ Ⓔ	20 Ⓕ Ⓖ Ⓗ Ⓙ Ⓚ	35 Ⓐ Ⓑ Ⓒ Ⓓ Ⓔ	50 Ⓕ Ⓖ Ⓗ Ⓙ Ⓚ
6 Ⓕ Ⓖ Ⓗ Ⓙ Ⓚ	21 Ⓐ Ⓑ Ⓒ Ⓓ Ⓔ	36 Ⓕ Ⓖ Ⓗ Ⓙ Ⓚ	51 Ⓐ Ⓑ Ⓒ Ⓓ Ⓔ
7 Ⓐ Ⓑ Ⓒ Ⓓ Ⓔ	22 Ⓕ Ⓖ Ⓗ Ⓙ Ⓚ	37 Ⓐ Ⓑ Ⓒ Ⓓ Ⓔ	52 Ⓕ Ⓖ Ⓗ Ⓙ Ⓚ
8 Ⓕ Ⓖ Ⓗ Ⓙ Ⓚ	23 Ⓐ Ⓑ Ⓒ Ⓓ Ⓔ	38 Ⓕ Ⓖ Ⓗ Ⓙ Ⓚ	53 Ⓐ Ⓑ Ⓒ Ⓓ Ⓔ
9 Ⓐ Ⓑ Ⓒ Ⓓ Ⓔ	24 Ⓕ Ⓖ Ⓗ Ⓙ Ⓚ	39 Ⓐ Ⓑ Ⓒ Ⓓ Ⓔ	54 Ⓕ Ⓖ Ⓗ Ⓙ Ⓚ
10 Ⓕ Ⓖ Ⓗ Ⓙ Ⓚ	25 Ⓐ Ⓑ Ⓒ Ⓓ Ⓔ	40 Ⓕ Ⓖ Ⓗ Ⓙ Ⓚ	55 Ⓐ Ⓑ Ⓒ Ⓓ Ⓔ
11 Ⓐ Ⓑ Ⓒ Ⓓ Ⓔ	26 Ⓕ Ⓖ Ⓗ Ⓙ Ⓚ	41 Ⓐ Ⓑ Ⓒ Ⓓ Ⓔ	56 Ⓕ Ⓖ Ⓗ Ⓙ Ⓚ
12 Ⓕ Ⓖ Ⓗ Ⓙ Ⓚ	27 Ⓐ Ⓑ Ⓒ Ⓓ Ⓔ	42 Ⓕ Ⓖ Ⓗ Ⓙ Ⓚ	57 Ⓐ Ⓑ Ⓒ Ⓓ Ⓔ
13 Ⓐ Ⓑ Ⓒ Ⓓ Ⓔ	28 Ⓕ Ⓖ Ⓗ Ⓙ Ⓚ	43 Ⓐ Ⓑ Ⓒ Ⓓ Ⓔ	58 Ⓕ Ⓖ Ⓗ Ⓙ Ⓚ
14 Ⓕ Ⓖ Ⓗ Ⓙ Ⓚ	29 Ⓐ Ⓑ Ⓒ Ⓓ Ⓔ	44 Ⓕ Ⓖ Ⓗ Ⓙ Ⓚ	59 Ⓐ Ⓑ Ⓒ Ⓓ Ⓔ
15 Ⓐ Ⓑ Ⓒ Ⓓ Ⓔ	30 Ⓕ Ⓖ Ⓗ Ⓙ Ⓚ	45 Ⓐ Ⓑ Ⓒ Ⓓ Ⓔ	60 Ⓕ Ⓖ Ⓗ Ⓙ Ⓚ

The Princeton Review
Diagnostic ACT Form

READING

1 Ⓐ Ⓑ Ⓒ Ⓓ	11 Ⓐ Ⓑ Ⓒ Ⓓ	21 Ⓐ Ⓑ Ⓒ Ⓓ	31 Ⓐ Ⓑ Ⓒ Ⓓ
2 Ⓕ Ⓖ Ⓗ Ⓙ	12 Ⓕ Ⓖ Ⓗ Ⓙ	22 Ⓕ Ⓖ Ⓗ Ⓙ	32 Ⓕ Ⓖ Ⓗ Ⓙ
3 Ⓐ Ⓑ Ⓒ Ⓓ	13 Ⓐ Ⓑ Ⓒ Ⓓ	23 Ⓐ Ⓑ Ⓒ Ⓓ	33 Ⓐ Ⓑ Ⓒ Ⓓ
4 Ⓕ Ⓖ Ⓗ Ⓙ	14 Ⓕ Ⓖ Ⓗ Ⓙ	24 Ⓕ Ⓖ Ⓗ Ⓙ	34 Ⓕ Ⓖ Ⓗ Ⓙ
5 Ⓐ Ⓑ Ⓒ Ⓓ	15 Ⓐ Ⓑ Ⓒ Ⓓ	25 Ⓐ Ⓑ Ⓒ Ⓓ	35 Ⓐ Ⓑ Ⓒ Ⓓ
6 Ⓕ Ⓖ Ⓗ Ⓙ	16 Ⓕ Ⓖ Ⓗ Ⓙ	26 Ⓕ Ⓖ Ⓗ Ⓙ	36 Ⓕ Ⓖ Ⓗ Ⓙ
7 Ⓐ Ⓑ Ⓒ Ⓓ	17 Ⓐ Ⓑ Ⓒ Ⓓ	27 Ⓐ Ⓑ Ⓒ Ⓓ	37 Ⓐ Ⓑ Ⓒ Ⓓ
8 Ⓕ Ⓖ Ⓗ Ⓙ	18 Ⓕ Ⓖ Ⓗ Ⓙ	28 Ⓕ Ⓖ Ⓗ Ⓙ	38 Ⓕ Ⓖ Ⓗ Ⓙ
9 Ⓐ Ⓑ Ⓒ Ⓓ	19 Ⓐ Ⓑ Ⓒ Ⓓ	29 Ⓐ Ⓑ Ⓒ Ⓓ	39 Ⓐ Ⓑ Ⓒ Ⓓ
10 Ⓕ Ⓖ Ⓗ Ⓙ	20 Ⓕ Ⓖ Ⓗ Ⓙ	30 Ⓕ Ⓖ Ⓗ Ⓙ	40 Ⓕ Ⓖ Ⓗ Ⓙ

SCIENCE REASONING

1 Ⓐ Ⓑ Ⓒ Ⓓ	11 Ⓐ Ⓑ Ⓒ Ⓓ	21 Ⓐ Ⓑ Ⓒ Ⓓ	31 Ⓐ Ⓑ Ⓒ Ⓓ
2 Ⓕ Ⓖ Ⓗ Ⓙ	12 Ⓕ Ⓖ Ⓗ Ⓙ	22 Ⓕ Ⓖ Ⓗ Ⓙ	32 Ⓕ Ⓖ Ⓗ Ⓙ
3 Ⓐ Ⓑ Ⓒ Ⓓ	13 Ⓐ Ⓑ Ⓒ Ⓓ	23 Ⓐ Ⓑ Ⓒ Ⓓ	33 Ⓐ Ⓑ Ⓒ Ⓓ
4 Ⓕ Ⓖ Ⓗ Ⓙ	14 Ⓕ Ⓖ Ⓗ Ⓙ	24 Ⓕ Ⓖ Ⓗ Ⓙ	34 Ⓕ Ⓖ Ⓗ Ⓙ
5 Ⓐ Ⓑ Ⓒ Ⓓ	15 Ⓐ Ⓑ Ⓒ Ⓓ	25 Ⓐ Ⓑ Ⓒ Ⓓ	35 Ⓐ Ⓑ Ⓒ Ⓓ
6 Ⓕ Ⓖ Ⓗ Ⓙ	16 Ⓕ Ⓖ Ⓗ Ⓙ	26 Ⓕ Ⓖ Ⓗ Ⓙ	36 Ⓕ Ⓖ Ⓗ Ⓙ
7 Ⓐ Ⓑ Ⓒ Ⓓ	17 Ⓐ Ⓑ Ⓒ Ⓓ	27 Ⓐ Ⓑ Ⓒ Ⓓ	37 Ⓐ Ⓑ Ⓒ Ⓓ
8 Ⓕ Ⓖ Ⓗ Ⓙ	18 Ⓕ Ⓖ Ⓗ Ⓙ	28 Ⓕ Ⓖ Ⓗ Ⓙ	38 Ⓕ Ⓖ Ⓗ Ⓙ
9 Ⓐ Ⓑ Ⓒ Ⓓ	19 Ⓐ Ⓑ Ⓒ Ⓓ	29 Ⓐ Ⓑ Ⓒ Ⓓ	39 Ⓐ Ⓑ Ⓒ Ⓓ
10 Ⓕ Ⓖ Ⓗ Ⓙ	20 Ⓕ Ⓖ Ⓗ Ⓙ	30 Ⓕ Ⓖ Ⓗ Ⓙ	40 Ⓕ Ⓖ Ⓗ Ⓙ

I hereby certify that I have truthfully identified myself on this form. I accept the consequences of falsifying my identity.

_____
Your signature

_____
Today's date

The Princeton Review
Diagnostic ACT Form

ESSAY

Begin your essay on this side. If necessary, continue on the opposite side.

Continue on the opposite side if necessary.

The Princeton Review
Diagnostic ACT Form

Continued from previous page.

_____

_____

_____

_____

_____

_____

_____

_____

_____

_____

_____

_____

_____

_____

_____

_____

_____

_____

_____

_____

_____

_____

_____

_____

_____

PLEASE PRINT
YOUR INITIALS

First	Middle	Last

Chapter 28
Practice Exam 2:
Answers
and Explanations

English		Math		Reading		Science	
1. D	40. J	1. A	40. H	1. C	40. J	1. C	40. H
2. F	41. A	2. H	41. C	2. F		2. F	
3. C	42. G	3. C	42. F	3. B		3. A	
4. F	43. C	4. J	43. B	4. G		4. H	
5. C	44. G	5. C	44. G	5. A		5. D	
6. H	45. B	6. K	45. B	6. H		6. G	
7. D	46. J	7. A	46. H	7. A		7. B	
8. F	47. C	8. K	47. D	8. J		8. F	
9. A	48. F	9. E	48. J	9. D		9. D	
10. G	49. C	10. J	49. B	10. J		10. G	
11. C	50. J	11. C	50. J	11. D		11. C	
12. H	51. C	12. K	51. D	12. G		12. G	
13. D	52. F	13. D	52. K	13. D		13. A	
14. F	53. A	14. G	53. C	14. G		14. H	
15. C	54. H	15. A	54. H	15. A		15. D	
16. G	55. A	16. H	55. C	16. G		16. G	
17. D	56. H	17. A	56. G	17. C		17. D	
18. H	57. D	18. K	57. A	18. F		18. F	
19. A	58. G	19. C	58. F	19. C		19. D	
20. G	59. D	20. H	59. D	20. G		20. J	
21. D	60. H	21. C	60. K	21. C		21. B	
22. F	61. B	22. F		22. G		22. H	
23. A	62. J	23. C		23. C		23. B	
24. F	63. C	24. G		24. G		24. F	
25. C	64. J	25. E		25. D		25. C	
26. G	65. C	26. G		26. J		26. G	
27. D	66. H	27. D		27. B		27. D	
28. H	67. D	28. F		28. J		28. H	
29. D	68. F	29. C		29. A		29. C	
30. J	69. A	30. H		30. H		30. F	
31. A	70. G	31. E		31. C		31. C	
32. F	71. A	32. J		32. H		32. J	
33. C	72. G	33. C		33. D		33. C	
34. F	73. B	34. K		34. G		34. G	
35. C	74. F	35. E		35. C		35. B	
36. J	75. D	36. K		36. J		36. J	
37. C		37. E		37. C		37. A	
38. J		38. J		38. H		38. F	
39. D		39. B		39. A		39. D	

ENGLISH TEST

1. **D** The verb *associate* requires the preposition *with*. None of the other choices are idiomatically correct.

2. **F** All the proposed substitutions essentially expand upon the word *genders* without adding any new information to the sentence. As a result, you can eliminate choices (G), (H), and (J) because they are all unnecessarily wordy.

3. **C** You can eliminate choices (A) and (B) right away because the proposed sentence is totally out of context with what you've read so far. Only choice (C) gives the correct reason why you shouldn't include the proposed sentence: the content of the sentence is irrelevant to the passage as a whole.

4. **F** Eliminate choices (H) and (J) immediately because these will not be correct under any circumstances. Only choice (F) uses the correct form of the past participle.

5. **C** Choices (A) and (B) contain punctuation that is used to separate independent clauses. Since *once you've learned a few basic stitches* is not an independent clause, neither answer choice can work. Instead, *once you've learned a few basic stitches* operates more as an introductory idea, which must be set off with a comma, as in choice (C).

6. **H** In this situation, choice (H) is the most concise answer that makes sense in the context. Notice all the other choices contain redundant words and phrases.

7. **D** This sentence is talking about the *completion of several projects*. Only choice (D) has the appropriate plural pronoun. If you picked choice (B), be careful: pronouns must agree in number.

8. **F** Since you can count the starter kits (there are three, as the passage says), use *fewer* rather than *less*. With that, you can eliminate choices (H) and (J). Next, you need to use *than*, which is a comparison word, rather than *then*, which is a word used to describe a sequence of events in time. Only choice (F) works in this sentence.

9. **A** No change is necessary here because no pause is needed after the word *types*. Choices (B) and (C) in particular use punctuation that is much too strong in this context.

10. **G** Use Process Of Elimination aggressively here. The idiomatic phrase *ranging from* should not be split up with a comma, so eliminate choices (F) and (J). Then, eliminate choice (H) because *ranging from very small to very large, with everything in between* is not an independent clause. Only choice (G) works in the context.

11. **C** This sentence talks about hooks that are *so big that you need to use two strands of yarn*, so it must be moved closer to other sentences that do the same. Only Sentence 3 works, because it talks about large hooks.

12. **H** Choices (F) and (G) don't make sense in the context. These are actually ideas with a negative slant and would be more appropriate in a sentence that was talking about some negative aspect of crocheting. Choice (J) might have worked better in the first paragraph. In this paragraph, however, choice (H) provides the most effective lead-in.

13. D   As written, this sentence contains a comma splice in its use of a comma to separate two independent clauses, so eliminate choice (A). Choices (C) and (D) both contain words that turn the first part of the sentence into a dependent clause, but choice (C) suggests a contrast where none exists. Choice (D) is the best answer because it fixes the dependency problem and contains the appropriate transition word.

14. F   Only choice (F) gives the idiomatically correct preposition. The others change the meaning of the sentence or use incorrect idioms.

15. C   The essay is clearly in favor of crocheting, but it has not discussed the commercial potential of crocheting at all, so you can eliminate choices (A) and (B). Neither has it talked about the commercial potential of any other hobby, so you can eliminate choice (D).

16. G   The verbs in this sentence are fairly complex, so use Process of Elimination aggressively. You can eliminate choices (F), (H), and (J) because all would be used in a situation in which the author *had seen* the painting. In the context of this sentence, however, the author is trying to suggest that she never believed that she *would see* the painting, so only choice (G) can work.

17. D   This sentence may sound correct as written, but be careful. If you're going to use the *chance to* construction, you must complete the infinitive. In other words, in this situation, the sentence would have to read, *I finally got my chance to see the painting*. In this case, the only possible solution is to delete the underlined portion. Note that this is the most concise answer that works. Always give these deletions and omissions special consideration—they can often get some of the tangled logic out of the sentences as written.

18. H   This sentence refers to the *grandeur* of the *painting*. In other words, you need the possessive pronoun *its* when describing the painting's grandeur. Only choice (H) works.

19. A   The verbs in this sentence form a kind of list, so make sure all the verbs in the sentence are consistent (or "parallel") with one another. The verbs should read *packed*, *jumped*, and *headed*. Only choice (A) keeps all three verbs consistent with one another.

20. G   The proposed insertion has the word *her* right at the beginning, which means that you need to find the sentence that contains its antecedent. Notice the clause in Sentence 3, *I met someone else who loved the painting as much as I did*. This *someone else* is the best available antecedent for *her* in the paragraph.

21. D   There are dependent clauses on either side of this sentence, so you can't use either a colon or a semi-colon. Even a comma gives the sentence a pause where none is necessary. Only choice (D) gives the sentence its appropriate flow and does not break up the compound subject and its verb.

22. F   Notice the word *impossible* directly before the underlined portion. Since this word is not underlined, it can't be changed, thus making choices (G), (H), and (J) redundant.

23. A   Sentence 1 does talk about the size of the canvas, but Sentence 2 is out of context in this paragraph. This paragraph is about the author's impressions of the painting; the kind of technical detail presented in Sentence 2 is not part of these impressions.

24. F Remember that transitions are used to connect the ideas in paragraphs. The previous paragraph is about the author's impression of the painting, particularly relating to the size of the painting. The new paragraph goes on to present the author's impression of another element of the painting, which she finds *even more impressive*, as in choice (F). Choices (G), (H), and (J) might work in a different context, but they don't connect these paragraphs as well as choice (F).

25. C Notice that choices (A), (B), (D), and the underlined portion of the original sentence all contain the subordinating conjunctions *as* and *when*. The absence of any of these conjunctions in choice (C) creates a comma splice, and choice (C) is therefore NOT an acceptable substitution.

26. G *From a distance* is the first part of the contrast in this sentence, the second part of which is *up close*. If you were to delete the prepositional phrase *from a distance*, this contrast would be unclear.

27. D The subjects of these paragraphs have been the author and her friend, so of all the answer choices, only choice (D), which contains the first-person plural pronoun *we*, could work here.

28. H This essay has been about the author's love of a single painting, so there is no need to mention other paintings at this point in the essay; eliminate choices (F) and (G). You can also eliminate choice (J) because this information is not contradicted elsewhere in the passage.

29. D No pause is necessary between *sights* and *on our trip*, so eliminate all answer choices that suggest this pause with unnecessary punctuation.

30. J The only clear placement for the underlined portion is after the word *bought*, completing the phrase *bought at the museum gift shop*. The other answer choices make the sentence unclear.

31. A The clause *cats have developed* is not an independent clause, so a semicolon can't be used after it. Eliminate choice (D). In fact, no pause is needed anywhere in this sentence, so any of the choices that introduce unnecessary commas can be deleted. Choice (A) is the only choice that does not contain unnecessary pauses.

32. F Make sure you read the question carefully. It's asking for something that expresses the *ownership* relationship between people and cats. Choice (H) can be eliminated because it talks about dogs, and choices (G) and (J) can be eliminated because they don't express the ownership relationship for which the question is asking.

33. C In this sentence, the phrase *When communicating with each other* is a misplaced modifier. As written it sounds like the "*talk*" is somehow *communicating with each other*. It is of course the *cats* that are communicating with each other, which means that only choice (C) fixes the misplaced modifier.

34. F First, since this question is testing changes in verb tense, identify the subject of the verb. In this case, the subject is the plural noun *tails*, which requires a plural verb. You can eliminate choice (H) immediately, and choice (G) makes the sentence incomplete. Choice (J) changes the meaning of the sentence and uses a wordy passive construction. Given the new mistakes in all the proposed substitutions, the best answer is choice (F), NO CHANGE.

35.　C　The paragraph has been discussing the ways that cats communicate nonverbally. The sentence gives an exception to this rule, which only choice (C) adequately describes.

36.　J　You'll want to begin a new paragraph here, because the focus of the essay changes with the introduction of the word *human*. Because this sentence is not describing a step in a process, and there's no first idea for which this can be the *next*, you can eliminate choice (H). Only choice (J) works.

37.　C　Use context. The previous sentence is describing plural cats, so this sentence should do the same. Only choice (C) gives the correct possessive form of the plural, *cats'*.

38.　J　Choices (F) and (G) are redundant. The word *logical* alone gets the point across here. Choice (H) modifies *logical*, but it does so unnecessarily—*to a startling degree* is not specific. Only choice (J) is concise while preserving the meaning of the sentence.

39.　D　*Clear* is an adjective, which modifies a noun; *clearly* is an adverb, which can modify a verb, an adjective, or another adverb. The word being modified here is *demonstrated*, which is a verb, so you'll need the adverb *clearly* and can eliminate choices (A) and (B). Choice (C) can't work because the subordinating conjunction *since* is not the appropriate transition between ideas in the sentence. Only choice (D) contains the correct adverb with the proper subordinating conjunction *when*.

40.　J　The information given is true and may be interesting, but in the context of this passage, it would be out of context. Remember, this is a passage about cats, so it is not at all likely that a sentence about birds will contribute to the main idea of the passage.

41.　A　The structure of this sentence is clumsy, but you can change only what appears in the underlined portion. In this instance, your most important clue is the comma after the word *examples*. This comma suggests that the infinitive phrase *to name only a few examples* is being set off as unnecessary to the meaning of the sentence. The sentence as written is the only choice that does not contain a grammatical error.

42.　G　Of all the possibilities listed here, only choice (G) establishes any kind of link between *cats* and *their owners*. Other answer choices talk about *mammals*, but this question asks specifically about *cats*.

43.　C　The underlined portion must be parallel with the rest of the sentence. Early in the sentence, the author speaks of *communicating as every bit as important as forging good relationships*. A second *as* will be needed to complete the comparison, and any verb used will need the same conjugation as *forging*. Choices (B) and (C) both meet these criteria, but of the two, choice (C) is more concise.

44.　G　Choice (G) is the most concise substitution that maintains the meaning of the sentence. Choices (F), (H), and (J) are redundant because they contain some form of the word *senseless* and other words that mean the same thing.

45. B   Some of the transition words offered in the answer choices may seem similar, so it is best in this situation to compare what comes after those transition words. Again, you need an answer that expresses the relationship between *cats* and their *owners*. Although the word *human* does not appear in it, choice (B) is the only one of the answer choices that talks about a relationship between cats and humans.

46. J   Choices (F), (G), and (H) all give redundant constructions. Only choice (J) gives a concise construction and maintains the meaning of the sentence.

47. C   The *houses* described here are not in possession of anything, so you can eliminate choices (A) and (B). You can also eliminate choice (D) because it introduces an unnecessary pause after the word *houses*.

48. F   Only choice (F) maintains the meaning of the subject without introducing new, unnecessary information. Choice (J) might look appealing, but choice (F) is still more concise. Think of it this way: to say the same thing, choice (F) takes one word and choice (J) takes two. Go with the most concise choice that works.

49. C   *Michigan island* is a compound noun in this case, so the adjective *isolated* should not be set off from *Michigan* with a comma. Eliminate choices (A) and (D). Then, notice the coordinating conjunction *so* directly after the underlined portion. If a coordinating conjunction is being used to link two independent clauses, it must be preceded by a comma. Only choice (C) works.

50. J   All items in a list must be parallel. In this sentence, the list should read *by horse, carriage, or bicycle*. Choices (F), (G), and (H) are not within this parallel structure.

51. C   As written, this sentence creates a comma splice. The clause that ends with the word *necessary* and the clause that begins with the word *Mackinac* are both independent, so of the different possible punctuation marks in the answer choices, only a period can be used to separate them.

52. F   If the end of this sentence were deleted, the meaning of the sentence would not fundamentally change, but you would lose an interesting detail about Arch Rock, as choice (F) suggests. Choice (G) is misleading in that it suggests the geological descriptions of multiple tourist attractions, where the underlined portion gives the geological description of only one attraction. There is no contrast with the governor's mansion, so eliminate choice (H); the information is not detailed elsewhere in the passage, so eliminate choice (J).

53. A   The next sentence discusses *fudge*, and only choice (A) contains any mention of stores that might sell this product.

54. H   This question is testing the idiom *for sale*. The only viable alternative to this would be *on sale*, but that doesn't appear in the answer choices. Choices (F), (G), and (J) all suggest incorrect idioms.

55. A   Choices (B), (C), and (D) are all grammatically correct while preserving the basic meaning of the sentence. Choice (A), *which*, is neither grammatically correct nor consistent with the meaning of the sentence. Therefore, choice (A) would NOT be an acceptable alternative.

56. **H** Only choice (H) removes the redundancy problem and maintains the meaning of the sentence.

57. **D** The pronoun in this portion of the sentence should refer back to the *local residents*. As such, it should be a third-person plural. Only choice (D) has the appropriate pronoun, *they*.

58. **G** Of all the answer choices, only choice (G) reduces the wordiness of the sentence while clarifying its meaning.

59. **D** The subject of this sentence is *privacy*, so the verb in the underlined portion must agree with a singular noun. Eliminate choice (A). Choices (B) and (C) change the meaning of the sentence by changing the tense of the auxiliary verbs. Only choice (D) maintains the meaning of the sentence and fixes the verb-conjugation problem.

60. **H** This passage discusses Mackinac Island as a tourist destination and mentions cars only in the beginning of this essay. If the writer's intention is to show the difficulties residents have with cars, this essay has not succeeded; its subject has been the island itself and its many tourist attractions.

61. **B** The two nouns *friends* and *peers* are not part of a list or separate ideas. Instead, they are both the objects of the prepositional phrase *in front of*, and they should thus not be separated with any punctuation.

62. **J** Choice (J) is grammatically incorrect because it makes the sentence unable to stand on its own (i.e., it changes the sentence from an independent to a dependent clause). It is therefore NOT an acceptable alternative to the underlined portion.

63. **C** Sentence 2 refers to something that *defies understanding*, and the word *though* suggests that something in a previous sentence does not defy understanding. Sentence 4 reads, *It is understandable that people would enjoy singing in the privacy of their homes.* Sentence 2 should follow this sentence because it describes, by way of a contrast, something that is not so understandable.

64. **J** Notice the other verb in this sentence, *see*. These verbs should be parallel; the basic subjects and verbs of each part of the sentence should read *look and you'll see*. Only choice (J) contains the parallel verb and maintains the meaning of the sentence.

65. **C** The *even though* at the beginning of this sentence operates as a subordinating conjunction, thus making everything up to *busy restaurants* part of a single dependent clause. Choices (A) and (C) set this dependent clause off with a comma correctly, but choice (A) has the coordinating conjunction *but*. A coordinating conjunction preceded by a comma can only be used to separate two independent clauses.

66. **H** The phrase *such staples as* should not be divided with any punctuation. Only choice (H) gives the appropriate absence of punctuation. In order to use a colon, the clause before the colon must be independent. This one is not, so you can eliminate choice (G).

67. D The verb in the underlined portion must be parallel with the other major verb in this sentence, *responds*. Only choice (D) establishes this parallelism. Choices (A) and (C) are in the wrong tense, and choice (B) makes for an awkward construction.

68. F The beginning of the next paragraph speaks of *another, more obvious reason*. The underlined portion, therefore, must contain a reason of some kind. Only choice (F) contains anything close, particularly in the final clause, *this is not the only reason for its enduring popularity*. The other answer choices do not link these two paragraphs, nor do they make sense in the larger context of the passage.

69. A This sentence should be in contrast with the previous sentence, and the sentence as written signals this contrast. The others give adverbs that suggest a comparison rather than a contrast.

70. G This sentence needs something that will suggest that the quality of people's voices doesn't matter. Only choice (G) does this with the word *regardless*. The prepositional phrase *in lieu of* suggests a substitution, but nothing is being substituted here; rather, the poor singing of many of karaoke's participants is being disregarded in consideration of other, more important things.

71. A Choice (D) gives the contraction *who is*, which does not work here, so you can eliminate that immediately. Choices (B) and (C) are not grammatically correct in this situation. The sentence as written contains the appropriate possessive pronoun and should therefore not be changed.

72. G The clause *who are ordinarily shy* is important in its modification of the word *people*. It would be incorrect to say that karaoke brings people in general out of their shells. The clause is necessary because it clarifies that the sentence is talking about people not normally inclined to perform in public.

73. B The word *first* indicates that the underlined portion will need to have something to do with time. Choice (D) suggests a place, so you can eliminate it. Choices (A) and (C) suggest a cause and effect that is not substantiated in the rest of the sentence. Only choice (B), *when*, gives the appropriate time word.

74. F If you are not sure how to use *less* and *fewer*, look at the second word in each underlined portion. *Then* refers to a sequence of events; *than* is a comparison word. In this sentence, the author is making a comparison, so you need *than*. Eliminate choice (H). Now choice (F) is the only choice that makes the sentence grammatically correct. As a general note, *less* is used with general quantities (e.g., less money) and *fewer* is used with quantities that can be counted (e.g., fewer dollars). This question actually tests an exception to the rule in which both adjectives can work depending on the context; if were you to expand this sentence, it would read *less money than $7 billion* rather than *fewer than 7 billion dollars*.

75. D This passage deals with the international popularity of karaoke. At no point does the passage discuss specific regions. Therefore, the proposed insertion would not be appropriate at any point in the passage.

MATHEMATICS TEST

1. **A** The midpoint of segment XY is the average of X and Y, so add them up and divide by 2:
    $$\frac{-15-11}{2} = \frac{-26}{2} = -13.$$

2. **H** Use the Pythagorean theorem ($a^2 + b^2 = c^2$) to find the length of DE: $8^2 + (DE)^2 = 10^2$, so $64 + (DE)^2 = 100$, $(DE)^2 = 36$, $DE = \sqrt{36} = 6$. Also note that this is a Pythagorean triple with sides of 6, 8, and 10.

3. **C** The phrase *double the volume of the ant farm* means your equation must contain the expression $2V$, so eliminate choices (A), (B), and (E). The second sentence also says that the number of ants *is close to 50 more*, so your expression will have to contain the expression $2V + 50$; choice (C) is correct because it adds 50. Choice (D) is incorrect because, when the 2 is distributed, it becomes $2V + 100$.

4. **J** The probability that Lisa will take a fiction book can be defined as a fraction: the number of fiction books divided by the total number of books. Therefore, the probability of Lisa taking a fiction book is $\frac{5}{5+7} = \frac{5}{12}$: choice (J). (K) is the probability that she will take a nonfiction book; choice (G) is the ratio of fiction books to nonfiction books.

5. **C** To find the average, add up all the test scores and divide by the number of tests: $\frac{108+81+79+99+85+82}{6} = \frac{534}{6} = 89$, choice (C). You can eliminate choices (A) and (B) because the average must be less than the highest test score.

6. **K** Angles 3 and 5 are alternate interior angles and therefore congruent. Angles 1 and 3 look congruent only because the triangle appears to be isosceles—the problem does not give any indication that it is, so eliminate choice (G).

7. **A** If p is Gregor's monthly pay, write an equation that represents Gregor's deposit. He spends 20% and deposits the rest, so $p - (0.2)p = 3200$ or $(0.8)p = 3200$. Divide through by the (0.8) to find that $p = 4000$. If you're not sure how to set up the equation, you could also try out the answer choices as possibilities for Gregor's monthly pay to see which gives a deposit value of $3200.

8. **K** By definition, similar polygons have equal corresponding angles, making choice (K) the correct response. Two similar polygons are really the same figure on different scales: smaller or larger versions of each other. Therefore, their dimensions are not necessarily the same, making choices (F), (G), (H), and (J) incorrect.

9. **E** Work through this word problem one step at a time. $\$60 \times .30 = \$18$, so the dress is discounted \$18. $\$60 - \$18 = \$42$, the sale price. Now calculate Victoria's second discount: $\$42 \times .10 = \$4.20$. $\$42 - \$4.20 = \$37.80$, the price Victoria pays. Choice (D) incorrectly discounts the dress 40%; this is wrong because Victoria gets 10% off the *reduced price*, not the original price.

10.   J   Erin begins with x chips, which means (according to the second sentence of the question) Amy has $x - 3$. When Erin wins 4 of Amy's chips, Erin's total increases to $x + 4$ while Amy's drops to $x - 7$. Subtract $(x + 4) - (x - 7) = 11$, the difference in their chip totals.

11.   C   Since absolute value must always be greater than or equal to zero, you can eliminate choices (A) and (B). Substitute $y = 4$ into the expression $|1 - y| = |1 - 4| = |-3| = 3$.

12.   K   FOIL: multiply the First terms $3a \times a = 3a^2$, the Outer terms $3a \times (-b^2) = (-3ab^2)$, the Inner terms $2b \times a = 2ab$, and the Last terms $2b \times (-b^2) = -2b^3$. Add these terms to get $3a^2 - 3ab^2 + 2ab - 2b^3$, choice (K).

13.   D   Simplify the expression: $3 - 2(4 - y) = 3 - 8 + 2y = -5 + 2y$, which is the same as choice (D). Be careful when you multiply two negative values, such as $(-2) \times (-y)$: you should get a positive value.

14.   G   When raising a number with an exponent to another power, you multiply the exponents; therefore, $(y^3)^8 = y^{3 \times 8} = y^{24}$.

15.   A   Sketch out a little calendar until you see a pattern: Day 1 is Monday, 2 is Tuesday, 3 Wednesday, 4 Thursday, 5 Friday, 6 Saturday, 7 Sunday, 8 Monday, and so on. Notice that Sundays are always multiples of 7. Pick a multiple of 7 close to 260, such as 259. That means Day 259 is a Sunday, so Day 260 is a Monday.

16.   H   Draw yourself a figure to see the relationship between the two shapes. Since the formula for area of a square is $A = s^2$ (where s is the side length of the square), you can find that a square with area 64 has side length 8, which would also be the diameter of the circle inscribed in this square, meaning the circle's radius would be 4. The formula for the area of a circle is $A = \pi r^2$, so $A = \pi(4)^2 = 16\pi$.

17.   A   Factor $x^2 - 5x - 14 = 0$ to $(x - 7)(x + 2) = 0$; therefore, the solutions (the values of x that make this true) are 7 and -2. Their product: $7 \times -2 = -14$. Also, note than in the standard formula $ax^2 + bx + c$, the product of the solutions will always be c/a.

18.   K   Factor $x^{12} - 9$ to $(x^6 - 3)(x^6 + 3)$; eliminate choices (F) and (G). Factor $(x^6 - 3)$ to $(x^3 - \sqrt{3})(x^3 + \sqrt{3})$; eliminate choices (H) and (J).

19.   C   Plug $x = \dfrac{1}{6}$ into the expression: $\dfrac{2x + 4}{3x} = \dfrac{2 \times \frac{1}{6} + 4}{3 \times \frac{1}{6}} = \dfrac{\frac{2}{6} + \frac{24}{6}}{\frac{3}{6}} = \dfrac{\frac{26}{6}}{\frac{3}{6}} = \dfrac{26}{3}$.

20.   H   Use the formula Distance = Rate $\times$ Time. Substitute the values from the problem: $60 = 90 \times t$. Therefore, $t = \dfrac{60}{90} = \dfrac{2}{3}$ hours. To convert from hours into minutes, multiply 60 minutes by $\dfrac{2}{3}$ hours: $60 \times \dfrac{2}{3} = 40$ minutes.

21.   C   Begin by drawing a perpendicular height by drawing vertical lines from the top vertices straight down to the base: these segments are the height of the trapezoid, and your figure should now look like a rectangle and two right triangles. Since the bottom base of the trapezoid is 11" and the top

base is 5", the difference is 6". Assume the two triangles you've created are the same size, which means the base of each is 3" (and the base of your rectangle is 5"). Use the Pythagorean theorem $(a^2 + b^2 = c^2)$ to find the height (which we'll call h) of one of the triangles: $h^2 + 3^2 = (3\sqrt{2})^2$, so $h^2 + 9 = 18$, $h^2 = 9$, and $h = 3$. This is also the height of the trapezoid, so plug these values (height and two bases) into the formula in the question: $A = h\left(\frac{b_1 + b_2}{2}\right) = 3\left(\frac{5+11}{2}\right) = 3\left(\frac{16}{2}\right) = 3(8) = 24$. If you hadn't been given the formula for the area of a trapezoid, or if you just find the formula too confusing, notice that the vertical heights split this figure into three familiar shapes: two triangles and a rectangle. You can find the area of each of these smaller pieces and add them together.

22. F   By definition, the roots of a quadratic equation are the values for the variable that cause the equation to equal zero. Starting with the first answer choice, set each factor equal to zero and solve for x: $3x + 2 = 0$ yields $x = -\frac{2}{3}$, and $4x - 1 = 0$ yields $x = \frac{1}{4}$. None of the other answer choices yields both roots given in the problem.

23. C   Draw the line segments $\overline{AC}$ and $\overline{BD}$; these are the diagonals. By definition, the diagonals of a rhombus bisect each other; therefore, the two halves of $\overline{AC}$ are 3 each and the two halves of $\overline{BD}$ are 4 each. The diagonals of a rhombus also (by definition) are perpendicular; this means that each of the four triangles inside this rhombus are right triangles. Use the Pythagorean theorem to find the length of the side of the rhombus: $3^2 + 4^2 = s^2$, so $9 + 16 = s^2$, $25 = s^2$, and $5 = s$. Note that these sides create a 3:4:5 Pythagorean triple.

24. G   The formula for the area of a rectangle is $A = lw$. Fill in what you know: $80 = l(l - 2) = l^2 - 2l$. Solve the quadratic to find solutions $l = 10$ and $l = -8$. You can't have a negative side, so the length of the rectangle must be 10. Since this is a tough algebraic problem, you can also work backwards from the answer choices. Try choice (H) first: if the length is 16, then the width (2 shorter) is 14. Area of a rectangle formula is $A = lw$, so $A = 16 \times 14 = 224$. That's too big, so eliminate choices (H), (J), and (K). Try choice (G) next: if the length is 10, the width is 8, then the area is $10 \times 8 = 80$.

25. E   Don't be intimidated by the Cartesian plane: it's the same (x,y) coordinate plane you're used to. Slope is defined as $\frac{rise}{run}$, so use the two points given in the slope formula: $\frac{y_2 - y_1}{x_2 - x_1} = \frac{10 - (-5)}{5 - 1} = \frac{10 + 5}{4} = \frac{15}{4}$.

26. G   The equation of a circle is $(x - h)^2 + (y - k)^2 = r^2$, where (h,k) is the center of the circle and r is the radius. The first part of the equation tells you that the x-coordinate of the center is -5, since $(x + 5)^2 = (x - [-5])^2$, so $h = -5$. The second part more clearly matches the formula, so it's easier to see that the y-coordinate of the center is 5. Therefore, the center of the circle is $(-5,5)$.

27. D The open circles at $x = 0$ and $x = 4$ mean that $x \neq 0$ and $x \neq 4$; therefore, eliminate choices (A), (B), and (E). The solid line between $x = 0$ and $x = 4$ means that x can be any value between 0 and 4, so eliminate choice (C). Make sure you read the question carefully. If you selected choice (C), you may have mistaken it for the range.

28. F The *point exactly halfway between* is another way to describe the midpoint, so plug the two points into the midpoint formula: $\left(\dfrac{x_1 + x_2}{2}, \dfrac{y_1 + y_2}{2} \right)$. This gives you $\left(\dfrac{-1+3}{2}, \dfrac{-5+3}{2} \right)$, which simplifies to $\left(\dfrac{2}{2}, \dfrac{-2}{2} \right)$, or $(1, -1)$.

29. C To find the *average rate of change*, begin by finding the total change: the liquid begins at $0°$ and eventually reaches $80°$, so the total change is the difference, $80°$. The question asks for the rate of change *during the times in which Sanjay is applying* heat to the container. Sanjay applies heat from minutes 0 to 5, $7\dfrac{1}{2}$ to 10, and 15 to $17\dfrac{1}{2}$. Find the difference in each of these pairs of numbers to see that Sanjay applied heat for 5 minutes, then 2.5 minutes, then another 2.5 minutes, or 10 minutes total. Therefore, the average rate of change in degrees per minute is $\dfrac{80°}{10 \, \text{min}} = 8$ degrees/min.

30. H When you divide exponentials with the same base, you subtract the exponents, so $\dfrac{a^x}{a^y} = a^{x-y}$; therefore, $a^{x-y} = a^5$ and $x - y = 5$.

31. E The slope of a line in standard form $(Ax + By = C)$ is $-\dfrac{A}{B}$; therefore, the slope of $-5x + 3y = 8$ is $-\left(\dfrac{-5}{3} \right) = \dfrac{5}{3}$. Or, if you prefer, rearrange the equation into slope-intercept form $(y = mx + b)$. $8 - 3y = 5x$ becomes $3y = 5x + 8$, or $y = \dfrac{5}{3}x + \dfrac{8}{3}$. In slope-intercept form, m is the slope; in this case, $\dfrac{5}{3}$.

32. J The least common denominator (LCD) must be a multiple of the denominator of each of the three given fractions. Take the factors of each denominator (3, 5, 7, 11) to the highest powers they appear: 3^2 (first fraction), 5^2 (second fraction), 7 (second fraction), and 11^3 (third fraction). This results in $3^2 \cdot 5^2 \cdot 7 \cdot 11^3$, choice (J). Choice (K) is the product of all three denominators and is wrong because choice (J) is smaller and still a multiple of all three denominators; in other words, both are common denominators but choice (J) is the "least."

33. C To multiply fractions, you multiply all the numbers on top of the fractions and all the numbers on the bottom of the fractions: $\dfrac{1}{4} \times \dfrac{2}{5} \times \dfrac{3}{6} \times \dfrac{4}{7} \times \dfrac{5}{8} \times \dfrac{6}{9} \times \dfrac{7}{10} = \dfrac{1 \times 2 \times 3 \times 4 \times 5 \times 6 \times 7}{4 \times 5 \times 6 \times 7 \times 8 \times 9 \times 10}$. Now, before you pull out the calculator, you can cancel out numbers that appear on both the top and bottom (4, 5, 6, and 7) because a number divided by itself (such as $\dfrac{4}{4}$) is 1, which doesn't affect the final product. After canceling, you get $\dfrac{1 \times 2 \times 3}{8 \times 9 \times 10} = \dfrac{6}{720}$, which reduces to $\dfrac{1}{120}$.

34. K   The figure provided is a right triangle, so use the Pythagorean theorem ($a^2 + b^2 = c^2$) to find the distance asked for. $110^2 + 200^2 = c^2$, so $12{,}100 + 40{,}000 = c^2$, $52{,}100 = c^2$, and $\sqrt{52{,}100} = c$.

35. E   The key phrase in this question is *at most*. It's possible that the second pentagon is the same size and is laid directly over the original pentagon. Because all points of one pentagon are the same as the other, select choice (E).

36. K   When assigning employees to duties, there are 10 available to reserve a venue (the first duty). That leaves 9 remaining to arrange catering (because no one can be assigned more than one duty) and then 8 to plan activities. Then, multiply $10 \times 9 \times 8$ to find how many different ways these duties can be assigned. Note the format of the answer choices—don't do more work than you have to.

37. E   The easiest way to work this problem is to sketch it out. Draw $\overline{PQ}$, then draw the line perpendicular to $\overline{PQ}$ at Q; R is somewhere on this line. All of the answer choices have x-values greater than 1 and you can see the line rising to the right of Q (1,4) in your sketch. This means that the y-value of R must be greater than 4, which leaves only choice (E). Alternatively, you could find the slope of $\overline{PQ}$: the slope formula is $\frac{y_2 - y_1}{x_2 - x_1}$, so $\frac{2-4}{6-1} = \frac{-2}{5}$. Since $\angle PQR$ is a right angle, $\overline{PQ} \perp \overline{QR}$. In the coordinate plane, the slopes of perpendicular lines are negative reciprocals, which makes the slope of $\overline{QR}$ $\frac{5}{2}$. Then use the points given in each answer choice to see which gives you the correct slope. It's (E): $\frac{9-4}{3-1} = \frac{5}{2}$.

38. J   Solve the given equation for y. Start with $y = 0.25(100 - y)$. You can either distribute the 0.25 or divide both sides by the 0.25. In this case, it is easier to divide by 0.25. After doing this your equation becomes: $4y = 100 - y$. Add y to both sides to get $5y = 100$. Divide both sides by 5 to get $y = 20$. If you chose to begin the problem by distributing the 0.25, you should have gotten the same answer.

39. B   Since $4\cos^2 x = 1$, $\cos^2 x = 0.25$ and $\cos x = 0.5$. You want to know x, the degree measure whose cosine is 0.5. A scientific/graphing calculator can help you calculate that: the $\cos^{-1}$ key will tell you the degree measure that yields the cosine you give it. $\cos^{-1}(0.5) = 60°$, so choice (B) is correct. If you prefer, you can try each of the answers in your scientific/graphing calculator. When you plug in choice (B), you can find that $\cos 60° = 0.5$, so $\cos^2 60° = 0.25$, and $4\cos^2 60° = 1$. Make sure your calculator is in degree mode!

40. H   Sketch the rug over the floor to help you visualize the situation. The area of the exposed floor is the difference between the area of the entire floor and the area of the rug. First, find the area of the entire floor: area of a rectangle formula is $A = lw$, so $A = 16 \times 18 = 288$. Area of a circle formula is $A = \pi r^2$, where r is the radius. The diameter is 12, so $r = 6$. Therefore, $A = \pi \times 6^2 = \pi \times 36$, which is approximately 113. The difference: $288 - 113 = 175$. If you got a negative number when you did the calculation, you may have used the diameter of the circle in the Area of a circle formula rather than the radius.

41. C The equation of the given line is in slope-intercept form: $y = mx + b$, where m is the slope and b is the y-intercept. That tells you the slope of this line is -2. Since the slopes of perpendicular lines are negative reciprocals, the slope of the line in the credited answer choice must be $\frac{1}{2}$: eliminate choices (A), (B), and (E). The question says that the line you're looking for passes through the point $(0,-3)$: that makes the y-intercept (by definition) -3, so eliminate choice (D).

42. F Draw a vertical line from the point $\left(2\sqrt{3}, 2\right)$ straight down to the x-axis; this creates a right triangle with base $2\sqrt{3}$ and height 2. Use the Pythagorean theorem $(a^2 + b^2 = c^2)$ to find the hypotenuse: $(2\sqrt{3})^2 + 2^2 = c^2$, so $4 \times 3 + 4 = c^2$, $12 + 4 = c^2$, $16 = c^2$, so $4 = c$. (A shortcut is to recognize that this is a $30°$-$60°$-$90°$ triangle. Such a triangle has a ratio of side lengths $1 : \sqrt{3} : 2$, which means this triangle's sides are 2, $2\sqrt{3}$, and 4.) Since sine is the ratio of the opposite side to the hypotenuse, $\sin\theta = \frac{2}{4} = \frac{1}{2}$.

43. B Substitute $a = 5$ and $b = -\frac{1}{4}$ into the answer choices. Before you actually work each out, you can eliminate choices (C) and (D) because the product and quotient of a positive and a negative number will be negative. Now try choice (A): $5 + \left(-\frac{1}{4}\right) = 4\frac{3}{4}$. (B): $5 - \left(-\frac{1}{4}\right) = 5\frac{1}{4}$. (E): $\left|5 \times \left(-\frac{1}{4}\right)\right| = \left|-\frac{5}{4}\right| = \frac{5}{4}$. Choice (B) is the greatest.

44. G Solve for x: add 1 to both sides to get $\frac{x}{3} = -\frac{13}{12} + 1$, or $\frac{x}{3} = -\frac{13}{12} + \frac{12}{12}$. Simplify to $\frac{x}{3} = -\frac{1}{12}$. Multiply both sides by 3 to get $x = -\frac{1}{4}$. Only choice (G) is true.

45. B Because the statement includes an absolute value, you'll need to solve it twice: once assuming the expression inside is positive, once assuming it's negative. First, the positive assumption: $2z - 3 \geq 7$, so $2z \geq 10$ and $z \geq 5$. Eliminate choices (C), (D), and (E). Now, assume the expression is negative: you'd multiply a negative number by -1 to make it positive, so $-(2z - 3) \geq 7$. Solve by multiplying both sides by -1 (remember to flip the sign): $2z - 3 \leq -7$, so $2z \leq -4$ and $z \leq -2$. Eliminate choice (A). Alternatively, you could try substituting in values for z. Try $z = 4$: $|2 \times 4 - 3| = |8 - 3| = |5| = 5$. This expression is supposed to be ≥ 7; since it isn't, you can eliminate any answer choices that include $z = 4$, so eliminate choices (C), (D), and (E). Try $z = -3$: $|2 \times (-3) - 3| = |-6 - 3| = |-9| = 9$. This is ≥ 7, so z could be equal to -3; therefore, eliminate choice (A).

46. H To simplify this expression, recall the identity $\tan x = \frac{\sin x}{\cos x}$. Now $\frac{\sin^2 x}{\cos x \tan x} = \frac{\sin^2 x}{\cos x \left(\frac{\sin x}{\cos x}\right)}$. Simplify: $\frac{\sin^2 x}{\cos x \left(\frac{\sin x}{\cos x}\right)} = \frac{\sin^2 x}{\sin x} = \sin x$.

47. **D** Try the values of x given in the answer choices in the expression. Try $x = -4$:

$$\frac{a(-4)-b(-4)}{4a-4b} = \frac{-4a-(-4b)}{4a-4b} = \frac{-4a+4b}{4a-4b} = \frac{-(4a-4b)}{4a-4b}.$$ Since $\frac{4a-4b}{4a-4b} = 1$, $\frac{-(4a-4b)}{4a-4b}$

simplifies to -1. Since $-1 < 0$, $x = -4$ is valid: eliminate choices (B), (C), and (E). Now try $x = -\frac{1}{4}$:

$$\frac{a\left(-\frac{1}{4}\right)-b\left(-\frac{1}{4}\right)}{4a-4b} = \frac{-\frac{1}{4}a-\left(-\frac{1}{4}b\right)}{4a-4b} = \frac{-\frac{1}{4}a+\frac{1}{4}b}{4a-4b} = \frac{-\frac{1}{4}(a-b)}{4(a-b)} = \frac{-\frac{1}{4}}{4} = -\frac{1}{16}.$$ This is also less than

0, so eliminate choice (A).

48. **J** The original volume of the figure is described by the equation $V = \frac{1}{3}\pi r^2 h$. The new cylin-

der has had its radius halved and its height doubled, so the volume of the new cylinder will be

$V = \frac{1}{3}\pi\left(\frac{r}{2}\right)^2(2h) = \left(\frac{1}{3}\right)\pi\left(\frac{r^2}{4}\right)(2h) = \frac{1}{6}\pi r^2 h$. This volume is then one-half of the earlier volume,

and the ratio is 1:2. If you selected choice (H), be careful—you may have forgotten to square the new

radius value.

49. **B** Al's biking time going up the hill was m minutes, and because he went down the hill twice as fast,

his time going down was $\frac{1}{2}m$. His total time going up and down the hill was therefore $m + \frac{1}{2}m$

or $\frac{3}{2}m$. If you pick choice (D), be careful—you're not done here! The variable m represents the

time in minutes, and the question asks for the time in hours; therefore, you need to divide the total

value by 60: $\frac{\left(\frac{3}{2}m\right)}{60} = \frac{3}{120}m = \frac{m}{40}$.

50. **J** Since the wheel's diameter is 10, you can find the circumference ($C = \pi d$) of Pippin's wheel: $C = \pi d = 10\pi$. This means Pippin's wheel travels 10π inches in one rotation. Since her wheel rotated 15 times, multiply $10\pi \times 15 = 150\pi$.

51. **D** Draw a horizontal line, which is also the radius of the circle, from the center of the circle to the

right side of the square: this creates a 45°-45°-90° triangle. Recall that the ratio of sides in this type

of triangle is $s:s:s\sqrt{2}$. To find the length of the sides, and hence the radius, divide the hypotenuse

(x) by $\sqrt{2}$, giving $\frac{x}{\sqrt{2}}$, which, after multiplying by $\frac{\sqrt{2}}{\sqrt{2}}$ to rationalize the denominator, becomes

$\frac{x\sqrt{2}}{2}$, choice (D). You just found the radius, so choice (E) is wrong.

52. **K** No restrictions are needed because $f_{(x,y)} = f_{(y,x)}$ in all cases. Follow the same rules as the original function, just switch x and y. Because $-2yx = -2xy$, this is the same result that $f_{(x,y)}$ produced in the question and $f_{(y,x)} = -2yx + x + y - 4$. Therefore, all values of x and y will result in $f_{(x,y)} = f_{(y,x)}$, so choice (K) is correct. If you don't see this relationship immediately, you can use real numbers to test each of the answer choices. The question has already told you that $f_{(2,3)} = -11$, so see if $f_{(3,2)} = -11$ also. According to the original definition, $f_{(3,2)} = -2 \times 3 \times 2 + 2 + 3 - 4 = -12 + 1 = -11$. This means that $x = 2$ and $y = 3$ satisfy the goal $f_{(x,y)} = f_{(y,x)}$; therefore, eliminate choices (G), (H), and (J). Now you need to find out whether both variables must be positive, so try negative values: $x = -2$ and $y = -3$. $f_{(-2,-3)} = -2 \times -2 \times -3 + (-3) + (-2) - 4 = -12 - 3 - 2 - 4 = -21$ and $f_{(-3,-2)} = -2 \times -3 \times -2 + (-2) + (-3) - 4 = -12 - 2 - 3 - 4 = -21$. Since both are equal to -21, x and y don't have to be positive, so eliminate choice (F).

53. **C** *Each of the smaller pipes can handle exactly half as much water as the large pipe* means that the area of the cross-section of the small pipe is one-half the area of the cross-section of the large pipe. So start by finding the area of the circular cross-section of the large pipe: $A = \pi r^2$, so $A = \pi r^4 = 16\pi$. Therefore, the area of the cross-section of the smaller pipe is one-half that, or 8π. So for the smaller pipe's circular area $8\pi = \pi r^2$, $8 = r^2$, $r = \sqrt{8} = \sqrt{4} \times \sqrt{2} = 2\sqrt{2}$.

54. **H** The height (which we'll call h) divides this figure into two right triangles, each with base length of 3 feet. Tangent is the ratio of the opposite side to the adjacent side, so $\tan 40° = \dfrac{3}{h}$. Solve for h by multiplying both sides by h: $h(\tan 40°) = 3$, so $h = \dfrac{3}{\tan 40°}$.

55. **C** Sketch the girls' paths out on the coordinate plane. They start at school $(0,0)$, then Susan walks to $(-8,2)$ and Cindy walks to $(3,-1)$. Use the distance formula $\left(d = \sqrt{(x_1 - x_2)^2 + (y_1 - y_2)^2} \right)$ to find how far apart their homes are: $d = \sqrt{(-8-3)^2 + (2-[-1])^2} = \sqrt{(-11)^2 + 3^2} = \sqrt{121+9} = \sqrt{130} \approx 11.4$.

56. **G** If a is a positive integer and b is a negative integer, the only answer choice that will never yield a negative exponent (and therefore a fraction) is choice (G). If you're unsure, try substituting values for a and b. Let's say $a = 2$ and $b = -3$. Choice (F) becomes $3^{2-3} = 3^{-1} = \dfrac{1}{3}$; that's not an integer, so you can eliminate choice (F). Likewise, for choice (H), $3^{2(-3)} = 3^{-6} = \dfrac{1}{3^6} = \dfrac{1}{729}$, choice (J), $3^{-2} = \dfrac{1}{3^2} = \dfrac{1}{9}$, and (K), $3^{-\frac{2}{3}} = \dfrac{1}{3^{\frac{2}{3}}} = \dfrac{1}{\sqrt[3]{3^2}} = \dfrac{1}{\sqrt[3]{9}}$. Only choice (G) gives you an integer: $3^{2-(-3)} = 3^{2+3} = 3^5 = 243$.

57.   A   The question tells you that $0 < \frac{y}{x}$, which means $\frac{y}{x} \neq 0$, so eliminate choices (D) and (E). The only way $\frac{y}{x}$ could be larger than y itself is if $x < 1$ and $y \geq 1$. In other words, y could be 1 in this situation, and since we are told that $\frac{y}{x} > y$, $\frac{y}{x}$ must be greater than 1. This is a tough problem, and if you're not sure how to come up with these relationships, try to find numbers that make the initial relationship true and try them out on the number line. If $x = 0.5$ and $y = 1$, then $\frac{y}{x} = 2$, for example, so you can eliminate choice (C) [and (D) and (E), which you've already eliminated]. You'll find that you can't get a number less than 1 for $\frac{y}{x}$.

58.   F   Sketch out the rectangular 100-ft by 150-ft field described in the question. The 10-ft border within the field creates a new, smaller rectangle, 80 feet by 130 feet. The largest circle that can fit in this rectangle has a diameter of 80 feet, and therefore a radius of 40 feet. If you picked choice (G), be careful—you may have forgotten to subtract 10 feet on both sides of the track.

59.   D   Imagine cutting an orange: the first slice (one plane) cuts it into two pieces. If you hold those two pieces together and make another slice (the second plane), you cut both of those pieces, thereby creating 4 sections. Eliminate choices (A) and (C). Now, if you repeat this orange-slicing experiment, but your second slice is parallel to the first slice, it cuts a circular slice off only one piece, thereby creating 3 sections, so eliminate choice (B). The only way to keep the orange in two pieces after the first slice is for the second slice to repeat the first exactly. Since the question said the sphere was to be cut by two *different* planes, this cannot happen; therefore, it's impossible to get only 2 pieces, so eliminate choice (E).

60.   K   "Positive difference" means that when you subtract $a - b$ you can get $+5$ or -5. (That's also what the absolute value indicates.) Solve for a in both cases: $a - b = 5$, so $a = b + 5$; and $a - b = -5$, so $a = b - 5$. Now subtract these two values: $(b + 5) - (b - 5) = b + 5 - b + 5 = 10$, choice (K). Alternatively, you could substitute a number for b: let's say $b = 2$, so $|a - 2| = 5$. Then solve: $a - 2 = 5$, so $a = 7$; and $a - 2 = -5$, so $a = -3$. The positive difference is $7 - (-3) = 7 + 3 = 10$.

READING TEST

1.   C   When the narrator first sees her gift, her first response is confusion, followed by devastation that she won't be able to show her gift off to the other girls at school. Eliminate choice (A). She then recognizes that her father put a lot of effort into her gift and tries to be grateful. Eliminate choice (D). She then returns to being confused as to why they made her this house instead of buying her the real Barbie Dream House. Eliminate choice (B). That leaves choice (C), the correct answer. Disappointed and upset as the narrator is, the passage does not state that she hates the house.

2. **F** The narrator of the story explains that only when she and her sister could smell coffee were they allowed to go downstairs to start Christmas. Therefore, choice (F) is the best answer. Choice (G) incorrectly refers to breakfast, which is not mentioned in the passage. Choice (H) incorrectly refers to the narrator's father's preparation of a gift instead of general morning readiness. Choice (J) is incorrect because the passage explicitly states that the narrator was expected to wait in the kitchen for her parents; she just burst in ahead of them one year because she was too excited to wait.

3. **B** The narrator talks about her dream of owning the Dream House in the second paragraph, where she says "I knew that if I could only have a Dream House of my own, my life would be complete." Therefore, choice (B) is the best answer, as it is a good paraphrase of that statement. Choice (A) incorrectly refers to the other girl who owns the house and is not meant to be taken literally. Choice (C) confuses the actual result, based on her parents' hard work, with the narrator's dream, based on buying a particular toy. Choice (D) refers to the narrator's eventual comment that she will pass her gift on to her children someday, but that refers not to the Dream House but to her father's actual gift.

4. **G** The first paragraph describes the family's tradition of waiting until the parents have had a chance to wake up and make coffee before beginning to open the presents. Choice (G) is the best paraphrase of that summary and is the best answer. Choice (F) might be true but it is not mentioned in the passage and is not the best summary of the entire paragraph. Choice (H) states the opposite of what the passage says. Choice (J) is true, but is not the main point of the paragraph.

5. **A** When the narrator first sees her handmade doll house, she is confused and upset as she compares her house to her idealized Barbie Dream House. Choice (A) is the best paraphrase of her reaction. Choice (B) is incorrect because although the narrator does eventually try to be grateful, that is not her first response and she is not immediately successful in her attempt. Choice (C) goes against the passage—she compares the old-fashioned style of her house with the modern Barbie house and finds her house lacking. Choice (D) is incorrect because that was her goal before she saw her house, when she believed she would receive the official Barbie Dream House.

6. **H** The narrator's father is described in a few different places in the passage. First, he is overheard reassuring Mel, the mother, regarding Christmas. Then, when he is preparing to present his daughter with her gift, he is described as *smiling anxiously*. Finally, the narrator eventually realizes that her father had "spent countless hours working on the house." Therefore, choice (H) is the best characterization of the father in the story.

7. **A** In lines 25–30, the narrator overhears her parents discussing Christmas, wondering what they will do. This implies that there is some kind of problem. Her father then proceeds to make a homemade version of the Dream House that his daughter wants, implying that for some reason, he cannot give her the gift she wants but is willing to work very hard to give her something similar. Therefore, choice (A) is the best answer, because it explains what problem might cause him to act in such a manner. Choice (B) is incorrect because it refers to an early comment regarding a previous Christmas, not the one being described. Choice (C) is incorrect because there is no evidence

that the father made the dollhouse because he had always wanted to do so. Choice (D) is incorrect because the fact that the father put so much time and effort into making the dollhouse implies that they do in fact want their daughter to be happy.

8. J   At the end of the passage, the narrator comments that she still has the dollhouse and that she hopes to someday tell her own children the story of how she got it. Therefore, choice (J) is the best answer, since it refers only to her hopes of passing on the story. Choice (F) incorrectly refers to the narrator's initial hopes of impressing other children with an official Barbie Dream House. Choice (G) focuses on the possible value of the house, which is not discussed in the passage. Choice (H) is incorrect because the narrator did not in fact appreciate the gift initially.

9. D   The narrator concludes, at the time of the gifting, that although she does not like her dollhouse as much as she would have liked a Barbie Dream House, it must have taken her father a lot of time and effort to build. Therefore, choice (D) is the best answer. Choice (A) is incorrect because she refers to the dollhouse as a crude approximation of what she wanted. Choice (B) is incorrect because the absence of an elevator is not mentioned in the passage. Choice (C) is incorrect because there is no evidence that her eventual decision to pass the house on to her children was anticipated by her or her parents at the time when it was given to her.

10. J   The last paragraph is told as if the narrator is looking back on her childhood and having trouble remembering the events that followed the previous part of the passage. She reflects that she now more fully understands her parents' actions and wishes she could go back in time and explain things to her younger self. Therefore, the best answer is choice (J). Choice (F) might be true, but the focus of the last paragraph is on the narrator as an adult, not as a child. Choice (G) is incorrect because the passage does not discuss the narrator's sister's gift. Choice (H) is too negative—the narrator is looking back on the events with greater wisdom and understanding, not bitterness.

11. D   This passage describes the formation and activities of the CCC. No one was "forced" to work in the CCC, so you can eliminate choice (A). The CCC did employee many veterans, but nothing in the passage supports the claim that veterans had suitable employment "only after" the creation of the CCC.

12. G   While (F) is true, it isn't the main idea of the paragraph. Choice (H) is incorrect because the bonuses were never paid. For (J), the paragraph says that the age restriction was waived, but at no point does it say how many of these veterans were over the age limit. Only choice (G) gives a reasonable summation of the content of the paragraph.

13. D   The passage states that Roosevelt "also cared about the fate of trees, having practiced the art of silviculture on his Hyde Park estate with such enthusiasm that on various official forms he was fond of listing his occupation as 'tree farmer.'" Choice (A) makes an assumption that is not supported in the passage; there is nothing to suggest that his interest in silviculture predated his political life. Choices (B) and (C) are not supported in the passage. Only choice (D) is supported by the sentence cited above.

14. **G** Read this question carefully. The lines you need are 61–63: "For the National Park Service, they built roads, campgrounds, bridges, and recreation and administration facilities." This clearly supports choice (G). The other activities in the answer choices are mentioned in the passage, but not as things the CCC did *for the National Park Service*.

15. **A** Starting on line 72, the passage reads, "the program taught more than a hundred thousand to read and write, passed out twenty-five thousand eighth-grade diplomas and five-thousand high-school diplomas." This line most clearly supports choice (A). Choices (B) and (D) contain deceptive language from elsewhere in the passage, but they do not describe the CCC. Choice (C) is a trap because of the placement of the word *only*. As written, choice (C) means that all men the CCC accepted were those with six teeth.

16. **G** Lines 24–25 describe the terms of payment in the CCC, so eliminate choice (F). Line 58 describes the "4.1 million man-hours" spent fighting forest fires; it does NOT say that the CCC employed 4.1 million men, so eliminate choice (H). The states referred to in choice (J) are described in the passage as the sites of "flood control projects," not firefighting projects. Only choice (G) has support in the passage.

17. **C** Lines 60–61 describe the "first major reforestation campaign in the country's history." Although the specific years during which this reforestation campaign took place are unclear, the campaign must have taken place after the establishment of the CCC in 1933. It can therefore be inferred, since this was the "first," that the nation had not undergone a major reforestation campaign before, as choice (C) suggests.

18. **F** Lines 11–16 state the following: "When he went to Congress for authorization of the program, he called the new agency the Civilian Corps Reforestation Youth Rehabilitation Movement, but before sinking under the weight of an acronym like CCRYRM, it was soon changed to the Civilian Conservation Corps (known forever after as the CCC)." These lines describe the change, and only choice (F) is supported by the time of these events. The only other answer that might work chronologically would be choice (G), but nothing in the passage supports the claim that Congress complained about the length of the name.

19. **C** Lines 29–30 state that the "men had to be US citizens between the ages of seventeen and twenty-seven (later twenty-four)." Since the question asks about enrollees when the CCC was founded, you can disregard the "later" age; choice (C) gives the correct age range.

20. **G** Lines 21–24 state that "the Departments of Agriculture and Interior... would design and supervise projects in regional and national forests, national parks, and other public lands." These lines give direct support to choice (G), and show that the others are incorrect or inadequate responses to the question.

21. **C** This passage deals with the importance of the totem pole and the role the totem pole plays in Native American culture. Even with this very general overview of the passage, the only answer that fits is choice (C). The others are too specific or suggest incorrectly that the tone of the passage is negative.

22. G   The question in choice (F) is answered in lines 2–3. The question in choice (H) is answered in line 65–66. The question in choice (J) is answered in lines 8–9. Only the question posed in choice (G) goes unanswered in the passage. The discussion in the fourth paragraph is distracting, but notice this paragraph does not claim that the pole in Pioneer Square is the largest.

23. C   Note the opening sentence of the fifth paragraph on line 39: "Poles serve the important purpose of recording the lore of a clan, much as a book would." The other choices describe some minor functions of totem poles, but only the function described in choice (C) is described as "important."

24. G   This paragraph describes the meanings of some of the symbols used on totem poles. Choice (F) would be fine if it did not contain the word "every." Clearly, a short paragraph cannot describe *every* possible symbol. There are no regional comparisons, so you can eliminate choice (H). Choice (J) is too limited. Think in terms of the larger point of this paragraph; it describes figures other than the Raven. Only choice (G) adequately describes the main idea of the paragraph.

25. D   Choice (A) is addressed in lines 40–41. Choice (B) is addressed just after this in lines 42–44. Choice (C) is addressed in lines 64–66. Choice (D) may seem like it is addressed in the passage, but read this part of the passage carefully. There is no reference to the importance of this pole in Native American culture; after all, the group that took it, according to line 33, were "Seattle businessmen," not the Tlingit.

26. J   Choice (F) is addressed in lines 13–15. Choice (G) is addressed in line 12. Choice (H) is addressed in line 17. Choice (J) is not addressed in the passage; the "family crest" is mentioned in line 16, but there is no evidence in the passage that the poles were constructed exclusively by clans who had family crests.

27. B   As lines 39–41 indicate, one of the main functions of the poles is to identify the lore of a clan. The points mentioned in choices (A), (C), and (D) are mentioned, but none could be described as a "main point." Only choice (B) is general enough to be described as a "main point."

28. J   When the Tlingit are introduced in line 31, they are described as coming from "the southeastern coast of Alaska." Only choice (J) could work. Don't be distracted by the other places mentioned in this paragraph; those places may have some significance for the Tlingit, but could not be described as the "home of the Tlingit."

29. A   This paragraph is used to conclude some of the ideas in the preceding paragraphs and to suggest the broader importance of totem poles beyond their physical beauty. Choices (B), (C), and (D) all use words from the passage, but they use those words in misleading ways. Only choice (A) can be supported by evidence from the passage.

30. H   All we know about the employers is that they "complained that their Indian workers were unreliable when a pole was being carved or a potlatch planned" (lines 27–28). Because this is the only reference the author gives to these employers, we can only infer that the employers were "irritated," as choice (H) suggests.

31. **C** Lines 14–16 state, "…in the present climate of fiscal austerity, there is no telling when humans will next get a good look at the earth's nearest planetary neighbor." Choice (A) can be eliminated because the author is clearly not cheerful and optimistic. Choice (B) can be eliminated because the author's tone does not suggest sarcasm or condescension. Choice (D) can be eliminated because of the word *withdrawn*. Only choice (C) is supported by the lines quoted above: he is doubtful ("there is no telling") and pragmatic ("in the present climate of fiscal austerity").

32. **H** Lines 28–33 discuss the state of scientific knowledge before the arrival of *Pioneer Venus*. The paragraph discusses in detail the differences in surface temperatures and atmospheric pressures. Choice (G) is too strong: the two planets are not "twins," but the passage does not say that they are anything like "polar opposites." The best answer is choice (H), because the paragraph details the objections to the term *twins*.

33. **D** This question asks about the same portion of the passage as question 32. Lines 28–33 detail some of the ways in which the "twin" characterization of Earth and Venus was reconsidered. The main evidence in this paragraph relates to surface temperature and atmosphere.

34. **G** The paragraph in question concerns the *Magellan* and *Pioneer Venus* missions. Each mission studied different elements of Venus's physical composition, and the information from each can be used in tandem with the other. The missions are contrasted, but neither is cast in a negative light, so you can eliminate choices (F) and (H), and choice (J) is too narrow in that it does not include the findings of the *Magellan*. Only choice (G) adequately summarizes the paragraph.

35. **C** Lines 34–35 state, "Even aside from the heat and the pressure, the air of Venus would be utterly unbreathable to humans." It then goes on to discuss the atmospheric conditions in more detail. Choice (C) is the only one of the answer choices that addresses these issues. Choices (B) and (D) describe the physical properties of the planet, but they do not give any indication why human survival would not be possible. Eliminate (A) because it is not the mistaken belief that makes survival impossible—the belief is mistaken because survival would be impossible.

36. **J** Choice (J) is supported in lines 31–32, which say that Venus's "surface temperature of 450 degrees Celsius is hotter than the melting point of lead." Choice (H) is misleading; these physical properties describe the Earth. Choice (F) can be eliminated because "lead" is introduced as a point of comparison, not as one of the constitutive elements of Venus's surface. Choice (G) can be eliminated because it does not contain any mention of Venus.

37. **C** The full sentence in lines 56–57 reads as follows: "Unlike the Earth, Venus harbors little if any molecular oxygen in its lower atmosphere." In other words, Venus contains or holds or has little if any molecular oxygen in its lower atmosphere.

38. **H** The word *primordial* appears in line 65. The lines that follow state that Venus is "more primordial" than Earth because it "has held on to a far greater fraction of its earliest atmosphere." Only choice (H) contains the appropriate reference to these early formations.

39. A The full sentence starting on line 57 establishes a clear link between the activity of these plants (i.e., living things) and the composition of the earth's atmosphere. The only answer that even mentions the earth is choice (A), and this choice provides a reasonable paraphrase of the passage.

40. J Choice (J) is the only answer that accurately paraphrases lines 20–22.

SCIENCE TEST

1. C Looking at Table 1 and examining the trials with coin samples II and IV shows that electric current is held constant at 2000 mA. The current does not change, eliminating choices (A) and (B). The variable that does change is the identity of precious metal solution. For coin sample II exposed to silver nitrate, 4.0 mg of precious metal plates. For coin sample IV exposed to copper sulfate, only 2.4 mg of precious metal plates. Therefore, choice (D) is eliminated and choice (C) is correct.

2. F The precious metal solutions react with zinc to form a coating of pure precious metal on the coin samples. If the available surface area exposed to the solutions decreased, the amount of precious metal coating is expected to decrease. There is no specific evidence in the passage to support the plating amount remaining constant or increasing.

3. A Table 2 shows that increasing the exposure time of a zinc coin to silver nitrate results in higher concentrations of zinc nitrate in the surrounding solution. Therefore, choices (C) and (D) are eliminated. The passage states that *silver nitrate, formed when silver dissolves in nitric acid, reacts with zinc to form solid silver and zinc nitrate.* Therefore, increasing the amount of silver nitrate available to react with zinc is expected to result in higher concentrations of zinc nitrate. This eliminates choice (B) and makes choice (A) the best answer.

4. H The question describes using the same sized sample of zinc and same exposure time as Experiment 1. Table 1 shows that when electric current is increased from 1000 to 2000 mA for zinc coins exposed to copper sulfate for 30 minutes, the plated copper increases from 1.2 to 2.4 mg. 1580 mA is between 1000 and 2000 mA, so the amount of plated copper should fall between 1.2 and 2.4 mg.

5. D In the description of Experiment 1, all coin samples were stated to have a radius of 1 cm. Table 1 shows that the change in mass from precious metal plating, electric current applied, and identity of precious metal solution used were not constant for samples I–IV.

6. G The passage states that *silver nitrate, formed when silver dissolves in nitric acid, reacts with zinc to form solid silver and zinc nitrate.* Therefore, when zinc is plated with solid silver, zinc nitrate is also formed as a product. Choices (F), (H), and (J) are not involved in this reaction.

7. B   Melting point is the temperature at which a substance changes from a solid to a liquid. Any compound with a melting point above 215 K will still be a solid at that temperature. For alkanes, according to Table 2, only octane will still be a solid at 215 K. Octane must be in the answer, and on this basis alone, choices (A), (C), and (D) can all be eliminated, leaving only choice (B). The remaining data in choice (B) are supported in Table 2 as well.

8. F   According to Table 3, the 8-carbon alcohol has the highest value for viscosity. Referring to Table 1 for the prefix and suffix of the compound's name, the structure is called octanol.

9. D   Reading across any single row of Table 3 demonstrates that for a fixed number of carbons in the molecule, the alcohol has the highest viscosity. This eliminates choices (A) and (B). Further, for any given row, the alkane has the lowest viscosity, eliminating choice (C).

10. G   Reading down any single column in Table 2 demonstrates that as the number of carbons in the molecule increases, the melting point increases. Therefore, choices (F) and (J) are eliminated. Reading down any single column in Table 3 demonstrates that as the number of carbons in the molecule increases, the viscosity increases as well, eliminating choice (H) and making choice (G) the correct answer.

11. C   Compare the melting points of the alkanes and alcohols in Table 2. For any given number of carbons in the molecule, the melting points between these two types of compounds differ by varying but similar amounts between 41 and 57 K. Of the possible answer choices, choice (C) is the best approximation of the average of these differences.

12. G   When testing the effects of different variables, all variables must be held constant except those being tested. To determine the effects of drag force or air resistance, therefore, all variables except drag force and air resistance must be held constant. Altering the apparatus to use a spring makes this into a completely different experiment, so choices (F) and (H) are eliminated. To negate the effects of air resistance, using a vacuum with no air pressure would be best, making choice (G) the best answer.

13. A   In experiments, more precision is nearly always better. A timer that reads to the nearest second can give only whole number results. Therefore, it would read either "1" or "2" for each trial. This would not greatly alter the results for the tin cube (Trials 1 and 5 would be 2 sec, and Trials 2–4 would be 1 sec for an average of 1.4 sec). However, all of the trials for the lead cube would round down to 1 sec for an average of 1 sec. This is significantly different from the 1.46 sec obtained with the more precise timer, eliminating choices (C) and (D). Choice (B) is eliminated because the period of both pendulums is greater than 1 sec, meaning they would travel a shorter distance in 1 second than they would in the time it takes them to complete a cycle.

14. **H** Choices (F) and (G) are true statements, but they do not explain why forces other than gravity must be acting on the pendulums. The passage states that for a *simple gravity pendulum, gravity is the only force acting on the mass causing an acceleration of 9.8 m/sec²*. The times obtained in Experiments 1 and 2 resulted in acceleration calculations less than this, indicating some other force was slowing the pendulum down (air resistance and friction). This eliminates choice (J) and makes choice (H) the best answer.

15. **D** Comparing the results of Experiments 1 and 2 presented in Tables 1 and 2, doubling the length of the thread from 0.5 m to 1.0 m increases the observed period. Since the average period observed for the tin cube in Experiment 2 (pendulum length of 1.0 m) was 2.09 sec, doubling the length of the thread once again would be expected to result in an increase in average period observed.

16. **G** The text below Table 2 states that the average period for the lead cube in Experiment 2 was 2.06 sec. An additional trial of the same experiment would be expected to give a result closest to this value.

17. **D** For both Experiments 1 and 2, comparisons between the lead and tin pendulums held length and starting angle constant, eliminating choices (A), (B), and (C). The mass and density of the lead and tin cubes were different. The main difference noted in the text of the passage is that between the masses of the two objects, so choice (D) provides the best-supported option.

18. **F** In the description of the Coevolution Hypothesis, the passage states that *RNA sequences developed enzyme-like abilities including the ability to self-replicate*. Development of capsids was mentioned in the Regressive Evolution Hypothesis, but not in Coevolution, eliminating choice (G). DNA was not mentioned in the Coevolution Hypothesis, eliminating choice (H). Cell membrane transit was mentioned only in the Cellular Origin Hypothesis, eliminating choice (J).

19. **D** The first paragraph states that biologists agree that viruses originated from nucleic acid. Choice (A) is eliminated because the Coevolution Hypothesis does not provide an explanation for viruses evolving from bacteria. Choice (B) is eliminated because according to the passage, viruses cannot replicate unless they first infect a cell. Choice (C) is eliminated because only the Regressive Evolution Hypothesis and Coevolution Hypothesis mentions anything about viruses having membranes or envelopes.

20. **J** The Coevolution Hypothesis specifically mentions that the first virus particles were RNA nucleotides with enzyme-like activity that incorporated into protein structures. Therefore, choices (F), (G), and (H) are all eliminated. DNA is not mentioned as a component of the earliest virus particles in this hypothesis.

21. B   The Cellular Origin Hypothesis states that viruses originated from cellular-organism ancestors. They could have come from prokaryotic or eukaryotic organisms, and the type of ancestor cell does not necessarily determine what type of cell they will evolve to infect. Therefore, choices (C) and (D) are eliminated because this cannot necessarily be determined from the information given. Given that both T4 and PP7 infect bacteria, they likely contain genetic material similar to the bacteria they infect. However, given that one is a DNA virus and one is an RNA virus, if they are related at all it is likely through a very distant ancestor virus that escaped a cellular organism long ago. This eliminates choice (A) and makes choice (B) the best answer.

22. H   Since the Regressive Evolution Hypothesis suggests that viruses originated from obligate intracellular parasites, one would expect that they would share features of these ancestors. The hypothesis specifically states that intracellular parasites evolved into viruses, eliminating choices (F) and (G). Between the remaining choices, finding a parasite with DNA similar to a known virus could suggest that this organism and the known virus evolved from a common ancestor, making choice (H) the best answer.

23. B   The passage states that viruses cannot replicate unless they first infect a cell. Therefore, the first viruses were unlikely to originate before cells, making choice (B) the best answer. There is nothing in the passage to support that viral capsids are similar to bacterial cell walls, and the word "capsid" does not even appear in the first hypothesis, eliminating choice (A). Choice (C) is eliminated because the differences in RNA and DNA viruses are not elaborated in the passage. Moreover, given that RNA viruses are mentioned in the Coevolution Hypothesis and DNA viruses are mentioned in the hypotheses that relate to more complex cellular organisms, it seems unlikely that RNA viruses would be considered more advanced than DNA viruses. Choice (D) is eliminated because the Coevolution Hypothesis specifically states that the first viruses contained RNA.

24. F   The incorporation of RNA sequences into protein structures versus cell structures is specifically mentioned in the Coevolution Hypothesis. Choices (G) and (J) relate to the Regressive Evolution Hypothesis and choice (H) relates to the Cellular Origin Hypothesis.

25. C   Table 1 shows that as organic cover percentage increases, erosion from topsoil deflation decreases, eliminating choices (A) and (B). Choices (C) and (D) both state that increased rainfall will reduce erosion as shown in Table 3. The choice comes down to the type of topsoil. Tables 1 and 3 consistently show that Soil Y resists erosion more than Soil X does, eliminating choice (D).

26. G   Soil X contains 5% clay and Soil Y contains 40% clay. A soil with 10% clay should have topsoil deflation between the values for X and Y with 0% organic cover in Table 1, eliminating choices (F) and (J). Since 10% clay is most similar to the 5% clay found in Soil X, the topsoil deflation value is expected to be closer to 105,000 kg/ha than to 65,000 kg/ha, eliminating choice (H) and making choice (G) the best answer.

27. **D** Only Experiment 2 involved a variation in water content, eliminating choices (A) and (B). Between choices (C) and (D), only choice (D) provides a clear manner of comparing soils with different water contents.

28. **H** Experiment 1 investigates wind erosion of different types of topsoil with varying amounts of organic cover. If the fans did not adequately simulate the effects of real wind, it would be difficult to apply the findings to any practical situation, making choice (H) the best answer. Choice (F) is not an assumption but a variable being tested by the experiment. Choice (G) is the opposite of an assumption made in the experiment, that compost and straw do adequately simulate vegetation and organic cover. Choice (J) is not addressed in Experiment 1 because water content is not varied.

29. **C** Table 3 demonstrates that regardless of the water content, Soil X with the smaller clay percentage is more prone to topsoil deflation, making choice (C) the correct answer. Table 3 shows that erosion is related to water content for both soils, eliminating choice (A). Further, erosion takes place in the presence of water content, eliminating choice (B). Finally, Table 3 demonstrates that increased water content tends to decrease topsoil deflation, eliminating choice (D).

30. **F** Soil X contains 5% clay and Soil Y contains 40% clay. A soil with 10% clay should have water content and topsoil deflation in Tables 2 and 3 that are between the values for Soils X and Y after 8 hours of sprinkling. Choices (H) and (J) have water contents that are too low, and choice (G) has an erosion value that is too low. Therefore, only choice (F) can be correct.

31. **C** According to Figure 1, bathypelagic, mesopelagic, and epipelagic zones are all within mutually exclusive depth ranges. In other words, none of them overlap, so answer choices (A), (B), and (D) are all eliminated and only choice (C) is possible. Depths between 100 and 200 m can be categorized in either the epipelagic or thermocline zone according to Figure 1.

32. **J** According to Figure 1, when total pressure is 1,200 kPa, the ocean zone can be classified as epipelagic, continental shelf, or thermocline. Therefore, choice (J) is the best answer. Choices (F) and (G) are at higher pressures, and choice (H) is at a lower pressure.

33. **C** The points on Figure 2 where the two oceans would be indistinguishable for any temperature and depth combination would be where the two lines intersect. The tropical and temperate lines on Figure 2 intersect at two points, at depths of approximately 125 m and 625 m. This makes choice (C) the best answer. All other answer choices give depths where the two lines would yield different values of temperature and would thus be distinguishable from one another.

34. **G** The general trend for both regions in Table 1 is a decrease in ocean temperature with an increase in depth. This eliminates choices (F) and (H). However, Region 2 had a temperature of 8°C at a depth of both 39.7 m and 49.6 m whereas Region 1 showed a decrease in temperature for every increased depth. Therefore, only Region 1 showed a consistent decrease in ocean temperature with increasing depth.

35. **B**   Both Figure 1 and Table 1 demonstrate that as depth increases, total pressure increases. If the pressure at 79.5 m is 900 kPa, it would be expected to increase beyond 900 kPa at greater depth. Only choice (B) is possible. Note that choice (D) is eliminated because it is impossible to increase from 900 to 101 kPa.

36. **J**   Looking at Figure 1, since 800 mg of sulfamethoxazole results in greater bacterial elimination than 400 mg over time, choices (F) and (G) are both eliminated. Table 1 provides insight to the mechanism of action of sulfamethoxazole, so choice (H) is also eliminated. According to Figure 1, combining sulfamethoxazole (SMX) with either doxycycline or azithromycin increases overall elimination of a common skin infection bacterium, making choice (J) the best answer.

37. **A**   According to Figure 1, it takes 120 minutes for an 800 mg dose of sulfamethoxazole to achieve 80% bacterial elimination and hence 20% original bacterial survival. At the same time, the 400 mg dose only achieves between 40–50% elimination. A 600 mg dose would be expected to give results between these two values at the 120 minute mark. Therefore, only choice (A) is possible because the time required to reach 20% survival would be greater than 120 minutes for a 600 mg dose.

38. **F**   According to the passage and the data in Figure 1, penicillin is not very effective against the bacterium studied, but it does eliminate some bacteria, eliminating choices (H) and (J). In the experiment in the passage, less than 10% of the bacteria are eliminated by penicillin after 120 minutes (2 hours), meaning most survived. Therefore, choice (F) is better than choice (G).

39. **D**   Figure 1 shows greater bacterial elimination by doxycycline and azithromycin when compounded with sulfamethoxazole (SMX). This eliminates choices (A) and (B). Choice (C) is a true statement. However, even though sulfamethoxazole 800 mg is more effective than SMX/azithromycin according to the figure, this does not answer the question of whether or not azithromycin is more effective when *combined with* sulfamethoxazole. Therefore, choice (D) is the best answer.

40. **H**   The passage describes the goal of antibiotics as eliminating bacteria, so choices (F) and (G) are incorrect. From the data in Figure 1, it can be inferred that antibiotics that eliminate a large amount of bacteria in a short amount of time are most effective. This eliminates choice (J) and makes choice (H) the best answer.

WRITING TEST

To grade your essay, see the Essay Checklist on the following page. The following is an example of a top-scoring essay for the prompt given in this test. Note that it's not perfect, but it still follows an organized outline and has a strong introductory paragraph, a concluding paragraph, and transitions throughout.

The traditional academic calendar of school in the fall, winter, and spring, with summers off, was developed to accommodate the needs of an agrarian society. Simply put, children were needed to work in the fields during the summer. There is an argument that spring break existed to allow for help with planting, and fall break to help with the harvests. Although the shape of our nation has changed dramatically since the academic calendar was created, there are still powerful reasons for keeping it in place: School has become much more stressful, and students need the break during summer; colleges have become much more expensive, and students need the chance to earn money in the summer; childhood is something special, and the things which make it special should not be casually stripped from the young simply because we're no longer a nation of farmers.

Contrary to high school in years past, high school is no longer a gentle nine-month trek through classes. High school today is a very difficult academic exercise designed to prepare students for college, not just for getting a job when they graduate. Consequently, the classes have become harder, and the amount of homework and other preparation has increased. Every student has heard his or her parents comment that they never worked so hard when they were in school. The fact is, this is the truth. Students today have to take AP classes (which are really college-level classes in high school) if they are serious about getting into a top college. These classes run all year and end with a very difficult exam in May. The amount of work being demanded from students is so high that during the year many students need help coping with the stress. If summer vacation did not exist and students had to go at this pace all the time, it would be disasterous.

Furthermore, summer is also for more than just recovering from the school year. Most students today have jobs in the summer, which are critically important to their ability to pay for college. Because college has become more expensive, and because financial aid is so hard to get, many high school students work during the summers. The money they earn is usually for their college savings, although some of them even give this money to their families to help support them. If this flow of money were cut off, perhaps some students would not be able to afford college, or their families would suffer.

Also, we should be cautious about altering the academic calendar in high school because summer vacation is one of those things that make being a child special. Every parent has fond memories of their summers playing, and tells those stories to his or her children. Teachers talk about this in classes as well. The truth is, there is a difference between children and adults, and we should not act rashly to take away those things which mark that difference. We should be cautious when considering decisions that will make childhood less like childhood and more like the "real world" inhabited by adults. Although it is hard to explain in a concrete way exactly how this is a damaging thing to do, that difficulty makes it no less damaging. The simple pleasures mean a lot and should be protected, not eliminated in the name of efficiency.

For a wide variety of reasons, from the very concrete to the somewhat abstract, it would be a bad idea to force students to go to school year-round. Although there may be problems like overcrowding, which cause administrators to consider abolishing the academic calendar and going to a year-round calendar, the proper solution is not changing the calendar, the proper solution is spending more money on education. Because students need a break from the rigors of the classroom, a chance to earn much needed money, and a childhood full of memories to pass on to their own kids, the academic calendar should remain the way it is.

WRITING TEST

Essay Checklist

1. The Introduction
   Did you
   o start with a topic sentence that paraphrases or restates the prompt?
   o clearly state your position on the issue?

2. Body Paragraph 1
   Did you
   o start with a transition/topic sentence that discusses the opposing side of the argument?
   o give an example of a reason that one might agree with the opposing side of the argument?
   o clearly state that the opposing side of the argument is wrong or flawed?
   o show what is wrong with the opposing side's example or position?

3. Body Paragraphs 2 and 3
   Did you
   o start with a transition/topic sentence that discusses your position on the prompt?
   o give one example or reason to support your position?
   o show the grader how your example supports your position?
   o end the paragraph by restating your thesis?

4. Conclusion
   Did you
   o restate your position on the issue?
   o end with a flourish?

5. Overall
   Did you
   o write neatly?
   o avoid multiple spelling and grammar mistakes?
   o try to vary your sentence structure?
   o use a few impressive-sounding words?

SCORING YOUR PRACTICE EXAM

Step A

Count the number of correct answers for each section and record the number in the space provided for your raw score on the Score Conversion Worksheet below.

Step B

Using the Score Conversion Chart on the next page, convert your raw scores on each section to scaled scores. Then compute your composite ACT score by averaging the four subject scores. Add them up and divide by four. Don't worry about the essay score; it is not included in your composite score.

Score Conversion Worksheet		
Section	Raw Score	Scaled Score
1	_____/75	_____
2	_____/60	_____
3	_____/40	_____
4	_____/40	_____

SCORE CONVERSION CHART

Scaled Score	Raw Scores			
	Test 1 Engish	Test 2 Math	Test 3 Reading	Test 4 Science
36	75	60	40	40
35	73–74	59	39	39
34	72	58	38	---
33	71	57	37	38
32	70	54–56	36	37
31	69	52–53	35	36
30	68	50–51	34	---
29	66–67	48–49	33	35
28	65	46–47	32	33–34
27	63–64	44–45	30–31	32
26	61–62	42–43	29	31
25	59–60	40–41	28	29–30
24	57–58	37–39	26–27	28
23	55–56	35–36	25	26–27
22	52–54	33–34	24	24–25
21	49–51	31–32	23	23
20	46–48	29–30	21–22	21–22
19	44–45	26–28	20	19–20
18	41–43	23–25	19	17–18
17	39–40	20–22	18	14–16
16	36–38	17–19	16–17	13
15	33–35	14–16	15	11–12
14	31–32	12–13	14	09–10
13	29–30	10–11	12–13	08
12	27–28	08–09	10–11	06–07
11	25–26	06–07	09	05
10	23–24	05	07–08	---
09	22	04	06	04
08	18–21	---	---	03
07	15–17	03	05	02
06	12–14	02	04	---
05	09–11	---	03	---
04	07	---	---	01
03	05–06	01	02	---
02	03–04	---	01	---
01	00–02	00	00	00

Part X
Paying for College 101

If you're reading this book, you've already made an investment in your education. You may have shelled out some cold hard cash for this book, and you've definitely invested time in reading it. It's probably even safe to say that this is one of the smaller investments you've made in your future so far. You put in the hours and hard work needed to keep up your GPA. You've paid test fees and applications fees, perhaps even travel expenses. You have probably committed time and effort to a host of extracurricular activities to make sure colleges know that you're a well-rounded student.

But after you get in, there's one more issue to think about: How do you pay for college?

More Great Titles from The Princeton Review
Paying for College Without Going Broke,
The Best 377 Colleges

Let's be honest, college is not cheap. The average tuition for a private four-year college is over $33,000 a year. The average tuition of a four-year public school is about $6,695 a year. And the cost is rising. Every year the sticker price of college education bumps up about 6 percent.

Like many of us, your family may not have 33 grand sitting around in a shoebox. With such a hefty price tag, you might be wondering: "Is a college education really worth it? The short answer: Yes! No question about it. According to a 2010 report by the College Board, the median earnings of full-time workers with bachelor's degrees were $55,700 in 2008—$21,900 more than those of workers who finished only high school.

Still, the cost of college is no joke. It's said that a college education ultimately pays for itself; however, some colleges pay better than others. It's best to be prudent when determining the amount of debt that is reasonable for you to take on.

Here's the good news. Even in the wake of the current financial crisis, financial aid is available to almost any student who wants it. There is an estimated $177 billion—that's right, billion!—in financial aid offered to students annually. This comes in the form of federal grants, scholarships, state financed aid, loans, and other programs.

We know that financial aid can seem like an overwhelmingly complex issue, but the introductory information in this chapter should help you grasp what's available and get you started in your search.

How Much Does College Really Cost?

When most people think about the price of a college education, they think of one thing and one thing alone: tuition. It's time to get that notion out of your head. While tuition is a significant portion of the cost of a college education, you need to think of all the other things that factor into the final price tag.

Let's break it down.

- Tuition and fees
- Room and board
- Books and supplies
- Personal expenses
- Travel expenses

Collectively, these things contribute to your total Cost of Attendance (COA) for one year at a college or university.

Understanding the distinction between tuition and COA is crucial because it will help you understand this simple equation:

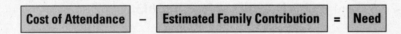

Cost of Attendance − Estimated Family Contribution = Need

When you begin the financial aid process, you will see this equation again and again. We've already talked about the COA, so let's talk about the Estimated Family Contribution, or EFC. The EFC simply means, "How much you and your family can afford to pay for college." Sounds obvious right?

Here's the catch: What you think you can afford to pay for college, what the government thinks you can afford to pay for college, and what a college or university thinks you can afford to pay for college are, unfortunately, three different things. Keep that in mind as we discuss financing options later on.

The final term in the equation is self-explanatory. Anything that's left after what you and your family have contributed, still needs to be covered. That's where financial aid packages come in.

Check out our Financial Aid Library
PrincetonReview.com/
FinancialAidAdvice.aspx

WHAT'S IN A FINANCIAL AID PACKAGE?

A typical financial aid package contains money—from the school, federal government, or state—in various forms: grants, scholarships, work-study programs, and loans.

Let's look at the non-loan options first. Non-loan options include grants, scholarships, and work-study programs. The crucial thing about them is that they involve monetary assistance that you won't be asked to pay back. They are as close as you'll get to "free money."

Grants

Grants are basically gifts. They are funds given to you by the federal government, state agencies, or individual colleges. They are usually need-based, and you are not required to pay them back.

One of the most important grants is the Pell Grant. Pell Grants are provided by the federal government but administered through individual schools. Amounts can change yearly. The maximum Federal Pell Grant award is $5,550 for the 2012–2013 award year (July 1, 2012 to June 30, 2013).

You apply for a Pell Grant by filling out the Free Application for Federal Student Aid (FAFSA). Remember that acronym because you'll be seeing it again. Completing the FAFSA is the first step in applying for any federal aid. The FAFSA can be found online at www.fafsa.ed.gov.

There are several other major federal grant programs that hand out grants ranging from $100 to thousands of dollars annually. Some of these grants are given to students entering a specific field of study and others are need-based, but all of them amount to money that you never have to pay back. Check out the FAFSA website for complete information about qualifying and applying for government grants.

The federal government isn't the only source of grant money. State governments and specific schools also offer grants. Use the Internet, your guidance counselor, and your library to see what non-federal grants you might be eligible for.

Scholarships

Like grants, you never have to pay a scholarship back. But the requirements and terms of a scholarship might vary wildly. Most scholarships are merit- or need-based, but they can be based on almost anything. There are scholarships based on academic performance, athletic achievements, musical or artistic talent, religious affiliation, ethnicity, and so on.

Believe It or Not...
The Chick and Sophie Major Memorial Duck Calling Contest, held annually by the Chamber of Commerce of Stuggart, Arkansas, gives out college scholarships totaling $4,250 (in 2011) to those high school seniors who can master hailing, feeding, comeback, and mating duck calls.

When hunting for scholarships, one great place to start is the U.S. Department of Labor's "Scholarship Search," available at www.careerinfonet.org/scholarshipsearch. It includes over 5,000 scholarships, fellowships, loans, and other opportunities.

There is one important caveat about taking scholarship money. Some, but not all, schools think of scholarship money as income and will reduce the amount of aid they offer you accordingly. Know your school's policy on scholarship awards.

Federal Work-Study (FWS)

One of the ways Uncle Sam disperses aid money is by subsidizing part-time jobs, usually on campus, for students who need financial aid. Because your school will administer the money, they get to decide what your work-study job will be. Work-study participants are paid by the hour, and federal law requires that they cannot be paid less than the federal minimum wage.

One of the benefits of a work-study program is that you get a paycheck just like you would at a normal job. The money is intended to go toward school expenses, but there are no controls over exactly how you spend it.

Colleges and universities determine how to administer work-study programs on their own campuses.

LOANS

Most likely, your entire COA won't be covered by scholarships, grants, and work-study income. The next step in gathering the necessary funds is securing a loan. Broadly speaking, there are two routes to go: federal loans and private loans. Once upon a time, which route to choose might be open for debate. But these days the choice is clear: *Always* try to secure federal loans first. Almost without exception, federal loans provide unbeatable low fixed-interest rates; they come with generous repayment terms; and, although they have lending limits, these limits are quite generous and will take you a long way toward your goal. We'll talk about the benefits of private loans later, but they really can't measure up to what the government can provide and should be considered a last resort.

Stafford Loans

The Stafford loan is the primary form of federal student loan. Loans can be subsidized or unsubsidized. Students with demonstrated financial need may qualify for subsidized loans. This means that the government pays interest accumulated during the time the student is in school. Students with unsubsidized Stafford loans are responsible for the interest accumulated while in school. You can qualify for a subsidized Stafford loan, an unsubsidized Stafford loan, or a mixture of the two.

Check out the Financial Aid Library
PrincetonReview.com/scholarships-financial-aid.aspx

The Bottom Line? Not So Fast!
It is possible to appeal the amount of the financial aid package a school awards you. To learn more about how to do that, check out "Appealing Your Award Package" at PrincetonReview.com/appealing-your-award.aspx

Stafford loans are available to all full-time students and most part-time students. Though the terms of the loan are based on demonstrated financial need, lack of need is not considered grounds for rejection. No payment is expected while the student is attending school. The interest rate on your Stafford loan will depend on when your first disbursement is. The chart below shows the fixed rates set by the government.

First disbursement made on or after	Interest rate on unpaid balance
July 1, 2009 to July 1, 2010	5.6 percent
July 1, 2010 to July 1, 2011	4.5 percent
July 1, 2011 to July 1, 2012	3.4 percent
July 1, 2012 to July 1, 2013	6.8 percent

As with grants, you must start by completing the Free Application for Federal Student Aid (FAFSA) to apply for a Stafford loan.

PLUS Loans

Another important federal loan is the PLUS loan. This loan is designed to help parents and guardians put dependent students through college. Unlike the Stafford loan, the PLUS has no fixed limits or fixed interest rates. The annual limit on a PLUS loan is equal to your COA minus any other financial aid you are already receiving. It may be used on top of a Stafford loan. The interest rates on PLUS loans are variable though often comparable to, or even lower than, the interest rates on Stafford loans. Your PLUS Loan enters repayment once your loan is fully disbursed (paid out).

To become eligible for a PLUS loan, you need only complete a Free Application for Federal Student Aid (FAFSA). There are no other special requirements or forms to fill out.

Perkins Loans

A third and final federal loan you should be aware of is the Perkins loan. Intended to help out students in extreme need, the Perkins loan is a government-subsidized loan that is administered only through college and university financial aid offices. Under the terms of a Perkins loan, you may borrow up to $5,500 a year of undergraduate study, up to $27,500. The Perkins loan has a fixed interest rate of just 5 percent. Payments against the loan don't start until nine months after you graduate. Apply for Perkins loans through your school's financial aid office. More information about Perkins Loans can be found on their website, www.studentaid .ed.gov/types/loans/perkins.

Private Lenders

We said it before, and we'll say it again: DO NOT get a private loan until you've exhausted all other options.

That said, there are some benefits to securing a private loan. First off, many students find that non-loan and federal loan options don't end up covering the entire bill. If that's the case, then private lenders might just save the day. Second, loans from private sources generally offer you greater flexibility with how you use the funds. Third, private loans can be taken out at anytime during your academic career. Unlike most non-loan and government-backed financial options, you can turn to private lenders whenever you need them.

All private lenders are not the same! As the old song says, "You better shop around." Every lender is going to offer you a different package of terms. What you need to do is find the package that best fits your needs and plans. Aside from low interest rates, which are crucially important, there are other terms and conditions you will want to look out for.

Low origination fees Origination fees are fees that lenders charge you for taking out a loan. Usually the fee is simply deducted automatically from your loan checks. Obviously, the lower the origination fee, the better.

Minimal guaranty fees A guaranty fee is an amount you pay to a third-party who agrees to insure your loan. That way, if the borrower—that is you—can't pay the loan back, the guarantor steps in and pays the difference. Again, if you can minimize or eliminate this fee, all the better.

Interest rate reductions Some lenders will reduce your interest rates if you're reliable with your payments. Some will even agree to knock a little off the interest rate if you agree to pay your loans through a direct deposit system. When shopping for the best loan, pay careful attention to factors that might help you curb your interest rates.

Flexible payment plans One of the great things about most federal loans is the fact that you don't have to start paying them off until you leave school. In order to compete, many private lenders have been forced to adopt similarly flexible payment plans. Before saying yes to a private loan, make sure that it comes with a payment timetable you can live with.

IT'S YOUR CALL

Only you (and your parents or guardians) can make the decision of what is right for you. Before deciding to attend college or selecting a school, you should attempt to secure as much assistance (in the form of financial aid: grants, scholarships, work study) as you can, then weigh your options. Thankfully, there are plenty of excellent financing options out there. With a little effort (and a lot of form-filling!) you'll be able to pay your way through school without breaking the bank.

NOTES

About the Authors

Geoff Martz attended Dartmouth College and Columbia University before joining The Princeton Review in 1985 as a teacher and writer. His first book for The Princeton Review was *Cracking the GMAT*, published in 1989. He is also the author or coauthor of *Cracking the GED* and *Paying for College Without Going Broke*.

Kim Magloire is a graduate of Princeton University with a master's degree from Columbia University where she is currently completing her doctorate in Epidemiology. She joined The Princeton Review in 1984 as an SAT teacher and has since taught SAT, MCAT, GMAT, LSAT, GRE, and science SAT Subject tests.

Ted Silver is a graduate of Yale University, the Yale University School of Medicine, and the law school at the University of Connecticut. He has been intensely involved in the fields of education and testing since 1976 and has written several books and computer tutorials pertaining to those fields. He became affiliated with The Princeton Review in 1988 as the chief architect of The Princeton Review's MCAT course. Dr. Silver's full-time profession is as Associate Professor of Law at Touro College Jacob D. Fuchsberg Law Center.

Navigate the admissions process with more guidance from the experts.

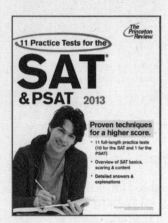

Get the scores you need:

11 Practice Tests for the SAT and PSAT, 2013 Edition
978-0-307-94481-8 • $24.99/$28.99 Can.

ACT or SAT?
978-0-375-42924-8 • $15.99/$19.99 Can.

College Essays that Made a Difference, 5th Edition
978-0-307-94521-1 • $13.99/$16.99 Can.
eBook: 978-0-307-94522-8

Cracking the ACT, 2013 Edition
978-0-307-94535-8 • $19.99/$23.99 Can.
eBook: 978-0-307-94540-2

Cracking the ACT with DVD, 2013 Edition
978-0-307-94536-5 • $31.99/$37.99 Can.

Cracking the SAT, 2013 Edition
978-0-307-94478-8 • $21.99/$25.99 Can.
eBook: 978-0-307-94479-5

Cracking the SAT with DVD, 2013 Edition
978-0-307-94480-1 • $34.99/$41.99 Can.

Reading and Writing Workout for the SAT, 2nd Edition
978-0-375-42832-6 • $16.99/$18.99 Can.

Essential ACT (Flashcards)
978-0-375-42806-7 • $17.99/$19.99 Can.

Essential SAT Vocabulary (Flashcards)
978-0-375-42964-4 • $16.99/$21.99 Can.

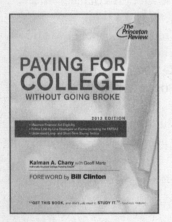

Find and fund the best school for you:

The Best 377 Colleges, 2013 Edition
978-0-307-94487-0 • $23.99/$27.99 Can.
Enhanced eBook: 978-0-307-94601-0
Enhanced (iPad only) eBook:
978-0-307-94600-3

The Complete Book of Colleges, 2013 Edition
978-0-307-94492-4 • $26.99/$32.00 Can.

Paying for College Without Going Broke, 2013 Edition
978-0-307-94532-7 • $20.00/$24.00 Can.
eBook: 978-0-307-94533-4

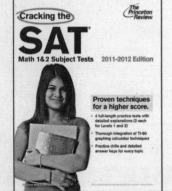

Boost your scores on the SAT Subject Tests:

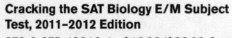

Cracking the SAT Biology E/M Subject Test, 2011-2012 Edition
978-0-375-42810-4 • $19.99/$22.99 Can.

Cracking the SAT Chemistry Subject Test, 2011-2012 Edition
978-0-375-42814-2 • $19.99/$22.99 Can.

Cracking the SAT French Subject Test, 2011-2012 Edition
978-0-375-42815-9 • $19.99/$22.99 Can.

Cracking the SAT Literature Subject Test, 2011-2012 Edition
978-0-375-42811-1 • $19.99/$22.99 Can.

Cracking the SAT Math 1 & 2 Subject Tests, 2011-2012 Edition
978-0-375-42812-8 • $19.99/$22.99 Can.

Cracking the SAT Physics Subject Test, 2011-2012 Edition
978-0-375-42813-5 • $19.99/$22.99 Can.

Cracking the SAT Spanish Subject Test, 2011-2012 Edition
978-0-375-42817-3 • $19.99/$22.99 Can.

Cracking the SAT U.S. & World History Tests, 2011-2012 Edition
978-0-375-42816-6 • $19.99/$22.99 Can.

Ace the APs:

Cracking the AP Biology Exam, 2013 Edition (Revised)
978-0-307-94633-1 • $18.99/$21.99 Can.
eBook: 978-0-307-94580-8

Cracking the AP Calculus AB & BC Exams, 2013 Edition
978-0-307-94486-3 • $19.99/$23.99 Can.
eBook: 978-0-307-94451-1

Cracking the AP Chemistry Exam, 2013 Edition
978-0-307-94488-7 • $18.99/$21.99 Can.
eBook: 978-0-307-94452-8

Cracking the AP Economics Macro & Micro Exams, 2013 Edition
978-0-307-94509-9 • $18.00/$21.00 Can.
eBook: 978-0-307-94581-5

Cracking the AP English Language & Composition Exam, 2013 Edition
978-0-307-94511-2 • $18.00/$21.00 Can.
eBook: 978-0-307-94582-2

Cracking the AP English Literature & Composition Exam, 2013 Edition
978-0-307-94512-9 • $18.00/$21.00 Can.
eBook: 978-0-307-94583-9

Cracking the AP Environmental Science Exam, 2013 Edition
978-0-307-94513-6 • $18.99/$21.99 Can.
eBook: 978-0-307-94584-6

Cracking the AP European History Exam, 2013 Edition
978-0-307-94489-4 • $18.99/$21.99 Can.
eBook: 978-0-307-94453-5

Cracking the AP Human Geography Exam, 2013 Edition
978-0-307-94514-3 • $18.00/$21.00 Can.

Cracking the AP Physics B Exam, 2013 Edition
978-0-307-94515-0 • $18.99/$21.99 Can.
eBook: 978-0-307-94585-3

Cracking the AP Physics C Exam, 2013 Edition
978-0-307-94516-7 • $18.99/$21.99 Can.

Cracking the AP Psychology Exam, 2013 Edition
978-0-307-94517-4 • $18.00/$21.00 Can.
eBook: 978-0-307-94586-0

Cracking the AP Spanish Exam with Audio CD, 2013 Edition
978-0-307-94518-1 • $24.99/$28.99 Can.

Cracking the AP Statistics Exam, 2013 Edition
978-0-307-94519-8 • $19.99/$23.99 Can.

Cracking the AP U.S. Government & Politics Exam, 2013 Edition
978-0-307-94520-4 • $18.99/$21.99 Can.
eBook: 978-0-307-94587-7

Cracking the AP U.S. History Exam, 2013 Edition
978-0-307-94490-7 • $18.99/$21.99 Can.
eBook: 978-0-307-94447-4

Cracking the AP World History Exam, 2013 Edition
978-0-307-94491-7 • $18.99/$21.99 Can.
eBook: 978-0-307-94445-0

Essential AP Biology (Flashcards)
978-0-375-42803-6 • $18.99/$20.99 Can.

Essential AP Psychology (Flashcards)
978-0-375-42801-2 • $18.99/$20.99 Can.

Essential AP U.S. Government & Politics (Flashcards)
978-0-375-42804-3 • $18.99/$20.99 Can.

Essential AP U.S. History (Flashcards)
978-0-375-42800-5 • $18.99/$20.99 Can.

Essential AP World History (Flashcards)
978-0-375-42802-9 • $18.99/$20.99 Can.

**Available everywhere books are sold
and at PrincetonReviewBooks.com**